Lecture Notes in Computer Science 12513

More information about this subseries at http://www.springer.com/series/7410

Quanyan Zhu · John S. Baras ·
Radha Poovendran · Juntao Chen (Eds.)

Decision and Game Theory for Security

11th International Conference, GameSec 2020
College Park, MD, USA, October 28–30, 2020
Proceedings

 Springer

Editors
Quanyan Zhu 🆔
Tandon School of Engineering
New York University
Brooklyn, NY, USA

John S. Baras 🆔
ISR
University of Maryland
College Park, MD, USA

Radha Poovendran 🆔
Electrical Engineering
University of Washington
Seattle, WA, USA

Juntao Chen 🆔
New York University
New York, NY, USA

ISSN 0302-9743 ISSN 1611-3349 (electronic)
Lecture Notes in Computer Science
ISBN 978-3-030-64792-6 ISBN 978-3-030-64793-3 (eBook)
https://doi.org/10.1007/978-3-030-64793-3

LNCS Sublibrary: SL4 – Security and Cryptology

This Springer imprint is published by the registered company Springer Nature Switzerland AG
The registered company address is: Gewerbestrasse 11, 6330 Cham, Switzerland

Preface

Cybersecurity is a major challenge of today's connected world as we are becoming increasingly connected by the recent advances in information and communication technologies. This challenge is exacerbated by the ubiquitous digitalization which is affecting every aspect of society, life, and work. Traditional ways to address network security issues rely on cryptography, firewalls, and intrusion detection systems. As attackers are becoming more and more sophisticated, these solutions are not sufficient to guarantee the security of the network. There is an inevitable need to shift to a new security paradigm where security solutions take into account the strategic behaviors and the constraints on the attack-and-defense resources. We need to understand the fundamental tradeoffs in the design of secure systems instead of hoping for a panacea that can be effective in all security scenarios. Game theory is a mathematical science that studies strategic interaction among rational decision-makers. It can naturally capture the competitive and strategic behaviors between an attacker and a defender, and a promising baseline framework for the analysis and design of system security. In the past years, we have witnessed the success of applications of game theory to multiple security domains, including wireless community, cloud computing, industrial control systems, Internet of Things, and national homeland security. This year's GameSec conference is a continuing celebration of this success.

This volume contains the papers presented at the 11th conference on Decision and Game Theory for Security (GameSec 2020), held virtually during October 28–30, 2020. This conference was planned to take place at College Park, Maryland, USA. Due to COVID-19, this conference was the first virtual conference since GameSec was inaugurated in 2010 in Berlin, Germany. The previous conferences were held in College Park (Maryland, USA, 2011), Budapest (Hungary, 2012), Fort Worth (Texas, USA, 2013), Los Angeles (USA, 2014), London (UK, 2015), New York (USA, 2016), Vienna (Austria, 2017), Seattle (Washington, USA, 2018), and Stockholm (Sweden, 2019). For the past 11 years, GameSec has been widely recognized as a prominent venue for interdisciplinary research in security and privacy.

The conference program this year included 21 full paper presentations and 2 short papers. We have seen the applications of game theory to security issues in cyber-physical systems, computer networks, and machine learning. One special session of this conference is on the confluences between machine learning and game theory for cybersecurity. The presented papers not only explore new attack mechanisms but also aim to develop defense solutions to deter and mitigate the attacks. Another session of this conference is on the theoretical foundations of security games. Presentations in this session discuss new modeling frameworks, analytical methods, and algorithmic solutions that bridge cognitive science, decision and control theory, data science, and network science to solidify the foundations of security games.

An additional special feature of this year's program for GameSec are several invited papers and presentations. The purpose of these invited lectures is to provide to the

GameSec participants a broader and richer set of problems and challenges, where interdisciplinary research involving security, trust, privacy, and various forms of game theory holds great promise.

Thanks to the support of the National Science Foundation, New York University, the University of Maryland, Springer, we were able to make this year's conference completely free of charge, allowing students and researchers from all over the world to participate in the discussions of research. We sincerely hope that this conference will continue to bridge between theory and practice, and offer useful resources for cybersecurity practitioners and researchers.

October 2020

Quanyan Zhu
John S. Baras
Radha Poovendran
Juntao Chen

Organization

General Chairs

John S. Baras   University of Maryland, USA
Radha Poovendran   University of Washington, USA

Program Committee Chair

Quanyan Zhu   New York University, USA

Steering Committee

Tansu Alpcan   The University of Melbourne, Australia
John S. Baras   University of Maryland, USA
Tamer Başar   University of Illinois at Urbana-Champaign, USA
Anthony Ephremides   University of Maryland, USA
Radha Poovendran   University of Washington, USA
Milind Tambe   Harvard University, USA

Program Committee

Habtamu Abie   Norwegian Computing Centre, Norway
Konstantin Avratchenkov   Inria, France
Svetlana Boudko   Norwegian Computing Centre, Norway
Ahmet Cetinkaya   National Institute of Informatics, Japan
Andrew Clark   Worcester Polytechnic Institute, USA
Prithviraj Dasgupta   U.S. Naval Research Laboratory, USA
Jie Fu   Worcester Polytechnic Institute, USA
Jens Grossklags   Technical University of Munich, Germany
Yezekael Hayel   University of Avignon, France
Hideaki Ishii   Tokyo Institute of Technology, Japan
Murat Kantarcioglu   The University of Texas at Dallas, USA
Christopher Kiekintveld   The University of Texas at El Paso, USA
Sandra König   Austrian Institute of Technology, Austria
Aron Laszka   Vanderbilt University, USA
Yee Wei Law   University of South Australia, Australia
M. Hossein Manshaei   Isfahan University of Technology, Iran
Katerina Mitrokotsa   Chalmers University of Technology, Sweden
Shana Moothedath   University of Washington, USA
Mehrdad Nojoumian   Florida Atlantic University, USA
Manos Panaousis   University of Surrey, UK
Sakshyam Panda   University of Surrey, UK

David Pym	University College London, UK
Bhaskar Ramasubramanian	University of Washington, USA
Stefan Rass	Klagenfurt University, Austria
Henrik Sandberg	KTH Royal Institute of Technology, Sweden
Stefan Schauer	Austrian Institute of Technology, Austria
George Theodorakopoulos	Cardiff University, UK
Jun Zhuang	University at Buffalo, USA

Additional Reviewers

Svetlana Boudko
Sadegh Farhang
Marcus Gutierrez
Linan Huang
Kyle Hunt
Yunhan Huang
Tao Li
Mohammad Miah
Dinuka Sahabandu
Hampei Sasahara
Nazia Sharmin
Xiaojun Shan
Jasmin Wachter

Contents

Theoretic Foundations of Security Games

Emerging Topics

Short Paper

Machine Learning and Security

Academic Learning and Security

Distributed Generative Adversarial Networks for Anomaly Detection

Marc Katzef[1]($\boxtimes$) ⓘ, Andrew C. Cullen[2] ⓘ, Tansu Alpcan[1] ⓘ,
Christopher Leckie[2] ⓘ, and Justin Kopacz[3] ⓘ

[1] Department of Electrical and Electronic Engineering, University of Melbourne,
Melbourne, Australia
marc.katzef@student.unimelb.edu.au
[2] School of Computing and Information Systems, University of Melbourne,
Melbourne, Australia
[3] Northrop Grumman Corporation, Denver, USA

Abstract. Cognitive radio networks can be used to detect anomalous and adversarial communications to achieve situational awareness on the radio frequency spectrum. This paper proposes a distributed anomaly detection scheme based on adversarially-trained data models. While many anomaly detection methods typically depend on a central decision-making server, our distributed approach makes better use of decentralized resources, and decreases reliance on a single point of failure. Using a novel combination of generative adversarial network (GAN) elements, participating cognitive radio devices learn a representation of local network activity data through a non-cooperative (strategic) game. Deviations from this expected network activity are flagged as anomalies and treated as possible network security threats, improving situational awareness. Tested on a range of time series datasets, the performance of the proposed distributed scheme matches that of state-of-the-art, centralized anomaly detection methods.

Keywords: Anomaly detection · Distributed · Generative adversarial networks · Cognitive radio networks

1 Introduction

Cognitive Radio (CR) is a communication architecture that strives to shift decision-making to network-connected devices themselves [1]. Originally envisioned to improve spectral efficiency (by intelligently hopping to unused frequencies), the devices composing CR Networks (CRNs) are autonomous, general-purpose computing resources. While the spectral efficiency aspect of CR has gathered great attention, the alternative benefits of device autonomy (such as increased situational awareness) are often overlooked.

Cognitive radio networks can be used to detect anomalous and adversarial communications to achieve situational awareness on the radio frequency spectrum. One of the objectives here is to identify potentially malicious communications by identifying unusual patterns. A secondary objective, as outlined in [2,3],

Q. Zhu et al. (Eds.): GameSec 2020, LNCS 12513, pp. 3–22, 2020.
https://doi.org/10.1007/978-3-030-64793-3_1

is to defend CRNs against a range of attacks spanning multiple network layers. These attacks include denial of service, firmware tampering, primary user emulation, false sensing reports, and spectrum data poisoning, as well as the standard wireless attacks of jamming and eavesdropping. In each of these attack scenarios, individual devices can collect unique, local data that can be used to identify unusual activity. The task of identifying these attacks has been treated as an anomaly detection problem and approached from different fields, as Sect. 2.1 explains.

Anomaly detection is the task of identifying outlying elements in a collection. Given a set of data samples (such as historical readings of network activity), anomaly detection can be formulated as the task of identifying the samples $x \in \mathbb{R}^d$ that were unlikely to be drawn from the same distribution as the remaining samples, $p_X(x)$. In a network security context, the samples being considered are typically feature vectors containing recent network traffic statistics, such as mean packet size, mean inter-arrival time and counts of each packet type. While many methods exist to approximate $p_X(x)$, few methods consider the resource constraints imposed by low-power devices in the CRN setting. With limitations on battery life, computation power, memory and storage, a CR device sharing all of its local observations with the entire CRN is infeasible. Shifting to a distributed anomaly detector would reduce the workload of any individual device and allow for arbitrary scalability.

This paper explores anomaly detection using GANs—adversarially-trained Machine Learning (ML) models with a strong data-generating ability and a high level of modularity—against test-time attacks. Recognizing that GANs learn the distribution of a given dataset, anomaly detection is a natural extension by identifying if a sample lies outside of the learned distribution. Recognizing that GANs are composed of several independent neural networks, exchanging these modules is a comparatively low-cost method to transfer learned experiences. Using these features, the contributions of this paper are (1) a game-theoretic evaluation and interpretation of a novel combination of GAN components (referred to as Peer-GAN), (2) a distributed formulation of Peer-GAN, applied to anomaly detection and (3) a framework for testing arbitrary anomaly detection methods in a distributed setting.

2   Related Work

Existing anomaly detection methods draw on a variety of related fields, with ML becoming the most prevalent in recent years. This section summarizes popular methods and one ML method in particular—the GAN.

2.1   Anomaly Detection

The task of anomaly detection has been explored using the fields of information theory, signal processing and a variety of ML methods. These methods all make a trade-off between storage requirements, computational requirements and manual feature engineering. With minimal feature engineering and methods that balance storage and computation, ML has been a popular approach. When labelled training data is available, supervised ML methods often model anomaly detection as a binary classification problem. Supervised model-based works like [4] have used support vector machines to classify spectrum sensing fingerprints during a transmission. The approach in [5] used clustering and reinforcement learning. However, a significant performance improvement in terms of the Area Under Receiver Operating Characteristic (AUROC) curve was found by moving to the field of deep learning [6].

When signal class information is not known (e.g., when a network is under a novel attack), unsupervised ML methods may be used. As shown in [7], the field of unsupervised ML anomaly detection includes the well-established methods of k-Nearest Neighbor (kNN), isolation forest, feature bagging, Principal Component Analysis (PCA), auto-encoders and GANs. These methods can be divided into categories of distance-based (including kNN, isolation forests and feature bagging) and reconstruction-based (including PCA, auto-encoders and GANs). Distance-based methods measure some distance from a given sample to historical samples, which may be compared with a threshold to identify anomalies. For kNN, this distance is the norm of the difference between a sample and the k-th nearest historical sample. While the benchmarks in [7] show these methods perform well (in terms of AUROC), they depend on all N historical samples—giving $\mathcal{O}(N)$ storage requirements and $\mathcal{O}(\log(N))$ computational complexity for tree-based sample lookup. This storage requirement makes distance-based anomaly detection methods infeasible for use on storage-constrained devices such as CRs. To address these constraints, works like [8] have reduced the memory footprint of kNN by creating representative samples for each class. However, this decreased memory comes with decreased performance resulting in single hidden layer neural networks and support vector machines achieving higher classification accuracy.

The remaining, reconstruction-based anomaly detection methods do not depend on the entire training dataset for each subsequent classification. Instead, PCA and auto-encoders learn to reconstruct a given sample x to obtain $\hat{x}$ to then calculate a reconstruction error, $||x - \hat{x}||$, which may be compared with a threshold. These methods expect unfamiliar samples to give larger reconstruction errors. PCA (typically used as a dimensionality-reduction operation) reconstructs a sample by projecting a sample from the sample space to a lower-dimensional space (using a subset of the training dataset's eigen-vectors as the basis) and back. As these projections are two linear transformations, PCA reconstruction offers low fitting/training complexity and low storage requirements (only storing eigen-vectors) after training. Furthermore, [9] show that the PCA method may be approximated in a distributed environment. However, due to PCA's use of linear transformations, [9] states that PCA cannot represent data distributions with multiple data clusters.

Using deep neural networks (DNNs), auto-encoders overcome PCA's linearity constraint by performing arbitrary transformations to and from a low-dimensional auxiliary (code) space. After training, auto-encoders can update their representation online (by training on additional samples) without the need to store the dataset after training. However, to initially form this representation, an auto-encoder must be trained on a centralized dataset, with collaboration hindered by the fact the auto-encoder's coded sample representation is arbitrary. As the following subsection explains, the GAN follows a similar pattern but the GAN imposes structure to the coded sample representation allowing for collaborative training.

2.2   GANs for Anomaly Detection

A GAN is composed of two ML models, the generator and discriminator, which are the players of a min-max game (see Sect. 3.1 for details). The tasks for the generator and discriminator are to, respectively, approximate $p_X(x)$ with a parameterized distribution, $p_G(x)$ and to discriminate between samples from $p_X(x)$ and $p_G(x)$. Existing works have applied GANs to the domain of anomaly detection by separating the GAN into its constituent components to achieve better performance than PCA, kNN and feature bagging on multiple datasets [10]. GANs have been applied to anomaly detection by either using discriminator output directly, measuring some distance between a sample x and $p_G(x)$, such as $\min_{\hat{x} \sim p_G} ||x - \hat{x}||$, or a combination of the two [10,11]. One issue identified with using $p_G(x)$ is the large computation requirement to calculate the generator's anomaly score for individual samples. To speed up the required projection from sample space to the generator's output space, the Bidirectional GAN (BiGAN) is utilised in [12,13] to produce the *Efficient AnoGAN* and *Fast AnoGAN*. These BiGAN-based models introduce an additional player, the encoder, in the GAN game to learn the inverse to the generator's mapping, avoiding the need for an iteration-based projection to find $\hat{x}$.

Recognizing that GAN training involves separate, modular components—the players—recent research has considered collaborative configurations combining multiple generators (as in the MO-GAAL, [14]), multiple discriminators (as in the MD-GAN, [15]), or both. Previous studies [15–18] have shown that distributed GAN formulations learn a distribution that is closer to the real distribution (as measured by Fréchet inception distance) than that of a standalone GAN. When applied to anomaly detection in [16], a distributed GAN-based anomaly detector (using multiple discriminators and only discriminator-based anomaly scores) achieved a significantly higher accuracy at a given false positive rate.

3   Game-Theoretic Model of Generative Adversarial Networks

The GAN is a non-cooperative game between two ML models—a generator and a discriminator—in which the generator learns to approximate the distribution of a given dataset and the discriminator learns to distinguish between real data samples and the generator's synthetic output samples [19]. Through a zero-sum (min-max) game between adversarially-trained ML models, a GAN can map points from an auxiliary data space to points from the same distribution as those in the given dataset as described in the following subsections.

3.1 GAN Games

The two independent ML models—a generator and a discriminator—are the players of the GAN engaged in a zero-sum non-cooperative (strategic) game denoted formally by the following tuple of players, action spaces and utility functions: $\mathcal{M} = \langle \{G, D\}, \{\Theta_G, \Theta_D\}, \{u_G, u_D\} \rangle$ where

- G is the generator player, which uses a θ_G-parametrized function approximator, $G(z; \theta_G)$ or $G(z)$ (for brevity) with $G : \mathbb{R}^l \mapsto \mathbb{R}^d$, to choose its actions,
- D is the discriminator player, which uses a θ_D-parametrized function approximator, $D(x; \theta_D)$ or $D(x)$ with $D : \mathbb{R}^d \mapsto \mathbb{R}$, to choose its actions,
- Θ_G is the generator's action/decision space, $\theta_G \in \Theta_G$.
- Θ_D is the discriminator's action/decision space, $\theta_D \in \Theta_D$,
- u_G and u_D are the generator and discriminator utility functions, respectively.

The typical choices for the above function approximators are DNNs, where Θ_G and Θ_D are the possible values for each network's weights. The selection of u_G and u_D define the type of GAN. In all GAN formulations, the goals of the generator and discriminator are to maximize their own utility function (or minimize their loss, the negative of utility). For the original GAN zero-sum game formulation and many subsequent variants, the player objective functions are $u_D = -u_G = u$ and take the form of

$$u(\theta_G, \theta_D) = \mathop{\mathbb{E}}_{x \sim p_X} \left[\phi(\hat{D}(x)) \right] + \mathop{\mathbb{E}}_{z \sim p_Z} \left[\phi(1 - \hat{D}(G(z))) \right].$$

Here $p_X(x)$ is the distribution of the given data samples, $x \in \mathbb{R}^d$, $p_Z(z)$ is the distribution of the noise samples for the generator (the generator's *latent space*), $z \in \mathbb{R}^l$, and ϕ is a measuring function.

In the original GAN definition (referred to as the min-max GAN), $\phi(x) = \log(x)$ and $\hat{D}(x) = \sigma(D(x))$ using the sigmoid function $\sigma(x) = (1 + e^{-x})^{-1}$ [19]. With these parameters, [19] shows that the shared utility function is equivalent to the Jensen-Shannon (JS) divergence $JS(p_G \| p_X)$. In the Wasserstein GAN— a popular alternative to the min-max GAN—$\phi(x) = x$ and $\hat{D}(x) = D(x)$, which produces a shared objective function that is equivalent to the Wasserstein metric/earth-mover distance [20] (the significance of which is explained in Sect. 3.2).

To avoid the (computationally-intensive) projection method used in [11,21] the BiGAN trains an additional ML model [22]. Instead of training one neural network (the generator) to learn $p_X(x)$, the BiGAN structure trains two neural networks (a generator and a θ_E-parameterized encoder, $E(x)$) simultaneously to collaboratively learn the conditional probability distributions $p_G(x|z)$ and $p_E(z|x)$ that define the joint probability distributions $p_{GZ}(x, z) = p_G(x|z)p_Z(z)$

and $p_{EX}(x, z) = p_E(z|x)p_X(x)$. These distributions are learned in a version of the min-max GAN game where a modified discriminator, $D(x, z)$, discriminates over data-noise tuples, $(G(z), z)$ and $(x, E(x))$, from both adversaries. The standard-form game for the BiGAN is represented by the tuple $\langle\{G, E, D\}, \{\Theta_G, \Theta_E, \Theta_D\}, \{u_G, u_E, u_D\}\rangle$ where the objective function shared by all three neural networks is $u_D = -u_G = -u_E = u$, defined as

$$u(\theta_G, \theta_E, \theta_D) = \mathop{\mathbb{E}}_{x \sim p_X} \left[\phi(D(x, E(x)))\right]$$
$$+ \mathop{\mathbb{E}}_{z \sim p_Z} \left[\phi(1 - D(G(z), z))\right].$$

In a BiGAN, the players have the complementary roles of generating synthetic data or noise, $(G(z), z)$ or $(x, E(x))$, and discriminating between (data, noise vector) tuples. These players pass data as shown in Fig. 1, where the generator receives input from an auxiliary space (the generator's latent space), the encoder receives data samples, $x \in p_X$ and the discriminator receives input from either the generator or the encoder.

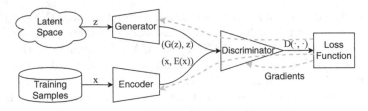

Fig. 1. ML model connections in the BiGAN game (with arrows labelled "Gradients" showing the path for back-propagation when updating player actions).

3.2   GAN Training Methods and Challenges

Using the BiGAN formulation, GAN training is the search for a Nash equilibrium, $(\theta_G^*, \theta_E^*, \theta_D^*)$, at the intersection of player best responses. One such Nash equilibrium is achieved when the generator's and encoder's joint probability distributions are equal, $p_{GZ}(x, z) = p_{EX}(x, z)$, and the discriminator can no longer distinguish between generator and encoder tuples. From [19], the discriminator model's output is

$$\sigma(D(x, z))\bigg|_{x \sim p_X, z \sim p_Z} = \frac{p_{EX}(x, z)}{p_{GZ}(x, z) + p_{EX}(x, z)} = \frac{1}{2}. \tag{1}$$

Due to the non-convexity of GAN utility functions and the high-dimensional action spaces, finding a Nash equilibrium in GANs is challenging. The search for Nash equilibrium in a GAN game is performed by updating each player's action iteratively through stochastic gradient-based optimization to maximize their respective utilities. It has been shown that the use of two different learning rates in player updates guarantees convergence to a Nash equilibrium [23]. However, [24] shows simply that (regardless of utility function) if one equilibrium exists, that equilibrium belongs to a family of equilibria achieved by permuting neurons to produce equivalent neural networks. With the existence of multiple Nash equilibria, a common problem in training GANs is convergence to suboptimal solutions where the generator learns a small selection of samples (a problem termed *mode collapse*) or fails to learn any valid output before $\nabla_{\theta_G} u_G$ decays to 0 (a problem termed *vanishing gradient*).

The problem of vanishing gradients was identified in [19], prompting a revision to the generator's utility function (referred to as the non-saturating loss), in which the $\log(1-\sigma(D(\cdot)))$ term is replaced by $-\log(\sigma(D(\cdot)))$. In doing so, $\nabla_{\theta_G} u_G$ remains non-zero after improvements in the discriminator's action while leaving the equilibrium that is characterized by (1) unchanged. Another, more significant GAN modification is made in [20], which presented the Wasserstein loss for GANs to address mode collapse. This loss is shown to provide training gradients that vary smoothly with the difference between p_X and p_G, preventing the generator from getting trapped representing only a subset of data modes. While the Wasserstein loss-trained generators represent more modes of the training data, generators trained with the original min-max loss (and its non-saturating variant) generate higher fidelity samples of the modes they learn [25].

While the generator of a trained GAN can map noise samples, $z \sim p_Z$, to data samples, $x \sim p_G$, how these elements are linked is set arbitrarily during training. This arbitrary assignment is one additional hurdle for reconstruction using GANs. The study in [22] shows that in the presence of a perfect discriminator, the optimal generator and encoder are inverses (i.e., $E(G(z)) = z$ and $G(E(x)) = x$). Again due to the non-convexity of GAN utility functions, the BiGAN generator and encoder are unlikely to produce exact inverses in practice [22]. This problem is addressed by the GAN variants referred to as *CycleGAN* and *ALICE BiGAN* which add regularization terms based upon reconstruction error to u_G and u_E [26,27]. CycleGAN implements this regularization with an $l1$-norm-based penalty in both directions, while ALICE BiGAN applies regularization only to the forward direction, but by using an additional, resource-intensive adversarially-trained model. These regularization terms ensure that player actions are updated such that $||G(E(x)) - x||$ and $||E(G(z)) - z||$ remain small.

4   A Novel Distributed GAN Framework

In this section, we present a novel GAN game combining non-saturating GAN loss for high-fidelity samples, Wasserstein loss to avoid mode collapse and ALICE BiGAN structure for cyclically-consistent mapping, referred to as *Peer-GAN*. As this section explains, this combination of existing GAN features are extended to a distributed training environment and used for anomaly detection.

4.1 Peer-GAN Game

Peer-GAN combines non-saturating loss, Wasserstein loss and ALICE BiGAN-like structure for a data flow given in Fig. 2. This combination of GAN elements targets accurate data representation, data reconstruction and straightforward extension to a distributed environment. Like BiGAN, the strategic-form game for a single instance, n, of Peer-GAN is represented by the tuple $\mathcal{M}_n = \langle \{G_n, E_n, D_n\}, \{\Theta_G, \Theta_E, \Theta_D\}, \{u_G, u_E, u_D\}\rangle$. Note that unlike classical GANs, this is a three player non-cooperative game with non-convex utility functions. In a distributed Peer-GAN, each instance comprises an independent generator, encoder and discriminator. Discriminator n, for example, chooses a strategy $\theta_{D,n} \in \Theta_{D,n}$ independently from $D_{i \neq n}$. The utility function for D_n,

$$u_D(\theta_G, \theta_E, \theta_D) = \mathop{\mathbb{E}}_{x \sim p_X} [\log(\sigma(D(x, E(x)))) + D(x, E(x))]$$
$$+ \mathop{\mathbb{E}}_{z \sim p_Z} [\log(1 - \sigma(D(G(z), z))) - D(G(z), z)], \qquad (2)$$

is the sum of Wasserstein and non-saturating loss functions. With the remaining players both assigned the utility function, $u_G = u_E = u$, given as

$$u(\theta_G, \theta_E, \theta_D) = - \mathop{\mathbb{E}}_{x \sim p_X} [\log(\sigma(D(x, E(x)))) + D(x, E(x))]$$
$$+ \mathop{\mathbb{E}}_{z \sim p_Z} [\log(\sigma(D(G(z), z))) + D(G(z), z)] - \mathop{\mathbb{E}}_{x \sim p_X} [\|G(E(x)) - x\|_2] \qquad (3)$$

which opposes u_D by having maxima where u_D has minima, while incorporating non-saturating generator loss and the expected data reconstruction error.

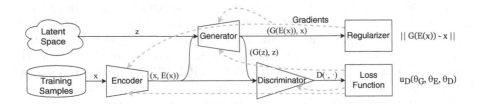

Fig. 2. Connections between ML models/players in the Peer-GAN game. Using BiGAN as a base, Peer-GAN adds a reconstruction-based regularizer in the generator and encoder loss functions to ensure G and E are inverses at game solutions.

With utility functions as above, players G, E and D seek to maximize u_G, u_E and u_D. Combining utility functions and regularizers in this way alters some fixed points of the games mentioned in the previous sections. The one fixed point that remains unchanged is that of the desired Nash equilibrium—where $p_{GZ}(x, z) = p_{EX}(x, z)$ and $\mathbb{E}_{x \sim p_X, z \sim p_Z} [\sigma(D(x, z))] = \frac{1}{2}$. At this optimum, both the JS divergence and Wasserstein distance between p_{GZ} and p_{EX} are minimal and the discriminator can no longer discern between generator and encoder samples. However, the regularization in these utilities adds an additional objective; at the global optimum, the generator and encoder are required to be exact inverses of each other on $\text{supp}(p_X)$. This property is the foundation of Peer-GAN-based anomaly detection, allowing for an anomaly score, $a_G(x)$, to be calculated as

$$a_G(x) = ||G(E(x)) - x||_2.$$

After evaluating $a_G(x)$ for a collection of test samples, a threshold may be chosen to classify future samples as anomalous. This threshold is typically chosen as n standard deviations greater than the mean $a_G(x)$ from the test set. Instead of defining a single threshold, our results in Sect. 5.3 capture anomaly detection performance for all possible thresholds using the AUROC.

4.2   Peer-GAN Distributed Training and Convergence

Using the Peer-GAN game definition above, the players G_n, E_n and D_n of a single Peer-GAN instance may be trained as described in Sect. 3.2. This section extends the formulation and analysis of Peer-GAN training to a distributed setting.

Distributed Training. Peer-GAN's modular architecture allows for collaborative training in the form of parameter exchange. The proposed distribution strategy is to swap the discriminator player in each Peer-GAN instance with a neighboring instance after a chosen number of training steps while the generator and encoder remain in-place. As per Algorithm 1, in the proposed distributed framework, each of N participating devices is trained locally to determine $(\theta^*_{G,n}, \theta^*_{E,n}, \theta^*_{D,n})$ for local data, $p_{X,n}(x)$. For each of these obtained equilibria, the discriminator is no longer able to discern between generator and encoder output and adopts the strategy of outputting a constant

$$\mathbb{E}_{x \sim p_{X,n}}[\sigma(D_n(x, E(x)))] = \frac{1}{2}$$

as explained in Sect. 3.2. If the training data at device n is different from that at device $n + 1$, $p_{X,n} \neq p_{X,n+1}$, the discriminator at device $n + 1$ is expected to label unrecognized samples in $p_{X,n}$ as fake, giving

$$\mathbb{E}_{x \sim p_{X,n}}[\sigma(D_{n+1}(x, E(x)))] \leq \frac{1}{2}.$$

This discriminator output indicates that D_{n+1} has not yet/recently been trained to label $\text{supp}(p_{X,n})$ as real. The pairing $(\theta_{G,n}, \theta_{E,n}, \theta_{D,n+1})$ therefore gives G_n and E_n an opportunity to increase their respective utilities by outputting $p_G(x|z)$ and $p_E(z|x)$, the distributions learned by D_{n+1}. As performed in [16,17] for the min-max GAN, the distributed Peer-GAN uses this pairing by swapping all discriminators in the framework such that $\mathcal{M}_n$ receives D_{n+1} after every T training epochs. This cyclic swapping scheme ensures that each discriminator is trained on all available devices, avoiding any model bias from training on a subset of devices more than the others.

Algorithm 1: Distributed Peer-GAN training

Result: $(\theta_{G,n}, \theta_{E,n}, \theta_{D,n}),\ n = 1, 2, ..., N$

$\theta_{G,n}, \theta_{E,n}, \theta_{D,n} \leftarrow$ GlorotUniform, $n = 1, 2, ..., N$;

for $t = 1, 2, ..., num\_epochs$ **do**

    for $n = 1, 2, ..., N$ **do**

        for *minibatch in minibatches* **do**

            $\theta_{G,n} \leftarrow \theta_{G,n} - \alpha_G \nabla_{\theta_G} u_G(\theta_{G,n}, \theta_{E,n}, \theta_{D,n})$;

            $\theta_{E,n} \leftarrow \theta_{E,n} - \alpha_E \nabla_{\theta_E} u_E(\theta_{G,n}, \theta_{E,n}, \theta_{D,n})$;

            $\theta_{D,n} \leftarrow \theta_{D,n} + \alpha_D \nabla_{\theta_D} u_D(\theta_{G,n}, \theta_{E,n}, \theta_{D,n})$;

        end

    end

    if $(t \mod T) = 0$ **then**

        tmp $\leftarrow \theta_{D,1}$;

        for $i = 1, 2, ..., N\text{-}1$ **do**

            $\theta_{D,i} \leftarrow \theta_{D,i+1}$;

        end

        $\theta_{D,N} \leftarrow$ tmp;

    end

end

After a set number of training updates (or once training gradients drop below a chosen threshold) an optional final step is to measure anomaly detection performance on a held-out test set and broadcast the best-performing player parameters. In an environment where multiple Peer-GANs are being trained simultaneously, exchanging the current state of parameters between instances (as shown in Fig. 3) may be seen as both a method of compressed data transfer and as an additional form of regularization. This compressed data transfer view is from transmitting the result of training instead of the training data itself. The regularization view is from sudden changes in paired adversaries, which requires generalization for all models to maintain their current utility. The effect of this compression is shown in Table 1. By exchanging parameters instead of data samples, the required communication between devices (both transmission and reception) is altered and no longer dependent on the dataset's size. Where each device collects a large number of samples—which is expected from CRs—this reformulation keeps communication resource usage low and modifiable by changing the underlying discriminator model's size P and/or the exchange period T.

Training Convergence. Distributed Peer-GAN training builds on centralized GAN training (in Sect. 3.2) by exchanging discriminator model parameters. These parameter exchanges may be seen as a compressed data transfer and a form of regularization, preventing overfitting to local data. This section explains the effect of these exchanges during training. Assuming each of N distributed Peer-GANs had reached an equilibrium before a parameter exchange, generator and encoder pairs have learned conditional distributions of the joint distribution $p_{GZ,n}(x, z) = p_{EX,n}(x, z)$ and the generator and encoder conditional

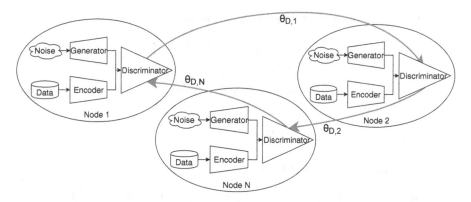

Fig. 3. Distributed Peer-GAN architecture, showing a cyclic swap of discriminator model parameters between three participating devices.

Table 1. The number of elements (e.g., floating point numbers) exchanged while training an anomaly detector using CRN-collected data where S is the dataset size, d is the sample length, N is the number of devices, P is the number of parameters in the model being exchanged, E is the number of training epochs, and T is the distributed strategy's swapping period.

Usage stat (per-device)	Centralized	Distributed
Transmitted data	$\frac{Sd}{N}$	$\left(\lfloor \frac{E}{T} \rfloor + 1\right) P$
Received data	P	$\left(\lfloor \frac{E}{T} \rfloor + 1\right) P$

distributions match the distribution of that device's training data, $p_{G,n}(x|z) = p_{X,n}(x)$. After the first parameter exchange, the generator and encoder joint distribution no longer match the distribution of discriminator's training data, $p_{X,n+1}(x)$ and the new discriminator labels generator and encoder outputs using its previous strategy. Any samples from $\text{supp}(p_{G,n})\backslash\text{supp}(p_{X,n+1})$ are determined less likely to be real by D_{n+1}, worsening the generator's utility. However, any samples from $\text{supp}(p_{X,n+1})\backslash\text{supp}(p_{G,n})$ are opportunities for the generator to improve its utility.

For each player to obtain their optimal utility in a steady state, G_n must approximate the conditional probability

$$p_{G,n}(x|z) = \frac{1}{N} \sum_{i=1}^{N} p_{X,i}(x)$$

which is the mean of data distributions of all individual devices. At the same time, E_n must learn a representation of $p_{X,n}(x)$ that matches G_n's mapping from the latent space. In this state, the optimal discriminator output is

$$\mathbb{E}_{x \sim p_X, z \sim p_Z} \left[\sigma(D_n(x, z)) \right] = \frac{1}{2}$$

which, using (2), gives a discriminator loss (negative of utility) of

$$-u_D^* = -\left(\log\left(\frac{1}{2}\right) + 0 + \log\left(\frac{1}{2}\right) + 0\right) = \log(4).$$

Considering the first and second terms in (3) independently, the loss component contributed by G_n is

$$-u_G^* = -\mathop{\mathbb{E}}_{z \sim p_Z}[\log(\sigma(D_n(G_n(z), z))) + D_n(G_n(z), z)] = \log(2)$$

and the component contributed by E_n is

$$-u_E^* = \mathop{\mathbb{E}}_{x \sim p_{X,n}}[\log(\sigma(D_n(x, E_n(x)))) + D_n(x, E_n(x))] = -\log(2).$$

These are the ideal losses for each of the Peer-GAN players at a desired Nash equilibrium. In the limit as the discriminator swapping frequency increases, the distributed training scheme approaches the mini-batch training of N parallel Peer-GANs on $p_X(x)$, where all instances learn mappings between z and x that are compatible with other instances. Unfortunately, approaching this mini-batch training requires more frequent transmissions of $\theta_{D,n}$ and so a balance must be found between transmission overhead and distribution approximation accuracy.

5   Anomaly Detection and Simulation Results

To evaluate the performance of Peer-GAN as an anomaly detection system, a Peer-GAN was trained (along with its distributed counterpart) on a range of 1D datasets focusing on signals and compared with existing techniques. The proposed Peer-GAN anomaly detector and its distributed counterpart were implemented in Keras and Tensorflow using artificial neural networks for all three players, G, E and D, with ReLU as the activation functions for the two hidden layers in the generator and encoder, leaky ReLU for the three hidden layers in the discriminator, and linear activations for all model outputs. The Adam optimizer was used for all models, with learning rates set to $\alpha_G = \alpha_E = 10^{-4}$ and $\alpha_D = 10^{-5}$ for two time-scale separation allowing G and E to make use of D's learned modes after discriminator swaps. The datasets used here to evaluate Peer-GAN and other anomaly detectors are shown in Table 2.

To represent distributed network environments, the first two stated datasets contain measured data from simulated and real-world communication networks under attack. Each sample in the CRN dataset is a time-series window of received packet sizes, inter-arrival times and transmission durations averaged over five minute intervals in an OMNeT++ simulation (with occasional activity from adversaries) [28]. In contrast, KDD'99 was collected from real-world network activity—from an Ethernet testbed exposed to attacks including denial of service and port scanning [29]. The samples in each of these datasets are vectors of features derived from received packet metadata (such as size, protocol and inter-arrival time) over discrete time windows. The MNIST dataset used here

Table 2. Anomaly detection evaluation datasets.

Dataset	Sample count	Anomaly %	Feature count
CRN	4,190	50.0	111
KDD'99	445,372	11.0	121
MNIST	7,603	9.2	100
Synthetic	60,000	8.3	111

is a pre-processed version of the MNIST handwritten digit dataset where 100 significant features are retained from the original 28×28 images, available at [7]. Furthermore, this pre-processed dataset contains only the digit "0" as the typical sample, with samples from the "6" class added as anomalies. The final dataset (listed as *synthetic*) is a collection of randomly-generated time series signals with step changes and additive white Gaussian noise (with a higher power for generated anomalous samples). Each sample consists of 111 elements set at one of two distinct levels, flipping between the two at intervals of 35–40 indices, with additive noise with standard deviation of 10% and 50% of the difference between the two levels for typical and anomalous signals respectively. All sample elements were linearly shifted and scaled such that each feature in the training set fell in $[0, 1]$ and any categorical features were one-hot encoded before being embedded in feature vectors. Together, these datasets represent diverse use cases that could benefit from distributed anomaly detection.

Peer-GAN was evaluated by training two configurations; one with a single device which can access all data (the centralized case) and one consisting of three devices each with one third of the dataset (the distributed case). The distributed configuration trained each Peer-GAN with a fixed swapping interval of once per epoch. For effective anomaly detection, the desired trends during Peer-GAN training are:

- All model losses converge to steady-state values stated in Sect. 4.2,
- All model loss gradients (as measured by $l2$-norm) decay to 0,
- Reconstruction error decreases for typical samples (seen as a low final value for G and E losses),
- Reconstruction error for typical samples becomes reliably smaller than that for anomalous samples (measured as AUROC using a dedicated test dataset).

The above training trends are addressed in the following subsections.

5.1   Peer-GAN Convergence

Throughout Peer-GAN training, each ML model's losses (negative of utility) and loss gradients were recorded for each parameter update step, for each device. Using the KDD'99 dataset for demonstration, the losses and gradients for the centralized and distributed cases (averaged over each epoch) are shown in Figs. 4a and 4b respectively. In these tests, both Peer-GAN variants initially show large variations in losses (a typical feature of the Wasserstein training loss) but both converge to a relatively steady state after 30 training epochs (a state more stable than with Wasserstein loss by itself).

While the loss values shown in Figs. 4a and 4b do not settle to constant values, the losses each remain in narrow bands. Notably, each of these bands match the expected losses explained in Sect. 4.2; $-u_D \approx \log(4)$, $u_G \approx \log(2)$ and $u_E \approx -\log(2)$. The visible instability in losses is expected to result from the use of stochastic gradient action updates for each player. Because of the inherent randomness in these update strategies, player loss gradients remain non-zero throughout training. However, Figs. 4a and 4b show that these loss gradients decrease significantly after 20 training epochs, again indicating that a Peer-GAN game solution was found. One key difference between the two tested configurations is the height of each case's peak gradient. With a lower peak gradient, parameter swapping acts like regularization with training less prone to any player over-fitting and causing instability in other players' action updates. This better stability early in distributed training comes at the cost of a slight increase in variation later on—both effects of the initial model mismatch after a discriminator swap.

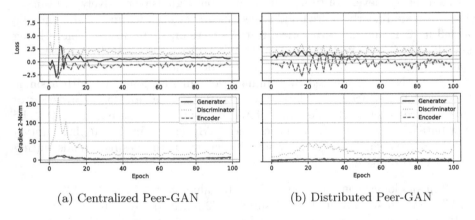

(a) Centralized Peer-GAN   (b) Distributed Peer-GAN

Fig. 4. Player losses, $-u_P$, and gradients, $\|\nabla_{\theta_P}\|_2$, when training Peer-GAN on the KDD'99 dataset. After an initial period of instability, model losses approach the expected values from Sect. 4.2 (overlaid as solid, horizontal lines) indicating that a Nash equilibrium was found.

5.2   Sample Reconstruction

As Sect. 2.1 explains, the proposed Peer-GAN anomaly detector relies on sample reconstruction to identify anomalies. Reconstruction accuracy is therefore implicitly measured in anomaly detection performance. However, only the relative reconstruction accuracy is used to distinguish between samples from distributions. This section presents example reconstructions to observe Peer-GAN absolute reconstruction accuracy for both typical and anomalous samples.

Using the CRN dataset, random samples (both typical and anomalous) from the test set were passed through trained Peer-GAN models. Figures 5 and 6 show x values with $G(E(x))$ superimposed, where the ideal generator/encoder pair would satisfy $G(E(x)) = x, \forall x \in \operatorname{supp}(p_X)$. From this small selection of typical samples, both the centralized and distributed Peer-GANs show accurate reconstruction in Fig. 5 (with neither model significantly outperforming the other). For anomalous samples (in Fig. 6) each model reverts to outputting noise (sometimes outside the bounds of the signal), mismatching the anomalous CRN signals. Together, these results indicate that Peer-GAN reconstructions are suitable for separating typical samples from anomalies and that distributed Peer-GANs perform similar reconstructions to centralized Peer-GANs.

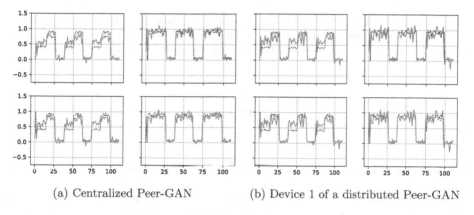

(a) Centralized Peer-GAN   (b) Device 1 of a distributed Peer-GAN

Fig. 5. Peer-GAN reconstruction of typical CRN samples, $x \sim p_X$. Dotted lines represent the typical samples, solid lines the reconstructions, $G(E(x))$. For both models, the reconstruction visibly matches the given, typical samples.

5.3 Anomaly Detection Comparison

This section combines the previous section results of convergence and accurate reconstruction by applying Peer-GANs to anomaly detection. For each of the datasets in Table 2, the previously mentioned centralized Peer-GAN and distributed Peer-GAN were trained using shuffled and evenly-divided training datasets across participating devices. The shuffling in this dataset preparation breaks up any clusters of time-correlated data that may be present. Both Peer-GANs were trained using mini-batches of 500 samples for 100 epochs and (for the distributed Peer-GAN) a swapping period set as $T = 1$.

Performance. Once trained, each Peer-GAN was evaluated by calculating AUROC on the complete test dataset. The highest AUROC of all devices was collected for three trials of both Peer-GANs. The means of these trials are presented in Table 3 along with the performance of existing methods. The competing

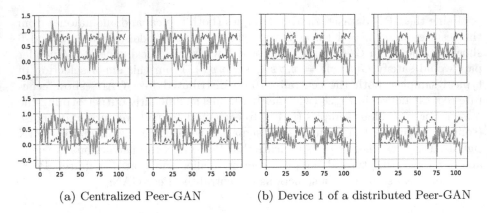

(a) Centralized Peer-GAN   (b) Device 1 of a distributed Peer-GAN

Fig. 6. Peer-GAN reconstruction of anomalous CRN samples. Dashed lines represent the anomalous samples, solid lines the reconstructions, $G(E(x))$. Unlike the typical samples in Fig. 5, Peer-GAN reconstructions do not match anomalous samples.

methods shown are those with low feature engineering, storage and computational requirements as discussed in Sect. 2.1, using the default parameters from the python outlier detection library, [7] and the Efficient AnoGAN, [12].

Table 3. Anomaly detection AUROCs for the distributed Peer-GAN and competing methods on the datasets listed in Table 2 with the highest AUROC per dataset in bold. The competing methods are Auto-Encoders (AE), Principal Component Analysis (PCA), MO-GAAL (MG), Efficient AnoGAN (EA), centralized Peer-GAN (C-Peer-GAN) and, separated as the only distributed anomaly detector, the distributed Peer-GAN (D-Peer-GAN).

Dataset	AE	PCA	MG	EA	C-Peer-GAN	D-Peer-GAN
CRN	**1.0**	**1.0**	0.0	0.0	**1.0**	**1.0**
KDD'99	0.97	0.97	0.37	0.71	**0.99**	**0.99**
MNIST	**0.91**	**0.91**	0.55	0.29	0.83	0.88
Synthetic	0.51	0.51	0.19	0.54	0.98	**1.0**

As shown in Table 3, anomaly detection performance varied from reliably correct (an AUROC of 1.0) to reliably incorrect (an AUROC of 0.0). With an anomaly detector that randomly assigns labels expected to achieve an AUROC of 0.5, this performance range gives an insight into how each method handles different types of anomalies. For the CRN dataset, low performance is the result of the average energy in anomalous samples being lower than that of typical samples (as seen in Figs. 5 and 6). For the CRN dataset, zero-mean, low-energy, random sample reconstructions would achieve an AUROC close to 0. Low performance on the synthetic dataset is the result of reconstructed sample noise exceeding the noise in typical test samples. For the remaining datasets, KDD'99 and MNIST, more sophisticated patterns must be learnt to reconstruct typical samples.

Of the tested methods, no one anomaly detector outperformed the competition for every dataset. For the CRN dataset, all anomaly detectors were either reliably correct or reliably incorrect for reasons explained above. For the synthetic dataset, the only anomaly detectors to perform better than random selection are the Peer-GAN variants. For the remaining datasets, auto-encoders, PCA and Peer-GAN variants achieved high performance. Compared to the remaining methods, both Peer-GAN variants were the only with AUROCs consistently above 0.51, showing a higher level of flexibility—being able to model both structural and fine-level detail in data samples—than PCA, auto-encoders and the remaining GAN-based methods. Notably, the performance of the distributed Peer-GAN was equal to or better than that of the centralized case. This counter-intuitive result may be explained by each Peer-GAN better learning the features of a small dataset—typically considered over-fitting—before sharing these results through discriminator exchanges.

Also tested were the methods kNN, feature bagging and isolation forest. With these methods, kNN was found to perform the best (or tied-best) across all datasets. kNN's high performance was followed closely by feature bagging, isolation forest and our distributed Peer-GAN. However, as explained in Sect. 2.1, the methods kNN, feature bagging and isolation forest have significant storage and computation requirements in use after training, making them unsuitable for resource-constrained devices.

Resource Usage. Compared with the centralized methods of kNN, feature bagging and isolation forest, Peer-GAN does not need to load samples into memory for anomaly detection and replaces the transmission of data samples to a central server with transmission of model parameters. Using Table 1, the communication resource usage (summing transmissions and receptions) for each participating device in the distributed scheme is only 58% of a typical collaborative scheme for our discriminator model (where $P = 51,585$), the KDD'99 dataset (where $S = 445,372$ and $d = 121$), and three devices training for 100 epochs with a swapping period of 1 (giving $N = 3$, $E = 100$ and $T = 1$).

Training Stability. As shown in Sect. 5.1, discriminator training gradients do not consistently decay to zero with additional Peer-GAN training epochs. The impact of these gradients was observed by evaluating each Peer-GAN's anomaly detection performance at the end of each training epoch. Results on the MNIST dataset (presented in Fig. 7) show that both centralized and distributed Peer-GAN performance remains stable in that their AUROC increases with additional training. The distributed Peer-GAN is seen to require additional training epochs to achieve the same performance as the centralized case. This delay is due to each distributed Peer-GAN training on a smaller dataset, which results in fewer parameter updates per epoch. Once identified, Peer-GAN retains its method of separating samples (in MNIST and additional datasets) after additional training

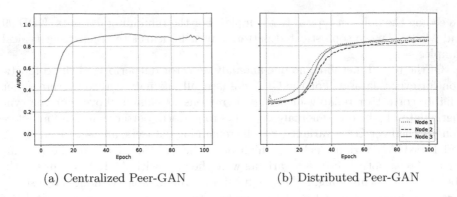

(a) Centralized Peer-GAN   (b) Distributed Peer-GAN

Fig. 7. Peer-GAN anomaly detection AUROC during training on the MNIST dataset. For the distributed case, AUROCs are shown using solid, dotted and dashed lines for devices 1–3. In both cases, the Peer-GAN AUROC increases dramatically at early training stages, before levelling out.

epochs, making Peer-GAN suitable for on-line training—updating each Peer-GAN model as more data becomes available.

6   Conclusion

In this paper, we presented Peer-GAN—a novel GAN-based anomaly detection scheme suitable for resource-constrained networked devices. Using a min-max game played locally on each device and collaboration between devices, Peer-GAN can accurately detect anomalies in 1D datasets while reducing data communication requirements for participating devices. Through theory and supporting simulation results, Peer-GAN was shown to converge to a Nash equilibrium wherein ML models—the players—achieve high reconstruction accuracy of dataset samples and, subsequently, anomaly detection performance to rival state-of-the art methods. In future work, we plan to investigate the effect of larger groups of devices and different swapping schemes (such as random pairing) in a distributed Peer-GAN as well as Peer-GAN's robustness in the presence of device failure or adversaries.

Acknowledgements. This work was supported in part by the Australian Research Council Linkage Project under the grant LP190101287, and by Northrop Grumman Mission Systems' University Research Program.

References

1. Mitola, J.: An Integrated Agent Architecture for Software Defined Radio. Ph.D. Dissertation, KTH, July 2000
2. Shi, Y., Erpek, T., Sagduyu, Y.E., Li, J.H.: Spectrum Data Poisoning with Adversarial Deep Learning. arXiv:1901.09247 [cs], January 2019

3. Chen, R., Park, J.-M., Reed, J.H.: Defense against primary user emulation attacks in cognitive radio networks. IEEE J. Sel. Areas Commun. **26**(1), 25–37 (2008)
4. Luo, Z., Lou, C., Chen, S., Zheng, S., Li, S.: Specific primary user sensing for wireless security in IEEE 802.22 network. In: 2011 11th International Symposium on Communications Information Technologies (ISCIT), pp. 18–22, October 2011
5. Srinivasan, S., Shivakumar, K.B., Mohammad, M.: Semi-supervised machine learning for primary user emulation attack detection and prevention through core-based analytics for cognitive radio networks. Int. J. Distrib. Sens. Netw. 15(9) (2019). https://doi.org/10.1177/1550147719860365
6. Pu, D., Shi, Y., Ilyashenko, A.V., Wyglinski, A.M.: Detecting primary user emulation attack in cognitive radio networks. In: 2011 IEEE Global Telecommunications Conference - GLOBECOM 2011, pp. 1–5, December 2011. ISSN: 1930–529X
7. Zhao, Y., Nasrullah, Z., Li, Z.: PyOD: A Python Toolbox for Scalable Outlier Detection. 20:7 (2019)
8. Gupta, C., et al.: ProtoNN: compressed and accurate kNN for resource-scarce devices. In: International Conference on Machine Learning, pp. 1331–1340. PMLR, July 2017. ISSN: 2640–3498
9. Lee, Y.J., Yeh, Y.R., Wang, Y.C.F.: Anomaly detection via online oversampling principal component analysis. IEEE Trans. Knowl. Data Eng. **25**(7), 1460–1470 (2013)
10. Li, D., Chen, D., Jin, B., Shi, L., Goh, J., Ng, S.-K.: MAD-GAN: Multivariate anomaly detection for time series data with generative adversarial networks. In: Tetko, I.V., Kůrková, V., Karpov, P., Theis, F. (eds.) ICANN 2019. LNCS, vol. 11730, pp. 703–716. Springer, Cham (2019). https://doi.org/10.1007/978-3-030-30490-4_56. arXiv:1901.04997
11. Schlegl, T., Seeböck, P., Waldstein, S.M., Schmidt-Erfurth, U., Langs, G.: Unsupervised anomaly detection with generative adversarial networks to guide marker discovery. In: Niethammer, M., et al. (eds.) IPMI 2017. LNCS, vol. 10265, pp. 146–157. Springer, Cham (2017). https://doi.org/10.1007/978-3-319-59050-9_12. arXiv:1703.05921
12. Zenati, H., Foo, C.S., Lecouat, B., Manek, G., Chandrasekhar, V.R.: Efficient GAN-Based Anomaly Detection. arXiv:1802.06222 [cs, stat], May 2019
13. Schlegl, T., Seebock, P., Waldstein, S.M., Langs, G., Schmidt-Erfurth, U.: f-AnoGAN: Fast unsupervised anomaly detection with generative adversarial networks. Med. Image Anal. **54**, 30–44 (2019)
14. Liu, Y., et al.: Generative adversarial active learning for unsupervised outlier detection. IEEE Trans. Knowl. Data Eng. **32**, 1517–1528 (2019). Conference Name: IEEE Transactions on Knowledge and Data Engineering
15. Hardy, C., Le Merrer, E., Sericola, B.: MD-GAN: Multi-Discriminator Generative Adversarial Networks for Distributed Datasets. arXiv:1811.03850 [cs, stat], February 2019
16. Ferdowsi, A., Saad, W.: Generative Adversarial Networks for Distributed Intrusion Detection in the Internet of Things. arXiv:1906.00567 [cs, stat], June 2019
17. Im, D.J., Ma, H., Kim, C.D., Taylor, G.: Generative Adversarial Parallelization. arXiv:1612.04021 [cs, stat], December 2016
18. Hoang, Q., Nguyen, T.D., Le, T., Phung, D.: MGAN: Training generative adversarial nets with multiple generators, p. 24 (2018)
19. Goodfellow, I.J., et al.: Generative Adversarial Networks. arXiv:1406.2661 [cs, stat], June 2014
20. Arjovsky, M., Chintala, S., Bottou, L.: Wasserstein generative adversarial networks. In: International Conference on Machine Learning, pp. 214–223, July 2017

21. Creswell, A., Bharath, A.A.: Inverting The Generator Of A Generative Adversarial Network (II). arXiv:1802.05701 [cs], February 2018
22. Donahue, J., Krähenbühl, P., Darrell, T.: Adversarial Feature Learning. arXiv:1605.09782 [cs, stat], April 2017
23. Heusel, M., Ramsauer, H., Unterthiner, T., Nessler, B., Hochreiter, S.: GANs Trained by a Two Time-Scale Update Rule Converge to a Local Nash Equilibrium. arXiv:1706.08500 [cs, stat], June 2017
24. Thierens, D.: Non-redundant genetic coding of neural networks. In: IEEE International Conference on Evolutionary Computation, pp. 571–575, May 1996
25. Lucic, M., Kurach, K., Michalski, M., Gelly, S., Bousquet, O.: Are GANs Created Equal? A Large-Scale Study. arXiv:1711.10337 [cs, stat], October 2018
26. Zhu, J.Y., Park, T., Isola, P., Efros, A.A.: Unpaired Image-to-Image Translation using Cycle-Consistent Adversarial Networks. arXiv:1703.10593 [cs], November 2018
27. Li, C., et al.: ALICE: Towards Understanding Adversarial Learning for Joint Distribution Matching. arXiv:1709.01215 [cs, stat], November 2017
28. Weerasinghe, S.: https://github.com/sandamal/omnet_simulation. Accessed 10 June 2020
29. The UCI KDD Archive. KDD Cup 1999 Data, October 1999

Learning and Planning in the Feature Deception Problem

Zheyuan Ryan Shi[1]([✉]), Ariel D. Procaccia[2], Kevin S. Chan[3],
Sridhar Venkatesan[4], Noam Ben-Asher[3], Nandi O. Leslie[3], Charles Kamhoua[3],
and Fei Fang[1]

[1] Carnegie Mellon University, Pittsburgh, USA
ryanshi@cmu.edu
[2] Harvard University, Cambridge, USA
[3] Army Research Laboratory, Adelphi, USA
[4] Perspecta Labs Inc., Basking Ridge, USA

Abstract. Today's high-stakes adversarial interactions feature attackers who constantly breach the ever-improving security measures. Deception mitigates the defender's loss by misleading the attacker to make suboptimal decisions. In order to formally reason about deception, we introduce the *feature deception problem (FDP)*, a domain-independent model and present a learning and planning framework for finding the optimal deception strategy, taking into account the adversary's preferences which are initially unknown to the defender. We make the following contributions. (1) We show that we can uniformly learn the adversary's preferences using data from a modest number of deception strategies. (2) We propose an approximation algorithm for finding the optimal deception strategy given the learned preferences and show that the problem is NP-hard. (3) We perform extensive experiments to validate our methods and results. In addition, we provide a case study of the credit bureau network to illustrate how FDP implements deception on a real-world problem.

1 Introduction

The world today poses more challenges to security than ever before. Consider the cyberspace or the financial world where a defender is protecting a collection of targets, e.g. servers or accounts. Despite the ever-improving security measures, malicious attackers work diligently and creatively to outstrip the defense [23]. Against an attacker with previously unseen exploits and abundant resources, the attempt to protect any target is almost surely a lost cause [10]. However, the defender could induce the attacker to attack a less harmful, or even fake, target. This can be seen as a case of deception.

Deception has been an important tactic in military operations for millenia [14]. More recently, it has been extensively studied in cybersecurity [9,13]. At the start of an attack campaign, attackers typically perform reconnaissance to learn the configuration of the machines in the network using tools such as

© Springer Nature Switzerland AG 2020
Q. Zhu et al. (Eds.): GameSec 2020, LNCS 12513, pp. 23–44, 2020.
https://doi.org/10.1007/978-3-030-64793-3_2

Table 1. Example features in cybersecurity

Feature	Observed value	Actual value
Operating system	Windows 2016	RHEL 7
Service version	v1.2	v1.4
IP address	10.0.1.2	10.0.2.1
Open ports	22, 445	22, 1433
Round trip time for probes [28]	16 ms	84 ms

Nmap [16]. Security researchers have proposed many deceptive measures to manipulate a machine's response to these probes [2,12], which could confound and mislead an attempt to attack. In addition, honey-X, such as honeypots, honey users, and honey files have been developed to attract the attackers to attack these fake targets [30]. For example, it is reported that country A once created encrypted but fake files with names of country B's military systems and marked them to be shared with country A's intelligence agency [18]. Using sensitive filenames as bait, country A successfully lured country B's hackers to these decoy targets.

Be it commanding an army or protecting a computer network, a common characteristic is that the attacker gathers information about the defender's system to make decisions, and the defender can (partly) control how her system appears to the surveillance. We formalize this view, abstract the collected information about the defender's system that is relevant to attacker's decision-making as features, and propose the *feature deception problem (FDP)* to model the strategic interaction between the defender and the attacker.

It is evident that the FDP model could be applied to many domains by appropriately defining the relevant set of features. To be concrete, we will ground our discussion in cybersecurity, where an attacker observes the features of each network node when attempting to fingerprint the machines (example features shown in the left column of Table 1) and then chooses a node to compromise. Attackers may have different preferences over feature value combinations when choosing targets to attack. If an intruder has an exploit for Windows machines, a Linux server might not be attractive. If the attacker is interested in exfiltration, he might choose a machine running database services. If the defender knows the attacker's preferences, she could strategically configure important machines appear undesirable or configure the honeypots to appear attractive to the attacker, by changing the observed value of the features, e.g. Table 1. However, to make an informed decision, she needs to first learn the attacker's preferences.

Our Contributions. Based on our proposed FDP model, we provide a learning and planning framework and make three key contributions. First, we analyze the sample complexity of learning attacker's preferences. We prove that to learn a classical subclass of preferences that is typically used in the inverse reinforcement learning and behavioral game theory literature, the defender needs to gather only a polynomial number of data points on a linear number of feature configurations. The proof leverages what we call the *inverse feature difference* matrix (IFD), and shows that the complexity depends on the norm of this matrix. If the attacker is aware of the learning, they may try to interfere with the learning process by launching the data-poisoning attack, a typical threat model in adversarial machine learning. Using the IFD, we demonstrate the robustness of learning in FDP against this kind of attack. Second, we study the planning problem of finding the optimal deception strategy against learned attacker's preferences. We show that it is NP-hard and propose an approximation algorithm. In addition, we perform extensive experiments to validate our results. We also conduct a case study to illustrate how our FDP framework implements deception on the network of a credit bureau.

2   The Feature Deception Problem

In an FDP, a defender aims to protect a set N of n targets from an adversary. Each target $i \in N$ has a set M of m features. The adversary observes these features and then chooses a target to attack. The defender incurs a loss $u_i \in [-1, 1]$ if the adversary chooses to attack target i.[1] The defender's objective is to minimize her expected loss. Now, we introduce several key elements in FDP. We provide further discussions on some of the assumptions in FDP in the final section.

Features. Features are the key element of the FDP model. Each feature has an *observed* value and an *actual* value. The actual value is given and fixed, while the defender can manipulate the observed value. Only the observed values are visible to the adversary. This ties into the notion of deception, where one may think of the actual value as representing the "ground truth" whereas the observed value is what the defender would like the attacker to see. Since deception means manipulating the attacker's perceived value of a target, not the actual value, changing the observable values does not affect the defender's loss u_i at each target.

Table 1 shows an example in cybersecurity. In practice, there are many ways to implement deception. For example, a node running Windows (actual feature) manages to reply to reconnaissance queries in Linux style using tools like OSfuscate. Then the attacker might think the node is running Linux (observed feature). For IP deception, Jafarian et al. [11] and Chiang et al. [4] demonstrate methods to present to the attacker a different IP from the actual one. In addition, when we "fake open" a port with no real vulnerable service runs on it, an attack on the underlying service will fail. This could be done with command line tools or existing technologies like Honeyd [24].

---

[1] Typically, the loss u_i is non-negative, but it might be negative if, for example, the target is set up as a decoy or honeypot, and allows the defender to gain information about the attacker.

Feature Representation. We represent the observed feature values of target i by a vector $x_i = (x_{ik})_{k \in M} \in [0,1]^m$. We denote their corresponding actual values as $\hat{x}_i \in [0,1]^m$. We allow for both continuous and discrete features. In practice, we may have categorical features, such as the type of operating system, and they can be represented using one-hot encoding with binary features.

Feasibility Constraints. For a feature k with actual value $\hat{x}_{ik}$, the defender can set its observed value $x_{ik} \in C(\hat{x}_{ik}) \subseteq [0,1]$, where the feasible set $C(\hat{x}_{ik})$ is determined by the actual value. For continuous features, we assume $C(\hat{x}_{ik})$ takes the form $[\hat{x}_{ik} - \tau_{ik}, \hat{x}_{ik} + \tau_{ik}] \cap [0,1]$ where $\tau_{ik} \in [0,1]$. This captures the feasibility constraint in setting up the observed value of a feature based on its actual value. Take the round trip time (RTT) as an example. Shamsi et al. fingerprint the OS using RTT of the SYN-ACK packets [28]. Typical RTTs are in the order of few seconds (Fig. 4 [28]), while a typical TCP session is 3–5 min. Thus, perturbing RTT within a few seconds is reasonable, but greater perturbation is dubious.

For binary features, $C(\hat{x}_{ik}) \subseteq \{0,1\}$. In addition to these feasibility constraints for individual features, we also allow for linear constraints over multiple features, which could encode natural constraints for categorical features with one-hot encoding, e.g. $\sum_{k \in M'} x_{ik} = 1$, with $M' \subseteq M$ being the subset of features that collectively represent one categorical feature. They may also encode the realistic considerations when setting up the observed features. For example, $x_{ik_1} + x_{ik_2} \leq 1$ could mean that a Linux machine ($x_{ik_1} = 1$) cannot possibly have ActiveX available ($x_{ik_2} = 1$).

Budget Constraint. Deception comes at a cost. We assume the cost is additive across targets and features: $c = \sum_{i \in N} \sum_{k \in M} c_{ik}$, where $c_{ik} = \eta_{ik}|x_{ik} - \hat{x}_{ik}|$. For a continuous feature k, η_{ik} represents the cost associated with unit of change from the actual value to the observable value. In the example of RTT deception, defender's cost is the packet delay which can be considered linear. If k is binary, η_{ik} defines the cost of switching states. The defender has a budget B to cover these costs. We note that, though we introduce these explicit forms of feasibility constraints and cost structure, our algorithms in the sequel are not specific to these forms.

Defender Strategies. The defender's strategy is an observed feature configuration $x = \{x_i\}_{i \in N}$. The defender uses only pure strategies.

Attacker Strategies. The attacker's pure strategy is to choose a target $i \in N$ to attack. Since human behavior is not perfectly rational and the attacker may have preferences that are unknown to the defender a priori, we reason about the adversary using a general class of bounded rationality models. We assume the attacker's utilities are characterized by a score function $f : [0,1]^m \to \mathbb{R}_{>0}$ over the observed feature values of a target. Given observed feature configuration $x = \{x_i\}_{i \in N}$, he attacks target i with probability $\frac{f(x_i)}{\sum_{j \in N} f(x_j)}$. f may take any form and in this paper, we assume that it can be parameterized by or approximated with a neural network with parameter w. In some of the theoretical analyses, we focus on a subclass of functions

$$f_w(x_i) = \exp\left(\sum\nolimits_{k \in M} w_k x_{ik}\right).$$ (1)

We omit the subscript w when there is no confusion. This functional form is commonly used to approximate the agent's reward or utility function in inverse reinforcement learning and behavioral game theory, and has been empirically shown to capture many attacker preferences in cybersecurity [1]. For example, the tactics of advanced persistent threat group APT10 [25] are driven by: (1) final goal: they aim at exfiltrating data from workstation machines; (2) expertise: they employ exploits against Windows workstations; (3) services available: their exploits operate against file sharing and remote desktop services. Thus, APT10 prefer to attack machines with Windows OS running a file-sharing service on the default port. Each of these properties is a "feature" in FDP and a score function f in Eq. (1) can assign a greater weight for each of these features. It can also capture more complex preferences by using hand-crafted features based on domain knowledge. For example, APT10 typically scan for NetBIOS services (i.e., ports 137 and 138), and Remote Desktop Protocol services (i.e., ports 445 and 3389) to identify systems that they might get onto [25]. Instead of treating the availability of ports as features, we may design a binary feature indicating whether each of the service is available (representing an "OR" relationship of the port availability features). We also show a more efficient way to approximately handle combinatorial preferences in Sect. 5.4. In addition, this score function also captures fully rational attackers in the limit.

The ultimate goal of the defender is to find the optimal feature configuration against an unknown attacker. This can be decomposed into two subtasks: *learning* the attacker's behavior model from attack data and *planning* how to manipulate the feature configuration to minimize her expected loss based on the learned preferences. In the following sections, we first analyze the sample complexity of the learning task and then propose algorithms for the planning task.

3   Learning the Adversary's Preferences

The defender learns the adversary's score function f from a set of d labeled data points each in the format of (N, x, y) where N is the set of targets and x is the observed feature configuration of all targets in N. The label $y \in N$ indicates that the adversary attacks target y.

In practice, there are two ways to carry out the learning stage. First, the defender can learn from historical data. Second, the defender can also actively collect data points while manipulating the observed features of the network. This is often done with honeynets [30], i.e. a network of honeypots.

No matter which learning mode we use, it is often the case, e.g. in cybersecurity, that the dataset contains multiple data points with the same x, since changing the defender configuration frequently leads to too much overhead.

In addition, at the learning stage, only the observed feature values x matter because the attacker does not observe the actual feature values $\hat{x}$. The feasibility constraints $C(\hat{x}_{ik})$ on each feature still apply. Yet, they are irrelevant during learning because we use either historical data that satisfy these constraints, or honeypots for which these constraints are vacuous.

To analyze the sample complexity of learning the adversary's preferences, we focus on the classical form score function f in Eq. (1). We show that, in an FDP with m features, the defender can learn the attacker's behavior model correctly with high probability, using only m observed feature configurations and a polynomial number of samples. We view this condition as very mild, because even if the network admin's historical dataset does not meet the requirement, she could set up a honeynet to elicit attacks, where she can control the feature configurations of each target [30]. It is still not free for the defender to change configurations, but attacks on honeynet do not lead to actual loss since it runs in parallel with the production network.

To capture the multiple features in FDP, we introduce the *inverse feature difference matrix* $(A^{st})^{-1}$. Specifically, given observed feature configurations $x^1, \ldots, x^m$, for any two targets $s, t \in N$, let A^{st} be the $m \times m$ matrix whose (i, j)-entry is $a_{ij}^{st} = x_{sj}^i - x_{tj}^i$. A^{st} captures the matrix-level correlation among feature configurations. We use the matrix norm of $(A^{st})^{-1}$ to bound the learning error.

For feature configuration x, let $D^x(t) = \frac{f(x_t)}{\sum_{i \in N} f(x_i)}$ be the attack probability on target t. We assume $\rho := \min_{x,t} D^x(t) > 0$. Let $\alpha = \min_{s \neq t} ||(A^{st})^{-1}||$, where $|| \cdot ||$ is the matrix norm induced by the L^1 vector norm, i.e. $||(A^{st})^{-1}|| = \sup_{y \neq 0} \frac{|(A^{st})^{-1}y|}{|y|}$. Our result is stated as the following theorem.

Theorem 1. *Consider m observed feature configurations $x^1, x^2, \ldots, x^m \in [0,1]^{mn}$. With $\Omega(\frac{\alpha^4 m^4}{\rho \epsilon^2} \log \frac{nm}{\delta})$ samples for each of the m feature configurations, with probability $1 - \delta$, we can learn a score function $\hat{f}(\cdot)$ with uniform multiplicative error ϵ of the true $f(\cdot)$, i.e., $\frac{1}{1+\epsilon} \leq \frac{f(x_i)}{\hat{f}(x_i)} \leq 1 + \epsilon, \forall x_i$.*

Proof. Let $\hat{D}^x(t) = \frac{\hat{f}(x_t)}{\sum_{i \in N} \hat{f}(x_i)}$. We leverage a known result from behavioral game theory [8]. It cannot be directly translated to sample complexity guarantee in FDP because of the correlation among feature configurations, but we use it to reason about attack probabilities in proving Theorem 1.

Lemma 1. *[8] Given observable features $x \in [0,1]^{mn}$, and $\Omega(\frac{1}{\rho \epsilon^2} \log \frac{n}{\delta})$ samples, we have $\frac{1}{1+\epsilon} \leq \frac{\hat{D}^x(t)}{D^x(t)} \leq 1 + \epsilon$ with probability $1 - \delta$, for all $t \in N$.*

Fix $\epsilon, \delta > 0$. From Eq. (1), for each x^i where $i = 1, 2, \ldots, m$, we have

$$\sum_{j=1}^m w_j(x_{sj}^i - x_{tj}^i) = \ln \frac{D^{x^i}(s)}{D^{x^i}(t)}, \quad \forall s, t \in N, s \neq t$$

Let

$$b^{st} = (\ln \frac{D^{x^1}(s)}{D^{x^1}(t)}, \dots, \ln \frac{D^{x^m}(s)}{D^{x^m}(t)})^T.$$

The system of equations above can be represented by $A^{st}w = b^{st}$. It is known that $\|A^{st}\| = \max_{1 \le j \le m} \sum_{i=1}^{m} |a_{ij}^{st}|$. In our case, the feature values are bounded in $[0,1]$ and thus $|a_{ij}^{st}| \le 1$. This yields $\|A^{st}\| \le m$. Now, choose s, t such that $\|(A^{st})^{-1}\| = \alpha$. Suppose A^{st} is invertible.

Let $\epsilon' = \frac{\epsilon}{4\alpha^2 m^2}$ and $\delta' = \frac{\delta}{m}$. Suppose we have $\Omega(\frac{1}{p\epsilon'^2} \log \frac{n}{\delta'})$ samples. From Lemma 1, for any node $r \in N$ and any feature configuration x^i where $i = 1, 2, \dots, m$, $\frac{1}{1+\epsilon'} \le \frac{\hat{D}^{x^i}(r)}{D^{x^i}(r)} \le 1 + \epsilon'$ with probability $1 - \delta'$. The bound holds for all strategies simultaneously with probability at least $1 - m\delta' = 1 - \delta$, using a union bound argument. In particular, for our chosen nodes s and t, we have

$$\frac{1}{(1+\epsilon')^2} \le \frac{\hat{D}^{x^i}(s)}{\hat{D}^{x^i}(t)} \frac{D^{x^i}(t)}{D^{x^i}(s)} \le (1+\epsilon')^2, \quad \forall i = 1, \dots, m$$

Define $\hat{b}^{st}$ similarly as b^{st} but using empirical distribution $\hat{D}$ instead of true distribution D. Let $e = \hat{b}^{st} - b^{st}$. Then, for each $i = 1, \dots, m$, we have

$$-2\epsilon' \le 2\ln \frac{1}{1+\epsilon'} \le e_i = \ln \frac{\hat{D}^{x^i}(s) D^{x^i}(t)}{\hat{D}^{x^i}(t) D^{x^i}(s)} \le 2\ln(1+\epsilon') \le 2\epsilon'$$

Therefore, we have $|e| \le 2\epsilon'm$. Let $\hat{w}$ be such that $A^{st}\hat{w} = \hat{b}^{st}$, i.e. $\hat{w} - w = (A^{st})^{-1}e$. Observe that

$$\frac{|(A^{st})^{-1}e|/|(A^{st})^{-1}b^{st}|}{|e|/|b^{st}|} \le \max_{\tilde{e}, \tilde{b}^{st} \ne 0} \frac{|(A^{st})^{-1}\tilde{e}|/|(A^{st})^{-1}\tilde{b}^{st}|}{|\tilde{e}|/|\tilde{b}^{st}|}$$

$$= \max_{\tilde{e} \ne 0} \frac{|(A^{st})^{-1}\tilde{e}|}{|\tilde{e}|} \max_{\tilde{b}^{st} \ne 0} \frac{|\tilde{b}^{st}|}{|(A^{st})^{-1}\tilde{b}^{st}|} = \max_{\tilde{e} \ne 0} \frac{|(A^{st})^{-1}\tilde{e}|}{|\tilde{e}|} \max_{y \ne 0} \frac{|A^{st}y|}{|y|} = \|(A^{st})^{-1}\| \cdot \|A^{st}\|$$

This leads to

$$|(A^{st})^{-1}e| \le \|(A^{st})^{-1}\| \cdot \|A^{st}\| \cdot |e| \cdot \frac{|(A^{st})^{-1}b^{st}|}{|b^{st}|}$$

$$\le \|(A^{st})^{-1}\| \cdot \|A^{st}\| \cdot |e| \cdot \max_{\tilde{b}^{st} \ne 0} \frac{|(A^{st})^{-1}\tilde{b}^{st}|}{|\tilde{b}^{st}|}$$

$$= \|(A^{st})^{-1}\|^2 \cdot \|A^{st}\| \cdot |e| \le \alpha^2 m(2\epsilon'm)$$

For any observable feature configuration x,

$$\left| \left(\sum_{j=1}^{m} w_j x_{ij} \right) - \left(\sum_{j=1}^{m} \hat{w}_j x_{ij} \right) \right| \le \sum_{j=1}^{m} |\hat{w}_j - w_j| = |(A^{st})^{-1}e| \le \alpha^2 m(2\epsilon'm) = \frac{\epsilon}{2}$$

Therefore,

$$\frac{1}{1+\epsilon} \le \frac{f(x_i)}{\hat{f}(x_i)} \le 1+\epsilon.$$

$\square$

It is easy to see that we do not have to use the same pair of targets (s,t) for every feature configuration. In fact, this result can be easily adapted to allow for each feature configuration being implemented on a different system with a different set and number of targets. Instead of defining A^{st} and b^{st}, we could define A and b, where row i of A and i-th entry of b correspond to feature configuration x^i and targets (s^i, t^i). If feature configuration x^i is implemented on a system with n_i targets, we need $\Omega(\frac{1}{\rho\epsilon'^2} \log \frac{n_i}{\delta'})$ samples from this system, and then the argument above still holds.

The α in Theorem 1 need not be large, especially if the defender can select the feature configurations to collect data and elicit preferences. Consider a sequence of m feature configurations $x^1, \ldots, x^m$, and focus on targets 1 and 2. For each x^j, let the features on target 1 be identical to target 2, except for the j-th feature, where $x^j_{1j} = 1$ and $x^j_{2j} = 0$. This leads to $A^{12} = I$, and $\alpha \le 1$. This also shows that it is not hard to set up the configurations such that A^{st} is nonsingular.

An adversary who is aware of the defender's learning procedure might sometimes intentionally attack without following his true score function f, to mislead the defender. The following theorem states that the defender can still learn an approximately correct f even if the attacker contaminates a γ fraction of the data.

Theorem 2. *In the setting of Theorem 1, if the attacker modifies a $\gamma \le \frac{\epsilon\rho}{4\alpha m}$ fraction of the data points for each feature configuration, the function f can be learned within multiplicative error 3ϵ.*

Proof. Fix two nodes s, t. Recall that in Theorem 1, without data poisoning, we learned the weights w by solving the linear equations $A^{st}\tilde{w} = \tilde{b}^{st}$ based on the empirical distribution of attacks, where $\tilde{b}^{st} = (\ln \frac{\tilde{D}^{x^1}(s)}{\tilde{D}^{x^1}(t)}, \ldots, \ln \frac{\tilde{D}^{x^m}(s)}{\tilde{D}^{x^m}(t)}).$[2] Denote a parallel system of equations $A^{st}\hat{w} = \hat{b}^{st}$ which uses the poisoned data. We are interested in bounding $|\hat{w} - \tilde{w}| = |(A^{st})^{-1}(\hat{b}^{st} - \tilde{b}^{st})|$. Consider the k-th entry in the vector $\hat{b}^{st} - \tilde{b}^{st}$:

$$|(\hat{b}^{st} - \tilde{b}^{st})_k| = \left| \ln \frac{\hat{D}^{x^k}(s)}{\hat{D}^{x^k}(t)} \frac{\tilde{D}^{x^k}(t)}{\tilde{D}^{x^k}(s)} \right|$$

To simplify the notations, we denote $\tilde{D}^{x^k}(t) = \gamma^k_t$ and $\tilde{D}^{x^k}(s) = \gamma^k_s$, and without loss of generality, assume $\gamma^k_t \le \gamma^k_s$. To find an upper bound of RHS of the above equation, we define function $g(\gamma_1, \gamma_2) = \frac{\gamma^k_t(\gamma^k_s + \gamma_1)}{\gamma^k_s(\gamma^k_t - \gamma_2)}$, and define function $h(\gamma_1, \gamma_2) = |\ln g(\gamma_1, \gamma_2)|$. The constraint that the attacker can only change γ fraction of the points translates into $|\gamma_1|, |\gamma_2|, |\gamma_1 - \gamma_2| \le \gamma$. Since g is increasing

---

[2] Refer to the proof of Theorem 1 for the notations used.

in γ_1 and γ_2, g attains maximum at $(\gamma_1, \gamma_2) = (\gamma, \gamma)$ and minimum at $(\gamma_1, \gamma_2) = (-\gamma, -\gamma)$, which are the only two possible maxima of h. Observe that $g(\gamma, \gamma) \geq 1$ and $g(-\gamma, -\gamma) \leq 1$. It then suffices to compare $g(\gamma, \gamma)$ with $1/g(-\gamma, -\gamma)$:

$$\frac{1/g(-\gamma, -\gamma)}{g(\gamma, \gamma)} = \frac{\gamma_s(\gamma_t + \gamma)}{\gamma_t(\gamma_s - \gamma)} \frac{\gamma_s(\gamma_t - \gamma)}{\gamma_t(\gamma_s + \gamma)} = \frac{\gamma_s^2 \gamma_t^2 - \gamma_s^2 \gamma^2}{\gamma_t^2 \gamma_s^2 - \gamma_t^2 \gamma^2} \leq 1$$

Therefore, $h(\gamma_1, \gamma_2)$ is maximized at $(\gamma_1, \gamma_2) = (\gamma, \gamma)$. From here, we obtain

$$|(\hat{b}^{st} - \tilde{b}^{st})_k| \leq \ln \frac{(\gamma_s^k + \gamma)\gamma_t^k}{(\gamma_t^k - \gamma)\gamma_s^k} = \ln\left(\left(1 + \frac{\gamma}{\gamma_s^k}\right)\left(1 + \frac{\gamma}{\gamma_t^k - \gamma}\right)\right) \leq \frac{\gamma}{\gamma_s^k} + \frac{\gamma}{\gamma_t^k - \gamma}.$$

Recall that

$$\frac{\left|(A^{st})^{-1}(\hat{b}^{st} - \tilde{b}^{st})\right|}{\left|\hat{b}^{st} - \tilde{b}^{st}\right|} \leq \sup_{y \neq 0} \frac{|(A^{st})^{-1} y|}{|y|} = \|(A^{st})^{-1}\| = \alpha$$

Thus, we get

$$|\hat{w} - \tilde{w}| = |(A^{st})^{-1}(\hat{b}^{st} - \tilde{b}^{st})| \leq \alpha \left|\hat{b}^{st} - \tilde{b}^{st}\right| \leq \alpha \sum_{k=1}^{m} \left(\frac{\gamma}{\gamma_s^k} + \frac{\gamma}{\gamma_t^k - \gamma}\right)$$

Note that by Lemma 1, we have $\gamma_t^k \geq \frac{\rho}{1+\epsilon'} \geq \frac{\rho}{2}$. Since we assumed that $\gamma \leq \frac{\epsilon\rho}{4\alpha m} \leq \frac{\epsilon\rho}{4}$, we know that $\gamma \leq \gamma_t/2$. Thus, we get

$$|\hat{w} - \tilde{w}| \leq \alpha \sum_{k=1}^{m} \left(\frac{\gamma}{\gamma_s^k} + \frac{2\gamma}{\gamma_t^k}\right) \leq \frac{3\epsilon(1 + \epsilon')}{4} \leq \frac{3}{4}\epsilon\left(1 + \frac{1}{4}\epsilon\right)$$

From here, using the triangle inequality, we have

$$|\hat{w} - w| \leq |\hat{w} - \tilde{w}| + |\tilde{w} - w| \leq \frac{3}{4}\epsilon\left(1 + \frac{1}{4}\epsilon\right) + \frac{\epsilon}{2} \leq \frac{3}{2}\epsilon$$

Thus, in the end, we get

$$\frac{1}{1 + 3\epsilon} \leq \frac{f(x_i)}{\hat{f}(x_i)} \leq 1 + 3\epsilon.$$

$\square$

For a general score function f_w, gradient-based optimizers such as RMSProp can be applied to learn w through maximum-likelihood estimation.

$$w = \arg\max_{w'} \sum_{j \in [d]} \left[L_{w'}^j(N^j, x^j, y^j)\right]$$

$$L_{w'}^j(N^j, x^j, y^j) = \log(f_{w'}(x_{y^j}^j)) - \log\left(\sum_{i \in N^j} f_{w'}(x_i^j)\right)$$

However, it is not guaranteed to find the optimal solution given the non-convexity of L.

4   Computing the Optimal Feature Configuration

We now embark on our second task: assuming the (learned) adversary's behavior model, compute the optimal observed feature configuration to minimize the defender's expected loss. For any score function, the problem can be formulated as the following mathematical program (MP).

$$\min_x \quad \frac{\sum_{i \in N} f(x_i) u_i}{\sum_{i \in N} f(x_i)} \tag{2}$$

$$s.t. \quad \sum_{i \in N} \sum_{k \in M} \eta_{ik} |x_{ik} - \hat{x}_{ik}| \leq B \tag{3}$$

$$\text{Categorical feature constraints} \tag{4}$$

$$x_{ik} \in C(\hat{x}_{ik}) \qquad \forall i \in N, k \in M \tag{5}$$

This MP is typically non-convex and very difficult to solve. We show that the decision version of FDP is NP-complete. Hence, finding the optimal feature configuration is NP-hard. In fact, this holds even when there is only a single binary feature and the score function f takes the form in Eq. (1).

Theorem 3. *FDP is NP-complete.*

Proof. We reduce from the Knapsack problem: given $v \in [0,1]^n$, $\omega \in \mathbb{R}_+^n$, $\Omega, V \in \mathbb{R}_+$, decide whether there exists $y \in \{0,1\}^n$ such that $\sum_{i=1}^n v_i y_i \geq V$ and $\sum_{i=1}^n \omega_i y_i \leq \Omega$.

We construct an instance of FDP. Let the set of targets be $N = \{1, \ldots, n+1\}$, and let there be a single binary feature, i.e. $M = \{1\}$ and $x_{i1} \in \{0,1\}$ for each $i \in N$. Since there is only one feature, we abuse the notation by using $x_i = x_{i1}$. Suppose each target's actual value of the feature is $\hat{x}_i = 0$. Consider a score function f with $f(0) = 1$ and $f(1) = 2$. For each $i \in N$, let $u_i = (1 - v_i)/\delta$ if $i \neq n+1$, and $u_{n+1} = (1 + V + \sum_{i=1}^n v_i)/\delta$. Choose a large enough $\delta \geq 1$ so that $u_{n+1} \leq 1$. For each $i \in N$, let $\eta_i = \omega_i$ if $i \neq n+1$, and $\eta_{n+1} = 0$. Finally, let the budget $B = \Omega$.

For a solution y to a Knapsack instance, we construct a solution x to the above FDP where $x_i = y_i$ for $i \neq n+1$, and $x_{n+1} = 0$. We know $\sum_{i \in N} \eta_i |x_i - \hat{x}_i| = \sum_{i \in N} \eta_i x_i \leq B$ if and only if $\sum_{i=1}^n \omega_i y_i \leq \Omega$. Since $f(x_i) > 0$ for all x_i, $\frac{\sum_{i \in N} f(x_i) u_i}{\sum_{i \in N} f(x_i)} \leq 1/\delta$ if and only if $\sum_{i \in N} (1 - \delta u_i) f(x_i) \geq 0$. Note that $\sum_{i \in N} (1 - \delta u_i) = \sum_{i=1}^n v_i (y_i + 1) - \sum_{i=1}^n v_i - V$. Thus, y is a certificate of Knapsack if and only if x is feasible for FDP and the defender's expected loss is at most $1/\delta$. $\square$

Despite the negative results for the general case, we design an approximation algorithm for the classical score function in Eq. (1) based on mixed integer linear programming (MILP) enhanced with binary search. As shown in Sect. 5, it can solve medium sized problems (up to 200 targets) efficiently. Given $f(x_i) = \exp(\sum_{k \in M} w_k x_{ik})$, scaling the score by a factor of e^{-W} does not affect the attack probability, where $W = |w|$ is the L^1 norm of $w = (w_1, \ldots, w_m)$. Thus, we treat the score function as $f(x_i) = \exp(\sum_{k \in M} w_k x_{ik} - W)$.

With slight abuse of notation, we denote the score of target i as f_i. Let $z_i = \sum_{k \in M} w_k x_{ik} - W \in [-2W, 0]$. We divide the interval $[-2W, 0]$ into $2W/\epsilon$ subintervals, each of length ϵ. On interval $[-l\epsilon, -(l-1)\epsilon]$ with $l = 0, 1, \ldots, 2W/\epsilon$, we approximate the function e^{z_i} with the line segment of slope γ_l connecting the points $(-l\epsilon, e^{-l\epsilon})$ and $(-(l-1)\epsilon, e^{-(l-1)\epsilon})$. We use this method to approximate f_i in the following mathematical program $\mathcal{MP}1$. We represent $z_i = -\sum_l z_{il}$, where each variable z_{il} indicates the quantity z_i takes up on the interval $[-l\epsilon, -(l-1)\epsilon]$. The constraints in Eqs. (9)–(10) ensure that $z_{i(l+1)} > 0$ only if $z_{il} = \epsilon$. While $\mathcal{MP}1$ is not technically a MILP, we can linearize the objective and the constraint involving absolute value following a standard procedure [31]. The full MILP formulation can be found in the full arXiv version of the paper.[3]

$$(\mathcal{MP}1) \quad \min_{f, z, x, y} \quad \frac{\sum_i f_i u_i}{\sum_i f_i} \tag{6}$$

$$\text{s.t.} \quad f_i = e^{-2W} + \sum_l \gamma_l (\epsilon - z_{il}), \quad \forall i \in N \tag{7}$$

$$\sum_{k \in M} w_k x_{ik} - W = -\sum_l z_{il}, \quad \forall i \in N \tag{8}$$

$$\epsilon y_{il} \leq z_{il}, z_{i(l+1)} \leq \epsilon y_{il}, \quad \forall l, \forall i \in N \tag{9}$$

$$z_{il} \in [0, \epsilon], y_{il} \in \{0, 1\}, \quad \forall l, \forall i \in N$$

$$\text{Constraints } (3) - (5) \tag{10}$$

We can now establish the following bound.

Theorem 4. *Given $\epsilon < 1$, the MILP is a $2\epsilon^2$-approximation to the original problem.*

Proof. To analyze the approximation bound of this MILP, we first need to analyze the tightness of the linear approximation. Consider two points s_1, s_2 where $s_2 - s_1 = \epsilon$. The line segment is $t(s) = \frac{1}{\epsilon}(e^{s_2} - e^{s_1})s - \frac{1}{\epsilon}(e^{s_2} - e^{s_1})s_1 + e^{s_1}$. Let $\Delta(s)$ be the ratio between the line and e^s on the interval $[s_1, s_2]$. Note that $\Delta(s)$ is maximized at

$$s^* = 1 + s_1 - \frac{\epsilon}{e^\epsilon - 1}, \qquad \text{with} \quad \Delta(s^*) = \frac{\frac{e^\epsilon - 1}{\epsilon}}{\exp\{1 - \frac{\epsilon}{e^\epsilon - 1}\}}.$$

Now, let $v = \frac{e^\epsilon - 1}{\epsilon}$. It is known that $v \in [1, 1 + \epsilon]$ when $\epsilon < 1.7$. Note that $\delta(x^*) = v \exp\{\frac{1}{v} - 1\} \leq 1 + (v - 1)^2/2$, which holds for all $v \geq 1$. Let $\hat{f}(\cdot)$ be the piecewise linear approximation. For any target i and observable feature configuration x_i, we have

$$\frac{\hat{f}(x_i)}{f(x_i)} \leq v \leq 1 + \frac{\epsilon^2}{2}.$$

---

[3] The full version of the paper is available at https://arxiv.org/abs/1905.04833.

Let x^* be the optimal observable features against the true score function f, and let x' be the optimal observable features to the above MILP. Let $U(\cdot)$ be the defender's expected loss, and $\hat{U}(\cdot)$ be the approximate defender's expected loss. For any observable feature configuration x, we have

$$|\hat{U}(x) - U(x)| = \left| \frac{\sum_i \hat{f}(x_i)u_i}{\sum_i \hat{f}(x_i)} - \frac{\sum_i f(x_i)u_i}{\sum_i f(x_i)} \right|$$

$$= \left| \frac{\sum_i \hat{f}(x_i)u_i}{\sum_i \hat{f}(x_i)} - \frac{\sum_i \hat{f}(x_i)u_i}{\sum_i f(x_i)} + \frac{\sum_i \hat{f}(x_i)u_i}{\sum_i f(x_i)} - \frac{\sum_i f(x_i)u_i}{\sum_i f(x_i)} \right|$$

$$\leq \frac{2}{\sum_i f(x_i)} \left| \sum_i f(x_i) - \sum_i \hat{f}(x_i) \right| = 2 \left(\frac{\sum_i \hat{f}(x_i)}{\sum_i f(x_i)} - 1 \right) \leq \epsilon^2$$

Therefore, we obtain

$$U(x') - U(x^*) = U(x') - \hat{U}(x') + \hat{U}(x') - U(x^*)$$

$$\leq U(x') - \hat{U}(x') + \hat{U}(x^*) - U(x^*) \leq 2\epsilon^2 \qquad \square$$

While $\mathcal{MP}1$ could be transformed into a MILP, the necessary linearization introduces many additional variables, increasing the size of the problem. To improve scalability, we perform binary search on the objective value δ. Specifically, the objective at each iteration of the binary search becomes

$$\min_{f,z,x,y} \quad \sum_i f_i u_i - \delta \sum_i f_i. \tag{11}$$

At each iteration, if the objective value of Eq. (11) is negative, we update the binary search upper bound, and update the lower bound if positive. We proceed to the next iteration until the gap between the bounds is smaller than tolerance ϵ_{bs} and then we output the solution x^{bs} when the upper bound was last updated. The complete procedure is given as Algorithm 1. Since Eq. (11) is linear itself, we no longer need to perform linearization on it to obtain a MILP. This leads to significant speedup as we show later. We also preserve the approximation bound using triangle inequalities.

Algorithm 1: MILP-BS

---

1 Initialize $L = -1, U = 1, \delta = 0, \epsilon_{bs}$
2 **while** $U - L > \epsilon_{bs}$ **do**
3 $\quad$ Solve the MILP $\mathcal{MP}1$ with objective in Eq. 11.
4 $\quad$ **if** *objective value* < 0 **then**
5 $\quad\quad \lfloor$ Let $U = \delta$
6 $\quad$ **else**
7 $\quad\quad \lfloor$ Let $L = \delta$

8 **return** U, the MILP solution when U was last updated.

Theorem 5. *Given $\epsilon < 1$ and tolerance ϵ_{bs}, binary search gives a $(2\epsilon^2 + \epsilon_{bs})$-approximation.*

Proof. Suppose binary search terminates with interval of length $U - L \leq \epsilon_{bs}$, and observable features x^{bs}. Both x^{bs} and the optimal observable features x' to the MILP lie in this interval. This means $U(x^{bs}, \tilde{f}) - U(x', \tilde{f}) \leq \epsilon_{bs}$. Recall that x^* is the optimal observable features against the true score function f. Therefore, we have

$$
\begin{aligned}
U(x^{bs}, f) - U(x^*, f) &= U(x^{bs}, f) - U(x^{bs}, \tilde{f}) + U(x^{bs}, \tilde{f}) - U(x^*, f) \\
&\leq U(x^{bs}, f) - U(x^{bs}, \tilde{f}) + U(x', \tilde{f}) + \epsilon_{bs} - U(x^*, f) \\
&\leq U(x^{bs}, f) - U(x^{bs}, \tilde{f}) + U(x^*, \tilde{f}) + \epsilon_{bs} - U(x^*, f) \\
&\leq 2\epsilon^2 + \epsilon_{bs}
\end{aligned}
$$

$\square$

Now, we connect the learning and planning results together. Suppose we learned an approximate score function $\hat{f}$ (Theorem 1), and we find an approximately optimal feature configuration (Theorem 4) assuming $\hat{f}$. The following result shows that we can still guarantee end-to-end approximate optimality.

Theorem 6. *Suppose for some $\epsilon \leq 1/4$, $\frac{1}{1+\epsilon} < \frac{\hat{f}(x_i)}{f(x_i)} < 1 + \epsilon$ for all x_i. Then, $|U(x, \hat{f}) - U(x, f)| \leq 4\epsilon$ for all x. Let $x^* = \arg\min_x U(x, f)$ and x'' be such that $U(x'', \hat{f}) \leq \min_x U(x, \hat{f}) + \eta$, then $U(x'', f) - U(x^*, f) \leq 8\epsilon + \eta$.*

Proof. Let $\hat{f}(x_i) = \exp(\sum_k \hat{w}_k x_{ik})$ and $f(x_i) = \exp(\sum_k w_k x_{ik})$. Since

$$
\frac{1}{1+\epsilon} < \frac{\hat{f}(x_i)}{f(x_i)} < 1 + \epsilon,
$$

we get

$$
-\epsilon \leq -\ln(1+\epsilon) < \sum_k (\hat{w}_k - w_k)x_{ik} = \ln \frac{\hat{f}(x_i)}{f(x_i)} < \ln(1+\epsilon) \leq \epsilon.
$$

That is, $|\sum_k (\hat{w}_k - w_k)x_{ik}| < \epsilon$. The proof of Theorem 3.7 in [8] now follows to prove the first part of Theorem 6 if we redefine their $u_i(p_i)$ as $\sum_{k \in M} w_k x_{ik}$ and $\hat{u}_i(p_i)$ as $\sum_{k \in M} \hat{w}_k x_{ik}$. For completeness, we adapt their proof below using our notations.

As defined in Sect. 3, $D^x(t) = \frac{f(x_t)}{\sum_i f(x_i)}$ and $\hat{D}^x(t) = \frac{\hat{f}(x_t)}{\sum_i \hat{f}(x_i)}$. We have

$$
\begin{aligned}
\left| \ln \frac{\hat{D}^x(t)}{D^x(t)} \right| &= \left| \left(\sum_k (\hat{w}_k - w_k)x_{tk} \right) - \ln \frac{\sum_i \exp\{\sum_k \hat{w}_k x_{ik}\}}{\sum_i \exp\{\sum_k w_k x_{ik}\}} \right| \\
&\leq \left| \sum_k (\hat{w}_k - w_k)x_{tk} \right| + \left| \ln \frac{\sum_i \exp\{\sum_k w_k x_{ik}\} \exp\{\sum_k (\hat{w}_k - w_k)x_{ik}\}}{\sum_i \exp\{\sum_k w_k x_{ik}\}} \right| \\
&< \epsilon + \max_i \left| \ln \exp\{\sum_k (\hat{w}_k - w_k)x_{ik}\} \right| < 2\epsilon
\end{aligned}
$$

Using a few inequalities we can bound $\left|\frac{\hat{D}^x(t)}{D^x(t)} - 1\right| \le 4\epsilon$. This leads to, for all x,

$$|U(x, \hat{f}) - U(x, f)| = \left|\sum_{i \in N}(\hat{D}^x(i) - D^x(i))u_i\right| \le \sum_{i \in N}\left|\hat{D}^x(i) - D^x(i)\right||u_i|$$

$$= \sum_{i \in N}\left|\frac{\hat{D}^x(i)}{D^x(i)} - 1\right||u_i|\, D^x(i) \le 4\epsilon \sum_{i \in N}|u_i|\, D^x(i) \le 4\epsilon \max_{i \in N}|u_i| \le 4\epsilon$$

Let $x^* = \arg\min_x U(x, f)$ be the true optimal feature configuration, $x' = \arg\min_x U(x, \hat{f})$ be the optimal configuration using the learned score function $\hat{f}$, and x'' be an approximate optimal configuration against $\hat{f}$, i.e., $U(x'', \hat{f}) \le U(x', \hat{f}) + \eta$. We have

$$U(x'', f) \le U(x'', \hat{f}) + 4\epsilon \le U(x', \hat{f}) + 4\epsilon + \eta \le U(x^*, \hat{f}) + 4\epsilon + \eta \le U(x^*, f) + 8\epsilon + \eta.$$

□

In addition, we propose two exact algorithms for special cases of FDP, which can be found in the arXiv version. When the deception cost is associated with discrete features only, we provide an exact MILP formulation. When there is no budget and feasibility constraints, we can find the optimal defender strategy in $O(n \log n + m)$ time using a greedy algorithm. Inspired by this greedy algorithm, we introduce a greedy heuristic for the general case. GREEDY (Algorithm 2 in the arXiv version) finds the feature vectors that maximize and minimize the score, respectively, using gradient descent-based algorithm. It then greedily applies these features to targets of extreme losses. We show its performance in the following section as well.

5   Experiments

We present the experimental results for our learning and planning algorithms separately, and then combine them to demonstrate the effectiveness of our learning and planning framework. All experiments are carried out on a 3.8 GHz Intel Core i5 CPU with 32 GB RAM. We use Ipopt as our non-convex solver and CPLEX 12.8 as the MILP solver. All results are averaged over 20 instances; error bars represent standard deviations. Details about hyper-parameters can be found in the arXiv version of the paper.

5.1   Learning

Classical Score Function. First, we assume the adversary uses the classical score function in Eq. (1). The defender learns this score function using the closed-form estimation (CF) in Theorem 1. We study how the learning accuracy changes with the size of training sample d. We sample the parameters of the true score

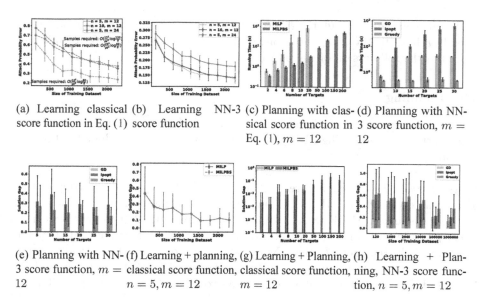

(a) Learning classical score function in Eq. (1) (b) Learning NN-3 score function (c) Planning with classical score function in Eq. (1), $m = 12$ (d) Planning with NN-3 score function, $m = 12$

(e) Planning with NN-3 score function, $m = 12$ (f) Learning + planning, classical score function, $n = 5, m = 12$ (g) Learning + Planning, classical score function, $m = 12$ (h) Learning + Planning, NN-3 score function, $n = 5, m = 12$

Fig. 1. Experimental results

function f uniformly at random from $[-0.5, 0.5]$. We then generate m feature configurations uniformly at random. For each of them, we sample the attacked target d/m times according to f, obtaining a training set of d samples. We generate a test set $\tilde{D}$ of 5×10^5 configurations sampled uniformly at random. We measure the learning error as the mean total variation distance between the attack distribution from the learned $\hat{f}$ and that of the true model f:

$$\frac{1}{|\tilde{D}|} \sum_{j=1}^{|\tilde{D}|} d_{TV}\left(\left(\frac{f(x_i^j)}{\sum_{t \in N} f(x_t^j)}\right)_{i \in N}, \left(\frac{\hat{f}(x_i^j)}{\sum_{t \in N} \hat{f}(x_t^j)}\right)_{i \in N}\right).$$

Figure 1a shows that the learning error decreases as we increase the number of samples. Theorem 1 provides a sample complexity bound, which we annotate in Fig. 1a as well. The experiment shows that we need much fewer samples to learn a relatively good score function, and smaller games exhibit smaller learning error.

3-layer NN Represented (NN-3) Score Function. We assume the adversary uses a 3-layer neural network score function, whose details are in the full version of the paper. We use the gradient descent-based (GD) learning algorithm RMSProp as described in Sect. 3, with learning rate 0.1. For each sample size d, we generate d feature configurations and sample an attacked target for each of them in the training set. Figure 1b shows GD can minimize the learning error to below 0.15. Note that the training data are different in Figs. 1a and b, thus the two figures are not directly comparable.

We also measured $|\hat{\theta}-\theta|$, the L_1 error in the score function parameter θ, which directly relates to the sample complexity bound in Theorem 1. We include the results in the full version of the paper.

5.2   Planning

We test our algorithms on finding the optimal feature configuration against a known attacker model. The FDP parameter distributions are included in the full version.

Classical Score Function. Figure 1c shows that the binary search version of the MILP based on $\mathcal{MP}1$ (MILPBS) runs faster than that without binary search on most instances. MILPBS scales up to problems with 200 targets, which is already at the scale of many real-world problems. MILP does not scale beyond problems with 20 targets. In the arXiv version, we show that MILPBS also scales better in terms of the number of features. We set the MILP's error bound at 0.005 and $\epsilon_{\mathrm{bs}} = 1e - 4$; the difference in the two algorithms' results is negligible.

NN-3 Score Function. When the features are continuous without feasibility constraints, planning becomes a non-convex optimization problem. We can apply the gradient-based optimizer or non-convex solver. Recall that $U(x)$ is the defender's expected loss using feature configuration x. We measure the solution gap of alg $\in$ {Ipopt, GD, GREEDY} as $\frac{U(x^{\mathrm{alg}})-U(x^{\mathrm{GD}})}{U(x^{\mathrm{GD}})}$, where x^{alg} is the solution from the corresponding algorithm.

Figures 1d and e show the running time and solution gap fixing $m = 12$. The running time of GD and GREEDY does not change much across different problem sizes, yet Ipopt runs slower than the former two on most problem instances. GD also has smaller solution gap than Ipopt and GREEDY. In the full version we show the number of features affect these metrics in a similar way.

5.3   Combining Learning and Planning

We integrate the learning and planning algorithms to examine our full framework. The defender learns a score function $\hat{f}$ using algorithm L. Then, she uses planning algorithm P to find an optimal configuration $x^{\mathrm{L,P}}$ assuming $\hat{f}$. We measure the solution gap as $\frac{U(x^{\mathrm{L,P}})-U(x^*)}{U(x^*)}$, where x^* is the optimal feature configuration against the true attacker model, computed using MILPBS or GD.

Classical Score Function. We test learning algorithm CF and planning algorithms P $\in$ {MILP, MILPBS}. Figure 1f shows how the solution gap changes with the size of the training dataset. With $n \leq 20$ targets, all algorithms yield solution gaps below 0.1 (Fig. 1g). The reader might note the overlapping error bars, which are expected since MILP and MILPBS should not differ much in solution quality. Indeed, the difference is negligible as the smallest p-value of the 6 paired t-tests (fixing the number of targets for which they are tested) is 0.16.

NN-3 Score Function. We test learning algorithm GD and planning algorithms P ∈ {GD, Ipopt, GREEDY}. Figure 1h shows how the solution gap changes with the size of training dataset d. Paired t-tests suggest that GD has significantly smaller solution gap than GREEDY ($p < 0.03$) at each size of training dataset except 1080. Ipopt also has significantly smaller solution gap than GREEDY ($p < 0.01$) when on large datasets with $d \geq 10^5$ samples. On the largest dataset $d = 10^6$, GD also performs significantly better than Ipopt ($p = 0.04$).

Compared to the case with classical score functions, more data are required here to achieve a small solution gap. Since learning error is small for both cases (Figs. 1a, b), this suggests planning is more sensitive to NN-3 score functions than classical score functions.

5.4   Case Study: Credit Bureau Network

The financial sector is a major victim of cyber attacks due to its large amount of valuable information and relatively low level of security measures. In this case study, we ground our FDP model in a credit bureau's network. We show how feature deception improves the network security when the attacker follows a domain-specific rule-based behavioral model.

We note that the purpose of this case study is not to show the scalability of our algorithm: all previous experiments fulfill that purpose. Instead, here we demonstrate why deception is useful, how our algorithm yields deception strategies reasonable in the real world, and how our algorithm capably handles an attacker which does not conform to our assumed score function.

As shown in Table 2, we consider a network of 10 nodes (i.e. targets) with 6 binary features: operating system (Windows/Linux) and the availability of SMTP, NetBIOS, HTTP, SQL, and Samba services. Each node has a type of server running on it, which determines the features available on that node. Some nodes would incur a high loss if attacked, like the database servers, because for a credit bureau the safety of users' credit information is of utmost importance. Others might incur a low loss, such as the mail servers and the web server. Nodes of the same type might lead to different losses. For example, some database servers might have access to more information than others. Each feature has different switching cost c_k. For the operating system, the cost is $c_k = 5$. For SQL, Samba, and HTTP services, the cost is 2. The cost is 1 for others. The defender has a budget of 10. There is no constraint on switching each individual feature, i.e. $C(\hat{x}_{ik}) = \{0, 1\}$. However, we impose that Windows + Samba and Linux + NetBIOS cannot be present on the same node, as it is technically impossible to do so.

We demonstrate the entire learning and planning pipeline. We use an attacker's behavior model common in the security analysis. The attacker cares about a subset $M' \subseteq M$ of the features, and we call each such feature $k \in M'$ a requirement. The attack is uniformly randomized among the targets that satisfy the most requirements. Although this decision rule does not fit our classical score function, we can approximate it by giving large weights w_k to the requirement features, and 0 to the rest.

Table 2. Feature configuration of a typical credit bureau computer network.

Node type	Node ID	Actual features $\hat{x}_i$	Loss u_i
Mail server	0, 1	Windows, SMTP, NetBIOS	0.1
Web server	2	Windows, HTTP	0.2
App server	3, 4	Windows, SQL, NetBIOS	0.3
Database server	5,6,7	Linux, SQL, SMTP, Samba	0.4
Database server	8,9	Linux, SQL, SMTP, Samba	0.8

Table 3. Learning + planning results for 2 types of attackers.

Attacker	Solution x_i	Attacked nodes	Loss
APT	Node 1: Windows → Linux	5,6,7,8,9 →1 ,5, 6, 7	0.56 → 0.325
	Node 1: SQL off → on		
	Node 1: NetBIOS on → off		
	Node 8, 9: SMTP on → off		
Botnet	Node 3: NetBIOS on → off	0,1,3,4 →0,1	0.2 → 0.1
	Node 4: NetBIOS on → off		

First, we consider an APT-like attacker, who wants to exfiltrate data by exploiting the SMTP service. They have expertise in Linux systems and want to maintain a high degree of stealth. Thus, their decision rule is based on the three requirement features: Linux, SMTP, and SQL. Without deception, the attacker would randomize attack over nodes 5–9, because these nodes satisfy 3 requirements and other nodes satisfy at most 2. As shown in Table 3, the optimal solution for the learning and planning problem leads to an expected defender's loss of 0.325, which is a 42% decrease from the loss with no deception. With limited budget, the defender makes the least harmful target, node 1, very attractive and the most harmful targets, nodes 8 and 9, less attractive.

We also consider a botnet attacker, who wants to create a bot by exploiting the NetBIOS service. They have expertise in Windows and want to maintain a moderate degree of stealth. Thus, their decision rule is based on two requirement features: Windows and NetBIOS. The results in Table 3 shows that the defender should set the NetBIOS observed value to be off for nodes 3 and 4, attracting the attacker to the least harmful nodes. This reduces the defender's expected loss by 50% compared to not using deception.

6   Related Work

Deception. Deception has been studied in many domains, and of immediate relevance is its use in cybersecurity [26]. Studies have suggested that deceptively responding to an attacker's scanning and probing could be a useful defensive measure [2,12]. Schlenker et al. [27] and Wang and Zeng [32] propose game-theoretic models where the defender manipulates the query response to a known attacker. Proposing a domain-independent model, we advance the state of the art by (1) providing a unified learning and planning framework with theoretical guarantee which can deal with unknown attackers, (2) extending the finite "type" space in both papers, where "type" is defined by the combination of feature values, to an infinite feature space that allows for both continuous and discrete features, and (3) incorporating a highly expressive bounded rationality model whereas both papers assume perfectly rational attackers.

For the more general case, Horak et al. [9] study a defender that engages an attacker in a sequential interaction. A complementary view where the attacker aims at deceiving the defender is provided in [6,19]. Different from them, we assume no knowledge of the set of possible attacker types. In [6,7,19,35] deception is defined as deceptively allocating defensive resources. We study feature deception where no effective tools can thwart an attack, which is arguably more realistic in high-stakes interactions. When such tools exist, feature deception is still valuable for strategic defense.

Learning in Stackelberg Games. Much work has been devoted to learning in Stackelberg games. Our work is most directly related to that of Haghtalab et al. [8]. They show that three defender strategies are sufficient to learn a SUQR-like adversary behavior model in Stackelberg security games. The only decision variable in their model, the coverage probability, may be viewed as a single feature in FDP. FDP allows for an arbitrary number of features, and this realistic extension makes their key technique inapplicable for analyzing the sample complexity. Our main learning result also removes the technical constraints on defender strategies present in their work. Sinha et al. [29] study learning adversary's preferences in a probably approximately correct (PAC) setting. However, their learning accuracy depends heavily on the quality of distribution from which they sample the defender's strategies. We provide a uniform guarantee in a distribution-free context. Other papers [3,15,17,21] study the online learning setting with rational attackers. As pointed out in [8], considering the more realistic bounded rationality scenario allows us to make use of historical data and use our algorithm more easily in practice.

Planning with Boundedly Rational Attackers. Yang et al. [34] propose a MILP-based solution in security games. Our planning algorithm goes beyond the coverage probability and determines the configuration of multiple features, and adopt a more expressive behavior model. The subsequent papers that incorporate learning with such bounded rationality models do not provide any theoretical guarantee [5,33]. A recent work develops a learning and planning pipeline in security games [22]. However, their algorithm requires the defender know a priori some parameters in the attacker's behavior model, and provides no global optimality guarantee.

7   Discussion

We conclude with a few remarks regarding the generality and limitations of our work. First, our model allows the attacker to have knowledge of deception if the knowledge is built into their behavior. For example, the attacker avoids attacking a target because it is "too good to be true". This can be captured by a score function that assigns a low score for such a target.

Second, our model can handle sophisticated attackers who can outstrip deception. A singleton feasible set $C(\hat{x}_{ik})$ implies the defender knows the attacker can find out the actual value of a feature. As an important next step, we will study the change of attacker's belief of deception over repeated interactions.

Third, typically, actual features on functional targets are environmental parameters beyond the defender's control, or at least have high cost of manipulation. Altering them and defender's losses u_i does not align conceptually with deception. Thus, we treat them as fixed. For a target with no fixed actual values, e.g., a honeypot, the defender's cost is just the cost of configuring the feature, e.g., installing Windows. For consistency, we can set $\hat{x}_{ik}$ as the feature value with the lowest configuration cost, and η_{ik} is the additional cost for a different feature value.

Fourth, the attacker's preference might shift when there is a major change in security landscape, e.g. a new vulnerability disclosed. In such case, a proactive defender will recalibrate the system: recompute the attacker's model and reconfigure the features. Moreover, exactly because the defender has learned the preferences before the change using our algorithms, the defender now knows better what qualifies as a major change. Our algorithms are fast enough for a proactive defender to run regularly.

Fifth, when faced with a group of attackers, in FDP we learn an average behavioral model of the population. To handle multiple attacker types, one could refer to the literature on Bayesian Stackelberg games [20].

Finally, in FDP the defender uses only pure strategies. In many domains such as cybersecurity, frequent system reconfiguration is often too costly. Thus, the system appears static to the attacker. We leave to future work to explore mixed strategies in applications where they are appropriate.

Acknowledgments. This research was sponsored by the Combat Capabilities Development Command Army Research Laboratory and was accomplished under Cooperative Agreement Number W911NF-13-2-0045 (ARL Cyber Security CRA). The views and conclusions contained in this document are those of the authors and should not be interpreted as representing the official policies, either expressed or implied, of the Combat Capabilities Development Command Army Research Laboratory or the U.S. Government. The U.S. Government is authorized to reproduce and distribute reprints for Government purposes not withstanding any copyright notation here on.

References

1. Abbasi, Y., et al.: Know your adversary: insights for a better adversarial behavioral model. In: CogSci (2016)

2. Albanese, M., Battista, E., Jajodia, S.: Deceiving attackers by creating a virtual attack surface. In: Jajodia, S., Subrahmanian, V.S.S., Swarup, V., Wang, C. (eds.) Cyber Deception, pp. 169–201. Springer, Cham (2016). https://doi.org/10.1007/978-3-319-32699-3_8
3. Blum, A., Haghtalab, N., Procaccia, A.D.: Learning optimal commitment to overcome insecurity. In: NIPS (2014)
4. Chiang, C.Y.J., et al.: ACyDS: An adaptive cyber deception system. In: MILCOM (2016)
5. Fang, F., Stone, P., Tambe, M.: When security games go green: designing defender strategies to prevent poaching and illegal fishing. In: IJCAI (2015)
6. Gan, J., Xu, H., Guo, Q., Tran-Thanh, L., Rabinovich, Z., Wooldridge, M.: Imitative follower deception in Stackelberg games. In: EC (2019)
7. Guo, Q., An, B., Bosanský, B., Kiekintveld, C.: Comparing strategic secrecy and Stackelberg commitment in security games. In: IJCAI, pp. 3691–3699 (2017)
8. Haghtalab, N., Fang, F., Nguyen, T.H., Sinha, A., Procaccia, A.D., Tambe, M.: Three strategies to success: learning adversary models in security games. In: IJCAI (2016)
9. Horák, K., Zhu, Q., Bošanský, B.: Manipulating adversary's belief: a dynamic game approach to deception by design for proactive network security. In: Rass, S., An, B., Kiekintveld, C., Fang, F., Schauer, S. (eds.) GameSec 2017. Lecture Notes in Computer Science, vol. 10575, pp. 273–294. Springer, Cham (2017). https://doi.org/10.1007/978-3-319-68711-7_15
10. Hurlburt, G.: "Good enough" security: the best we'll ever have. Computer **49**, 98–101 (2016)
11. Jafarian, J.H., Al-Shaer, E., Duan, Q.: Openflow random host mutation: transparent moving target defense using software defined networking. In: Proceedings of the First Workshop on Hot Topics in Software Defined Networks. ACM (2012)
12. Jajodia, S., et al.: A probabilistic logic of cyber deception. IEEE Trans. Inf. Forensics Secur. **12**(11), 2532–2544 (2017)
13. Jajodia, S., Subrahmanian, V., Swarup, V., Wang, C.: Cyber Deception. Springer, Heidelberg (2016). https://doi.org/10.1007/978-3-319-32699-3
14. Latimer, J.: Deception in War. John Murray, London (2001)
15. Letchford, J., Conitzer, V., Munagala, K.: Learning and approximating the optimal strategy to commit to. In: Mavronicolas, M., Papadopoulou, V.G. (eds.) SAGT 2009. LNCS, vol. 5814, pp. 250–262. Springer, Heidelberg (2009). https://doi.org/10.1007/978-3-642-04645-2_23
16. Lyon, G.F.: Nmap network scanning: The Official Nmap Project Guide to Network Discovery and Security Scanning. Insecure (2009)
17. Marecki, J., Tesauro, G., Segal, R.: Playing repeated Stackelberg games with unknown opponents. In: AAMAS (2012)
18. Nakashima, E.: To thwart hackers, firms salting their servers with fake data (2013)
19. Nguyen, T.H., Wang, Y., Sinha, A., Wellman, M.P.: Deception in finitely repeated security games. In: AAAI (2019)
20. Paruchuri, P., Pearce, J.P., Marecki, J., Tambe, M., Ordonez, F., Kraus, S.: Playing games for security: an efficient exact algorithm for solving Bayesian Stackelberg games. In: AAMAS (2008)
21. Peng, B., Shen, W., Tang, P., Zuo, S.: Learning optimal strategies to commit to. In: AAAI (2019)
22. Perrault, A., Wilder, B., Ewing, E., Mate, A., Dilkina, B., Tambe, M.: Decision-focused learning of adversary behavior in security games. arXiv preprint arXiv:1903.00958 (2019)

23. Potter, B., Day, G.: The effectiveness of anti-malware tools. Comput. Fraud Secur. **2009**, 12–13 (2009)
24. Provos, N., et al.: A virtual honeypot framework. In: USENIX Security Symposium (2004)
25. PwC: Operation Cloud Hopper Technical Annex
26. Rowe, N.C.: Deception in defense of computer systems from cyber attack. In: Cyber Warfare and Cyber Terrorism. IGI Global (2007)
27. Schlenker, A., et al.: Deceiving cyber adversaries: a game theoretic approach. In: AAMAS (2018)
28. Shamsi, Z., Nandwani, A., Leonard, D., Loguinov, D.: Hershel: single-packet OS fingerprinting. ACM SIGMETRICS Perform. Eval. Rev. **42**, 195–206 (2014)
29. Sinha, A., Kar, D., Tambe, M.: Learning adversary behavior in security games: A pac model perspective. In: AAMAS (2016)
30. Spitzner, L.: The honeynet project: trapping the hackers. IEEE Secur. Priv. **1**, 15–23 (2003)
31. Stancu-Minasian, I.M.: Fractional Programming: Theory, Methods and Applications, vol. 409. Springer, Heidelberg (2012). https://doi.org/10.1007/978-94-009-0035-6
32. Wang, W., Zeng, B.: A two-stage deception game for network defense. In: GameSec (2018)
33. Yang, R., Ford, B., Tambe, M., Lemieux, A.: Adaptive resource allocation for wildlife protection against illegal poachers. In: AAMAS (2014)
34. Yang, R., Ordonez, F., Tambe, M.: Computing optimal strategy against quantal response in security games. In: AAMAS (2012)
35. Yin, Y., An, B., Vorobeychik, Y., Zhuang, J.: Optimal deceptive strategies in security games: a preliminary study. In: AAAI Symposium on Applied Computational Game Theory (2014)

A Realistic Approach for Network Traffic Obfuscation Using Adversarial Machine Learning

Alonso Granados[1](✉), Mohammad Sujan Miah[2], Anthony Ortiz[3], and Christopher Kiekintveld[2]

[1] University of Arizona, Tucson, AZ 85721, USA
alonsog@email.arizona.edu
[2] University of Texas at El Paso, El Paso, TX 79968, USA
msmiah@miners.utep.edu, cdkiekintveld@utep.edu
[3] Microsoft AI for Good Research Lab, Redmond, WA 98052, USA
anthony.ortiz@microsoft.com

Abstract. Adversaries are becoming more sophisticated and standard countermeasures such as encryption are no longer enough to prevent traffic analysis from revealing important information about a network. Advanced encryption techniques are intended to mitigate network information exposure, but they remain vulnerable to statistical analysis of traffic features. An adversary can classify different applications and protocols from the observable statistical properties, especially from the meta-data (e.g. packet size, timing, flow directions, etc.). Several approaches are already being developed to protect computer network infrastructure from attacks using traffic analysis, but none of them are fully effective. We investigate solutions based on obfuscating the patterns in network traffic to make it more difficult to accurately use classification to extract information such as protocols or applications in use. A key problem of using obfuscation methods is to determine an appropriate algorithm that introduces minimal changes but preserves the functionality of the protocol. We apply Adversarial Machine Learning techniques to find realistic small perturbations that can improve the security and privacy of a network against traffic analysis. We introduce a novel approach for generating adversarial examples that obtains state-of-the-art performance compared to previous approaches, while considering more realistic constraints on perturbations.

Keywords: Network data analysis · Data obfuscation · Adversarial machine learning

1 Introduction

Heterogeneous network structure and the growing complexity of the IT environment introduce new vulnerabilities to computer networks. One evolving

---

The first author attended The University of Texas at El Paso during this work.

© Springer Nature Switzerland AG 2020
Q. Zhu et al. (Eds.): GameSec 2020, LNCS 12513, pp. 45–57, 2020.
https://doi.org/10.1007/978-3-030-64793-3_3

technique is using statistical traffic analysis to perform reconnaissance. Though advanced encryption techniques limit the information available to traffic analysis, encrypted network traffic can still have observable characteristics like packet sizes and inter-arrival times that reveal useful information to attackers that is a potential threat for network security [4, 12]. Sophisticated adversaries possess knowledge about communication types and maintain databases of well-known traffic patterns and protocols such as UDP, TCP, VoIP, ESP, among others. From the raw traffic, an adversary can determine likely features of the of source/destination without needing to decrypt sensitive information. They can also distinguish statistical characteristics used for communication by different protocols. There are currently no perfect methods to prevent traffic analysis completely. One approach to alleviate this issue is based on deceiving attackers by generating and sending false network traffic along with real traffic, but this can lead to costly overhead.

Recently Deep Packet Inspection (DPI) has become a common technique used by the network administrators to match specific byte patterns from a known database and to update it when unknown patterns are found. However, manually maintaining and updating a dynamic database from the immense network flows is a very tedious task. Machine learning methodologies perform a vital role in classifying network traffic and update the database if required. Similarly, attackers use different network classifiers to identify various applications and protocols. The performance of the classifier depends on the accuracy of collected information. Network traffic obfuscation is a technique where network traffic is manipulated (e.g. add dummy bytes with the packets in order to increase packet size) to limit the attacker's gathering of information by causing errors in the classification models. This obfuscation approach is effective at reducing the risk of passive reconnaissance where an attacker gathers traffic and uses statistical analysis to categorize different patterns (e.g. protocols, applications, user's information, etc.). A major issue of this approach is to determine the optimal algorithm for masking the features of the traffic effectively, but within the constraints of feasible modifications and limited resources or network overhead.

We propose solving this problem using Adversarial Machine Learning (AML), where a defender seeks to protect the network from an adversary by finding realistic small perturbations that are added to the network traffic to reduce the accuracy of machine learning traffic classifiers. Our contributions are three-fold:

- We introduce the Restricted Traffic Distribution Attack (RTDA), an algorithm for realistic adversarial traffic generation that can be applied in real-world networks.
- Our attack achieves state-of-the-art performance compared to previous approaches.
- We calculate the average perturbation cost for a real system and provide a comparative analysis between our proposed approach and previous work.

2   Motivation and Related Work

There are numerous reasons why network administrators need to use traffic obfuscation. For example, sometimes various internet resources are inaccessible due to an unavoidable circumstance but an administrator may want to meet performance benchmarks by shaping the network traffic. Encryption and mimicry are two basic obfuscation methods but they can not remove fingerprints from meta-data (e.g packet size, inter-arrival timing, etc.). Therefore, an adversary can classify encrypted traffic based on statistical features including packet and payload byte counts [6,14]. Using mimicry it is possible to shape a protocol to look like another, but statistical fingerprints of meta-data are still preserved [6,22]. We consider several data obfuscation methods that can be applied to network traffic. Our goal is to find more robust solutions for network administrators or defender in performing statistical obfuscation while minimizing unnecessary overhead using Adversarial Machine Learning (AML).

Several previous articles have proposed network obfuscation systems. Encryption and adding padding in traffic features at a variety of levels such as ciphertext formats, stateful protocol semantics, and statistical properties are effective ways of preventing statistical traffic analysis [7,21]. Guan et al. [10] show that sending dummy traffic with real traffic (called packet padding) can manipulate an adversary's observation to a particular traffic pattern and efficiently camouflage network traffic. However, this approach is usually inefficient and sometimes incurs immense network overhead. Anjum et al. [1] use fake flows to invalidate passive reconnaissance of an adversary and also propose a non-zero-sum game-theoretic model to deploy fake flow optimally which potentially reduces network overhead and confuses adversaries in identifying network vulnerabilities. Another approach is to pad real packets to make them uniform size instead of creating a dummy packet, but it can also delay packet transmission. Wright et al. [25] proposes a convex optimization algorithm to modify real-time VoIP and WEB traffics which is optimal in terms of padding cost and reduces the accuracy of different classifiers. Later, Ciftcioglu et al. [4] propose a water-filling optimizing algorithm for optimal chaff-aided trafc obfuscation where packet morphing is performed by either chaff byte or chaff packet and show that the algorithm can maximize obfuscation given a chaff budget.

Machine learning techniques are quite common to classify the various types of IP traffics [16]. Bar-Yanai et al. [2] presents a classifier that is robust to the statistical classification of real-time encrypted traffic data. Mapping network traffic from different applications to the preselected class of services (COS) is still a challenging task. One approach uses predetermined statistical application signatures which are associated connections, sessions, application-layer protocols to determine COS class for particular datagrams [5,22]. Zander et al. [26] use unsupervised machine learning technique to classify unknown and encrypted network protocols where flows are classified based on their network characteristics. Though classification methods are effective for statistical traffic analysis, many machine learning algorithms are vulnerable to adversarial attacks. An attacker can generate adversarial samples by adding small perturbation to the original inputs intent to mislead machine learning models [8,9]. They can also train their own model with adversarial samples and transfer the samples to victim model in order to produces incorrect output by the victim classifier [25]. Currently, no method is effective against adversarial examples [11,17,19]. Papernot et al. [19] introduces adversarial sample crafting techniques that can exploit adversarial sample transferability across many of the machine learning space. There are also several mathematical and ML methods for crafting adversarial example which can exploit the gradient of the loss function or the target of classification [3,9,18,20,23]. Verma et al. [24] proposed several loss functions and the "Carlini-Wagner L_2" (also called CW) algorithm to craft network traffic using a post-processing operation to the generated distributions. However, the proposed approach sometimes created invalid perturbations and distributions for each attack that does not match real-world settings. In our work, we impose more generalized constraints in generating adversarial network traffic samples; we generate a valid perturbation and distribution for every test sample that results in a more robust attack compare to previous work.

3   Experimental Setup

This section describes the classification model and dataset, building on the previous work in [24]. In Sect. 5 we discuss our proposed approach in detail. Also, the Table 1 shows the important notations used in this paper.

Table 1. Important notations

Notations	Description
τ	Original traffic
τ_θ	Modified traffic
δ	Perturbation amount
f_θ	Classification model
ρ	Application class set
x	Feature vector
x^{adv}	Adversarial feature vector
L_p	Distance metric

3.1   Dataset

We perform experiments on the Internet Traffic Network dataset used in [15]. This dataset was generated by monitoring a research-facility host with 1000 users connected via Gigabit Ethernet link. The objects to classify are traffic flows that represent the flow of one or more packets between the host and client during a complete TCP connection. Each flow was manually classified. Table 2 shows the class information, flow types per class, and flow count. Similarly to [24], we only include the classes with at least 2000 samples in our training set.

Table 2. Class composition and number used in this work from the dataset.

Classification	Flow Type	Number
Bulk	FTP	11539
Database	postgres, sqlnet, oracle, ingres	2648
Mail	imap, pop2/3, smtp	28567
Services	X11, dns, ident, ldap, ntp	2099
P2P	KaZaA, BitTorrent, GnuTella	2094
WWW	www	328091

3.2   Realistic Features

Each sample is composed of 249 features that were observed during generation time. In a real time traffic transmission, the defender only has the capability to increase the size of the packets. Therefore, we do not use inter arrival time as a feature. Our work shows that only using packet size is sufficient to attack a network. We select the 0, 25, 50, 75, 100 percentiles of the IP packets sizes from both client-to-server and server-to-client. We normalized these features to the range $(0, 1)$.

3.3   Classification Model

We replicate the training approach and neural network model used in the previous work [24]. The training model is a 3-layer neural network with 300, 200, and 100 hidden units and applies a rectified linear function in every layer. We process the data by randomly dividing it into three datasets—5000 validation samples, 5000 test samples, and the remaining samples as training. Due to large class imbalance, we randomly sample the training set so every class has equal number of examples. We train the network using mini-batches of size 1000 for 300 epochs. The results are found in Table 3.

Table 3. Neural network accuracy per class.

Class	Accuracy
Bulk	95%
Database	97%
Mail	95%
P2P	96%
Service	85%
WWW	91%

4   Adversarial Settings

We now formalize the models for the defender and the attacker. We also discuss some well-known approaches for generating adversarial examples.

4.1   Defender Model

We model the problem by considering an adversarial setting where a defender (d) tries to protect a network from an adversary (α). The goal of α is to observe d's network and classify its traffic flows (τ) by using statistical analysis, while d disguises τ by changing features. The new modified flow τ_θ can potentially lead α to misclassify τ_θ as relating to a different application or protocol class (σ) rather than the true one (ρ). We consider that d knows the attacker model f and observations O for training that implies d is capable to create a substitute model f_θ for τ_θ. The transferability property of AML supports that any adversarial example that can fool a machine learning algorithm can also fool other machine learning algorithms irrespective of the implementation [19]. Therefore, d uses AML technique to find an optimal way for generating τ_θ by considering that the traffic recipient has mechanisms for inverting the changes. However, in adding perturbations d must adhere to the following constraints:

- Basic rules of a protocol must be preserved such as packet size and timing can not be the negative, minimum or maximum range of size, etc.
- The network is be constrained by performance benchmarks meaning that the network supports a maximum threshold of latency
- The AML model should use small input perturbations for creating τ_θ since large alteration of τ can break down basic protocols and incur unnecessary network overhead

4.2   Adversary Model

We assume that α observes a particular flow between a source and destination where the flow is always bidirectional. It also has the required tools to analyze meta statistical signatures (e.g. packet size) and trains its classifier f_θ based on these features — 0, 25, 50, 75, 100 percentiles of the IP packets in both directions. The objective of α is to correctly classify the application set $\{\rho_1, \rho_2, ..., \rho_n\}$ observed in d's traffic τ where n is the possible number of classes. Therefore, α determines a probability distribution over n classes by using $f_\theta(x)$ where x is a feature vector of $\{x_1, x_2, ..., x_n\}$ obtained from O.

4.3   Obfuscation Approaches

Let $C(x)$ be the classification of x by a model and $C^*(x)$ be the true class. Then adversarial learning finds a perturbation δ such that when added to an input x, $C^*(x) \neq C(x + \delta)$. The value of δ should be small enough when added to x for producing $x^{adv} = x + \delta$ which implies that the difference between x^{adv}

and x should be almost imperceptible. While many approaches are common for generating adversarial examples, Szeged et al. [23] uses the L-BFGS optimization procedure for generating an adversarial example x^{adv} when input x is given and formulates the problem as:

$$min||x - x^{adv}||_2 + \lambda J(f_\theta(x^{adv}), t^{true})$$

The first term sets the penalty for large perturbations to x and the second one penalizes when classification deviates from the target class t^{true}. The loss function between t^{true} and output of the classifier $f_\theta(x^{adv})$ is denoted by J. $\lambda > 0$ is the model parameter.

The Carlini-Wagner L_2 attack is a robust iterative algorithm that creates adversarial examples with minimum perturbation [3]. This attack for a target class t is formalized as:

$$min||\frac{1}{2}(tanh(w) + 1) - x||_2 + \lambda f_\theta(\frac{1}{2}(tanh(w) + 1)$$
$$\text{such that}\ \ C^*(x) \neq t$$

where, f_θ is defined by

$$f_\theta(x^{adv}) = max(max\{Z(x^{adv})_i : i \neq t\} - Z(x^{adv})_t, -k)$$

and $\delta = \frac{1}{2}(tanh(w) + 1) - x$ is the perturbation of the adversarial sample. Here, λ is chosen empirically through binary search and k controls the confidence of misclassification occurrence.

For generating untargeted adversarial perturbations Goodfellow et al. [9] proposed a fast single-step method. This method determines an adversarial perturbation under L_∞ norm where the perturbation is bounded by the parameter ϵ that results in the highest increase in the linearized loss function. It can be obtained by performing one step in the gradient sign's direction with stepwidth ϵ

$$x^{adv} = x + \epsilon\ sign(\Delta_x J(f_\theta(x^{adv}), t^{true}))$$

Here, L_∞ computes the maximum change to any of the coordinates:

$$||x - x^{adv}||_\infty = max(|x_1 - x_1^{adv}|, |x_2 - x_2^{adv}|, ..., |x_n - x_n^{adv}|)$$

In [3], Szeged et al. used L_∞ distance metrics to generat CWL_∞ attack where the optimization functions is defined by following:

$$\lambda\ min f_\theta(x + \delta) + ||\delta||_\infty$$

and, $\delta = \frac{1}{2}(tanh(w) + 1) - x$. This method has a lower success rate but it is simple and computationally efficient [13].

5   Restricted Traffic Distribution Attack

We define an attack that can be translated more readily in a real-life setting. To ensure the perturbation yields a valid distribution, we have constrained our attack in two ways: the attack is not allowed to reduce the packet size, and the generated distribution should preserve the monotonic non-decreasing property. We solve this problem by enforcing these constraints directly in the adversarial optimization framework.

Notice that it is possible to reduce the packet size in a distribution by inserting small dummy packets into the traffic, but this approach introduces a larger overhead into the network than only appending dummy bytes.

5.1   Perturbation Constraints

Given a distribution x, a general adversarial algorithm finds a perturbation δ that it minimizes a distance metric L_p and changes the correct classification: $C^*(x) \neq C(x + \delta)$. This perturbation has no restrictions with respect to the direction that modifies the original distribution. Instead, we clip every value below zero in the perturbation during learning:

$$\text{minimize } L_p(x, x + (\delta)^+)$$
$$\text{such that } C(x + (\delta)^+) = t$$

where $(f)^+$ stands for $max(f, 0)$ and t is not the correct label.

5.2   Distribution Constraints

Given a batch of adversarial distributions A, we define an operation that identifies every adversarial sample with decreasing consecutive features.

Let (A_i, A_{i+1}) be consecutive features in the batch A, we compute the following operation:

$$diff := (A_i - A_{i+1})^+$$

We update our distribution based on this value: $A_{i+1} := A_{i+1} + diff$. For a valid sample the operation will result in 0, but for an invalid one it will compute the difference between features, so after the update we automatically get non-decreasing features. This operation is sequentially applied to every pair of consecutive features in the same distribution during the optimization of the attack.

5.3   Framework

These restrictions in an attack should generate a valid adversarial distribution if convergence is possible. In this work we choose the Carlini-Wagner attack for L_2 and L_∞ norm as our frameworks.

Implementation Details. We re-implement the Carlini-Wagner attack for L_2 and L_∞ norm. For the initial c we select 10^{-3} and 10^{-1}, respectively, and search for 5 steps with 1000 as the maximum number of iterations. In our algorithm, we clip the perturbation before adding to the batch, and then apply the series of operations to correct the distribution. We also replicate the method reported in [24] by applying a post-processing operation to the generated distributions from CW L_2 attack.

Table 4. Percentage of valid adversarial samples.

	Valid perturbation	Valid distribution
RTDA CW L_2	100%	100%
Post-processing CW L_2	0%	100%
CW L_2	0%	20%
RTDA CW L_∞	100%	100%
CW L_∞	0%	22%

6   Results

We test our two RTDA frameworks against previous adversarial approaches.

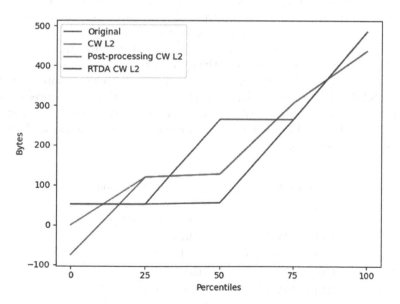

Fig. 1. A comparison of every L_2 adversarial example generated from the same distribution. Notice the negative packet size generated by CW L_2 and the reduction of 0th and 100th percentile by post-processing CW L_2. In contrast, RTDA generates an adversarial by only increasing the 50th percentile.

We compare the attacks by evaluating how realistic the generated distributions are, and the success rate for fooling the neural network. To evaluate how realistic an attack is we compare the ratios of valid perturbations and valid distributions for each attack. The results are shown in Table 4 for realistic attacks and Table 5 for success rate per class (Fig. 1).

Table 5. Success rate per class (Fraction of instances for which an adversarial was found).

	Database	Bulk	Mail	P2P	Services	WWW
RTDA CW L_2	100%	100%	95%	93%	100%	95%
Post-processing CW L_2	75%	33%	29%	50%	53%	84%
CW L_2	100%	100%	100%	100%	100%	100%
RTDA CW L_∞	100%	100%	74%	72%	67%	100%
CW L_∞	100%	100%	100%	100%	100%	100%

Prior work did not consider the limitations of a perturbation in real-world settings. Our algorithm is significantly more realistic than previous attacks. Both of our frameworks generate a valid perturbation and distribution for every test sample. Post-processing has the disadvantage that resultant distributions may no longer be adversarial examples. Our approach directly finds attacks in the valid space allowing to optimize towards the best attacks. Therefore, RTDA outperforms significantly the success rate of the previous post-processing CW L_2 attack in every class. Even with the additional constraints our attack L_2 and L_∞ are just 2% and 14% apart respectively from their unrestricted versions.

Both attacks have a larger norm in comparison to previous approaches. Surprisingly, RTDA L_2 has a smaller perturbation than the post-processed approach. On average, our attack can be applied to a system by increasing each packet by 14.5 bytes. Table 6 compares the corresponding norm and average perturbation for each approach.

Table 6. Average norm and perturbation.

	L_p	δ mean (Bytes)
RTDA CW L_2	0.015	14.5
Post-processing CW L_2	0.012	15.4
CW L_2	0.011	12.9
RTDA CW L_∞	0.033	19.41
CW L_∞	0.026	15.74

7   Conclusions and Future Work

Network traffic is vulnerable to statistical analysis in which an adversary can classify various types of applications and protocols by observing unencrypted meta signature of network packets. Adversarial machine learning techniques are very effective for obfuscating network traffic while introducing minimal network overhead. We proposed a novel network traffic obfuscating approach that is robust against network traffic attackers where we leverage adversarial attacks as a mechanism to obfuscate network traffic. Our algorithm outperforms previous approaches achieving state-of-the-art results and reduces the network overhead produced by the perturbation.

We plan to extend this work by testing our approach in a real world network and/or network traffic simulators. In addition, we are working on generating adversarial examples by using game-theoretic models where the defender adds various perturbation to the original features of different classes by paying variable cost to confuse the attacker in decision making. This game model seeks to simulate the AML approach's settings by initially imposing two general constraints—a positive perturbation and total perturbation bounded by a cost budget. We expect that similar approaches would also be effective in introducing other realistic constraints into the model, allowing simple but robust perturbations to limit traffic classification accuracy and reconnaissance value.

Acknowledgment. This work was supported by the Army Research Office under award W911NF-17-1-0370.

References

1. Anjum, I., Sujan Miah, M., Zhu, M., Sharmin, N., Kiekintveld, C., Enck, W., Singh, M.P.: Optimizing vulnerability-driven honey traffic using game theory. arXiv pp. arXiv-2002 (2020)
2. Bar-Yanai, R., Langberg, M., Peleg, D., Roditty, L.: Realtime classification for encrypted traffic. In: Festa, P. (ed.) SEA 2010. LNCS, vol. 6049, pp. 373–385. Springer, Heidelberg (2010). https://doi.org/10.1007/978-3-642-13193-6_32
3. Carlini, N., Wagner, D.: Towards evaluating the robustness of neural networks. In: 2017 IEEE Symposium on Security And Privacy (SP), pp. 39 57. IEEE (2017)
4. Ciftcioglu, E., Hardy, R., Chan, K., Scott, L., Oliveira, D., Verma, G.: Chaff allocation and performance for network traffic obfuscation. In: 2018 IEEE 38th International Conference on Distributed Computing Systems (ICDCS), pp. 1565–1568. IEEE (2018)
5. Duffield, N.G., Roughan, M., Sen, S., Spatscheck, O.: Statistical, signature-based approach to IP traffic classification (Feb 9 2010), US Patent 7,660,248
6. Dusi, M., Crotti, M., Gringoli, F., Salgarelli, L.: Tunnel hunter: detecting application-layer tunnels with statistical fingerprinting. Comput. Netw. **53**(1), 81–97 (2009)

7. Dyer, K.P., Coull, S.E., Shrimpton, T.: Marionette: A programmable network traffic obfuscation system. In: 24th USENIX Security Symposium (USENIX Security 15), pp. 367–382. USENIX Association, Washington, D.C. (Aug 2015). https://www.usenix.org/conference/usenixsecurity15/technical-sessions/presentation/dyer

8. Goodfellow, I., Papernot, N., McDaniel, P., Feinman, R., Faghri, F., Matyasko, A., Hambardzumyan, K., Juang, Y.L., Kurakin, A., Sheatsley, R., et al.: cleverhans v0. 1: an adversarial machine learning library, 1 (2016). arXiv preprint arXiv:1610.00768

9. Goodfellow, I.J., Shlens, J., Szegedy, C.: Explaining and harnessing adversarial examples (2014). arXiv preprint arXiv:1412.6572

10. Guan, Y., Fu, X., Xuan, D., Shenoy, P.U., Bettati, R., Zhao, W.: NetCamo: camouflaging network traffic for QOS-guaranteed mission critical applications. IEEE Trans. Syst. Man Cybern.-Part A: Syst. Humans **31**(4), 253–265 (2001)

11. He, W., Wei, J., Chen, X., Carlini, N., Song, D.: Adversarial example defense: Ensembles of weak defenses are not strong. In: 11th {USENIX} Workshop on Offensive Technologies ({WOOT} 17) (2017)

12. Karthika, C., Sreedhar, M.: Statistical traffic pattern discovery system for wireless mobile networks. Comput. Sci. Telecommun. **45**(1), 63–70 (2015)

13. Kurakin, A., Goodfellow, I., Bengio, S.: Adversarial examples in the physical world (2016). arXiv preprint arXiv:1607.02533

14. Mohajeri Moghaddam, H., Li, B., Derakhshani, M., Goldberg, I.: Skypemorph: Protocol obfuscation for tor bridges. In: Proceedings of the 2012 ACM Conference on Computer and Communications Security, pp. 97–108 (2012)

15. Moore, A.W., Zuev, D.: Internet traffic classification using Bayesian analysis techniques. In: Proceedings of the 2005 ACM SIGMETRICS International Conference on Measurement and Modeling of Computer Systems, pp. 50–60 (2005)

16. Nguyen, T.T., Armitage, G.: A survey of techniques for internet traffic classification using machine learning. IEEE Commun. Surv. Tutorials **10**(4), 56–76 (2008)

17. Ortiz, A., Fuentes, O., Rosario, D., Kiekintveld, C.: On the defense against adversarial examples beyond the visible spectrum. In: MILCOM 2018–2018 IEEE Military Communications Conference (MILCOM), pp. 1–5. IEEE (2018)

18. Ortiz, A., Granados, A., Fuentes, O., Kiekintveld, C., Rosario, D., Bell, Z.: Integrated learning and feature selection for deep neural networks in multispectral images. In: Proceedings of the IEEE Conference on Computer Vision and Pattern Recognition Workshops, pp. 1196–1205 (2018)

19. Papernot, N., McDaniel, P., Goodfellow, I.: Transferability in machine learning: from phenomena to black-box attacks using adversarial samples (2016). arXiv preprint arXiv:1605.07277

20. Papernot, N., McDaniel, P., Jha, S., Fredrikson, M., Celik, Z.B., Swami, A.: The limitations of deep learning in adversarial settings. In: 2016 IEEE European Symposium on Security and Privacy (EuroS&P), pp. 372–387. IEEE (2016)

21. Pinheiro, A.J., Bezerra, J.M., Campelo, D.R.: Packet padding for improving privacy in consumer IOT. In: 2018 IEEE Symposium on Computers and Communications (ISCC), pp. 00925–00929 (2018)

22. Roughan, M., Sen, S., Spatscheck, O., Duffield, N.: Class-of-service mapping for QOS: a statistical signature-based approach to IP traffic classification. In: Proceedings of the 4th ACM SIGCOMM Conference on Internet Measurement, pp. 135–148 (2004)

23. Szegedy, C., Zaremba, W., Sutskever, I., Bruna, J., Erhan, D., Goodfellow, I., Fergus, R.: Intriguing properties of neural networks (2013). arXiv preprint arXiv:1312.6199

24. Verma, G., Ciftcioglu, E., Sheatsley, R., Chan, K., Scott, L.: Network traffic obfuscation: an adversarial machine learning approach. In: MILCOM 2018 IEEE Military Communications Conference (MILCOM), pp. 1–6. IEEE (2018)

25. Wright, C.V., Coull, S.E., Monrose, F.: Traffic morphing: an efficient defense against statistical traffic analysis. In: NDSS, Vol. 9. Citeseer (2009)

26. Zander, S., Nguyen, T., Armitage, G.: Self-learning IP traffic classification based on statistical flow characteristics. In: Dovrolis, C. (ed.) PAM 2005. LNCS, vol. 3431, pp. 325–328. Springer, Heidelberg (2005). https://doi.org/10.1007/978-3-540-31966-5_26

Adversarial Deep Reinforcement Learning Based Adaptive Moving Target Defense

Taha Eghtesad[1(✉)], Yevgeniy Vorobeychik[2], and Aron Laszka[1]

[1] University of Houston, Houston, TX 77004, USA
teghtesad@uh.edu
[2] Washington University in St. Louis, St. Louis, MO 63130, USA

Abstract. Moving target defense (MTD) is a proactive defense approach that aims to thwart attacks by continuously changing the attack surface of a system (e.g., changing host or network configurations), thereby increasing the adversary's uncertainty and attack cost. To maximize the impact of MTD, a defender must strategically choose when and what changes to make, taking into account both the characteristics of its system as well as the adversary's observed activities. Finding an optimal strategy for MTD presents a significant challenge, especially when facing a resourceful and determined adversary who may respond to the defender's actions. In this paper, we propose a multi-agent partially-observable Markov Decision Process model of MTD and formulate a two-player general-sum game between the adversary and the defender. To solve this game, we propose a multi-agent reinforcement learning framework based on the double oracle algorithm. Finally, we provide experimental results to demonstrate the effectiveness of our framework in finding optimal policies.

1 Introduction

Traditional approaches for security focus on preventing intrusions (e.g., hardening systems to decrease the occurrence and impact of vulnerabilities) or on detecting and responding to intrusions (*e.g.,* restoring the configuration of compromised servers). While these passive and reactive approaches are useful, they cannot provide perfect security in practice. Further, these approaches let adversaries perform reconnaissance and planning unhindered, giving them a significant advantage in information and initiative. As adversaries are becoming more sophisticated and resourceful, it is imperative for defenders to augment traditional approaches with more proactive ones, which can give defenders the upper hand.

Moving Target Defense (MTD) is a proactive approach that changes the rules of the game in favor of the defenders. MTD techniques enable defenders to thwart cyber-attacks by continuously and randomly changing the configuration of their assets (*i.e.,* networks, hosts, etc.). These changes increase the uncertainty and complexity of attacks, making them computationally expensive for the adversary [32] or putting the adversary in an infinite loop of exploration [28].

Currently, system administrators typically have to manually select MTD configurations to be deployed on their networked systems based on their previous

ⓒ Springer Nature Switzerland AG 2020
Q. Zhu et al. (Eds.): GameSec 2020, LNCS 12513, pp. 58–79, 2020.
https://doi.org/10.1007/978-3-030-64793-3_4

experiences [9]. This approach has two main limitations. First, it can be very time consuming since (1) there are constraints on data locations, so that the system administrator must make sure that constraints are met before deploying MTD, (2) physical connectivity of servers cannot be easily changed, and (3) resources are limited. Second, it is difficult to capture the trade-off between security and efficiency since the most secure configuration is total randomization, but this has high performance overhead [5].

In light of this, it is crucial to provide automated approaches for deploying MTD, which maximize security benefits for the protected assets while preserves the efficiency of the system. The key ingredient to automation of MTD deployment is finding a design model that reflects multiple aspects of the MTD environment [2,13,22,32]. Further, we need a decision making algorithm for the model to select when to deploy an MTD technique and where to deploy it [28]. Finding optimal strategies for the deployment of MTD is computationally challenging since there can be huge number of applicable MTD deployment combinations even with trivial number of MTD configurations or in-control assets. Further, the adversary might adapt to these strategies.

One of the main approaches for finding decision making policies is *Independent Reinforcement Learning* (InRL). Recently, many research efforts have applied InRL to find the optimal action policies in fully or partially observable environments in various domains. These domains include: cybersecurity, hardware design, robotics, finance, and etc. In InRL, an agent learns to make optimal decisions by continuously interacting with its environment. In general, traditional reinforcement learning techniques use tabular approaches to store estimated rewards (*e.g.*, Q-Learning) [10]. To address challenges of reinforcement learning such as exploding state-action space, *Artificial Neural Networks* (ANN) have replaced table based approaches in many domains, thereby decreasing the training time and memory requirements. This led to the emergence of *deep reinforcement learning* (DRL) algorithms such as DQL [18].

Contributions. We formulate a multi-agent partially-observable Markov decision process for MTD, and based on this model, we propose a two-player general-sum game between the adversary and the defender. Then, we present a multi-agent deep reinforcement learning approach to solve this game. Our main contributions are as follows:

- We propose a multi-agent partially-observable Markov decision process for MTD.
- We propose a two-player general-sum game between the adversary and the defender based on this model.
- We formulate the problem of finding adaptive MTD policies as finding the mixed-strategy Nash equilibrium (MSNE) of this game.
- We propose a compact memory representation for the defender and adversary agents, which helps them to better operate in the partially-observable environment.
- We propose a computational approach for finding the optimal MTD policy using Deep Q-Learning and the Double Oracle algorithm.

- We evaluate our approach numerically while exploring various game parameters.
- We show that our approach is viable in terms of computational cost.

Organization. The rest of the paper is organized as follows. In Sect. 2, we describe preliminaries, including InRL (Sect. 2.1) and one specific InRL algorithm, Deep Q Learning (Sect. 2.2). In Sect. 3, we introduce a multi-agent partially-observable Markov decision process for MTD, which is used as the basis of the MARL. In Sect. 4, we formulate a two-player general-sum game between the adversary and the defender, and formulate the problem of finding adaptive MTD policies as finding the MSNE of the game. In Sect. 5, we propose our solution to solving the MTD game. In Sect. 6, we provide a thorough numerical analysis of our approach. In Sect. 7, we discuss the related work. Finally, in Sect. 8, we provide concluding remarks.

2   Preliminaries

In this section, we describe a family of reinforcement learning algorithms (Sect. 2.1), and one particular algorithm in this family, namely Deep Q-Learning (Sect. 2.2). Readers who are familiar with these concepts may skip this section and continue to Sect. 3.

2.1   Independent Reinforcement Learning

One of the primary approaches for finding a decision-making policy is *Independent Reinforcement Learning* (InRL), which focuses on interactions of a single agent and its environment to maximize the agent's gain (represented as rewards or utilities) from the environment. Figure 1 shows the interactions between different components of InRL. A basic InRL environment is a *Partially-Observable Markov Decision Process* (POMDP), which can be represented as a tuple:

$$POMDP = \langle \mathbb{S}, \mathbb{A}, \mathbb{T}, \mathbb{R}, \mathbb{O} \rangle. \tag{1}$$

where $\mathbb{S}$ is the set of all possible states of the environment, $\mathbb{A}$ is the set of all possible actions by the agent, $\mathbb{T}$ is the set of stochastic transition rules and, $\mathbb{R}$ is the immediate reward of a state transition, and $\mathbb{O}$ is the set of observation rules of the agent. For more detailed information on POMDP, please refer to [23].

The objective of InRL is to find a *policy* π, which is a mapping from observation space to action space, such that:

$$\pi(o_\tau) \mapsto a_\tau \tag{2}$$

$$\text{which maximizes } U_\tau^* = \mathbb{E}\left[\sum_{t=0}^{\infty} \gamma^t \cdot r_{t+\tau} \,\middle|\, \pi \right] \tag{3}$$

where o_τ is the observation received in time step τ, $a_{\tau+1}$ is the action taken after that observation, and r_τ is the reward received in time step τ after a state transition due to action a_τ. Also, the *discount factor* $\gamma \in [0, 1)$ prioritizes rewards received in the current time step over future rewards. When $\gamma = 0$, the agent cares only about the current reward; and when $\gamma = 1$, the agent cares about all future rewards equally. Note that in a partially-observable environment, the agent should consider its history of observations. However, considering the complete history of observations may be computationally challenging, so practical approaches limit the observation history (*e.g.*, limited number of recent observations [18], agent memory [21]). We propose a compact representation of history in Sect. 5.2, but for ease of presentation, we will treat policies as mappings from most recent observations until then.

The training is done in iterations called *steps*. In each step, the agent decides on an action to take which updates the state of the environment based on transition rules, and the agent receives the new observation from the environment and immediate reward of transition. To make sure that the majority of action/observation space is explored and the learning agent is not stuck in a locally optimal state, after an arbitrary number of

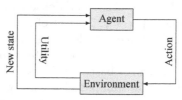

Fig. 1. Independent reinforcement learning.

steps, the environment state is *reset* to an arbitrary/random initial state and the agent receives the observation of the initial state. In the terms of RL, steps between one reset and the next one are called an *epoch* of training.

Algorithm 1: Deep-Q Learning
Result: policy σ
$Q \leftarrow$ random;
for N_e *episodes* **do**
$\quad O \leftarrow$ reset_game();
$\quad \epsilon_\tau \leftarrow 1$;
$\quad$ **for** $\tau \in \{0, \ldots, T_{epoch}\}$ **do**
$\qquad$ **if** $random[0,1] \leq \epsilon_\tau$ **then**
$\qquad\quad \mid$ $a \leftarrow$ random_action;
$\qquad$ **else**
$\qquad\quad \mid$ $a \leftarrow \mathrm{argmax}_{a'} Q(S, a')$;
$\qquad$ **end**
$\qquad (S', r) \leftarrow$ step_game(a);
$\qquad$ add $e = \langle S, S', a, r \rangle$ to E;
$\qquad$ sample X from E;
$\qquad$ update DQN based on X;
$\qquad S \leftarrow S'$;
$\qquad$ decay ϵ_τ;
$\quad$ **end**
end
$\sigma \leftarrow \langle S \mapsto \mathrm{argmax}_a Q(S, a) \rangle$;

Algorithm 2: Adaptive Solver
Result: set of pure policies Π^a and Π^d
$\Pi^a \leftarrow$ attacker heuristics;
$\Pi^d \leftarrow$ defender heuristics;
while $U^p(\sigma^p, \sigma^{\bar{p}})$ *not converged* **do**
$\quad \sigma^a, \sigma^d \leftarrow$ solve_MSNE(Π^a, Π^d);
$\quad \theta \leftarrow$ random;
$\quad \pi_+^a \leftarrow$ train($T \cdot N_e$, $env^a[\sigma^d], \theta$);
$\quad \Pi^a \leftarrow \Pi^a \cup \pi_+^a$;
$\quad$ assess π_+^a;
$\quad \sigma^a, \sigma^d \leftarrow$ solve_MSNE(Π^a, Π^d);
$\quad \theta \leftarrow$ random;
$\quad \pi_+^d \leftarrow$ train($T \cdot N_e$, $env^d[\sigma^a], \theta$);
$\quad \Pi^d \leftarrow \Pi^d \cup \pi_+^d$;
$\quad$ assess π_+^d;
end

Each *step* to the environment updates the state of the system based on the agent's action (a) and the current state of the environment (s), and returns a new observation (o), immediate utility given to agent (r), and whether the environment is finished or not. This new information and the previous observation of the agent forms an *experience*. Specifically, an experience is defined as a tuple of:

$$e = \langle o_\tau, a_\tau, o_{\tau+1}, r_\tau \rangle \tag{4}$$

where o_τ and a_τ are the agent's observation and action at time step τ; and $o_{\tau+1}$ and r_τ are the agent's observation and immediate utility received at the next time step $\tau + 1$. The set of recent experiences is used to update the policy.

Reinforcement learning aims to maximize the received utility of the agent (U_*) by trial and error: interacting with the environment (randomly, following heuristics, or based on the experiences that the agent has seen so far). Generally, during the training, there are two ways to find actions to be taken at each step: (1) *Exploitation*: we use the currently trained policy to choose actions, which helps the agent to more accurately find U_* values of states. (2) *Exploration*: to find actions that lead to higher utility by selecting actions at random and exploring the action/observation space. One of approaches for choosing between exploration or exploitation is the ϵ-greedy approach, where in each step the agent explores with probability ϵ, or takes the current optimal action with probability $1 - \epsilon$.

2.2   Deep-Q-Network Learning

The Deep-Q-Network Learning algorithm is described in Algorithm 1. Q-learning uses a Q function to estimate the expected future utilities of an action in an observation state (Eq. (3)):

$$Q(o_\tau, a_\tau) = U_\tau^* |_{\pi \leftarrow \text{argmax}_{a'} Q(o_\tau, a')} \tag{5}$$

With a tabular approach of storing the Q value for each observation/action, we can find the value of the Q function by applying the Bellman optimization equation:

$$Q(o_\tau, a_\tau) = (1 - \alpha_q) \cdot Q(o_\tau, a_\tau) + \alpha_q \cdot \underbrace{(r_\tau + \gamma \cdot \max_{a'} Q(o_{\tau+1}, a'))}_{\text{TD Target}} \tag{6}$$

where α_q is the learning rate of the Q function. The idea for updating the Q function is that the Q function should minimize the *temporal difference* (TD) error, *i.e.*, the difference between the predicted Q value, and the actual expected utility (U^* while following $\pi \leftarrow \text{argmax}_{a'} Q(O_\tau, a')$).

When we are dealing with environments with highly dimensional action/observation spaces, tabular based Q-learning is infeasible since: (1) the table for storing Q-values might not fit into memory, and (2) the action and observation spaces need to be enumerated many times for the algorithm to learn an optimal policy. To address these challenges, Mnih *et al.* [18] suggests to use *multi layer perceptrons* (MLP) as approximators for the Q function. Using MLP as Q-value approximator makes the deep Q-learning approach feasible for such environments since (1) at most thousands parameters are stored, and (2) MLP models can generalize the relation between observations and actions; as a result, learning agents need less time for exploring the observation/action space.

To optimize the parameters of MLP (θ), we can use gradient descent to minimize the TD error of the network. With the same TD target as Eq. (6), and taking optimal action as $\text{argmax}_{a'} Q(o_\tau, a'|\theta)$, the TD target will be:

$$q_\tau = r_\tau + \gamma \cdot Q(o_{\tau+1}, \text{argmax}_{a'} Q(o_\tau, a'|\theta))|\theta) \tag{7}$$

Suppose we have a batch of experiences X for updating the MLP parameters, then we can define a *mean squared error* (MSE) loss function and apply gradient descent with learning rate α_θ to optimise the MLP parameters:

$$L_\theta = \frac{1}{|X|} \sum_i^X (q_\tau - Q(o_\tau, a_\tau|\theta))^2 \tag{8}$$

3   Model

To model adaptive *Moving Target Defense*, we build a *Multi-Agent Partially-Observable Markov Decision Process* (MAPOMDP) based on the model of Prakash and Wellman [22]. A Multi-Agent POMDP is a generalization of POMDP to consider multiple agents influencing the environment simultaneously. Formally:

$$MAPOMDP = \langle \mathbb{S}, \{\mathbb{A}_i\}, \mathbb{T}, \{\mathbb{R}_i\}, \{\mathbb{O}_i\}\rangle \tag{9}$$

where $\mathbb{A}_i$ is the action space, $\mathbb{O}_i$ is the observation set of observation rules, and $\mathbb{R}_i$ is the immediate reward of a state transition for player i. In the following subsections (Sects. 3.1 through 3.5), we describe these sets in terms of an MTD model.

In this adversarial model, there are two players, a defender and an adversary ($p = a$ and $p = d$, resp.), who compete for control over a set of servers. At the beginning of the game, all servers are under the control of the defender. To take control of a server, the adversary can launch a *"probe"* against the server at any time, which either compromises the server or increases the success probability of subsequent probes. To keep the servers safe, the defender can *"reimage"* a server at any time, which takes the server offline for some time, but cancels the adversary's progress and control. The goal of the defender is to keep servers uncompromised (*i.e.,* under the defender's control) and available (*i.e.,* online). The goal of the adversary is to compromise the servers or make them unavailable. For a list of symbols used in this paper, see Table 1.

Table 1. List of symbols and experimental values

Symbol	Description	Baseline value
Environment, Agents, Actions		
M	Number of servers	10
Δ	Number of time steps for which a server is unavailable after reimaging	7
ν	Probability of the defender not observing a probe	0
α_θ	Knowledge gain of each probe	0.05
C_A	Attack (*probe*) cost	0.20
θ_{sl}^p	Slope of reward function for player p	5
θ_{th}^p	Steep point threshold of reward function for player p	0.2
w^p	Weighting of reward for having servers up and in control for player p	0/1
r_τ^p	Reward of player p in time step τ	
Heuristic strategies		
P_D	Period for defender's periodic strategies	4
P_A	Period for adversary's periodic strategies	1
π	Threshold of number of probes on a server for PCP defender	7
τ	Threshold for adversary's/defender's *Control-Threshold* strategy	0.5/0.8
Reinforcement learning		
T	Length of the game (number of time steps)	1000
γ	Temporal discount factor	0.99
ϵ_p	Exploration fraction	0.2
ϵ_f	Final exploration value	0.02
α_t	Learning rate	0.0005
$|E|$	Experience replay buffer size	5000
$|X|$	Training batch size	32
N_e	Number of training episodes	500

3.1 Environment and Players

There are M *servers* and two players, a *defender* and an *adversary*. The servers are independent of each other in the sense that they are independently attacked, defended, and controlled. The game environment is explained in detail in the following subsections.

3.2   State

Time is discrete, and in a given time step τ, the state of each server i is defined by tuple $s_i^\tau = \langle \rho, \chi, \upsilon \rangle$ where

- $\rho \in \mathbb{N}_0$ represents the number of probes lunched against server i since the last reimage,
- $\chi \in \{adv, def\}$ represents the player controlling the server, and
- $\upsilon \in \{up\} \cup \mathbb{N}_0$ represents if the server is online (*i.e.*, up) or if it is offline (*i.e.*, down) with the identifier of the time step in which the server was reimaged.

3.3   Actions

In each time step, a player may take either a single action or no action at all. The adversary's action is to select a server and *probe* it. Probing a server takes control of it with probability $1 - e^{-\alpha \cdot (\rho+1)}$ where ρ is the number of previous probes and α is a constant that determines how fast the probability of compromise grows with each additional probe, which captures how much information (or progress) the adversary gains from each probe. Also, by probing a server, the adversary learns whether it is up or down.

The defender's action is to select a server and *reimage* it. Reimaging a server takes the server offline for a fixed number Δ of time steps, after which the server goes online under the control of the defender and with the adversary's progress (*i.e.*, number of previous probes ρ) against that server erased (*i.e.*, reset to zero).

3.4   Rewards

Prakash and Wellman [22] define a family of utility functions. The exact utility function can be chosen by setting the values of preference parameters, which specify the goal of each player. The value of player p's utility function u^p at a particular, as described by Eqs. (10) and (11), depends on the number of servers in control of player p and the number of servers offline. Note that the exact relation depends on the scenario (*e.g.*, whether the primary goal is confidentiality or integrity), but in general, a higher number of controlled servers yields a higher utility.

$$u^p(n_c^p, n_d) = w^p \cdot f\left(\frac{n_c^p}{M}, \theta^p\right) + (1 - w^p) \cdot f\left(\frac{n_c^p + n_d}{M}, \theta^p\right) \tag{10}$$

where n_c^p is the number of servers which are up and in control of player p, n_d is the number of unavailable (down) servers, and f is a sigmoid function with parameters $\theta^p \leftarrow (\theta_{sl}^p, \theta_{th}^p)$:

$$f(x, \theta^p) = \frac{1}{e^{-\theta_{sl}^p \cdot (x - \theta_{th}^p)}} \tag{11}$$

where θ_{sl} and θ_{th} control the slope and position of the sigmoid's inflection point, respectively. Please note that, the value of variables used for computation of utility function (n_c^p, n_d), and therefore, the utility function depends on the time step. However, in the writing time step is removed explicitly from the formulation, since the time step can be understood from the context.

Reward weight (w^p) specifies the goal of each player. As described by Prakash and Wellman [22], there can be four extreme combinations of this parameter, which are summarized in Table 2. For example, in *control/availability*, both players gain reward by having the servers up and in their control. Or in *disrupt/availability*, which is the most interest-

Table 2. Utility environments

	Utility environment	w^a	w^d
0	Control/availability	1	1
1	Control/confidentiality	1	0
2	Disrupt/availability	0	1
3	Disrupt/confidentiality	0	0

ing case, the defender gains reward by having the servers up and in its control, while the adversary gains reward by bringing the servers down or having them in its control.

The defender's cost of action is implicitly defined by the utility function. In other words, the cost of reimaging a server comes from not receiving reward for the time steps when the server is "down." In contrast, the adversary's reward accounts for the cost of probing (C_A), which is a fixed costs that can be avoided by not taking any action.

The reward given to the adversary (r_τ^a) and defender (r_τ^d) at time τ is defined by:

$$r_\tau^d = u^d, \quad r_\tau^a = \begin{cases} u^a(n_c^a, n_d) - C_A & \text{adversary probed a server at } \tau \\ u^a(n_c^a, n_d) & \text{adversary did nothing at } \tau \end{cases} \tag{12}$$

3.5 Observations

A key aspect of the model is the players' uncertainty regarding the state of the servers. The defender does not know which servers have been compromised by the adversary. Further, the defender observes a probe only with a fixed probability $1 - \nu$ (with probability ν, the probe is undetected). Consequently, the defender can only estimate the number of probes against a server and whether a server is compromised. However, the defender knows the status of all servers (*i.e.*, whether the server is up or down; and if it is down, how many time steps it requires to be back up again).

The adversary always observes when the defender reimages a compromised server, but cannot observe reimaging an uncompromised server without probing it. Consequently, the adversary knows with certainty only which servers are compromised.

Observation of a player p is represented as a vector of tuples o_i^p, where o_i^p corresponds to player p's observation of server i:

$$o^p = \langle o_0^p, o_1^p, \cdots, o_{M-1}^p \rangle \tag{13}$$

The adversary knows which servers are compromised and knows how many probes it has initiated on each server. The adversary's observation of server i is defined as a tuple o_i^a:

$$\forall_{0 \leq i < M} : \qquad\qquad o_i^a = \langle \tilde{\rho}^a, \chi, \tilde{v}^a \rangle \tag{14}$$

where $\tilde{\rho}^a$ is the number of probes launched by the adversary since the last *observed* reimaging, χ is the player controlling of the server (always known by the adversary), and $\tilde{v}^a \in \{up, down\}$ is the observed state of the server.

Unlike the adversary, the defender does not know who controls the servers. Further, if ν is greater than 0, the defender can only estimate the number of probes. The observation state of the defender of each server i can be modeled with a tuple o_i^d:

$$\forall_{0 \leq i < M}: \qquad\qquad o_i^d = \langle \tilde{\rho}^d, v \rangle \qquad\qquad (15)$$

where $\tilde{\rho}^d$ is the number of probes *observed* since the last reimaging, and $v \in \{up\} \cup \mathbb{N}_0$ is the state of the server (always known by the defender).

4   Problem Formulation

In Sect. 3, we built an MTD model using a MAPOMDP. In this section, based on this model, we design an adversarial game between the adversary and the defender. In this setting, we assume that each player chooses a strategy to play, where a strategy is a policy function that maps an observation of the environment to an action to be taken. Since we assume that each strategy is a policy function, in the remainder of this paper, we use the terms *strategy* and *policy* interchangeably.

4.1   Pure Strategy

A pure strategy π^p for player p is a deterministic policy function $\pi^p(o^p) \mapsto a^p$, which given player p's current observation of the system o^p produces an action a^p to be taken by the player. We let Π^p denote the set of all pure strategies (*i.e.*, policies) of player p.

When the players are following pure policies $\pi^a \in \Pi^a$ and $\pi^d \in \Pi^d$, their expected cumulative utility can be expressed as the sum of discounted future rewards with discount factor γ. Formally, we can express player p's expected cumulative utility where $\bar{p}$ denotes player p's opponent as:

$$U^p(\pi^p, \pi^{\bar{p}}) = \mathbb{E}\left[\sum_{t=0}^{\infty} \gamma^\tau \cdot r_\tau^p \;\middle|\; \pi^p, \pi^{\bar{p}}\right] \qquad\qquad (16)$$

4.2   Mixed Strategy

One way to express stochastic policies is to use probability distributions over pure policies. A mixed strategy of player p is a probability distribution $\sigma^p = \{\sigma^p(\pi^p)\}_{\pi^p \in \Pi^p}$ over the player's pure strategies Π^p, where $\sigma^p(\pi^p)$ is the probability that player p chooses policy π^p.

We let Σ^p denote player p's mixed strategy space. The expected utility of the adversary and the defender when they are following mixed strategies $\sigma^a \in \Sigma^a$ and $\sigma^d \in \Sigma^d$, respectively, can be calculated as:

$$\forall_{p \in \{a,d\}} : \quad U^p(\sigma^p, \sigma^{\bar{p}}) = \sum_{\pi^p \in \Pi^p} \sum_{\pi^{\bar{p}} \in \Pi^{\bar{p}}} \sigma^p(\pi^p) \cdot \sigma^{\bar{p}}(\pi^{\bar{p}}) \cdot U^p(\pi^p, \pi^{\bar{p}}) \quad (17)$$

Note that we overloaded the notation for the players' pure-strategy utility to also denote their mixed-strategy utility since the distinction will always be clear from the context and function arguments.

4.3   Solution Concept

The aim of both players is to maximize their utility. As we are considering a rational adversary and defender, we can assume that they always pick a strategy that maximizes their own utility. A *best response* mixed strategy $\sigma_*^p(\sigma^{\bar{p}})$ provides maximum utility for player p given that its opponent $\bar{p}$ is using mixed strategy $\sigma^{\bar{p}}$. Formally, if the opponent $\bar{p}$ is using a mixed strategy $\sigma^{\bar{p}}$, then player p's best response σ_*^p is

$$\sigma_*^p(\sigma^{\bar{p}}) = \mathrm{argmax}_{\sigma^p} U^p(\sigma^p, \sigma^{\bar{p}}). \quad (18)$$

We optimize each player's strategy assuming that its opponent will always use a best-response strategy. This formulation is in fact equivalent to finding a *mixed-strategy Nash equilibrium* (MSNE) of the players' policy spaces Π^a and Π^d. Formally, a profile of mixed strategies (σ_*^a, σ_*^d) is a MSNE *iff*

$$\forall_{p \in \{a,d\}} \forall_{\sigma^p \in \Sigma^p} : U^p(\sigma_*^p, \sigma_*^{\bar{p}}) \geq U^p(\sigma^p, \sigma_*^{\bar{p}}) \quad (19)$$

That is, neither player can increase its expected utility by unilaterally changing its strategy. In the next section, we propose an approach for finding the MSNE of the MTD game, where Π^a and Π^d are the policy space of the players.

5   Framework

In Sect. 4, we proposed a general-sum game based on the MAPOMDP model described in Sect. 3. We concluded that finding an optimal action policy for the adversary and the defender in the MTD setting is equivalent to finding an MSNE of the game. In this section, we propose a computational approach and build a framework atop the double oracle (Sect. 5.1) and DQL (Sect. 2.2) algorithms to find optimal action policies for the adversary and the defender.

5.1   Solution Overview

The iterative *Double Oracle* (DO) algorithm [17] finds an MSNE of a game given an arbitrary initial subset Π_0^p of each player p's strategy set ($\Pi_0^p \subset \Pi^p$). The

DO algorithm extends these subsets iteratively by alternating between 1) finding MSNE of the game spanned by these subsets and 2) extending the subsets with best-response strategies against the latest MSNE.

We let Π_t^p denote player p's explored subset of strategies in iteration t of the DO algorithm. In each iteration, for each player, the DO algorithm refers to a *best response oracle*, an algorithm which finds a pure-strategy best response, to compute a best-response strategy against the opponent's MSNE strategy. Then, it adds this best response to the player's strategy set. Formally, in each iteration:

$$\forall_{p \in \{a,d\}} : \Pi_{t+1}^p \leftarrow \Pi_t^p \cup \left\{ \pi_*^p \left(\sigma_{*,t}^{\bar{p}} \right) \right\} \tag{20}$$

where $\sigma_{*,t}^p$ is the MSNE of the player p given the strategy sets Π_t^p. The DO algorithm guarantees [17] the convergence of the MSNE of these strategy sets to an MSNE of the game as long as the strategy sets are finite for both players. However, as the players' strategy sets are vast (even though they are finite) in our game model, enumeration of the strategy sets in search of the best response is infeasible.

For each player, we can use an InRL algorithm, such as Q-Learning [30], as a best-response oracle to find a best-response pure strategy against the opponent's MSNE strategy. Since the opponent's strategy is fixed, the player can use reinforcement learning by treating the opponent's actions as part of its localized environment.

5.2 Challenges

Solving the MAPOMDP model of Sect. 3 with the DO algorithm is not straightforward. In the following paragraphs, we discuss the issues faced while solving the MAPOMDP model and propose approaches for resolving these issues.

Partial Observability. For both players, state is only partially observable. This can pose a significant challenge for the defender, who does not even know whether a server is compromised or not. Consider, for example, the defender observing that a particular server has been probed only a few times: this may mean that the server is safe since it has not been probed enough times; but it may also mean that the adversary is not probing it because the server is already compromised. We can try to address this limitation by allowing the defender's policy to consider a long history of preceding observations; however, this poses computational challenges since the size of the policy's effective state space explodes.

Since partial observability poses a challenge for the defender, we let the defender's policy use information from preceding observations. To avoid state-space explosion, we feed this information into the policy in a compact form. In particular, we extend the observed state of each server (*i.e.*, number of observed probes and whether the server is online) with (a) the amount of time since the last reimaging r (always known by the defender) and (b) the amount of time since the last observed probe $\tilde{p}^d$. So, the actual state representation of the defender will be:

$$\forall_{0 \le i < M} : \qquad\qquad o_i^d = \langle \tilde{\rho}^d, v, \tilde{p}^d, r \rangle \qquad\qquad (21)$$

where $\tilde{p}^d$ is the time since the last *observed* probe of the server, and r is the time since the last reimage of the server.

Further, the adversary needs to make sure that the progress of the probes on the servers is not reset. Therefore, it is important that the adversary knows the amount of time since the last probe p of servers when deciding which server to probe. Hence, the observation state of the adversary becomes:

$$\forall_{0 \le i < M} : \qquad\qquad o_i^a = \langle \tilde{\rho}^a, \chi, \tilde{v}^a, p \rangle \qquad\qquad (22)$$

Complexity of MSNE Computation. In zero-sum games, computation of MSNE can be done in polynomial time (*e.g.*, linear programming). However, in general-sum games, the problem of finding the MSNE of given strategy sets of players is PPAD-complete [27], which makes computation of true MSNE infeasible for a game of non-trivial size. Therefore, we use an ϵ-*equilibrium* solver, which produces an approximate correct result. One such solver is the Global Newton solver [6].

Equilibrium Selection. Typically, the DO algorithm is used with zero-sum games, where all equilibria of a game yield the same expected payoffs. However, in general-sum games, there may exist multiple equilibria with significantly different payoffs. The DO algorithm in general-sum games converges to only one of these equilibria. The exact equilibrium to which the DO algorithm converges depends on the players' initial strategy sets and the output of the best-response oracle. However, in our experiments (Sect. 6.3), we show that in our game, this problem is not significant in practice, *i.e.*, all equilibria yield almost the same expected payoffs (Fig. 3) regardless of the initial strategy sets.

Model Complexity. Due to the complexity of our MAPOMDP model, computation of best response using tabular InRL approaches (*e.g.*, Q-Learning) is computationally infeasible. For example, the size of state space for the defender is $(2T^3)^M$ since each of $\hat{\rho}^d, \hat{p}^d$, and r can take any value between 0 and T, and v can only take two values. Although we expect that the values of $\hat{\rho}^d, \hat{p}^d$, and r be much smaller than T due to the dynamics of the game, it is still infeasible to explore each state even once or store a tabular policy in memory for a game of non-trivial size on a conventional computer. To address this challenge, we use computationally feasible *approximate best-response oracles* to find approximate best-response strategies instead of best responses. Lanctot *et al.* [11] show that deep reinforcement learning can be used as an approximate best-response oracle. However, when approximate best responses are used instead of true best responses, convergence guarantees are lost. In our experiments, we show that this algorithm does converge in only a few iterations (see Fig. 2b).

Short-Term Losses vs. Long-Term Rewards. For both players, taking an action has a negative short-term impact: for the defender, reimaging a server results in lower rewards while the server is offline; for the adversary, probing incurs a cost. While these actions can have positive long-term impact, benefits may not be experienced until much later: for the defender, a reimaged server remains offline for a long period of time; for the attacker, many probes may be needed until a server is finally compromised.

As a result, with typical temporal discount factors (*e.g.*, $\gamma = 0.9$), it may be an optimal policy for a player to never take any action since the short-term negative impact outweighs the long-term benefit. In light of this, we use higher temporal discount factors (*e.g.*, $\gamma = 0.99$). However, such high values can pose challenges for deep reinforcement learning since convergence will be much slower and less stable.

5.3 Solution Approach

Prakash and Wellman [22] proposed a set of heuristic strategies for each player (described in Sect. 6.1). However, as these strategies are only a subset of the agents' strategy sets, their MSNE is not necessarily an MSNE of the complete game. In Sect. 5.1, we showed how we can find the MSNE of the game, given a subset of strategy sets for each agent. In this section, based on our approach for resolving challenges of solving our MTD game with the DO algorithm (Sect. 5.2), we propose our framework to find the MSNE of the MTD game and therefore, the optimal decision making policy for the adversary and the defender. Algorithm 2 shows a pseudo-code of our framework.

We start by initializing the adversary's and defender's strategy sets Π_0^a and Π_0^d with heuristic policies (Sect. 6.1). From this stage, we proceed in iterations. In each iteration, first, we compute an MSNE (σ^a, σ^d) of the game restricted to the current strategy sets Π^a and Π^d, take the adversary's equilibrium mixed strategy σ^a and train an approximate best-response policy $(\pi_+^d(\sigma^a))$ for the defender assuming that the adversary uses σ^a. Next, we add this new policy to the defender's set of policies $(\Pi^d \leftarrow \Pi^d \cup \{\pi_+^d\})$.

Then, we do the same for the adversary. First, find the MSNE strategy of the defender (σ^d), and train an approximate best-response policy $(\pi_+^a(\sigma^d))$ for the adversary assuming that the defender uses σ^d. Then, we add this new policy to the adversary's set of policies $(\Pi^a \leftarrow \Pi^a \cup \{\pi_+^a\})$.

In both cases, when computing an approximate best response $(\pi_+(\sigma_*))$ for a player against its opponent's MSNE strategy σ_*, the opponent's strategy σ_* is fixed, so we may consider it to be part of the player's environment. As a result, we can cast the problem of finding an approximate best response as *Independent Reinforcement Learning* (InRL). Each invocation of InRL, denoted as `train()` in Algorithm 2, receives the limit on the number of training steps T of training and initial parameters θ. Moreover, we let $env^p[\sigma^{\bar{p}}]$ denote the InRL environment for player p when its opponent plays a mixed strategy $\sigma^{\bar{p}}$.

As we are dealing with discrete action and observation spaces in the MTD model, DQL [18] is a suitable InRL algorithm for finding an approximate best response. In each time step of the InRL, both players need to decide on an action. The learning agent either chooses an action randomly (*i.e.*, exploration), or follows its current policy. The opponent, whose strategy is a fixed mixed strategy $\sigma^{\bar{p}}$, refers to a pure strategy $\pi^{\bar{p}} \in \Pi^{\bar{p}}$ with probability distribution $\sigma^{\bar{p}}$ and follows that policy.

The MSNE payoff evolves over the iterations of the DO algorithm: whenever we add a new policy for an agent, which is trained against its opponent's best mixed strategy so far, the MSNE changes in favor of the agent. We continue these iterations until the MSNE payoff of the defender and the adversary $(U^p(\sigma_*^p, \sigma_*^{\bar{p}}))$ converges. Formally, we say that the MSNE is converged for both players *iff*

$$\forall_{p \in \{a,d\}} : U^p(\pi_+^p, \sigma^{\bar{p}}) \leq U^p(\sigma^p, \sigma^{\bar{p}}) \tag{23}$$

where σ^p is player p's current MSNE strategy and π_+^p is the approximate best response found for player p against its opponent's current MSNE strategy. Convergence of the algorithm means that neither the adversary nor defender could perform better by introducing a new policy.

6   Evaluation

In this section, we first describe the heuristic strategies of the MTD game (Sect. 6.1) proposed by Prakash and Wellman [22]. Next, we discuss our implementation of the framework (Sect. 6.2). Finally, we present the numerical results (Sect. 6.3).

6.1   Baseline Heuristic Strategies

Prakash and Wellman [22] proposed a set of heuristic strategies for both the adversary and the defender. Earlier, we used these strategies as our initial policy space for the DO algorithm. In this section, we describe these heuristics.

Adversary's Heuristic Strategies

- *Uniform-Uncompromised:* Adversary launches a probe every P_A time steps, always selecting the target server uniformly at random from the servers under the defender's control.
- *MaxProbe-Uncompromised:* Adversary launches a probe every P_A time steps, always targeting the server under the defender's control that has been probed the most since the last reimage (breaking ties uniformly at random).
- *Control-Threshold:* Adversary launches a probe if the adversary controls less than a threshold τ fraction of the servers, always targeting the server under the defender's control that has been probed the most since the last reimage (breaking ties uniformly at random).
- *No-Op:* Adversary never launches a probe.

Defender's Heuristic Strategies

- *Uniform:* Defender reimages a server every P_D time steps, always selecting a server that is up uniformly at random.

Table 3. Payoff table for heuristic and reinforcement learning based strategies

Adversary \ Defender	No-OP	ControlThreshold	PCP	Uniform	MaxProbe	Mixed-Strategy DQL
No-OP	98.20 / 26.89	98.20 / 26.89	98.20 / 26.89	95.83 / 46.03	98.20 / 26.89	97.47 / 33.23
MaxProbe	47.69 / 78.66	49.62 / 75.67	93.01 / 36.58	67.12 / 64.56	86.82 / 41.99	87.84 / 45.87
Uniform	46.74 / 79.08	51.58 / 70.97	89.48 / 44.43	76.23 / 56.83	75.21 / 57.14	88.16 / 45.91
ControlThreshold	85.98 / 63.64	85.35 / 65.58	88.81 / 46.38	81.32 / 59.54	80.09 / 60.43	87.91 / 45.91
Mixed-Strategy DQL	72.29 / 62.78	82.45 / 58.31	91.32 / 45.76	87.10 / 55.31	91.32 / 44.57	92.38 / 45.23

- *MaxProbe:* Defender reimages a server every P_D time steps, always selecting the server that has been probed the most (as observed by the defender) since the last reimage (breaking ties uniformly at random).
- *Probe-Count-or-Period (PCP):* Defender reimages a server which has not been probed in the last P time steps or has been probed more than π times (selecting uniformly at random if there are multiple such servers).
- *Control-Threshold:* Defender assumes that all of the observed probes on a server except the last one were unsuccessful. Then, it calculates the probability of a server being compromised by the last probe as $1 - e^{-\alpha \cdot (\rho+1)}$. Finally, if the expected number of servers in its control is below $\tau \cdot M$ and it has not reimaged any servers in P_D, then it reimages the server with the highest probability of being compromised (breaking ties uniformly at random). In other words, it reimages a server *iff* the last reimage was at least P_D time steps ago and $\mathbb{E}[n_c^d] \leq M \cdot \tau$.
- *No-Op:* Defender never reimages any servers.

6.2 Implementation

We implemented the MAPOMDP of Sect. 3 as an Open AI Gym [4] environment. We used Stable-Baselines' DQN [8] as the implementation of the DQL. Stable-Baselines internally uses TensorFlow [1] as the neural network framework. For the artificial neural network as our Q approximator, we used a feed forward network with two hidden layers of size 32, and *tanh* as our activation function. The rest of parameters are described in Table 1. We implemented the remainder of our framework in Python, including the double oracle algorithm. For computation of the mixed-strategy ϵ-equilibrium of a general-sum game, we used the Gambit-Project's Global Newton implementation [16].

We run the experiments on a computer cluster, where each node has two 14-core 2.4 GHz Intel Xeon CPUs and two NVIDIA P100 GPUs. Each node is capable of running $\approx$85 steps of DQL per second, which results in about 1.5 h of running time per each invocation of the best-response oracle (*i.e.*, DQL training for the adversary or defender). Note that the DQL algorithm is not distributed, so we use only one core of the CPU, and one GPU. It is important to note that in practice,

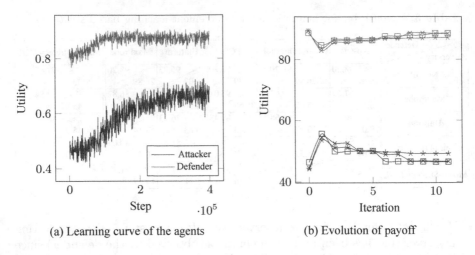

(a) Learning curve of the agents   (b) Evolution of payoff

Fig. 2. (a) shows the learning curve of the players. In (b), iteration 0 shows the MSNE payoff of the heuristics while each DQN training for adversary and defender happens at odd and even iterations, respectively.

optimal policies can be pre-computed, and then executed to mitigate attacks when needed. When policies are executed, inference takes only milliseconds.

6.3   Numerical Results

For acquiring the following results, our MTD model is always instantiated using baseline parameters from Table 1, unless explicitly specified otherwise.

DQL Convergence and Stability. Figure 2a shows the learning curve of the agents for their first iteration of the DO algorithm (Iteration 1 and 2). On average, the DQL algorithm converges in $3.88 \cdot 10^5$ steps (49.11 min) for the adversary, and $1.10 \cdot 10^5$ steps (18.13 min) for the defender. We can see that over the iterations of the DO algorithm, the speed of the training decreases. For example, in the first iteration of adversary training, DQL's speed is 131.67 steps per second, while for the first iteration of defender training, DQL's speed reduces to 101.12 steps per second. Further, in the fourth training of the adversary, training speed is decreased furthermore to 52.34 iterations per second.

Since over the iterations of the DO algorithm, the fraction of DQL strategies in both players MSNE increase (0% vs 51% for the first trainings), and inference from a DQL policy, which requires matrix multiplications, is slower than inference from a heuristic strategy, which requires only a few operations, we can conclude that DQL policies will be more dominant over the iterations. This means that DQL policies are performing better than heuristics over the iterations.

To measure the stability of the DQL algorithm, we extracted the first DQL trainings for both players. The DQL algorithm converges to almost the same expected cumulative reward with mean and standard deviation of 0.672 and 0.021 for the adversary and 0.878 and 0.011 for the defender. Table 3, which we will discuss in detail later, shows that these policies are significantly better than the heuristics.

DO Convergence and Stability.
Figure 2b shows the evolution of MSNE payoff over the iterations of the DO algorithm over three experiments with baseline values of Table 1. In this figure, each training for the adversary and defender happens at odd and even iterations, respectively, while iteration 0 is the equilibrium of heuristic policies. The figure shows that the DO algorithm indeed converges with ≈4 trainings for each player, *i.e.*, 6 h of training in total. Comparing multiple runs with the same configuration shows that the DO algorithm with multiple approximations (*e.g.*, approximation with deep networks, approximation on equilibrium computation) is stable since the average and standard

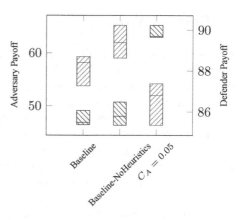

Fig. 3. Comparison of stability for different configurations. The blue and red boxes show the adversary's and defender's payoff, respectively. Each box shows the result of eight runs. (Color figure online)

deviation of the MSNE payoff is 47.81 and 1.77 for the adversary and 88.92 and 1.04 for the defender. For different configurations, the difference between final expected payoffs of eight DO runs is described in Fig. 3.

Equilibrium Selection. To analyze the impact of equilibrium selection on the MSNE payoff of the game, we executed Algorithm 2, but without heuristics as initial strategy sets. Instead, the initial strategy sets are set to only NoOP adversary and NoOP defender. As we can see in Fig. 3, regardless of the initial strategy sets, the resulting policies always converge to an MSNE with the same payoffs for both players. As a result, equilibrium selection is not an issue in practice since we always end with approximately the same equilibrium.

Heuristic Strategies. Table 3 shows the utilities for all combinations of heuristic defender and adversary strategies with baselines parameters. The optimal strategy given only heuristics as players' strategy sets are PCP for the defender, and control threshold for the adversary. This table also compares these heuristic strategies to mixed-strategy policies computed using DO and DQL. We can see that it is optimal for both players to commit to the mixed strategy DQL, since no player can receive more utility by committing to another policy, while the opponent still commits to the DQL policy.

Resiliency to Under/Over Estimation. One interesting observation of the DQL policies is their resiliency to under/over estimation of the opponent. As a showcase for when the defender underestimates the adversary, assume a defender who has trained with $C_A = 0.2$ plays with an adversary who is trained with $C_A = 0.05$. They receive 88.18 and 61.93 utility, respectively. For the defender, this utility is the same as when it correctly predicts the cost of attack (Fig. 3).

7   Related Work

In this work, we used multi-agent reinforcement learning to find optimal policies for the adversary and the defender in an MTD game model. In prior work, researchers have investigated both the application of reinforcement learning in cyber-security (Sect. 7.2) and game-theoretic models for MTD (Sect. 7.1). Perhaps the most closely related work on integration of reinforcement learning and moving target defense is the work of Sengupta and Kambhampati [24]. They propose a Bayesian Stackelberg game model to MTD and solve (*i.e.,* find the optimal action policy for the defender) it using Q-Learning. One main difference between our model and their model is that they assumed that the adversary is aware of the defender's policy, while in our model, not only both players are unaware of the opponent's strategy, they might not even observe the opponent's actions. One key advantage of our model is that we consider multiple target systems while they consider a single target system with four possible states. This makes a tabular approach (Q-Learning) feasible. However, tabular approaches scale poorly to more complex systems.

7.1   Moving Target Defense

One of the main research areas in moving target defense is to model interactions between the adversaries and the defenders. In the area of game-theoretic models for moving target defense, the most closely related work is from Prakash *et al.* [22], which introduces the model that our work uses. This model can also be used for defense against DDoS attacks [31], and defense for web applications [25]. Further, in this area, researchers have proposed MTD game models based on Stackelberg games [13], Markov Games [12,28], Markov Decision Process [32], and FlipIt game [20].

For solving a game model (*i.e.,* finding the optimal playing strategies), numerous approaches such as solving a min-max problem [13], non-linear programming [12], Bellman equation [28,32], Bayesian belief networks [2], and reinforcement learning [9,20] has been suggested.

7.2   Reinforcement Learning for Cybersecurity

Application of machine learning—especially *deep reinforcement learning* (DRL)—for cybersecurity has gained attention recently. Nguyen *et al.* [19] surveyed current literature on applications of DRL on cybersecurity. These applications include: DRL-based security methods for cyber-physical systems, autonomous intrusion detection techniques [10], and multi-agent DRL-based game-theoretic simulations for defense strategies against cyber attacks.

For example, Malialis [14,15] applied multi-agent deep reinforcement learning on network routers to throttle the processing rate in order to prevent *distributed denial of service* (DDoS) attacks. Bhosale *et al.* [3] proposed a cooperative multi-agent reinforcement learning for intelligent systems [7] to enable quick responses. Another example for multi-agent reinforcement learning is the fuzzy Q-Learning approach for detecting and preventing intrusions in *wireless sensor networks* (WSN) [26]. Furthermore, Tong *et al.* [29] proposed a multi-agent reinforcement learning framework for alert correlation based on double oracles.

8 Conclusion

Moving target defense tries to increase adversary's uncertainty and attack cost by dynamically changing host and network configurations. In this paper, we have proposed a multi-agent reinforcement learning approach for finding MTD strategies based on an adaptive MTD model. To improve the agents' performance in partially-observable environments, we proposed a compact memory presentation for the agents. Further, we showed that the double oracle algorithm with DQL as best-response oracle is a feasible and promising solution for finding optimal policies in general-sum adversarial games as it is stable and converges rapidly.

Acknowledgments. This research was partially supported by the NSF (CAREER Grant IIS-1905558) and ARO (W911NF1910241).

References

1. Abadi, M., et al.: TensorFlow: a system for large-scale machine learning. In: 12th USENIX Symposium on Operating Systems Design and Implementation (OSDI), pp. 265–283 (2016)
2. Albanese, M., Connell, W., Venkatesan, S., Cybenko, G.: Moving target defense quantification. In: Jajodia, S., Cybenko, G., Liu, P., Wang, C., Wellman, M. (eds.) Adversarial and Uncertain Reasoning for Adaptive Cyber Defense. LNCS, vol. 11830, pp. 94–111. Springer, Cham (2019). https://doi.org/10.1007/978-3-030-30719-6_5
3. Bhosale, R., Mahajan, S., Kulkarni, P.: Cooperative machine learning for intrusion detection system. Int. J. Sci. Eng. Res. **5**(1), 1780–1785 (2014)
4. Brockman, G., et al.: OpenAI gym (2016)
5. Chen, P., Xu, J., Lin, Z., Xu, D., Mao, B., Liu, P.: A practical approach for adaptive data structure layout randomization. In: Pernul, G., Ryan, P.Y.A., Weippl, E. (eds.) ESORICS 2015. LNCS, vol. 9326, pp. 69–89. Springer, Cham (2015). https://doi.org/10.1007/978-3-319-24174-6_4
6. Govindan, S., Wilson, R.: A global Newton method to compute Nash equilibria. J. Econ. Theory **110**(1), 65–86 (2003)
7. Herrero, Á., Corchado, E.: Multiagent systems for network intrusion detection: a review. In: Herrero, Á., Gastaldo, P., Zunino, R., Corchado, E. (eds.) Computational Intelligence in Security for Information Systems. AINSC, vol. 63, pp. 143–154. Springer, Heidelberg (2009). https://doi.org/10.1007/978-3-642-04091-7_18

8. Hill, A., et al.: Stable baselines (2018). https://github.com/hill-a/stable-baselines

9. Hu, Z., Chen, P., Zhu, M., Liu, P.: Reinforcement learning for adaptive cyber defense against zero-day attacks. In: Jajodia, S., Cybenko, G., Liu, P., Wang, C., Wellman, M. (eds.) Adversarial and Uncertain Reasoning for Adaptive Cyber Defense. LNCS, vol. 11830, pp. 54–93. Springer, Cham (2019). https://doi.org/10.1007/978-3-030-30719-6_4

10. Iannucci, S., Barba, O.D., Cardellini, V., Banicescu, I.: A performance evaluation of deep reinforcement learning for model-based intrusion response. In: 4th IEEE International Workshops on Foundations and Applications of Self* Systems (FAS* W), pp. 158–163 (2019)

11. Lanctot, M., et al.: A unified game-theoretic approach to multiagent reinforcement learning. In: Advances in Neural Information Processing Systems, pp. 4190–4203 (2017)

12. Lei, C., Ma, D.H., Zhang, H.Q.: Optimal strategy selection for moving target defense based on Markov game. IEEE Access **5**, 156–169 (2017)

13. Li, H., Zheng, Z.: Optimal timing of moving target defense: a Stackelberg game model. arXiv preprint arXiv:1905.13293 (2019)

14. Malialis, K., Devlin, S., Kudenko, D.: Distributed reinforcement learning for adaptive and robust network intrusion response. Connect. Sci. **27**(3), 234–252 (2015)

15. Malialis, K., Kudenko, D.: Distributed response to network intrusions using multiagent reinforcement learning. Eng. Appl. Artif. Intell. **41**, 270–284 (2015)

16. McKelvey, R.D., McLennan, A.M., Turocy, T.L.: Gambit: software tools for game theory (2006)

17. McMahan, H.B., Gordon, G.J., Blum, A.: Planning in the presence of cost functions controlled by an adversary. In: Proceedings of the 20th International Conference on Machine Learning (ICML 2003), pp. 536–543 (2003)

18. Mnih, V., et al.: Playing Atari with deep reinforcement learning. arXiv preprint arXiv:1312.5602 (2013)

19. Nguyen, T.T., Reddi, V.J.: Deep reinforcement learning for cyber security. arXiv preprint arXiv:1906.05799 (2019)

20. Oakley, L., Oprea, A.: Playing adaptively against stealthy opponents: a reinforcement learning strategy for the FlipIt security game. arXiv preprint arXiv:1906.11938 (2019)

21. Oh, J., Chockalingam, V., Singh, S., Lee, H.: Control of memory, active perception, and action in Minecraft. arXiv preprint arXiv:1605.09128 (2016)

22. Prakash, A., Wellman, M.P.: Empirical game-theoretic analysis for moving target defense. In: 2nd ACM Workshop on Moving Target Defense (MTD), pp. 57–65. ACM (2015)

23. Russell, S., Norvig, P.: Artificial Intelligence: A Modern Approach. Prentice Hall, Upper Saddle River (2002)

24. Sengupta, S., Kambhampati, S.: Multi-agent reinforcement learning in Bayesian Stackelberg Markov games for adaptive moving target defense. arXiv preprint arXiv:2007.10457 (2020)

25. Sengupta, S., et al.: A game theoretic approach to strategy generation for moving target defense in web applications. In: 16th Conference on Autonomous Agents and Multiagent Systems, pp. 178–186 (2017)

26. Shamshirband, S., Patel, A., Anuar, N.B., Kiah, M.L.M., Abraham, A.: Cooperative game theoretic approach using fuzzy Q-learning for detecting and preventing intrusions in wireless sensor networks. Eng. Appl. Artif. Intell. **32**, 228–241 (2014)

27. Shoham, Y., Leyton-Brown, K.: Multiagent Systems: Algorithmic, Game-Theoretic, and Logical Foundations. Cambridge University Press, Cambridge (2008)
28. Tan, J., Lei, C., Zhang, H., Cheng, Y.: Optimal strategy selection approach to moving target defense based on Markov robust game. Comput. Secur. $8(5)$, 63–76 (2019)
29. Tong, L., Laszka, A., Yan, C., Zhang, N., Vorobeychik, Y.: Finding needles in a moving haystack: prioritizing alerts with adversarial reinforcement learning. arXiv preprint arXiv:1906.08805 (2019)
30. Watkins, C.J., Dayan, P.: Q-learning. Mach. Learn. $8(3–4)$, 279–292 (1992)
31. Wright, M., Venkatesan, S., Albanese, M., Wellman, M.P.: Moving target defense against DDoS attacks: an empirical game-theoretic analysis. In: 3rd ACM Workshop on Moving Target Defense (MTD), pp. 93–104. ACM (2016)
32. Zheng, J., Namin, A.S.: Markov decision process to enforce moving target defense policies. arXiv preprint arXiv:1905.09222 (2019)

Lie Another Day: Demonstrating Bias in a Multi-round Cyber Deception Game of Questionable Veracity

Mark Bilinski[1]($\boxtimes$)(iD), Joe diVita[1](iD), Kimberly Ferguson-Walter[2](iD), Sunny Fugate[1](iD), Ryan Gabrys[1](iD), Justin Mauger[1](iD), and Brian Souza[1](iD)

[1] Naval Information Warfare Center Pacific, San Diego, CA, USA
{bilinski,divita,fugate,gabrys,jmauger,bsouza}@spawar.navy.mil
[2] Laboratory for Advanced Cybersecurity Research, Laurel, MD, USA
kjfergu@spawar.navy.mil

Abstract. Prior work has explored the use of defensive cyber deception to manipulate the information available to attackers and to proactively lie on behalf of both real and decoy systems. Such approaches can provide advantages to defenders by delaying attacker forward progress and thereby decreasing or eliminating attacker payoffs. In this work, we expand previous work by incorporating new parameters relating to attacker costs and choices. The extended model includes attacker costs for probing a system to learn its declared type ("real" or "fake") and allows an attacker to proactively choose to leave the game early by walking away. While these additional parameters represent extensions to our prior model, they are key to understanding attacker behavior when confronted with deceptive cyber defenses. We first present the extended model and an analysis of the expected rewards for rational players. We then present the behavior of an adaptive attacker in a Markov Decision Process (MDP) simulation. Lastly, we relate our analytic and empirical findings to cognitive bias effects and speculate on how the manipulation of game parameters may be used in future work to both estimate and trigger bias effects during defender-attacker interactions.

1 Introduction

There is a growing body of research exploring the defensive use of cyber deception through the direct manipulation of defender-controlled cyber environments [14]. In particular, cyber deception seeks to reverse traditional asymmetries present in the management and protection of computing systems and networks. While the theory guiding the proper application of cyber deception is still maturing, recent experimental results indicate that these techniques are not only effective, but that their impacts extend beyond their direct technical effects, leading to potentially lasting effects on the decision making of cyber attackers [8,9]. The implication of these findings is that the theories guiding the use of cyber deception should not be limited to the mechanical or procedural interactions

This is a U.S. government work and not under copyright protection in the U.S.;
foreign copyright protection may apply 2020
Q. Zhu et al. (Eds.): GameSec 2020, LNCS 12513, pp. 80–100, 2020.
https://doi.org/10.1007/978-3-030-64793-3_5

of competing entities, but should seek to encompass and exploit principles of human decision making under conditions of uncertainty and risk that have been revealed in the intersection of Cognitive Psychology and Behavioral Economics.

It is well-known that attackers will follow predetermined "rules of thumb" which may be implicit within known *Tactics, Techniques, and Procedures* (TTPs) or explicit and even mandated to ensure stealth or success of a particular cyber operation. Cataloguing and modeling the action spaces of various TTPs has been a widespread focus of cyber defense research to date [23]. While a comprehensive understanding of TTPs is necessary, the models do not currently extend to the behavioral or cognitive aspects of decision making. We believe it is these cognitive aspects which can have the most impact on the success of an attack. While traditional defenses are laser focused on defending against attacks, a human behavioral approach would defend against the human decision makers behind the attacks – bringing to bear not only the technical defenses already in play but tools designed to induce cognitive biases and cyber deterrence [20]. Recent research suggests that defenses which make use of cognitive bias effects can have immediate and lasting impacts against the human driving the attack [12,13].

As part of this ongoing effort, in this work we aim to further develop and analyze a cyber deception model whose framework is capable of incorporating cognitive and behavioral aspects of decision making. In [2], we introduced a simple masking game which abstracts away the mechanism of attacks and deceptive defenses and focuses on fundamental choices made by an attacker and a defender. In this game there are only two systems, one real and one fake. Each round the attacker may either probe or attack. When probed, a defended system sends a signal of questionable veracity indicating that it is either "real" or "fake." If a system's true type is masked by a false answer, then this is a deception. An attacker might even believe an honest response to be a deception. This interaction continues over many rounds until the attacker chooses to end the game by attacking, or the round limit is reached. The full parameters of this game are discussed in Sect. 3.1, as are the extensions – cost for probing and attacker action of walking away, allowing the defender to "lie another day."

Our initial work focused on the defender, resulting in a careful analysis of the optimal defender responses. A key assumption of the model was that the defender is unable to preemptively exit or end the game. This parallels the unfortunate scenario played out in many cyber attacks in which ejecting the attacker only informs the attacker of the observability of a particular technique, but does not prevent them from regaining access. A patient attacker might simply play sufficiently many repeated games to learn the defender's strategy. Indeed, in our initial study of the simplest forms of this game, an attacker has no incentive to attack prior to achieving sufficient confidence in the estimated defender characteristics. To reflect the "urgency" of an attacker in the face of opportunity costs for long enough games, we introduced an exponentially decaying multiplicative factor in the value of a system. Even with this rudimentary defensive model, the results of our preliminary work suggest both significant challenges for analysis as well as interesting and exploitable player behaviors. Our aim in this work is to consider a worst-case scenario from the point of view of the defender where the defender is heavily constrained in terms of their actions and where the attacker is aware of the costs associated with the defender's actions. Despite this advantage, we show that in many cases the attacker's best course of action is not always straightforward to determine.

Let τ_R, τ_F denote the probability the real and fake machines (respectively) tell the truth within our cyber deception model. In our initial work [2], we derived expressions for the optimal choices of τ_R, τ_F under the assumption that the defender pays a penalty for lying. The optimal choices were deterministic, i.e. for a reward maximizing defender, $\tau_R, \tau_F \in \{0, 1\}$. The natural question then is how should an attacker/defender behave if the defender is playing the game sub-optimally (and hence non-deterministically). This work aims to answer this question. Our main analytic result, which appears as Theorem 1, shows that the optimal number of rounds an attacker should play is at most sublinear with respect to the value V of the game. We then simulate the performance of a reinforcement learning (RL) agent operating within our game environment and show that in many cases the behavior of the agent aligns with our analysis.

The main contributions of this work are the following: (i) we generalize our previous game setup by incorporating a cost c_p to the attacker for probing; (ii) we allow the attacker to determine the round at which to attack; (iii) we derive an asymptotic result which shows that an attacker who seeks to maximize their expected reward should play the game for at most N rounds where N is sublinear in V; and (iv) we augment our framework by allowing the attacker the ability to exit the game early without attacking. This feature establishes a framework for investigating the role of human cognitive bias in our game of deception [12]; a topic which is discussed further in Sect. 4.4.

This paper is organized as follows. Section 2 discusses background work, highlighting where our model differs from existing art. Section 3 presents our analytic results on optimal attacker behavior. Section 4 simulates the interactions of an attacker and defender using a RL agent. Finally, Sect. 5 concludes the paper and proposes future work.

2   Related Work

Game theory is one of the methods that can be used to model cyber deception and the changes that deception drives for both the attacker and defender [1,7, 27]. This can lead to practical solutions that inform automatically adapting AI systems and advance the application of cyber deception techniques. One well-studied area related to cyber deception is the problem of deploying honeypots in a distributed environment. Under this setup, there are usually two players: (1) a defender and (2) an attacker. The defender, which is monitoring some collection of network resources, is able to deploy a certain number of honeypots, usually at some predetermined cost. The goal of the attacker then is to identify the locations of these honeypots, and to use this knowledge to expose system vulnerabilities. Typically these problems are modeled as two person, zero-sum games and such games have been studied extensively in the past [3,5,11].

Although the topic of deploying and configuring honeypots has received significant attention, there have been notably fewer works on the strategic use of honeypots and other forms of deception from a game-theoretic perspective. In [21], a model was proposed that included the interactions between the attacker and defender. This communication was then used by the attacker to determine whether a particular machine is a honeypot or not. In [6], and similar to [11], the interaction between the attacker and defender was modeled as a signaling game to mitigate denial of service attacks. Under this model, a defender can observe the attacker actions and subsequently improve their defenses.

Unlike previous work, our work does not allow the defender to change the underlying system configuration, but rather focuses on responses to the attacker's probes of the system. Our goal was to construct as simple a model as possible to capture the essence of deception. Similar to [22,28], we introduce a game with two repeated stages, where in the first stage the attacker probes the machines.

Due to the simplicity of our model and unlike [16,22], we were able to derive closed form expressions that represent optimal strategies for both the attacker and defender in [2]. In this work, we build upon this result and analyze the optimal behavior for the attacker provided that the defender is not playing the game optimally. In addition to the mathematical analysis, we simulate the interaction between players by using an RL agent as the attacker. Although our model does not allow direct manipulation of the cost signals for the RL agent as in [15], our model does provide insight into beneficial heuristics for the setup where an RL agent is operating in a deceptive environment. In addition, we discuss extensions to the existing model that incorporate possible cognitive bias.

3   Analysis of Optimal Attacker Strategies

In this section, we consider an attacker that wishes to maximize their expected reward. We begin by first describing our game before proceeding to the analysis.

3.1   Game Model

In this work, we study a generalization of the game model originally introduced in our preliminary work [2]. Our game model involves two players: an attacker and a defender. There are two machines, which we subsequently refer to as machine 1 and machine 2. One of these machines is real, and the other one is a decoy (fake). The identities of the machines are known to the defender, but not to the attacker, and the goal of the attacker is to attack the real machine.

The game is iterative and it proceeds in rounds where at every round, the attacker probes one of the two machines asking about its identity, or attacks. If the attacker probes a specific machine, then that machine–which is controlled by the defender–either responds truthfully about its identity or it lies. If the attacker chooses to attack, then the decision about which machine to target is resolved according to a hypothesis test which is described in Sect. 3.2. If the attacker ended up targeting the real machine, then he receives a reward of V, and otherwise he receives a reward of $-V$, where V is some positive number representing the value of the game. Each round of probing costs the attacker c_p. So if in round $i + 1$ the attacker attacks the real machine, they would get a reward of $V - ic_p$.

As in our previous work, we assume the attacker has accurate cost estimates of each defender action, but does not know the value of the real system. In a sense, our goal here was to consider the worst case scenario where, not only is the game itself simple so that the defender has limited options but also the attacker knows the costs to the defender for lying. We let the defender know the attacker's probing cost c_p. Similar to our earlier work, we also use the simplification that the real system's valuation, V, is the same for both attacker and defender. The parameters are summarized in Table 1.

Table 1. Summary of game parameters

M_R	Real machine	c_R	Defender cost of lying for real machine
M_F	Fake machine	c_F	Defender cost of lying for fake machine
N	Number of rounds	τ_R	Probability that real machine is truthful
V	Value of a real machine	τ_F	Probability that fake machine is truthful
c_p	Attacker cost of probing		

3.2   Cost Hypothesis

Next, we describe the hypothesis test [2] which will be used by the attacker to determine which of the two machines to attack. We assume a worst case scenario for the defender where the attacker knows the cost of lying on the fake machine and the cost of lying on the real machine – c_F and c_R, respectively.

Given that the attacker has knowledge of the defender costs, the attacker uses this knowledge to make its decision regarding which machine to attack. In particular, if the attacker wants to attack, they first compute the cost C_1 to the defender of lying under the hypothesis that machine 1 is the real machine:

$$C_1 = c_R(N_1 - R_1) + c_F R_2,$$

where N_1 and N_2 are the number of times the attacker queries machine 1 and 2 respectively; and R_1 and R_2 are the number of times that machine 1 and 2 respectively say it is the real machine. By symmetry, the calculation is analogous for the hypothesis where machine 1 is fake and 2 is real, giving the quantity C_2:

$$C_2 = c_F R_1 + c_R(N_2 - R_2)$$

When we refer to attacking according to the hypothesis test, we mean an attacker will attack machine 1 if $C_2 > C_1$ and attack machine 2 otherwise.

3.3   Analysis

In order to attack M_1 when it is real, the attacker needs $C_1 < C_2$. This implies:

$$c_R(N_1 - N_2) + (c_F + c_R)(R_2 - R_1) < 0.$$

Letting $\frac{c_R}{c_F} = \beta$, we can re-order terms to get

$$\beta(N_1 - N_2) + (1 + \beta)(R_2 - R_1) < 0. \tag{1}$$

If R_1 represents the sum of N_1 Bernoulli random variables each with parameter τ_R and R_2 represents the sum of N_2 Bernoulli random variables each with parameter $1 - \tau_F$, then the probability that (1) holds is

$$\sum_{k_2=0}^{N_2} \sum_{k_1=\frac{\beta}{1+\beta}(N_1-N_2)+k_2+1}^{N_1} \binom{N_2}{k_2}\binom{N_1}{k_1}(1 - \tau_F)^{k_2}\tau_F^{N_2-k_2}\tau_R^{k_1}(1 - \tau_R)^{N_1-k_1},$$

where we assume that $\frac{\beta}{1+\beta}(N_1 - N_2)$ is an integer.

Since we assume the attacker has no initial preference regarding the identities of the machines, we will focus on the setup where $N_1 = N_2$ so that N is even. For shorthand, let $\gamma(\tau_R, \tau_F)$ denote the probability that the attacker successfully attacks the correct machine so that according to our previous discussion,

$$\gamma = \sum_{k_2=0}^{N/2} \sum_{k_1=k_2+1}^{N/2} \binom{N/2}{k_2}\binom{N/2}{k_1}(1 - \tau_F)^{k_2}\tau_F^{N/2-k_2}\tau_R^{k_1}(1 - \tau_R)^{N/2-k_1}. \tag{2}$$

When clear from context, we will simply refer to $\gamma(\tau_R, \tau_F)$ as γ. Since $N_1 = N_2$, the lower limit of the inner summation simplifies with γ independent of β.

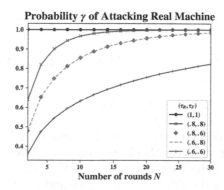

Fig. 1. Probability the attacker targets the real machine

Figure 1 plots γ versus N, for $2 \leq N \leq 30$ and for particular values of (τ_R, τ_F). First, note that all probabilities approach unity as N increases. This reflects that more probing can only help the attacker. Second, notice that the curves for $(\tau_R, \tau_F) = (0.8, 0.6)$ and $(\tau_R, \tau_F) = (0.6, 0.8)$ coincide. We will prove in Lemma 1 that this property holds in general, and a bound on the probability the attacker chooses the correct machine depends on the difference between τ_R and $(1 - \tau_F)$. Thus, from the attacker's point of view, it does not matter which machine is being untruthful. If there are different costs associated with lying for the defender, then it is more beneficial for the defender to lie more frequently at the less costly (with the same effect on the hypothesis test).

We now analyze the attacker's expected reward. Suppose that the penalty for probing at each round is c_p. Then, if the game proceeds for N rounds, it follows that the expected value (reward) of the game is:

$$R(N) = \gamma(V - Nc_p) + (1 - \gamma)(-V - Nc_p) = V(2\gamma - 1) - Nc_p. \tag{3}$$

It will be informative to plot the expected reward as a fraction of V. This has the effect of expressing the dependency of Eq. (3) on the parameters V and c_p in terms of the dimensionless ratio V/c_p. In Fig. 2 we plot the quantity

$$\frac{R(N)}{V} = 2\gamma - 1 - \frac{N}{V/c_p} \tag{4}$$

for the setup where $V \in 10, 20, 100$, $c_p = 1$, and $N \in 20, 40, 50$.

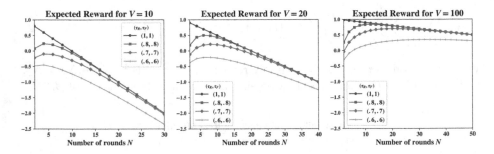

Fig. 2. Expected rewards for increasing ratios V/c_p.

There are a few patterns which can be observed in these plots. Whenever there is deception present, the expected reward starts increasing, then decreases as N gets large. This is due to the interplay between γ increasing with N, and the costs of continuing to probe also increasing. The effect is most pronounced the less truthful the machines are, and the larger V is relative to c_p. The location of the peak increases as the ratio V/c_p increases and τ_R, τ_F decrease.

This motivates the question of determining the relationship between the parameters V, N, τ_R, τ_F, and c_p. In particular, for fixed V, τ_R, τ_F, and c_p, let $N^* = \mathrm{argmax}_N(R(N))$ denote the optimal number of rounds the attacker should play. Without loss of generality, we may assume $c_p = 1$. Certainly, the attacker has no reason to probe more than V times, since then the largest reward they could get is negative – worse than just attacking immediately. Can they do better? Figure 3 plots the value of N^* as a function of V for different pairs of (τ_R, τ_F). For low levels of deception, the growth of N^* appears logarithmic in V. For high levels, growth is larger. We next turn to computing this value.

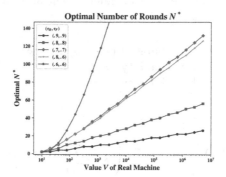

Fig. 3. Growth of N^* as a function of V

Due to the convolution, computing (2) for a large number of rounds N quickly becomes intractable; so we turn to analyzing the effects of increasing V on the expression (2) in this regime using probabilistic bounds. Our goal is to study the relationship between N and V as both parameters become large. The main result, which is presented in Theorem 1, shows that in the asymptotic regime $(N, V$ large), the optimal number of rounds that should be played by the attacker is at most sublinear with respect to V. We begin by bounding the value of γ from (2), which is the probability the attacker attacks the correct machine.

Lemma 1. *Suppose that $\tau_F, \tau_R > \frac{1}{2}$. Then, the probability that the hypothesis test fails is at most*

$$1 - \gamma \leq \exp\left(-\frac{N}{4}(1 - \tau_F - \tau_R)^2\right),$$

and the probability the hypothesis test succeeds is at most

$$\gamma \leq 1 - \binom{N/2}{N/4}^2 \left(\tau_R \tau_F (1 - \tau_R)(1 - \tau_F)\right)^{N/4}.$$

Furthermore, $\gamma(\tau_R, \tau_F) = \gamma(\tau_F, \tau_R)$.

Proof. From (2),

$$1 - \gamma = \sum_{k_2=0}^{N/2} \sum_{k_1=0}^{k_2} \binom{N/2}{k_2}\binom{N/2}{k_1}(1 - \tau_F)^{k_2}\tau_F^{N/2-k_2}\tau_R^{k_1}(1 - \tau_R)^{N/2-k_1}.$$

Let Y_1 and Y_2 be binomial random variables with parameters $(N/2, \tau_R)$ and $(N/2, 1 - \tau_F)$ respectively. Then the previous expression is equivalent to

$$\Pr(Y_2 \geq Y_1).$$

Let $X_1, X_2, \ldots, X_{\frac{N}{2}}$ denote a set of independent and identically distributed random variables where for $i \in \frac{N}{2}$, we have

$$X_i = \begin{cases} 1, & \text{with probability } (1 - \tau_R)(1 - \tau_F), \\ 0, & \text{with probability } \tau_R(1 - \tau_F) + (1 - \tau_R)\tau_F, \\ -1, & \text{with probability } \tau_R \tau_F \end{cases}.$$

Note that

$$1 - \gamma(\tau_R, \tau_F) = \Pr(Y_2 \geq Y_1) = \Pr\left(\frac{1}{N/2} \sum_{i=1}^{N/2} X_i \geq 0\right) \tag{5}$$

$$= \Pr\left(\frac{1}{N/2} \sum_{i=1}^{N/2} X_i - [(1 - \tau_F) - \tau_R] \geq [\tau_R - (1 - \tau_F)]\right).$$

Note that since $\tau_R, \tau_F > \frac{1}{2}$ by assumption, $\tau_R - (1 - \tau_F) > 0$. Since $E\left[\frac{1}{N/2} \sum_{i=1}^{N/2} X_i\right] = (1 - \tau_F) - \tau_R$, we can apply a generalization of Hoeffding's inequality where X_i are strictly bound by the intervals $[-1, 1]$ to get

$$\Pr(Y_2 \geq Y_1) \leq \exp\left(\frac{-2(N/2)^2(1 - \tau_R - \tau_F)^2}{\sum_{i=1}^{N/2}[1 - -1]^2}\right) \leq \exp\left(-\frac{N}{4}(1 - \tau_F - \tau_R)^2\right),$$

which implies the first statement in the lemma.

Next, we upper bound the probability the quantity that the hypothesis test succeeds, which is equal to $\Pr(Y_1 > Y_2)$. For this quantity, we note that it is at least as large as the largest individual term in the expression

$$\Pr(Y_2 \geq Y_1) > \binom{N/2}{N/4}(1 - \tau_F)^{N/4}\tau_F^{N/4}\binom{N/2}{N/4}(\tau_R)^{N/4}\tau_R^{N/4},$$

which implies the following and gives the second statement of the lemma:

$$\gamma(\tau_R, \tau_F) = \Pr(Y_1 > Y_2) \leq 1 - \binom{N/2}{N/4}^2 \left(\tau_R \tau_F(1 - \tau_R)(1 - \tau_F)\right)^{N/4}.$$

To prove the last statement, note that by switching τ_R, τ_F in (5), we get

$$1 - \gamma(\tau_F, \tau_R) = \Pr\left(\frac{1}{N/2} \sum_{i=1}^{N/2} \widehat{X}_i\right) \geq 0,$$

where

$$\widehat{X}_i = \begin{cases} 1, & \text{with probability } (1 - \tau_F)(1 - \tau_R), \\ 0, & \text{with probability } \tau_F(1 - \tau_R) + (1 - \tau_F)\tau_R, \\ -1, & \text{with probability } \tau_F\tau_R \end{cases}.$$

Since $\widehat{X}_i = X_i$, it follows that $\gamma(\tau_F, \tau_R) = \gamma(\tau_R, \tau_F)$, and the result follows.

An immediate consequence of the previous lemma is provided in the following corollary, which follows by substituting the upper/lower bounds on γ into (3).

Corollary 1. *The expected reward $\widehat{R}(N)$ of a game with N rounds is at most*

$$V\left(1 - 2\binom{N/2}{N/4}^2 \zeta^{-N/4}\right) - Nc_p,$$

where $\zeta = \frac{1}{\tau_R\tau_F(1-\tau_R)(1-\tau_F)}$, and at least

$$V\left(1 - 2\exp\left(-\frac{N}{4}(1 - \tau_F - \tau_R)^2\right)\right) - Nc_p.$$

As a result of the previous corollary, we can determine the relationship between N and V. This is made precise in the following theorem, which represents the main contribution of this section. Recall that we assume $N_1 = N_2 = \frac{N}{2}$.

Theorem 1. *Assuming ζ is a constant with respect to V and $\frac{1}{2} < \tau_R, \tau_F < 1$, the expected reward of the game is maximized when the number of rounds played by the attacker is at most proportional to $\sqrt{V}$.*

Proof. The proof is organized as follows. We bound the expected reward $\widehat{R}(N)$ between lower bound $R_{LB}(N)$ and upper bound $R_{UB}(N)$. We show that R_{UB} is non-increasing after at most $\mathcal{O}(\log V)$ rounds. Then, we consider the value of our upper and lower bound at two different values of N. We show that when $N_U = C\sqrt{V}$ and $N_L = \sqrt{V}$, $R_{LB}(N_L) > R_{UB}(N_U)$ for an appropriate choice of constant $C > 1$. Since R_{UB} is decreasing after round N_U, the attacker cannot increase their reward if they play more than N_U rounds, giving the desired result.

From Corollary 1, we have that the expected reward of the game is at most $V\left(1 - 2\binom{N/2}{N/4}^2\zeta^{-N/4}\right) - Nc_p$. Using the fact that $\binom{n}{k} \geq \left(\frac{n}{k}\right)^k$, this implies that the expected reward of the game is bounded above by

$$R_{UB}(N) = V\left(1 - 2 \cdot 2^{N/2}\zeta^{-N/4}\right) - Nc_p = V\left(1 - 2(\zeta/4)^{-N/4}\right) - Nc_p. \quad (6)$$

Taking the derivative of $R_{UB}(N)$ with respect to N, we get

$$-c_p + 2V(\zeta/4)^{-N/4}\log(\zeta/4) \cdot 1/4. \quad (7)$$

Setting the previous expression equal to zero and solving for N, gives

$$N^* = \frac{4}{\log(\zeta/4)}\log\left(\frac{V\log(\zeta/4)}{2c_p}\right). \quad (8)$$

From (7), it is easy to verify that the second derivative of $R_{UB}(N)$ is negative, implying that $R_{UB}(N)$ is concave. Thus, our upper bound on the expected reward of the game reaches its maximum at N^* and is decreasing for $N > N^*$. Since ζ is assumed to be a constant with respect to V, we have $N^* = \mathcal{O}(\log V)$.

From Corollary 1, the expected reward of the game after N rounds is at least

$$R_{LB}(N) = V\left(1 - 2\exp\left(-\frac{N}{4}(1 - \tau_F - \tau_R)^2\right)\right) - Nc_p.$$

In the following, we want to get a lower bound on the quantity $R_{LB}(N)$. To do this, we bound the term $(1 - \tau_R - \tau_F)^2$ from below. Let $\delta = \min\{1 - \tau_R, 1 - \tau_F, \tau_R, \tau_F\}$. Note that either $\delta = 1 - \tau_R$ or $\delta = 1 - \tau_F$ since $\tau_R, \tau_F > \frac{1}{2}$ by assumption. Without loss of generality, assume that $\delta = 1 - \tau_R$. Then $(1 - \tau_R - \tau_F)^2 = (\delta - \tau_F)^2$, from simple substitution. Now since $\delta < \frac{1}{2}$ and $\tau_F > \frac{1}{2}$,

$$(1 - \tau_R - \tau_F)^2 = (\delta - \tau_F)^2 \geq \left(\delta - \tfrac{1}{2}\right)^2,$$

which implies

$$R_{LB}(N) \geq V\left(1 - 2\exp\left(-\frac{N}{4}\left(\delta - \tfrac{1}{2}\right)^2\right)\right) - Nc_p. \tag{9}$$

It is straightforward to verify that

$$16 < \zeta \leq \frac{1}{\delta^4},$$

where ζ is as defined in Corollary 1. Then, since $\zeta \leq \frac{1}{\delta^4}$, we have

$$R_{UB}(N) \leq V\left(1 - 2\left(\frac{1}{4\delta^4}\right)^{-N/4}\right) - Nc_p. \tag{10}$$

Substituting $N = \sqrt{V}$ into (9) and $N = C\sqrt{V}$ into (10), where $C > 1$ is a constant, we get that $R_{LB}(\sqrt{V}) - R_{UB}(C\sqrt{V}) \geq$

$$c_p(C - 1)\sqrt{V} + 2V\left(\exp\left(C\sqrt{V}\frac{\log 2}{2} + C\sqrt{V}\log\delta\right) - \exp\left(-\tfrac{1}{4}(\delta - \tfrac{1}{2})^2\sqrt{V}\right)\right).$$

Clearly, if $c_p(C - 1) \geq 3$ and $\exp\left(-\tfrac{1}{4}(\delta - \tfrac{1}{2})^2\sqrt{V}\right) \leq V^{-\frac{1}{2}}$, then $R_{LB}(\sqrt{V}) - R_{UB}(C\sqrt{V}) \geq 0$, which would complete the proof. Note that $\exp\left(-\tfrac{1}{4}(\delta - \tfrac{1}{2})^2\sqrt{V}\right) \leq V^{-\frac{1}{2}}$, if

$$\sqrt{V} \cdot \exp\left(-\tfrac{1}{4}(\delta - \tfrac{1}{2})^2\sqrt{V}\right) \leq 1,$$

which (by a change of logs) holds when $\exp\left(\tfrac{1}{2}\log V - \tfrac{1}{4}(\delta - \tfrac{1}{2})^2\sqrt{V}\right) \leq 1$ or

$$\tfrac{1}{2}\log V - \tfrac{1}{4}(\delta - \tfrac{1}{2})^2\sqrt{V} \leq 0,$$

which holds for V large enough, and this completes the proof.

In the next section, we consider the performance of an RL agent under a similar setup. It will be shown that although in many cases the agent behaves in a manner which reflects the analysis discussed here, there are some circumstances under which the agent will behave sub-optimally.

4   Simulation

In this work we extend our simulation results from [2]. In certain scenarios, we previously found that the attacker would choose to continually probe and never attack, indirectly signaling a desire to not play the game. In the following, we consider the setup where the attacker is able to leave the game prematurely which we refer to as the action "walk away". Under this setup, we investigate how the value V of the game influences the length of the game and compare it to the results from Sect. 3. In studying this setup, we identify certain interesting behaviors from the RL agent, and lay the ground work for considering both human and algorithmic biases that could potentially be exploited by a defender.

4.1   Simulation Model

The game model, which is a generalization of the model described in Sect. 3, largely borrows from our earlier prototype established in [2]. The game is a turn based Stackelberg Game, in which the attacker plays first and the defender responds. There are two machines M_1 and M_2, one real and the other fake. The game proceeds in rounds where the attacker probes a machine and the defender responds real or fake – potentially untruthfully. At the beginning of every round, the attacker has four actions, to probe one of the two machines, attack, or walk away. The game ends after at most N rounds. The game proceeds as follows:

1. The game begins at round $i = 1$ with the game initially in state $s = [0, 0, 0, 0]$.
2. Each round begins with the attacker choosing an action from the set:

$$\{P_1, P_2, A, W\}.$$

   If the attacker chooses W, they walk away with 0 reward for the round and the game ends. If the attacker chooses A, then they attack a machine and the game ends. The attacker's choice of which machine to attack is based on the hypothesis test described in Sect. 3.2. If the attacker chooses P_j, then the attacker probes M_j and the game continues.
3. If the attacker probes M_j, then the defender responds with one of the following actions:

$$\{R_j, F_j\}.$$

   For example, if M_1 is probed, it can respond with the signal R_1 indicating to the attacker that it is a real machine. Otherwise, the response F_1 would indicate to the attacker that it is a fake machine.
4. We update the game state vector s according to the response by incrementing the corresponding entry in the state vector $s = [R_1, F_1, R_2, F_2]$. For example, if in the first round the response was R_2, s would be $[0, 0, 1, 0]$. Next, the round number i is incremented. If $i < N$, then another turn is played so that steps 2–4 are repeated. Otherwise the game terminates.

The reward function for the attacker is as follows, where c_p is the cost for probing each round:

$$R = \begin{cases} -(i-1)c_p, & \text{if the attacker walks away or } i = N+1 \\ V - (i-1)c_p, & \text{for attacking the real machine, and} \\ -V - (i-1)c_p, & \text{for attacking the fake machine.} \end{cases}$$

There are three notable differences in this version compared with the model in [2]. First, in each round the attacker now has the additional action W of walking away. This new W action can be enabled or disabled in a particular run of the simulation. The second is the introduction of a cost of c_p for probing each round. The third addresses state space explosion by changing how the state vector s is defined. Specifically in Step 4, we no longer append an element from the set $\{R_1, F_1, R_2, F_2\}$ to the state vector and instead just increment the corresponding counter. In essence, this ignores order and significantly collapses the state space. This updated implementation gives results consistent with those from [2], with $c_p = 0$ and W disabled.

4.2   Parameters

The number of rounds and episodes were chosen together to empirically demonstrate convergence. Recall that at the start of each episode, the simulation chooses which of the machines is real, uniformly at random. Unless otherwise specified, the parameters in simulation are:

Max number of rounds: $N = 10$,	Value of the real machine: $V = 10$
Defender cost when real lies: $c_R = 2$	Defender cost when fake lies: $c_F = 1$
Discount of value per round: $\beta = 1$	Cost of probing per round: $c_p = 1$

Similar to before, the attacker pays a cost of $-V$ if they attack the fake machine. The defender's strategy was fixed by choosing parameters (τ_F, τ_R) which determine the probability of telling the truth on the fake and real machines respectively. The attacker is a RL agent trained using tabular q-learning with an epsilon greedy approach in a novel environment using the Open AI Gym framework [4], using the parameters for $100,000$ episodes:

Discount factor: $\gamma = 1$,	Learning Rate: $\alpha = 0.1$
Defender cost when real lies: $c_R = 2$	Defender cost when fake lies: $c_F = 1$
Exploration Parameter: $\epsilon = 1$	Epsilon Decay Rate $= 0.9999$

Let w be an indicator for whether W is enabled (1) or disabled (0) in the simulation. The simulation was run for values of (τ_F, τ_R, w) in the set $\{(1,1,1), (0,0,0), (0,0,1), (0.9,0.9,1), (0.7,0.7,1), (0.7,0.7,0)\}$.

The choice of fixed learning rate, while not standard, is intentional. Slower decay rates mean an agent is slower to accept the information they are gathering from the environment. To us, that is of particular interest since adversaries have been shown to be more cautious in exploring systems where they believe there is deception present [10]. A constant learning rate reflects an adversary that remains skeptical throughout.

4.3   Results

First, in Fig. 4, we consider the cases where both machines always tell the truth or always lie. Our initial work [2] found these to be optimal strategies for the defender depending on the relationship between V and c_R, c_F and they serve as good first examples to consider in the simulation. When both machines always tell the truth $(\tau_R, \tau_F) = (1, 1)$, adding walk away does not have much of an effect as seen in Fig. 4a. However, in the case where they always lie $(\tau_R, \tau_F) = (0, 0)$, walk away has a dramatic impact as seen comparing Figs. 4b and c. Since the machines always lie, a human adversary can intuit which is real. But as lying is costlier on the real machine, the cost hypothesis forces attacks on the fake machine in this setup. Without walk away, the adversary learns to avoid attacking, eventually exceeding the max number of rounds and never attacking. Given the option to walk away, the adversary chooses to walk away from the

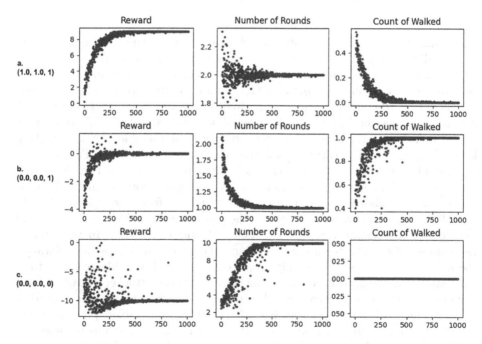

Fig. 4. Average rewards, rounds, and walk away fraction (grouped by 100 episodes) evolved over $100,000$ episodes for $(\tau_F, \tau_R, w) = (1, 1, 1), (0, 0, 1), (0, 0, 0)$

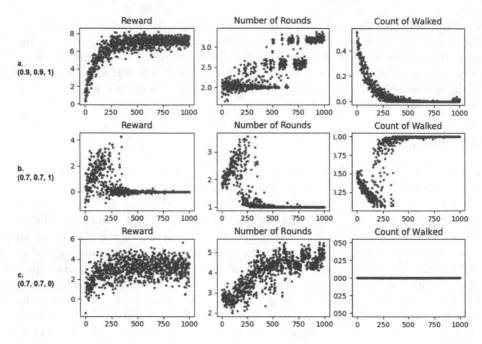

Fig. 5. Average rewards, rounds, and walk away fraction (grouped by 100 episodes) evolved over $100,000$ episodes for $(\tau_F, \tau_R, w) = (0.9, 0.9, 1), (0.7, 0.7, 1), (0.7, 0.7, 0)$

game immediately. This suggests that simulation using the cost hypothesis is only applicable where $\tau > \frac{1}{2}$ – hence we focus our attention there.

Consider next the case where $(\tau_R, \tau_F) = (0.9, 0.9)$ as seen in Fig. 5a. The behavior is very similar to $(\tau_R, \tau_F) = (1, 1)$ and the only notable difference from Fig. 4a is that the number of rounds gradually increases to 2.5 then 3 instead of 2. Intuitively a second probe provides corroboration – the first could have been untruthful. The reward converges to nearly the best possible of 8 and slightly lower than in the fully truthful case. The attacker learns to not walk away.

Consider next the case where $(\tau_R, \tau_F) = (0.7, 0.7)$ as seen in Fig. 5b. In this case, the truthfulness of both machines has dropped more significantly. One might expect similar but more pronounced changes as from the $(\tau_R, \tau_F) = (1, 1)$ to $(0.9, 0.9)$ case. However, that is not the case as seen in Fig. 5b. Instead the reward increases steadily to about 4 then suddenly drops to 0. In these plots, the number of rounds steadily increases and then suddenly drops to 1. Notably, the fraction of walk away gradually drops to near 0 until it suddenly spikes to 1. There is a near asymptotic change in the behavior as the attacker converges from a strategy that has a positive reward to purely walking away with no reward.

Analyzing the same scenario, but with walk away disabled provides some insight. In Fig. 5c, the fraction that walks away naturally remains 0. However, reward climbs to 4, and number of rounds climbs then oscillates in a narrow range around 5. This is a natural progression of decreased truthfulness on both machines and what we would have expected. However, the attacker learns to walk away when presented with the option by the defender, achieving cyber deterrence [20]! The q-tables reveal that after sufficiently many episodes of evolution, states with positive expected rewards for attacking have only negative values. Walk away, with value of 0, dominates. We refer to this type of scenario as a *trap*.

In a given state s, once the Attack action is chosen, the target machine is chosen based on the cost hypothesis. However, even if all probing agrees the machine is real, there is always a chance that the machine is actually fake and has been deceptive the entire time. This event, albeit unlikely, has nonzero probability and will eventually occur, giving a large negative reward. The resulting update to the q-table turns the value of attacking negative while walk away always maintains a q-table value of 0. Whenever an action's value dips below 0, it will never be revisited during on-policy play. Given enough episodes of evolution, eventually all actions other than walk away are no longer viable.

Further, the RL agent seems to be able to fall into this kind of *trap* even in different learning schemes. Consider for example the scenario as in Fig. 5b, except where α initially is 1 and has a decay rate, which is a more standard RL setup. With α decay $= 0.999953$, the RL usually does not abruptly change behavior and fall into the *trap*. But if you run it repeatedly, it happens about 1/10 of the time. Alternately if you slow the decay rate to 0.999965, the *trap* becomes far more common, about 9/10 of the time. Since we are interested in studying this behavior and there is a risk of missing it with different decays, that motivated our choice to consider a constant learning rate of $\alpha = 0.1$.

Given that RL agents can fall into these kinds of *traps*, knowing the optimal behavior is helpful in identifying such scenarios. So we turn to identifying the optimal strategy for an attacker given a fixed defender profile. To estimate this, we modified our simulation to force the agent to probe a certain number of rounds before being forced to attack. For a given fixed number of rounds, we ran the simulation 100, 000 times and calculated the expected reward according to (3) in Sect. 3. Figure 6 plots the expected rewards for different fixed numbers of rounds with fixed defender profile $(\tau_R, \tau_F) = (0.7, 0.7)$. Each of the plots corresponds to a different value of V. These plots show that there clearly is a maximum number of rounds and further that the maximum tends to shift to the right as the value of V increases. For $V = 10^1, 10^2, 10^4$ they are about 2,

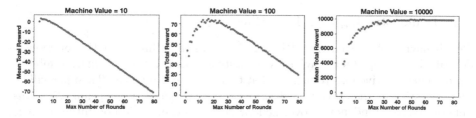

Fig. 6. Attacker is forced to play max number of rounds. Plots of average reward over 100, 000 episodes against rounds for different $V = 10^1, 10^2, 10^4$. $(\tau_R, \tau_F) = (0.7, 0.7)$.

18, 80 respectively – while the analytically derived maximums are not far off, respectively: 4, 20, 60. Intuitively this makes sense as c_p remains fixed at 1 per round. So, as the value of the game increases, gaining additional certainty about the outcome from another round of probing is relatively inexpensive.

We now turn our attention towards overcoming the *trap* as the attacker. The fundamental issue is that due to a string of bad luck, an otherwise "good" action gets a q-table value that makes it never get revisited during on-policy play. Recall we saw this in Fig. 5b where anything worse than walk away's 0 reward would never get played. Intuitively, the most natural counter would be to introduce randomness back into the attacker's profile. Specifically this only affects on-policy play, so if there is still some amount of exploration that takes place, the attacker agent should be resilient.

To this end, we modify the simulation to force a minimum amount of exploration. Specifically, ϵ decays as normal until exploration hits that threshold T and then never drops below that point. To highlight the impact of this random play, in the last 10% of episodes, we revert back to strictly on-policy play. We recreate both scenarios that resulted in the RL agent falling into the *trap*, but with $T > 0$. In Fig. 7a, we have the first scenario with $T = 0.2$ and no longer see a sudden change in strategy (until the end when we revert to on-policy play). Figure 7b and c are the second scenario with $T = 0.2$ and 0.5 respectively. Figure 7b, still suffers from the *trap* but Fig. 7c does not. While maintaining random exploration does seem to confer some resilience to the *trap*, the required amount to be effective can also be costly to the attacker.

Fig. 7. Average rewards (grouped by 100 episodes) evolved over 100,000 episodes for $(\tau_R, \tau_F) = (0.7, 0.7)$, $w = 1$. a. $V = 10$, $\alpha = 0.1$, $T = 0.2$. b. $V = 10^4$, $\alpha = 0.8$, $T = 0.2$. c. $V = 10^4$, $\alpha = 0.8$, $T = 0.5$

4.4 Demonstrating Cognitive Bias

The behavior of the current RL algorithm when falling into the previously described *trap* appears behaviorally consistent with the "law of small numbers" – a human cognitive bias to believe that the outcome from a small sample will be representative of the statistical distribution of the larger population [25]. This belief leads to a tendency to over-generalize the interpretation of initial findings and is indicative that people are not aware that small sample sizes may exhibit greater variability. In the first instance of the *trap*, the agent uses the negative reward of a single outcome and learns to always walk away. In this sense it is blind to the variability that is inherent in any single outcome. The algorithm is learning a statistical prior but is mistakenly predisposed to treating each new observation disproportionately. Based on prior efforts in studying cognitive biases, humans are likely to be similarly susceptible to the law of small numbers when presented with such choices. Exploration of game parameters seeks to associate the outcome of algorithms to that of human decision-making biases.

Demonstrating such behaviors in a RL algorithm has also led us to speculate on whether other decision making bias might be explored by our current model. For our RL agent, the disproportionate importance given to a small number of bad outcomes seems to lead to loss aversion – an irrational tendency to judge losses as having greater weight than gains [19]. Once the algorithm selects walking away with zero reward as preferred, the algorithm becomes rigidly averse to "bad" outcomes (the *trap* as we call it). As a corollary, it may be possible to arrange the game parameters and operation to trigger risk seeking in the form of gambler's fallacy [24] – belief that a particular outcome is more or less likely based on earlier events even though they are independent. While we have not yet pursued this line of reasoning in earnest, this might be achieved by extending our model to allow the defender to randomly vary the final round, allowing "easy" wins but penalizing "hard" losses – forcing the attacker to use small sample sizes in estimating the likelihood of win conditions and prevent learning from games of significant length. This would exacerbate the law of small numbers effects and may also lead to additional biases that could be exploited by a defender.

In a similar line of reasoning, changes in the implementation of walk away may present another way [17] to explore sunk cost fallacy effects – the tendency for individuals to persist in a venture as a result of previous investments even though cutting their losses and walking away would be optimal. In the current game, attacker costs incurred are proportional to the number of probes. This may be viewed as creating a deficit in the internal mental ledger that the attacker keeps while playing the game. Tversky and Kahneman [26] have argued that decision-making is contingent on the framing of outcomes, which are perceived as positive or negative relative to some neutral reference point that is set, or framed, by the decision maker. It bears to reason that if our model imposed a cost for walk away and made this cost dependent on the number of rounds played that an attacker's tendency to continue the game rather than attack or walk away might be disproportionately affected. An increasing cost for walk away should result in an increasing reluctance to leave the game early. An attacker may therefore choose to attack when they would have otherwise fled. If however, (τ_R, τ_F) are low, the attacker may not have sufficient evidence for making a correct prediction and may still have a positive estimate of the outcome in continuing play even though the rational solution should be to accept the loss of walk away.

In general, cognitive biases relating to decisions involving gains result in risk averse behaviors whereas decisions involving losses result in risk seeking behaviors [19]. From this perspective, sunk cost can be viewed as relationship between risk tolerance and the negative or positive balance in the decisions maker's ledger. In order to break even, a risk-seeking decision maker may be willing to engage in further play even when not the rational strategy. While we have not yet assessed the feasibility of adjusting the game model to this end, our present results suggest ample room for exploration. If we can incentivize longer games in spite of increasing cumulative attacker costs, this would represent a radical departure of the learning attacker's behavior from our results to date. Researchers have begun to investigate which cognitive biases are most relevant to cyber operations [18] and as that research matures, AI models that help examine them will be critical.

5   Conclusion

In Sect. 3, we derived expressions and bounds relating the value of the machine with the number of rounds played. The central result, Theorem 1, shows there is a sublinear relationship between value and optimal rounds played. In Sect. 4, we corroborated our analytic results, analyzed a potential *trap* for algorithmic opponents, and laid groundwork for analysis of human cognitive biases.

Adding the walk away action and a cost to probing uncovered a very simple but effective *trap* against some types of algorithmic attackers. The *trap* in particular presents both the attacker and defender with interesting design decisions. For the attacker, maintaining randomness builds resilience against the *trap*. However, any amount of randomness potentially leads to suboptimal play compared to the ideal strategy. The amount of randomness needed depends on the environment itself and might be a challenge to guess or learn correctly.

From the defender's perspective, they have two or three mechanisms to possibly trigger this *trap*. First, the less honest the defender, the more likely an individual game ends poorly for the attacker. Second, if there are alternative actions available to the attacker, the more valuable those alternatives are, the more likely it is that the attacker will never revisit a given action. In the example of walking away, an attacker technically always has the option of not playing the game, but may be too focused on the game itself to realize it. Third, the cost of probing matters relative to the value of the machine. While this likely plays a minor role, the smaller the cost of probing is, the smaller the gap is going to be between the worst possible result in probing versus attacking.

References

1. Aggarwal, P., Dutt, V., Gonzalez, C.: Cyber-security: role of deception in cyber-attack detection. In: Nicholson, D. (ed.) Advances in Human Factors in Cybersecurity. AISC, vol. 501, pp. 85–96. Springer, Cham (2016). https://doi.org/10.1007/978-3-319-41932-9_8
2. Bilinski, M., Ferguson-Walter, K., Fugate, S., Gabrys, R., Mauger, J., Souza, B.: You only lie twice: a multi-round cyber deception game of questionable veracity. In: Alpcan, T., Vorobeychik, Y., Baras, J.S., Dán, G. (eds.) GameSec 2019. LNCS, vol. 11836, pp. 65–84. Springer, Cham (2019). https://doi.org/10.1007/978-3-030-32430-8_5

3. Bilinski, M., Gabrys, R., Mauger, J.: Optimal placement of honeypots for network defense. In: Bushnell, L., Poovendran, R., Başar, T. (eds.) GameSec 2018. LNCS, vol. 11199, pp. 115–126. Springer, Cham (2018). https://doi.org/10.1007/978-3-030-01554-1_7

4. Brockman, G., et al.: Open AI gym. https://arxiv.org/abs/1606.01540s (2016)

5. Carroll, T.E., Grosu, D.: A game theoretic investigation of deception in network security. Secur. Commun. Netw. 4(10), 1162–1172 (2011)

6. Çeker, H., Zhuang, J., Upadhyaya, S., La, Q.D., Soong, B.-H.: Deception-based game theoretical approach to mitigate DoS attacks. In: Zhu, Q., Alpcan, T., Panaousis, E., Tambe, M., Casey, W. (eds.) GameSec 2016. LNCS, vol. 9996, pp. 18–38. Springer, Cham (2016). https://doi.org/10.1007/978-3-319-47413-7_2

7. Cifranic, N., Romero-Mariona, J., Souza, B., Hallman, R.: Decepti-SCADA: a framework for actively defending networked critical infrastructures (2020). https://doi.org/10.5220/0009343300690077

8. Ferguson-Walter, K.: An empirical assessment of the effectiveness of deception for cyber defense. Ph.D. thesis (2020). https://doi.org/10.7275/z0rb-ek46

9. Ferguson-Walter, K.J., et al.: The tularosa study: an experimental design and implementation to quantify the effectiveness of cyber deception, Maui, HI (2019)

10. Ferguson-Walter, K.J., LaFon, D., Shade, T.: Friend or Faux: deception for cyber defense. J. Inf. Warfare 16, 28–42 (2017)

11. Garg, N., Grosu, D.: Deception in honeynets: a game-theoretic analysis. In: 2007 IEEE SMC Information Assurance And Security Workshop, pp. 107–113 (2007)

12. Gutzwiller, R., Ferguson-Walter, K.J., Fugate, S., Rogers, A.: Oh, look, a butterfly!. A framework for distracting attackers to improve cyber defense, Philadelphia, Pennsylvania (2018)

13. Gutzwiller, R.S., Ferguson-Walter, K.J., Fugate, S.J.: Are cyber attackers thinking fast and slow? Exploratory analysis reveals evidence of decision-making biases in red teamers. In: Proceedings of the Human Factors and Ergonomics Society Annual Meeting, vol. 63, pp. 427–431. SAGE Publications (2019)

14. Heckman, K.E., Stech, F.J., Thomas, R.K., Schmoker, B., Tsow, A.W.: Cyber Denial, Deception and Counter Deception: A Framework for Supporting Active Cyber Defense. AIS. Springer, Cham (2015). https://doi.org/10.1007/978-3-319-25133-2. www.springer.com/us/book/9783319251318

15. Huang, Y., Zhu, Q.: Deceptive reinforcement learning under adversarial manipulations on cost signals. In: Alpcan, T., Vorobeychik, Y., Baras, J.S., Dán, G. (eds.) GameSec 2019. LNCS, vol. 11836, pp. 217–237. Springer, Cham (2019). https://doi.org/10.1007/978-3-030-32430-8_14

16. Jajodia, S., et al.: A probabilistic logic of cyber deception. IEEE Trans. Inf. Forensics Secur. 12(11), 2532–2544 (2017)

17. Johnson, C.: Measuring the impact of the sunk cost fallacy to delay and disrupt attacker behavior. Doctoral dissertation in preparation, Arizona State University

18. Johnson, C., Gutzwiller, R., Ferguson-Walter, K.J., Fugate, S.: A cyber-relevant table of decision making biases and their definitions. https://doi.org/10.13140/RG.2.2.14891.87846

19. Kahneman, D., Tversky, A.: Prospect theory: an analysis of decision under risk. Econometrica 47(2), 363–391 (1979)

20. Libicki, M.: Cyberdeterrence and Cyberwar. RAND Corporation, Santa Monica (2009)

21. Píbil, R., Lisý, V., Kiekintveld, C., Bošanský, B., Pěchouček, M.: Game theoretic model of strategic honeypot selection in computer networks. In: Grossklags, J., Walrand, J. (eds.) GameSec 2012. LNCS, vol. 7638, pp. 201–220. Springer, Heidelberg (2012). https://doi.org/10.1007/978-3-642-34266-0_12

22. Schlenker, A., et al.: Deceiving cyber adversaries: a game theoretic approach. In: Proceedings of the 17th International Conference on Autonomous Agents and MultiAgent Systems, pp. 892–900 (2018)

23. Strom, B.E., Applebaum, A., Miller, D.P., Nickels, K.C., Pennington, A.G., Thomas, C.B.: MITRE ATT&CK: design and philosophy. Technical report (2018)

24. Terrell, D.: A test of the gambler's fallacy: evidence from pari-mutuel games. J. Risk Uncertainty 8(2), 309–317 (1994)

25. Tversky, A., Kahneman, D.: Belief in the law of small numbers. Psychol. Bull. 76(2), 105 (1971)

26. Tversky, A., Kahneman, D.: Judgment under uncertainty: heuristics and biases. Science 185(4157), 1124–1131 (1974)

27. Wagener, G., State, R., Dulaunoy, A., Engel, T.: Self adaptive high interaction honeypots driven by game theory. In: Guerraoui, R., Petit, F. (eds.) SSS 2009. LNCS, vol. 5873, pp. 741–755. Springer, Heidelberg (2009). https://doi.org/10.1007/978-3-642-05118-0_51

28. Wang, W., Zeng, B.: A two-stage deception game for network defense. In: Bushnell, L., Poovendran, R., Başar, T. (eds.) GameSec 2018. LNCS, vol. 11199, pp. 569–582. Springer, Cham (2018). https://doi.org/10.1007/978-3-030-01554-1_33

Cyber Deception

Exploiting Bounded Rationality in Risk-Based Cyber Camouflage Games

Omkar Thakoor[1]($\boxtimes$), Shahin Jabbari[2], Palvi Aggarwal[3], Cleotilde Gonzalez[3], Milind Tambe[2], and Phebe Vayanos[1]

[1] University of Southern California, Los Angeles, CA 90007, USA
{othakoor,phebe.vayanos}@usc.edu
[2] Harvard University, Cambridge, MA 02138, USA
jabbari@seas.harvard.edu, milind_tambe@harvard.edu
[3] Carnegie Mellon University, Pittsburgh, PA 15213, USA
palvia@andrew.cmu.edu, coty@cmu.edu

Abstract. Recent works have growingly shown that *Cyber deception* can effectively impede the reconnaissance efforts of intelligent cyber attackers. Recently proposed models to optimize a deceptive defense based on camouflaging network and system attributes, have shown effective numerical results on simulated data. However, these models possess a fundamental drawback due to the assumption that an attempted attack is always successful—as a direct consequence of the deceptive strategies being deployed, the attacker runs a significant risk that the attack fails. Further, this risk or uncertainty in the rewards magnifies the boundedly rational behavior in humans which the previous models do not handle. To that end, we present Risk-based Cyber Camouflage Games—a general-sum game model that captures the uncertainty in the attack's success. In case of the rational attackers, we show that optimal defender strategy computation is NP-hard even in the zero-sum case. We provide an MILP formulation for the general problem with constraints on cost and feasibility, along with a pseudo-polynomial time algorithm for the special *unconstrained* setting. Second, for risk-averse attackers, we present a solution based on Prospect theoretic modeling along with a robust variant that minimizes regret. Third, we propose a solution that does not rely on the attacker behavior model or past data, and effective for the broad setting of *strictly competitive games* where previous solutions against bounded rationality prove ineffective. Finally, we provide numerical results that our solutions effectively lower the defender loss.

Keywords: Game theory · Cyber deception · Rationality

1 Introduction

Rapidly growing cybercrime [13,15,24], has elicited effective defense against adept attackers. Many recent works have proposed *Cyber deception* techniques to thwart the reconnaissance – typically a crucial phase prior to attacking [17,21].

© Springer Nature Switzerland AG 2020
Q. Zhu et al. (Eds.): GameSec 2020, LNCS 12513, pp. 103–124, 2020.
https://doi.org/10.1007/978-3-030-64793-3_6

One deception approach is to camouflage the network by attribute obfuscation [7,10,35] to render an attacker's information incomplete or incorrect, creating indecision over their infiltration plan [4,10,12,28]. Optimizing such a deceptive strategy is challenging due to many practical constraints on feasibility and costs of deploying, as well as critically dependent on the attacker's decision-making governed by his behavioral profile, and attacking motives and capabilities. Game theory offers an effective framework for tackling both these aspects and has been successfully adopted in security problems [2,20,29,31].

Attacking a machine amounts to launching an exploit for a particular system configuration – information that is concealed or distorted due to the deceptive defense, thus, an attempted attack may not succeed. Recent game theoretic models for deception via attribute obfuscation [30,34] have a major shortcoming in ignoring this risk of attack failure as they assume that an attempted attack is guaranteed to provide utility to the attacker. Further, results from recent human subject studies [1] suggest that this risk may unveil risk-aversion in human attackers rather than a perfectly rational behavior of maximizing expected utility that the models assume. Apart from risk-aversion, other behavioral models, e.g., the Quantal response theory [22], also assert that humans exhibit bounded rationality. This can severely affect the performance of a deployed strategy, which has not been considered by the previous works.

As our first main contribution, we present Risk-based Cyber Camouflage Games (RCCG)—a crucial refinement over previous models via redefined strategy space and rewards to explicitly capture the uncertainty in attack success. As foundation, we first consider rational attackers and show analytical results including NP-hardness of optimal strategy computation and its MILP formulation which, while akin to previous models, largely require independent reasoning. Further, we consider risk-averse attackers modeled using Prospect theory [36] and present a solution (PT) that estimates model parameters from data to compute optimal defense. To circumvent the limitations of parametrization and learning errors, we also present a robust solution (MMR) that minimizes worst-case regret for a general prospect theoretic attacker. Finally, we propose a solution ($GEBRA$) free of behavioral modeling assumptions and avoiding reliance on data altogether, that can exploit arbitrary deviations from rationality. Our numerical results show the efficacy of our solutions summarized at the end.

1.1   Related Work

Cyber Deception Games [30], and Cyber Camouflage Games (CCG) [34] are game-theoretic models for Cyber deception via attribute obfuscation. In these, the defender can mask the *true configuration* of a machine, creating an uncertainty in the associated reward the attacker receives for attacking the machine. These have a fundamental limitation, namely, the assumption that the attacked machine is guaranteed to provide utility to the attacker. Further, they do not consider that human agents tend to deviate from rationality, particularly when making decisions under risk. Our refined model handles both these crucial issues.

A model using Prospect theory is proposed in [38] for boundedly rational attackers in Stackelberg security games (SSG) [33]. However, it relies on using model parameters from previous literature, discounting the fact that they can largely vary for the specific experimental setups. We provide a solution that learns the parameters from data, as well as a robust solution to deal with uncertainty in the degree of risk-aversion and broadly the parametrization hypothesis. A robust solution for unknown risk-averse attackers has been proposed for SSGs in [27], however, it aims to minimize the worst-case utility, whereas, we take the less conservative approach of minimizing worst-case regret. Previous works on uncertainty in security games consider Bayesian [18], interval-based [19], and regret-based approaches [23], however, these do not directly apply due to fundamental differences between RCCGs and SSGs as explained in [34].

Another approach in [38] is based on the Quantal Response model [22]. However, the attack probabilities therein involve terms that are exponential in rewards, which in turn are non-linear functions of integer variables in our model, leading to an intractable formulation. However, we show effectiveness of our model-free solution for this behavior model as well.

Machine learning models such as Decision Tree and Neural Networks have been used for estimating human behavior [8]. However, the predictive power of such models typically comes with an indispensable complexity (non-linear kernels, functions and deep hidden layers of neural nets, sizeable depth and branching factor of decision trees etc.). This does not allow the predicted human response to be written as a simple closed-form expression of the instance features, viz, the strategy decision variables, preventing a concise optimization problem formulation. This is particularly problematic since the alternative of searching for an optimal solution via strategy enumeration is also non-viable—due to the compact input representation via a *polytopal* strategy space [16] in our model.

MATCH [25] and COBRA [26] aim to tackle human attackers in SSGs that avoid the complex task of modeling human decision-making and provide robustness against deviations from rationality. However, their applicability is limited— in *Strictly Competitive* games where deviation from rationality always benefits the defender, they reduce to the standard minimax solution. Our model-free solution GEBRA on the other hand, achieves better computational results than minimax, and MATCH can be seen as its conservative derivative.

2   Risk-Based Cyber Camouflage Games (RCCG) Model

Here, we describe the components of the RCCG model, explicitly highlighting the key differences with respect to the CCG model [34].

Network Configurations. The network is a set of k machines $\mathcal{K} := \{1, \ldots, k\}$. Each machine has a *true configuration* (TC), which is simply an exhaustive tuple of attributes so that machines having the same TC are identical. $\mathcal{S} := \{1, \ldots, s\}$ is the set of all TCs. The *true state of the network* (TSN) is a vector $\boldsymbol{n} = (n_i)_{i \in \mathcal{S}}$ with n_i denoting the number of machines with TC i. Note that $\sum_{i \in \mathcal{S}} n_i = k$.

The defender can disguise the TCs using deception techniques. Each machine is "masked" with an *observed configuration* (OC). The set of OCs is denoted by $\mathcal{T}$. Similar to a TC, an OC corresponds to an attribute tuple that fully comprises the attacker view, so that machines with the same OC are indistinguishable.

Deception Strategies. We represent the defender strategy as an integer matrix Φ, where Φ_{ij} is the no. of machines with TC i, masked with OC j. The *observed state of the network* (OSN) is a function of Φ, denoted as $m(\Phi) := (m_j(\Phi))_{j \in \mathcal{T}}$, where $m_j(\Phi) = \sum_i \Phi_{ij}$ denotes the no. of machines under OC j for strategy Φ.

Deception Feasibility and Costs. Achieving deception is often costly and not arbitrarily feasible. We have *feasibility* constraints given by a (0,1)-matrix Π, where $\Pi_{ij} = 1$ if a machine with TC i can be masked with OC j. Next, we assume that masking a TC i with an OC j (if so feasible), has a cost of c_{ij} incurred by the defender, denoting the aggregated cost from deployment, maintenance, degraded functionality, etc. We assume the total cost is to be bounded by a *budget B*.

These translate to linear constraints to define the valid defender strategy set:

$$\mathcal{F} = \left\{ \Phi \middle| \begin{array}{l} \Phi_{ij} \in \mathbb{Z}_{\geq 0}, \quad \Phi_{ij} \leq \Pi_{ij} n_i \; \forall (i,j) \in \mathcal{S} \times \mathcal{T}, \\ \sum_{j \in \mathcal{T}} \Phi_{ij} = n_i \; \forall i \in \mathcal{S}, \quad \sum_{i \in \mathcal{S}} \sum_{j \in \mathcal{T}} \Phi_{ij} \, c_{ij} \leq B \end{array} \right\}$$

The first and the third constraints follow from the definitions of Φ and n. The second imposes the feasibility constraints, and the fourth, the budget constraint.

Remark 1. The budget constraint can encode feasibility constraints as a special case by setting a cost higher than the budget for an infeasible masking. The latter are still stated explicitly for the useful interpretation and practical significance.

Defender and Attacker Valuations. A machine with TC i gets successfully attacked if the attacker uncovers the disguised OC and uses the correct exploit corresponding to TC i. In such a case, the attacker gets a utility v_i—his *valuation* of TC i. Collectively, these are represented as a vector v. Analogously, we define valuations u representing the defender's loss.

Remark 2. For ease of interpretation, we assign a 0 utility to the players when the attack is unsuccessful, which sets a constant reference point. Hence, unlike CCGs, valuations cannot be freely shifted. Further, a successful attack typically is undesirable for the defender (except, e.g., honeypots), and to let the valuations be typically positive values, they represent the defender's loss; its minimization is the defender objective unlike maximization in CCGs.

Attacker Strategies. As the attacker cannot distinguish between machines with the same OC, he chooses an OC from which to attack a random machine. Attacking a machine requires choosing an exploit to launch for a particular TC. Thus, the attack can be described as a pair of decisions $(i, j) \in \mathcal{S} \times \mathcal{T}$. This significant difference in attack strategy space definition and the imminent player utility definitions as a consequence, cause the fundamental distinction in the practical scope as well as the technical solutions of the RCCG model.

We model the interaction as a Stackelberg game to capture the order of player decisions. The defender is the leader who knows the TSN n and can deploy a deception strategy Φ, and the attacker chooses a pair $(i, j) \in \mathcal{S} \times \mathcal{T}$. The defender can only play a pure strategy since it is typically not possible to change the network frequently, making the attacker's view of the network static. As in Schlenker et al. [30], Thakoor et al. [34], we assume the attacker can use the defender's strategy Φ to perfectly compute the utilities from different attacks, which is justified via insider information leakage or other means of surveillance.

Suppose the defender plays a strategy Φ, and the attacker attacks using an exploit for TC i on a machine masked with OC j. Among $m_j(\Phi)$ machines masked by OC j, Φ_{ij} are of TC i. Hence, the attack is successful with a probability $\frac{\Phi_{ij}}{m_j(\Phi)}$. Consequently, the player utilities are given by

$$U^{\mathrm{a}}(\Phi, i, j) = \frac{\Phi_{ij}}{m_j(\Phi)} v_i \quad , \quad U^{\mathrm{d}}(\Phi, i, j) = \frac{\Phi_{ij}}{m_j(\Phi)} u_i. \tag{1}$$

Note that these expressions imply that if the player valuations (v or u) are simultaneously scaled by a positive constant (for normalization etc.), it preserves the relative order of player utilities, and in particular, the best responses to any strategies, thus keeping the problem equivalent.

Next, we show analytical results on optimal strategy computation for a rational attacker, which lay the foundation for further tackling bounded rationality.

3   Rational Attackers

The attacker having to choose a TC-OC pair as an attack here rather than just an OC as in the CCG model [34], requires entirely new techniques for our analytical results, despite close resemblance in the optimization problem as below.

Optimization Problem. Previous work on general-sum Stackelberg games has typically used *Strong Stackelberg equilibria* (SSE). This assumes that in case of multiple best responses, the follower breaks ties in favor of the leader (i.e., minimizing defender loss). The leader can *induce* this with mixed strategies, which is not possible in RCCGs as the defender is restricted to pure strategies [14].

Hence, we consider the worst-case assumption that the attacker breaks ties against the defender, leading to *Weak Stackelberg Equilibria* (WSE) [6]. WSE may not always exist [37], but it does when the leader can only play a finite set of pure strategies as in CCG. Hence, we assume that the attacker chooses a best response to the defender strategy Φ, maximizing the defender loss in case of a ti.e. This defender utility is denoted as $U^{\mathrm{wse}}(\Phi)$, defined as the optimal value of the inner Optimization Problem (OP) in the following, while the defender aims to compute a strategy to minimize $U^{\mathrm{wse}}(\Phi)$ as given by the outer objective.

$$\text{argmin}_{\Phi} \ \max_{i,j} U^{\text{d}}(\Phi, i, j)$$
$$\text{s.t. } U^{\text{a}}(\Phi, i, j) \geq U^{\text{a}}(\Phi, i', j') \ \ \forall i' \in \mathcal{S}, \ \forall j' \in \mathcal{T}. \tag{2}$$

Next, we show results on optimal strategy computation shown for the important special cases—the zero-sum and *unconstrained* settings. While similar results have been shown for CCG, independent proof techniques are needed herein due to a distinctive model structure (see Appendix for omitted proofs).

3.1   Zero-Sum RCCG

In the zero-sum setting, the defender loss equals the attacker reward, i.e. $v = u$.

Theorem 1. *Zero-sum RCCG is NP-hard.*

Proof Sketc.h. We reduce from the problem "Exact Cover by 3-Sets" (*ExC3* for brevity) which is known to be NP-complete. Given an instance of *ExC3*, we construct an instance of RCCG for which the minimum defender loss is precisely equal to a certain value if and only if the given *ExC3* instance is YES.   □

For the special unconstrained setting[1] (i.e. with no feasibility or budget constraints), we show the following.

Proposition 1. *Unconstrained zero-sum RCCG always has an optimal strategy that uses just one OC, thus computable in $O(1)$ time.*

Thus, both these results hold for RCCG, same as for CCG (albeit, they do not follow from the latter, requiring independent derivation).

3.2   Unconstrained General-Sum RCCG

Proposition 2. *Unconstrained RCCG always has an optimal strategy that uses just two OCs.*

This result is crucial for an efficient algorithm to compute an optimal strategy (Algorithm 1), named Strategy Optimization by Best Response Enumeration (SOBRE). SOBRE constructs an optimal strategy with two OCs, due to Proposition 2, with attacker best response being (say) OC 1 (Note: this is without loss of generality in the unconstrained setting). It classifies the candidate strategies by triplets (i, n, m) (Line 2) where the attacker best response is $(i, 1)$, and OC 1 masks n machines of TC i, and m machines in total. It uses a subroutine DPBRF (Dynamic Programming for Best Response Feasibility) to construct a strategy yieldsing the desired best response (Line 6) if it exists, and then compares the defender utility from all such feasible candidates, to compute the optimal (Lines 7,8). For details on DPBRF and runtime analysis, refer to the Appendix.

---

[1] The *unconstrained* setting accents the inherent challenge of strategic deception even when sophisticated techniques can arbitrarily mask TCs with any OCs at low cost.

Algorithm 1: SOBRE

---

1 **Initialize** $minUtil \leftarrow \infty$
2 **for** $i = 1, \ldots, s; n = 0, \ldots n_i; m = n, \ldots, k$ **do**
3   **if** $(n/m < (n_i - n)/(|K| - m))$ **continue**
4     $util \leftarrow (n/m)u_i$
5   **if** $(util \geq minUtil)$ **continue**
6   **if** $DPBRF(i, n, m)$
7   **Update** $minUtil \leftarrow util$
8 **Return** $minUtil$

Theorem 2. *The optimal strategy in an unconstrained RCCG can be computed in time $O(k)^4$.*

Remark 3. Note that the input can be expressed in $O(st)$ bits, which makes this algorithm pseudo-polynomial. However, it becomes a poly-time algorithm under the practical assumption of constant-bounded no. of machines per TC, (so that, $k = O(s)$, or more generally, if k in terms of s is polynomially bounded). In contrast, unconstrained CCG is NP-hard even under this restriction. This distinction arises since in RCCG, the best response utility given the attack strategy and the no. of machines masked by the corresponding OC, depends on only the count of attacked TC as opposed to all the TCs in CCG.

3.3 Constrained General-Sum RCCG

For this general setting of RCCG, $U^{\text{wse}}(\Phi)$ is given by OP (2), and thus, computing its minimum is a bilevel OP. Reducing to a single-level Mixed Integer Linear Program (MILP) is typically hard [32]. (in particular, computing an SSE allows such a reduction due to attacker's tiebreaking favoring the defender's objective therein, however, the worst-case tiebreaking of WSE does not). Notwithstanding the redefined attack strategies, a single-level OP can be formulated analogous to CCGs by assuming an ϵ-rational attacker instead of fully rational (as it can be shown that for sufficiently small ϵ, it gives the optimal solution for rationality):

$$\min_{\Phi, q, \gamma, \alpha} \gamma \tag{3}$$

$$\text{s.t.} \quad \alpha, \gamma \in \mathbb{R}, \ \Phi \in \mathcal{F}, \ q \in \{0, 1\}^{|\mathcal{I}| \times |\mathcal{J}|}$$

$$q_{11} + \ldots + q_{st} \geq 1 \tag{3a}$$

$$\epsilon(1 - q_{ij}) \leq \alpha - U^{\text{a}}(\Phi, j, i) \qquad \forall i \in \mathcal{S} \ \forall j \in \mathcal{T} \tag{3b}$$

$$M(1 - q_{ij}) \geq \alpha - U^{\text{a}}(\Phi, j, i) \qquad \forall i \in \mathcal{S} \ \forall j \in \mathcal{T} \tag{3c}$$

$$U^{\text{d}}(\Phi, j, i) \leq \gamma + M(1 - q_{ij}) \qquad \forall i \in \mathcal{S} \ \forall j \in \mathcal{T} \tag{3d}$$

$$q_{ij} \leq \Phi_{ij} \qquad \forall i \in \mathcal{S} \ \forall j \in \mathcal{T}. \tag{3e}$$

The defender aims to minimize the objective γ which captures the defender's optimal utility. The binary variables q_{ij} indicate if attacking (i, j) is an optimal attacker strategy, and as specified by (3a), there must be at least one. As per (3b) and (3c), α is the optimal attacker utility, and this enforces $q_{ij} = 1$ for all the ϵ-optimal attacker strategies (using a big-M constant). (3e) ensures that only the OCs which actually mask a machine are considered as valid attacker responses. Finally, (3d) captures the worst-case tie-breaking by requiring that γ is the highest defender loss from a possible ϵ-optimal attacker response. Using an alternate strategy representation with binary decision variables enables linearization to an MILP, that can be sped up with *symmetry-breaking* cuts [34].

Next, we consider human attackers who typically exhibit bounded rationality.

4   A Model-Driven Approach with Prospect Theory

A well-studied model for the risk-behavior of humans is Prospect theory [36]. As per this, humans under risk make decisions to maximize the *prospect*, which differs from the utilitarian approach in that the reward value and the probability of any event are transformed as follows. We have a value transformation function R that is monotone increasing and concave, s.t., the outcome reward v (value of the machine attacked), gets perceived as $R(v)$ by the attacker. A parameterization of the form $R_\lambda(v) = c(v/c)^\lambda$ is commonly considered in the literature, with $\lambda < 1$ capturing the risk-aversion of the attacker[2], and we use $c = \max_i v_i$ so that the perceived values are normalized to the same range as true values. Prospect theory also proposes a probability weighting function Π, such that the probability p of an event is perceived as $\Pi(p)$. A function of the form $\Pi_\delta(p) = p^\delta/(p^\delta + (1-p)^\delta)^{1/\delta}$ has been previously proposed in literature, parametrized by δ. In our problem, the attack success probability p is a non-linear non-convex function of the decision variables Φ_{ij} and applying a function as above loses tractability. For simplicity, we omit the probability weighting from our solution which shows effective results regardless. Future work could explore the benefits of incorporating this additional complexity.

Thus, each of the attacker's strategies (i, j) has a prospect

$$f_\lambda(\Phi, i, j) = \frac{\Phi_{ij}}{m_\Phi(j)} R_\lambda(v_i) \tag{4}$$

as a function of the player strategies, parametrized by λ. This value transformation makes the problem inherently harder (even in the simpler zero-sum setting).

Learning the parameter λ is a key challenge. Once λ is estimated, the defender computes an optimal strategy for the prospect theoretic attacker, by simply modifying (3), replacing the valuations v_i with the transformed values $R_\lambda(v_i)$. More generally, with this replacement, all results from Sect. 3 for rational attackers apply here too.

---

[2] The conventional usage of the symbol λ in prospect theoretic models is different.

4.1   Learning Model Parameters from Data

Suppose we have data consisting of a set of instances $\mathcal{N}$ from a study such as [1]. A particular instance $n \in \mathcal{N}$ corresponds to a particular human subject that plays against a particular defense strategy Φ_n, and decides to attack (i_n, j_n) having the maximum prospect. The instances come from different subjects who may have a different parameter λ, however, at the time of deployment, the defender cannot estimate the risk-averseness of an individual in advance and play a different strategy accordingly. Hence, we aim to compute a strategy against a particular λ that works well for the whole population[3]. Due to different subjects, different instances may have different attack responses for the same defender strategy, and requiring a strict prospect-maximization may not yield any feasible λ. Hence, we define the likelihood of an instance, by considering a soft-max function instead, so that the probability of attacking (i_n, j_n) is[4]

$$P_n(\lambda) = \frac{\exp(f_\lambda(\Phi_n, i_n, j_n))}{\sum_{i,j} \exp(f_\lambda(\Phi_n, i, j))}.$$

Using the Maximum Likelihood Estimation approach, we choose λ which maximizes the likelihood $\prod_n P_n(\lambda)$, or, log likelihood $\sum_n \log P_n(\lambda)$. (Note: Manually eliminating anomalous instances from data which indicate complete irrationality can help avoid over-fitting). Finding such a solution via the standard approach of *Gradient Descent* does not have the convergence guarantee due to the likelihood being non-convex and we resort to *Grid Search* instead.

4.2   Robust Solution with Prospect Theory

The learning error can be sizeable if the subject population has a high variance of λ or if limited data is available (for sensitivity analysis, see Appendix). Further, the parameterization hypothesis may not fit well, degrading solution quality. To circumvent both these issues, we propose a solution offering robustness when the attacker behavior cannot be predicted with certainty. We assume a prospect-theoretic attacker, but with no assumption of a parametrized model or data availability. Thus, the defender knowledge of value transformations has uncertainty, which we handle with the minimax regret framework [5,9], seen to be less conservative in contrast with a purely maximin approach that focuses on the worst cases of uncertainty.

Value transformation and Uncertainty modelling. We assume the attacker has the transformed values $\boldsymbol{w}$. Defender does not precisely know $\boldsymbol{w}$ which can be anything from a set $\mathcal{W} \subseteq \mathbb{R}^s$ which we call the *uncertainty set* [3]. $\mathcal{W}$ is obtained by requiring that the transformation from $\boldsymbol{v}$ to $\boldsymbol{w}$ is a monotone increasing and

---

[3] This avoids learning a complex distribution of λ from limited data, and the subsequent need for a Bayesian game formulation with attackers coming from a continuous distribution which is not expressible as an MILP.

[4] When considering a continuous range of λ for payoff transformations, the degenerate cases of tie-breaking between strategies are zero-probability events and thus ignored.

concave function with $\boldsymbol{w}$ normalized to the same range as valuations $\boldsymbol{v}$. WLOG, let v be sorted increasingly in the index. Then, $\mathcal{W}$ is defined by the constraints

$$\mathcal{W} = \left\{ w \left| \begin{array}{c} 0 \leq w_1 \leq w_2 \ldots w_s = v_s \\ \frac{w_1}{v_1} \geq \frac{w_2}{v_2} \geq \ldots \geq \frac{w_s}{v_s} = 1 \end{array} \right. \right\}$$

The first constraints ensure monotonicity, and the second ones convexity. An equivalent formulation can also be obtained by adapting constraints used in [27].

Minmax Regret Formulation. Let $U^{\mathrm{a}}(\Phi, i, j, \boldsymbol{w})$ denote the attacker's prospect in terms of $\boldsymbol{w}$ and the player strategies. Similarly, let the defender's wse utility in terms of $\boldsymbol{w}$ be denoted by $U^{\mathrm{wse}}(\Phi, \boldsymbol{w})$ defined analogous to $U^{\mathrm{wse}}(\Phi)$ in (2):

$$\max_{i,j} U^{\mathrm{d}}(\Phi, i, j) \mid U^{\mathrm{a}}(\Phi, i, j, \boldsymbol{w}) \geq U^{\mathrm{a}}(\Phi, i', j', \boldsymbol{w}) \ \forall i' \in \mathcal{S} \ \forall j' \in \mathcal{T}. \qquad (5)$$

Then, the *max regret* (MR) of Φ is the worst-case value over all $\boldsymbol{w} \in \mathcal{W}$ of the decrements in defender loss that the optimal $\hat{\Phi}$ achieves over Φ for valuations $\boldsymbol{w}$:

$$\mathrm{MR}(\Phi) = \max_{\boldsymbol{w} \in \mathcal{W}} \max_{\hat{\Phi} \in \mathcal{F}} \left[U^{\mathrm{wse}}(\Phi, \boldsymbol{w}) - U^{\mathrm{wse}}(\hat{\Phi}, \boldsymbol{w}) \right]. \qquad (6)$$

The minmax regret (MMR) approach looks to compute the Φ that minimizes $\mathrm{MR}(\Phi)$, i.e., solving the following OP:

$$\min_{\Phi \in \mathcal{F}, \beta} \ \beta \mid \beta \geq U^{\mathrm{wse}}(\Phi, \boldsymbol{w}) - U^{wse}(\hat{\Phi}, \boldsymbol{w}) \ \ \forall (\boldsymbol{w}, \hat{\Phi}) \in \mathcal{W} \times \mathcal{F}. \qquad (7)$$

OP (7) has a constraint for each $(\boldsymbol{w}, \hat{\Phi}) \in \mathcal{W} \times \mathcal{F}$ making it a *semi-infinite program* as $\mathcal{W}$ is infinite, and difficult to solve also due to $\mathcal{F}$ being large. Hence, we adopt the well-studied approach of using *constraint sampling* [9] with *constraint generation* [5], to devise Algorithm 2. It iteratively computes successively tighter upper and lower bounds on MMR until they converge to the objective value. For the lower bound, we compute a relaxed version of OP (7), i.e., *relaxed MMR* by computing its objective subject to constraints corresponding to a sampled subset $\mathcal{S} = \{(\boldsymbol{w}_{(n)}, \hat{\Phi}_{(n)})\}_n$ instead of $\mathcal{W} \times \mathcal{F}$ directly, giving an interim solution Φ (line 4). Since only partial constraints were considered, the regret thus computed must be a lower bound on the true MMR. Next, if this interim solution is not optimal, there must be a constraint of OP (7) not satisfied by Φ. In particular, such a violated constraint can be found by computing the max regret (MR) of the interim solution Φ (as per OP (6)) and by definition of max regret, must be an upper bound on the overall MMR (line 5). We use the new sample $(\boldsymbol{w}, \hat{\Phi})$ thus computed and add to $\mathcal{S}$ (line 6) and repeat. We get successively tighter lower bounds as $\mathcal{S}$ grows and finally meets the tightest upper bound so far, which marks the convergence of the algorithm (line 3).

Algorithm 2: minmax regret computation

---

1 **Initialize** $u \leftarrow \infty, l \leftarrow 0$
2 Randomly generate samples $\mathcal{S} = \{(\boldsymbol{w}_{(n)}, \hat{\boldsymbol{\Phi}}_{(n)})\}_n$
3 **while** $u > l$ **do**
4     $l \leftarrow$ relaxed MMR w.r.t $\mathcal{S}$; giving interim solution $\boldsymbol{\Phi}$.
5     $u \leftarrow$ MR for $\boldsymbol{\Phi}$; giving a new sample $s = (\boldsymbol{w}, \hat{\boldsymbol{\Phi}})$.
6   **Update** $\mathcal{S} = \mathcal{S} \cup \{s\}$
7 **Return** incumbent solution as the true solution.

Next, we look at the two main subroutines of the algorithm.

(i) Relaxed MMR Computation. OP (7) has constraints for each $(\boldsymbol{w}, \hat{\boldsymbol{\Phi}}) \in \mathcal{W} \times \mathcal{F}$. Instead, considering a small subset of samples $\{(\hat{\boldsymbol{\Phi}}_{(n)}, \boldsymbol{w}_{(n)})\}_n \subseteq \mathcal{W} \times \mathcal{F}$ to generate a subset of constraints in (7) yields

$$\min_{\beta \in \mathbb{R}, \boldsymbol{\Phi} \in \mathcal{F}} \beta \mid \beta \geq U^{\mathrm{wse}}(\boldsymbol{\Phi}, \boldsymbol{w}_{(n)}) - U^{\mathrm{wse}}(\hat{\boldsymbol{\Phi}}_{(n)}, \boldsymbol{w}_{(n)}) \;\; \forall n. \tag{8}$$

This yields a lower bound on MMR since we consider fewer constraints. For sample n, let $\gamma_n = U^{\mathrm{wse}}(\boldsymbol{\Phi}, \boldsymbol{w}_{(n)})$. Then, minimizing β translates to minimizing γ_n and this can be achieved by adding constraints analogous to (3a)–(3e) corresponding to each n, to obtain the following OP:

$$
\begin{aligned}
\min_{\boldsymbol{\Phi}, \beta} \;\; & \beta \\
\text{s.t.} \;\; & \beta \in \mathbb{R}, \;\; \boldsymbol{\Phi} \in \mathcal{F} \\
& \left. \begin{array}{l}
q_n \in \{0,1\}^{s \times t}, \; \alpha_n, \gamma_n \in \mathbb{R} \\
\beta \geq \gamma_n - U^{\mathrm{wse}}(\hat{\boldsymbol{\Phi}}_{(n)}, \boldsymbol{w}_{(n)}) \\
\sum_{i,j} q_{nij} \geq 1
\end{array} \right\} \quad \forall n \\
& \left. \begin{array}{l}
\epsilon(1 - q_{nij}) \leq \alpha_n - U^{\mathrm{a}}(\boldsymbol{\Phi}, i, j, \boldsymbol{w}_{(n)}) \\
M(1 - q_{nij}) \geq \alpha_n - U^{\mathrm{a}}(\boldsymbol{\Phi}, i, j, \boldsymbol{w}_{(n)}) \\
U^{\mathrm{d}}(\boldsymbol{\Phi}, i, j) \leq \gamma_n + (1 - q_{nij})M \\
q_{nij} \leq m_j(\boldsymbol{\Phi}).
\end{array} \right\} \quad \forall i \in \mathcal{S} \;\; \forall j \in \mathcal{T} \;\; \forall n
\end{aligned}
$$

(ii) Max Regret Computation. Here, we consider a candidate solution $\boldsymbol{\Phi}$, and compute a sample $(\boldsymbol{\Phi}', \boldsymbol{w})$ which yields $MR(\boldsymbol{\Phi})$ as per (6), giving an upper bound on MMR by definition. Since $U^{\mathrm{wse}}(\boldsymbol{\Phi}, \boldsymbol{w})$ is defined via an optimization problem itself (given by (5)), (6) becomes a bilevel problem. To reduce it to single-level problems, we let $(i', j'), (i'', j'')$ be the attacked targets at WSE for the two defender strategies $\boldsymbol{\Phi}'$ and $\boldsymbol{\Phi}$ (the candidate solution) resp. Introducing these allows us to write the required defender utility expressions simply as:

$$U^{\mathrm{wse}}(\boldsymbol{\Phi}', \boldsymbol{w}) = U^{\mathrm{d}}(\boldsymbol{\Phi}', i', j') \quad \text{and} \quad U^{\mathrm{wse}}(\boldsymbol{\Phi}, \boldsymbol{w}) = U^{\mathrm{d}}(\boldsymbol{\Phi}, i'', j'').$$

We then iterate over all tuples (i', j', i'', j'') ($O(s^2 t^2)$ many of them) to compute the max regret corresponding to each pair (via OP described momentarily), and the tuple leading to maximum objective gives the solution to (6).

Previous works using a similar approach, such as, [23] assume mixed strategies and compute the SSE. In our model, however, computing WSE presents the challenge of capturing the worst-case tiebreaking, requiring an entirely different formulation. For given pair of targets $(i', j'), (i'', j'')$ as described above and for input strategy Φ, we compute the regret maximizing sample $(\Phi', \boldsymbol{w})$ as follows:

$$
\begin{aligned}
\max_{\Phi', \boldsymbol{w}, \beta} \quad & \beta \\
\text{s.t.} \quad & \Phi' \in \mathcal{F}, \ \boldsymbol{w} \in \mathcal{W}, \ \beta \in \mathbb{R}, \ \boldsymbol{q} \in \{0, 1\}^{s \times t} \\
& \beta \leq U^{\mathrm{d}}(\Phi, i'', j'') - U^{\mathrm{d}}(\Phi', i', j') \\
& \left. \begin{aligned}
& Mq_{ij} \geq U^{\mathrm{d}}(\Phi', i, j) - U^{\mathrm{d}}(\Phi', i', j') \\
& U^{\mathrm{a}}(\Phi', i', j', \boldsymbol{w}) \geq U^{\mathrm{a}}(\Phi', i, j, \boldsymbol{w}) + \epsilon q_{ij} \\
& U^{\mathrm{a}}(\Phi, i'', j'', \boldsymbol{w}) \geq U^{\mathrm{a}}(\Phi, i, j, \boldsymbol{w}).
\end{aligned} \right\} \forall \, i \in \mathcal{S}, j \in \mathcal{T}
\end{aligned}
$$

The objective β is the the regret to be maximized, while the remaining constraints ensure that $(i', j'), (i'', j'')$ are indeed the respective attacked targets, as follows. The fourth constraint requires (i'', j'') to be the attacker best-response against Φ, and the worst-case tiebreaking is ensured by the first constraint since maximizing objective β requires maximizing $U^{\mathrm{d}}(\Phi, i'', j'')$. For (i', j') on the other hand, the third constraint ensures that it is a best response to Φ'. Moreover, ϵ is a small positive constant used there which sets $q_{ij} = 0$ for each ϵ-optimal OC j. As explained previously for computing (3), choosing a small enough ϵ sets $q_{ij} = 0$ for precisely every optimal attack j. Consequently, the defender loss for every such (i, j) is more than for (i', j') (by the second constraint, where M is a large positive constant), thus capturing the worst-case tiebreaking.

5   GEBRA: Exploiting Bounded Rationality Model-Free

Here, we aim to tackle bounded rationality without any assumptions on the attacker model. One simple approach is to use (3) (where ϵ was set very small for full rationality), and set an appropriate ϵ to reflect the extent of sub-optimality—akin to the COBRA algorithm [26] for SSGs. Another previous approach for SSGs is MATCH [25] which bounds the defender's loss due to attacker's deviation from rationality, by a (pre-set) constant β times the attacker's utility reduction. Thus, it guarantees that if the attacker is *close* to rationality, the defender is *close* to optimal utility. We adapt this principle to propose our solution GEBRA (Guaranteed Exploitation against Boundedly Rational Attackers).

Strictly Competitive Games. In the security domain, having attack choices favorable to both the attacker and the defender is rather unlikely. A very practical class of games here is the *Strictly competitive games* [11], where all outcomes are pareto optimal. In particular, if the attacker deviates to lower utility, the defender gets a smaller loss, thus, the attacker playing rationally is the worst case for the defender. Hence, the previous approaches COBRA and MATCH merely reduce to the conservative Minimax solution, rendering them unavailing as the desired robustness is intrinsically present. Hence, we aim to exploit bounded rationality in this setting, by requiring that the defender loss must improve by at least (a factor of) the reduction in the attacker utility, as explained momentarily.

Note that, checking if a game is strictly competitive is challenging due to the compact representation via polytopal strategy spaces in our game. We show an MILP formulation to determine if a game is strictly competitive (see Appendix).

Optimization problem for GEBRA: In the strictly competitive setting, if the attacker deviates from his optimal utility, the defender is guaranteed to get a smaller loss. To have guaranteed exploitation, we require that the decrement in defender's loss, is lower-bounded by β times the decrement in attacker utility, where β is a positive constant. Then, this can be computed by modifying (3) as:

$$\min_{\Phi, q, h, \gamma, \alpha} \quad \gamma \tag{9}$$

$$\text{s.t.} \quad \alpha, \gamma \in \mathbb{R}, \ \Phi \in \mathcal{F}, \ q, r \in \{0,1\}^{s \times t}$$

$$q_{11} + \ldots + q_{st} \geq 1 \tag{9a}$$

$$r_{11} + \ldots + r_{st} \geq 1 \tag{9b}$$

$$\left.\begin{aligned}
\epsilon(1 - q_{ij}) &\leq \alpha - U^{\mathrm{a}}(\Phi, j, i) & \text{(9c)} \\
M(1 - q_{ij}) &\geq \alpha - U^{\mathrm{a}}(\Phi, j, i) & \text{(9d)} \\
U^{\mathrm{d}}(\Phi, j, i) &\leq \gamma + M(1 - q_{ij}) & \text{(9e)} \\
\gamma &\leq U^{\mathrm{d}}(\Phi, j, i) + M(1 - r_{ij}) & \text{(9f)} \\
r_{ij} &\leq q_{ij} \leq \Phi_{ij} & \text{(9g)} \\
M(1 - h_{ij}) + \gamma - U^{\mathrm{d}}(\Phi, j, i) &\geq \beta(\alpha - U^{\mathrm{a}}(\Phi, j, i)) & \text{(9h)} \\
h_{ij} &\leq \Phi_{ij} \leq M h_{ij}. & \text{(9i)}
\end{aligned}\right\} \forall i \in \mathcal{S}, j \in \mathcal{T}$$

Similar to (3a)–(3e), constraints (9a)–(9g) enforce α, γ as wse utilities. Here, we have binary variables h_{ij} for any attack (i, j) the attacker can deviate to instead of the best response. Constraint (9i) ensures $h_{ij} = 1$ iff Φ_{ij} is nonzero, i.e., (i, j) is a valid attack (for a deviation). The gist of GEBRA is captured by (9h). For any deviation (i, j), the attacker's utility decreases by $\alpha - U^{\mathrm{a}}(\Phi, j, i)$ relative to optimal. The corresponding decrease in defender loss is $\gamma - U^{\mathrm{d}}(\Phi, j, i)$ which we require to be at least β-fold (whenever $h_{ij} = 1$, i.e. for every valid deviation). The constant β represents the magnitude of exploitation guarantee.

Remark 4. Setting $\beta = 0$ makes the key constraint of GEBRA always true, and the last constraint is redundant (since h is not tied to any other variables). Hence, GEBRA reduces to computing WSE which always exists in this case.

Note that for strictly competitive games (by definition), (9) is guaranteed to have a feasible solution for some β strictly positive. Importantly, however, the converse is not true, and in fact, in our numerical results, we use a class of games that generalizes strictly competitive games, and GEBRA still always finds a feasible solution. Further, setting $\beta < 0$ in (9), we can rearrange and reinterpret it as to require that the increase in defender loss is at most $|\beta|$ times the attacker's utility decrement—same robustness guarantee as MATCH, which we resort to in games where attacker suboptimality can severely increase defender loss.

6   Numerical Results

Setup We keep the game parameters small[5] for numerical analysis and it suffices to clearly highlight their efficacy. We use 5 TCs, OCs each and 15 machines. A game instance is created by randomly creating constraints, player valuations for TCs and the assignment of machines to TCs. To compute aggregates or averages across games or attacker populations, we keep the sample size 50 in each case.

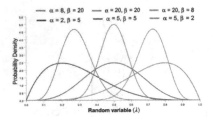

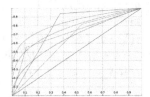

Fig. 1. Distributions $Beta(\alpha, \beta)$

Fig. 2. Two-piecewise Linear (in green) Vs Polynomial (in red) transformations (normalized to be from $[0, 1]$ to $[0, 1]$) (Color figure online)

Parametrized Prospect Theoretic Model. Here, we compare our Prospect theory based solution (PT) against WSE (i.e., the solution assuming a rational attacker with worst-case tiebreaking). We consider a population of risk-averse attackers governed by a parameter λ drawn from a distribution $Beta(\alpha, \beta)$ (density functions as shown in Fig. 1). PT estimates λ by computing the MLE and best-responds to it. We vary the parameters α, β so as to cover a spectrum of the average degree of risk-aversion (captured by distribution mean $\frac{\alpha}{\alpha+\beta}$), and the homogeneity (captured by distribution variance $\approx \frac{\alpha\beta}{(\alpha+\beta)^3}$) of the population.

As shown in Table 1, PT does significantly better for populations with low variance, as compared to high variance. Intuitively, this is because the learned parameter λ can represent the population better when there is more homogeneity (i.e., low variance). Within each of the Sub-Tables 1c, 1b, 1a, when the degree of risk-aversion is high (i.e., low mean λ; left column), the improvement of WSE over PT is higher, than when the population mean is high (i.e., smaller overall risk-aversion; right column), as expected. At the extreme with small risk-aversion

---

[5] Essential for quickly solving many instances (to get averaged numbers). Bigger parameters can be handled when solving a specific instance for real-world deployment.

Table 1. Average Defender loss of WSE and PT

	Distribution				Distribution				Distribution		
	(32,80)	(80,80)	(80,32)		(8,20)	(20,20)	(20,8)		(2,5)	(5,5)	(5,2)
WSE	2.712	2.827	2.941		2.724	2.832	2.919		2.710	2.829	**2.892**
PT	**2.178**	**2.432**	**2.580**		**2.272**	**2.662**	**2.739**		**2.396**	**2.749**	3.093
	(a) Low variance				(b) Medium variance				(c) High variance		

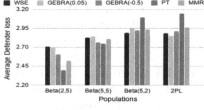 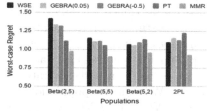

(a) Comparing Average Defender Loss   (b) Comparing Worst-case Regret

Fig. 3. Comparing PT, MMR, GEBRA and WSE for prospect theoretic attackers

on average and low homogeneity, PT does worse than WSE (Table 1c - column 3). For such cases, and others where the parametrization hypothesis may not be accurate, we show that the model-free algorithms are valuable as shown next.

Prospect-Theoretic Attackers with Arbitrary Transformations: PT relies on the assumption of polynomial transformations and homogeneous populations, which may not hold. Here, we consider a family of *Two-piecewise linear* (2PL) payoff transformations shown in Fig. 2 in contrast with the polynomial transformations that PT hypothesizes for parametrization. We compare the average defender loss of PT, MMR and GEBRA (with overall best parameters $\beta = 0.05$ among positive, and $\beta = -0.5$ among negative), against attacker populations with 2PL transformations, and polynomial transformations with high variance.

Figure 3a shows that against $Beta(5,2)$ and $2PL$, PT has a much higher loss than WSE which is greatly mitigated with MMR and GEBRA. For $Beta(2,5)$ and $Beta(5,5)$, PT has a smaller loss than WSE as seen before, and so do MMR and GEBRA(-0.5), even though the reduction margin is lower, while GEBRA(0.05) does not show much difference. In conclusion, in populations with high risk-aversion and parametrized populations, PT has an edge, however, in other cases where PT suffers, MMR and GEBRA perform much better. To compare the robustness quality, we compare the worst-case regret. Figure 3b shows that the worst-case regret is reduced with MMR compared to WSE and PT in all 4 cases, by up to 40%, 30% respectively, while GEBRA has a worst-case regret a little lower for $Beta(2,5)$ and not much different than WSE in other cases.

Exploiting Bounded Rationality with GEBRA: We want to consider the aforementioned class of strictly competitive games, however, checking this property is non-trivial (requiring to solve an MILP for each game, rather than defined via closed-form constraints). Hence, we consider a slightly more general class of games with *strictly conflicting valuations* - for TCs i and j, $u_i \geq u_j \iff v_i \geq v_j$, i.e. if the attacker gets a higher reward from a TC than the other, the defender suffers a higher loss and vice versa. Unsurprisingly, even for this class, MATCH (i.e., GEBRA with $\beta < 0$) and COBRA achieve an output that differs little from that of WSE. Hence, we only compare GEBRA (with $\beta > 0$) against WSE here.

Having studied risk-averse attackers, we consider a different form of bounded rationality as given by the *Quantal Response* (QR) model—an attacker with a QR parameter ϵ chooses an attack having utility u, with a probability $\propto \exp(\epsilon u)$. Thus, $\epsilon \to \infty$ for a perfectly rational attacker, while $\epsilon = 0$ for a fully random attacker. We consider populations of attackers with varying distributions of ϵ, namely $LN(-2,1)$, $LN(-1,1)$, $LN(0,1)$ where $LN(\alpha,\beta)$ denotes a LogNormal Distribution with parameters (α, β). These three distributions have an increasing order of means and thus, increasing average degree of rationality.

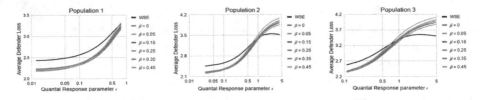

Fig. 4. Average Defender Loss comparison between GEBRA and WSE

Figure 4 shows the performance of GEBRA for various settings of β (for illustration, we only show a range for β with sizeable loss reduction). For $LN(-2,1)$ with least average rationality, GEBRA reduces the absolute loss by about 10%. However, the loss gets higher by 10% than WSE for attackers nearly rational.

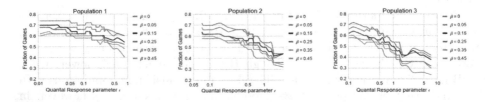

Fig. 5. Fraction of games where GEBRA does at least as good as WSE

We also measure the fraction of games in which GEBRA surpasses WSE, shown in Fig. 5. With $\beta = 0.05$, it does at least as good as WSE in 75% games for attackers nearly random and over 60% for the ones more rational. As degree of rationality rises, however, this percentage drops in other two populations.

7   Summary

In this paper, we present Risk-based Cyber Camouflage Games (RCCG) to capture the crucial uncertainty in the attack success. First, for rational attackers, we show NP-hardness of equilibrium computation, a pseudo-polynomial time algorithm for the special *unconstrained* setting, and an MILP formulation for the general *constrained* problem. Further, to tackle risk-averse attackers, we propose a Prospect theory based approach (PT) that estimates the attacker behavior from data and a variant that is robust against arbitrary payoff transformations based on Min-Max Regret (MMR). Finally, we also propose a model-free approach (GEBRA) that can exploit arbitrary deviations from rationality.

Our numerical results show that PT shows significant improvement for homogeneous populations and for a high risk-aversion, however, for heterogeneous populations, MMR moderately improves the defender loss while also achieving much lower regret. Finally, GEBRA is valuable in the *Strictly Competitive* [11] setting where previous model-free approaches for handling bounded rationality prove ineffective, particularly for attackers with a high deviation from rationality.

Acknowledgements. This work is sponsored by the Army Research Office (grant W911NF-17-1-0370).

A   RCCG for Rational Attackers

Lemma 1. *Under a given defender strategy Φ, let j_1, j_2 be OCs which are masking subsets of machines $\mathcal{K}_1$ and $\mathcal{K}_2$ respectively. Let Φ' be constructed from Φ by merging the machines in $\mathcal{K}_1$ and $\mathcal{K}_2$ and masking with a single OC, say j'. Then, $U^{\mathrm{a}}(\Phi', i, j') \leq \max(U^{\mathrm{a}}(\Phi, i, j_1), U^{\mathrm{a}}(\Phi, i, j_2)) \ \forall \ i \in \mathcal{S}$.*

Proof. For an arbitrary TC i, for brevity, let's denote $a = \Phi_{i,j_1}$, $b = \Phi_{i,j_2}$. WLOG, let $a/|\mathcal{K}_1| \leq b/|\mathcal{K}_2|$ (these are the probabilities that the attacks on (i, j_1), (i, j_2) are successful, resp.). Then,

$$U^{\mathrm{a}}(\Phi', i, j') = \frac{(a+b)}{|\mathcal{K}_1| + |\mathcal{K}_2|} v_i \leq \frac{b}{|\mathcal{K}_2|} v_i = U^{\mathrm{a}}(\Phi, i, j_2).$$

$\square$

This shows that merging the machines in any two OCs under one, cannot increase the attacker utility for any target, which prompts the following results.

Proposition 1. *Unconstrained zero-sum RCCG always has an optimal strategy that uses just one OCs.*

Proof. Consider an optimal strategy Φ that uses two or more OCs, with i^*, j^* being the attacker best response. In the unconstrained setting, OCs can be freely merged. Say we merge machines from OC $\hat{j}$ to j^* to obtain Φ'. By Lemma 1, the attacker utility from any (i, j^*) under Φ' is at most the utility from (i, j^*) or

$(i, \hat{j})$ under Φ, and thus, at most the best response attacker utility against Φ. As the remaining attack options have an unchanged utility, it follows that the best response attacker utility against Φ' is at most that against Φ. Since the game is zero-sum, the same applies for the defender loss, making Φ' also optimal while it uses fewer OCs. It follows via inductive reasoning that there exists an optimal strategy which uses a single OC to mask all the machines.   □

Theorem 1. *Zero-sum RCCG is NP-hard.*

Proof. We reduce from the problem "Exact Cover by 3-Sets" (*ExC3* for brevity) which is NP-complete. In this problem, we are given a set X, with $|X| = 3q$ (so, the size of X is a multiple of 3), and a collection C of 3-element subsets of X. The decision problem is whether $\exists C' \subset C$ where every element of X occurs in exactly one member of C'. Given such an instance, construct an RCCG instance as follows. Construct TCs $1, \ldots, 3q$ corresponding to elements of X. Let the value of each TC be 0 and let there be exactly one machine of each. Let there be TC $3q + 1$ of value $V > 0$ and q machines of it. Let there be $|C|$ OCs corresponding the subsets in C. Suppose OC corresponding to any $S \in C$ can mask exactly the 3 TCs in S & TC $3q + 1$. Let al.l costs be 0. This is a poly-time reduction by construction. We claim that an *ExC3* instance is YES iff the minimum defender loss in the constructed RCCG is exactly $V/4$.

Consider a strategy Φ. Let $J' \subseteq J$ be the OCs which mask at least one machine of some TC $i \in \{1, \ldots, 3q\}$. By construction, J' must have q OCs. Further, machines of TC $3q + 1$ must be masked by OCs in j' to minimize the defender loss since otherwise the defender loss is V. Now, for an OC j that masks a machine of TC $3q+1$, it must mask only one to minimize the defender loss. For each such OC j, if it masks $x_j (\leq 3)$ machines from TCs $1, \ldots, 3q$, we can write $U^d(\Phi, 3q+1, j) = \frac{1}{1+x_j} V \geq V/4$ which attains the minimum of $V/4$ when $x_j = 3$. Since the attacker chooses to attack (i, j) which maximizes it , the defender loss is lower bounded by $v/4$. Now, if the given instance of *ExC3* is a YES instance, it is possible to find q OCs which cover all the TCs, and use them to mask the 3 machines of the corresponding TCs along with one machine of TC $3q + 1$ each, thus achieving the minimum loss of $V/4$. Conversely, if the minimum defender loss is $V/4$, the defender loss when attacked at any OC and TC $3q + 1$ (if so valid) must be at most $V/4$, which implies that it must contain only 1 machine of $3q+1$, and thus i) there should be q such OCs used, and ii) each of them must have at least 3 machines of TCs $1, \ldots, 3q$. So, there must be exactly q such OCs each with exactly 3 machines. Hence, the subsets corresponding to these OCs form the exact cover of the given *ExC3* making it a YES instance.   □

Proposition 2. *Unconstrained RCCG always has an optimal strategy that uses just two OCs.*

Proof. Consider an optimal strategy Φ that uses three or more OCs, with i^*, j^* being the attacker best response. In the unconstrained setting, OCs can be freely merged. Say we merge machines from OC j_1 to j_2 (with $j_1, j_2 \neq j^*$) to obtain Φ'. By Lemma 1, the attacker utility of any (i, j_2) under Φ' is at most the utility of (i, j_1) or (i, j_2) under Φ, and thus, i^*, j^* must still be the best response for the attacker against Φ. In particular, this also ensures that it remains the worst-case for the defender in case of tie-breaks. It follows via inductive reasoning that given an optimal strategy with two or more OCs, another using fewer OCs can be constructed. Thus, there exists an optimal strategy which uses a single OC.

$\square$

SOBRE Algorithm

SOBRE uses the subroutine DPBRF (Dynamic Programming for Best Response Feasibility) which given the input (i, n^*, m^*), computes if the machines can be masked so that OC 1 has m^* total machines with n^* of TC i^*, and $(i^*, 1)$ is the attacker best response. Function $f(i, m)$, (memoized: Line 2), computes if such a strategy exists with additional property that TCs $1, \ldots, i$ in total have m machines in $OC1$. To compute $f(i, m)$, we consider n out of n_i machines of TC $i(\neq i^*)$ to be put in OC 1 (Line 7). If doing so keeps $(i^*, 1)$ at a higher utility than $(i, 1), (i, 2)$ (Line 8), and similarly recursively for all smaller-indexed TCs (Line 9), $f(i, m)$ is true. Lines 5,6 mark the base cases. DPBRF returns true if $f(s, m^*)$ is true (Line 3) by definition.

$f(i, m)$ is computable in $O(n_i)$ (Line 7), hence, DPBRF takes $O(km^*)$ using $\sum_{i=1}^{s} n_i = k$. Summing over the loops of SOBRE gives its runtime as $O(k^4)$.

Algorithm 3: DPBRF(i^*, n^*, m^*)

---

1 **for** $i = 1, \ldots, s; m = 0, \ldots, m^*$
2      $A[i, m] \leftarrow f(i, m)$
3 **Return** $A[s, m^*]$

4 **Function** $f(i, m)$
5   **if** $(i = 0)$ **Return** $m = 0$
6   **if** $(i = i^*)$ **Return** $A[i - 1, m - n^*]$
7   **for** $n = 0, \ldots, n_i$
8   **if** $(\max\{\frac{n}{m^*} v_i, \frac{n_i - n}{k - m^*} v_i\} < \frac{n^*}{m^*} v_{i^*})$ // '<=' if lower defender loss
9   **if** $(A[i - 1, m - n])$ **Return** $true$
10   **Return** $false$

B   Sensitivity to Learning Error

Suppose the estimated parameter is λ^* and the computed optimal solution is Φ, yielding a defender utility u^*. We want to provide an error interval around λ^* s.t. the defender loss does not increase (at all, or beyond a desired margin ϵ), if the true λ is within this interval. Equivalently, we compute the least perturbation needed s.t. the defender loss increases. We consider all pairs (i, j) s.t.

$U^{\mathrm{d}}(\Phi, i, j) > u^* + \epsilon$. Thus, if the attacker best response is any such (i, j), then the defender loss increases beyond the desired threshold. We compute the minimum deviation (of true λ from estimated λ^*) that causes this (if it exists) by solving

$$\min_{\lambda} \ |\lambda - \lambda^*| \quad \text{s.t.} \ \log f_\lambda(i, j) \geq \log f_\lambda(i', j') \ \forall \, i' \in \mathcal{S} \ \forall \, j' \in \mathcal{T} \qquad (10)$$

The constraint here ensures that (i, j) is indeed the prospect-maximizing response, where we use log on both sides to get an LP, for efficient computation. Then, solving (10) for all (i, j) pairs for which $U^{\mathrm{d}}(\Phi, i, j) > u^* + \epsilon$, and taking the minimum of all the perturbations, gives us the required tolerance.

C Computing Strict Competitiveness

We formulate an MILP that is feasible iff for a strategy Φ, deviating from some (i, j) to (i', j') is beneficial to both players—game is not strictly competitive.

$$\left.\begin{array}{ll} M(1 - q_{ij}) + U^{\mathrm{a}}(\Phi, i, j) > \alpha, & M(1 - r_{ij}) + \alpha > U^{\mathrm{a}}(\Phi, i, j) \\ M(1 - r_{ij}) + U^{\mathrm{d}}(\Phi, i, j) > \beta, & M(1 - q_{ij}) + \beta > U^{\mathrm{d}}(\Phi, i, j) \\ r_{ij} \leq \Phi_{ij} \leq M r_{ij}, & q_{ij} \leq \Phi_{ij} \leq M q_{ij} \end{array}\right\} \forall \, i \in \mathcal{S}, j \in \mathcal{T}$$

$$\Phi \in \mathcal{F}, \ \boldsymbol{q}, \boldsymbol{r} \in \{0, 1\}^{s \times t}, \quad q_{11} + \ldots + q_{st} = 1, \quad r_{11} + \ldots + r_{st} = 1$$

Here, binary variables q, r capture (i, j) and (i', j') respectively which define the aforementioned attacker deviation. Line 4 ensures they are unique and Line 3 ensures they are valid attacks. Attacker and defender both prefer (i, j) over (i', j') as per Lines 1,2 respectively.

References

1. Aggarwal, P., et al.: An exploratory study of a masking strategy of cyberdeception using cybervan. In: HFES (2020)
2. Alpcan, T., Başar, T.: Network Security: A Decision and Game-Theoretic Approach. Cambridge University Press, Cambridge (2010)
3. Ben-Tal, A., El Ghaoui, L., Nemirovski, A.: Robust optimization. Princeton University Press, Princeton (2009)
4. Berrueta, D.: A Practical Approach for Defeating Nmap OS- Fingerprinting (2003)
5. Boutilier, C., Patrascu, R., Poupart, P., Schuurmans, D.: Constraint-based optimization and utility elicitation using the minimax decision criterion. Artif. Intell. **170**(8–9), 686–713 (2006)
6. Breton, M., Alj, A., Haurie, A.: Sequential stackelberg equilibria in two-person games. J. Optim. Theory Appl. **59**, 71–97 (1988). https://doi.org/10.1007/BF00939867
7. Chadha, R., et al.: Cybervan: a cyber security virtual assured network testbed. In: MILCOM 2016–2016 IEEE Military Communications Conference (Nov 2016). https://doi.org/10.1109/MILCOM.2016.7795481
8. Cooney, S., Wang, K., Bondi, E., Nguyen, T., Vayanos, P., et al.: Learning to signal in the goldilocks zone: improving adversary compliance in security games. In: ECML/PKDD (2019)

9. de Farias, D.P., Van Roy, B.: On constraint sampling in the linear programming approach to approximate linear programming. In: CDC (2003)
10. De Gaspari, F., Jajodia, S., Mancini, L.V., Panico, A.: Ahead: a new architecture for active defense. In: SafeConfig (2016)
11. Eatwell, J., Milgate, M., Newman, P.: The New Palgrave: A Dictionary of Economics. Palgrave Macmillan, London (1987)
12. Ferguson-Walter, K., LaFon, D., Shade, T.: Friend or faux: deception for cyber defense. J. Info. Warfare 16(2), 28–42 (2017)
13. Goel, V., Perlroth, N.: Yahoo Says 1 Billion User Accounts Were Hacked. (December 2016). https://www.nytimes.com/2016/12/14/technology/yahoo-hack.html
14. Guo, Q., Gan, J., Fang, F., Tran-Thanh, L., Tambe, M., An, B.: On the inducibility of stackelberg equilibrium for security games. CoRR, abs/1811.03823 (2018)
15. Gutzmer, I.: Equifax Announces Cybersecurity Incident Involving Consumer Information (2017). https://investor.equifax.com/news-and-events/news/2017/09-07-2017-213000628
16. Xin Jiang, A., Chan, H., Leyton-Brown, K.: Resource graph games: a compact representation for games with structured strategy spaces. In: AAAI (2017)
17. Joyce, R.: Disrupting Nation State Hackers. USENIX Association, San Francisco (2016)
18. Kiekintveld, C., Marecki, J., Tambe, M.: Approximation methods for infinite bayesian stackelberg games: modeling distributional payoff uncertainty. In: AAMAS (2011)
19. Kiekintveld, C., Islam, T., Kreinovich, V.: Security games with interval uncertainty. In: AAMAS (2013)
20. Laszka, A., Vorobeychik, Y., Koutsoukos, X.D.: Optimal personalized filtering against spear-phishing attacks. In: AAAI (2015)
21. Mandiant: Apt1: exposing one of china's cyber espionage units (2013)
22. McKelvey, R., Palfrey, T.: Quantal response equilibria for normal form games. Games Econ. Behav. 10(1), 6–38 (1995)
23. Nguyen, T.H., Yadav, A., An, B., Tambe, M., Boutilier, C.: Regret-based optimization and preference elicitation for stackelberg security games with uncertainty. In: AAAI (2014)
24. Peterson, A.: OPM says 5.6 million fingerprints stolen in cyberattack, five times as many as previously thought (September 2015). https://www.washingtonpost.com/news/the-switch/wp/2015/09/23/opm-now-says-more-than-five-million-fingerprints-compromised-in-breaches
25. Pita, J., John, R., Maheswaran, R., Tambe, M., Kraus, S.: A robust approach to addressing human adversaries in security games. In: ECAI, pp. 660–665 (2012a)
26. Pita, J., John, R., Maheswaran, R., Tambe, M., Yang, R., Kraus, S.: A robust approach to addressing human adversaries in security games. In: AAMAS, pp. 1297–1298 (2012)
27. Qian, Y., Haskell, W., Tambe, M.: Robust strategy against unknown risk-averse attackers in security games. In: AAMAS (2015)
28. Rahman, M., Manshaei, M., Al-Shaer, E.: A game-theoretic approach for deceiving remote operating system fingerprinting. In: CNS, pp. 73–81 (2013)
29. Schlenker, A., et al.: Don't bury your head in warnings: A game-theoretic approach for intelligent allocation of cyber-security alerts (2017)
30. Schlenker, A., et al.: Deceiving cyber adversaries: a game theoretic approach. In: AAMAS (2018)

31. Serra, E., Jajodia, S., Pugliese, A., Rullo, A., Subrahmanian, V.S.: Pareto-optimal adversarial defense of enterprise systems. ACM Trans. Inf. Syst. Secur. (TISSEC) **17**(3), 11 (2015)
32. Sinha, A., Malo, P., Deb, K.: A review on bilevel optimization: from classical to evolutionary approaches and applications. IEEE Trans. Evol. Comput. **22**(2), 276–295 (2018)
33. Tambe, M.: Security and game theory: algorithms, deployed systems, lessons learned (2011)
34. Thakoor, O., Tambe, M., Vayanos, P., Xu, H., Kiekintveld, C., Fang, F.: Cyber camouflage games for strategic deception. In: GameSec (2019)
35. Thinkst. Canary (2015). https://canary.tools/
36. Tversky, A., Kahneman, D.: Prospect theory: an analysis of decision under risk. Econometrica **47**(2), 263–291 (1979)
37. von Stengel, B., Zamir, S.: Leadership with commitment to mixed strategies. Technical report (2004)
38. Yang, R., Kiekintveld, C., Ordonez, F., Tambe, M., John, R.: Improving resource allocation strategy against human adversaries in security games. In: ICJAI (2011)

Farsighted Risk Mitigation of Lateral Movement Using Dynamic Cognitive Honeypots

Linan Huang[✉] and Quanyan Zhu

Department of Electrical and Computer Engineering, New York University,
2 MetroTech Center, Brooklyn, NY 11201, USA
{lh2328,qz494}@nyu.edu

Abstract. Lateral movement of advanced persistent threats has posed a severe security challenge. Due to the stealthy and persistent nature of the lateral movement, defenders need to consider time and spatial locations holistically to discover latent attack paths across a large time-scale and achieve long-term security for the target assets. In this work, we propose a time-expanded random network to model the stochastic service links in the user-host enterprise network and the adversarial lateral movement. We design cognitive honeypots at idle production nodes and disguise honey links as service links to detect and deter the adversarial lateral movement. The location of the honeypot changes randomly at different times and increases the honeypots' stealthiness. Since the defender does not know whether, when, and where the initial intrusion and the lateral movement occur, the honeypot policy aims to reduce the target assets' Long-Term Vulnerability (LTV) for proactive and persistent protection. We further characterize three tradeoffs, i.e., the probability of interference, the stealthiness level, and the roaming cost. To counter the curse of multiple attack paths, we propose an iterative algorithm and approximate the LTV with the union bound for computationally efficient deployment of cognitive honeypots. The results of the vulnerability analysis illustrate the bounds, trends, and a residue of LTV when the adversarial lateral movement has infinite duration. Besides honeypot policies, we obtain a critical threshold of compromisability to guide the design and modification of the current system parameters for a higher level of long-term security. We show that the target node can achieve zero vulnerability under infinite stages of lateral movement if the probability of movement deterrence is not less than the threshold.

Keywords: Advanced persistent threats · Lateral movement · Time-expanded network · Attack graph · Cognitive security · Long-term security · Risk analysis

Q. Zhu—This research is partially supported by awards ECCS-1847056, CNS-1544782, CNS-2027884, and SES-1541164 from National Science of Foundation (NSF), and grant W911NF-19-1-0041 from Army Research Office (ARO).

© Springer Nature Switzerland AG 2020
Q. Zhu et al. (Eds.): GameSec 2020, LNCS 12513, pp. 125–146, 2020.
https://doi.org/10.1007/978-3-030-64793-3_7

1   Introduction

Advanced Persistent Threats (APTs) have recently emerged as a critical security challenge to enterprise networks. Their stealthy, persistent, and sophisticated nature has made it difficult to prevent, detect, and deter them. The life cycle of APT attacks consists of multiple stages and phases [1,2]. After the initial intrusion by phishing emails, social engineering, or an infected USB, an attacker can enter the enterprise network from an external network domain. Then, the attacker establishes a foothold, escalates privileges, and moves laterally in the enterprise network to search for valuable assets as his final target. The targeted assets can be either a database with confidential information or a controller in an industrial plant as shown in the instance of APT27 [3] and Stuxnet, respectively. Valuable assets are usually segregated and cannot be compromised by an attacker directly from the external domain in the initial intrusion phase. Therefore, it is indispensable for the attacker to exploit the internal network flows of legitimate service links between hosts and users to move laterally from the location of the initial intrusion to the final target of valuable assets.

Early detection of the adversarial lateral movement is challenging. First, an APT attacker is persistent. The long duration between the initial intrusion and the final target compromise makes it difficult for the defender to relate alarms over a time scale of years and piece together shreds of evidence to identify the attack path. Second, an APT attack is stealthy. Each time the attacker has compromised a new network entity, such as a host, and obtained its root privilege, he does not take any subversive actions on the compromised entity and remains "under the radar". These entities are only used as the attacker's stepping stones toward the final target. Third, the high volume of network traffic during regular operation generates a considerable number of false alarms, and thus significantly delays and reduces the accuracy of adversary detection. Without an accurate and timely detection of adversarial lateral movement, defensive methods, such as patching and frequent resetting of suspicious entities, become cost-prohibitive and significantly reduce operational efficiency as those entities become unavailable for the incoming service links.

Honeypot is a promising active defense method of deception. A honeypot is a monitored and regulated trap that is disguised to be a valuable asset for the attacker to compromise. Since legitimate users do not have the motivation to access a honeypot, any inbound network traffic directly reveals the attack with negligible false alarms. The off-the-shelf honeypots are applied at fixed locations and on isolated machines that are not involved in the regular operation. Honeypots at fixed locations are easy to implement. Isolating the honeypot completely from the production system can reduce the risk that an attacker uses the honeypot as a pivot node to penetrate the production system [4]. Despite the advantages, honeypots at fixed and isolated locations can be easily identified by sophisticated attackers [5] and become ineffective. Motivated by the concept of cognitive radio [6] and roaming honeypots [7], we develop the concept of cognitive honeypots to mitigate the Long-Term Vulnerability (LTV) of a target asset during the adversarial lateral movement. Contrary to the off-the-shelf honeypots, the cognitive honeypots aim to leverage idle machines of the production system and configure them into honeypots to make the deception indecipherable and unpredictable for the attacker. Since the defender reconfigures part of the production systems into honeypots, she needs to guarantee that the honeypot configuration does not interfere with service links. Also, the defender needs to balance the utility of security with the cost of reconfiguration. We manage to consider the above three factors, i.e., the level of stealthiness/indecipherability, the probability of interference, and the cost of roaming, in determining the optimal honeypot policy that minimizes the target asset's LTV.

In this work, we model the adversarial lateral movement in the enterprise network as a time-expanded network [8], where the additional temporal links connect the isolated spatial service links across a long time to reveal persistent attack paths explicitly. We consider the scenario where service links occur randomly at each stage and the attacker can exploit these service links for lateral movement with a success probability. Due to the *curse of multiple attack paths*, the computation complexity increases dramatically with the network size and the number of stages. To efficiently compute the optimal policy for the cognitive honeypot, we propose an iterative algorithm and approximate the LTV by its upper and lower bounds, which result in the optimal conservative and risky honeypot policies, respectively. The results of the vulnerability analysis illustrate the limit and the bounds of LTV when the duration of lateral movement goes to infinity under direct and indirect policies, respectively. Without proper mitigation strategies, vulnerability never decreases over stages and the target node is doom to be compromised. Under the improved honeypot strategies, a *vulnerability residue* exists and LTV cannot be reduced to 0. Besides honeypot policies, we further investigate the possibility of changing the frequency of service links and the probability of successful compromise for *long-term security*. We manage to character a critical threshold for the *Probability of Movement Deterrence* (**PoMD**) and prove that the target node can achieve zero vulnerability even when the adversarial lateral movement last for infinite stages if POMD is not less than the threshold.

1.1   Related Works

Lateral Movement Detection and Mitigation. Various methods have been proposed for lateral movement detection [9–11]. However, most of them rely on accurate and timely identification of the initial intrusion, which may be challenging to achieve. Mitigation methods of network topology change have also been proposed to delay lateral movement [12] and reduce its adversarial impact [13]. Authors in [14,15] have proposed a proactive defense-in-depth model against the multi-stage multi-phase attacks. Previous works have also analyzed security metrics, such as reachability [13], enforceability [16], and survivability [17], to reduce risk and loss under lateral movement attacks. Compared to these works, our work applies honeypots and honey links to detect and mitigate lateral movement. Moreover, we enable the analysis of the target's LTV under an undetected initial intrusion and an arbitrary duration of lateral movement.

Cognitive Honeypots. Honeypots as a defensive deception method have been widely studied in the literature. The authors in [18–20] have investigated the optimal timing and actions to attract and engage attackers in the honeypot. The authors in [21] have investigated the optimal honeypot configuration and the signaling mechanism to simultaneously incentivize attackers and disincentivize legitimate users to access a honeypot. All these honeypots are assumed to be placed at fixed and segregated locations. In this work, we consider cognitive honeypots that use the idle machines of the production system to increase the stealthiness of honeypots. The terminology of "cognitive honeypots" has appeared in [22] but refers to a cognition of the suspicion level. The authors in [23] have investigated the optimal honeypot locations during the adversarial lateral movement to prevent the attacker from compromising the target node. Their honeypot policy requires a partial observation of the state, which may not be available as a result of the attacker's stealthiness. Our work assumes that the defender does not know whether, when, or where the initial intrusion and the lateral movement occur in the network. Without real-time feedback information such as alerts of node compromise, the cognitive honeypot provides proactive and persistent protection of the valuable asset.

Time-Expanded Network. Time-expanded networks have been applied in transportation [24], satellite communications [25], and network security [26]. Since the transportation planning and satellite communications follow a timetable, the time-expanded networks in these applications usually have time-varying links that are deterministic and known at all stages. In enterprise networks, the defender does not know which service links will be used in the ensuing stages. Thus, we consider a time-expanded network with random topology. Compared to attack graphs (e.g., [27]), which focus on capturing the paths of an attack, the time-expanded network explicitly portrays the timing of the attacks and captures the temporal information of the legitimate network flows and the adversarial lateral movement.

1.2   Notation and Organization of the Paper

Throughout this paper, we use the pronoun 'he' for the attacker and 'she' for the defender. The superscript represents the time index. The calligraphic letter $\mathscr{V}$ represents a set and $\mathscr{V} \setminus \mathscr{V}_I$ means the set of elements in $\mathscr{V}$ but not in $\mathscr{V}_I$. We summarize important notations in Table 1 for readers' convenience.

The rest of the paper is organized as follows. Section 2 introduces the time-expanded network to model the random arrival of the service links, the adversarial lateral movement, and the implementation of cognitive honeypots. In Sect. 3, we compute the optimal honeypot policy dependent on the level of stealthiness, the probability of interference, and the cost of roaming. The LTV of the target node is then analyzed. Section 4 concludes the paper.

Table 1. Summary of notations.

Variable	Meaning
$\mathscr{V} = \{\mathscr{V}_U, \mathscr{V}_H\}$	Node set of users and hosts
$N = \|\mathscr{V}\|$	Number of user and host nodes
$\mathscr{V}_I \subseteq \mathscr{V}$	Demilitarized Zone (DMZ), i.e., the node-set of potential initial intrusion
$\mathscr{V}_D \subseteq \mathscr{V}$	The node-set that can be reconfigured as honeypots
$\mathscr{V}_S$	The set of all the subsets of $\mathscr{V}$
$n_{j_0} \in \mathscr{V} \setminus \mathscr{V}_I$	The target node that contains valuable assets
$\Delta k \in \mathbb{Z}_0^+$	The length of the adversarial lateral movement
ρ_i	The probability that the initial intrusion occurs at node $n_i \in \mathscr{V}_I$
β	The probability/frequency of service links
λ	The probability of a successful compromise
γ	The probability of honey links
$q_{i,j}$	The probability that the attacker identifies the honey link from n_i to n_j

2 Chronological Enterprise Network Model

We model the normal operation of an enterprise network over a continuous period as a sequence of user-host networks in chronological order. As shown in Fig. 1, nodes U1 and U2 represent the two users' client computers. Nodes H1, H2, and H3 represent three hosts in the network. In particular, host H3 stores confidential information or controls a critical actuator, thus the defender needs to protect H3 from attacks. Define $\mathscr{V} := \{\mathscr{V}_U, \mathscr{V}_H\}$ as the node set where $\mathscr{V}_U, \mathscr{V}_H$ are the sets of the user nodes and hosts, respectively. The solid arrows represent two types of service links, i.e., the user-host connections and the host-host communications through an application such as HTTP [28]. Users such as U1 and U2 can access non-confidential hosts, such as H1 and H2, through their client computers for upload and/or download. However, to prevent data theft and physical damages, host H3 is inaccessible to users; e.g., there are no service links from U1 or U2 to H3 at any stage k. Since the normal operation requires data exchanges among hosts, directed network flows exist among hosts at different stages; e.g., H3 has an outbound connection to H2 at stage $k = k_0$ and an inbound connection from H2 at stage $k = k_0 + 3$. We assume that both types of service links occur randomly and last for a random but finite duration. Whenever there is a change of network topology, i.e., adding or deleting the user-host and host-host links, we define it as a new stage. We can characterize the chronological network as a series of user-host networks at discrete stages $k = k_0, k_0 + 1, \cdots, k_0 + \Delta k$, where the initial stage $k_0 \in \mathbb{Z}^+$ and $\Delta k \in \mathbb{Z}_0^+$. Since APTs are stealthy, the defender may not know the value of k_0, i.e., when the initial intrusion happens or has already happened. The lack of accurate and timely identification of the initial intrusion brings a significant challenge to detect and deter the lateral movement.

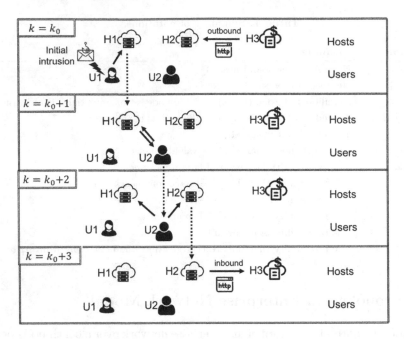

Fig. 1. A sequence of user-host networks with service links in chronological order under discrete stage-index k. The initial stage k_0 is the stage of the attacker's initial intrusion yet the defender does not know the value of k_0. The solid arrows show the direction of the user-host and host-host network flows. By incorporating part of temporal links denoted by the dashed arrows, we reveal the attack path over a long period explicitly.

2.1   Time-Expanded Network and Random Service Links

We abstract the discrete series of networks in Fig. 1 from $k \in \{k_0, \cdots, k_0 + \Delta k\}$ as a time-expanded network $\mathscr{G} = (\mathscr{V}, \mathscr{E}, \Delta k)$ in Fig. 2.   In the time-expanded network, we distinguish the same user or host node by the stage k and define $n_i^k \in \mathscr{V}$ as the i-th node in set $\mathscr{V}$ at stage $k \in \{k_0, \cdots, k_0 + \Delta k\}$. We drop the superscript k if we refer to the node rather than the node at stage k or the time does not matter. We can assume without loss of generality that the number of nodes $N := |\mathscr{V}|$ does not change with time as we can let $\mathscr{V}$ contain all the potential users and hosts in the enterprise network over Δk stages. The link set $\mathscr{E} := \{\mathscr{E}^{k_0}, \cdots, \mathscr{E}^{k_0 + \Delta k}\} \cup \{\mathscr{E}_C^{k_0}, \cdots, \mathscr{E}_C^{k_0 + \Delta k - 1}\}$ consists of two parts. On the one hand, the user-host and host-host connections at each stage $k \in \{k_0, \cdots, k_0 + \Delta k\}$ are represented by the set $\mathscr{E}^k = \{e(n_i^k, n_j^k) \in \{0, 1\} | n_i^k, n_j^k \in \mathscr{V}, i \neq j, \forall i, j \in \{1, \cdots, N\}\}$. On the other hand, set $\mathscr{E}_C^k := \{e(n_i^k, n_i^{k+1}) = 1 | n_i^k, n_i^{k+1} \in \mathscr{V}, \forall i \in \{1, \cdots, N\}\}$ contains the virtual temporal links from stage k to $k+1$. A link exists if $e(\cdot, \cdot) = 1$ and does not if $e(\cdot, \cdot) = 0$. The time-expanded network $\mathscr{G}$ is a directed graph due to the temporal causality represented by the set $\mathscr{E}_C^k, k \in \{k_0, \cdots, k_0 + \Delta k - 1\}$.

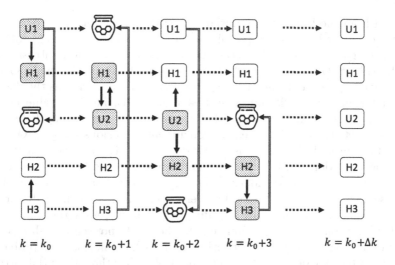

$$k = k_0 \qquad k = k_0+1 \qquad k = k_0+2 \qquad k = k_0+3 \qquad k = k_0+\Delta k$$

Fig. 2. Time-expanded network $\mathscr{G} = \{\mathscr{V}, \mathscr{E}, \Delta k\}$ for the adversarial lateral movement and the cognitive honeypot configuration. The solid, dashed, double-lined arrows represent the service links, the temporal connections, and the honey links to honeypots, respectively. The shadowed nodes reveal the attack path from U1 to H3 explicitly over $\Delta k = 3$ stages.

Since the user-host and the host-host connections happen randomly at each stage, we assume that a service link from node $n_i^k \in \mathscr{V}$ to node $n_j^k \in \mathscr{V} \setminus \{n_i^k\}$ exists with probability $\beta_{i,j} \in [0,1]$ for any stage $k \in \{k_0, \cdots, k_0 + \Delta k\}$. If a connection from node n_i^k to n_j^k is prohibitive; e.g., U1 cannot access H3 in Fig. 1, then $\beta_{i,j} = 0$. We can define $\beta := \{\beta_{i,j}\}, i, j \in \{1, \cdots, N\}$, as the service-link generating matrix without loss of generality by letting $\beta_{i,i} = 0, \forall i \in \{1, \cdots, N\}$. In this work, we consider a time-invariant β whose value can be estimated empirically from long-term historical data[1]. The service links at each stage may only involve a small number of nodes and leave other nodes idle.

Definition 1. *A node $n_i^k \in \mathscr{V}$ is said to be **idle** at stage k if it is neither the source nor the sink node of any service link at stage k, i.e., $e(n_i^k, n_j^k) = 0, e(n_j^k, n_i^k) = 0, \forall n_j^k \in \mathscr{V}$.*

2.2   Attack Model of Lateral Movement over a Long Duration

We assume that the initial intrusion can only happen at a subset of N nodes $\mathscr{V}_I \subseteq \mathscr{V}$ due to the network segregation. We can refer to $\mathscr{V}_I$ as the Demilitarized Zone (DMZ). Take Fig. 1 as an example, if all hosts in the enterprise network are

---

[1] For example, we can use the user-computer authentication dataset from the Los Alamos National Laboratory enterprise network [29] to estimate the probability of user-host service links over a long period. The dataset is available at https://csr. lanl.gov/data/auth/.

segregated from the Internet, the initial intrusion can only happen to the client computer of U1 or U2 through phishing emails or social engineering. Although network segregation narrows down the potential location of initial intrusion from $\mathcal{V}$ to the subset $\mathcal{V}_I$ that may contain only one node, it is still challenging for the defender to prevent the nodes in $\mathcal{V}_I$ from an initial intrusion as the defender cannot determine *when* the initial intrusion happens; i.e., the value of k_0 is unknown. In this work, we assume that the initial intrusion only happens to one node in set $\mathcal{V}_I$ at a time; i.e., no concurrent intrusions happen. Once the attacker has entered the enterprise network via the initial intrusion from an external network domain, he does not launch new intrusions from the external domain to compromise more nodes in $\mathcal{V}_I$. Instead, the attacker can exploit the internal service links to move laterally over time, which is much stealthier than intrusions from external network domains. For example, after the attacker has controlled U1's computer by phishing emails, he would not send phishing emails to other users from the external network domain, which increases his probability of being detected. We define $\rho_i \in [0, 1]$ as the probability that the initial intrusion happens at node $n_i^{k_0} \in \mathcal{V}_I, \forall k_0 \in \mathbb{Z}^+$. The probability satisfies $\sum_{i \in \mathcal{V}_I} \rho_i = 1$ and is assumed to be independent of the stage k_0. This probability of initial intrusion can be estimated based on the node's vulnerability assessed by historical data, red team exercises, and the Common Vulnerability Scoring System (CVSS) [30].

After the initial intrusion, the attacker can exploit service links at different stages by various techniques to move laterally, such as Pass the Hash (PtH), taint shared content, and remote service session hijacking [1]. Take PtH as an example, when a user enters the password and logs into host H1 from a compromised client computer U1 at stage k_0 as shown in Fig. 1, the attacker at U1 can capture the valid password hashes for accessing host H1 by credential access technique. Then, the attacker can use the captured hashes to access the host H1 for all the future stage $k > k_0$. The attacker can also compromise a user node from a compromised host by tainting the shared content, i.e., adding malicious scripts to valid files in the host. Then, the malicious code can be executed when user U2 downloads those files from H1 at stage $k_0 + 1$. PtH (resp. tainting shared content) enables an adversarial lateral movement from a user node (resp. host node) to a host node (resp. user node). The attacker can also use remote service session hijacking, such as Secure Shell (SSH) hijacking and Remote Desktop Protocol (RDP) hijacking, to move laterally between hosts by hijacking the inbound or outbound network flows. In this work, we assume that once the attacker compromises a node, he retains the control of the node for the given length of time window Δk determined by the defender. For example, the defender can require users to update their password every Δk days to invalidate the PtH attack. During the time window, i.e., from the initial intrusion $k = k_0$ to $k = k_0 + \Delta k$, the attacker can launch simultaneous attacks from all the compromised nodes to move laterally whenever there are outbound service links from them. If there are multiple service links from one compromised node, the attacker can also compromise all the sink nodes of these service links within the stage. Note that the only objective of the attacker is to search for valuable nodes (e.g., H3), compromise it, and then launch subversive attacks for data theft and physical damages. Thus, we assume that the attack does not launch any subversive attacks in all the compromised nodes except at the target node to remain stealthy. That is, even though the attacker retains the control of the compromised nodes, he only uses them as stepping stones to reach the target node.

The persistent lateral movement over a long time period enables the attacker to reach and compromise segregated nodes that are not in the DMZ $\mathcal{V}_I$. In both Fig. 1 and Fig. 2, although the network has no direct service links, represented by solid arrows, from U1 to H3 at each stage, the cascade of *static security* in all stages does not result in *long-term security* over $\Delta k = 3$ stages. After we add the temporal links represented by the dashed arrows and consider stages and spatial locations holistically, we can see the attack path from the initial intrusion node U1 to the target node H3 over $\Delta k = 3$ stages as highlighted by the shadows in Fig. 2. The temporal order of the service links affects the likelihood that the attacker can compromise the target node. For example, if we exchange the services links that happen at stage $k_0 + 1$ and stage $k_0 + 2$, then the attacker from node U1 cannot reach H3 in $\Delta k = 3$ stages. Since the attacker can launch simultaneous attacks from multiple compromised nodes to move laterally, there can exist multiple attack paths from an initial intrusion node to the target node.

The adversarial exploitation of service links is not always successful due to the defender's mitigation technologies against lateral movement techniques [1]. For example, the firewall rules to block RDP traffic between hosts can invalidate RDP hijacking. If the attacker has compromised nodes $n_i^{k'} \in \mathcal{V}$ before stage $k > k'$ and a service link from n_i^k to $n_j^k \in \mathcal{V} \setminus \{n_i^k\}$ exists at stage k, i.e., $e(n_i^k, n_j^k) = 1$, we can define $\lambda_{i,j} \in [0, 1]$ as the probability that the attacker at node n_i^k successfully compromises node n_j^k, which is assumed to be independent of stage k.

2.3   Cognitive Honeypot

The lateral movement of persistent and stealthy attacks makes the enterprise network insecure in the long run. The high rates of false alarms and the miss detection of both the initial external intrusion and the following internal compromise make it challenging for the defender to identify the set of nodes that have been compromised. Thus, the defender needs to patch and reset all suspicious nodes at all stages to deter the attacks, which can be cost-prohibitive.

Honeypots are a promising active defense method to detect and deter these persistent and stealthy attacks by deception [31]. In this paper, the connection from a service node to a honeypot is referred to as a honey link. The defender disguises a honey link as a service link to attract attackers. For example, the defender can start a session with remote services from a host to a honeypot. The attacker who has compromised the host will be detected once he hijacks the remote service session and carries out actions in the honeypots. Since regular honeypots are implemented at fixed locations and on machines that are never involved in the regular operation, advanced attacks like APTs can identify the honeypots and avoid accessing them. Motivated by the roaming honeypot [7] and the fact that the service links at each stage only involve a small number of nodes, we develop the following cognitive honeypot configuration that utilizes and reconfigures different idle nodes at different stages as honeypots. Let $\mathcal{V}_D \subseteq \mathcal{V}$ be the subset of nodes that can be reconfigured as honeypots when idle. At each stage k, the defender randomly selects a node $n_w^k \in \mathcal{V}_D$ to be the potential honeypot and creates a random honey link from other nodes to n_w^k. Since disguising a honeypot as a normal node requires emulating massive services and the continuous monitoring of all inbound network flows are costly, we assume that the defender sets up at most one honeypot and monitors one honey link at each stage.

As shown in Fig. 2, U1, H2, and H3 are idle at stage $k_0 + 1$ and U1 is reconfigured as the honeypot. The link from H3 to U1 is the honey link which is monitored by the defender. At stage k_0, U2 is the only idle node and is reconfigured as the honeypot with a honey link from U1 to U2. As stated in Sect. 2.2, the attacker who has compromised U1 at stage k_0 remains stealthy and does not sabotage any normal operations. Thus, the defender can reconfigure U1 as a honeypot at stage $k_0 + 1$. However, the honeypot of U1 at stage $k_0 + 1$ cannot identify the attacker by monitoring all the inbound traffic as he has already compromised U1. On the contrary, the honeypots at stage k_0 and $k_0 + 2$ can trap the attackers who have compromised U1 and mistaken the honey links as service links[2]. Theoretically, the honeypot can achieve zero false alarms as the legitimate network flows should occur only at the service links. For example, although the existence of the honey link at stage k_0 enables legitimate users at U1 to access another user's computer U2, a legitimate user aiming to finish the service link from U1 to H1 should not access any irrelevant nodes other than host H1. On the other hand, an attacker at U1 cannot tell whether the links from U1 to H1 and U2 are service links or honey links. Thus, only an attacker at U1 can access the honeypot U2 at stage k_0.

Random Honeypot Configuration and Detection Since the defender can neither predict future service links nor determine the set of compromised nodes at the current stage, she needs to develop a time-independent policy $\gamma := \{\gamma_{l,w}\}, \forall n_l^k, n_w^k \in \mathcal{V}$, to determine the honeypot location and the honey link at each stage k to minimize the risk that an attacker from the node of the initial intrusion can compromise the target node after Δk stages. Each policy element $\gamma_{l,w}$ is the probability that the honeypot is node n_w^k and the honey link is from node n_l^k to n_w^k at stage $k \in \{k_0, \cdots, k_0 + \Delta k\}$. Note that $\gamma_{i,i} = 0, \forall i \in \mathcal{V}$, and we can let n_l, n_w belong to the entire node set $\mathcal{V}$ without loss of generality

---

[2] The defender would avoid configuring honey links from the target node to the honeypot. If the attacker has not compromised the target node H3 as shown in stage $k_0 + 1$, the honeypot cannot capture the attacker. If the attacker has compromised the target node as shown in stage $k_0 + 3$, then the late detection cannot reduce the loss that has already been made.

because if a node $n_w \notin \mathcal{V}_D$ is not reconfigurable, then we can let the proba-bility $\gamma_{l,w}$ be zero. Define $n_{j_0} \in \mathcal{V} \setminus \mathcal{V}_I$ as the target node to protect for all stages and the target node is segregated from the set of potential initial intru-sion. Then, defender should avoid honey links from node n_{j_0} for all stages, i.e., $\gamma_{j_0,w} = 0, \forall n_w \in \mathcal{V}$. If a honey link from n_l to n_w, e.g., the link from U1 to H3, is not available for all stages due to segregation, then $\gamma_{l,w} = 0$. Since at most one link is allowed, we have the constraint $\sum_{n_l, n_w \in \mathcal{V}} \gamma_{l,w} = 1$. In this work, we assume that the honeypot policy γ is not affected by the realization of the service links at each stage and thus can interfere with the service links that are not idle as defined in Definition 1. If the honeypot n_w^k selected by the policy γ is interfering, i.e., not *idle*, then the defender neither monitors nor filters the inbound network flows to avoid any interference with the normal operation.

Although we increase the difficulty for the attacker to identify the honeypot by applying it to idle nodes in the network and change its location at every stage, we cannot eliminate the possibility of advanced attackers identifying the honeypot [5]. If the attacker has compromised node n_i before stage k and there is a honey link from node n_i^k to n_j^k at stage k, then we assume that the attacker has probability $q_{i,j} \in [0,1]$ to identify the honey link and choose not to access the honeypot. If the honeypot is not identified, then the attacker accesses the honeypot and he is detected by the defender. We assume the defender can deter the lateral movement completely after a detection from any single honeypot by patching or resetting all nodes at that stage. As stated in Sect. 2.2, the attacker can move simultaneously from all the compromised nodes to multiple nodes through service links that connect them. For example, the attacker at stage k_0+2 can compromise H2 and H1 through the two service links and may also reach the honeypot if the attacker attempts to compromise H3 from U1. However, we assume that the attacker at a compromised node does not move consecutively through multiple service links (or honey links defined in Sect. 2.3 as the attacker cannot distinguish honey links from service ones) in a single stage to remain stealthy. Contrary to the persistent lateral movement over a long time period, consecutive attack moves within one stage make it easier for the defender to connect all the indicators of compromise (IoCs) and attribute the attacker. Take Fig. 2 as an example. Suppose that there are two links, e.g., H1 to U2 and U2 to H2 at a stage k, where each link can be either a service link or a honey link. If the attacker has only compromised H1 among these three nodes, then he only attempts to compromise node U2 rather than both U2 and H2 during stage k.

Interference, Stealthiness, and Cost of Roaming In this section, we define three critical security metrics for a cognitive honeypot to achieve low interfer-ence, low cost, and high stealthiness. Define $\mathcal{V}_S$ as the set of all the subsets of $\mathcal{V}$. Define a series of binary random variables $x_{v,w,v'}^k \in \{0,1\}, v, v' \in \mathcal{V}_S, n_w^k \in \mathcal{V}$, where $x_{v,w,v'}^k = 1$ means that there are no direct service links from any node $n_l^k \in v$ to node n_w^k and from n_w^k to $n_l^k \in v'$ at stage k. Thus, $\Pr(x_{v,w,v'}^k = 1) = \prod_{n_l^k \in v}(1 - \beta_{l,w}) \prod_{n_{l'}^k \in v'}(1 - \beta_{w,l'})$ represents the probability that the honeypot at n_w^k does not interfere with any service link whose source node is in set v and sink node is in v'. Then, we can define $H_{PoI}(\gamma)$ as the probability of interference in Definition 2. Since the defender can only apply cognitive honeypots to idle nodes, a low probability of interfering can increase efficiency. To reduce $H_{PoI}(\gamma)$, the defender can design γ based on the value of β, i.e., the frequency/probability of all potential service links.

Definition 2. *The **probability of interference** (PoI) for any honeypot policy* γ *is*

$$H_{PoI}(\gamma) := \sum_{n_h \in \mathcal{V}} \sum_{n_w \in \mathcal{V} \setminus \{n_h\}} \gamma_{h,w}(1 - \Pr(x^k_{\mathcal{V} \setminus \{n_w\}, w, \mathcal{V} \setminus \{n_w\}} = 1))$$

$$= \sum_{n_w \in \mathcal{V}} (1 - \Pr(x^k_{\mathcal{V} \setminus \{n_w\}, w, \mathcal{V} \setminus \{n_w\}} = 1)) \sum_{n_h \in \mathcal{V} \setminus \{n_w\}} \gamma_{h,w}. \tag{1}$$

Since the attacker can learn the honeypot policy γ, the defender prefers the policy to be as random as possible to increase the stealthiness of the honeypot. A fully random policy that assigns equal probability to all possible honey links provides forward and backward security; i.e., even if an attacker identifies the honeypot at stage k, he cannot use that information to deduce the location of the honeypots in the following and previous stages. We use $H_{SL}(\gamma)$, the entropy of γ in Definition 3 as a measure for the stealthiness level of the honeypot policy where we define $0 \cdot \log 0 = 0$.

Definition 3. *The **stealthiness level** (SL) for any* γ *is* $H_{SL}(\gamma) := \sum_{n_h, n_w \in \mathcal{V}} \gamma_{h,w} \log(\gamma_{h,w})$.

A tradeoff of roaming honeypots hinges on the cost to reconfigure the idle nodes when the defender changes the location of the honeypot and the honey link. Define the term $C(\gamma_{h_1, w_1}, \gamma_{h_2, w_2}), \forall n_{h_1}, n_{h_2}, n_{w_1}, n_{w_2} \in \mathcal{V}$, as the cost of changing a $(n_{h_1} - n_{w_1})$ honey link to a $(n_{h_2} - n_{w_2})$ honey link. Note that this cost captures the cost of changing the honeypot location from w_1 to w_2. If only the location change of honeypots incurs a cost, we can let $C(\gamma_{h_1, w}, \gamma_{h_2, w}) = 0, \forall h_1 \neq h_2, \forall n_w \in \mathcal{V}$, without loss of generality. We define the cost of roaming in Definition 4.

Definition 4. *The **cost of roaming** (CoR) for any honeypot policy* γ *is*

$$H_{CoR}(\gamma) := \sum_{n_{h_1} \in \mathcal{V}} \sum_{n_{w_1} \in \mathcal{V} \setminus \{n_{h_1}\}} \gamma_{h_1, w_1}(1 - \Pr(x^k_{\mathcal{V} \setminus \{n_{w_1}\}, w_1, \mathcal{V} \setminus \{n_{w_1}\}} = 1))$$

$$\cdot \sum_{n_{h_2} \in \mathcal{V}} \sum_{n_{w_2} \in \mathcal{V} \setminus \{h_2\}} \gamma_{h_2, w_2}(1 - \Pr(x^k_{\mathcal{V} \setminus \{n_{w_2}\}, w_2, \mathcal{V} \setminus \{n_{w_2}\}} = 1)) \cdot C(\gamma_{h_1, w_1}, \gamma_{h_2, w_2})$$

$$\tag{2}$$

3   Farsighted Vulnerability Mitigation for Long-Term Security

Throughout the entire operation of the enterprise network, the defender does not know whether, when, and where the initial intrusion has happened. The defender also cannot know attack paths until a honeypot detects the lateral movement attack. Therefore, instead of reactive policies to mitigate attacks that have happened at known stages, we aim at proactive and persistent policies that prepare for the initial intrusion at any stage k_0 over a time window of length Δk. That means that the honeypot should roam persistently at all stages according to the policy γ to reduce LTV, i.e., the probability that an initial intrusion can reach and compromise the target node within Δk stages.

Given the target node $n_{j_0} \in \mathscr{V} \setminus \mathscr{V}_I$, a subset $v \in \mathscr{V}_S$, and the defender's honeypot policy γ, we define $g_{j_0}(v, \gamma, \Delta k)$ as the probability that an attacker who has compromised the set of nodes v can compromise the target node n_{j_0} within Δk stages. Since the initial intrusion happens to a single node $n_i \in \mathscr{V}_I$ with probability ρ_i as argued in Sect. 2.2, the Δk-stage vulnerability of the target node n_{j_0} defined in Definition 5 equals $\bar{g}_{j_0,\mathscr{V}_I}^{\Delta k}(\gamma) := \sum_{n_i \in \mathscr{V}_I} \rho_i g_{j_0}(\{n_i\}, \gamma, \Delta k)$. In this paper, we refer to Δk-stage vulnerability as LTV when $\Delta k > 1$.

Definition 5. *(Long-Term Vulnerability) The Δk-**stage vulnerability** of the target node n_{j_0} is the probability that an attacker in the DMZ $\mathscr{V}_I$ can compromise the target node n_{j_0} within a time window of Δk stages.*

The length of the time window represents the attack's time-effectiveness which is determined by the system setting and the defender's detection efficiency. For example, Δk can be the time-to-live (typically on the order of days [13]) for re-authentication to invalidate the PtH attack. For another example, suppose that the defender can detect and deter the attacker after the initial intrusion yet with a delay due to the high rate of false alarms. If the delay can be contained within Δk_0 stages, then the defender should choose the honeypot policy to minimize the Δk_0-stage vulnerability. Consider a given threshold $T_0 \in [0, 1]$, we define the concept of level-T_0 stage-Δk security for node n_{j_0} and honeypot policy γ in Definition 6.

Definition 6. *(Long-Term Security) Policy γ achieves **level-T_0 stage-Δk security** for node n_{j_0} if the Δk-stage vulnerability is less than the threshold, i.e., $\bar{g}_{j_0,\mathscr{V}_I}^{\Delta k}(\gamma) \leq T_0$.*

Finally, we define the defender's decision problem of a cognitive honeypot that can minimize the LTV for the target node with a low PoI, a high SL, and a low CoR in (3). The coefficients $\alpha_{PoI}, \alpha_{SL}, \alpha_{CoR}$ represent the tradeoffs of Δk-stage vulnerabilities with PoI, SL, and CoR, respectively.

$$\min_{\gamma} \quad \bar{g}_{j_0,\mathscr{V}_I}^{\Delta k}(\gamma) + \alpha_{PoI} H_{PoI}(\gamma) - \alpha_{SL} H_{SL}(\gamma) + \alpha_{CoR} H_{CoR}(\gamma)$$

$$\text{s.t.} \quad \sum_{n_h, n_w \in \mathscr{V}} \gamma_{h,w} = 1, \tag{3}$$

$$\gamma_{h,w} = 0, \forall n_h \in \mathscr{V}, n_w \in \mathscr{V} \setminus \mathscr{V}_D.$$

3.1 Imminent Vulnerability

We first compute the probability that an initial intrusion at node $n_i \in \mathscr{V}_I$ can compromise the target node $n_{j_0} \in \mathscr{V} \setminus \mathscr{V}_I$ within $\Delta k = 0$ stages. The term

$\gamma_{i,w}(1 - q_{i,w})$ is the *Probability of Immediate Capture* (**PoIC**), i.e., the attacker with initial intrusion at node n_i is directly trapped by the honeypot n_w. Since the attacker does not take consecutive movements in one stage to remain stealthy as stated in Sect. 2.2, $g_{j_0}(\{n_i\}, \gamma, 0)$ equals the product of the probability that attacker exploits the service link from n_i to n_{j_0} successfully and the probability that the attacker is not trapped by the honeypot, i.e., $\forall n_i \in \mathcal{V}_I$,

$$g_{j_0}(\{n_i\}, \gamma, 0) = \beta_{i,j_0} \lambda_{i,j_0} (1 - \sum_{w \neq i,j_0} \gamma_{i,w}(1 - q_{i,w}) \Pr(x^k_{\mathcal{V} \setminus \{n_w\}, w, \mathcal{V} \setminus \{n_w\}} = 1)).$$

$$(4)$$

3.2 Δk-stage Vulnerability

Define $\mathcal{V}_{i,j_0} \subseteq \mathcal{V}_S$ as the set of all the subsets of $\mathcal{V} \setminus \{n_i, n_{j_0}\}$. For each $v \in \mathcal{V}_{i,j_0}$, define $\mathcal{V}^v_{i,j_0}$ as the set of all the subsets of $\mathcal{V} \setminus \{n_i, n_{j_0}, v\}$. Define the shorthand notation $f_{v,u}(\beta, \lambda) := \prod_{n_{h_1} \in v} \beta_{i,h_1} \lambda_{i,h_1} \prod_{n_{h_2} \in u} \beta_{i,h_2} (1 - \lambda_{i,h_2}) \prod_{n_{h_3} \in \mathcal{V} \setminus \{n_i, n_{j_0}, v, u\}} (1 - \beta_{i,h_3})$ as the *probability of partial compromise*, i.e., the attacker with initial intrusion at node n_i has compromised the service links from n_i to all nodes in set $v \in \mathcal{V}_{i,j_0}$, yet fails to compromise the remaining service links from n_i to all nodes in set $u \in \mathcal{V}^v_{i,j_0}$. We can compute $g_{j_0}(\{n_i\}, \gamma, \Delta k)$ based on the following induction, i.e.,

$$g_{j_0}(\{n_i\}, \gamma, \Delta k) = g_{j_0}(\{n_i\}, \gamma, 0) + (1 - \beta_{i,j_0} \lambda_{i,j_0}) \sum_{v \in \mathcal{V}_{i,j_0}} \sum_{u \in \mathcal{V}^v_{i,j_0}} f_{v,u}(\beta, \lambda)(1 -$$

$$\sum_{n_w \in \mathcal{V} \setminus \{n_i, v, u\}} \gamma_{i,w}(1 - q_{i,w}) \Pr(x^k_{\mathcal{V} \setminus \{n_i, n_w\}, w, \mathcal{V} \setminus \{n_w\}} = 1)) g_{j_0}(\{n_i\} \cup v, \gamma, \Delta k - 1).$$

$$(5)$$

3.3 Curse of Multiple Attack Paths and Two Sub-Optimal Honeypot Policies

For a given γ, we can write out the explicit form of $g_{j_0}(\{n_i\} \cup v, \gamma, \Delta k - 1)$ for all $\Delta k \in \mathbb{Z}^+$ as in (4) and (5). However, the complexity increases dramatically with the cardinality of set v due to the *curse of multiple attack paths*; i.e., the event that the attacker can compromise target node n_{j_0} within Δk stages from node n_i is not independent of the event that the attacker can achieve the same compromise from node $n_h \neq n_i$. Thus, we use the union bound

$$g_{j_0}(\{n_i\} \cup v, \gamma, \Delta k) \geq \max_{n_j \in \{n_i\} \cup v} g_{j_0}(\{n_j\}, \gamma, \Delta k),$$

$$g_{j_0}(\{n_i\} \cup v, \gamma, \Delta k) \leq \min(1, \sum_{n_j \in \{n_i\} \cup v} g_{j_0}(\{n_j\}, \gamma, \Delta k)),$$

to simplify the computation and provide an upper bound and a lower bound for $g_{j_0}(\{n_i\} \cup v, \gamma, \Delta k), v \neq \emptyset, \forall \Delta k \in \mathbb{Z}^+$, in (6) and (7), respectively.

$$g_{j_0}^{lower}(\{n_i\}, \gamma, \Delta k) = g_{j_0}(\{n_i\}, \gamma, 0) + (1 - \beta_{i,j_0}\lambda_{i,j_0}) \sum_{v \in \mathscr{V}_{i,j_0}} \sum_{u \in \mathscr{V}_{i,j_0}^v} f_{v,u}(\beta, \lambda)(1-$$

$$\sum_{n_w \in \mathscr{V} \setminus \{n_i, v, u\}} \gamma_{i,w}(1 - q_{i,w}) \Pr(x_{\mathscr{V} \setminus \{n_i, n_w\}, w, \mathscr{V} \setminus \{n_w\}}^k = 1)) \max_{n_j \in \{n_i\} \cup v} g_{j_0}^{lower}(\{n_j\}, \gamma, \Delta k - 1).$$

$$(6)$$

$$g_{j_0}^{upper}(\{n_i\}, \gamma, \Delta k) = g_{j_0}(\{n_i\}, \gamma, 0) + (1 - \beta_{i,j_0}\lambda_{i,j_0}) \sum_{v \in \mathscr{V}_{i,j_0}} \sum_{u \in \mathscr{V}_{i,j_0}^v} f_{v,u}(\beta, \lambda)$$

$$\cdot (1 - \sum_{n_w \in \mathscr{V} \setminus \{n_i, v, u\}} \gamma_{i,w}(1 - q_{i,w}) \Pr(x_{\mathscr{V} \setminus \{n_i, n_w\}, w, \mathscr{V} \setminus \{n_w\}}^k = 1)) \quad (7)$$

$$\cdot \min(1, \sum_{n_j \in \{n_i\} \cup v} g_{j_0}^{upper}(\{n_j\}, \gamma, \Delta k - 1)).$$

The initial condition at $\Delta k = 0$ is $g_{j_0}^{lower}(\{n_j\}, \gamma, 0) = g_{j_0}^{upper}(\{n_j\}, \gamma, 0) = g_{j_0}(\{n_j\}, \gamma, 0), \forall n_j \in \{n_i\} \cup v$. Define $\bar{g}_{j_0, \mathscr{V}_I}^{\Delta k, lower}(\gamma) := \sum_{n_i \in \mathscr{V}_I} \rho_i g_{j_0}^{lower}(\{n_i\}, \gamma, \Delta k)$ and $\bar{g}_{j_0, \mathscr{V}_I}^{\Delta k, upper}(\gamma) := \sum_{n_i \in \mathscr{V}_I} \rho_i g_{j_0}^{upper}(\{n_i\}, \gamma, \Delta k)$ as the lower and upper bounds of the Δk-stage vulnerability of the target node n_{j_0} under any given policy γ, respectively. Then, replacing $\bar{g}_{j_0, \mathscr{V}_I}^{\Delta k}(\gamma)$ in (3) with $\bar{g}_{j_0, \mathscr{V}_I}^{\Delta k, lower}(\gamma)$ and $\bar{g}_{j_0, \mathscr{V}_I}^{\Delta k, upper}(\gamma)$, we obtain the optimal risky and conservative honeypot policy $\gamma^{*, risky}$ and $\gamma^{*, cons}$, respectively. Both sub-optimal honeypot policies approximate the optimal policy that is hard to compute explicitly. A risky defender can choose $\gamma^{*, risky}$ to minimize the lower bound of LTV while a conservative defender can choose $\gamma^{*, cons}$ to minimize the upper bound.

We propose the following iterative algorithm to compute these two honeypot policies. We use $\gamma^{*, risky}$ as an example and $\gamma^{*, cons}$ can be computed in the same fashion. At iteration $t \in \mathbb{Z}_0^+$, we consider any feasible honeypot policy γ^t and compute $g_{j_0}^{lower}(\{n_i\}, \gamma^t, \Delta k'), \forall n_i \in \mathscr{V}_I, \forall \Delta k' \in \{1, \cdots, \Delta k\}$, via (6). Then, we solve (3) by replacing $\bar{g}_{j_0, \mathscr{V}_I}^{\Delta k}(\gamma^t)$ with $\bar{g}_{j_0, \mathscr{V}_I}^{\Delta k, lower}(\gamma^t)$ and plugging in $g_{j_0}^{lower}(\{n_i\}, \gamma^t, \Delta k), \forall n_i \in \mathscr{V}_I$, as constants. Since $\bar{g}_{j_0, \mathscr{V}_I}^{\Delta k, lower}(\gamma^t), H_{PoI}(\gamma^t), H_{CoR}(\gamma^t)$ are all linear with respect to γ^t, the objective function of the constrained optimization in (3) is a linear function of γ^t plus the entropy regularization $H_{SL}(\gamma^t)$. Then, we can solve the constrained optimization in closed form and update the honeypot policy from γ^t to γ^{t+1}. Given a small error threshold $\epsilon > 0$, the above iteration process can be repeated until there exists a $T_1 \in \mathbb{Z}_0^+$ such that a proper matrix norm is less than the error threshold, i.e., $||\gamma^{T_1+1} - \gamma^{T_1}|| \leq \epsilon$. Then, we can output γ^{T_1+1} as the optimal risky honeypot policy $\gamma^{*, risky}$.

3.4 LTV Analysis Under Two Heuristic Policies

In this section, we consider the scenario where the initial intrusion set $\mathscr{V}_I = \{n_i\}$ contains only one node n_i, i.e., the attacker cannot compromise other nodes directly from the external network at stage k_0. Then, a reasonable heuristic policy is to set up the honeypot at a fixed node $n_{w_0} \in \mathscr{V} \setminus \{n_i, n_{j_0}\}$ whenever

---

Algorithm 1: Optimal Risky (and Conservative) Honeypot Policy

---

1 Initialization $\mathscr{V}_I, n_{j_0} \in \mathscr{V} \setminus \mathscr{V}_I, \Delta k \in \mathbb{Z}^+, \epsilon > 0, \gamma^0, t = 0$;

2 **while** $\|\gamma^{t+1} - \gamma^t\| > \epsilon$ **do**

3   **for** $\Delta k' = 1, \cdots, \Delta k$ **do**

4   **for** $i \in \mathscr{V}_I$ **do**

5   Compute $g_{j_0}^{lower}(\{n_i\}, \gamma^t, \Delta k')$ via (6);

6   **end**

7   **end**

8   Replace $\bar{g}_{j_0, \mathscr{V}_I}^{\Delta k}(\gamma^t)$ with $\bar{g}_{j_0, \mathscr{V}_I}^{\Delta k, lower}(\gamma^t)$ and plug in $g_{j_0}^{lower}(\{n_i\}, \gamma^t, \Delta k), \forall n_i \in \mathscr{V}_I$;

9   Obtain γ^{t+1} as the solution of (3);

10   **if** $\|\gamma^{t+1} - \gamma^t\| \leq \epsilon$ **then**

11         $T_1 = t$;

12   **Terminate**

13     $t := t + 1$;

14 **end**

15 **Output** $\gamma^{*, risky} = \gamma^{T_1+1}$.

---

the node is idle and also a direct honey link from n_i to n_{w_0}. We refer to these deterministic policies with $\gamma_{i,w_0} = 1$ as the direct policies in Sect. 3.4.

In the second scenario, the defender further segregates node n_i from the external network to form a *air gap* so that she chooses to apply no direct honey links from n_i to any honeypot at all stages, i.e., $\gamma_{i,w} = 0, \forall n_w \in \mathscr{V}$. However, advanced attacks, such as Stuxnet, can cross the air gap by an infected USB flash drive to accomplish the initial intrusion to the air-gap node n_i and then move laterally to the entire network $\mathscr{V}$. Although the defender mistakenly sets up no honey links from n_i to the honeypot at all stages, other indirect honey links with source nodes other than n_i may also detect the lateral movement in Δk stages. Unlike the deterministic direct policies, we refer to these stochastic policies with $\gamma_{i,w} = 0, \forall n_w \in \mathscr{V}$, as the indirect policies in Sect. 3.4.

Since the defender may adopt these heuristic policies in the listed scenarios, this section aims to analyze the LTV under the direct and indirect policies to answer the following security questions. How effective is the lateral movement for a different length of duration time under heuristic policies? What are the limit and the bounds of the vulnerability when the window length goes to infinity? How much additional vulnerability is introduced by adopting improper indirect policies rather than the direct policies? How to change the value of parameters, such as β and λ, to reduce LTV if they are designable?

Indirect Honeypot Policies Since the defender overestimates the effectiveness of air gap and chooses the improper honeypot policies that $\gamma_{i,w} = 0, \forall n_w \in \mathscr{V}$, the vulnerability of any target node n_{j_0} is non-decreasing with the length of the time window as shown in Proposition 1.

Proposition 1. (Non-Decreasing Vulnerability over Stages) If the PoIC is zero, i.e., $\gamma_{i,w}(1-q_{i,w}) = 0, \forall n_w \in \mathcal{V}$, then the vulnerability $g_{j_0}(\{n_i\}, \gamma, \Delta k) \in [0,1]$ is an non-decreasing function regarding Δk for all target node $n_{j_0} \in \mathcal{V} \setminus \mathcal{V}_I, n_i \in \mathcal{V}_I$. The value of $g_{j_0}(\{n_i\}, \gamma, \Delta k)$ does not increase to 1 as Δk increases to infinity if and only if $\beta_{i,j_0}\lambda_{i,j_0} = 0$ and $g_{j_0}(\{n_i\} \cup v, \gamma, \Delta k - 1) = g_{j_0}(\{n_i\}, \gamma, \Delta k - 1), \forall v \in \mathcal{V}_S, \forall \Delta k \in \mathbb{Z}^+$.

Proof. If $\gamma_{i,w}(1 - q_{i,w}) = 0, \forall n_w \in \mathcal{V}$, we can use the facts that $g_{j_0}(\{n_i\} \cup v, \gamma, \Delta k - 1) \geq g_{j_0}(\{n_i\}, \gamma, \Delta k - 1), \forall \gamma, n_{j_0} \in \mathcal{V}, n_i \in \mathcal{V}_I, \Delta k \geq 0, \forall v \in \mathcal{V}_S$, and $\sum_{v \in \mathcal{V}_{i,j_0}} \sum_{u \in \mathcal{V}_{i,j_0}^v} f_{v,u}(\beta, \lambda) \equiv 1, \forall \beta, \lambda$, to obtain $g_{j_0}(\{n_i\}, \gamma, \Delta k)$ as

$$\beta_{i,j_0}\lambda_{i,j_0} + (1 - \beta_{i,j_0}\lambda_{i,j_0}) \sum_{v \in \mathcal{V}_{i,j_0}} \sum_{u \in \mathcal{V}_{i,j_0}^v} f_{v,u}(\beta, \lambda)g_{j_0}(\{n_i\} \cup v, \gamma, \Delta k - 1) \tag{8}$$
$$\geq \beta_{i,j_0}\lambda_{i,j_0} + (1 - \beta_{i,j_0}\lambda_{i,j_0})g_{j_0}(\{n_i\}, \gamma, \Delta k - 1) \geq g_{j_0}(\{n_i\}, \gamma, \Delta k - 1),$$

for all $\Delta k \in \mathbb{Z}^+$. The inequality is an equality if and only if $\beta_{i,j_0}\lambda_{i,j_0} = 0$ and $g_{j_0}(\{n_i\} \cup v, \gamma, \Delta k - 1) = g_{j_0}(\{n_i\}, \gamma, \Delta k - 1), \forall v \in \mathcal{V}_S, \forall \Delta k \in \mathbb{Z}^+$. □

The equation $g_{j_0}(\{n_i\} \cup v, \gamma, \Delta k - 1) = g_{j_0}(\{n_i\}, \gamma, \Delta k - 1), \forall v \in \mathcal{V}_S, \forall \Delta k \in \mathbb{Z}^+$, holds only under very unlikely conditions such as there is only one node in the network, i.e., $N = 1$ or service links occur only from node n_i, i.e., $\lambda_{i',j} = 0, \forall i' \neq i, \forall n_j \in \mathcal{V}$. Thus, except for these rare special cases, the vulnerability $g_{j_0}(\{n_i\}, \gamma, \Delta k)$ always increases to the maximum value of 1 under indirect policies.

Remark 1. Proposition 1 shows that without a proper mitigation strategy, e.g., no direct honey link from the initial intrusion node to the honeypot, the vulnerability of a target node never decreases over stages. Moreover, except from rare special cases, the target node will be compromised with probability 1 as time goes to infinity.

Proposition 1 demonstrates the disadvantaged position of the defender against persistent lateral movement without proper honeypot policies. Under these disadvantageous situations, the defender may need alternative security measures to mitigate the LTV. For example, the defender may reduce the arrival frequency of the service link from n_{j_1} to n_{j_2}, i.e., β_{j_1,j_2}, to delay lateral movement at the expenses of operational efficiency. Also, the defender may attempt to reduce the probability of a successful compromise from node n_{j_1} to n_{j_2}, i.e., λ_{j_1,j_2}, by filtering the service link from n_{j_1} to n_{j_2} with more stringent rules or demotivate the attacker to initiate the link compromise by disguising the service link as a honey link. In the rest of this subsection, we briefly investigate the influence of β and λ on the Δk-stage vulnerability under indirect policies.

The probability of no direct link from the initial intrusion node n_i to target n_{j_0}, i.e., $1 - \beta_{i,j_0}\lambda_{i,j_0}$, and the probability that the attacker at node n_i is demotivated to or fails to compromise the service links from node n_i, i.e., $\sum_{u \in \mathcal{V}_{i,j_0}^0} f_{\emptyset,u}(\beta, \lambda)$, defines the *Probability of Movement Deterrence* (**PoMD**)

$r := (1 - \beta_{i,j_0}\lambda_{i,j_0})\sum_{u \in \mathscr{V}_{i,j_0}^{\emptyset}} f_{\emptyset,u}(\beta, \lambda)$. In (8) where the PoIC is 0, i.e., $\gamma_{i,w}(1-q_{i,w}) = 0, \forall n_w \in \mathscr{V}$, we can upper bound the term $g_{j_0}(\{n_i\}\cup v, \gamma, \Delta k-1)$ by 1 for all $v \neq \emptyset$, which leads to

$$
\begin{aligned}
g_{j_0}(\{n_i\}, \gamma, \Delta k) &= (1 - r) \cdot g_{j_0}(\{n_i\} \cup v, \gamma, \Delta k - 1) + r \cdot g_{j_0}(\{n_i\}, \gamma, \Delta k - 1) \\
&\leq (1 - r) + r \cdot g_{j_0}(\{n_i\}, \gamma, \Delta k - 1) \\
&= 1 - r^{\Delta k} + r^{\Delta k} g_{j_0}(\{n_i\}, \gamma, 0) = 1 - r^{\Delta k}(1 - \beta_{i,j_0}\lambda_{i,j_0}),
\end{aligned}
$$
(9)

where the final line results from solving the first-order linear difference equation iteratively by $\Delta k - 1$ times.

Equation (9) shows that the upper bound of LTV increases exponentially concerning the duration of lateral movement Δk yet decreases in a polynomial growth rate as PoMD increases. Note that letting PoMD be 1 can completely deter lateral movement and achieve zero LTV for any $\Delta k \in \mathbb{Z}^+$. However, it is challenging to attain it as it requires the attacker do not succeed from n_i to any node n_j with probability 1, i.e., $\lambda_{i,j} = 0, \forall n_j \in \mathscr{V}$. Since increasing PoMD incurs a higher cost (e.g., reducing the compromise rate λ) and lower operational efficiency (e.g., reducing the frequency of service links β), we aim to find the minimum PoMD to mitigate LTV even when the duration of lateral movement Δk goes to infinity. In Proposition 2, we characterize the critical *Threshold of Compromisability* (***ToC***) $T_m^{ToC} := 1 - m/\Delta k$ for a positive $m \ll \Delta k$ to guarantee a level-$(\beta_{i,j_0}\lambda_{i,j_0})$, stage-$\infty$ security defined in Definition 6. The proof follows directly from a limit analysis based on (9).

Proposition 2. (*ToC*) *Consider the scenario where* $\gamma_{i,w}(1 - q_{i,w}) = 0, \forall n_w \in \mathscr{V}$, *and* r *as a function of* Δk *has the form* $r = 1 - m\Delta k^{-n}$, *where* $n, m \in \mathbb{R}^+$ *and* $m \ll \Delta k$.

(1). If $(1 - r)/m$ *is of the same order with* $1/\Delta k$, *i.e.,* $n = 1$, *then the limit of the upper bound* $\lim_{\Delta k \to \infty} 1 - r^{\Delta k}(1 - \beta_{i,j_0}\lambda_{i,j_0})$ *is a constant* $1 - e^{-m}(1 - \beta_{i,j_0}\lambda_{i,j_0})$.

(2). If $(1 - r)/m$ *is of higher order, i.e.,* $n > 1$, *then the limit of the upper bound is* $g_{j_0}(\{n_i\}, \gamma, 0) = \beta_{i,j_0}\lambda_{i,j_0}$. *If* $\beta_{i,j_0}\lambda_{i,j_0} = 0$, *zero LTV is achieved* $g_{j_0}(\{n_i\}, \gamma, \infty) = 0$.

(3). If $(1-r)/m$ *is of lower order, i.e.,* $n < 1$, *then the limit of the upper bound is 1.*

Based on the fact that $1 - e^{-m}(1 - \beta_{i,j_0}\lambda_{i,j_0}) \geq \beta_{i,j_0}\lambda_{i,j_0}$ where the equality holds if and only if $\beta_{i,j_0}\lambda_{i,j_0} = 1$, we can conclude that if $r \geq T_m^{ToC}$ for a positive $m \ll \Delta k$, then the ∞-stage vulnerability of target node n_{j_0} is upper bounded by $\beta_{i,j_0}\lambda_{i,j_0}$ and thus achieves the level-$(\beta_{i,j_0}\lambda_{i,j_0})$, stage-$\infty$ security as defined in Definition 6. Note that if the target node is segregated from nodes in DMZ $\mathscr{V}_I$ for the sake of security, then there is no direct service link from node n_i to the target node n_{j_0} and $\beta_{i,j_0}\lambda_{i,j_0} = 0$. In that case, the target node n_{j_0} can achieve a zero vulnerability for an infinite duration of lateral movement, i.e., $g_{j_0}(\{n_i\}, \gamma, \infty) = 0$, because the upper bound is 0 and LTV is always non-negative.

Direct Honeypot Policies For the direct policies $\gamma_{i,w_0} = 1, n_{w_0} \in \mathcal{V} \setminus \{n_i, n_{j_0}\}$, we obtain the corresponding Δk-stage vulnerability and an explicit lower bound in (10) based on (5) by using the inequality $g_{j_0}(\{n_i\} \cup v, \gamma, \Delta k - 1) \geq g_{j_0}(\{n_i\}, \gamma, \Delta k - 1)$. Define shorthand notations $k_1 := \prod_{l \neq w_0} (1 - \beta_{l,w_0})(1 - \beta_{w_0,l})(1 - q_{i,w_0}) \in [0,1]$ and $k_2 := \sum_{v \in \mathcal{V}_{i,j_0} \setminus \{n_{w_0}\}} \sum_{u \in \mathcal{V}_{i,j_0}^v \setminus \{w_0\}} f_{v,u}(\beta, \lambda) \leq \sum_{v \in \mathcal{V}_{i,j_0}} \sum_{u \in \mathcal{V}_{i,j_0}^v} f_{v,u}(\beta, \lambda) = 1$. Note that $k_1 = 0$ is a very restrictive condition as it requires that the honeypot n_{w_0} is not interfering, i.e., node n_{w_0} is *idle* and the attacker never identify the honey link from n_i to n_{w_0}, i.e., $q_{i,w_0} = 0$.

$$g_{j_0}(\{n_i\}, \gamma, \Delta k) = \beta_{i,j_0} \lambda_{i,j_0} [1 - \prod_{l \neq w_0} (1 - \beta_{l,w_0})(1 - \beta_{w_0,l})(1 - q_{i,w_0})] +$$

$$(1 - \beta_{i,j_0} \lambda_{i,j_0})[\sum_{v \in \mathcal{V}_{i,j_0}} \sum_{u \in \mathcal{V}_{i,j_0}^v} f_{v,u}(\beta, \lambda) g_{j_0}(\{n_i\} \cup v, \gamma, \Delta k - 1) - \sum_{v \in \mathcal{V}_{i,j_0} \setminus \{n_{w_0}\}} \sum_{u \in \mathcal{V}_{i,j_0}^v \setminus \{n_{w_0}\}}$$

$$f_{v,u}(\beta, \lambda) \cdot \prod_{l \neq i, w_0} (1 - \beta_{l,w_0}) \prod_{l' \neq w_0} (1 - \beta_{w_0,l'})(1 - q_{i,w_0}) g_{j_0}(\{n_i\} \cup v, \gamma, \Delta k - 1)]$$

$$\geq \beta_{i,j_0} \lambda_{i,j_0} (1 - k_1) + (1 - \beta_{i,j_0} \lambda_{i,j_0})[1 - k_1 k_2 (1 - \beta_{i,w_0})] g_{j_0}(\{n_i\}, \gamma, \Delta k - 1).$$

$$(10)$$

Define a shorthand notation $r_2 := (1 - \beta_{i,j_0} \lambda_{i,j_0})[1 - k_1 k_2 (1 - \beta_{i,w_0})]$, we can solve the linear difference equation in the final step of (10) to obtain an lower bound, i.e., $g_{j_0}(\{n_i\}, \gamma, \Delta k) \geq T_2^{lower,1} := \beta_{i,j_0} \lambda_{i,j_0} (1 - k_1) \frac{1 - (r_2)^{\Delta k + 1}}{1 - r_2}$ for all $\Delta k \in \mathbb{Z}^+$. According to the first equality in (10), we also obtain an upper bound T_2^{upper} for $g_{j_0}(\{n_i\}, \gamma, \Delta k), \forall \Delta k \in \mathbb{Z}^+$, in Lemma 1 by using the inequality $g_{j_0}(\{n_i\} \cup v, \gamma, \Delta k) \leq 1, \forall v \in \mathcal{V}_{i,j_0}$[3]. The bound $T_2^{upper} < 1$ is non-trivial if $\beta_{i,j_0} \lambda_{i,j_0} \neq 0, \beta_{i,j_0} \lambda_{i,j_0} \neq 1$, and $k_1 k_2 (1 - \beta_{i,w_0}) \neq 0$.

Lemma 1. *If* $\gamma_{i,w_0} = 1, w_0 \neq i, j_0$, *then* $g_{j_0}(\{n_i\}, \gamma, \Delta k)$ *is lower and upper bounded by* $T_2^{lower,1}$ *and* $T_2^{upper} := 1 - \beta_{i,j_0} \lambda_{i,j_0} k_1 - (1 - \beta_{i,j_0} \lambda_{i,j_0}) k_1 k_2 (1 - \beta_{i,w_0}) \in [0,1]$ *for all* $\Delta k \in \mathbb{Z}^+$, *respectively.*

Lemma 1 shows that if the defender applies a direct honeypot from n_i in a deterministic fashion, then the Δk-stage vulnerability is always upper bounded. However, these direct policies cannot reduce the ∞-stage vulnerability to zero as shown in Proposition 3.

Proposition 3. *(Vulnerability Residue) If* $\beta_{i,j_0} \lambda_{i,j_0} \neq 0$ *and* $\gamma_{i,w_0} = 1, w_0 \neq i, j_0$, *then*

(1). The term $T_2^{lower,2} := \frac{\beta_{i,j_0} \lambda_{i,j_0} (1 - k_1)}{(1 - \beta_{i,j_0} \lambda_{i,j_0}) k_1 k_2 (1 - \beta_{i,w_0}) + \beta_{i,j_0} \lambda_{i,j_0}} \in [0,1)$ *is strictly less than 1.*

(2). If $g_{j_0}(\{n_i\}, \gamma, \Delta k - 1) < T_2^{lower,2}$, *then* $g_{j_0}(\{n_i\}, \gamma, \Delta k) > g_{j_0}(\{n_i\}, \gamma, \Delta k - 1)$.

---

[3] Since we can compute $g_{j_0}(\{n_i\} \cup v, \gamma, \Delta k - 1)$ explicitly when v is empty, we can obtain a tighter upper bound by using the inequality $g_{j_0}(\{n_i\} \cup v, \gamma, \Delta k) \leq 1, \forall v \in \mathcal{V}_{i,j_0} \setminus \emptyset$.

(3). The term $\lim_{\Delta k \to \infty} g_{j_0}(\{n_i\}, \gamma, \Delta k)$ *is lower bounded by* $\max(T_2^{lower,1},$ $T_2^{lower,2})$.

Proof. Based on the inequality in (10), we obtain that if $g_{j_0}(\{n_i\}, \gamma, \Delta k - 1) < T_2^{lower,2}$, then $g_{j_0}(\{n_i\}, \gamma, \Delta k) > g_{j_0}(\{n_i\}, \gamma, \Delta k - 1)$. Since the above is true for all $\Delta k \in \mathbb{Z}^+$, we know that the Δk-stage vulnerability increases with Δk strictly until it has reach $T_2^{lower,2}$. If $\beta_{i,j_0} \lambda_{i,j_0} \neq 0$ and $k_1 \neq 1$, then $T_2^{lower,2} > 0$ is a non-trivial lower bound. The other lower bound $T_2^{lower,1}$ comes from Lemma 1. $\qquad\square$

Remark 2. Proposition 3 defines a *vulnerability residue* $T^{VR} := \max(T_2^{lower,1}, T_2^{lower,2})$ under direct honeypot policies. A nonzero T^{VR} characterizes the limitation of security policies against lateral movement attacks, i.e., LTV cannot be reduced to 0 as $\Delta k \to \infty$.

4 Conclusion

The stealthy and persistent lateral movement of APTs poses a severe security challenge to enterprise networks. Since APT attackers can remain undetected in compromised nodes for a long time, a network that is secure at any separate time may become insecure if the times and the spatial locations are considered holistically. Therefore, the defender needs to reduce the LTV of valuable assets. Honeypots, as a promising deceptive defense method, can detect lateral movement attacks at their early stages. Since advanced attackers, such as APTs, can identify the honeypots located at fixed machines that are segregated from the production system, we propose a cognitive honeypot mechanism which reconfigures idle production nodes as honeypot at different stages based on the probability of service links and successful compromise. The time-expanded network is used to model the time of the random service occurrence and the adversarial compromise explicitly. Besides the main objective of reducing the target node's LTV, we also consider the level of stealthiness, the probability of interference, and the cost of roaming as three tradeoffs. To reduce the computation complexity caused by the curse of multiple attack paths, we propose an iterative algorithm and approximate the vulnerability with the union bound. The analysis of the LTV under two heuristic honeypot policies illustrates that without proper mitigation strategies, vulnerability never decreases over stages and the target node is doom to be compromised given sufficient stages of adversarial lateral movement. Moreover, even under the improved honeypot strategies, a *vulnerability residue* exists. Thus, LTV cannot be reduced to 0 and perfect security does not exist. Besides honeypot policies, we investigate the influence of the frequency of service links and the probability of successful compromise on LTV and characterize a critical threshold to achieve *long-term security*. The target node can achieve zero vulnerability under infinite stages of lateral movement by a modification of the parameters β, λ to make PoMD not less than the ToC.

References

1. Corporation, T.M.: Enterprise matrix (2020). https://attack.mitre.org/matrices/enterprise/
2. Zhu, Q., Rass, S.: On multi-phase and multi-stage game-theoretic modeling of advanced persistent threats. IEEE Access **6**, 13:958–13:971 (2018)
3. Legezo, D.: LuckyMouse hits national data center to organize country-level water-holing campaign, June 13, 2018. https://securelist.com/luckymouse-hits-national-data-center/86083/
4. Spitzner, L.: Honeypots: Tracking Hackers. Addison-Wesley Reading, Boston (2003)
5. Krawetz, N.: Anti-honeypot technology. IEEE Secur. Priv. **2**(1), 76–79 (2004)
6. Mitola, J., Maguire, G.Q.: Cognitive radio: making software radios more personal. IEEE Pers. Commun. **6**(4), 13–18 (1999)
7. Khattab, S.M., Sangpachatanaruk, C., Mossé, D., Melhem, R., Znati, T.: Roaming honeypots for mitigating service-level denial-of-service attacks. In: Proceedings of the 24th International Conference on Distributed Computing Systems 2004, pp. 328–337. IEEE (2004)
8. Casteigts, A., Flocchini, P., Quattrociocchi, W., Santoro, N.: Time-varying graphs and dynamic networks. Int. J. Parallel Emergent Distrib. Syst. **27**(5), 387–408 (2012)
9. Liu, Q., Stokes, J.W., Mead, R., Burrell, T., Hellen, I., Lambert, J., Marochko, A., Cui, W.: Latte: Large-scale lateral movement detection. In: MILCOM 2018–2018 IEEE Military Communications Conference (MILCOM), pp. 1–6. IEEE (2018)
10. Tian, Z., Shi, W., Wang, Y., Zhu, C., Du, X., Su, S., Sun, Y., Guizani, N.: Real-time lateral movement detection based on evidence reasoning network for edge computing environment. IEEE Trans. Indust. Inform. **15**(7), 4285–4294 (2019)
11. Lah, A.A.A., Dziyauddin, R.A., Azmi, M.H.: Proposed framework for network lateral movement detection based on user risk scoring in siem. In: 2018 2nd International Conference on Telematics and Future Generation Networks (TAFGEN), pp. 149–154. IEEE (2018)
12. Noureddine, M.A., Fawaz, A., Sanders, W.H., Başar, T.: A game-theoretic approach to respond to attacker lateral movement. In: Zhu, Q., Alpcan, T., Panaousis, E., Tambe, M., Casey, W. (eds.) GameSec 2016. LNCS, vol. 9996, pp. 294–313. Springer, Cham (2016). https://doi.org/10.1007/978-3-319-47413-7_17
13. Purvine, E., Johnson, J.R., Lo, C.: A graph-based impact metric for mitigating lateral movement cyber attacks. In: Proceedings of the 2016 ACM Workshop on Automated Decision Making for Active Cyber Defense, pp. 45–52 (2016)
14. Huang, L., Zhu, Q.: A dynamic games approach to proactive defense strategies against advanced persistent threats in cyber-physical systems. Comput. Secur. **89**, 101660 (2020)
15. Huang, L., Zhu, Q.: Adaptive strategic cyber defense for advanced persistent threats in critical infrastructure networks. ACM SIGMETRICS Perform. Eval. Rev. (2018)
16. Alsaleh, M.N., Al-Shaer, E., Duan, Q.: Verifying the enforcement and effectiveness of network lateral movement resistance techniques (2018)
17. Shi, Y., Chang, X., Rodríguez, R.J., Zhang, Z., Trivedi, K.S.: Quantitative security analysis of a dynamic network system under lateral movement-based attacks. Reliab. Eng. Syst. Safety **183**, 213–225 (2019)

18. Pawlick, J., Nguyen, T.T.H., Colbert, E., Zhu, Q.: Optimal timing in dynamic and robust attacker engagement during advanced persistent threats. In: 2019 International Symposium on Modeling and Optimization in Mobile, Ad Hoc, and Wireless Networks (WiOPT), pp. 1-8. IEEE (2019)

19. Huang, L., Zhu, Q.: Adaptive honeypot engagement through reinforcement learning of semi-Markov decision processes. In: Alpcan, T., Vorobeychik, Y., Baras, J.S., Dán, G. (eds.) GameSec 2019. LNCS, vol. 11836, pp. 196–216. Springer, Cham (2019). https://doi.org/10.1007/978-3-030-32430-8_13

20. Huang, L., Zhu, Q.: Analysis and computation of adaptive defense strategies against advanced persistent threats for cyber-physical systems. In: Bushnell, L., Poovendran, R., Başar, T. (eds.) GameSec 2018. LNCS, vol. 11199, pp. 205–226. Springer, Cham (2018). https://doi.org/10.1007/978-3-030-01554-1_12

21. Huang, L., Zhu, Q.: Game of duplicity: a proactive automated defense mechanism by deception design (2020). arXiv preprint arXiv:2006.07942

22. Goldberg, I., Kozloski, J.R., Pickover, C.A., Sondhi, N., Vukovic, M.: Cognitive honeypot. 31 Jan 2017, uS Patent 9,560,075

23. Horák, K., Bošanský, B., Tomášek, P., Kiekintveld, C., Kamhoua, C.: Optimizing honeypot strategies against dynamic lateral movement using partially observable stochastic games. Comput. Secur. **87**, 101579 (2019)

24. Wang, S., Lin, W., Yang, Y., Xiao, X., Zhou, S.: Efficient route planning on public transportation networks: a labelling approach. In: Proceedings of the 2015 ACM SIGMOD International Conference on Management of Data, pp. 967–982 (2015)

25. Jiang, C., Zhu, X.: Reinforcement learning based capacity management in multilayer satellite networks. IEEE Trans. Wirel. Commun. (2020)

26. Xu, S.: Cybersecurity dynamics: a foundation for the science of cybersecurity. In: Wang, C., Lu, Z. (eds.) Proactive and Dynamic Network Defense. Advances in Information Security, vol. 74, pp. 1–31. Springer, Cham (2019)

27. Kaynar, K.: A taxonomy for attack graph generation and usage in network security. J. Inform. Secur. Appl. **29**, 27–56 (2016)

28. Chen, P.-Y., Choudhury, S., Rodriguez, L., Hero, A., Ray, I.: Enterprise cyber resiliency against lateral movement: a graph theoretic approach (2019). arXiv preprint arXiv:1905.01002

29. Hagberg, A., Kent, A., Lemons, N., Neil, J.: Credential hopping in authentication graphs. In: 2014 International Conference on Signal-Image Technology Internet-Based Systems (SITIS). IEEE Computer Society (2014)

30. Mell, P., Scarfone, K., Romanosky, S.: Common vulnerability scoring system. IEEE Secur. Priv. **4**(6), 85–89 (2006)

31. Nawrocki, M., Wählisch, M., Schmidt, T.C., Keil, C., Schönfelder, J.: A survey on honeypot software and data analysis (2016). arXiv preprint arXiv:1608.06249

Harnessing the Power of Deception in Attack Graph-Based Security Games

Stephanie Milani[1(✉)], Weiran Shen[1], Kevin S. Chan[2], Sridhar Venkatesan[3], Nandi O. Leslie[2], Charles Kamhoua[2], and Fei Fang[1]

[1] Carnegie Mellon University, 5000 Forbes Ave., Pittsburgh, PA 15213, USA
smilani@andrew.cmu.edu, emersonswr@gmail.com, feif@cs.cmu.edu
[2] Army Research Laboratory, 2800 Powder Mill Road, Adelphi, MD 20783, USA
kevin.s.chan.civ@mail.mil, nandi.o.leslie.ctr@mail.mil,
charles.a.kamhoua.civ@mail.mil
[3] Perspecta Labs Inc., 150 Mount Airy Road, Basking Ridge, NJ 07920, USA
svenkatesan@perspectalabs.com

Abstract. We study the use of deception in attack graph-based Stackelberg security games. In our setting, in addition to allocating defensive resources to protect important targets from attackers, the defender can strategically manipulate the attack graph through three main types of deceptive actions. We show that finding the optimal deception and defense strategy is at least NP-hard. We provide two techniques for efficiently solving this problem: a mixed-integer linear program for layered directed acyclic graphs (DAGs) and neural architecture search for general DAGs. We empirically demonstrate that using deception on attack graphs gives the defender a significant advantage, and the algorithms we develop scale gracefully to medium-sized problems.

Keywords: Deception · Attack graph · Security game

1 Introduction

Security is a serious worldwide issue, involving defending important infrastructure [62], protecting endangered wildlife species [14,25], securing computer networks [30,41,60], and more. Most security scenarios involve a defender who allocates limited security resources to protect targets from adversaries. To model and tackle these challenges, researchers have proposed game-theoretic approaches—especially those based on the Stackelberg security game (SSG) model. Many of these techniques have been successfully deployed in the real world [8,50,58,59].

Attack graphs [1,18,31,45,53] are a commonly-used, versatile modeling tool for security challenges in different domains. They can model the abstract state dependency and transition relations of any vulnerable system [7,19,35,44,46, 49,65], including a city's road system [33] and the topological structure of a company's computer network. Most existing work on attack graph-based SSGs

© Springer Nature Switzerland AG 2020
Q. Zhu et al. (Eds.): GameSec 2020, LNCS 12513, pp. 147–167, 2020.
https://doi.org/10.1007/978-3-030-64793-3_8

assumes the attack graph is given and unchangeable. Another widely-used security technique is defensive deception [5,48,66], where the defender can alter the appearance of targets or dynamically shift the attack surface. Commonly-used defensive deception mechanisms include honeypots [2,6,9,16,27,37] and honeytokens [12] in cybersecurity, as well as camouflaging [63] and moving target defense [34]. Existing work on deception in security does not consider attack graphs or ignores the defender's ability to strategically allocate security resources to mitigate attacks. Despite its significance, the use of deception alongside the allocation of security resources on attack graph-based SSGs has not been studied.

To address this gap, we propose a variant of the SSG, an *Attack Graph Deception Game*, in which the defender can take deceptive and protective actions on an attack graph. In our novel game model, the defender uses deception to modify the graph structure; a less capable attacker may observe the modified graph structure during reconnaissance. The attacker then attacks targets by moving between nodes on the graph, while the defender attempts to thwart the attacker by protecting edges with her limited security resources. To model different attackers' skill levels, we consider the Bayesian setting, where the attacker has a type representing his ability to perceive the true graph structure.

We focus on directed acyclic attack graphs (DAGs) and are particularly interested in layered DAGs, which are commonly used to model networks [29,38]. To solve layered DAGs, we propose a novel mixed-integer linear program (MILP)-based algorithm that builds upon the standard LP-based algorithm for solving Stackelberg games [17] and incorporates heuristic algorithms to significantly speed up computation. Our algorithm quickly finds the exact optimal solution for a special class of layered DAGs: bipartite DAGs. For general DAGs, we propose a neural architecture search (NAS)-based [23] algorithm, which uses a genetic algorithm to search for the modified attack graph and neural network optimization tools to find the remaining defense strategy. To our knowledge, this is the first use of NAS in SSGs. We conduct extensive experiments showing the scalability of our algorithms, and that using our algorithms and deception lead to significant increases in the defender's utility compared to baselines.

2 Game Model

An Attack Graph Deception Game is a two-player game on an attack graph. The defender chooses her strategy first; the attacker selects his strategy after surveillance. The attacker has a *type* $\theta \in \Theta$ drawn from a prior probability distribution. The defender knows the distribution, not the exact type. This type θ captures different skills and knowledge possessed by different attackers. For example, in cybersecurity, an attacker with superior reconnaissance skills has a greater chance of noticing honeypots and camouflage. In this section, we describe the attack graph, the players' strategy space, the players' payoff, and the solution concept. The notation that we use to describe our model is summarized in Table 1. We discuss the relaxation of some of our assumptions in Sect. 8.

Attack Graph. Attack graphs succinctly represent an attacker's possible attack paths. Of the many attack graph variants in the literature, we use a state-based Bayesian attack graph [21,39,55] $G = (N, E)$. The nodes N represent states in which attackers can be. The edges E represent actions that attackers can take to transition between states. In the urban security, each node can represent an intersection of a road network. In cybersecurity, a node can represent the attacker's intrusion status, including the compromised computers and accessed databases. Following the common *monotonicity* assumption [7] that attackers will not relinquish previously attained capabilities, we assume the graph is a DAG. Furthermore, we assume that the players share knowledge of potential attacker actions.

We assume that at most one edge connects two nodes. For an attacker type θ and an edge $e = (n, n') \in E$, $q^\theta(e)$ is the intrinsic success probability for a type-θ attacker to reach state n' from state n through edge e. When an attacker reaches n, he receives reward $r(n) \geq 0$. *Targets* are the set of nodes $T \subset S$ where $r(n) > 0$. *Entry points* are the set of nodes with no incoming edges and $r(n) = 0$. We create auxiliary nodes as entry points for problems without natural ones.

Layered DAGs are a special case of DAGs where nodes are partitioned into l layers. Let n_i^j be the j-th node in layer i and $L_i = \{n_i^j \mid \forall j\}$ be the set of all nodes in layer i. In a layered DAG, E only contains edges that connect nodes in L_i to nodes in $L_{i+1}, \forall 1 \leq i \leq l - 1$. Bipartite DAGs are special layered DAGs with $l = 2$. We are particularly interested in attack graphs that are layered DAGs because they are well-suited to model networks [29,38], and we can take advantage of their structure to design efficient algorithms. For layered attack DAGs, we assume all nodes except those in the first layer may be targets.

Defender Strategy. In our model, the defender's action space consists of two action types: *deceptive* and *protective* actions. Deceptive actions aim to make attackers plan their attack with a misunderstanding of the game structure. Using her *deception budget* B^d, the defender can take three classes of deceptive actions: (i) hiding a real edge with a cost $c^h(e)$, (ii) adding a fake edge in a given set E_d with a cost $c^a(e)$, and (iii) modifying the perceived reward of a non-entry-point node with a cost $c^\delta(n)$ per unit of change. We assume the deceptive actions only change an attacker's *perception* of the attack graph (called the *induced* attack graph) and do not modify the true attack graph. Thus, a hidden edge is not truly removed; it is simply hidden from some attackers. An added fake edge is *virtual*: attackers cannot successfully move along that edge.

Each edge in the set E_d has perceived success probabilities $q^\theta(e)$ for each attacker type. These values are given as input. For the last action class, we assume a type-θ attacker's perceived reward of a node n is $r^\theta(n) = r(n) + \beta^\theta \Delta(n)$, where β^θ is the probability of observing the associated (perceived) change to the node reward $\Delta(n)$. The defender chooses the value of $\Delta(n)$ with a cost of $c^\delta(n)|\Delta(n)|$. In cybersecurity, a defender can hide edges by masking connections between physical machines or modifying the perceived routing table, add edges by faking network traffic or vulnerabilities, and change perceived rewards by manipulating outgoing traffic [3,4] to make machines look like something else

Table 1. Notation table.

Notation	Definition
$\theta \in \Theta$	Attacker type from the set of attacker types
$G = (N, E)$	Attack graph, with set of a set of states N and set of edges E
$e = (n, n') \in E$	An edge in the set of edges
$q^\theta(e)$	Probability of type-θ attacker reaching n' from n using e
$r(n)$	Attacker reward for reaching n
$T \subset N$	Set of targets where $r(n) > 0$
B^d	Defender's deception budget
B^a	Defender's effort budget
$c^h(e)$	Cost of hiding edge
$c^a(e)$	Cost of adding fake edge
$c^\delta(n)$	Cost per change to node reward
E_d	Set of fake edges that can be added
$\Delta(n)$	Perceived change to node reward
$r^\theta(n) = r(n) + \beta^\theta \Delta(n)$	Type-θ attacker's perceived reward of n
β^θ	Probability of observing $\Delta(n)$
$x(e)$	Interruption probability
C	Attacker's penalty if interrupted by defender
s_d	Defender's strategy
U_d	Defender's expected utility
BR^Θ	Best response(s) of the attacker type(s)

(e.g., an unimportant relay device). In physical security, she can hide and add edges by spreading misinformation about road closures or traffic [15], and change perceived rewards by signaling to attackers—either by spreading misinformation or transforming targets to make them look like something else (e.g., through "uglification" [32]).

To deploy *protective* measures, the defender allocates effort $x(e)$ to edges with an effort budget B^a, increasing the chance of interrupting an attack. This effort can have different, domain-dependent meaning. $x(e)$ may represent the marginal probability of setting up a checkpoint on edge e [33] in urban security, or the time spent monitoring edge e in cybersecurity. We assume the probability that the defender will interrupt the attacker's movement on e is proportional to her allocated effort. Without loss of generality, we assume the coefficient to be 1. Thus, the interruption probability is $x(e)$. A defender's strategy includes a set of deceptive actions and a protective strategy x. We consider a deterministic deception strategy because the attacker observes the induced graph before choosing his strategy, so randomized deception does not benefit the defender [52].

Attacker Strategy. After observing the graph induced by the defender's deception strategy and the defender's protective strategy x, an attacker chooses a pure strategy. Following the literature [51], this strategy is an attack path on his

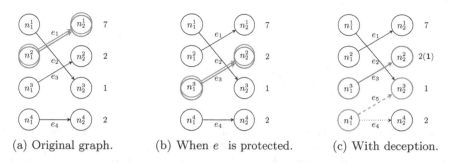

(a) Original graph.   (b) When e is protected.   (c) With deception.

Fig. 1. Influence of defender strategy on attackers' best responses (blue for weak attacker, red for powerful attacker) on a bipartite DAG. The dashed line represents an *added* edge; the dotted line represents a *hidden* edge. The numbers next to a node show the true reward and the modified reward (parenthesized). (Color figure online)

perceived attack graph. It is either null (the attacker chooses not to attack) or consists of a sequence of nodes or edges on the graph, starting from an entry point. To execute this strategy, the attacker starts from the entry point and moves along the edges as planned until he fails or successfully reaches the last node in the path. The attacker can fail to move along an edge for three reasons: (i) he fails due to the intrinsic possibility of failure (with probability $1 - q^\theta(e)$), (ii) the defender interrupts his movement (with probability $q^\theta(e)(1-x(e))$), (iii) the edge is fake ($e \in E_d$). The game ends when the attacker's movement fails or he reaches the last node along the planned path. We assume the attacker is best responding based on his available information, including $q^\theta(e)$ and $r^\theta(n)$, and chooses a path that maximizes his total expected utility.

Player's Utility. When the attacker executes his attack strategy, he receives reward (or penalty) at each step. His total utility is the accumulated undiscounted reward (or penalty). Since the perceived reward and perceived success probability governs the attacker's response, we only discuss the attacker's perceived (expected) utility. If the attacker arrives at node n, he receives reward $r^\theta(n)$. If the defender interrupts the attack in one step of movement, the attacker pays a penalty C in that step, and the game ends. If the defender interrupts an attack before the attacker reaches any target, she gets 0. If the attacker successfully reaches a set of target nodes $T' \subset T$, the defender's utility is $-\sum_{n \in T'} r(n)$.

Solution Concept. We want to find the optimal defender strategy assuming that attackers best respond based on their induced attack graphs: $s_d^* = \arg\max_{s_d}\{U_d(s_d, BR^\Theta(s_d))\}$, where s_d is the defender's strategy containing both deceptive and protective actions, U_d is the defender's expected utility, and BR^Θ denotes the best response(s) of the attacker type(s) with defender-favoring tiebreaking. Our game model can be viewed as a two-stage problem: in stage one, the defender takes deceptive actions and stage two is a Bayesian Stackelberg game. We want to optimize the choice of deceptive actions in stage one and find a Strong Bayesian Stackelberg equilibrium in stage two.

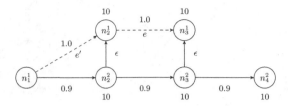

Fig. 2. Non-submodularity example. The edge labels show the success probabilities; the node labels show the rewards. ϵ is a sufficiently small positive number. Adding either edge e or e' will not affect the attacker's choice of the lower path; adding both will make the attacker choose the upper path.

For expository purpose, we consider two extreme attacker types: attackers who believe all and no deceptive actions, referred to as *weak* attackers W (w. p. γ) and *powerful* attackers P (w. p. $1 - \gamma$), respectively. A type-P attacker will not be deceived, i.e., $q^P(e) = 0$, $\forall e \in E_d$ and $\beta^P = 0$. Our theoretical results and algorithms can be applied to the multiple attacker type setting.

Example Game Instance. To further elucidate our game model, we illustrate an example game instance on a bipartite DAG (Fig. 1) and show how the defender can use both deceptive and protective actions to improve her utility. We set the costs and deception budget so that the defender can at most take the following deceptive actions: adding edge e_5 from n_1^4 to n_2^3, hiding edge e_4, and changing the weak attacker's perceived reward of n_2^2 from 2 to 1. We set the effort budget B^a to 1 and the success probabilities to satisfy $q^\theta(e_2) < q^\theta(e_4) < q^\theta(e_3) < 1$ and $q^\theta(e) = 1$ for other edges. Here $\gamma = 0.5$, i.e., the defender encounters the two attacker types with equal probability.

Figure 1a shows the best responses of both attackers BR^Θ on the graph with no defender actions taken. The defender's expected utility U_d is -7. Figure 1b shows BR^Θ after the defender allocates all protective effort to e_1. Here $U_d = \sum_\theta -q^\theta(e_3)$. Figure 1c shows BR^Θ when the defender takes all possible deceptive actions and protects e_1. Here $U_d = -q^P(e_3)$, as the weak attacker will fail due to the fake edge. This example shows that deception can benefit the defender.

3   Theoretical Analysis

In this section, we show that the defender's optimal utility as a function of added or hidden edges is not submodular and the problem of finding the optimal defender strategy is NP-hard.

Non-submodularity Results. Let $f(D)$, where $D \subset E_d$, denote the defender's optimal expected utility when she adds a set of fake edges D. $f(D)$ is submodular if $\forall D \subset D', e \in E_d \setminus D', f(D \cup \{e\}) - f(D) \geq f(D' \cup \{e\}) - f(D')$. Submodular functions enjoy desirable properties and often have efficient approximation algorithms [26]. However, as shown by the example in Fig. 2, $f(D)$ in our game model is not submodular[1].

In Fig. 2, the original graph contains all nodes and solid edges. Node n_1^1 is the entry point. We set $B^d = 7$, $c^\delta(n) = c^a(e) = 1, \forall e, n$, and $c^h(e) > 7, \forall e$, so the defender cannot hide any edges. We set $B^a = 0$ and $\gamma = 1$. Let $D = \emptyset$ and $D' = \{e'\}$. If the defender does not add an edge (the set of added edges is D) or adds only one dashed line (D' or $D \cup \{e\}$), then no matter how she changes the node rewards, the attacker's best response is path $(n_1^1, n_2^2, n_3^2, n_4^2)$, resulting in $U_d = -24.39$. If the defender adds both edges e' and e, then she can change the reward of n_3^1 to 15 with the remaining budget 5. The attacker then chooses path (n_1^1, n_2^1, n_3^1) as he believes that it yields a higher utility (25) than the lower path. Here $U_d = 0$, as the fake edges will cause the attacker to fail. Thus, $f(D \cup \{e\}) - f(D) = 0$ and $f(D' \cup \{e\}) - f(D') = 24.39$, contradicting the definition of submodularity. The non-submodularity indicates that it may be hard to find efficient approximation algorithms for our problem.

Hardness Results. Our main result is that the problem is NP-hard when the defender can perform both protective and deceptive actions, even when restricted to layered DAGs.

Theorem 1. *The problem of finding the optimal deceptive actions is NP-hard even in layered DAGs.*

Proof. We prove the theorem by providing a polynomial time reduction from the knapsack problem (KP). In a typical KP, there are k items. Each item i is associated with a weight w_i and a value z_i. We want to find a subset of the items, such that $\sum_i z_i$ is maximized and $\sum_i w_i \leq W$, where W is given. Here we only consider cases where $w_i \in \mathbb{Z}, \forall i$, which are still NP-hard problems.

Given any KP instance with parameters w, z, W, we construct a problem instance with a layered DAG as follows. First, create a source node n_0 and k other *milestone* nodes $n_1, n_2, \ldots, n_{k+1}$. Second, for each $1 \leq i \leq k$, create two sets of nodes $\{u_i^j\}_{j=1}^{w_i}$ and $\{l_i^j\}_{j=1}^{W+1}$, respectively called upper and lower nodes. Third, for each upper node u_i^j, add edges (n_{i-1}, u_i^j) and (u_i^j, n_i). For each lower node l_i^j, add (n_{i-1}, l_i^j) and (l_i^j, n_i). Fourth, add nodes $\{l^j\}_{j=1}^{W+1}$ and edges $(n_k, l^j), (l^j, n_{k+1}), \forall j$. Last, set $r(u_i^j) = z_i$ for each upper node, $r(n_{k+1}) = M$, where M is sufficiently large: $M > \sum_{i=1}^k z_i$. For all other nodes n, set $r(n) = 0$.

Constructing this layered DAG with the above construction takes polynomial time. We consider the case where $\gamma = 1$ and $q^w(e) = 1, \forall e$. We set $B^d = W$ and $B^a = 0$. Let $c^h(e) = 1, \forall e$, $c^a(e) > W, \forall e$, and $c^\delta(n), \forall n$ be sufficiently large, such that the defender can only hide edges. Since there are more than W ways go from one milestone node to the next, there is always a path from n_0 to n_{k+1}. Because the attacker selects the highest-valued path, the attacker will choose to go through an upper node to reach n_i from n_{i-1}, if able.

Let x_i be the binary variable indicating if the attacker's path from n_{i-1} to n_i contains an upper node. The attacker's utility is $M + \sum_{i=1}^k z_i x_i$, so the

---

[1] For space, we omit the full proof for hiding edges. We follow a similar construction.

defender's goal is to hide edges to minimize $M + \sum_{i=1}^{k} z_i x_i$. If the defender wants to prevent the attacker from reaching the upper nodes, she must hide at least w_i edges at a cost of w_i. Let y_i indicate whether the defender hides these w_i edges. Since $x_i = 1 - y_i$, we can rewrite the defender's problem as an integer program that minimizes $M + \sum_{i=1}^{k} z_i(1 - y_i)$, subject to $\sum_{i=1}^{k} w_i y_i \leq W$ and $y_i \in \{0, 1\}$, which is equivalent to maximizing $\sum_{i=1}^{k} z_i y_i$, subject to $\sum_{i=1}^{k} w_i y_i \leq W$ and $y_i \in \{0, 1\}$. $\qquad\square$

4 The MILP Approach for Layered DAGs

Here we provide an MILP-based algorithm for layered DAGs. We first describe our approach for bipartite DAGs and then extend it to general layered DAGs.

4.1 Bipartite DAG

We describe our MILP-based approach for bipartite DAGs. We begin with the following important observation.

Observation 1. *In the defender's optimal strategy, any edge added by the defender must be in the optimal path chosen by the weak attackers.*

Proof. Because the powerful attackers know that the edges are fake, only weak attackers will choose them. The statement trivially follows; otherwise, adding these edges would cause the attackers' optimal path to stay the same, and the defender would obtain the same expected utility. $\qquad\square$

Here any attacker's action contains a single edge. According to Observation 1, the defender will add at most one edge in her optimal strategy: that edge must be the weak attacker's best response. Thus, we have $E_d = \{(n_1, n_2) \notin E \mid n_1 \in L_1, n_2 \in L_2\}$. Denote by e_0 the choice to not attack. Let $e_W \in E \cup E_d \cup \{e_0\}$ and $e_P \in E \cup \{e_0\}$ be the choices of the weak and powerful attacker, respectively. Let $x^m(e) \in \{0, 1\}$ indicate if $e \in E \cup E_d$ is in the perceived graph. Denote by $n_{end}(e)$ the endpoint of edge e. As with prior work [17], we must enumerate all possible action profiles (e_W, e_P) and for each profile solve a mathematical program:

$$
\begin{aligned}
\text{Maximize} \quad & U_d^W + U_d^P \\
\text{Subject to} \quad & U_d^W = -\gamma \mathbb{1}[e_W \in E] q^W(e_W)(1 - x(e_W)) r(n_{end}(e_W)), \\
& U_d^P = -(1 - \gamma) \mathbb{1}[e_P \in E] q^P(e_P)(1 - x(e_P)) r(n_{end}(e_P)), \\
& U_a^W(e) = q^W(e)[(1 - x(e)) r^W(n_{end}(e)) - x(e)C], \forall e \in E \cup E_d, \\
& U_a^W(e_0) = 0, \\
& U_a^W(e_W) \geq \max\{U_a^W(e) - (1 - x^m(e))M, 0\}, \forall e \in E \cup E_d, \qquad (1) \\
& U_a^P(e) = q^P(e)[(1 - x(e)) r^P(n_{end}(e)) - x(e)C], \forall e \in E, \\
& U_a^P(e_0) = 0,
\end{aligned}
$$

$$U_a^P(e_P) \geq \max\{U_a^P(e), 0\}, \forall e \in E, \tag{2}$$

$$\sum_{e \in E \cup E_d} x^m(e)x(e) \leq r, \tag{3}$$

$$\sum_{n \in L_2} c^\delta(n)|r(n) - r^W(n)| + \sum_{e \in E} c^h(e)\left[1 - x^m(e)\right]$$

$$+ c^a(e_W)(1 - \mathbb{1}[e_W \in E]) \leq B^d,$$

$$0 \leq x(e) \leq 1, \forall e \in E \cup E_d,$$

$$x^m(e_W) = 1, \text{ if } e_W \neq e_0,$$

$$x^m(e) = 0, \forall e \in E_d \setminus \{e_W\},$$

$$x^m(e) \in \{0, 1\}, \forall e \in E,$$

$$l_k^+(n), l_k^-(n) \in \{0, 1\}, \forall n \in L_2,$$

$$0 \leq m_k^+(e) \leq l_k^+(n_{end}(e)), \forall e \in E \cup E_d,$$

$$x(e) - [1 - l_k^+(n_{end}(e))] \leq m_k^+(e) \leq x(e), \forall e \in E \cup E_d,$$

$$0 \leq m_k^-(e) \leq l_k^-(n_{end}(e)), \forall e \in E \cup E_d,$$

$$x(e) - [1 - l_k^-(n_{end}(e))] \leq m_k^-(e) \leq x(e), \forall e \in E \cup E_d, \tag{4}$$

where U_a^W and U_a^P are the utilities of the weak and powerful attacker, U_d^W and U_d^P are the defender's utilities from the weak and powerful attacker, and M is a sufficiently large positive number.

We safely remove $x^m(e)$ from constraint (3). To handle the absolute terms in constraint (4), we introduce two variables for each target $n \in L_2$: $r^+(n) = \max\{r^W(n) - r(n), 0\}$ and $r^-(n) = \max\{r(n) - r^W(n), 0\}$. Thus, we have: $r^W(n) - r(n) = r^+(n) - r^-(n)$ and $|r^W(n) - r(n)| = r^+(n) + r^-(n)$. For the quadratic term in constraints (1), we use similar techniques from previous work [57] to find approximate solutions. We first focus on solutions where $r^W(n) - r(n)$ is a multiple of a basic step r_0 and use binary representations for $r^+(n)$ and $r^-(n)$. We introduce binary variables $l_k^+(n)$ and $l_k^-(n)$ and let $r^+(n) = r_0 \sum_k 2^k l_k^+(n)$ and $r^-(n) = r_0 \sum_k 2^k l_k^-(n)$. We introduce two new variables $m_k^+(e) = x(e)l_k^+(n_{end}(e))$ and $m_k^-(e) = x(e)l_k^-(n_{end}(e))$ to replace all possible quadratic terms:

$$0 \leq m_k^+(e) \leq l_k^+(n_{end}(e)) \quad \text{and} \quad x(e) - [1 - l_k^+(n_{end}(e))] \leq m_k^+(e) \leq x(e),$$

$$0 \leq m_k^-(e) \leq l_k^-(n_{end}(e)) \quad \text{and} \quad x(e) - [1 - l_k^-(n_{end}(e))] \leq m_k^-(e) \leq x(e).$$

We improve the algorithm's scalability in two ways. First, we track the best solution U^* so far and add a constraint to each MILP: $U_d^W + U_d^P \geq U^*$. In addition to not affecting the final solution, this constraint speeds up the algorithm by rendering many MILPs infeasible. We can efficiently decide a MILP's feasibility. Second, we build a two-layer search tree: the first layer corresponds to the powerful attacker's choice; the second layer corresponds to the weak attacker's choice. We compute each node's upper and lower bounds and prune a branch if its upper bound is less than the lower bound of other branches. To compute the lower bound, we set $B^d = 0$, so the perceived graph of all attacker types is the same as the true attack graph. Because all attacker types choose the same attack, we view them as a single attacker.

We use two methods to compute the upper bound. In the first method, we set $B^d = \infty$ in the original game, so the defender can hide all edges. The weak attacker will not attack; thus, we need only consider the powerful attacker. In the second method, we relax the original MILP to yield a tighter bound. We remove the binary constraints, transforming the MILP into a linear program (LP). We relax the LP by randomly adding a fraction of the constraints described in Eqs. (1) and (2). Solving the new relaxed LP is much faster. Initially, we compute both global lower ($B^d = 0$) and upper ($B^d = \infty$) bounds. For each leaf node, we compute a new upper bound using the second method described above, and update the lower bounds and upper bounds for other related nodes.

4.2   Layered DAG

Now we consider general layered DAGs, where an attacker's pure strategy is to choose a state from each layer to form a path. The number of possible pure strategies is $\prod_{i=1}^{l} |L_i|$, which can be exponential in the number of states. Using the multiple-LP method [17], we would need to solve exponentially many MILPs. Instead, we provide a different formulation by simulating backward induction.

For simplicity, we describe our formulation for weak attackers; handling powerful attackers is simpler. Let $x^m(e)$ indicate if e is in the weak attacker's perceived graph. For each node, we introduce variables $V^W(n_i^j)$ and $V^P(n_i^j)$, one for each attacker type, to represent the expected utilities of starting from n_i^j:

$$V^W(n_i^j) = r^W(n_i^j) + \max_{e:x^m(e)=1, n_{start}(e)=n_i^j} q^W(e)[(1 - x(e))V^W(n_{end}(e)) + x(e)C],$$

where $n_{start}(e)$ is the start state of edge e. To handle the quadratic terms, we use their binary representations [57]. To handle the max operator, we introduce a binary variable $a^W(e)$ indicating the attacker's choice if he starts from $n_{start}(e)$. We guarantee that only existing edges are chosen and, among all edges starting from the same state, at most one of them is selected: $a^W(e) \leq x^m(e)$ and $\sum_{x^m(e)=1, n_{start}(e)=n_i^j} a^W(e) \leq 1$.

With $a^W(e) = 1$, the defender's expected utility $U_d^W(n_i^j)$ from weak attackers starting from n_i^j is:

$$U_d^W(n_{start}(e)) = -r(n_{start}(e)) + q^W(e)[(1 - x(e))U_d^W(n_{end}(e)) + x(e)C].$$

We apply similar techniques to obtain the defender's utility for powerful attackers. The defender's overall objective is $\gamma \sum_j U_d^W(n_1^j) + (1-\gamma) \sum_j U_d^P(n_1^j)$. We omit the complete MILPs for layered DAGs, as they can be obtained by modifying the MILPs for bipartite graphs using the above steps.

5   The NAS Approach for General DAGs

In this section, we present our neural architecture search (NAS) algorithm for general DAGs. We first describe how we find the attacker's best response. The rest of this section is devoted to solving the defender's problem.

Given the defender's strategy, let $V^\theta(n)$ be a type θ attacker's highest expected utility starting from node n, and E^θ be the set of edges in the perceived graph for that attacker type. From the definition of best response, we have:

$$V^\theta(n) = \max_{n':(n,n')\in E^\theta} \left\{ r^\theta(n) + q^\theta(n,n')[(1 - x(n,n'))V^\theta(n') + x(n,n')C] \right\}.$$

We can equivalently view V^θ as a Bellman equation, so it can be solved with dynamic programming or, because we focus on DAGs, backward induction on the reversed topological order.

Fig. 3. The neural architecture search algorithm. The left figure is the DAG, where the dashed line is the added edge. The right figure is the corresponding neural network, where U_d is the defender's total utility: the sum of utilities from both types of attackers. The two dashed boxes correspond to the networks for the weak (top) and powerful (bottom) attackers.

We now describe our NAS approach for solving the defender's problem. We leverage the insight that the defender's actions can be divided into two categories: actions that change the attack graph structure (e.g., adding and hiding edges) and actions that change the parameter values of the graph (e.g., changing node values and protecting edges). Because the attack graph is a DAG, it naturally can be viewed as a feedforward neural network (NN). Thus, we redefine the problem as a NAS problem [23], in which we first use a search strategy to find a NN structure, then use machine learning techniques to optimize the parameter values. We use a genetic algorithm to propose architectures and a modified gradient-based technique to optimize the parameter values and evaluate the quality of each architecture.

We cast the defender's utility as the objective function in the optimization problem of training a NN. To optimize the parameter values, we use the forward pass to simulate the attacker's decision-making process (backward induction). Thus, we reverse the DAG and start from the end nodes. We build a network for each attacker type based on their perceived graphs and obtain the defender's expected utility by aggregating the utilities obtained from different attacker types.

However, we still need to address the following issues. First, the rational attacker chooses a single, deterministic path from the set of possible paths. Thus, small changes in a state's value may not change the attacker's decision, and, by extension, the defender's utility. Therefore, the gradients of the defender's utility with respect to these variables are 0. Second, the defender has budgets B^d and B^a. To solve these problems, we borrow techniques from prior work [54]. For the first problem, we slightly relax the assumption of rational attackers and use the quantal response model [40]. Thus, the probability of choosing an edge (n, n') is:

$$
\Pr^\theta\{n'|n\} = \begin{cases} \dfrac{e^{\lambda V^\theta(n,n')}}{\sum_{m:(n,m)\in E^\theta} e^{\lambda V^\theta(n,m)}} & \text{if } (n, n') \in E^\theta; \\ 0 & \text{otherwise}, \end{cases}
$$

where E^θ is the set of edges in the perceived graph for a type θ attacker, and λ is a parameter that controls the rationality of the attackers. The term $V^\theta(n, n')$ is defined as the expected utility of a type θ attacker moving through edge (n, n'): $V^\theta(n, n') = r^\theta(n) + q^\theta(n, n')[(1 - x(n, n'))V^\theta(n') - x(n, n')C]$, where

$$
V^\theta(n) = \begin{cases} r^\theta(n) & \text{if } n \text{ has no outgoing edges;} \\ \sum_{m:(n,m)\in E^\theta} \Pr^\theta\{m|n\}V^\theta(n, m) & \text{otherwise.} \end{cases}
$$

Thus, $U_d^\theta(n) = \sum_{m:(n,m)\in E} \Pr^\theta\{m|n\}U_d^\theta(m)$ captures the defender's utility from a type θ attacker. Instead of a regularization term, which cannot guarantee that the budget constraints are strictly satisfied, we use another method that "distributes" the budgets to different nodes and edges. We introduce a variable $z(e)$ for each edge $e \in E$ and two variables $y(n)$ and $d(n)$ for each target. Define:

$$
x(e) = \min\left\{1.0, \frac{B_r^d e^{z(e)}}{\sum_{e'\in E} e^{z(e')}}\right\} \text{ and } r^W(n) - r(n) = \frac{B^a e^{y(n)}}{c^\delta(n)\sum_n e^{y(n)}} \frac{e^{d(n)} - 1}{e^{d(n)} + 1},
$$

where B_r^d is the remaining deceptive budget after adding and hiding edges. The feasibility $0 \le x(e) \le 1$ and budget constraints are always satisfied for all possible combinations of $z(e)$, $y(n)$, and $d(n)$. The quantities $\Pr^\theta\{n'|n\}$, $x(e)$, and $r^W(n)$ can be represented in all major deep learning packages using the sigmoid and softmax functions.

6 Experiments

We conduct experiments on both bipartite and general DAGs. We generate the graphs using the random Erdös-Renyi method [24]. To ensure the DAG property for general graphs, each node has a unique number; only edges (s, t) s.t. $s < t$ can be added. Edge density ρ denotes the probability that an edge is added to the original graph when constructed. We sample the edge success probabilities and the attacker's penalty C uniformly at random from the interval $(0,1]$ for all experiments. We set $B^a = 1$. As hiding or adding an edge is more difficult in reality than changing node rewards, we set the costs of deceptive actions to $c^h(e) = c^a(e) = 1, \forall e$ and $c^\delta(n) = 0.1, \forall n$ (unless otherwise noted). We generate the target rewards by sampling uniformly at random from the interval $[5,10]$. We generate 20 instances for each point in all plots. Because differential evolution [61], a population-based evolutionary algorithm (EA), works well on many problems, we use a modified $DE/rand/1/bin$ variant [42] as a baseline (see Appendix for details). The EA uses `differential_evolution` from the `scipy` package [64]. We use Gurobi [28] to solve the MILPs and PyTorch [47] for NAS. We run all experiments on a machine with a Core i7 CPU at 4.2GHz.

With our experiments, we seek to answer the following questions: 1) What is the effect of different deception budgets on the defender's utility?, 2) What is the solution quality obtained by our algorithms?, 3) How well do our algorithms scale?, and 4) How do our algorithms allocate the deceptive budget?

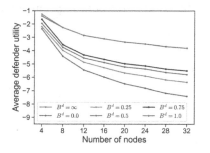
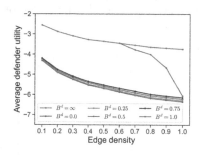

(a) Defender utility vs. number of nodes   (b) Defender utility vs. edge density

Fig. 4. Change in defender's utility versus graph size. The utility decreases as the deceptive budget decreases and as the graph size increases.

6.1 Bipartite DAGs

Effect of Different Deception Budgets. We investigate how different deceptive budgets and graph sizes affect the defender's utility U_d in a bipartite DAG setting with the following experiments. In the first experiment, we fix the edge density ρ to 0.5, vary the number of nodes N from 4 to 32 (from 2 to 16 on each side), and solve each game with a different B^d. In the second experiment, we fix $N = 16$, vary D in increments of 0.1, and solve each game with a different B^d. We only use the MILP algorithm for both experiments.

Figure 4 shows that U_d decreases as the graph size increases and as B^d decreases. Figure 4a depicts the first experiment's results. When $B^d = 1$, the defender achieves nearly the same U_d as $B^d = \infty$. Because the cost of adding or hiding an edge is 1, the defender can afford to manipulate the graph structure instead of only changing the perceived node rewards. This result shows that, in the bipartite DAG case, adding one edge can typically yield the best solution. Figure 4b depicts the second experiment's results. When $B^d < 1$, there is a small utility improvement from an increased B^d; in contrast, U_d sharply increases when $B^d = 1$. When ρ increases, the performance when $B^d = 1$ quickly decreases. When ρ is large, few edges are available to add, so the effect of adding edges quickly diminishes.

Algorithm Performance. In our first experiment, we show the scalability of our improved MILP algorithm (we omit NAS since it is not guaranteed to produce the optimal solution). In the second experiment, we compare the solution quality of our MILP and NAS algorithms with the EA baseline. For the first experiment, we vary N from 4 to 80 in increments of 4. For the second experiment, we vary N from 10 to 60 in increments of 10. We set the maximum running time for the EA and NAS to 5 minutes, as the MILP algorithm terminates within 5 min for all instances. We set the population size to 60 for the EA and NAS's genetic algorithm part. We set the EA's recombination and mutation parameters to the `scipy` package's default values. For NAS, we set $\lambda = 5$ and use the Adam optimizer [36] with a learning rate of 0.2. We fix $\rho = 0.5$ for both experiments.

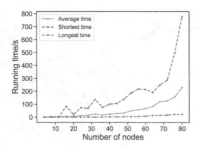

(a) Running time of MILP algorithm

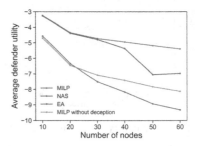

(b) Solution quality of all algorithms

Fig. 5. Scalability and performance on bipartite graphs

Figure 5a depicts the results of the first experiment: our MILP algorithm scales well. The average running time for solving an instance with 80 nodes is less than 4 min; the longest individual running time is about 13 min. The standard multiple-MILP [17] algorithm would need to solve about $(40 \times 40 \times 0.5) \times (40 \times 40) = 1,280,000$ MILPs. With our heuristic algorithm, we only need to solve 4.6 MILPs on average.

Figure 5b shows the results of the second experiment. To examine the effect of the various algorithms on the defender's utility U_d, we conduct a one-way repeated measures ANOVA on all graph sizes. The results show that the algorithm used leads to a statistically significant difference in U_d ($F(3, 177) = 189.18, p = 5.66 \times 10^{-55}, \alpha = .05$). We conduct pairwise paired t-tests with the Bonferroni correction to determine which algorithms result in significant increases in U_d. We find that all algorithm pairs have a significant difference in U_d. In fact, NAS ($M = -3.0151, SD = 7.1396$), the MILP algorithm with no deception ($M = -6.8458, SD = 1.7518$), and the MILP algorithm with deception ($M = -2.2892, SD = 2.8603$) significantly outperform the EA ($M = -7.1396, SD = 3.3582$), $p = 7.8 \times 10^{-20}, .0012, 1.6 \times 10^{-24}$, respectively.

Budget Expenditure of the MILP Algorithm. We show how the MILP allocates B^d. In this experiment, each graph has $N = 16$ and $\rho = 0.5$. For each instance, we increase B^d from 0 to 2 and track how each budget is spent. Figure 6a shows the results. The defender never hides an edge in any of the optimal solutions, suggesting that adding edges may be more useful than hiding edges. This suggestion is further strengthened when $B^d = 1$: we see a sudden increase in spending on adding edges. We also see that changing the node rewards may not be as useful as other deceptive actions: the unused budget generally occupies a large area. However, when $B^d > 1$, changing the node rewards is more frequently used than when $B^d \leq 1$. This result suggests that changing the node rewards is more useful when combined with adding edges, as it makes the fake path appear more valuable (and, thus, more attractive) to a weak attacker.

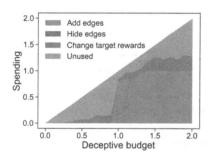

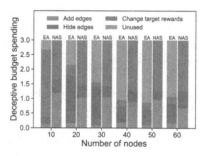

(a) Spending on bipartite DAGs   (b) Spending on general DAGs

Fig. 6. Deceptive budget expenditure of the MILP (left), and EA and NAS (right)

6.2   General DAGs

Algorithm Performance

We compare the performance of NAS and three baselines on general DAGs. We omit the MILP algorithm: it is not applicable. For the baselines, we use a random strategy (RAND), and a no-action strategy (NA), and EA. We fix $\rho = 0.5$ and vary N from 10 to 50 in increments of 10. We set $B^d = 3$ and sample $c^a(e)$ and $c^h(e)$ from the interval $[0.5, 1.5]$, such that $c^a(e_i) = c^a(e_j), \forall e_i, e_j$ and $c^h(e_i) = c^h(e_j), \forall e_i, e_j$. EA and NAS use the same parameters as before, but the maximum running time is $1.5 \times N$ minutes.

NAS leads to significantly higher defender utility U_d than all other algorithms (Fig. 7a). We perform a one-way repeated measures ANOVA on all graph sizes to examine different algorithms' effect on U_d. We find that the choice of algorithm produces statistically significant differences in U_d ($F(3, 357) = 1286.9, p = 1.7 \times 10^{-106}, \alpha = .05$). We conduct pairwise paired t-tests with the Bonferroni correction to determine which algorithms result in these significant increases. We find that all algorithm pairs have significant differences in U_d. Importantly, NAS ($M = -3.3453, SD = 6.3247$) leads to a significant increase in U_d compared to all algorithms: RAND ($M = -10.067, SD = 12.369$), NA ($M = -10.435, SD = 12.246$), and the EA ($M = -8.5974, SD = 15.220$), $p = 6.77 \times 10^{-47}, 7.83 \times 10^{-48}, 6.56 \times 10^{-38}$, respectively.

We are interested in how quickly NAS reaches solutions with high U_d. Figure 7b shows how the NAS and EA solutions evolve. On average, NAS quickly ($< 20 \, \text{min}$) finds high-quality solutions and successfully refines the solution quality; in contrast, the EA struggles to improve the utility from its initial solution.

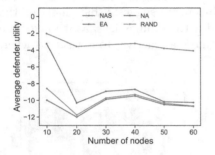 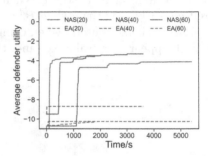

(a) Average defender utility achieved vs. the size of the graph

(b) Performance over time. The graph's number of nodes is parenthesized.

Fig. 7. Performance of different algorithms on general graphs

Budget Expenditure of Different Algorithms. We show how the EA and NAS allocate B^d. This experiment uses the same graphs as in Sect. 6.2. Figure 6b shows how the EA and NAS spend B^d. On average, NAS allocates more of B^d to adding edges and changing the node rewards, indicating that the EA struggles to find solutions that involve adding edges and to determine the appropriate changes in the node rewards. We believe this is due to how the EA performs recombination and mutation.

7   Related Work

In addition to the related literature mentioned throughout the paper, we introduce and discuss some additional related works. Some SSG variants enable the defender to manipulate the game's payoff structure [13,52,57] or alter a system's observable features to influence the attacker's attack choice [43,56]). However, these works do not capture the graphical structure of security problems.

In contrast, in our work, the defender manipulates the attacker's perceived payoff structure, allocates defensive resources, and manipulates the attacker's perceived graphical structure of the game (including the actions that the attacker believes that he can take). Previous work that combines defensive deception and attack graph games typically only focuses on deploying honeypots or fake vulnerabilities in a network [10,11,19,20,22,51]. Our model is more general in the sense that it can model these deception techniques by allowing the defender to manipulate the edges and perceived reward of targets. In addition, we consider the protective actions the defender may take to interrupt an attack. Another related work [29] uses a model of defensive deception to manipulate the attacker's belief; however, it abstracts away specific deceptive actions, and does not account for non-deterministic transitions between states, which are considered in our model.

8   Discussion and Conclusion

Our techniques can be applied to more general settings. For example, when the attacker's reward depends on the edge, not the node, we can replace the term $r(s_{end}(e))$ with $r(e)$ in the MILP and NAS algorithms. We can also easily relax the assumption that the probability of catching an attacker at edge e is $q^{\theta}(e)x(e)$. Our MILP algorithm works if all constraints are linear in the defender's protection effort; the NAS algorithm works for any differentiable function.

We introduced a novel variant of Stackelberg attack graph games, in which the defender can alter the perceived structure of the attack graph and the perceived reward of the nodes in the graph, as well as allocate protective effort along the graph's edges. We proved the hardness of this problem and proposed two algorithms to solve special but important subcases of this game: a MILP algorithm with novel heuristics and a NAS algorithm in which the attack graph structure is the neural network architecture. We performed extensive experiments that show the effectiveness of deception and of our algorithms.

Acknowledgements. This research was sponsored by the U.S. Army Combat Capabilities Development Command Army Research Laboratory and was accomplished under Cooperative Agreement Number W911NF-13-2-0045 (ARL Cyber Security CRA). The views and conclusions contained in this document are those of the authors and should not be interpreted as representing the official policies, either expressed or implied, of the Combat Capabilities Development Command Army Research Laboratory or the U.S. Government. The U.S. Government is authorized to reproduce and distribute reprints for Government purposes notwithstanding any copyright notation here on.

Appendix

We modify the DE [61] variant *DE/rand/1/bin* [42]. To initialize the population, we randomly choose the sequence of deceptive actions to consider. For each type, we determine the maximum number of components that can be altered (e.g., edges to add) for this individual. If allowed, we then modify the graph with randomly-selected modifications of that type. We also add a new termination condition based on the known optimal utility (0) for the defender if the defender has infinite protective and deceptive budgets. If any solution yields this utility, then we stop early and select it as the final solution. We also use a more compact solution representation: the full solution takes space $m_e(2|N| + 1) + |N| + 2|E|$, where m_e indicates the maximum number of edges that can be added to the graph given B^d. Each edge to be added takes space $2|N|$. To indicate that an edge is to be added, we take the arg max over the effort allocated in the first N and last N slots. The resulting indices i, j indicate the endpoints of the edge. If the summed effort at i, j is greater than a threshold, the edge is added. We further compact the representation when the defender cannot add or hide any edges without violating constraints by removing these parts of the solution, so each strategy uses space $|E| + |N|$.

References

1. Abdallah, M., Naghizadeh, P., Hota, A.R., Cason, T., Bagchi, S., Sundaram, S.: Behavioral and game-theoretic security investments in interdependent systems modeled by attack graphs. IEEE Trans. Control Netw. Syst. (2020)
2. Achleitner, S., La Porta, T., McDaniel, P., Sugrim, S., Krishnamurthy, S.V., Chadha, R.: Cyber deception: virtual networks to defend insider reconnaissance. In: International Workshop Managing Insider security Threats (2016)
3. Albanese, M., Battista, E., Jajodia, S.: A deception based approach for defeating OS and service fingerprinting. In: Conference on Communications and Network Security (CNS) (2015)
4. Albanese, M., Battista, E., Jajodia, S.: Deceiving attackers by creating a virtual attack surface. In: Cyber Deception (2016)
5. Almeshekah, M., Spafford, E.: Planning and integrating deception into computer security defenses. In: New Security Paradigms Workshop (2014)
6. Almeshekah, M., Spafford, E.: Cyber security deception. In: Cyber Deception (2016)
7. Ammann, P., Wijesekera, D., Kaushik, S.: Scalable, graph-based network vulnerability analysis. In: Conference on Computer and Communications Security (2002)
8. An, B., Ordóñez, F., Tambe, M., Shieh, E., Yang, R., Baldwin, C., et al.: A deployed quantal response-based patrol planning system for the US coast guard. Interfaces **43**(5) (2013)
9. Anwar, A.H., Kamhoua, C., Leslie, N.: A game-theoretic framework for dynamic cyber deception in internet of battlefield things. In: International Conference on Mobile and Ubiquitous Systems: Computing, Networking and Services (2019)
10. Anwar, A.H., Kamhoua, C., Leslie, N.: Honeypot allocation over attack graphs in cyber deception games. In: International Conference on Computing, Networking and Communications (2020)
11. Basak, A., Kamhoua, C., Venkatesan, S., Gutierrez, M., Anwar, A.H., Kiekintveld, C.: Identifying stealthy attackers in a game theoretic framework using deception. In: Alpcan, T., Vorobeychik, Y., Baras, J.S., Dán, G. (eds.) GameSec 2019. LNCS, vol. 11836, pp. 21–32. Springer, Cham (2019). https://doi.org/10.1007/978-3-030-32430-8_2

12. Bercovitch, M., Renford, M., Hasson, L., Shabtai, A., Rokach, L., Elovici, Y.: HoneyGen: an automated honeytokens generator. In: IEEE ISI (2011)
13. Blocki, J., Christin, N., Datta, A., Procaccia, A.D., Sinha, A.: Audit games. In: International Joint Conference on Artificial Intelligence (2013)
14. Bondi, E., Oh, H., Xu, H., Fang, F., Dilkina, B., Tambe, M.: Broken signals in security games: coordinating patrollers and sensors in the real world. In: International Conference on Autonomous Agents and MultiAgent Systems (2019)
15. Car and Driver: artist shows google maps' control over our lives by creating a fake traffic jam (2020)
16. Cohen, F.: The use of deception techniques: honeypots and decoys. In: Handbook Information Security, vol. 3(1) (2006)
17. Conitzer, V., Sandholm, T.: Computing the optimal strategy to commit to. In: conference on Electronic commerce (2006)
18. Dong, C., Zhao, L.: Sensor network security defense strategy based on attack graph and improved binary PSO. Saf. Sci. **117**, 81–87 (2019)
19. Durkota, K., Lisý, V., Bošanský, B., Kiekintveld, C.: Approximate solutions for attack graph games with imperfect information. In: Khouzani, M.H.R., Panaousis, E., Theodorakopoulos, G. (eds.) GameSec 2015. LNCS, vol. 9406, pp. 228–249. Springer, Cham (2015). https://doi.org/10.1007/978-3-319-25594-1_13
20. Durkota, K., Lisẏ, V., Bošanskẏ, B., Kiekintveld, C.: Optimal network security hardening using attack graph games. In: International Joint Conference on Artificial Intelligence (2015)
21. Durkota, K., Lisẏ, V., Bošanskẏ, B., Kiekintveld, C., Pěchouček, M.: Hardening networks against strategic attackers using attack graph games. Comput. Secur. **87**, 101578 (2019)
22. Durkota, K., Lisẏ, V., Kiekintveld, C., Bošanskẏ, B., Pěchouček, M.: Case studies of network defense with attack graph games. Intell. Syst. **31**(5), 24–30 (2016)
23. Elsken, T., Metzen, J.H., Hutter, F.: Neural architecture search: a survey. J. Mach. Learn. Res. **20** (2019)
24. Erdős, P., Rényi, A.: On Random Graphs. Publicationes Mathematicae Debrecen, vol. 6 (1959)
25. Fang, F., et al.: PAWS-a deployed game-theoretic application to combat poaching. AI Mag. **38**(1), 23–36 (2017)
26. Feldman, M., Naor, J., Schwartz, R.: A unified continuous greedy algorithm for submodular maximization. In: Annual Symposium on Foundations of Computer Science (2011)
27. Garg, N., Grosu, D.: Deception in honeynets: a game-theoretic analysis. In: Information Assurance and Security Workshop (2007)
28. Gurobi Optimization, LLC: Gurobi optimizer reference manual (2020)
29. Horák, K., Zhu, Q., Bošanskẏ, B.: Manipulating adversary's belief: a dynamic game approach to deception by design for proactive network security. In: Conference on Decision and Game Theory for Security (2017)
30. IBM Security: Cost of a data breach report 2019 (2019). https://ibm.co/2CPsVnV
31. Ingols, K., Lippmann, R., Piwowarski, K.: Practical attack graph generation for network defense. In: Annual Computer Security Applications Conference (2006)
32. Instructables: how to make your bike look an ugly discouragement for thieves (2015). https://rb.gy/kb384b
33. Jain, M., Korzhyk, D., Vaněk, O., Conitzer, V., Pěchouček, M., Tambe, M.: A double oracle algorithm for zero-sum security games on graphs. In: International Conference on Autonomous Agents and Multiagent Systems (2011)

34. Jajodia, S., Ghosh, A.K., Swarup, V., Wang, C., Wang, X.S.: Moving Target Defense: Creating Asymmetric Uncertainty for Cyber Threats, vol. 54. Springer Science & Business Media (2011)
35. Jajodia, S., Noel, S., O'berry, B.: Topological analysis of network attack vulnerability. In: Managing Cyber Threats (2005)
36. Kingma, D.P., Ba, J.: Adam: a method for stochastic optimization. arXiv preprint arXiv:1412.6980 (2014)
37. Kreibich, C., Crowcroft, J.: Honeycomb: creating intrusion detection signatures using honeypots. Comput. Commun. Rev. **34**(1), 51–56 (2004)
38. Kuipers, D., Fabro, M.: Control systems cyber security: defense in depth strategies. Technical report, Idaho Nat. Labo. (2006)
39. Liu, Y., Man, H.: Network vulnerability assessment using Bayesian networks. In: Data Mining, Intrusion Detection, Information Assurance, and Data Networks Security (2005)
40. McKelvey, R.D., Palfrey, T.R.: Quantal response equilibria for normal form games. Games Econ. Behav. **10**(1), 6–38 (1995)
41. Mee, P., Schuermann, T.: How a cyber attack could cause the next financial crisis (2018). https://bit.ly/3f2lOFP
42. Mezura-Montes, E., Velázquez-Reyes, J., Coello Coello, C.A.: A comparative study of differential evolution variants for global optimization. In: Annual Conference on Genetic and Evolutionary Computation (2006)
43. Miah, M.S., Gutierrez, M., Veliz, O., Thakoor, O., Kiekintveld, C.: Concealing cyber-decoys using two-sided feature deception games. In: International Conference on System Sciences (2020)
44. Nguyen, T.H., Wright, M., Wellman, M.P., Baveja, S.: Multi-stage attack graph security games: Heuristic strategies, with empirical game-theoretic analysis. Secur. Commun. Netw. (2018)
45. Noel, S., Jajodia, S.: Managing attack graph complexity through visual hierarchical aggregation. In: Workshop on Visualization and Data Mining for Computer Security (2004)
46. Noel, S., Jajodia, S., O'Berry, B., Jacobs, M.: Efficient minimum-cost network hardening via exploit dependency graphs. In: Computer Security Applications Conference (2003)
47. Paszke, A., et al.: Pytorch: an imperative style, high-performance deep learning library. In: Advances in Neural Information Processing Systems (2019)
48. Pawlick, J., Colbert, E., Zhu, Q.: A game-theoretic taxonomy and survey of defensive deception for cybersecurity and privacy. Comput. Surv. **52**(4), 1–28 (2019)
49. Phillips, C., Swiler, L.P.: A graph-based system for network-vulnerability analysis. In: Workshop on New Security Paradigms (1998)
50. Pita, J., Jain, M., Ordónez, F., Portway, C., Tambe, M., Western, C., et al.: Armor security for Los Angeles International Airport. In: AAAI Conference on AI (2008)
51. Polad, H., Puzis, R., Shapira, B.: Attack graph obfuscation. In: Dolev, S., Lodha, S. (eds.) CSCML 2017. LNCS, vol. 10332, pp. 269–287. Springer, Cham (2017). https://doi.org/10.1007/978-3-319-60080-2_20
52. Schlenker, A., et al.: Deceiving cyber adversaries: a game theoretic approach. In: International Conference on Autonomous Agents and Multiagent Systems (2018)
53. Schneier, B.: Attack trees. Dr. Dobb's J. **24**, 12 (1999)
54. Shen, W., Tang, P., Zuo, S.: Automated mechanism design via neural networks. In: International Conference on Autonomous Agents and Multiagent Systems (2019)
55. Sheyner, O., Haines, J., Jha, S., Lippmann, R., Wing, J.M.: Automated generation and analysis of attack graphs. In: IEEE Symposium on Security and Privacy (2002)

56. Shi, Z.R., et al.: Learning and planning in feature deception games. arXiv preprint arXiv:1905.04833 (2019)
57. Shi, Z.R., Tang, Z., Tran-Thanh, L., Singh, R., Fang, F.: Designing the game to play: optimizing payoff structure in security games. In: International Joint Conference on Artificial Intelligence (2018)
58. Shieh, E., et al.: Protect: a deployed game theoretic system to protect the ports of the United States. In: International Conference on Autonomous Agents and Multiagent Systems (2012)
59. Shieh, E., et al.: Protect in the ports of Boston, New York and beyond: experiences in deploying Stackelberg security games with quantal response. In: Handbook Computational Approaches to Counterterrorism (2013)
60. Stallings, W., Brown, L., Bauer, M.D., Bhattacharjee, A.K.: Computer Security: Principles and Practice (2012)
61. Storn, R., Price, K.: Differential evolution-a simple and efficient heuristic for global optimization over continuous spaces. J. Global Optim. **11**(4), 341–359 (1997)
62. Tambe, M.: Security and Game Theory: Algorithms, Deployed Systems. Lessons Learned. Cambridge University Press, Cambridge (2011)
63. Thakoor, O., Tambe, M., Vayanos, P., Xu, H., Kiekintveld, C., Fang, F.: Cyber camouflage games for strategic deception. In: Alpcan, T., Vorobeychik, Y., Baras, J.S., Dán, G. (eds.) GameSec 2019. LNCS, vol. 11836, pp. 525–541. Springer, Cham (2019). https://doi.org/10.1007/978-3-030-32430-8_31
64. Virtanen, P., et al.: Scipy 1.0: fundamental algorithms for scientific computing in python. Nat. Methods **17**(3), 261–272 (2020)
65. Wright, M., Wang, Y., Wellman, M.P.: Iterated deep reinforcement learning in games: history-aware training for improved stability. In: ACM Conference on Economics and Computation (2019)
66. Zhuang, J., Bier, V.M.: Reasons for secrecy and deception in homeland-security resource allocation. Risk Anal. Int. J. **30**(12), 1737–1743 (2010)

Decoy Allocation Games on Graphs with Temporal Logic Objectives

Abhishek N. Kulkarni[1]([✉]) [iD], Jie Fu[1] [iD], Huan Luo[1] [iD], Charles A. Kamhoua[2] [iD], and Nandi O. Leslie[2] [iD]

[1] Worceter Polytechnic Institute, Worcester, MA 01609, USA
{ankulkarni,jfu2}@wpi.edu, hluo12@126.com
[2] U.S. Army Research Laboratory, Adelphi, MD 20783, USA
{charles.a.kamhoua.civ,nandi.o.leslie.ctr}@mail.mil

Abstract. We study a class of games, in which the adversary (attacker) is to satisfy a complex mission specified in linear temporal logic, and the defender is to prevent the adversary from achieving its goal. A deceptive defender can allocate decoys, in addition to defense actions, to create disinformation for the attacker. Thus, we focus on the problem of jointly synthesizing a decoy placement strategy and a deceptive defense strategy that maximally exploits the incomplete information the attacker about the decoy locations. We introduce a model of hypergames on graphs with temporal logic objectives to capture such adversarial interactions with asymmetric information. Using the hypergame model, we analyze the effectiveness of a given decoy placement, quantified by the set of deceptive winning states where the defender can prevent the attacker from satisfying the attack objective given its incomplete information about decoy locations. Then, we investigate how to place decoys to maximize the defender's deceptive winning region. Considering the large search space for all possible decoy allocation strategies, we incorporate the idea of compositional synthesis from formal methods and show that the objective function in the class of decoy allocation problem is monotone and non-decreasing. We derive the sufficient conditions under which the objective function for the decoy allocation problem is submodular, or supermodular, respectively. We show a sub-optimal allocation can be efficiently computed by iteratively composing the solutions of hypergames with a subset of decoys and the solution of a hypergame given a single decoy. We use a running example to illustrate the proposed method.

Keywords: Games on graphs · Hypergames · Deception · Temporal logic

1 Introduction

In security and defense applications, deception plays a key role to mitigate the information and strategic disadvantages of the defender against adversaries. In this paper, we investigate the design of active defense with deception for a class

© Springer Nature Switzerland AG 2020
Q. Zhu et al. (Eds.): GameSec 2020, LNCS 12513, pp. 168–187, 2020.
https://doi.org/10.1007/978-3-030-64793-3_9

of games on graphs, also known as ω-regular games [7,8,11]. A game in this class captures the attack-defend sequential interaction in which the attacker is to complete an attack mission specified in temporal logic [19] and the defender is to mitigate attacks by selecting counter-actions and allocating decoys to create a disinformation to the attacker. We are interested in the following question: How to design the decoy allocation strategy so that the defender can influence the attacker into taking (or not taking) certain actions that minimize the set of attacker's winning region? The winning region is defined as the set of game states from which the attacker has a strategy to successfully complete its attack mission irrespective of the defender's counter-strategy.

Games on graphs with temporal logic objectives have been studied extensively in the synthesis of reactive programs [7]. In a reactive program, the system (player 1) is to synthesize a program (a finite-memory strategy) to provably satisfy a desired behavior specification, no matter which actions are taken by the uncontrollable environment (player 2). In these games, players' payoffs are temporal goals and constraints, described using linear temporal logic formulas and a labeling function. A player receives a payoff equal to one if the *labeling* over the outcome (state-sequence) of the game satisfies its temporal logic formula. In our recent work [17], we have shown that a class of decoy-based deception can be captured by assuming that the defender has the true labels of game states but the attacker has incorrect labels. For example, a state labeled "unsafe" by the defender may be mislabeled as "safe" for the attacker. By modeling the interactions between the defender and the attacker as a hypergame, we developed the solutions of subjective rationalizable strategies for both players in this class of hypergames. The defender's subjective rationalizable strategy is by nature deceptive, as it ensures the security temporal logic specification to be satisfied by exploiting the attacker's misperception and mistakes in the attacker's subjective rationalizable strategy. We introduced deceptive winning region as the set of states (or finite game histories) from which the defender can ensure to satisfy a security specification in this hypergame.

However, an important problem remains: How to *control the attacker's misinformation in the labeling function* so as to maximize the deceptive winning region? To restrict the freedom in crafting the disinformation, we formulate a class of *decoy-based deception game*: In this game, the defender can allocate a subset of states as hidden decoys or "traps", unknown to the attacker. During these interactions, the defender is to strategically select actions to lure the attacker into the traps, whereas the attacker plays rationally to satisfy her temporal logic objective given her subjective view of the interaction. In addition, the defender strategy should be *stealthy*, in the sense that the attacker cannot realize a misperception exists before getting caught by one of the traps. To determine the decoy allocation, we employ the aforementioned solutions of hypergames [17] to calculate the defender's deceptive sure-winning region given each individual decoys. The selection of decoy locations is based on compositional synthesis [10,18], which answers, given the two deceptive sure-winning regions for decoys allocated at two different states s and s', what is the deceptive sure-winning region when both states are allocated as decoys simultaneously? We derive the sufficient conditions when the objective function for the decoy allocation problem is submodular, or supermodular, respectively. Based on this, we can construct an under-approximation of the deceptive sure-winning regions incrementally (in polynomial time), instead of having to solve a combinatorially large number of hypergames for all possible decoy configurations.

Related Work. Decoy allocation, also called honeypot allocation and camouflage, has been studied in recent years with applications to cyber- and physical security problems. In [16,22], the authors propose a game-theoretic method to place honeypots in a network so as to maximize the probability that the attacker attacks a honeypot and not a real system. In their game formulation, the defender decides where to insert honeypots in a network, and the attacker chooses one server to attack and receives different payoffs when attacking a real system (positive reward) or a honeypot (zero reward). The game is imperfect information as the real systems and honeypots are indistinguishable for the attacker. By the solution of imperfect information games, the defender's honeypot placement strategy is solved to minimize the attacker's rewards.

Security games [15,24] are another class of important models for resource allocation in adversarial environments. In [25], the authors formulate a security game (Stackelberg game) to allocate limited decoy resources in a cybernetwork to mask network configurations from the attacker. This class of deception manipulates the adversary's perception of the payoffs and thus causes the adversary to take (or not to take) certain actions that aid the objective of the defender. In [9], the authors formulate an Markov decision process to assess the effectiveness of a fixed honeypot allocation in an attack graph, which captures multi-stage lateral movement attacks in a cybernetwork and dependencies between vulnerabilities [13,21]. In [2], the authors analyze the honeypot allocation problem for attack graphs using normal-form games, where the defender allocates honeypots that changes the payoffs matrix of players. The optimal allocation strategy is determined using the minimax theorem. The attack graph is closely related to our game on graph model, which generalizes the attack graph to *attack-defend game graphs* [3,14] by incorporating the defender counter-actions in active defense.

There are several key distinctions between our work and the prior work. First, our work focuses on a qualitative approach to decoy allocation instead of a quantitative one, which often requires solving an optimization problem over a well-defined reward/cost function. In the qualitative approach, we represent the attacker's goal using a linear temporal logic formula, which captures rich, qualitative behavioral objectives such as reachability, safety, recurrence, persistence or a combination of these. Second, we show how to incorporate the attacker's misinformation about decoy locations into a ω-regular hypergame model by representing it as labeling misperception. Hypergames [6,23,27] are a class of games with asymmetric (one-sided incomplete) information in which different players might play according to different perceptual games that capture the information and higher-order information known to that player. While the underlying idea behind our game model is similar to "indistinguishable honeypots" discussed in [22], we are able to leverage the solution approaches for hypergames to address decoy allocation problem. Third, we solve for a stealthy strategy for the defender, which ensures that defender's actions will not inform the attacker that deceptive tactics are being used. Lastly, we borrow the idea of compositional reasoning from formal methods to find approximately optimal solutions for the decoy allocation problem for this class of hypergames.

The paper is structured as follows. In Sect. 2, we discuss the preliminaries of attack-defend game on graph model and define the problem statement. In Sect. 3, we present the main results of this paper including an algorithm for the decoy allocation based on the ideas of deceptive synthesis and compositional synthesis. We employ a running example to provide intuition and illustrate the correctness as well as (near-)optimality of the proposed algorithm. Section 4 concludes the paper and discusses the future directions.

2   Problem Formulation

2.1   Attack-Defend Games on Graph

In a zero-sum two-player *game on graph*, player 1 (P1, pronoun 'he') plays against player 2 (P2, pronoun 'she') to satisfy a given temporal logic formula. Formally, a game on graph consists of a tuple $\mathcal{G} = \langle G, \varphi \rangle$, where G is a *game arena* modeling the dynamics of the interaction between P1 and P2, and φ is the temporal logic specification of P1. As the game is zero-sum, the temporal logic specification of P2 is $\neg\varphi$, that is, the negation of P1's specification.

Definition 1 (Game Arena). *A two-player turn-based, deterministic game arena between P1 and P2 is a tuple*

$$G = \langle S, Act, T, AP, L \rangle,$$

where

- $S = S_1 \cup S_2$ *is a finite set of states partitioned into two sets S_1 and S_2. At a state in S_1, P1 chooses an action. At a state in S_2, P2 selects an action;*
- $Act = Act_1 \cup Act_2$ *is the set of actions. Act_1 (resp., Act_2) is the set of actions for P1 (resp., P2);*
- $T : (S_1 \times Act_1) \cup (S_2 \times Act_2) \to S$ *is a deterministic transition function that maps a state-action pair to a next state;*
- AP *is a set of atomic propositions;*
- $L : S \to 2^{AP}$ *is the labeling function that maps each state $s \in S$ to a set $L(s) \subseteq AP$ of atomic propositions that evaluate to true at that state.*

A *run* in G is a (finite/infinite) ordered sequence of states $\rho = (s_0, s_1, \ldots)$ such that for any $i > 0$, $s_i = T(s_{i-1}, a)$ for some $a \in Act$. Given the labeling function L, every run ρ in G can be mapped to a word over an alphabet $\Sigma = 2^{AP}$ as $w = L(\rho) = L(s_0)L(s_1)\ldots$.

In this paper, we use Linear Temporal Logic (LTL) [19] to define the objectives of P1 and P2. Formally, an LTL formula is defined as

$$\varphi ::= p \mid \neg\varphi \mid \varphi \wedge \varphi \mid \varphi \vee \varphi \mid \bigcirc\varphi \mid \varphi\,\mathsf{U}\,\varphi \mid \varphi\,\mathsf{W}\,\varphi$$

where $p \in AP$ is an atomic proposition, $\neg$ (negation), $\wedge$ (and), and $\vee$ (or) are Boolean operators, and $\bigcirc$ (next), U (strong until) and W (weak until) are temporal operators. Formula $\bigcirc\varphi$ means that the formula φ will be true in the next state. Formula $\varphi_1\mathsf{U}\,\varphi_2$ means that φ_2 will be true in some future time step, and before that φ_1 holds true for every time step. Formula $\varphi_1\mathsf{W}\,\varphi_2$ means that φ_1 holds true until φ_2 is true, but does not require that φ_2 becomes true. We define two additional temporal operators: $\lozenge$ (eventually) and $\square$ (always) as follows: $\lozenge\,\varphi = \mathsf{T}\,\mathsf{U}\,\varphi$ and $\square\,\varphi = \neg\lozenge\,\neg\varphi$.

Given a word $w \in \Sigma^\omega$, let $w[i]$ be the i-th element in the word and $w[i\ldots]$ be the subsequence of w starting from the i-th element. For example, for a word $w = abc$, $w[0] = a$ and $w[1\ldots] = bc$. We write $w \models \varphi$ if the word w satisfies the temporal logic formula φ. The semantics of LTL are defined as follows.

- $w \models p$ if $p \in w[0]$;
- $w \models \neg\varphi$ if $w \not\models \varphi$;
- $w \models \varphi_1 \wedge \varphi_2$ if $w \models \varphi_1$ and $w \models \varphi_2$;
- $w \models \bigcirc\varphi$ if $w[1\ldots] \models \varphi$;
- $w \models \varphi\mathsf{U}\,\psi$ if $\exists i \geq 0$, $w[i\ldots] \models \psi$ and $\forall 0 \leq j < i$, $w[j\ldots] \models \varphi$.
- $w \models \varphi\mathsf{W}\,\psi$ if either $w \models \varphi\mathsf{U}\,\psi$ or $\forall 0 \leq j$, $w[j\ldots] \models \varphi$.

A subclass of LTL formula, called syntactically cosafe LTL (scLTL), does not include the weak until operator W and allows the negation operator $\neg$ to only occur before an atomic proposition. An scLTL formula can be equivalently represented by a finite-state deterministic automaton with regular acceptance conditions, defined as follows.

Definition 2 (Specification DFA). *Given an scLTL formula φ, its corresponding specification Deterministic Finite Automaton (DFA) is a tuple*

$$\mathcal{A} = \langle Q, \Sigma, \delta, \iota, Q_F \rangle,$$

which includes a finite set Q of states, a finite set $\Sigma = 2^{AP}$ of symbols, a deterministic transition function $\delta : Q \times \Sigma \rightarrow Q$, a unique initial state $\iota \in Q$, and a set $Q_F \subseteq Q$ of final states.

The transition function is recursively extended as $\delta(q, aw) = \delta(\delta(q, a), w)$ for given $a \in \Sigma$ and $w \in \Sigma^*$, where Σ^* is the set of all finite words (also known as the Kleene closure of Σ). A word w is *accepted* by the DFA if and only if $\delta(q, u) \in Q_F$ and u is a prefix of w, i.e., $w = uv$ for $u \in \Sigma^*$ and $v \in \Sigma^\omega$, where Σ^ω is the set of all infinite words defined over Σ. A word is accepted by the specification DFA $\mathcal{A}$ if and only if it satisfies the LTL formula φ.

Putting together the game arena G and the scLTL objective φ of P1, we can formally define a graphical model for the zero-sum game $\mathcal{G}$.

Definition 3 (Product game). *Let $G = \langle S, Act, T, AP, L \rangle$ be a game arena and let $\mathcal{A} = \langle Q, \Sigma, \delta, \iota, Q_F \rangle$ be the specification DFA given the LTL formula φ. Then, the product game $\mathcal{G} = G \otimes \mathcal{A}$ is the tuple,*

$$\mathcal{G} = \langle S \times Q, Act, \Delta, F \rangle,$$

where

- *$S \times Q$ is a set of states partitioned into P1's states $S_1 \times Q$ and P2's states $S_2 \times Q$.*
- *$\Delta : (S_1 \times Q \times Act_1) \cup (S_2 \times Q \times Act_2) \to S \times Q$ is a deterministic transition function that maps a game state $(s, q) \in S \times Q$ and an action $a \in Act$ to a next state $(s', q') \in S \times Q$ such that $s' = T(s, a)$ and $q' = \delta(q, L(s'))$;*
- *$F = S \times Q_F$ is the set of final states in $\mathcal{G}$.*

It is noted that we did not include an initial state in the definition of the game arena. This is because any state in S can be selected to be the initial state. Let $s_0 \in S$ be the initial state of the game arena, the corresponding initial state in the product game is $q_0 = \delta(\iota, L(s_0))$. By construction, for each run $\rho = (s_0, s_1, \dots)$ in G, there is a unique run $\hat{\rho} = (s_0, q_0), (s_1, q_1), \dots$ in the product game, where $q_0 = \delta(\iota, L(s_0))$ for $i = 0$ and $q_i = \delta(q_{i-1}, L(s_i))$ for $i \geq 1$. The run ρ satisfies the scLTL formula φ if and only if $L(\rho) \models \varphi$ and as a result of construction, there exists $(s_i, q_i) \in \hat{\rho}$ for some $i \geq 0$ such that $(s_i, q_i) \in F$. Thus, P1's objective of satisfying an scLTL specification over the game arena G is reduced to that of reaching one of the final states F in product game $\mathcal{G}$. In the zero-sum game, P2's objective of satisfying $\neg\varphi$ is reduced to preventing P1 from reaching any final states in F.

A memoryless, randomized *strategy* for i-th player, for $i \in \{1, 2\}$, is a function $\pi_i : S_i \times Q \to \mathcal{D}(Act_i)$, where $\mathcal{D}(Act_i)$ is the set of discrete probability distributions over Act_i. It is noted that a memoryless strategy in a product game is a finite-memory strategy in game arena. A strategy is deterministic if $\pi_i(\rho)$ is a Dirac delta function. We say that player i commits to (or follows) a strategy π_i if and only if for a given state (s, q), if $\pi_i(s, q)$ is defined, then an action is sampled from the distribution $\pi_i(s, q)$, otherwise, player i selects an action at random. Let Π_i be the set of memoryless strategies of player i in the product game.

A strategy $\pi_1 \in \Pi_1$ is said to be sure-winning for P1 if, for every P2's strategy $\pi_2 \in \Pi_2$, P1 can ensure to reach F in finitely many steps. A strategy $\pi_2 \in \Pi_2$ is sure-winning for P2 if for every P1's strategy $\pi_1 \in \Pi_1$, P2 can ensure the game to stay in $(S \times Q) \setminus F$ for infinitely many steps. The product game is known to be determined [11, 20]. That is, at any state (s, q), only one of the players has a winning strategy and the winning strategy is memoryless.

The set of states in the product game $\mathcal{G}$ from which P1 (resp. P2) has a sure-winning strategy are called the *sure-winning region* for P1 (resp. P2), denoted as Win_1 (resp. Win_2). Players' sure-winning regions can be computed by using the Algorithm 1 by letting $S_i \times Q$ to be V_i, Act_i to be A_i, the transition function

---

Algorithm 1: SURE-WIN: Compute Player's Sure-Winning Regions of Zero-Sum Product Games with Reachability Objective [11, 20].

Input: A reachability game $\langle V = V_1 \cup V_2, A_1 \cup A_2, \Delta, F \rangle$ where V_i are states
     where player i takes an action, A_i are player i's actions,
     $\Delta : V \times A \to V$ and P1's goal is to reach the set F and P2's goal is to
     stay within $V \setminus F$.

Output: The winning regions Win_1 and Win_2 for P1 and P2.

$Z_0 \leftarrow F$, $Z_1 \leftarrow \emptyset$, $k \leftarrow 0$;

while $Z_{k+1} \neq Z_k$ **do**
    | $\mathsf{Pre}_1(Z_k) \leftarrow \{v \in V_1 \mid \exists a \in A_1 \text{ s.t. } \Delta(v, a) \in Z_k\}$;
    | $\mathsf{Pre}_2(Z_k) \leftarrow \{v \in V_2 \mid \forall b \in A_2 \text{ s.t. } \Delta(v, b) \in Z_k\}$;
    | $Z_{k+1} \leftarrow Z_k \cup \mathsf{Pre}_1(Z_k) \cup \mathsf{Pre}_2(Z_k)$;
    | $k \leftarrow k + 1$;

end

$\mathsf{Win}_1 \leftarrow Z_k$, $\mathsf{Win}_2 \leftarrow (V_1 \cup V_2) \setminus \mathsf{Win}_1$;

return $\mathsf{Win}_1, \mathsf{Win}_2$.

Δ and F are the same components in $\mathcal{G}$. The interested readers are referred to Chap 2 of [11] for more details.

The sure-winning strategy is defined for P1 as follows: Let $Z_1, Z_2, \ldots Z_k$ be the sequence of sets generated by Algorithm 1, for a state $v \in (Z_i \setminus Z_{i-1}) \cap V_1$, let a be the action that $\Delta(v, a) \in Z_{i-1}$, then $\pi_1(v) = a$ (by construction, such an action a exists). P2's sure-winning strategy is constructed as: For each $v \in \mathsf{Win}_2$, $\pi_2(v) = a$ such that $\Delta(v, a) \in \mathsf{Win}_2$. Clearly, there may exist more than one sure-winning strategies for each player.

2.2 Formulating the Decoy Allocation Problem

We consider an interaction between the defender (P1, pronoun 'he') and the attacker (P2, pronoun 'she') in which the defender can use decoys to introduce incorrect information to the attacker about the game. Our goal is to investigate *how to create the attacker's misinformation by allocating the decoys so as to minimize the size of the sure-winning region of the attacker.*

We now formalize the problem of decoy allocation using the game arena (Definition 1). Let **decoy** be an atomic proposition that evaluates to true at a state if the state is equipped with a decoy.

Assumption 1. *In P2's knowledge of the game arena, no state is labeled as decoy, i.e.,* **decoy** $\notin L(s)$ *for all* $s \in S$.

Assumption 1 captures one important function of decoys—*concealing fictions* [12]. The idea behind *concealing fictions* is that P1 simulates the decoy states to function like a real system. As a result, P1 and P2 play with different subjective views of their interaction. With this in mind, we formalize the notion of *perceptual game arena* of the players to characterize these subjective views.

Perceptual Game Arena. Given that P2 does not know about the decoys, we distinguish between her view of the game arena from P1's view by introducing a different labeling function for P2. Let P1's perceptual game arena be $G^1 = G = \langle S, Act, T, AP, L \rangle$. That is, P1 knows the ground truth. And, let P2's perceptual game arena be $G^2 = \langle S, Act, T, AP, L^2 \rangle$ such that for any $s \in S$, we have $L_2(s) = L(s) \setminus \{\text{decoy}\}$. In other words, if a state is not a decoy, then P1 and P2 share the same label for that state. If it is a decoy, then P1 knows that the proposition decoy evaluates to true at that state, but P2 does not.

The Attacker and Defender Temporal Logic Objectives. Over the perceptual game arenas G and G^2, P1 and P2 aim to satisfy their LTL objectives. We consider that P2's objective is specified by an scLTL formula φ_2, whose specification DFA is $\mathcal{A}_2 = \langle Q, \Sigma, \delta_2, \iota, Q_F \rangle$.

Given P2's perceptual game arena G^2 and the specification DFA $\mathcal{A}_2$, we can construct a perceptual product game of P2 as $\mathcal{G}_2 = G^2 \otimes \mathcal{A}_2$. P1's objective is an LTL formula $\neg \varphi_2 \mathsf{W}\, \text{decoy}$. That is, P1 satisfies the goal by preventing P2 from satisfying φ_2 before reaching a decoy. However, reaching a decoy is not necessary due to the semantics of the "weak until" operator.

Example 2 (Part 1). Consider a game arena as shown in Fig. 1a consisting of 15 states. At a circle state, P1 takes an action, and at a square state, P2 takes an action. As the actions are deterministic, we use edges to indicate players' actions. For example, $(c, f), (c, g), (c, h)$ are possible actions for P2 at the state c. Over this game arena, P2 wants to satisfy an scLTL specification $\varphi_2 = \Diamond (n \vee o) \wedge (f \implies \Diamond n) \wedge (g \implies \Diamond o)$, which, in words, means that P2 must reach either the state n or o with the condition that whenever she visits the state f, she must visit n and whenever she visits g, she must visit o. If she does not visit either f or g, then she can visit either n or o to successfully complete her objective. The DFA equivalent to φ_2 is shown in Fig. 2a.

Suppose that P1 allocates the states $D = \{h, k\}$ as decoys. The perceptual game arenas of P1 and P2 under decoy allocation D are now different. P1's perceptual game arena in Fig. 1b has the same underlying graph as the perceptual game arena of P2 shown in Fig. 1a but P1 has the knowledge of where the decoys are placed. We have decoy $\in L(h)$ and decoy $\in L(k)$ but decoy $\notin L(s)$ for any state s except $s = h, k$. Figure 2b shows the perceptual product games of P2. A transition $(c, 0) \to (f, 1)$ is based on the transition $c \to f$ and $\delta_2(0, L(f)) = 1$ in the DFA $\mathcal{A}_2$ (shown in Fig. 2a). We omit all nodes that do not have a path leading to $(n, 3)$ or $(o, 3)$.

We now formalize our problem statement.

Problem 1. Given a set of k decoys and a set $\mathcal{D} \subseteq S$ of states at which decoys can be placed, identify the decoy locations $D \subseteq \mathcal{D}$ with $|D| \leq k$ such that by letting decoy $\in L(s)$ for each $s \in D$, the number of states in the product game $\mathcal{G}_1$ from which P1 has a strategy to satisfy the security specification φ_1 is maximized, given that P2 may choose any counter-strategy that she considers rational in her perceptual game, $\mathcal{G}_2$.

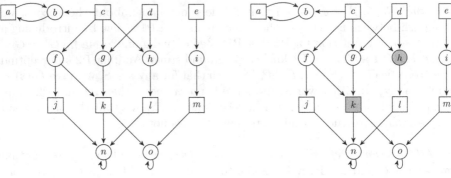

(a) Perceptual Game Arena of P2   (b) Perceptual Game Arena of P2
                                              (Ground-Truth)

Fig. 1. Perceptual Game Arenas of P1 and P2 in Example 2.

The objective of P1 is intuitively understood as to maximize the set of system states protected by the defense strategy.

3   Main Result

Our proposed solution to Problem 1 is based upon two key ideas from formal methods and hypergame theory, namely (a) deceptive synthesis, and (b) compositional synthesis. In Sect. 3.1, we introduce deceptive synthesis to construct a strategy for P1 to deceive P2 into reaching a pre-defined decoy set in finitely many steps by exploiting the incomplete information of P2. The strategy is called *deceptive sure-winning strategy* and depends on the chosen set of decoys. Then, in Sect. 3.2, we introduce a compositional synthesis approach to identify an approximately optimal allocation of decoys.

3.1   Deceptive Synthesis: Hypergames on Graphs

Consider a set $D \subseteq S$ of states are allocated with decoys, unknown to P2. In such an interaction, as seen in Sect. 2.2, the players have different perceptual game arenas that share the same set of states, actions, and transitions but different labeling functions. We introduce a model of hypergame on graph to integrate the games $\mathcal{G}_1$ of P1 and $\mathcal{G}_2$ of P2 into a single graphical model.

Definition 4 (Hypergame on Graph (modified from [17][1]). *Given the perceptual game arenas* $G = \langle S, Act, T, AP, L \rangle$ *and* $G^2 = \langle S, Act, T, AP, L^2 \rangle$, *and P2's specification DFA* $\mathcal{A}_2 = \langle Q, 2^{AP}, \delta_2, \iota, Q_F \rangle$, *let* $D \subsetneq S$ *be a set of states*

---

[1] Definition 4 is a simplified version of [17, Def. 6], which considers the general case when P1 and P2's objectives are both general scLTL formulas, not necessarily in the current form.

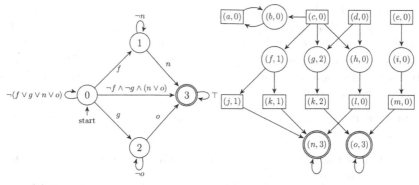

(a) Specification DFA for φ_2 (b) Perceptual Product Game of P2

Fig. 2. P2's specification DFA and the perceptual product game in Example 2.

such that $\mathsf{decoy} \in L(s)$. The hypergame on graph given the players' objectives $\neg\varphi_2 \mathsf{W}\,\mathsf{decoy}$ for P1 and φ_2 for P2 is a transition system

$$\mathcal{H}_D = \langle S \times Q, Act, \Delta, F_D, F_2 \rangle,$$

where

- $S \times Q$ is the set of states;
- $\Delta : (S_1 \times Q \times Act_1) \cup (S_2 \times Q \times Act_2) \to S \times Q$ is a deterministic transition function such that $\Delta((s,q),a) = (s',q')$ if and only if $s' = T(s,a)$ and $q' = \delta_2(q, L_2(s'))$;
- $F_D = \{(s,q) \mid \mathsf{decoy} \in L(s)\}$ is the set of states which P1 must reach in order to satisfy $\neg\varphi_2 \mathsf{W}\,\mathsf{decoy}$;
- $F_2 = \{(s,q) \mid q \in Q_F\}$ is the set of final states which P2 must reach in order to satisfy φ_2.

It is noted that the sets of states, actions, transitions, and P2's final states F_2 in $\mathcal{H}_D$ are defined exactly as these components in P2's perceptual product game $\mathcal{G}_2$ (see Definition 3). The additional set F_D is introduced to represent P1's objective.

Let us denote the sure-winning region of player i in player j's perceptual game $\mathcal{G}_j$ by Win_i^j. The attacker's perceptual winning regions can be solved with the attacker's reachability game using Algorithm 1 by letting $V_1 := S_2 \times Q, V_2 := S_1 \times Q, A_1 := Act_2, A_2 := Act_1, \Delta$ is the same as in $\mathcal{H}_D$, and $F := F_2$. The following observations are noted:

- For every state $(s,q) \in \mathsf{Win}_1^2$ (P1's sure-winning region perceived by P2), P1 can ensure to satisfy $\neg\varphi_2$ no matter which strategy P2 uses. Decoys are not needed for states within Win_1^2.
- For every state $(s,q) \in \mathsf{Win}_2^2$ (P2's sure-winning region perceived by P2), P2 can ensure satisfying φ_2 when no decoy is used. However, when decoys are introduced, P1 can exploit P2's lack of knowledge about the decoys and lure P2 into reaching decoys before P2 is able to satisfy φ_2.

It is known [5] that we can rewrite $\neg\varphi_2 W\,\mathtt{decoy}$ using the temporal operators: U (until) and $\Box$ (always), as $(\neg\varphi_2 U\,\mathtt{decoy}) \vee \Box\neg\varphi_2$, where $\Box\varphi = \neg\Diamond\neg\varphi$. When the game state is within P2's perceptual winning region Win_2^2, then P1 does not have a strategy to ensure $\Box\neg\varphi_2$ (reads "always φ_2 is false") and can only satisfy his specification by enforcing P2 to visit a decoy. The following Lemma formalizes this statement.

Lemma 1. *For any state* $(s, q) \in \mathsf{Win}_2^2$, *any strategy* π_1 *of P1 that satisfies* $\neg\varphi_2 W\,\mathtt{decoy}$ *also satisfies* $\neg\varphi_2 U\,\mathtt{decoy}$.

We omit the proof noting that it follows from the definition of weak until and the property of winning region.

Thus, when we focus our attention on the region Win_2^2, P1's objective is equivalently $\neg\varphi_2 U\,\mathtt{decoy}$. Before addressing the decoy allocation problem, we must answer: From which states in Win_2^2, P1 can ensure to satisfy $\neg\varphi_2 U\,\mathtt{decoy}$ by exploiting P2's lack of knowledge about the decoy states, *i.e.*, F_D?

To answer this question, we formulate a deceptive game for P1. We first restrict P1's actions to those considered rational for P2 in her perceptual game. At the same time, P2's irrational actions are removed as P1 knows a rational P2 will not use these actions. As the rational actions are based on P2's subjective view of the game, we formalize this notion of rationality using the concept of *subjective rationalizability* from game theory (we refer the interested readers to [17] for rigorous treatment).

Definition 5. (Subjectively Rationalizable Actions in $\mathcal{G}_2$). *Given P2's perceptual product game* $\mathcal{G}_2 = \langle S \times Q, Act, \Delta, F_2 \rangle$, *a player* i*'s action* $a \in Act_i$ *is said to be* subjectively rationalizable *at his/her winning state* $(s, q) \in \mathsf{Win}_i^2$ *in* $\mathcal{G}_2$ *if and only if* $\Delta((s, q), a) \in \mathsf{Win}_i^2$. *At player* i*'s losing state* $(s, q) \notin \mathsf{Win}_i^2$, *any action of player* i *is assumed to be subjectively rationalizable for player* i.

Based on Definition 5, we define the set of subjectively rationalizable actions of player i at a state $(s, q) \in S \times Q$ as follows:

$$\mathsf{SRActs}_i^2(s, q) = \{a \in Act_i \mid (s, q) \in \mathsf{Win}_i^2 \text{ and } \Delta((s, q), a) \in \mathsf{Win}_i^2\} \cup$$
$$\{a \in Act_i \mid (s, q) \notin \mathsf{Win}_i^2 \text{ and } \Delta((s, q), a) \text{ is defined}\} \quad (1)$$

Assumption 2. *Subjective rationalizability is a common knowledge between P1 and P2.*

Assumption 2 means that both players know that their opponent is subjectively rational and that the opponent is aware of this fact. Thus, P2 would become aware of her misperception in the game arena, when P1 uses an action which is not subjectively rationalizable in P2's perceptual game, $\mathcal{G}_2$. We can refine the hypergame on graph $\mathcal{H}_D$ to eliminate: 1) states that do not require decoys: This is the set Win_1^2 from which P1 has a sure-winning strategy for $\neg\varphi_2$; 2) actions that contradict P2's perception. After this elimination, we obtain a deceptive reachability game for P1, for synthesizing P1's deceptive strategy.

Definition 6 (P1's deceptive reachability game). *Given the hypergame on graph* $\mathcal{H}_D = \langle S \times Q, Act, \Delta, F_D, F_2 \rangle$, *P1's deceptive reachability game is*

$$\widehat{\mathcal{H}}_D = \langle \mathsf{Win}_2^2, Act, \widehat{\Delta}, F_D \rangle,$$

where

- Win_2^2 *is a set of P2's perceptual winning states, and game state space for P1's deceptive reachability game.*
- $\widehat{\Delta} : S \times Q \times Act \to S \times Q$ *is a* deterministic *transition function such that*
    • *if* $(s,q) \notin F_2$ *then* $\widehat{\Delta}((s,q),a) = \Delta((s,q),a)$ *whenever* $s \in S_i$ *and* $a \in \mathsf{SRActs}_i^2(s,q)$ *for* $i = 1,2$. *Otherwise,* $\widehat{\Delta}((s,q),a)$ *is undefined.*
    • *if* $(s,q) \in F_2$, *then for any action* $a \in Act$, $\widehat{\Delta}((s,q),a) = (s,q)$. *That is, the set* F_2 *are modified into sink states.*
- F_D *is the set of states that P1 aims to reach.*

Lemma 2. *For a given state* (s,q), *if P1 has a sure-winning strategy in* $\widehat{\mathcal{H}}_D$ *starting from* (s,q), *then P1 can ensure to satisfy* $\neg\varphi_2 \mathsf{U}$ decoy *by following this sure-winning strategy in* $\widehat{\mathcal{H}}_D$.

Proof. A path satisfies $\neg\varphi_2 \mathsf{U}$ decoy if it reaches F_D and before reaching F_D, it does not visit any state in F_2. By construction of $\widehat{\mathcal{H}}_D$, if any path reaches F_D, it must not have visited F_2 because if F_2 is reached prior to F_D, then the game stays in the sink state and will never reach F_D. Thus, P1's sure-winning strategy that ensures a path to reach F_D alone satisfies $\neg\varphi_2 \mathsf{U}$ decoy. □

Formally, P1's sure-winning strategy π_1 in the deceptive reachability game is said to be *deceptively sure winning*. A state from which P1 has a deceptive sure-winning strategy is called a *deceptively sure-winning state*. The set of all deceptively sure-winning states of P1 in $\widehat{\mathcal{H}}_D$ is called P1's *deceptive sure-winning region*. The deceptive sure-winning region for P1 can be computed by using Algorithm 1 with $\widehat{\mathcal{H}}_D$ by letting $V_1 := (S_1 \times Q) \cap \mathsf{Win}_2^2$, $V_2 := (S_2 \times Q) \cap \mathsf{Win}_2^2$, $\Delta := \widehat{\Delta}$, and $F := F_D$ (see the description of terms in Algorithm 1). We denote the deceptive sure-winning region for P1 as DSWin_D.

It is noted that the deception is induced by the set F_D which is hidden from P2, and the fact that during the interaction, P1 does not choose any action that contradicts P2's misperception. Additionally, we note that deceptive sure-winning region is not defined for P2, as she is unaware of her lack of information until a decoy is reached.

We now continue with the running example to illustrate the hypergame and P1's deceptive reachability game.

Example 2 (Part 3). From Definition 4, we note that the hypergame on graph $\mathcal{H}_D$ shares the same underlying graph as P2's perceptual game, $\mathcal{G}_2$. That is, in our example, $\mathcal{H}_D$ would have the same graph as Fig. 2b but has the states $(h,0), (k,1)$ and $(k,2)$ labeled as the sink states (shown in red). Now, let us understand the construction of $\widehat{\mathcal{H}}_D$ from $\mathcal{H}_D$. We start by computing Win_2^2 using

Algorithm 1 over the model $\mathcal{G}_2$ by letting $V_1 := S_2 \times Q, V_2 := S_1 \times Q, \Delta := \Delta$ and $F := F_2$. This results in Win_2^2 to include all states except $(a,0), (b,0)$. Intuitively, at the state $(b,0)$, P1 can always choose the transition $b \to a$ to reach $(a,0)$ and keep the game state within $\{(a,0), (b,0)\}$. Consequently, any action that leads to $(a,0), (b,0)$ is **not** subjectively rationalizable for P2 and thereby removed. Additionally, the states $(a,0)$ and $(b,0)$ are also removed from $\mathcal{H}_D$ to get $\widehat{\mathcal{H}}_D$, which is shown in Fig. 3.

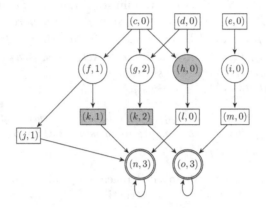

Fig. 3. P1's deceptive reachability game.

3.2   Compositional Synthesis for Decoy Allocation

Given a subset $\mathcal{D} \subseteq S$ of states that can be allocated as decoys, for every different choice of decoy allocation $D \subseteq \mathcal{D}$ we have a different hypergame, $\widehat{\mathcal{H}}_D$. In this context, solving Problem 1 is equivalent to identifying one hypergame that has the largest deceptive sure-winning region $|\mathsf{DSWin}_D|$ for P1. A naïve approach to solve this problem would be to compute DSWin_D for each $D \subseteq \mathcal{D}$ and then select a set D for which $|\mathsf{DSWin}_D|$ is the largest. However, this approach is not scalable because the number of subsets increases combinatorially with the size of game. To address this issue, we introduce a compositional approach to decoy allocation in which we show that when certain conditions hold, the decoy allocation problem can be formulated as a sub or supermodular optimization problem. We propose an algorithm to approximate the optimal decoy allocation.

Proposition 1. *Let* $\mathsf{DSWin}_{\{s_1\}}$ *and* $\mathsf{DSWin}_{\{s_2\}}$ *be P1's deceptive sure-winning regions in the hypergames* $\widehat{\mathcal{H}}_{\{s_1\}}$ *and* $\widehat{\mathcal{H}}_{\{s_2\}}$ *respectively. Then, P1's deceptive sure-winning region* $\mathsf{DSWin}_{\{s_1,s_2\}}$ *in the reachability game* $\widehat{\mathcal{H}}_{\{s_1,s_2\}}$ *is equal to the sure-winning region for P1 in the following zero-sum, reachability game:*

$$\widehat{\mathcal{H}}_{\{s_1,s_2\}} = \langle \mathsf{Win}_2^2, Act, \widehat{\Delta}, \mathsf{DSWin}_{\{s_1\}} \cup \mathsf{DSWin}_{\{s_2\}} \rangle,$$

where P1's goal is to reach the target set $\mathsf{DSWin}_{\{s_1\}} \cup \mathsf{DSWin}_{\{s_2\}}$ *and P2's goal is to prevent P1 from reaching the target set.*

Proof. First, it is noted that all the three deceptive reachability games: $\widehat{\mathcal{H}}_{\{s_1\}}$, $\widehat{\mathcal{H}}_{\{s_2\}}$ and $\widehat{\mathcal{H}}_{\{s_1,s_2\}}$, share the same underlying graphs but different reachability objectives for P1: $F_{\{s_1\}}, F_{\{s_2\}}$, and $F_{\{s_1,s_2\}}$. In addition, $F_{\{s_1\}} \cup F_{\{s_2\}} = F_{\{s_1,s_2\}}$. By definition of sure-winning regions, from every state $(s,q) \in \mathsf{DSWin}_{\{s_i\}}$ for $i = 1, 2$, there exists a deceptive sure-winning strategy $\pi^*_{\{s_i\}}$ for P1 to ensure $F_{\{s_i\}}$ is reached in finitely many steps, for any subjectively rationalizable counter-strategy of P2.

In $\widehat{\mathcal{H}}_{\{s_1,s_2\}}$, let $W^* \subseteq \mathsf{Win}_2^2$ be the sure-winning region for P1 and π^* be the sure-winning strategy of P1. From a state (s,q) in W^*, P1 can ensure to reach a state, say $(s',q') \in \mathsf{DSWin}_{\{s_1\}} \cup \mathsf{DSWin}_{\{s_2\}}$ by following π^*. Upon reaching a state (s',q'), P1 can ensure to reach a state in either $F_{\{s_1\}}$ or $F_{\{s_2\}}$—that is, P1 can ensure to reach a state in $F_{\{s_1,s_2\}}$. Hence, a sure-winning state (s,q) in the above reachability game is deceptive sure-winning in $\widehat{\mathcal{H}}_{\{s_1,s_2\}}$ in which $F_{\{s_1,s_2\}}$ is P1's reachability objective. The deceptive sure-winning strategy is sequentially composed of strategies π^*, $\pi^*_{\{s_1\}}$, and $\pi^*_{\{s_1\}}$ as follows: From a state $(s,q) \in W^*$, P1 uses π^* until a state in $\mathsf{DSWin}_{\{s_1\}} \cup \mathsf{DSWin}_{\{s_2\}}$ is reached. If $\mathsf{DSWin}_{\{s_1\}} \setminus \mathsf{DSWin}_{\{s_2\}}$ is reached, P1 uses the sure-winning strategy $\pi^*_{\{s_1\}}$; If $\mathsf{DSWin}_{\{s_2\}} \setminus \mathsf{DSWin}_{\{s_1\}}$ is reached, P1 uses the sure-winning strategy $\pi^*_{\{s_2\}}$; if $\mathsf{DSWin}_{\{s_1\}} \cap \mathsf{DSWin}_{\{s_2\}}$, P1 selects one of $\pi^*_{\{s_1\}}$ and $\pi^*_{\{s_2\}}$ arbitrarily.   □

Proposition 1 provides us a way for composing the deceptive sure-winning regions of two deceptive reachability games $\widehat{\mathcal{H}}_{s_1}$ and $\widehat{\mathcal{H}}_{s_2}$ to compute the deceptive sure-winning region in the deceptive reachability game $\widehat{\mathcal{H}}_{\{s_1,s_2\}}$ where both s_1 and s_2 are allocated as decoys. A more general result can be obtained by applying Proposition 1 repeatedly.

Corollary 1. *Given* DSWin_D *and* $\mathsf{DSWin}_{\{s\}}$ *as P1's deceptive sure-winning regions in hypergames* $\widehat{\mathcal{H}}_D$ *and* $\widehat{\mathcal{H}}_{\{s\}}$ *respectively, P1's deceptive sure-winning region* $\mathsf{DSWin}_{D \cup \{s\}}$ *in the deceptive reachability game* $\widehat{\mathcal{H}}_{D \cup \{s\}}$ *equals the sure-winning region for P1 in the following zero-sum, reachability game:*

$$\langle \mathsf{Win}_2^2, Act, \widehat{\Delta}, \mathsf{DSWin}_D \cup \mathsf{DSWin}_{\{s\}} \rangle$$

where P1's goal is to reach the target set $\mathsf{DSWin}_D \cup \mathsf{DSWin}_{\{s\}}$ *and P2's goal is to prevent P1 from reaching the target set.*

Corollary 2. *Given a set* $D \subseteq \mathcal{D}$ *and a state* $s \in \mathcal{D}$, *we have*

$$\mathsf{DSWin}_D \cup \mathsf{DSWin}_{\{s\}} \subseteq \mathsf{DSWin}_{D \cup \{s\}}$$

Corollary 2 follows immediately from Proposition 1 and Algorithm 1. To see this, consider a P1 state $s \in \mathcal{D}$ which is neither in DSWin_D nor in $\mathsf{DSWin}_{\{s\}}$ but has exactly two transitions: one leading to s and another leading to a state in DSWin_D. Clearly, the new state will be added to $\mathsf{DSWin}_{D \cup \{s\}}$. Thus, if we consider the size of DSWin_D to be a measure of effectiveness of allocating the states in $D \subseteq \mathcal{D}$ as decoys, then Corollary 2 states that the effectiveness of adding a new state to a set of decoys is greater than or equal to the sum of their individual effectiveness.

Example 2 (Part 4). Given the underlying graph of P1's reachability game $\widehat{\mathcal{H}}_D$ from Fig. 3, let us observe the effect of choosing different D on P1's deceptive sure-winning region, DSWin_D. Letting $k = 2$, Fig. 4 shows the DSWin_D for $D = \{h, k\}$ (Fig. 4a) and $D = \{l, m\}$ (Fig. 4b). In the figure, the colored states represent P1's deceptive sure-winning region, DSWin_D. The states in F_D are colored red and the states from which P1 has deceptive sure-winning strategy to reach a state in F_D are colored blue. For instance, for $D = \{h, k\}$, a P1 state $(f, 1)$ is included in $F_{\{h,k\}}$ because there exists an action for P1 that leads to $(k, 1)$, which is in $F_{\{h,k\}}$. Similarly, a P2 state $(d, 0)$ is included in $\mathsf{DSWin}_{\{h,k\}}$ because both the outgoing transitions from $(d, 0)$ lead to a deceptively sure-winning state. We also notice that the states $(c, 0)$ and $(d, 0)$ from $\mathsf{DSWin}_{\{h,k\}}$ are *not* included in either $\mathsf{DSWin}_{\{h\}} = \{(h, 0)\}$ or $\mathsf{DSWin}_{\{k\}} = \{(k, 1), (k, 2), (f, 1), (g, 2)\}$ because both the states have at least one transition that does not lead to deceptive sure-winning state. For instance, the transition $(d, 0) \to (g, 2)$ prevents the state $(d, 0)$ to be added to DSWin_h.

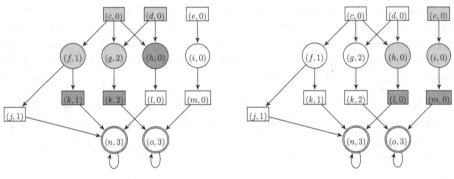

(a) Deceptive sure-winning region of P1 when $D = \{h, k\}$

(b) Deceptive sure-winning region of P1 when $D = \{l, m\}$

Fig. 4. Deceptive sure-winning region of P1 under different choice of D.

We now define a composition operator $\uplus$ over deceptive sure-winning regions which represent the true effect of adding a new state to a given set of decoys. That is, given $D \subseteq \mathcal{D}$ and $s \in \mathcal{D}$, let $\uplus$ be an operator such that

$$\mathsf{DSWin}_D \uplus \mathsf{DSWin}_{\{s\}} = \mathsf{DSWin}_{D \cup \{s\}}.$$

That is, the composition operator returns the deceptive sure-winning region in the reachability game $\langle \text{Win}_2^2, Act, \widehat{\Delta}, \text{DSWin}_D \cup \text{DSWin}_{\{s\}} \rangle$, which equals P1's deceptive sure-winning region when the set $D \cup \{s\}$ are selected to be decoys.

With this notation, Problem 1 becomes equivalent to identifying a set $D^* \subseteq \mathcal{D}$ such that

$$D^* = \arg\max_{D \subseteq \mathcal{D}} \left| \biguplus_{s \in D} \text{DSWin}_{\{s\}} \right| \quad \text{subject to: } |D| \leq k. \tag{2}$$

It is noted that if we replace the composition operator $\biguplus$ with the union operator $\cup$ in (2), then the problem becomes

$$\max_{D \subseteq \mathcal{D}} \left| \bigcup_{s \in D} \text{DSWin}_{\{s\}} \right| \quad \text{subject to: } |D| \leq k. \tag{3}$$

which is a maximum set-cover problem. The maximum set-cover problem is well-known submodular optimization problem and can be solved using a greedy algorithm: Given the current choice D_i of decoys at iteration i, the greedy algorithm selects a new decoy $s \in \mathcal{D} \setminus D_i$ that covers the greatest number of uncovered states in Win_2^2. This selection iterates until k decoys are selected. It is also known that the greedy algorithm is $(1 - 1/e)$-approximate. The reader is referred to [26] for more details.

Let $f^\cup(D) = \left| \bigcup_{s \in D} \text{DSWin}_{\{s\}} \right|$ and $f^\uplus(D) = \left| \biguplus_{s \in D} \text{DSWin}_{\{s\}} \right|$. It follows from Corollary 2 that $f^\cup(D) \leq f^\uplus(D)$ for all $D \subseteq \mathcal{D}$. In other words, $f^\cup(D)$ underapproximates the effectiveness of allocating the states in D as decoys, which is captured by $f^\uplus(D)$.

While the function $f^\cup$ is submodular, a similar sub/supermodularity condition does not necessarily hold for the function $f^\uplus$. In the sequel, we provide sufficient conditions on when $f^\uplus$ is submodular and when it is supermodular.

Theorem 1. *The following statements about* $f^\uplus(D) = \left| \biguplus_{s \in D} \text{DSWin}_{\{s\}} \right|$ *are true.*

(a) $f^\uplus$ *is monotone and non-decreasing.*
(b) $f^\uplus$ *is submodular if* $\text{DSWin}_{D \cup \{s\}} = \text{DSWin}_D \cup \text{DSWin}_{\{s\}}$ *for all* $D \subseteq \mathcal{D}$ *and* $s \in \mathcal{D}$.
(c) $f^\uplus$ *is supermodular if* $\text{DSWin}_D = \text{DSWin}_{D \cup \{s_1\}} \cap \text{DSWin}_{D \cup \{s_2\}}$ *for all* $D \subseteq \mathcal{D}$ *and all* $s_1, s_2, \in \mathcal{D}$.

Proof.   **(a).** Based on Corollary 2, for any set $D \subseteq \mathcal{D}$ and a state $s \in \mathcal{D} \setminus D$, $f^\uplus(D) = |\text{DSWin}_D|$ and $f^\uplus(D \cup \{s\}) = |\text{DSWin}_{D \cup \{s\}}|$, because $\text{DSWin}_D \subseteq \text{DSWin}_{D \cup \{s\}}$, $f^\uplus(D) \leq f^\uplus(D \cup \{s\})$.
     (b). When $\text{DSWin}_{D \cup \{s\}} = \text{DSWin}_D \cup \text{DSWin}_{\{s\}}$, we can write $f^\uplus(D) = \left| \biguplus_{s \in D} \text{DSWin}_{\{s\}} \right| = \left| \bigcup_{s \in D} \text{DSWin}_{\{s\}} \right| = f^\cup(D)$, which is submodular.

(c). We will show that

$$LHS := f^\uplus(D \cup \{s_1\}) + f^\uplus(D \cup \{s_2\}) - f^\uplus(D) \leq f^\uplus(D \cup \{s_1, s_2\}) := RHS$$

for all $D \subseteq \mathcal{D}$ and all $s_1, s_2 \in \mathcal{D}$. Given that $\mathsf{DSWin}_D = \mathsf{DSWin}_{D \cup \{s_1\}} \cap \mathsf{DSWin}_{D \cup \{s_2\}}$ holds for any $D \subseteq \mathcal{D}$ and any $s_1, s_2 \in \mathcal{D}$, we have that $f^\uplus(D \cup \{s_1\}) + f^\uplus(D \cup \{s_2\}) - f^\uplus(D)$ counts every state in $\mathsf{DSWin}_{D \cup \{s_1\}} \cup \mathsf{DSWin}_{D \cup \{s_2\}}$ exactly once. On the other hand, we have $f^\uplus(D \cup \{s_1, s_2\}) = |\mathsf{DSWin}_{D \cup \{s_1, s_2\}}|$ and $\mathsf{DSWin}_{D \cup \{s_1, s_2\}} \supseteq \mathsf{DSWin}_{D \cup \{s_1\}} \cup \mathsf{DSWin}_{D \cup \{s_2\}}$, by Corollary 2. Thus, there may exist a state in $\mathsf{DSWin}_{D \cup \{s_1, s_2\}}$ which is not included in either $\mathsf{DSWin}_{D \cup \{s_1\}}$ or $\mathsf{DSWin}_{D \cup \{s_2\}}$. In other words, RHS may be greater than or equal to LHS and the statement follows.   □

Based on Theorem 1, we now propose a greedy algorithm described in Algorithm 2. This greedy algorithm is an extension of the GreedyMax algorithm for maximizing monotone submodular-supermodular functions in [4]. It starts with an empty set of states labeled with **decoy** and incrementally adds new decoys in the game arena. At each step, given the deceptive winning region of the chosen decoys, a new decoy is selected such that by adding the new decoy into the chosen decoys, P1's deceptive sure-winning region covers the largest number of states in Win_2^2. The algorithm iterates until k decoys are added, where k is the upper bound on the number of decoys.

Algorithm 2: GreedyMax Algorithm for Decoy Allocation

Input: P1's deceptive reachability game $\langle \mathsf{Win}_2^2, Act, \widehat{\Delta}, F_D = \emptyset \rangle$, the set $\mathcal{D} \subseteq S$, the bound k on the number of decoys.

Output: An approximate solution $\overline{D}$ for the optimization problem in Eq. 2.

$\overline{D} \leftarrow \emptyset$;

$\mathsf{DSWin}_{\overline{D}} \leftarrow \emptyset$;

while $|\overline{D}| < k$ **do**

    for $s \in \mathcal{D} \setminus \overline{D}$ **do**

        $\mathcal{G}_s \leftarrow \langle \mathsf{Win}_2^2, Act, \widehat{\Delta}, \mathsf{DSWin}_{\{s\}} \cup \mathsf{DSWin}_{\overline{D}} \rangle$;

        $\mathsf{DSWin}_{\{s\} \cup \overline{D}} \leftarrow \mathsf{Sure\text{-}Win}(\mathcal{G}_s)$;   ... by Alg. 1;

    end

    $s^* \leftarrow \arg\max_{s \in \mathcal{D} \setminus \overline{D}} |\mathsf{DSWin}_{\{s\} \cup \overline{D}}|$;

    $\overline{D} \leftarrow s^* \cup \overline{D}$;

end

return $\overline{D}$

Complexity Analysis. The complexity of Algorithm 2 is $\mathcal{O}(k|\mathcal{D}|N)$ where N is the number of state-action pairs in P1's deceptive reachability game. This is because to add $(i + 1)$-th state to $\overline{D}$, we update deceptive sure-winning regions of $|\mathcal{D}| - i$ states. The complexity of solving a reachability game is linear in the size N of the game, measured by the number of state-action pairs.

Example 2 (Part 5). We maximize $|\mathsf{DSWin}_D|$, under the constraint that a maximal two decoys to be placed within the set $\mathcal{D} = \{j, k, l, m\}$. Following the compositional approach, we compute the following deceptive sure-winning regions: $\mathsf{DSWin}_{\{j\}} = \{(j, 1), (f, 1)\}$, $\mathsf{DSWin}_{\{k\}} = \{(k, 1), (k, 2), (f, 1), (g, 2)\}$, $\mathsf{DSWin}_{\{l\}} = \{(l, 0), (h, 0)\}$ and $\mathsf{DSWin}_{\{m\}} = \{(m, 0), (i, 0), (e, 0)\}$.

First, we use the greedy algorithm for maximum set-cover to solve for $D \subseteq \mathcal{D}$ that maximizes $f^{\cup}(D)$ under the constraint $|D| \leq 2$. In the first iteration, the greedy algorithm selects the largest the state corresponding to $|\mathsf{DSWin}_{\{s\}}|$, which is $s = k$. In the second iteration, it selects the set that has the largest number of states not already included in $\mathsf{DSWin}_{\{k\}}$. Thus, it selects m as the second state to place the decoy. In conclusion, it selects $D = \{k, m\}$ as solution to decoy allocation problem, for which $|\mathsf{DSWin}_{\{k,m\}}| = 7$.

Second, we use Algorithm 2 to solve for $D \subseteq \mathcal{D}$ that maximizes $f^{\uplus}(D)$ under the constraint $|D| \leq 2$. In the first iteration, s^* is selected to be k because $|\mathsf{DSWin}_{\{k\}}|$ is the largest. In the second iteration, s^* is selected to be l because $\mathsf{DSWin}_{\{l\} \cup \overline{D}} = \{(l, 0), (h, 0), (k, 1), (k, 2), (f, 1), (g, 2), (c, 0), (d, 0)\}$. In conclusion, it selects $D = \{k, l\}$ as solution to decoy allocation problem, for which $|\mathsf{DSWin}_{\{k,l\}}| = 8$, which coincidentally in this example is also the globally optimal solution for the problem. We note the improvement in the solution is attributed to incremental computation of $\mathsf{DSWin}_{D \cup \{s\}}$ in Algorithm 2.

Due to space limitation, we omit other examples with larger game arena. But the interested readers can find more examples in which the decoy allocation problems are solved with both the greedy algorithm for submodular optimization and Algorithm 2 in https://github.com/abhibp1993/decoy-allocation-problem.

4   Conclusion

In this paper, we investigated the optimal decoy allocation problems in a class of games where players' objectives are specified in temporal logic and players have asymmetric information. The contributions of the paper are twofold: First, we develop a hypergame on graph model to capture the deceivee (the adversary)'s incomplete and incorrect information due to the decoys and the deceiver (the defender)'s information about the deceivee's information. Using decoy-based deception, we designed algorithms to compute a deceptive sure-winning strategy with which the defender can take actions deceptively and lure the adversary into decoys, from a state where the adversary perceives herself a winner (*i.e.*, has a strategy to achieve the attack objective). Second, to compute the optimal choice of decoy locations, we employed compositional synthesis from formal methods and proved that the optimal decoy allocation problem is monotone, and non-decreasing. However, the problem can be submodular or supermodular or neither in different games. We design two greedy algorithms, one is based on maximizing an under-approximation of the deceptive winning regions given the effectiveness of individual decoys using maximum set cover, another is to use submodular-supermodular optimization to find approximate solutions of the optimal decoy placement.

Future work include the study of decoy allocation with other types of decoy-induced misperception. In this scope, the decoys are set up as "traps" for the adversary. But it is possible to use decoys as "fake targets" for distracting the adversary. We intend to explore a mixture of types of decoys given their functionalities in cyber-physical defense and the respective deceptive synthesis problems and decoy-allocation problems. Also, we are interested in deceptive planning for other class of games, for example, concurrent (*i.e.*, simultaneous-move) reachability games [1]. We intend to implement a toolbox for the proposed algorithm and apply the methods to practical network security problems.

References

1. de Alfaro, L., Henzinger, T.A., Kupferman, O.: Concurrent reachability games. Theoret. Comput. Sci. **386**(3), 188–217 (2007)
2. Anwar, A.H., Kamhoua, C., Leslie, N.: Honeypot allocation over attack graphs in cyber deception games. In: 2020 International Conference on Computing, Networking and Communications (ICNC), pp. 502–506 (2020)
3. Aslanyan, Z., Nielson, F., Parker, D.: Quantitative verification and synthesis of attack-defence scenarios. In: 2016 IEEE 29th Computer Security Foundations Symposium (CSF), pp. 105–119. IEEE, June 2016
4. Bai, W., Bilmes, J.A.: Greed is still good: maximizing monotone submodular+ supermodular functions. arXiv preprint arXiv:1801.07413 (2018)
5. Baier, C., Katoen, J.P.: Principles of Model Checking. MIT Press, Cambridge (2008)
6. Bennett, P.G., Bussel, R.R.: Hypergame theory and methodology: the current "state of the art". In: Wilkin, L. (ed.) The Management of Uncertainty: Approaches, Methods and Applications. NATO ASI Series, vol. 32, pp. 158–181. Springer, Dordrecht (1986). https://doi.org/10.1007/978-94-009-4458-9_7
7. Bloem, R., Chatterjee, K., Jobstmann, B.: Graph games and reactive synthesis. In: Handbook of Model Checking, pp. 921–962. Springer, Cham (2018). https://doi.org/10.1007/978-3-319-10575-8_27
8. Chatterjee, K., Henzinger, T.A.: A survey of stochastic omega-regular games. J. Comput. Syst. Sci. **78**(2), 394–413 (2012)
9. Durkota, K., Lisy, V., Bosansky, B., Kiekintveld, C.: Optimal network security hardening using attack graph games. In: Twenty-Fourth International Joint Conference on Artificial Intelligence (2015)
10. Filiot, E., Jin, N., Raskin, J.F.: Antichains and compositional algorithms for LTL synthesis. Formal Methods Syst. Des. **39**, 261–296 (2011). https://doi.org/10.1007/s10703-011-0115-3
11. Mazala, R.: Infinite games. In: Grädel, E., Thomas, W., Wilke, T. (eds.) Automata Logics, and Infinite Games. LNCS, vol. 2500, pp. 23–38. Springer, Heidelberg (2002). https://doi.org/10.1007/3-540-36387-4_2
12. Heckman, K.E., Stech, F.J., Thomas, R.K., Schmoker, B., Tsow, A.W.: Bridging the classical D&D and cyber security domains. In: Cyber Denial, Deception and Counter Deception. AIS, pp. 5–29. Springer, Cham (2015). https://doi.org/10.1007/978-3-319-25133-2_2

13. Jha, S., Sheyner, O., Wing, J.: Two formal analyses of attack graphs. In: Proceedings 15th IEEE Computer Security Foundations Workshop, CSFW-15, pp. 49–63 (2002)
14. Jiang, W., Fang, B.x., Zhang, H.l., Tian, Z.h., Song, X.f.: Optimal network security strengthening using attack-defense game model. In: 2009 Sixth International Conference on Information Technology: New Generations, pp. 475–480 (2009)
15. Kiekintveld, C., Jain, M., Tsai, J., Pita, J., Ordóñez, F., Tambe, M.: Computing optimal randomized resource allocations for massive security games. In: Proceedings of the 8th International Conference on Autonomous Agents and Multiagent Systems-Volume 1, pp. 689–696 (2009)
16. Kiekintveld, C., Lisý, V., Píbil, R.: Game-theoretic foundations for the strategic use of honeypots in network security. In: Jajodia, S., Shakarian, P., Subrahmanian, V.S., Swarup, V., Wang, C. (eds.) Cyber Warfare. AIS, vol. 56, pp. 81–101. Springer, Cham (2015). https://doi.org/10.1007/978-3-319-14039-1_5
17. Kulkarni, A.N., Luo, H., Leslie, N.O., Kamhoua, C.A., Fu, J.: Deceptive labeling: hypergames on graphs for stealthy deception. IEEE Control Syst. Lett. 5(3), 977–982 (2021)
18. Kulkarni, A.N., Fu, J.: A compositional approach to reactive games under temporal logic specifications. In: 2018 Annual American Control Conference (ACC), pp. 2356–2362. IEEE (2018)
19. Manna, Z., Pnueli, A.: The Temporal Logic of Reactive and Concurrent Systems: Specification. Springer, New York (1992). https://doi.org/10.1007/978-1-4612-0931-7
20. McNaughton, R.: Infinite games played on finite graphs. Ann. Pure Appl. Logic 65(2), 149–184 (1993)
21. Ou, X., Boyer, W.F., McQueen, M.A.: A scalable approach to attack graph generation. In: Proceedings of the 13th ACM Conference on Computer and Communications Security - CCS 2006, Alexandria, Virginia, USA, pp. 336–345. ACM Press (2006)
22. Píbil, R., Lisý, V., Kiekintveld, C., Bošanský, B., Pěchouček, M.: Game theoretic model of strategic honeypot selection in computer networks. In: Grossklags, J., Walrand, J. (eds.) GameSec 2012. LNCS, vol. 7638, pp. 201–220. Springer, Heidelberg (2012). https://doi.org/10.1007/978-3-642-34266-0_12
23. Sasaki, Y., Kijima, K.: Hierarchical hypergames and Bayesian games: a generalization of the theoretical comparison of hypergames and Bayesian games considering hierarchy of perceptions. J. Syst. Sci. Complex. 29(1), 187–201 (2016)
24. Sinha, A., Fang, F., An, B., Kiekintveld, C., Tambe, M.: Stackelberg security games: looking beyond a decade of success. In: Proceedings of the Twenty-Seventh International Joint Conference on Artificial Intelligence, pp. 5494–5501. International Joint Conferences on Artificial Intelligence Organization (2018)
25. Thakoor, O., Tambe, M., Vayanos, P., Xu, H., Kiekintveld, C., Fang, F.: Cyber camouflage games for strategic deception. In: Alpcan, T., Vorobeychik, Y., Baras, J.S., Dán, G. (eds.) GameSec 2019. LNCS, vol. 11836, pp. 525–541. Springer, Cham (2019). https://doi.org/10.1007/978-3-030-32430-8_31
26. Vazirani, V.V.: Approximation Algorithms. Springer, Heidelberg (2003). https://doi.org/10.1007/978-3-662-04565-7
27. Wang, M., Hipel, K.W., Fraser, N.M.: Solution concepts in hypergames. Appl. Math. Comput. 34(3), 147–171 (1989)

Popular Imperceptibility Measures in Visual Adversarial Attacks are Far from Human Perception

Ayon Sen[1]($\boxtimes$), Xiaojin Zhu[1], Erin Marshall[2], and Robert Nowak[2]

[1] Computer Sciences Department, University of Wisconsin-Madison, Madison, USA
asen6@wisc.edu, jerryzhu@cs.wisc.edu
[2] Department of Electrical and Computer Engineering,
University of Wisconsin-Madison, Madison, USA
{limarshall,rdnowak}@wisc.edu

Abstract. Adversarial attacks on image classification aim to make visually imperceptible changes to induce misclassification. Popular computational definitions of imperceptibility are largely based on mathematical convenience such as pixel p-norms. We perform a behavioral study that allows us to quantitatively demonstrate the mismatch between human perception and popular imperceptibility measures such as pixel p-norms, earth mover's distance, structural similarity index, and deep net embedding. Our results call for a reassessment of current adversarial attack formulation.

Keywords: Adversarial machine learning · Imperceptibility · Just noticeable difference

1 Introduction

Recent visual adversarial attack research frequently uses the following formulation [10,17]. Let $\mathbf{x}_0$ be an image in an appropriate vector space, y be its true class label, θ a trained classifier, and ℓ the learner's loss function. The attacker seeks a perturbed image $\mathbf{x}$ to make the true label y seem unlikely (by maximizing the loss):

$$\max_{\mathbf{x}} \ \ell(\mathbf{x}, y, \theta)$$
$$\text{s.t.} \ \ d(\mathbf{x}, \mathbf{x}_0) \leq \epsilon. \tag{1}$$

The feasible set is defined by a distance function $d()$ and a threshold ϵ. A common choice for $d()$ is the infinite norm in the pixel space: $d(\mathbf{x}, \mathbf{x}_0) := \|\mathbf{x} - \mathbf{x}_0\|_\infty$, although other p-norms (especially for $p = 1, 2$) and several other measures (defined in the next section) are popular, too. An alternative formulation minimizes the distance function $d(\mathbf{x}, \mathbf{x}_0)$ subject to wrong label prediction.

Implicit in such formulations is the assumption that the feasible set defined by $d(\mathbf{x}, \mathbf{x}_0) \leq \epsilon$ coincides with imperceptible perturbations as

© Springer Nature Switzerland AG 2020
Q. Zhu et al. (Eds.): GameSec 2020, LNCS 12513, pp. 188–199, 2020.
https://doi.org/10.1007/978-3-030-64793-3_10

observed by human inspectors [3,7,15,20,26,27]. Then perhaps the attacker can wreck havoc against the classifier without being noticed by humans. This assumption has been criticized for its over-simplification of the threat model [6,21]. Indeed, many adversarial learning researchers readily admit that popular choices of $d()$ are more of a mathematical convenience, and may not correspond well with human perception. Disconcertingly, a large number of papers keep making this assumption without verifying how good or bad the assumption really is: Out of 32 recent papers we surveyed, 27 papers (each with over 100 citations) used pixel p-norms for $d()$. Among these 27, 20% assumed p-norms are a good match to human perception without providing evidence; 50% used them because other papers did; and the rest used them without justification. Given the recent prominence of visual adversarial learning research, there is a need to quantitatively study this assumption to refine the threat model.

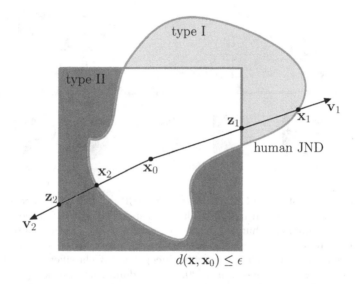

Fig. 1. Mismatches between human perception and distance function d

What is the harm if $d()$ and human perception differ? Consider the image space around image $\mathbf{x}_0$ in Fig. 1. The feasible set $\{\mathbf{x} : d(\mathbf{x}, \mathbf{x}_0) \leq \epsilon\}$ is the region within the gray contour, while the human imperceptibility region is within the green contour: intuitively, any image in this region looks like $\mathbf{x}_0$ to an average human (precise definition below).

– The yellow region is type I error: humans perceive images there, e.g. $\mathbf{x}_1$, the same as $\mathbf{x}_0$ but the feasible set by definition thinks otherwise. Type I errors are dangerous because it lets the machine's guard down: the machine does not even consider $\mathbf{x}_1$ to be a valid attack (while $\mathbf{x}_1$ may in fact change the label prediction), *and* human inspection will not notice the attack.

– The blue region is type II error: humans perceive images there, e.g. z_2, as noticeably different from x_0 but the feasible set thinks they cannot be distinguished. Type II errors waste the machine's resources by defending against fictitious threats.

Both types of error have occurred in practice, as shown in Fig. 2. In both examples we used $d(x, x_0) = \|x - x_0\|_\infty$ and $\epsilon = 8$ (out of pixel value 0–255), as is commonly used in adversarial machine learning [1,31].

Our main contribution is a new human experiment design that allows us to quantitatively gauge the mismatch between human perception and popular imperceptibility measures $d()$, specifically pixel p-norms, EMD, 1-SSIM, and DNN representation p-norms. Our results call for a reassessment of the adversarial attack formulation (1) vis-à-vis real threats.

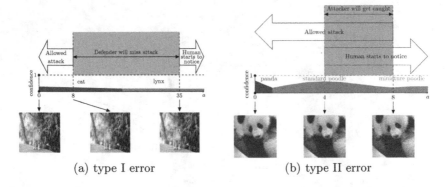

(a) type I error   (b) type II error

Fig. 2. (a) x_0=cat photo, v=M_RGB_Box (see Sect. 3), $x = x_0 + av$. $d(x, x_0) = \|x - x_0\|_\infty$ and $\epsilon = 8$ as in the literature [1,31]; this corresponds to $a = 8$. On the other hand, our experiments showed that human JND is not until $a = 35$. The images produced by $a \in (8, 35)$ are type I errors: a machine defender will not consider them, and humans cannot tell them apart from x_0. Critically, Inception V3 classifier [25] will classify $a \geq 20$ as lynx, meaning images in $a \in [20, 35)$ are dangerous attacks. (b) x_0=panda photo, v=FGSM [7] attack direction. Again d is the infinite norm, and $\epsilon = 8$. Along this direction humans are good at detecting changes: our experiments showed that human JND happens at $\|x - x_0\|_\infty = 4$ already. An attack produced by FGSM with $\|x - x_0\|_\infty \in \{4, 5, \ldots, 8\}$ will get caught. Therefore, the specific FGSM attack will likely be detected by humans. The issue on the surface may look like an inappropriate ϵ threshold used by FGSM, but keep in mind that along different directions v the human JND threshold can vary, and there may not be a correct global ϵ. The root cause is an inappropriate $d()$ used by adversarial attacks.

2   Study Overview

Our study is designed to facilitate human experiments. Given a natural image x_0, consider an arbitrary direction v as shown in Fig. 1. The ray centered at x_0 in the direction $\mathbf{v}$ is parametrized as $\{\mathbf{x} := \mathbf{x}_0 + a\mathbf{v} \mid a \geq 0\}$ with a scalar parameter a. Larger a leads to more changes to $\mathbf{x}_0$. We expect to find a threshold value a_v for direction $\mathbf{v}$, above which an average human inspector will notice the difference between $\mathbf{x}_0$ and $\mathbf{x}_0 + a_v\mathbf{v}$. These are images $\mathbf{x}_1, \mathbf{x}_2$ in Fig. 1 for directions $\mathbf{v}_1, \mathbf{v}_2$, respectively.

Now, an adversarial attack feasible set in (1) is defined by distance measure $d()$ and threshold ϵ. Our primary interest is the appropriateness of $d()$ compared to human perception. ϵ is a nuisance parameter; fortunately, we do not need to know its value. The **key insight** is that, if $d()$ correctly models human perception, then under this measure the distance

$$d(\mathbf{x}_0 + a_v\mathbf{v}, \mathbf{x}_0) \tag{2}$$

is a constant for all directions $\mathbf{v}$. In other words, the "just noticeably different" images by humans form a sphere around $\mathbf{x}_0$ under the correct $d()$. Conversely, we may summarize how far off some $d()$ is from human perception by the *condition number*

$$\kappa(d) := \frac{\max_{\mathbf{v}} d(\mathbf{x}_0 + a_v\mathbf{v}, \mathbf{x}_0)}{\min_{\mathbf{v}} d(\mathbf{x}_0 + a_v\mathbf{v}, \mathbf{x}_0)}. \tag{3}$$

The larger $\kappa(d)$ is, the worse $d()$ is. The smallest possible value of $\kappa(d)$ is 1. It is analogous to the ratio of major vs. minor axes for an ellipsoid. Note $\kappa(d)$ is center-image $\mathbf{x}_0$ dependent.

We will empirically estimate $\kappa(d)$ for popular $d()$'s. Because this involves human experiments, practically we can only consider a finite, small number of center images $\mathbf{x}_0$. Furthermore, for each $\mathbf{x}_0$ we can only consider a small number of directions $V = \{\mathbf{v}_1, \ldots, \mathbf{v}_k\}$. From these, we obtain an empirical estimate of condition number

$$\hat{\kappa}(d) := \frac{\max_{\mathbf{v} \in V} d(\mathbf{x}_0 + a_v\mathbf{v}, \mathbf{x}_0)}{\min_{\mathbf{v} \in V} d(\mathbf{x}_0 + a_v\mathbf{v}, \mathbf{x}_0)}, \tag{4}$$

where max and min only go over the directions in V. Clearly, this is an underestimate: $\hat{\kappa}(d) \leq \kappa(d)$. If our measured $\hat{\kappa}(d)$ is large (and thus $\kappa(d)$ potentially even larger), we conclude that $d()$ is inappropriate.

2.1   Human Just Noticeable Difference (JND)

We define the just noticeable difference (JND) [5,32] with respect to a center image $\mathbf{x}_0$ and direction $\mathbf{v}$ as the image $\mathbf{x}_0 + a_v\mathbf{v}$ where an average human observer starts to perceive a difference. Equivalently, human JND is characterized by the scalar a_v. We discuss how to empirically measure human JND in Sect. 3.

2.2   Popular Imperceptibility Measures $d()$

Pixel p-Norm. For any $p \in [0, \infty]$ it measures the amount of perturbation by $\|\mathbf{x} - \mathbf{x}_0\|_p := \left(\sum_{i=1}^d |x_i - x_{0,i}|^p\right)^{1/p}$. We define the 0-norm to be the number of nonzero elements.

Earth Mover's Distance (EMD). Also known as Wasserstein distance, it is a distance function defined between two probability distributions on a given metric space. The metric computes the minimum cost of converting one distribution to the other one. EMD has been used as a distance metric in the image space also, e.g. for image retrieval [19]. Given two images $\mathbf{x}_0$ and $\mathbf{x}$, EMD is calculated as $EMD(\mathbf{x}_0, \mathbf{x}) = \inf_{\gamma \in \Gamma(\mathbf{x}_0, \mathbf{x})} \int_{\mathbb{R} \times \mathbb{R}} |a - b| d\gamma(a, b)$. Here, $\Gamma(\mathbf{x}_0, \mathbf{x})$ is the set of joint distributions whose marginals are $\mathbf{x}_0$ and $\mathbf{x}$ (treated as histograms), respectively.

Structural Similarity (SSIM). This measure is intended to be a perceptual similarity measure that quantifies image quality loss due to compression [29], and used as a signal fidelity measure with respect to humans in multiple research works [22,28]. SSIM has three elements: luminance, contrast and similarity of local structure. Given two images $\mathbf{x}_0$ and $\mathbf{x}$, SSIM is defined by $SSIM(\mathbf{x}_0, \mathbf{x}) = \left(\frac{2\mu_{\mathbf{x}_0}\mu_{\mathbf{x}} + C_1}{\mu_{\mathbf{x}_0}^2 + \mu_{\mathbf{x}}^2 + C_1} \right) \left(\frac{2\sigma_{\mathbf{x}_0}\sigma_{\mathbf{x}} + C_2}{\sigma_{\mathbf{x}_0}^2 + \sigma_{\mathbf{x}}^2 + C_2} \right) \left(\frac{\sigma_{\mathbf{x}_0\mathbf{x}} + C_3}{\sigma_{\mathbf{x}_0}\sigma_{\mathbf{x}} + C_3} \right)$. $\mu_{\mathbf{x}_0}$ and $\mu_{\mathbf{x}}$ are the sample means; $\sigma_{\mathbf{x}_0}$, $\sigma_{\mathbf{x}}$ and $\sigma_{\mathbf{x}_0\mathbf{x}}$ are the standard deviation and sample cross correlation of $\mathbf{x}_0$ and $\mathbf{x}$ (after subtracting the mean) respectively. To compute SSIM we use window size 7 without Gaussian weights. Since SSIM is a similarity score, we define $d(\mathbf{x}, \mathbf{x}_0) = 1 - SSIM(\mathbf{x}, \mathbf{x}_0)$.

Deep Neural Network (DNN) Representation. Even though DNNs are designed with engineering goals in mind, studies comparing their internal representations to primate brains have found similarities [11]. Let $\xi(\mathbf{x}) \in \mathbb{R}^D$ denote the last hidden layer representation of input image $\mathbf{x}$ in a DNN. We define $d(\mathbf{x}, \mathbf{x}_0) = \|\xi(\mathbf{x}) - \xi(\mathbf{x}_0)\|_p$ as a potential distance metric for our purpose. We use Inception V3 [25] representations with $D = 2048$.

3   Human JND Experiments

Center Images $\mathbf{x}_0$ and Perturbation Directions $\mathbf{v}$: We chose three natural images (from the Imagenet dataset [4]) popular in adversarial research: a panda [7], a macaw [16] and a cat [1] as $\mathbf{x}_0$ in our experiments. We resized the images to 299×299 to match the input dimension of the Inception V3 image classification network [25].

As indicated in Fig. 1, we consider $\mathbf{x}$ generated along the ray defined by a perturbation direction $\mathbf{v} \in \mathbb{R}^d$ with a perturbation scale $a > 0$. To render the image for display, we project it to the image space: $\mathbf{x} = \Pi(\mathbf{x}_0 + a\mathbf{v})$, namely, clipping pixel values to $[0, 255]$ and rounding to integers.

For each natural image $\mathbf{x}_0$ we considered 10 perturbation directions $\mathbf{v}$, see Fig. 3. Eight are specially crafted ± 1-perturbation (i.e., $\mathbf{v}$ has elements -1, 0, 1) directions varying in three attributes (Table 1). Specifically, the nonzero elements v_i depend on the value of the corresponding element $x_{0,i}$ in $\mathbf{x}_0$: $v_i = 1$ if $x_{0,i} < 128$, and -1 otherwise. For ± 1-perturbations $\mathbf{v}$ and integer $a \in \{1, \dots, 128\}$ it is easy to see that the projection Π is not needed: $\mathbf{x} = \Pi(\mathbf{x}_0 + a\mathbf{v}) = \mathbf{x}_0 + a\mathbf{v}$.

Fig. 3. All 10 perturbation directions **v** with severe perturbation scale $a = 128$. (a) S_Red_Box: the red channel of the center pixel. (b) S_Red_Dot: a randomly selected red channel. (c) M_Red_Dot: 288 randomly selected red channels. (d) M_RGB_Dot: all three color channels of 96 randomly selected pixels ($s = 3 \times 96 = 288$). (c) M_Red_Eye: 288 red channels around the eyes of the animals. (f) M_RGB_Box: all colors of a centered 8×12 rectangle. (g) L_RGB_Box: all colors of a centered 101×101 rectangle. (h) X_RGB_Box: all dimensions. (i) FGSM. (j) PGD.

The remaining two perturbation directions are adversarial directions. We used Fast Gradient Sign Method (FGSM) [7] and Projected Gradient Descent (PGD) [14] to generate two adversarial images $\mathbf{x}^{FGSM}, \mathbf{x}^{PGD}$ for each $\mathbf{x}_0$, with Inception V3 as the victim network. All attack parameters are set as suggested in the methods' respective papers. PGD is a directed attack and requires a target label; we choose gibbon (on panda) and guacamole (on cat) following the papers, and cleaver (on macaw) arbitrarily. We then define the adversarial perturbation directions by $\mathbf{v}^{FGSM} = 127.5(\mathbf{x}^{FGSM} - \mathbf{x}_0)/\|\mathbf{x}^{FGSM} - \mathbf{x}_0\|_2$ and $\mathbf{v}^{PGD} = 127.5(\mathbf{x}^{PGD} - \mathbf{x}_0)/\|\mathbf{x}^{PGD} - \mathbf{x}_0\|_2$. We use the factor 127.5 based on a pilot study to ensure that changes between consecutive images in the adversarial perturbation directions are not too small or too big.

Table 1. Naming convention for perturbation directions **v**

# Dimensions changed	S = 1, M = 288
	L = 30603, X = 268203
	(mnemonic: garment size)
Color channels affected	Red = only the red channel of a pixel
	RGB = all three channels of a pixel
Shape of perturbed pixels	Box = a centered rectangle
	Dot = scattered random dots
	Eye = on the eye of the animal

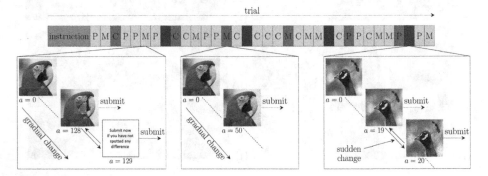

Fig. 4. Experiment procedure. The green, red and blue cells denote ±1-perturbation, adversarial, and guard trials, respectively. The letters P, M and C denote the panda, macaw and cat $\mathbf{x}_0$, respectively. (Color figure online)

Experimental Procedure : See Fig. 4. Each participant was first presented with instructions and then completed a sequence of 34 trials, of which 30 were ±1-perturbation or adversarial trials, and 4 were guard trials. The order of these trials was randomized then fixed (see figure). During each trial the participants were presented with an image $\mathbf{x}_0$. They were instructed to increase (decrease) perturbations to this image by using right/left arrow keys or buttons. Moving right (left) incremented (decremented) a by 1, and the subject was then presented with the new perturbed image $\mathbf{x} = \Pi(\mathbf{x}_0 + a\mathbf{v})$. We did not divulge the nature of the perturbations **v** beforehand, nor the current perturbation scale a the participant had added to $\mathbf{x}_0$ at any step of the trial. **The participants were instructed to submit the perturbed image x when they think it became just noticeably different from the original image $\mathbf{x}_0$.** The participants had to hold $\mathbf{x}_0$ in memory, though they could also go all the way left back to see $\mathbf{x}_0$ again. We hosted the experiment using the NEXT platform [9,23].

In a ±1-perturbation trial, the perturbation direction **v** is one of the eight ±1-perturbations. We allowed the participants to vary a within $\{0, 1, \ldots, 128\}$ to avoid value cropping. If a participant was not able to detect any change even after $a = 128$, then they were encouraged to "give up".

In an adversarial trial, the perturbation direction is $\mathbf{v}^{FGSM}$ or $\mathbf{v}^{PGD}$. We allowed the participants to increment a indefinitely, though no one went beyond $a = 80$.

The guard trials were designed to filter out participates who clicked through the experiment without performing the task. In a guard trial, we showed a novel fixed natural image (not panda, macaw or cat) for $a < 20$. Then for $a \geq 20$, a highly noisy version of that image is displayed. An attentive participant should readily notice this sudden change at $a = 20$ and submit it. We disregarded guard trials in our analysis.

Participants and Data Inclusion Criterion : We enrolled 68 participants using Amazon Mechanical Turk [2] master workers. A master worker is a person who has consistently displayed a high degree of success in performing a wide range of tasks. All participants used a desktop, laptop or a tablet device; none used a mobile device where the screen would be too small. On average the participants took 33 minutes to finish the experiment. Each participant was paid $5. As mentioned before, we use guard trials to identify inattentive participants. While the change happens at exactly $a = 20$ in a guard trial, our data indicates a natural spread in participant submissions around 20 with sharp decays. We speculate that the spread was due to keyboard/mouse auto repeat. We set a range for an acceptable guard trial if a participant submitted $a \in \{18, 19, 20, 21, 22\}$. A participant is deemed inattentive if any one of the four guard trials was outside the acceptable range. Only $n = 42$ out of 68 participants survived this stringent inclusion condition. All our analyses below are on these 42 participants.

4   Results

For each center image $\mathbf{x}_0$ and perturbation direction $\mathbf{v}$, the jth participant ($j = 1 \ldots n$) gave us their individual JND threshold scale parameter $a_v^{(j)}$. That is, the image $\mathbf{x}^{(j)} = \Pi(\mathbf{x}_0 + a_v^{(j)} \mathbf{v})$ is the one participant j thinks has just-noticeable-difference to $\mathbf{x}_0$ along direction $\mathbf{v}$.

Because our participants can sometimes choose to "give up" if they did not notice a change, we have *right censored data* on a_v. All we know from a given-up trial is that $a \geq 129$, but not what larger a value will cause the participant to noticed a difference. For example, many participants failed to notice a difference along the S_Red_Box and S_Red_Dot perturbation directions, thus many a_v's in those directions (50.8% and 51.6% respectively) were censored. A total of 13.2% a_v's were censored along all directions.

4.1   Qualitative Assessment

Recall if a distance measure $d()$ is a good match to human perception, then by (2) along any direction $\mathbf{v}$ the human JND image $\mathbf{x} = \mathbf{x}_0 + a_v \mathbf{v}$ has the same $d(\mathbf{x}, \mathbf{x}_0)$. We present box plots to qualitatively assess the different $d()$'s in Figs. 5 and 6. We selectively show only one center image $\mathbf{x}_0$ for each of the measures for

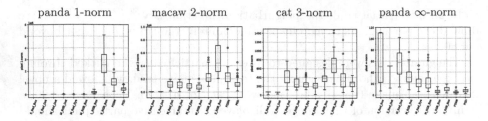

Fig. 5. Participant JND **x**'s pixel norm $\|\mathbf{x} - \mathbf{x}_0\|_p$. Within a plot, each vertical box is for a perturbation direction **v**. The box plot depicts the median, quartiles, and outliers.

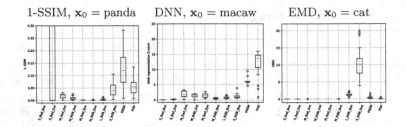

Fig. 6. Box plots of different measures ρ on human JND images.

the interest of space. We will show all plots in an extended version of this paper. The perturbation directions **v** are indicated on the x-axis. The y-axis shows the median, quartiles, and outliers of the participants' JND images, measured in the specific $d()$ indicated in the plots. The **main qualitative observation** is that none of the popular distance measure $d()$ has a flat median across the directions we tested. For example, for pixel 2-norm on $\mathbf{x}_0$=macaw, the median is 1049 and 4402 along the PGD and X_RGB_Box directions respectively. Similarly for DNN 2-norm on $\mathbf{x}_0$=macaw, the median is 1.8 and 13.6 respectively along the M_Red_Dot and PGD directions respectively. This indicates that none of these measures is a good fit to human JND.

4.2   Quantitative Assessment

Now we report the empirical estimate of condition number $\hat{\kappa}$ for each distance measure $d()$ and center image $\mathbf{x}_0$. Recall that $\hat{\kappa}(d)$ must be close to 1 for a distance measure $d()$ to have the possibility to be a good fit to human perception. Due to the large number of censored data along some directions, we estimate $\hat{\kappa}(d)$ in two ways.

- Non-censored median: We discarded all "given up" data. We then estimated the human JND distance using the median value along a direction **v**. This is shown in Table 2.
- First quartile: In the second procedure, we do not discard the "given up" values but consider those distances to be infinity. Then we estimate the human

Table 2. Estimated $\hat{\kappa}(d)$ using non-censored median.

Center Image	1-norm	2-norm	3-norm	∞-norm	EMD	1 - SSIM	DNN 1-norm	DNN 2-norm	DNN ∞-norm
panda	73853	142.6	17.8	**14**	68457	27913	476	512	575
macaw	499559	95.7	**11.9**	14.3	48210	56933	854	683	627
Cat	46460	89.7	**11.2**	14	42919	11786	389	381	355

Table 3. Estimated $\hat{\kappa}(d)$ using the first quartile.

Center Image	1-norm	2-norm	3-norm	∞-norm	EMD	1 - SSIM	DNN 1-norm	DNN 2-norm	DNN ∞-norm
panda	84379	163	20.3	**17.1**	79777	16353	577	704	496
macaw	23752	45.9	**5.7**	21.6	23300	255502	442	355	341
Cat	31787	61.4	**7.6**	24.2	30031	68609	341	329	297

JND along a direction by the first quartile. The median would have fallen in censored values for some directions. The first quartile is a biased estimate of human JND $d(\mathbf{x}, \mathbf{x}_0)$, but has the benefit of not hitting any censored values. This is shown in Table 3.

We highlight the smallest estimated condition number $\hat{\kappa}$ in each table. All of these values are much larger than 1. This quantitatively shows that popular imperceptibility measures in visual adversarial attacks are far from human perception.

5   Discussions and Conclusion

We quantitatively show that pixel p-norms, EMD, 1 - SSIM, and DNN representation p-norms are not good matches to human perception. This paper thus calls for a rethinking of adversarial attack formulation. The closest work to ours is [21], which also conducted human experiments on adversarial attacks and human perception. That study was limited in design: they only tested pixel 0-, 2-, ∞-norms but not other p-norms or measures. Their test also relies on the knowledge of the feasible set radius ϵ, and depended on humans (mis)-categorizing a low resolution thumbnail (MNIST [13], CIFAR10 [12]). Instead, humans may notice small changes in a normal-sized image well before their categorization of the image changes. The present paper addresses these issues.

We also mention some limitations of our own work: (1) We used only three center images $\mathbf{x}_0$ in our human experiments. This is due to the fact that running human experiments is time consuming and expensive. (2) We still cannot answer "what is the correct measure $d()$", noting that computationally modeling human visual perception is still an open question in psychology [8, 18, 24, 30]. (3) We used a "show $\mathbf{x}_0$ then perturb" experiment paradigm, while in real applications the human inspector may not have access to $\mathbf{x}_0$. (4) We limited ourselves to the visual domain. Addressing these limitations remain future work.

Acknowledgments. Acknowledgments: This work is supported in part by NSF grants 1545481, 1623605, 1704117, 1836978 and the MADLab AF Center of Excellence FA9550-18-1-0166.

References

1. Athalye, A., Carlini, N., Wagner, D.: Obfuscated gradients give a false sense of security: Circumventing defenses to adversarial examples. arXiv preprint arXiv:1802.00420 (2018)
2. Buhrmester, M., Kwang, T., Gosling, S.D.: Amazon's mechanical turk: a new source of inexpensive, yet high-quality, data? Perspect. Psychol. Sci. **6**(1), 3–5 (2011)
3. Carlini, N., Wagner, D.: Adversarial examples are not easily detected: bypassing ten detection methods. In: Proceedings of the 10th ACM Workshop on Artificial Intelligence and Security, pp. 3–14. ACM (2017)
4. Deng, J., Dong, W., Socher, R., Li, L.J., Li, K., Fei-Fei, L.: Imagenet: a large-scale hierarchical image database. In: Proceedings of the IEEE Conference on Computer Vision and Pattern Recognition, pp. 248–255. IEEE (2009)
5. Fechner, G.T., Boring, E.G., Howes, D.H., Adler, H.E.: Elements of Psychophysics. Translated by Helmut E. Adler. Edited by Davis H. Howes And Edwin G. Boring, With an Introd. by Edwin G. Boring. Holt, Rinehart and Winston (1966)
6. Gilmer, J., Adams, R.P., Goodfellow, I., Andersen, D., Dahl, G.E.: Motivating the rules of the game for adversarial example research. arXiv preprint arXiv:1807.06732 (2018)
7. Goodfellow, I.J., Shlens, J., Szegedy, C.: Explaining and harnessing adversarial examples (2014). arXiv preprint arXiv:1412.6572
8. Itti, L., Koch, C.: Computational modelling of visual attention. Nat. Rev. Neurosci. **2**(3), 194 (2001)
9. Jamieson, K.G., Jain, L., Fernandez, C., Glattard, N.J., Nowak, R.: Next: a system for real-world development, evaluation, and application of active learning. In: Cortes, C., Lawrence, N.D., Lee, D.D., Sugiyama, M., Garnett, R. (eds.) Advances in Neural Information Processing Systems, vol. 28, pp. 2656–2664. Curran Associates Inc., Red Hook (2015)
10. Kolter, Z., Madry, A.: Adversarial robustness: theory and practice. In: Tutorial at NeurIPS (2018)
11. Kriegeskorte, N.: Deep neural networks: a new framework for modeling biological vision and brain information processing. Ann. Rev. Vis. Sci. **1**, 417–446 (2015)
12. Krizhevsky, A., Hinton, G.: Learning multiple layers of features from tiny images. Technical report, Citeseer (2009)
13. LeCun, Y.: The mnist database of handwritten digits (1998). http://yann.lecun.com/exdb/mnist/
14. Madry, A., Makelov, A., Schmidt, L., Tsipras, D., Vladu, A.: Towards deep learning models resistant to adversarial attacks. arXiv preprint arXiv:1706.06083 (2017)
15. Moosavi-Dezfooli, S.M., Fawzi, A., Fawzi, O., Frossard, P.: Universal adversarial perturbations. In: Proceedings of the IEEE Conference on Computer Vision and Pattern Recognition, pp. 1765–1773 (2017)

16. Moosavi-Dezfooli, S.M., Fawzi, A., Frossard, P.: Deepfool: a simple and accurate method to fool deep neural networks. In: Proceedings of the IEEE Conference on Computer Vision and Pattern Recognition, pp. 2574–2582 (2016)
17. Papernot, N., McDaniel, P., Sinha, A., Wellman, M.: Towards the science of security and privacy in machine learning. arXiv preprint arXiv:1611.03814 (2016)
18. Rensink, R.A.: Change detection. Ann. Rev. Psychol. **53**(1), 245–277 (2002)
19. Rubner, Y., Tomasi, C., Guibas, L.J.: The earth mover's distance as a metric for image retrieval. Int. J. Comput. Vis. **40**(2), 99–121 (2000)
20. Salamati, M., Soudjani, S., Majumdar, R.: Perception-in-the-loop adversarial examples. arXiv preprint arXiv:1901.06834 (2019)
21. Sharif, M., Bauer, L., Reiter, M.K.: On the suitability of lp-norms for creating and preventing adversarial examples. In: The Bright and Dark Sides of Computer Vision: Challenges and Opportunities for Privacy and Security (CVPR Workshop) (2018)
22. Sheikh, H.R., Sabir, M.F., Bovik, A.C.: A statistical evaluation of recent full reference image quality assessment algorithms. IEEE Trans. Image Process. **15**(11), 3440–3451 (2006)
23. Sievert, S., Ross, D., Jain, L., Jamieson, K., Nowak, R., Mankoff, R.: Next: a system to easily connect crowdsourcing and adaptive data collection. In: Proceedings of the 16th Python in Science Conference, pp. 113–119 (2017)
24. Simons, D.J., Ambinder, M.S.: Change blindness: theory and consequences. Curr. Direct. Psychol. Sci. **14**(1), 44–48 (2005)
25. Szegedy, C., Vanhoucke, V., Ioffe, S., Shlens, J., Wojna, Z.: Rethinking the inception architecture for computer vision. In: Proceedings of the IEEE Conference on Computer Vision and Pattern Recognition, pp. 2818–2826 (2016)
26. Szegedy, C., et al.: Intriguing properties of neural networks. arXiv preprint arXiv:1312.6199 (2013)
27. Tramèr, F., Dupré, P., Rusak, G., Pellegrino, G., Boneh, D.: Adversarial: Perceptual ad blocking meets adversarial machine learning. In: Proceedings of the 2019 ACM SIGSAC Conference on Computer and Communications Security, pp. 2005–2021 (2019)
28. Wang, Z., Bovik, A.C.: Mean squared error: love it or leave it? a new look at signal fidelity measures. IEEE Signal Process. Mag. **26**(1), 98–117 (2009)
29. Wang, Z., Bovik, A.C., Sheikh, H.R., Simoncelli, E.P.: Image quality assessment: from error visibility to structural similarity. IEEE Trans. Image Process. **13**(4), 600–612 (2004)
30. Wolfe, J.M.: Visual search. Curr.Biol. **20**(8), R346–R349 (2010)
31. Yuan, X., He, P., Zhu, Q., Li, X.: Adversarial examples: attacks and defenses for deep learning. IEEE Trans. Neural Netw. Learn. Syst. **30**, 2805–2824 (2019)
32. Zhang, X., Lin, W., Xue, P.: Just-noticeable difference estimation with pixels in images. J. Vis. Commun. Image Representation **19**(1), 30–41 (2008)

Cyber-Physical System Security

Secure Discrete-Time Linear-Quadratic Mean-Field Games

Muhammad Aneeq uz Zaman$^{(\boxtimes)}$, Sujay Bhatt, and Tamer Başar

Coordinated Science Laboratory, University of Illinois at Urbana-Champaign,
Urbana, IL 61801-2307, USA
mazaman2@illinois.edu

Abstract. In this paper, we propose a framework for strategic interaction among a large population of agents. The agents are linear stochastic control systems having a communication channel between the sensor and the controller for each agent. The strategic interaction is modeled as a Secure Linear-Quadratic Mean-Field Game (SLQ-MFG), within a consensus framework, where the communication channel is noiseless, but, is susceptible to eavesdropping by adversaries. For the purposes of security, the sensor shares only a sketch of the states using a private key. The controller for each agent has the knowledge of the private key, and has fast access to the sketches of states from the sensor. We propose a secure communication mechanism between the sensor and controller, and a state reconstruction procedure using multi-rate sensor output sampling at the controller. We establish that the state reconstruction is noisy, and hence the Mean-Field Equilibrium (MFE) of the SLQ-MFG does not exist in the class of linear controllers. We introduce the notion of an approximate MFE (ϵ-MFE) and prove that the MFE of the standard (non-secure) LQ-MFG is an ϵ-MFE of the SLQ-MFG. Also, we show that $\epsilon \to 0$ as the estimation error in state reconstruction approaches 0. Furthermore, we show that the MFE of LQ-MFG is also an $(\epsilon + \varepsilon)$-Nash equilibrium for the finite population version of the SLQ-MFG; and $(\epsilon + \varepsilon) \to 0$ as the estimation error approaches 0 and the number of agents $n \to \infty$. We empirically investigate the performance sensitivity of the $(\epsilon + \varepsilon)$-Nash equilibrium to perturbations in sampling rate, model parameters, and private keys.

1 Introduction

In this paper, we study large scale multi-agent interaction, where a large number of *sensing systems* (a.k.a agents) interact with each other, to solve a *consensus problem* in a decentralized manner. The individual agents in such a multi-agent system comprise of a sensor and a controller with a communication channel between them. The communication channel is noiseless, but, is susceptible to eavesdropping by adversaries; so a secure communication mechanism is desired.

Research support in part by Grant FA9550-19-1-0353 from AFOSR, and in part by US Army Research Laboratory (ARL) Cooperative Agreement W911NF-17-2-0196.

© Springer Nature Switzerland AG 2020
Q. Zhu et al. (Eds.): GameSec 2020, LNCS 12513, pp. 203–222, 2020.
https://doi.org/10.1007/978-3-030-64793-3_11

The eavesdropping adversary is not a strategic player, and hence there is no game being played against the adversary, as in robust MFGs [1]. The sensors collect and/or generate various sensory data over time and the controllers analyze the data streams to discover new information, derive future insights, and take sequential control decisions.

Mean-Field Games (MFGs) are a framework for analyzing large scale strategic interaction between rational agents optimizing their accumulated returns over time. Estimating the solution of finite population games with a large number of agents is prohibitive in most cases, being exponential in the number of agents [2,3]. Mean-field games was proposed to address this scalability issue in the seminal works of [4] and [5]. In the mean-field setting, a generic agent interacts with a mass of infinitely many agents, modeled as an exogenous signal, also called the mean-field trajectory. The solution concept analogous to the Nash equilibrium in MFGs is that of the mean-field equilibrium, where the generic agent reacts optimally to the mean-field trajectory and the mean-field trajectory in turn models the *average* behavior of the agent.

Linear Quadratic MFGs (LQ-MFGs) [6–8] are a significant benchmark in the area of MFGs which inherit much of the advantages of the MFG formalism, while allowing analytical expressions for MFE. While there have been several works on the continuous time formulation of LQ-MFGs [6–8], the discrete-time setting has recently gained momentum due to its application to digital systems [9] and reinforcement learning [10–12]. Following this line of work, we adopt a discrete-time LQ framework to study the secure multi-agent interaction.

1.1 Agent Model and Objective

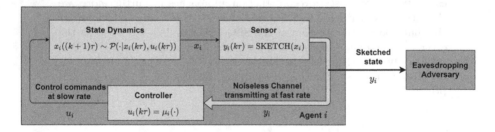

Fig. 1. Schematic representation of an agent in the multi-agent system. The sensor measures the state and provides a multi-rate access to the controller over the noiseless communication channel. The channel is susceptible to eavesdropping by adversaries. Hence, the sensor and controller employ a secure communication mechanism (sketching and multi-rate sampling) for decision making.

Figure 1 shows the schematic representation of an agent in the multi-agent system under consideration. The agents aim to solve a consensus problem in a decentralized manner. Namely, the cost function of each agent penalizes (i) deviation of the agent's state from the aggregate behavior, and (ii) high control effort. For each agent, the communication link between the sensor and the controller is assumed to be noiseless, but susceptible to eavesdropping by adversaries. The sensor collects information on the underlying high-dimensional stochastic process, modelled as a state, and the controller takes actions to affect the evolution of the stochastic process. However, for the purposes of security and fast communication, the sensor shares only a *sketch* of the high-dimensional states. Sketches obfuscate the original data using a transformation (called the *private key*) and thus have the flexibility to reduce the dimensionality of the shared data while providing privacy features [13,14]. The controller reconstructs the states, using the private key and multi-rate sensor output sampling, for decision making. We assume that there is a finite set of private keys that the agents in the multi-agent system can choose from. Each agent chooses a key from the set randomly for the purposes of secure sketching and state reconstruction.

In this paper, we model the agents as *linear* control systems perturbed by a noise process, which is not necessarily Gaussian. For ease of implementation, we restrict the controllers of the secure LQ game to the class of linear controllers. There is a communication channel between the sensor and the controller; a model similar to [15]. However, unlike [15], the channel is noiseless but susceptible to eavesdropping by adversaries, and the sensor provides the controller with multi-rate (fast with respect to the rate of control input) access to the linear sketch of the underlying states. The controller reconstructs the state, which is noisy owing to finite-sampling rates, and decides the course of action guided by a decentralized feedback control law. In a multi-agent system made up of agents as in Fig. 1, we consider the following problem: *How do rational agents solve a consensus problem in a decentralized manner, when they have security concerns?*

1.2 A Motivating Application

Internet of Battlefield Things (IoBT) is a paradigm that is becoming increasingly important, partly due to the advantages it can offer in battlefield scenarios and largely due to the success of Internet of Things. Entities ("things") are more useful and effective when they are smarter, and even more so when they can interact with each other [16].

Multi-agent systems can model the interaction of entities and their capabilities including controlled sensing and processing of information, undertaking coordinated defensive actions against adversaries, and effecting offensive measures to achieve desired objectives. This is achieved by coordinating, jointly planning and executing the decisions of the agents that constitute the Internet of Battlefield Things. Successful leverage of large scale multi-agent systems to build battlefield solutions requires learning optimal policies in a *secure* and *decentralized* manner; which increases reliability, decreases computational overhead, and facilitates interaction of heterogeneous agents.

1.3   Main Results and Organization

The paper is organized as follows:

1. In Sect. 2, we propose a Secure Linear Quadratic Mean-Field Game (SLQ-MFG), for studying the multi-agent interaction with possibly infinitely many agents solving a consensus problem. We also derive insights in the secure (finite) $n-$agent dynamic game using this analysis.
2. In Sect. 3, we discuss a secure communication mechanism for information transfer between the sensor and the controller for each agent; see Fig. 1. This (noisy) reconstructed state, obtained using multi-rate sensor output sampling, is used by the controller for decentralized decision making.
3. In Sect. 4, we establish that Mean-Field Equilibrium (MFE), a notion that formalizes the notion of consensus in multi-agent systems, does not exist in SLQ-MFGs in the class of linear controllers. Hence, we introduce the notion of ϵ-MFE and ($\epsilon+\varepsilon$)-Nash equilibrium to characterize consensus in secure multi-agent interactions. We prove that MFE of (standard) LQ-MFG, in which the controller has perfect state information, corresponds to ϵ-MFE of the SLQ-MFG, and an ($\epsilon+\varepsilon$)-Nash equilibrium for the secure $n-$agent dynamic game.
4. In Sect. 5 we empirically investigate the performance of ($\epsilon + \varepsilon$)-Nash equilibrium (deduced in Sect. 4) and its sensitivity to perturbations in sampling rate, model parameters and private keys.

2   Secure LQ-MFG: Model and Objective

In this section, we discuss the model and objective for dynamic games considered in this paper for analyzing the multi-agent interaction. Section 2.1 discusses the model and objective of Secure n-agent LQ game and Sect. 2.2 discusses the model and objective of Secure LQ-MFG.

2.1   Secure n-agent Linear Quadratic (LQ) Game

We formulate the secure n-agent LQ game by defining the state dynamics and objectives of the agents, where the agents are coupled by a consensus-like term in their objectives.

Consider the following secure $n-$agent discrete-time Linear Quadratic (LQ) game [17]. Each agent i, $i \in \{1, 2, \cdots, n\}$ in the game has the following dynamics:

$$x_i(k\tau + (j+1)\Delta) = Ax_i(k\tau + j\Delta) + Bu_i(k\tau) + \tilde{w}_i(k\tau + j\Delta),$$
$$y_i(k\tau + j\Delta) = \text{SKETCH}(x_i(k\tau + j\Delta)) = C_i x_i(k\tau + j\Delta), \qquad (1)$$

where $j \in \{0, 1, \ldots, N-1\}$ is the index of the fast time scale and $k \in \{0, 1, 2, \ldots\}$ is the index of the slow time scale. We denote by $x_i \in \mathbb{R}^m$ the state of agent i, by $u_i \in \mathbb{R}^p$ the control action and by $y_i \in \mathbb{R}^q$ the garbled state (a sketch a.k.a. observation) which is revealed to the agent. The initial state $x_i(0)$ has mean ν_0 and covariance matrix Ξ_0. A and B are state transition and control matrices of appropriate dimensions, and $\tilde{w}_i$ are i.i.d random vectors generated by distribution with mean zero and covariance $\tilde{\Sigma}$, denoted by $\mathcal{D}(0, \tilde{\Sigma})$. Note that since we are restricting our attention to linear controllers we don't require the noise to be necessarily Gaussian. At time $k\tau$ each agent has access to knowledge $I_i(k\tau)$, which corresponds to observations and actions of the agent i and the observations of all other agents upto time $k\tau$. Here SKETCH($\cdot$) is any function that obfuscates the data. In this paper, we choose a random linear sketch [13] as a private key to transmit the state from the sensor to the controller. Sketching has been used for dimensionality reduction by using random projections [13] and providing privacy features [14]. In this paper, sketching is employed to obfuscate the data by making it hard for any adversary to guess/reconstruct the states.

Let the set of private keys available for each agent be denoted by:

$$\mathcal{C} = \{C^{(i)} | i \in \{1, 2, \ldots, M\}, M < \infty, C^{(i)} \in \mathbb{R}^{q \times m}\}, \tag{2}$$

We assume that the each agent chooses a private key $C^{(i)}$ from $\mathcal{C}$, uniformly at random. In Sect. 4.4 we discuss how careful construction of $\mathcal{C}$ positively impacts the performance of the proposed control strategies.

Multi-rate Setup: It is assumed that the sensor and hence the controller has multi-rate (fast) $1/\Delta$ access to the states, while the system is controlled at a slower rate $1/\tau$, such that $\tau = N\Delta$ for an integer $N > 0$. The motivation for this two time-scaled approach is that the obfuscated state received by the controller is not readily amenable for decision making as the private key C_i is not invertible. So using ideas as in [17], we use multi-rate sensor output sampling approach to reconstruct the state. Note that this approach is different from using filtering [13] which is not applicable in this context as there is no observation noise due to the channel being noiseless. In [17], it is shown that for the controller to be able to reconstruct the state using the observations, N should be greater than the observability index of the system (A, C_i).

The cost of agent i is a consensus like cost which couples the agent with the other agents by penalizing deviation from the aggregate behavior of the other agents while minimizing control effort. This is the standard objective function for the original LQ-MFGs problem [6] and has been used as a framework in many follow-up studies, such as [1]. The cost of agent i in the n-agent game under policy $\pi^i \in \Pi^i$, where Π^i is the set of all policies $\pi^i : I_i \to \mathbb{R}^p$, while other agents are following the set of policies $\pi^{-i} \in \Pi^{-i}, \Pi^{-i} := \{\Pi^j\}_{j \neq i}$ is given by,

$$J_i^n(\pi^i, \pi^{-i}) = \limsup_{T \to \infty} \frac{1}{T} \mathbb{E}_\pi \left\{ \sum_{k=0}^{T-1} \|x_i(k\tau) - \bar{x}_i^n(k\tau)\|_Q^2 + \|u_i(k\tau)\|_R^2 \right\}, \tag{3}$$

where

$$\bar{x}_i^n(k\tau) = \frac{1}{n-1} \sum_{j \neq i} x_j(k\tau), \tag{4}$$

and $Q \geq 0$ and $R > 0$ are symmetric matrices of appropriate dimensions and I_i is the information set of agent i. The expectation $\mathbb{E}_\pi$ is with respect to the joint control law $\pi = (\pi^i, \pi^{-i})$. The quantity $\bar{x}_i^n$ captures the aggregate behavior of agents other than i and is also called the *empirical mean-field trajectory*.

2.2 Secure Linear Quadratic Mean-Field Game (SLQ-MFG)

Owing to the difficulty of finding ϵ-Nash equilibria in n–agent games, we now introduce a limiting case of infinite population game, called the mean-field game [4,5]. Specifically, we formulate SLQ-MFG by describing the state dynamics and objective of the generic agent interacting with the mass of infinitely many agents, referred to as the *mean-field trajectory* [6].

The dynamics of a generic agent are

$$x(k\tau + (j+1)\Delta) = Ax(k\tau + j\Delta) + Bu(k\tau) + \tilde{w}(k\tau + j\Delta),$$
$$y(k\tau + j\Delta) = Cx(k\tau + j\Delta) \tag{5}$$

where $x \in \mathbb{R}^m$ denotes the state, $u \in \mathbb{R}^p$ the control action and $y \in \mathbb{R}^q$ the observation of the generic agent. As in the finite population game (Sect. 2.1), j is the index of the fast time scale and k is the index of the slow time scale. Matrices A and B denote the state transition and control matrices of appropriate dimensions and C belongs to the finite set $\mathcal{C}$ as defined in (2). As the generic agent in the SLQ-MFG has the same structure as the agent shown in Fig. 1, it is susceptible to surveillance and hence it is necessary to sketch the state of the agent. As a result, the multi-rate setup is required to reconstruct the sketched state. The initial condition $x(0)$ has mean ν_0 and covariance matrix Ξ_0. The noise process $\tilde{w}$ is generated i.i.d. with distribution $\mathcal{D}(0, \tilde{\Sigma})$. The generic agent's controller μ at time t depends on the observations and actions of the agent upto time $k\tau$ and the mean-field trajectory. The set of all such controllers is denoted by $\mathcal{M}$. The generic agent's cost under controller μ and mean-field trajectory $\bar{x} = (\bar{x}(0), \bar{x}(\tau), \bar{x}(2\tau) \ldots)$ is

$$J(\mu, \bar{x}) = \limsup_{T \to \infty} \frac{1}{T} \mathbb{E}_\mu \left\{ \sum_{k=0}^{T-1} \|x(k\tau) - \bar{x}(k\tau)\|_Q^2 + \|u(k\tau)\|_R^2 \right\}, \tag{6}$$

The mean-field trajectory is assumed to belong to the set of bounded sequences ℓ^∞. In the context of MFGs, the appropriate solution concept is that of Mean-Field Equilibrium (MFE), which is the infinite population analog of Nash equilibrium. To define the mean-field equilibirium (MFE) we use an operator $\Lambda : \mathcal{M} \to \ell^\infty$ (as defined in [18]) which maps a controller μ to a mean-field trajectory $\bar{x}$. If $\bar{x} = \Lambda(\mu)$, $\bar{x}$ is also referred to as being *generated* by controller μ. Now we state the definition of MFE.

Definition 1. *The tuple $(\mu^*, \bar{x}^*) \in \mathcal{M} \times \ell^\infty$ is an MFE if $\bar{x}^* = \Lambda(\mu^*)$ and*

$$J(\mu^*, \bar{x}^*) \leq J(\mu, \bar{x}^*), \quad \forall \mu \in \mathcal{M}$$

MFE is the infinite population analog to the Nash equilibrium where any agent (represented by the generic agent) has no incentive to deviate from the MFE given all other agents are following the same policy.

3   State Reconstruction Using Multi-rate Sensor Output Sampling

Since the multi-rate setup plays a crucial role in state reconstruction, we describe the reconstruction mechanism (inspired by [17]) employed by the controller to reconstruct the state of the agent. The method in [17] is for deterministic dynamic systems, and we extend it to the case where the agent dynamics are stochastic. This reconstruction is shown to reproduce the state of the agent with some estimation error.

In the multi-rate setup, the observation rate is faster than the control rate. We suppress subscripts for clarity in this subsection. As a consequence of (5),

$$x(k\tau + j\Delta) = A^j x(k\tau) + \sum_{i=0}^{j-1} A^i B u(k\tau) + \sum_{i=0}^{j-1} A^i \tilde{w}(k\tau + (j-1-i)\Delta)$$

and since $x((k+1)\tau) = x(k\tau + N\Delta)$ we can deduce the dynamics of the state at the slower input rate $1/\tau$,

$$x((k+1)\tau) = A^N x(k\tau) + \sum_{i=0}^{N-1} A^i B u(k\tau) + \sum_{i=0}^{N-1} A^i \tilde{w}(k\tau + (N-1-i)\Delta)$$

$$= A_0 x(k\tau) + B_0 u(k\tau) + w^0(k\tau) \tag{7}$$

where $A_0 = A^N$, $B_0 = \sum_{i=0}^{N-1} A^i B$ and $w^0(k\tau)$ is an i.i.d. random vectors such that $w^0(k\tau) = \sigma w_{[k]}$ where $\sigma = [A^{N-1}, A^{N-2}, \ldots, I]$ and $w_{[k]} = [\tilde{w}^T(k\tau), \tilde{w}^T(k\tau+\Delta), \ldots, \tilde{w}^T(k\tau+(N-1)\Delta)]^T$. The vectors $w^0(k\tau)$ and $w_{[k]}$ have distributions $w_{[k]} \sim \mathcal{D}(0, I \otimes \tilde{\Sigma})$ and $w^0 \sim \mathcal{D}(0, \Sigma^0)$ where $\Sigma^0 = \sigma(I \otimes \tilde{\Sigma})\sigma^T$. Let us define $y_{[k]}$ such that $y_{[k]} := [y^T((k-1)\tau), y^T((k-1)\tau + \Delta), \ldots, y^T((k-1)\tau + (N-1)\Delta)]^T$. The vector $y_{[k+1]}$ can be written down as,

$$y_{[k+1]} = C_0 x(k\tau) + D_0 u(k\tau) + C_d w_{[k]} \tag{8}$$

where

$$C_0 = \begin{bmatrix} C \\ CA \\ CA^2 \\ \vdots \\ CA^{N-1} \end{bmatrix}, D_0 = \begin{bmatrix} 0 \\ CB \\ C(AB+B) \\ \vdots \\ C\sum_{i=0}^{N-2} A^i B \end{bmatrix}, C_d = \begin{bmatrix} 0 & 0 & 0 & \ldots 0 \\ C & 0 & 0 & \ldots 0 \\ CA & C & 0 & \ldots 0 \\ \vdots & \vdots & \vdots & \ddots \vdots \\ CA^{N-2} & CA^{N-3} & CA^{N-4} & \ldots 0 \end{bmatrix}$$

Multiplying C_0^T on both sides of (8) we get,

$$C_0^T y_{[k+1]} = C_0^T (C_0 x(k\tau) + D_0 u(k\tau) + C_d w_{[k]})$$

As N is greater than the observability index of the system, $C_0^T C_0$ is invertible. Hence,

$$x(k\tau) = (C_0^T C_0)^{-1} C_0^T \left[y_{[k+1]} - D_0 u(k\tau) - C_d w_{[k]} \right] \tag{9}$$

Using (7) and (9) we get,

$$x((k+1)\tau) = A_0 (C_0^T C_0)^{-1} C_0^T \left[y_{[k+1]} - D_0 u(k\tau) \right] + B_0 u(k\tau) + E_C w_{[k]}$$

where $E_C = \sigma - A_0 (C_0^T C_0)^{-1} C_0^T C_d$. Thus the state $x(k\tau)$ can be expressed as,

$$x(k\tau) = L_y y_{[k]} + L_u u((k-1)\tau) + w(k\tau)$$

where $L_y = A_0 (C_0^T C_0)^{-1} C_0^T$, $L_u = B_0 - L_y D_0$ and $w(k\tau) = E_C w_{[k-1]}$ is a zero mean random vector with covariance matrix

$$\Sigma_C = E_C (I \otimes \tilde{\Sigma}) E_C^T. \tag{10}$$

As the controller has access to $y_{[k]}$ and $u((k-1)\tau)$ at time $(k\tau)^-$ it can reconstruct the state as,

$$\hat{x}(k\tau) = L_y y_{[k]} + L_u u((k-1)\tau)$$

Hence the estimation error $\hat{x}(k\tau) - x(k\tau) = -w(k\tau)$ is a zero mean random vector with covariance matrix Σ_C. Note that since Σ_C depends on the key C, it belongs to a finite set. We denote this set by $\mathcal{E}_C$, which has one-to-one correspondence with C and hence has cardinality M.

4   Equilibria of Secure LQ Games

In this section, we establish the equilibrium notions and derive the (approximately) optimal policies for the agents in the multi-agent system. Section 4.1 shows that the optimal control problem (which is a part of the MFE) is a nonstandard optimal control problem. Due to this non-standard problem, the SLQ-MFG does not permit an MFE in the class of linear controllers. Section 4.2 introduces the concept of ϵ-MFE and establishes that the MFE of the LQ-MFG is an ϵ-MFE for the SLQ-MFG. The variable ϵ depends on the estimation error in the state reconstruction. Section 4.3 shows that MFE for LQ-MFG is also an $(\epsilon + \varepsilon)$-Nash equilibrium for the secure n-agent LQ game, where ϵ and ε depend on the estimation error and the number of agents n.

4.1   MFE of the SLQ-MFG

We will show that the MFE of the SLQ-MFG does not exist in the class of linear controllers. As is common in the stochastic LQ setting [18], we restrict the controllers to the class of linear feedback controllers μ_K. The controller has the form

$$u(k\tau) = K_1 \hat{x}(k\tau) + K_2 \bar{x}(k\tau)$$

where $\hat{x}(k\tau)$ is the reconstructed state of the agent and $\bar{x}(k\tau)$ is the mean-field trajectory.

The choice of the controller is similar to [18], where the MFE of the LQ-MFG was derived. See in Appendix (Sect. 7.1) for a brief overview of the results. These controllers generate mean-field trajectories which follow linear dynamics [18], formally if $\bar{x} = \Lambda(\mu_K)$ where $K = [K_1^T, K_2^T]^T \in \mathbb{R}^{p \times 2m}$, then $\bar{x}((k+1)\tau) = F\bar{x}(k\tau)$ where $F = A_0 - B_0(K_1 + K_2)$. So for this paper we focus our attention on linear feedback controllers and mean-field trajectories with linear dynamics. Moreover, with some slight abuse of notation $J(\mu, \bar{x})$ will be referred to by $J(K, F)$ and $\bar{x} = \Lambda(\mu_K) \iff F = \Lambda(K)$, since a linear feedback controller μ_K is completely characterized by K and a linear mean-field trajectory $\bar{x}$ by F.

Let us define an augmented state by $z(k\tau) = [x^T(k\tau), \bar{x}^T(k\tau)]^T$ where $\bar{x}^T(k\tau)$ is the mean-field trajectory. Assuming that the mean-field trajectory has linear dynamics given by state matrix F, using (7) the augmented system can be written down as,

$$z((k+1)\tau) = \bar{A}z(k\tau) + \bar{B}u(k\tau) + \bar{w}(k\tau)$$

where,

$$\bar{A} = \begin{bmatrix} A_0 & 0 \\ 0 & F \end{bmatrix}, \bar{B} = \begin{bmatrix} B_0 \\ 0 \end{bmatrix}, \bar{w}(k\tau) = \begin{bmatrix} w^0(k\tau) \\ 0 \end{bmatrix} \tag{11}$$

The random variable $\bar{w}(k\tau)$ has distribution $\mathcal{D}(0, \bar{\Sigma})$ where $\bar{\Sigma} = \begin{bmatrix} \Sigma^0 & 0 \\ 0 & 0 \end{bmatrix}$. Similarly using (6) the cost function of the generic agent can be expressed as,

$$J(K, F) = \limsup_{T \to \infty} \frac{1}{T} \mathbb{E}_K \left\{ \sum_{k=0}^{T-1} \|z(k\tau)\|_{\bar{Q}}^2 + \|u(k\tau)\|_R^2 \right\}, \text{where } \bar{Q} = \begin{bmatrix} Q & -Q \\ -Q & Q \end{bmatrix} \geq 0 \tag{12}$$

Now we investigate the MFE of the SLQ-MFG (Definition 1). As per the definition, one part of finding the MFE corresponds to finding the K which minimizes cost (12) for a given F.

In what follows we show that such a K does not exist. For stabilizing linear feedback controllers $u(k\tau) = -K\hat{z}(k\tau) = -K(z(k\tau) - \hat{w}(k\tau))$ where $\hat{w}(k\tau) = [w^T(k\tau), 0]^T$, the closed-loop dynamics of a system $z(k\tau)$ are

$$z((k+1)\tau) = \bar{A}z(k\tau) + \bar{B}u(k\tau) + \bar{w}(k\tau) = (\bar{A} - \bar{B}K)z(k\tau) + \bar{B}K\hat{w}(k\tau) + \bar{w}(k\tau) \tag{13}$$

where $\hat{w}(k\tau) \sim \mathcal{D}(0, \hat{\Sigma}_C)$, with

$$\hat{\Sigma}_C = \begin{bmatrix} \Sigma_C & 0 \\ 0 & 0 \end{bmatrix} \tag{14}$$

As Σ_C (as given in Eq. (10)) belongs to the finite set $\mathcal{E}_C$, $\hat{\Sigma}_C$ also belongs to the finite set $\hat{\mathcal{E}}_C$ which has the same cardinality M and has one-to-one correspondence with $\mathcal{E}_C$. Using the definitions of $\hat{w}(k\tau)$ and $\bar{w}(k\tau)$, the random vector $(BK\hat{w}(k\tau) + \bar{w}(k\tau)) \sim \mathcal{D}(0, \Psi_K)$, where $\Psi_K = \bar{\Sigma} + BK\hat{\Sigma}_C(BK)^T$. The stationary distribution of the closed-loop system (13) is $\mathcal{D}(0, \Sigma_K)$, where Σ_K satisfies

$$\Sigma_K = \Psi_K + (\bar{A} - \bar{B}K)\Sigma_K(\bar{A} - \bar{B}K)^T$$

and is guaranteed to be positive semi-definite and unique for any stabilizing K. Using techniques similar to [19] the cost of controller K is

$$
\begin{aligned}
J(K, F) &= \mathbb{E}_{z(k\tau) \sim \mathcal{D}(0, \Sigma_K)}[z^T(k\tau)(\bar{Q} + K^T RK)z(k\tau)] + \text{Tr}\,(K\hat{\Sigma}_C K^T R), \\
&= \text{Tr}\,((\bar{Q} + K^T RK)\Sigma_K) + \text{Tr}\,(K\hat{\Sigma}_C K^T R) \\
&= \text{Tr}\,((\bar{Q} + K^T RK)\mathcal{T}_K^T(\Psi_K)) + \text{Tr}\,(K\hat{\Sigma}_C K^T R), \\
&= \text{Tr}\,(\mathcal{T}_K(\bar{Q} + K^T RK)\Psi_K) + \text{Tr}\,(K\hat{\Sigma}_C K^T R), \\
&= \text{Tr}\,(P_K\bar{\Sigma}) + \text{Tr}\,((B^T P_K B + R)K\hat{\Sigma}_C K^T) \quad\quad (15)
\end{aligned}
$$

where the operators $\mathcal{T}_K(M)$ and $\mathcal{T}_K^T(M)$ are defined as

$$\mathcal{T}_K(M) = \sum_{i=0}^{\infty}((\bar{A} - \bar{B}K)^T)^i M(\bar{A} - \bar{B}K)^i,$$

$$\mathcal{T}_K^T(M) = \sum_{i=0}^{\infty}(\bar{A} - \bar{B}K)^i M((\bar{A} - \bar{B}K)^T)^i$$

and P_K is the solution to the Lyapunov equation,

$$
\begin{aligned}
P_K &= (\bar{A} - \bar{B}K)^T P_K(\bar{A} - \bar{B}K) + (\bar{Q} + K^T RK) \\
&= \bar{A}^T P_K \bar{A} + \bar{Q} + K^T(\bar{B}^T P_K \bar{B} + R)K - \bar{A}^T P_K \bar{B}K - (\bar{B}K)^T P_K \bar{A} \quad (16)
\end{aligned}
$$

To find the K which minimizes cost (15), we define the Hamiltonian,

$$H = \text{Tr}\,(P_K\bar{\Sigma}) + \text{Tr}\,((B^T P_K B + R)K\hat{\Sigma}_C K^T) + \text{Tr}\,(GS)$$

where

$$G = -P_K + (\bar{A} - \bar{B}K)^T P_K(\bar{A} - \bar{B}K) + (\bar{Q} + K^T RK) = 0$$

Using the minimum principle,

$$\frac{\partial H}{\partial S} = -P_K + (\bar{A} - \bar{B}K)^T P_K(\bar{A} - \bar{B}K) + (\bar{Q} + K^T RK) = 0 \quad\quad (17)$$

$$\frac{\partial H}{\partial P_K} = \Psi_K - S + (\bar{A} - \bar{B}K)S(\bar{A} - \bar{B}K)^T = 0 \quad\quad (18)$$

$$
\begin{aligned}
\frac{\partial H}{\partial K} &= \frac{\partial}{\partial K}[\text{Tr}\,(K^T(\bar{B}^T P_K \bar{B} + R)K\hat{\Sigma}_C) + \text{Tr}\,(GS)] \\
&= \frac{\partial}{\partial K}[\text{Tr}\,((-\bar{A}^T P_K \bar{A} + P_K - \bar{Q} + \bar{A}^T P_K \bar{B}K + (\bar{B}K)^T P_K \bar{A})\hat{\Sigma}_C) \\
&\quad\quad\quad\quad\quad\quad\quad\quad\quad\quad + \text{Tr}\,(GS)] \text{ (using equation (16))} \\
&= \bar{B}^T P_K \bar{A}(\hat{\Sigma}_C - \Sigma_K) + (\bar{B}^T P_K \bar{B} + R)K\Sigma_K = 0 \quad\quad (19)
\end{aligned}
$$

Equation (17) recovers the Lyapunov Eq. (16), and from Eq. (18) we can deduce that $S \equiv \Sigma_K$ since K is a stabilizing controller. Equation (19) gives the form of the optimal controller (if it exists) for a given F

$$\hat{K}_F = (\bar{B}^T \hat{P} \bar{B} + R)^{-1} \bar{B}^T \hat{P} \bar{A} (I - \hat{\Sigma}_C \Sigma_{\hat{K}_F}^{-1})$$

where $\hat{P}$ is the solution to the Lyapunov equation,

$$\hat{P} = (\bar{A} - \bar{B}\hat{K}_F)^T \hat{P} (\bar{A} - \bar{B}\hat{K}_F) + (\bar{Q} + \hat{K}_F^T R \hat{K}_F) \tag{20}$$

Since

$$\Sigma_K = T_K^T(\Psi_K)$$
$$= \sum_{i=0}^{\infty} \begin{bmatrix} A_0 - B_0 K_1 & -B_0 K_2 \\ 0 & F \end{bmatrix}^i \begin{bmatrix} B_0 K_1 \Sigma_C (B_0 K_1)^T + \Sigma^0 & 0 \\ 0 & 0 \end{bmatrix} \begin{bmatrix} A_0 - B_0 K_1 & -B_0 K_2 \\ 0 & F \end{bmatrix}^{Ti}$$

it is clear that Σ_K will be a block diagonal matrix with the second block as all zeros. Hence Σ_K is guaranteed to have at least a zero eigenvalue which results in Σ_K being non-invertible. This means that $\hat{K}_F$ does not exist and as a result the MFE does not exist within the class of linear controllers.

To formulate useful strategies for the SLQ-MFG its useful to recall the MFE for the LQ-MFG. The MFE of the LQ-MFG is defined by the tuple (K^*, F^*) where K^* is the controller and F^* is the matrix which defines the mean-field trajectory $\bar{x}^*$. These results are obtained from a previous work [18] and the reader can refer to the Appendix (Sect. 7.1) for details of the MFE of LQ-MFG.

4.2 ϵ-MFE of the SLQ-MFG

We introduce the concept of ϵ-MFE for the SLQ-MFG and the MFE of LQ-MFG is shown to satisfy this definition. We start by formally proposing the ϵ-MFE of the SLQ-MFG. This is followed by the result that the MFE of the LQ-MFG is also the ϵ-MFE of the SLQ-MFG where $\epsilon \to 0$ as estimation error due to state reconstruction approaches 0. Consequently, if the state sketching is performed in a manner that estimation error is minimized (while obfuscating the state) the MFE of LQ-MFG is a close-to-optimal strategy for the SLQ-MFG.

Definition 2. *The tuple* $(K', F') \in \mathbb{R}^{p \times 2m} \times \mathbb{R}^{m \times m}$ *is an ϵ-MFE if* $F' = \Lambda(K')$ *and*

$$J(K', F') \leq J(K, F') + \epsilon, \quad \forall K \in \mathbb{R}^{p \times 2m}, \epsilon > 0$$

This is the analog of the ϵ-Nash equilibrium for the infinite population case. An ϵ-MFE proposes strategies where an agent has at most ϵ incentive to deviate from the ϵ-MFE. Now we note the conditions required for the existence and uniqueness of the MFE, which are a carry-over from previous work [18].

Assumption 1. *With P given as the unique positive definite solution to the Discrete-Time Riccati Equation (DARE),*

$$P = A_0^T P A_0 + Q - A_0^T P B_0 (R + B_0^T P B_0)^{-1} B_0^T P A_0$$

and furthermore that $G_P := -(R + B_0^T P B_0)^{-1} B_0^T$ and $H_P := A_0^T (I + P B_0 G_P)$, we have

$$\|H_P\|_2 + \frac{\|B_0 G_P\|_2 \|Q\|_2}{(1 - \|H_P\|_2)^2} < 1$$

Now we present the result that the MFE of LQ-MFG is also the ϵ-MFE of the SLQ-MFG. Moreover $\epsilon \to 0$ if estimation error approaches 0.

Theorem 1. *Under Assumption 1, the MFE of LQ-MFG (K^*, F^*) is also the ϵ-MFE of the SLQ-MFG where $\epsilon = \mathcal{O}(\mathrm{Tr}(\hat{\Sigma}_C))$ and $\hat{\Sigma}_C$ (as given in Eq. (14)) belongs to the finite set $\hat{\mathcal{E}}_C$.*

Proof. We start by defining the cost of the tuple (K, F) in the LQ-MFG. From Eq. (28), we have

$$\tilde{J}(K, F) = \mathrm{Tr}(P_K \bar{\Sigma}),$$

where P_K satisfies the Lyapunov Eq. (16). Hence, $J(K, F) \geq \tilde{J}(K, F)$ for a given K and F and as a consequence $\inf_K J(K, F) \geq \inf_K \tilde{J}(K, F)$. Trying to characterize ϵ-MFE,

$$J(K^*, F^*) - \inf_K J(K, F^*)$$

$$\leq J(K^*, F^*) - \inf_K \tilde{J}(K, F^*) = J(K^*, F^*) - \tilde{J}(K^*, F^*)$$

$$= \mathrm{Tr}(P^* \bar{\Sigma}) + \mathrm{Tr}((B^T P^* B + R) K^* \hat{\Sigma}_C K^{*T}) - \mathrm{Tr}(P^* \bar{\Sigma})$$

$$= \mathrm{Tr}\left((\bar{A}^T P^* \bar{B}(R + \bar{B}^T P^* \bar{B})^{-1} \bar{B}^T P^* \bar{A})\hat{\Sigma}_C\right)$$

The first equality in the above equation is due to Eq. (29), the second one is obtained by using (15), (28), (16) and the third equality is a result of using the definition of K^* (26). Hence,

$$J(K^*, F^*) - \inf_K J(K, F^*) \leq \mathrm{Tr}\left((\bar{A}^T P^* \bar{B}(R + \bar{B}^T P^* \bar{B})^{-1} \bar{B}^T P^* \bar{A})\hat{\Sigma}_C\right)$$

$$= \epsilon = \mathcal{O}(\mathrm{Tr}(\hat{\Sigma}_C))$$

Now we prove that F^* is generated by controller K^*. A generic agent using controller K^* will have closed-loop dynamics,

$$x((k+1)\tau) = (A_0 - B_0 K_1^*)x(k\tau) - B_0 K_2^* \bar{x}^*(k\tau) + B_0 K_1^* w(k\tau) + w^0(k\tau),$$

where $\bar{x}^*(k\tau)$ is the mean-field at time t generated by the controller K^*. Aggregating the closed-loop dynamics we get the dynamics of $\bar{x}^*$,

$$\bar{x}^*((k+1)\tau) = (A_0 - B_0(K_1^* + K_2^*))\bar{x}^*(k\tau) = F^* \bar{x}^*(k\tau)$$

Hence we have completed the proof of the second part of the ϵ-MFE definition, that is F^* is generated by controller K^*. $\qquad\square$

4.3 $(\epsilon + \varepsilon)$-Nash Equilibrium of the Secure n-Agent LQ Game

We prove that the MFE of the LQ-MFG is also an $(\epsilon + \varepsilon)$-Nash Equilibrium of the secure n-agent LQ game. We refer to the control law generated by MFE of LQ-MFG (F^*, K^*) by μ^*. We now show that for the n-agent game μ^* is an $(\epsilon + \varepsilon)$-Nash equilibrium where $\epsilon \to 0$ if the estimation error goes to zero and $\varepsilon \to 0$ if number of agents $n \to \infty$. As a result, if the state sketching is performed so that the estimation error is minimized (while obfuscating the state) and the number of agents is large enough, then the MFE of the LQ-MFG is close-to-optimal strategy for the secure n-agent LQ game. Before stating the theorem, since we are considering linear controllers, we define the set $\Pi_K^i \subset \Pi^i$, which is the set of controllers π^i that are linear in their arguments.

Theorem 2. *Under Assumption 1, let the cost of secure n-agent LQ game under controller μ^* be $J_i^n(\mu^{*i}, \mu^{*-i})$, then*

$$J_i^n(\mu^{*i}, \mu^{*-i}) - \inf_{\pi^i \in \Pi_K^i} J_i^n(\pi^i, \mu^{*-i}) < \epsilon + \varepsilon$$

where $\epsilon = \mathcal{O}(\hat{\sigma}_{max})$ and $\hat{\sigma}_{max} := \max_{\hat{\Sigma}_C \in \hat{\mathcal{E}}_C} \mathrm{Tr}(\hat{\Sigma}_C)$ and $\varepsilon = \mathcal{O}(\hat{\sigma}_{max}/\sqrt{n-1})$.

Proof. For an agent i,

$$J_i^n(\mu^{*i}, \mu^{*-i}) - \inf_{\pi^i \in \Pi_K^i} J_i^n(\pi^i, \mu^{*-i}) =$$

$$J_i^n(\mu^{*i}, \mu^{*-i}) - J(K^*, F^*) + J(K^*, F^*) - \inf_{\pi^i \in \Pi_K^i} J_i^n(\pi^i, \mu^{*-i}) \qquad (21)$$

We start by bounding the first expression on the RHS of (21). Let us define $\bar{x}^*(k\tau)$ as the linear mean-field trajectory defined by the state matrix F^* (also by definition generated by controller K^*) and $\bar{x}_i^{n*}(k\tau)$ as the empirical mean-field trajectory if all agents are following controller μ^*. From [9] we obtain the expression,

$$J_i^n(\mu^{*i}, \mu^{*-i}) - J(K^*, F^*) = \mathcal{O}\left(\sqrt{\limsup_{T\to\infty} \sum_{k=0}^{T-1} \mathbb{E}_\mu\left(\|\bar{x}_i^{n*}(k\tau) - \bar{x}^*(k\tau)\|_2^2\right)/T}\right) \qquad (22)$$

To upper bound the expression, we write the dynamics of $\bar{x}_i^{n*}$,

$$\bar{x}_i^{n*}((k+1)\tau) = (A_0 - B_0 K_1^*)\bar{x}_i^{n*}(k\tau) - B_0 K_2 \bar{x}(k\tau) + \bar{w}_i^n(k\tau)$$

where $\bar{w}_i^n(k\tau) = \sum_{j\neq i}(\bar{w}_j(k\tau) + B_0 K^* \hat{w}_j(k\tau))/(n-1)$ with distribution $\bar{w}_i^n(k\tau) \sim \mathcal{D}(0, \bar{\Sigma}_i^n)$ where,

$$\bar{\Sigma}_i^n = \sum_{j\neq i} \frac{\bar{\Sigma}}{(n-1)^2} + \sum_{j\neq i} \frac{BK^*\hat{\Sigma}_{C_j}(BK^*)^T}{(n-1)^2} = \frac{\bar{\Sigma}}{n-1} + \sum_{j\neq i} \frac{BK^*\hat{\Sigma}_{C_j}(BK^*)^T}{(n-1)^2}$$

Since $\hat{\Sigma}_{C_j}$ belongs to the finite set $\hat{\mathcal{E}}_C$, we define a constant $\hat{\sigma}_{max} :=$ $\max_{\hat{\Sigma}_C \in \hat{\mathcal{E}}_C} \text{Tr}\,(\hat{\Sigma}_C)$. Using this constant we can bound $\text{Tr}\,(\bar{\Sigma}_i^n)$

$$\text{Tr}\,(\bar{\Sigma}_i^n) \leq \frac{\text{Tr}\,(\bar{\Sigma})}{n-1} + \frac{m_1 \hat{\sigma}_{max}}{n-1}$$

where m_1 is a constant. Using the same techniques as [18] the expression on RHS of (22) is $\mathcal{O}(\hat{\Sigma}_{max}/\sqrt{n-1})$. Now we bound the second expression on the RHS in (21). Using techniques used in [18] for any $\pi^i \in \Pi_K^i$,

$$J_i^n(\pi^i, \mu^{*-i}) \geq J(\pi^i, \bar{x}^*) + \lim_{T \to \infty} \frac{2}{T} \sum_{k=0}^{T-1} \mathbb{E}[(x_i(k\tau) - \bar{x}^*(k\tau))^T C_Z (\bar{x}^*(k\tau) - \bar{x}_i^{n*}(k\tau))]$$

$$\geq J(K^*, F^*) - \epsilon_i + \lim_{T \to \infty} \frac{2}{T} \sum_{k=0}^{T-1} \mathbb{E}[(x_i(k\tau) - \bar{x}^*(k\tau))^T C_Z (\bar{x}^*(k\tau) - \bar{x}_i^{n*}(k\tau))]$$

$$\geq J(K^*, F^*) - \epsilon + \lim_{T \to \infty} \frac{2}{T} \sum_{k=0}^{T-1} \mathbb{E}[(x_i(k\tau) - \bar{x}^*(k\tau))^T C_Z (\bar{x}^*(k\tau) - \bar{x}_i^{n*}(k\tau))]$$

where ϵ_i is obtained from Theorem 1 and $\epsilon_i = \mathcal{O}(\text{Tr}\,(\hat{\Sigma}_{C_i}))$, and hence $\max_i \epsilon_i =:$ $\epsilon = \mathcal{O}(\hat{\Sigma}_{max})$. Moreover using techniques similar to [18]

$$\lim_{T \to \infty} \frac{2}{T} \sum_{k=0}^{T-1} \mathbb{E}[(x_i(k\tau) - \bar{x}^*(k\tau))^T C_Z (\bar{x}^*(k\tau) - \bar{x}_i^{n*}(k\tau))] = \mathcal{O}(\hat{\Sigma}_{max}/\sqrt{n-1}) \quad (23)$$

Using (22)–(23) we get

$$J_i^n(\mu^{*i}, \mu^{*-i}) - \inf_{\pi^i \in \Pi_K^i} J_i^n(\pi^i, \mu^{*-i}) < \epsilon + \varepsilon$$

where $\epsilon = \mathcal{O}(\hat{\Sigma}_{max})$ and $\varepsilon = \mathcal{O}(\hat{\Sigma}_{max}/\sqrt{n-1})$. $\qquad \square$

4.4 Summary and Discussion

The results in Sect. 4 provide decentralized feedback control laws for the agents in the multi-agent system, and provide conditions under which they are approximately optimal for the Secure LQ games. For ease of implementation, we restrict the controllers of the secure LQ game to the class of linear controllers. The approximation is characterized in terms of the estimation error and the number of agents.

In Sect. 4.1, we have shown that for the class of linear controllers, the MFE does not exist for the SLQ-MFG, as the estimation error in state reconstruction leads to a non-standard optimal control problem. This problem is overcome by proposing the idea of an ε-MFE (approximate MFE) in Sect. 4.2. Then the MFE of the (standard) LQ-MFG is shown to be an ε-MFE of the SLQ-MFG.

It is shown that, $\epsilon = \mathcal{O}(\text{Tr}\,(\hat{\Sigma}_C))$. As $\hat{\Sigma}_C$ is dependent on the private key C chosen uniformly from set $\mathcal{C}$, by careful choice of $\mathcal{C}$ in (2) the estimation error can be minimized (while obfuscating the state) resulting in close-to-optimal strategies for the agent.

In Sect. 4.3, the MFE of LQG has been shown to be $(\epsilon + \varepsilon)$-Nash Equilibrium of the secure n-agent LQ game. Moreover, $\epsilon = \mathcal{O}(\hat{\Sigma}_{max})$ where $\hat{\Sigma}_{max} :=$ $\max_{\hat{\Sigma}_j \in \hat{\mathcal{E}}_C} \text{Tr}\,(\hat{\Sigma}_j)$ and $\varepsilon = \mathcal{O}(\hat{\Sigma}_{max}/\sqrt{n-1})$. Similar to Sect. 4.2, through a careful choice of set $\mathcal{C}$ in (2), ϵ can be minimized. It can also be seen that if the number of agents n is large enough, ε is also small. Hence, MFE of LQ-MFG will be close-to-optimal for the secure n-agent LQ game.

In the IoBT setting (Sect. 1.2) for example, owing to the scale of the multi-agent systems, the computation of optimal (Nash) decentralized feedback laws for the agents is prohibitive. Results in Sect. 4 provide a way to design decentralized feedback control laws by first deriving the results for the infinite agent case, which is computationally tractable, and then establishing that the same control laws perform well (are approximately optimal) for the considered large scale finite agent setting.

5   Empirical Studies

In this section, we empirically investigate the performance and sensitivity of the $(\epsilon + \varepsilon)$-Nash policies (Sect. 4) to perturbations in the parameters: (i) Sampling rate (N), (ii) Model parameters (A, B), and (iii) Private keys $(\mathcal{C})$.

We use the *average accumulated cost* [20] as a metric to measure the performance of the $(\epsilon + \varepsilon)$-Nash policies. The average accumulated cost, $J^{n,T}$ is obtained by first simulating the secure n-agent LQ game, under the $(\epsilon + \varepsilon)$-Nash policies. The average accumulated cost is then defined as [20]:

$$J^{n,T} = \frac{1}{T} \sum_{i=1}^{n} \frac{1}{n} \Big\{ \sum_{k=0}^{T-1} ||x_i(k\tau) - \bar{x}_i^n(k\tau)||_Q^2 + ||u_i(k\tau)||_R^2 \Big\},$$

where x_i and u_i are the state and control trajectories of agent i and $\bar{x}_i^n$ is the empirical mean-field trajectory defined in Eq. (4).

The cost $J^{n,T}$ is an empirical approximation of the cost per agent J_i^n (Sect. 2), for T sufficiently large. Hence (for high enough T) a low value of $J^{n,T}$ implies a low value of J_i^n and hence indicates good performance by the $(\epsilon + \varepsilon)$-Nash policies.

5.1   Performance Sensitivity w.r.t. Sampling Rate

First we explore the effect of increasing the sampling rate N on the cost $J^{n,T}$. As shown in (15), the effect of N on the cost per agent (through the covariance matrix $\bar{\Sigma}_C$) is quite involved and hence hard to analyze in closed form. Due to this reason, we examine this effect using empirical studies.

We simulate the behavior of $n = 500$ agents, where each agent follows linear dynamics with states $x_i \in \mathbb{R}^{10}$, control actions $u_i \in \mathbb{R}^4$ and sketched state $y_i \in \mathbb{R}^2$, using a fixed set of private keys $\mathcal{C}$ (generated randomly with $m = 4$) and the

$(\epsilon + \varepsilon)$-Nash policies stated in Sect. 4.3. Figure 2 presents the effect of sampling rate N on the average accumulated cost $J^{n,T}$ for $T = \{400, 425, 450, 475, 500\}$. The values of $J^{n,T}$ reach steady-state for $T > 500$.

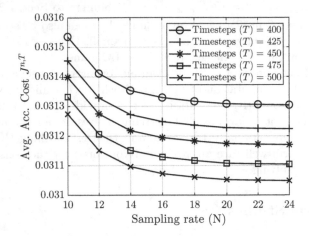

Fig. 2. Average accumulated cost w.r.t. change in sampling rate N.

Observations: Figure 2 shows that for a fixed sampling rate N, the cost $J^{n,T}$ decreases to a steady state value, as T increases. This decrease is due to the stabilizing nature of the $(\epsilon + \varepsilon)$-Nash policies. Furthermore, from Fig. 2 we also observe that for a fixed T and increasing N, the cost $J^{n,T}$ decreases to a steady state value. This suggests that higher sampling rates, N, lead to better performance by the $(\epsilon + \varepsilon)$-Nash policies, but high sampling rates may not be achievable due to limited bandwidth available at the channel (see Fig. 1). This indicates a trade-off between reduction in cost and limitations of the channel, which calls for a judicious choice.

5.2   Performance Sensitivity w.r.t. Model Parameters and Private Keys

Using the same setup as before, we next investigate the average accumulated cost, under perturbations in model parameters (A, B) (Fig. 3a) and set of private keys $\mathcal{C}$ (Fig. 3b). In the simulation, the perturbed parameters are obtained by adding randomly generated matrices to A, B and $C^{(i)}$ for $i \in [M]$. Figure 3a shows the boxplot[1] for perturbation of model parameters (A, B) and Fig. 3b for perturbation of set of private keys $\mathcal{C}$. The boxes in these figures are ordered by increasing perturbation magnitude, where perturbation magnitude is defined as

---

[1] The red line in the boxplot represents the median, the box represents the 1st and 3rd quartile and the whiskers represent the max and min values, with outliers shown as red crosses.

the Frobenius norm of the perturbation. The x-axes of Figs. 3a and b show the perturbation magnitudes, for their respective boxplots.

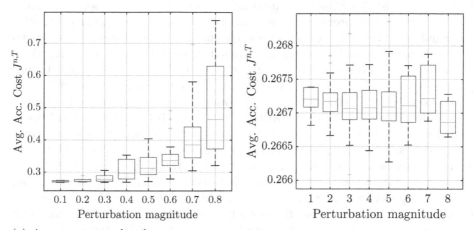

(a) Average accumulated cost w.r.t. per-   (b) Average accumulated cost w.r.t. perturbation of the A and B matrices.   turbation of the set of keys $\mathcal{C}$.

Fig. 3. Distribution of average accumulated cost $J^{n,T}$ w.r.t. magnitude of perturbation of model parameters (A, B) and set of keys $\mathcal{C}$, with $T = 500$. (Color figure online)

Observations: Figure 3a shows that as the perturbation in the model parameters (A, B) increases, the median and variance of the cost $J^{n,T}$ increases as well, signifying a decrease in performance. The increase in median cost $J^{n,T}$ is quite intuitive, as the $(\epsilon + \varepsilon)$-Nash policies have been generated for the model parameters (A, B) and any perturbation of these parameters should cause a loss in performance. The increase in variance of cost $J^{n,T}$ is due to random nature of the perturbation, higher perturbation magnitudes result in a bigger spread of the perturbations, resulting in a bigger spread of the average accumulated cost $J^{n,T}$. On the other hand, the median and variance of cost $J^{n,T}$ is shown to be quite insensitive to small perturbations of the set of keys $\mathcal{C}$ (Fig. 3b). This result is quite interesting and opens a path for future studies to investigate online methods to maintain security in the face of adapting adversaries.

In this section, we have empirically investigated the performance of the $(\epsilon + \varepsilon)$-Nash policies and inferred the following. There is a clear trade-off when choosing the sampling rate N, as the performance improves for higher N but it might be bounded from above due to channel limitations. Furthermore, we have discovered that the performance of $(\epsilon + \varepsilon)$-Nash policies deteriorates with perturbations in model parameters (A, B) but is insensitive to perturbations in the set of private keys $\mathcal{C}$.

6   Conclusion

In this paper, we have proposed the framework of Secure Linear Quadratic Mean-Field Games (SLQ-MFGs) to analyze multi-agent interactions between agents solving a consensus problem. Each agent has a sensor and a controller, with communication carried out over a noiseless channel, which however is susceptible to eavesdropping. The agents are coupled through their objective functions as in consensus problems. We have proposed a multi-rate sensor output sampling mechanism for the controller to reconstruct the state, albeit with some estimation error. We showed that this estimation error results in non-existence of the Mean-Field Equilibrium (MFE) of the SLQ-MFG for the class of linear controllers, and hence introduced the notions of ϵ-MFE and $(\epsilon + \varepsilon)$-Nash equilibria to characterize consensus in secure multi-agent interactions. Moreover, we have established that MFE of (standard) LQ-MFG, in which the controller has perfect state information, corresponds to ϵ-MFE of the SLQ-MFG, and an $(\epsilon + \varepsilon)$-Nash equilibrium for the secure $n-$agent dynamic game. Finally, we have empirically demonstrated that the performance of the $(\epsilon + \varepsilon)$-Nash equilibrium improves with increasing sampling rate N, deteriorates with variations in model parameters (A, B), and is insensitive to small perturbations in the set of private keys $\mathcal{C}$.

A number of extensions are being considered for future work: (i) A secure and robust n-agent LQ game where the adversary is strategic and can inject malicious signals into the communication channels of the agents to manipulate them into desired behavior, (ii) Design of the set of private keys $\mathcal{C}$ such that the estimation error is minimized while ensuring the obfuscation of the state from the adversary,(iii) Optimal state reconstruction (e.g. MMSE) strategy for the multi-rate setup with noise, (iv) Learning in secure n-agent LQ games where the agents have incomplete knowledge of its dynamic system and/or cost function.

7   Appendix

In this section, we provide some necessary background material for completeness.

7.1   MFE of the LQ-MFG

Here we briefly discuss the MFE of the LQ-MFG which has been developed in a previous work [18]. We note from [18] that the dynamics of the generic agent in the LQ-MFG are given by,

$$x((k + 1)\tau) = A_0 x(k\tau) + B_0 u(k\tau) + w^0(k\tau) \tag{24}$$

Although w^0 is assumed to be non-Gaussian (Sect. 2.2) the results of [18] (which assume Gaussian distribution) still hold, since we restrict our attention to the class of linear controllers. In the standard LQ-MFG, the multi-rate setup is not required since the controller has access to the true state of the agent. The generic agent aims to minimize the cost function,

$$\tilde{J}(\mu, \bar{x}) = \limsup_{T \to \infty} \frac{1}{T} \mathbb{E}_\mu \left\{ \sum_{k=0}^{T-1} ||x(k\tau) - \bar{x}(k\tau)||_Q^2 + ||u(k\tau)||_R^2 \right\}, \qquad (25)$$

where $\bar{x}$ is the mean-field trajectory. Next we restate the existence and uniqueness guarantees of MFE for the LQ-MFG.

Proposition 1. ([18]). *Under Assumption 1 the LQ-MFG ((24)–(25)) admits the unique MFE given by the tuple* $(K^*, F^*) \in \mathbb{R}^{p \times 2m} \times \mathbb{R}^{m \times m}$. *The matrix* $F^* = \Lambda(K^*) = A_0 - B_0(K_1^* + K_2^*)$, *and controller* K^* *is defined as,*

$$K^* = (\bar{B}^T P^* \bar{B} + R)^{-1} \bar{B}^T P^* \bar{A}^*, \ where \ \bar{A}^* = \begin{bmatrix} A_0 & 0 \\ 0 & F^* \end{bmatrix} \qquad (26)$$

and P^* *is the solution to the DARE,*

$$P^* = \bar{A}^{*T} P^* \bar{A}^* + \bar{Q} - \bar{A}^{*T} P^* \bar{B} (R + \bar{B}^T P^* \bar{B})^{-1} \bar{B}^T P^* \bar{A}^* \qquad (27)$$

and $\bar{B}$ *and* $\bar{Q}$ *as defined in* (11) *and* (12), *respectively.*

The DARE is obtained by substituting K^* in the Lyapunov Eq. (16) hence $P^* = P_{K^*}$. An important point to note is that in the LQ-MFG the estimation error is 0, as the controller has perfect access to the state of the agent. This translates to the covariance matrix of estimation error $\Sigma_C = 0$ and hence $\hat{\Sigma}_C = 0$ for LQ-MFG. Using (15) the cost of linear controller K and linear trajectory defined by matrix F for the LQ-MFG will be

$$\tilde{J}(K, F) = \text{Tr}\,(P_K \bar{\Sigma}) \qquad (28)$$

where P_K is the solution to the Lyapunov Eq. (15). Furthermore it can also be verified that

$$K^* = \text{argmin}_K \tilde{J}(K, F^*) \qquad (29)$$

This MFE (K^*, F^*) can be obtained by using the mean-field update operator as discussed in [18].

References

1. Moon, J., Başar, T.: Linear quadratic risk-sensitive and robust mean field games. IEEE Trans. Autom. Control **62**(3), 1062–1077 (2016)
2. Breban, R., Vardavas, R., Blower, S.: Mean-field analysis of an inductive reasoning game: application to influenza vaccination. Phys. Rev. E **76**(3), 031127 (2007)
3. Couillet, R., Perlaza, S.M., Tembine, H., Debbah, M.: Electrical vehicles in the smart grid: a mean field game analysis. IEEE J. Sel. Areas Commun. **30**(6), 1086–1096 (2012)

4. Huang, M., Malhamé, R.P., Caines, P.E., et al.: Large population stochastic dynamic games: closed-loop Mckean-Vlasov systems and the Nash certainty equivalence principle. Commun. Inf. Syst. **6**(3), 221–252 (2006)
5. Lasry, J.-M., Lions, P.-L.: Mean field games. Japan. J. Math. **2**(1), 229–260 (2007)
6. Huang, M., Caines, P.E., Malhamé, R.P.: Large-population cost-coupled LQG problems with nonuniform agents: individual-mass behavior and decentralized ε-Nash equilibria. IEEE Trans. Autom. Control **52**(9), 1560–1571 (2007)
7. Bensoussan, A., Sung, K., Yam, S.C.P., Yung, S.-P.: Linear-quadratic mean field games. J. Optim. Theory Appl. **169**(2), 496–529 (2016)
8. Huang, M., Zhou, M.: Linear quadratic mean field games-part I: the asymptotic solvability problem. arXiv preprint arXiv:1811.00522 (2018)
9. Moon, J., Başar, T.: Discrete-time LQG mean field games with unreliable communication. In: 53rd IEEE Conference on Decision and Control, pp. 2697–2702. IEEE (2014)
10. Guo, X., Hu, A., Xu, R., Zhang, J.: Learning mean-field games. In: Advances in Neural Information Processing Systems (2019)
11. Fu, Z., Yang, Z., Chen, Y., Wang, Z.: Actor-critic provably finds Nash equilibria of linear-quadratic mean-field games. In: International Conference on Learning Representation (2020)
12. Elie, R., Pérolat, J., Laurière, M., Geist, M., Pietquin, O.: Approximate fictitious play for mean field games. arXiv preprint arXiv:1907.02633 (2019)
13. Berberidis, D., Giannakis, G.B.: Data sketching for large-scale Kalman filtering. IEEE Trans. Signal Process. **65**(14), 3688–3701 (2017)
14. Blocki, J., Blum, A., Datta, A., Sheffet, O.: The Johnson-Lindenstrauss transform itself preserves differential privacy. In: 2012 IEEE 53rd Annual Symposium on Foundations of Computer Science, pp. 410–419. IEEE (2012)
15. Tatikonda, S., Sahai, A., Mitter, S.: Stochastic linear control over a communication channel. IEEE Trans. Autom. Control **49**(9), 1549–1561 (2004)
16. Kott, A., Swami, A., West, B.J.: The internet of battle things. Computer **49**(12), 70–75 (2016)
17. Janardhanan, S., Bandyopadhyay, B.: Output feedback sliding-mode control for uncertain systems using fast output sampling technique. IEEE Trans. Industr. Electron. **53**(5), 1677–1682 (2006)
18. Zaman, M., Zhang, K., Miehling, E., Başar, T.: Reinforcement learning in nonstationary discrete-time linear-quadratic mean-field games. In: 59th IEEE Conference on Decision and Control (2020, to appear)
19. Yang, Z., Chen, Y., Hong, M., Wang, Z.: Provably global convergence of actor-critic: a case for linear quadratic regulator with ergodic cost. In: Advances in Neural Information Processing Systems, pp. 8351–8363 (2019)
20. Zaman, M., Zhang, K., Miehling, E., Başar, T.: Approximate equilibrium computation for discrete-time linear-quadratic mean-field games. arXiv preprint arXiv:2003.13195 (2020)

Detection of Dynamically Changing Leaders in Complex Swarms from Observed Dynamic Data

Christos N. Mavridis[(✉)], Nilesh Suriyarachchi, and John S. Baras

Department of Electrical and Computer Engineering and Institute
for Systems Research, University of Maryland, College Park, MD 20742, USA
{mavridis,nileshs,baras}@umd.edu

Abstract. In this work we consider the problem of defending against adversarial attacks from UAV swarms performing complex maneuvers, driven by multiple, dynamically changing, leaders. We rely on short-time observations of the trajectories of the UAVs and develop a leader detection scheme based on the notion of Granger causality. We proceed with the estimation of the swarm's coordination laws, modeled by a generalized Cucker-Smale model with non-local repulsive potential functions and dynamically changing leaders, through an appropriately defined iterative optimization algorithm. Similar problems exist in communication and computer networks, as well as social networks over the Internet. Thus, the methodology and algorithms proposed can be applied to many types of network swarms including detection of influential malevolent "sources" of attacks and "miss-information". The proposed algorithms are robust to missing data and noise. We validate our methodology using simulation data of complex swarm movements.

Keywords: Leader detection · Anti-UAV defense · Identification of swarm coordination laws

1 Introduction

Air defense systems have been forced to constantly adapt and evolve over time to combat various new types of aerial threats. Today's air defense systems are highly capable of taking out single targets with ever increasing levels of precision. However, the advent and proliferation of the use of Unmanned Aerial Vehicles (UAV's) now poses new challenges to air defense systems. With the increase in computing capabilities in low cost hardware components, it has become feasible for adversarial forces to employ UAV swarms to be used for activities ranging from surveillance to deadly payload delivery and targeted attacks. While modern

This work was partially supported by the Defense Advanced Research Projects Agency (DARPA) under Agreement No. HR00111990027, by ONR grant N00014-17-1-2622, and by a grant from Northrop Grumman Corporation.

Q. Zhu et al. (Eds.): GameSec 2020, LNCS 12513, pp. 223–240, 2020.
https://doi.org/10.1007/978-3-030-64793-3_12

high-precision targeting anti-air defenses are capable of taking down a single UAV, when it comes to a large swarm of UAV's attacking simultaneously, these defences can be rendered ineffective. These problems are even more challenging when in UAV swarms, a few units are managed by humans (we refer to them as "leaders", while most units "follow", leading to very effective management of large swarms. When the role of leaders can be dynamically re-assigned the monitoring and defense against such swarms becomes even more difficult.

The first question that needs to be addressed in creating a defense against a hostile UAV swarm is understanding the control (coordination) and communication laws governing how the drones move and interact with each other. In large swarms it is unlikely that all the interacting drones have independent control and motion planning algorithms (of the kind found in the single robot planning literature [24]). Instead, flocking models have been proposed to study animal flocks and artificial swarm dynamics [1,2,8,9,20,25,27]. The investigation of these biological swarms have provided inspiration and useful modeling abstractions for addressing these challenging problems.

However, when studying complex swarm maneuvers, autonomous models such as the Cucker-Smale model [8,11] or the Boids model [27] cannot capture the behavior of the swarm, and leadership is often incorporated in the flocking model [31]. Having understood the flocking nature of the swarm, one key idea for creating a defense strategy in order to combat the swarm involves accurately identifying the leaders and the underlying dynamics of particle interactions in the swarm. The first step requires the clear identification of the leaders in the hostile swarm. If the leaders can be identified in real time then modern air defense systems such as high precision laser weapons which are aimed at combating UAV's can be used to take out these leaders, thus disrupting the operation of the entire swarm. Recent work into leader detection has looked into the use of Markov Chain Monte Carlo based group tracking methods [6]. However, in order to handle real time leader detection in high particle count swarms this paper proposes a Granger causality based detection method.

In this paper we will use the terms agents and particles interchangeably. Extracting the laws of interaction (or coordination) between agents is the next requirement for creating a defense strategy against large hostile swarms. Understanding the governing dynamics of the hostile swarm will enable the defense system to plan ahead and anticipate how the swarm would react to different strategies such as the focused removal of the agents identified as leaders. Multiple methods exist in order to identify the underlying interactions and dynamics of particle swarms. Statistical [5,16], and, mainly, model-based [8,20,27] learning approaches have been used to infer interaction rules between particles. In [4] symbolic equations are generated from the numerically calculated derivatives of the system variables, in [19] the constitutive equations of physical components composing the system are learned, while in [18] the order of a fractional differential system of equations, which models the system, is estimated. Recently, Matei et al. in [20], and Mavridis et al. in [22] have modeled the networked swarm as a port-Hamiltonian system [29] and have accurately reconstructed the laws of interaction (or coordination) of the swarm and its dynamical properties, from observed trajectories of the individual agents. Furthermore in these recent works [20, 22, 23] we have also demonstrated the robustness of the associated algorithms to both noisy observations as well as missing data.

Similar problems are found in many other types of large networked systems, including communication and computer networks, sensor networks, networked cyber-physical systems, biological systems, and social networks over the Internet. In such systems there are corresponding notions of leaders, such as initiators of a malicious attack, or coordinators of malevolent behavior, or initiators of a biological cell-malfunction, or influential sources of miss-information or untrustworthiness [30]. In all these problems fast identification of the leaders and the associated followers groups (or influence groups) is essential for defending and correcting such malevolent actions and functions. Thus the applicability of the ideas and methods proposed in this work is very broad, with the appropriate modeling and semantic changes for the various domains.

In this work, we focus on observations of complex swarm maneuvers driven by multiple dynamically changing leaders, and propose a leader detection scheme, based on the notion of Granger causality, that allows for the online estimation of the particle interaction laws through an appropriately defined iterative optimization algorithm. In the learning process, we assume a generalized Cucker-Smale model with non-local repulsive potential functions and dynamically changing leaders [31]. We validate our methodology using simulation data of complex swarm movements. Similar problems exist in communication and computer networks, as well as social networks over the Internet. Thus the methodology and algorithms proposed can be applied to many types of network swarms including detection of influential malevolent "sources" of attacks and "miss-information".

The rest of the manuscript is organized as follows: Sect. 2 describes the models used to describe the swarm dynamics, and Sects. 3 and 4 introduce the leader detection algorithm. In Sect. 5 the learning algorithm for the swarm's interaction laws is formulated. Finally, Sect. 6 presents the experimental results, and Sect. 7 concludes the paper.

2 Modeling Complex Swarm Maneuvers

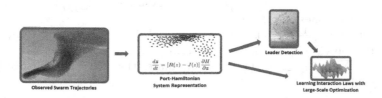

Fig. 1. Reconstructing complex swarm dynamics. The agents' trajectories are observed and used to detect leaders and identify a port-Hamiltonian networked system modeling their interaction rules.

We view the interconnected problems of modeling and learning the interaction laws of a swarm as one problem that can be analyzed in the microscopic scale as a port-Hamiltonian networked system. We extend existing simulation models, such as the Boids and the Cucker-Smale models, to incorporate interaction, communication and dynamics terms that can capture realistic complex swarm maneuvers and develop corresponding simulation models in the macroscopic domain. Specifically, we introduce

- a scalable simulation algorithm, based on the Boids model, that can capture interaction laws and communication protocols of complex swarm maneuvers, including (a) velocity alignment, (b) spatial cohesion, (c) collision avoidance, and (d) response to dynamically changing leaders.
- a large-scale learning algorithm, based on the generalized Cucker-Smale model and automatic differentiation, designed to work on state-of-the-art deep learning platforms that can identify the interaction laws (a)–(d) by observing particle trajectories of position and velocity (Fig. 1).

2.1 Extended Boids Model

The Boids algorithm is a widely used artificial flocking simulation algorithm based on three basic rules [27].

1. *Cohesion*: Boids are steered in such a way that they move towards the average position (perceived center of mass) of local flockmates. The radius of attraction is a parameter than can be tuned in this section.
2. *Alignment*: Boids are steered towards the average heading and average speed of local flockmates.
3. *Separation*: Boids are steered in such a way that they avoid crowding local flockmates. This acts as a collision avoidance strategy between particles.

The Boids model can be written as a dynamical system:

$$\begin{cases} \dot{x}_i &= v_i \\ \dot{v}_i &= -c\nabla U_c(x) - a\nabla U_a(x,v) + s\nabla U_s(x) \end{cases} \tag{1}$$

where

- $\nabla U_c(x) = x_i - \frac{1}{N_c}\sum_{j\neq i} \mathbb{1}_{[x_i-x_j\leq r_c]}x_j = \frac{1}{2}\nabla\|x_i - \frac{1}{N_c}\sum_{j\neq i} \mathbb{1}_{[x_i-x_j\leq r_c]}x_j\|^2$, simulates the cohesion rule,
- $\nabla U_a(x,v) = v_i - \frac{1}{N_a}\sum_{j\neq i} \mathbb{1}_{[x_i-x_j\leq r_a]}v_j = \frac{1}{2}\nabla\|v_i - \frac{1}{N_a}\sum_{j\neq i} \mathbb{1}_{[x_i-x_j\leq r_a]}v_j\|^2$, simulates the velocity alignment rule, and
- $\nabla U_s(x) = \sum_{j\neq i} \mathbb{1}_{[x_i-x_j\leq r_s]}(x_i - x_j)$, simulates the collision avoidance (separation) rule.

In addition to these rules, the interacting agents (boids) may be modeled to have a tendency towards a particular place, by adding an attractive term with respect to a possibly time-dependent potential function

$$-w\nabla U_w(x,x_w) = -w\mathbb{1}_{[x_i-x_w\leq r_w]}(x_i - x_w) = -\frac{1}{2}w\mathbb{1}_{[x_i-x_w\leq r_w]}\nabla\|x_i - x_w\|^2$$

simulating strong wind or leadership.

Although the Boids model is widely adapted in many simulations due to its simplicity, the fact that the interaction of each particle with its neighbors is local, i.e., the existence of the neighborhood radii r_a, r_s, r_c etc., introduces problems with the differentiability of the cost function of the learning problem. In order to preserve differentiability and be able to utilize existing large-scale optimization frameworks for deep learning to work, we need to replace the indicator function of belonging to a neighborhood with a smooth interaction function ψ that defines the grade of membership of a particle to the neighborhood of another.

2.2   Cucker-Smale Model with Leadership

When focused on the learning algorithm, we model the swarm with the Cucker-Smale model [7,8]. In order to model complex flock maneuvers, we borrow from the theory of flock leadership (see e.g. [31]) and incorporate leadership to the Cucker-Smale model as follows:

Definition 1. *Consider an interacting system of N particles. The leader sets $\mathcal{L}(i)$, $1 \le i \le N$ of cardinality $|\mathcal{L}(i)| = 1$ are assigned to each particle representing the index of the leader particle that it is following. Then the Cucker-Smale (CS) model with leadership is defined in the following:*

$$\begin{cases} \dot{x}_i & = v_i \\ \dot{v}_i & = \frac{K}{N} \sum_{j=1}^{N} \psi_{ij}(x(t), v(t)) \end{cases} \tag{2}$$

where

$$\psi_{ij}(x) = \begin{cases} -\nabla U(\|x_i - x_j\|), & j \notin \mathcal{L}(i), j \ne i \\ G(\|x_i - x_j\|)(v_j(t) - v_i(t)) - \nabla U(\|x_i - x_j\|), & j \in \mathcal{L}(i) \end{cases} \tag{3}$$

with a typical choice for the interaction function G that provably results in flocking behavior being $G(r) = \frac{1}{(1+r^2)^\gamma}$ and the potential function usually taking the form $U(r) = -C_A e^{-r/l_A} + C_R e^{-r/l_R}$, with C_A, C_R, l_A, l_R positive scalars.

It has been shown in [20] that the Cucker-Smale model with potentials is equivalent to a fully connected N-dimensional network of generalized mass-spring-dampers with appropriately defined Hamiltonian functions, that can be written in a port-Hamiltonian form

$$\dot{z} = [\mathbf{J}(\mathbf{z}) - \mathbf{R}(\mathbf{z})] \frac{\partial \mathbf{H}z)}{\partial \mathbf{z}} \tag{4}$$

where $z = (q, p)$, with $q, p \in \mathbb{R}^{\frac{N(N-1)}{2}}$ being the vectors of relative distances and momenta between each pair of particles, and the quantities $J = -J^\mathrm{T}$, H and R are appropriately defined. The dependence of (5) on the interaction function ψ is introduced by the resistive term $R = R(\psi)$ [20].

It is straightforward to show that the CS model with leadership is equivalent to an input-state-output port-Hamiltonian system of the form

$$\dot{\mathbf{z}} = [\mathbf{J}(\mathbf{z}) - \mathbf{R}(\mathbf{z})]\frac{\partial \mathbf{H}(\mathbf{z})}{\partial \mathbf{z}} + \mathbf{g}(\mathbf{z})\mathbf{u}, \tag{5}$$

where $g(z)$ is appropriately defined, and u is an external control input that affects only the leader particles and is responsible for their trajectories.

The intuitive difference in the interaction function is actually the sole difference between the Boids model and the Cucker-Smale model with potentials. This also justifies why we may use the Boids model to simulate and the CS model to learn, and why approaching the simulation and learning problems with a single dynamical system is important for reconstructing the dynamics of complex swarm maneuvers. The difference in the interaction functions is illustrated in Fig. 2.

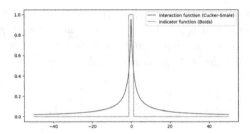

Fig. 2. The indicator "neighborhood" function in Boids model and the interaction function in Cucker-Smale model.

We would like to emphasize that all the models proposed in our work including port-Hamiltonian systems, Boids, CS interaction potentials, are useful abstractions inspired from biology and physics. However the underlying systems do not have to be biological or physical. The validity of the abstraction is measured by the degree with which these abstract models can generate dynamic trajectories very similar to the observed ones (or the observed time varying data series). Therefore these abstractions can be used, and have been used, to model the various networked systems we mentioned earlier.

3   Leader Detection

We adopt a majority vote criterion for leader detection, where each particle i votes for the particle j to be the leader, according to a measure related to the observed trajectories of the particles.

3.1 Granger Causality

Clive Granger in [10] defined a causality relationship based on two principles:

i. The cause happens prior to its effect
ii. The cause has unique information about the future values of its effect.

Given these assumptions, we say that a time series Y Granger-causes X if the past values of Y provide statistically significant information about the future values of X. In other words, we associate the existence of a causal effect of Y on X with the following *Hypothesis Test*:

Definition 2. *Let Y, X be stationary random processes, and consider the following two auto-regression models*

$$x_t = \alpha_0 + \sum_{i=1}^{p} \alpha_i x_{t-i} + \epsilon_t^1, \ t > p \tag{6}$$

$$x_t = \alpha_0 + \sum_{i=1}^{p} \alpha_i x_{t-i} + \sum_{i=1}^{q} \beta_i y_{t-i} + \epsilon_t^2, \ t > \max\{p,q\} \tag{7}$$

where $\epsilon_t \sim N(0, \sigma^2)$ is white noise. Then the non-causality null Hypothesis:

$$H_0 : \beta_i = 0, \forall i \in \{1, \ldots, q\}$$

is rejected if model (7) fits the data $\{x_t\}_{t=T}^{T+n}$, $T > \max\{p,q\}$, in a window of n samples, significantly better than model (6), i.e. if

$$p \triangleq \mathbb{P}\left[F > \hat{F}|H_0\right] < a$$

for a given confidence level a, e.g. $a \leq 0.05$, where

$$\hat{F} = \frac{\dfrac{\sum_{t=T}^{T+n} \epsilon_t^1 - \sum_{t=T}^{T+n} \epsilon_t^2}{q}}{\dfrac{\sum_{t=T}^{T+n} \epsilon_t^2}{n - (p+q+1)}} \tag{8}$$

We note that if (6) and (7) were simple regression models, the random variable F would be defined such that it follows an $F(q, n-(p+q+1))$ distribution. Because of the autoregression nature of (6), (7), it can be shown (e.g. Ch. 8 of [12]), that qF asymptotically follows a $\chi^2(q)$ distribution as $n \to \infty$. In case of non-stationary processes X, Y, one can apply the AR models to the n-th order differences, resulting in ARIMA models.

3.2   Leader Detection Based on Granger Causality

The leader-particle relationship is causal, satisfying both assumptions of Granger Causality. In order to make sure that we capture causality, and not merely correlation, we follow the hypothesis test described in Sect. 3.1 for each pair of particles (i, j).

As a result, a particle i votes for j to be the leader, where each vote takes the value G_{ij}, with $G = \mathbb{1}_{[p<\alpha]}$ indicating Granger Causality, where p is the p-value according to the χ^2 distribution as argued in Sect. 3.1.

However, because of the high correlation between the trajectories of the particles-followers, it is often the case that $G_{ij} \simeq 1$ even between two followers. In order to avoid such confusion, we bypass the last quantization step $G_{ij} = \mathbb{1}_{[p<\alpha]}$, and compare directly the p-values. Going one step further, we can see that the lowest p-value, corresponds to the highest $\hat{F}$-value. Moreover, the profile of the $\hat{F}_{ij}$ values is such that $\hat{F}_{ij}$ is *consistently* higher (i.e. lower variance) for every i, when j is the leader. In other words, even though for a follower j, a set of $\hat{F}_{ij}$ values may be high, indicating that particles with different indices i may be leaders, for each i, a high fluctuation on the observed values $\hat{F}_{ij}$ is indicative of a false positive, i.e. that particle i is not a leader. Therefore, we define the proposed leader detection algorithm to be based on the measure

$$F_{v,j} = \frac{\hat{\mu}_{\hat{F}_{\cdot j}}}{\hat{\sigma}_{\hat{F}_{\cdot j}}} = \frac{\sum_{i \neq j} \hat{F}_{ij}}{\sqrt{N \sum_{i \neq j} \hat{F}_{ij}^2 - \left(\sum_{i \neq j} \hat{F}_{ij}\right)^2}}$$

for each j. The measure $F_{v,j}$ can be thought of as the *inverse coefficient of variation*, and is designed such that particles i with high variation on the observed values $\hat{F}_{ij}$, for different followers-voters j, are not selected as leaders. The detection algorithm is shown in Algorithm 1.

Algorithm 1. F-Based Leader Detection Algorithm

Require: w(big enough), t, λ
  for i in $\{1, \ldots, N + 1\}$ **do**
    for $j \neq i$ **do**
      In the window $[t - w, t]$:
      Compute $\hat{F}_{ij}$
      Compute $F_{v,j} = F_{v,j} = \dfrac{\hat{\mu}_{\hat{F}_{\cdot j}}}{\hat{\sigma}_{\hat{F}_{\cdot j}}}$
    end for
  end for
  Select the leader: $L_F \leftarrow \arg\max_j F_{v,j}$

---

4   Estimating the Number of Leaders

The first question one needs to answer when dealing with leader detection is the number of leaders that the algorithm is trying to find. We view this problem as a clustering problem given a window of position and velocity observations of the particles, since it is reasonable to assume that particle trajectories will be more 'similar' to each other if they are following the same leader.

However, the number of the clusters is not known a priori, which makes standard clustering algorithms based on Vector Quantization (e.g. k-means) inappropriate for this application. Instead, we need an unsupervised learning algorithm that progressively estimates the number of clusters by adding new clusters only when some measure of distortion is high enough to support this decision. In this regard, the Deterministic Annealing algorithm [28] is a fitting clustering algorithm for estimating the number of leaders and is presented in the next Section.

4.1   Deterministic Annealing

The observation of annealing processes in physical chemistry motivated the use of similar concepts to avoid local minima of the optimization cost. Certain chemical systems can be driven to their low-energy states by annealing, which is a gradual reduction of temperature, spending a long time at the vicinity of the phase transition points.

Deterministic Annealing (DA), proposed by Rose [28], is an annealing optimization method that tries to achieve a good compromise between the world of stochastic relaxation, or simulated annealing [15], and the world of deterministic optimization. On the one hand it is deterministic, meaning that we do not want to be wandering randomly on the energy surface while making incremental progress on the average, as is the case for stochastic relaxation. On the other hand, it is still an annealing method and aims at the global minimum, instead of getting greedily attracted to a nearby local minimum. One can view DA as replacing stochastic simulations by the use of expectation. An effective energy function, which is parameterized by a (pseudo) temperature, is derived through expectation and is deterministically optimized at successively reduced temperatures.

The Optimization Problem. The problem of divergence-based Vector Quantization can be stated as an optimization problem:

Problem 1. Let $X : \Omega \to S$ be a random variable defined in the probability space $(\Omega, \mathcal{F}, \mathbb{P})$, and $d : S \times ri(S) \to [0, \infty)$ be a divergence measure, with $ri(S)$ representing the relative interior of S. Let $V := \{S_h\}_{h=1}^{k}$ be a partition of S with respect to d and $M := \{\mu_h\}_{h=1}^{k}$, such that $\mu_h \in ri(S_h)$, $h \in K$, $K := \{1, \ldots, k\}$, and define the quantizer $Q : S \to S$ such that $Q(X) = \sum_{h=1}^{k} \mu_h \mathbb{1}_{[X \in S_h]}$.

Then the problem is formulated as

$$\min_{M,V} \ J(Q) := \mathbb{E}_X \left[d\left(X, Q(X) \right) \right]$$

The distortion function J is typically non convex and riddled with poor local minima. In order to deal with this phenomenon, soft-clustering approaches have been proposed as a probabilistic framework for clustering, where input vectors are assigned to clusters in probability.

For the randomized partition we can rewrite the expected distortion as

$$D = \mathbb{E}\left[d_\phi(X, M)\right]$$
$$= \mathbb{E}\left[\mathbb{E}\left[d_\phi(X, M)|X\right]\right]$$
$$= \sum_x p(x) \sum_\mu p(\mu|x) d_\phi(x, \mu)$$

where $p(\mu|x)$ is the association probability relating the input vector x with the codevector μ. At the limit where the association probabilities are hard and each input vector is assigned to a unique codevector with probability one, this becomes identical with the traditional hard clustering distortion.

We seek the distribution that minimizes D subject to a specified level of randomness, measured by the Shannon entropy

$$H(X, M) = \mathbb{E}\left[-\log p(X, M)\right]$$
$$= H(X) + H(M|X)$$
$$= \mathbb{E}\left[-\log p(X)\right] + \mathbb{E}\left[\mathbb{E}\left[-\log p(M|X)|X\right]\right]$$
$$= H(X) - \sum_x p(x) \sum_\mu p(\mu|x) \log p(\mu|x)$$

by appealing to Jaynes's maximum entropy principle [13] which states: of all the probability distributions that satisfy a given set of constraints, choose the one that maximizes the entropy.

The optimization is conveniently formulated as the minimization of the Lagrangian

$$F = D - TH \tag{9}$$

where F represents the free energy and T is the temperature parameter that acts as a Lagrange multiplier. Clearly, for large values of T we maximize the entropy, and, as T is lowered, we trade entropy for reduction in distortion.

As in the case of Vector Quantization, we form a coordinate block optimization algorithm by successively minimizing with respect to the association probabilities $p(\mu|x)$ and the codevector locations μ. Minimizing F with respect to the association probabilities $p(\mu|x)$ is straightforward and gives the Gibbs distribution

$$p(\mu|x) = \frac{e^{-\frac{d_\phi(x,\mu)}{T}}}{\sum_\mu e^{-\frac{d_\phi(x,\mu)}{T}}}$$

while, in order to minimize F with respect to the codevector locations μ we set the gradients to zero

$$\frac{d}{d\mu}D = 0 \implies \frac{d}{d\mu}\mathbb{E}\left[\mathbb{E}\left[d_\phi(X, \mu)|X\right]\right] = 0$$
$$\implies \sum_x p(x)p(\mu|x)\frac{d}{d\mu}d_\phi(x, \mu) = 0$$

Remark 1. If d_ϕ is a Bregman divergence [3,21], such as the Euclidean distance or the Kulback-Leibler divergence, we get $\frac{d}{d\mu}d_\phi(x,\mu) = \frac{d\phi}{d\mu}(\mu)(x-\mu)$, which allows for the direct computation of the optimal solution μ as the convenient centroid form

$$\mu = \mathbb{E}\left[x|\mu\right] = \frac{\sum_x xp(x)p(\mu|x)}{p(\mu)}$$

This deterministic optimization procedure takes place for decreasing values of the temperature T such that DA maintains minimum free energy (thermal equilibrium) while gradually lowering the temperature. Adding to the physical analogy, it is significant that, as the temperature is lowered, the system undergoes a sequence of "phase transitions", which consists of natural cluster splits where the cardinality of the codebook (number of clusters) increases. This is a bifurcation phenomenon and provides a useful tool for controlling the size of the clustering model relating it to the scale of the solution. At very high temperature $(T \to \infty)$ the optimization yields uniform association probabilities

$$p(\mu|x) = \lim_{T \to \infty} \frac{e^{-\frac{d_\phi(x,\mu)}{T}}}{\sum_\mu e^{-\frac{d_\phi(x,\mu)}{T}}} = \frac{1}{K}$$

and all the codevectors are located at the same point

$$\mu = \mathbb{E}\left[X\right]$$

which is the expected value of X (in practice we get the sample mean of the N realizations of X that we observe). As we lower the temperature, the cardinality of the codebook changes. The bifurcation occurs when a set of coincident codevectors splits into separate subsets, which can be traced when the Hessian of F loses its positive definite property. In other words, the effective number of codevector depends only on the temperature parameter which is the Lagrange multiplier of the multi-objective minimization problem (9).

We can approach the bifurcation using perturbation analysis. At each temperature, we can generate a perturbed pair of codevectors for each effective cluster which, after convergence, can either merge together or separate depending on whether a phase transition has occurred.

The Algorithm. A computationally efficient implementation of the DA algorithm for clustering can be constructed in this way. The complete algorithm is shown in Algorithm 2 and constitutes a batch unsupervised learning algorithm that provides the ability to trade complexity for accuracy by progressively increasing the model size (number of efficient clusters) when needed (when a critical temperature has been reached). Furthermore, as argued in Remark 1, when d_ϕ is a Bregman divergence [3,21], such as the Euclidean distance or the Kulback-Leibler divergence, the optimization steps can be solved analytically providing a computationally efficient implementation.

Algorithm 2. Deterministic Annealing Algorithm

Require: Dataset $\mathcal{X}$ $\triangleright\ |\mathcal{X}| = N$

Set parameters:

    K_{max} $\triangleright$ maximum number of codevectors

    $T_{max},\ T_{min}$ $\triangleright$ maximum and minimum temperatures

Initialize:

    $K = 1$ $\triangleright$ number of codevectors

    $T = T_{max} > 2\lambda_{max}(C_x)$ $\triangleright$ temperature

    $\mu_1 = \sum_x xp(x),\ p(\mu_1) = 1$ $\triangleright\ 1^{st}$ codevector

while $K < K_{max}$ **and** $T > T_{min}$ **do**

    Replace each μ_i with a perturbed pair $\{\mu_i', \mu_i''\}$

    Update:

    $p(\mu_i') = p(\mu_i'') = p(\mu_i)/2$

    $K \leftarrow 2K$

    repeat $\triangleright$ Step (O)

        for $i = 1, \ldots, K$ **do**

            Update:

            $p(\mu_i|x) \leftarrow \dfrac{p(\mu_i)e^{-\frac{d_\phi(x,\mu_i)}{T}}}{\sum_i p(\mu_i)e^{-\frac{d_\phi(x,\mu_i)}{T}}},\ \forall x$ $\triangleright$ Step (E)

            $p(\mu_i) \leftarrow \sum_{x \in \mathcal{X}} p(x)p(\mu_i|x)$ $\triangleright$ Step (M_1)

            $\mu_i \leftarrow \dfrac{\sum_{x \in \mathcal{X}} xp(x)p(\mu_i|x)}{p(\mu_i)}$ $\triangleright$ Step (M_2)

        end for

    until Convergence $\triangleright\ \|\Delta\mu_i\| < \epsilon_c,\ \forall i$

    Keep only effective codevectors:

    if $\|\mu_i - \mu_j\| < \epsilon_n$ **then**

        discard μ_j

        set $p(\mu_i) \leftarrow p(\mu_i) + p(\mu_j),\ \forall i \neq j$

    end if

    Update K

    Lower the temperature $\triangleright\ T \leftarrow \gamma T$

end while

Do one hard-clustering loop $\triangleright$ Step (O) with $T = 0$

---

5   Learning the Particle Interaction Laws

For the learning task we model the networked system of interacting agents as a port-Hamiltonian system representing a general Cucker-Smale model (5) [20]. We make use of the position and velocity trajectories of the particles to recover the resistive terms $R(z)$ and the Hamiltonian $H(z)$, which is equivalent to recovering the interaction functions $\psi_{ij}(x, v)$ of a general Cucker-Smale model (2).

The components of the interaction model (resistive element and the spring Hamiltonian) are modeled as neural-networks with one hidden layer, and the following optimization problem with a mean square error (MSE) loss function is formulated

$$\min_w \frac{1}{n} \sum_{i=1}^n \|\dot{\mathbf{z}}(t_i) - \dot{\hat{\mathbf{z}}}(t_i; w)\|^2 \tag{10}$$

$$\text{s.t.} \qquad \dot{\mathbf{z}}(t_i) = [\mathbf{J}(\mathbf{z}(t_i)) - \mathbf{R}(\mathbf{z}(t_i))] \frac{\partial \mathbf{H}(\mathbf{z}(t_i))}{\partial \mathbf{z}} + \mathbf{g}(z)\mathbf{u} \tag{11}$$

$$\dot{\hat{\mathbf{z}}}(\mathbf{t_i}; \mathbf{w}) = \left[\mathbf{J}(\mathbf{z}(\mathbf{t_i})) - \hat{\mathbf{R}}(\mathbf{z}(\mathbf{t_i}; \mathbf{w}))\right] \frac{\partial \hat{\mathbf{H}}(\mathbf{z}(\mathbf{t_i}; \mathbf{w}))}{\partial \mathbf{z}} + \mathbf{g}(z)\mathbf{u}, \tag{12}$$

where n is the number of time samples, $w = \{W^{[0]}, b^{[0]}, W^{[1]}, b^{[1]}\}$ is the set of optimization variables, and $(\hat{\cdot})$ represents quantities estimated by the neural networks.

We approach the solution w^* of (10) with respect to

$$V_p(\theta) := \sum_{\tau=t_0}^{t_f} \|\dot{z}^*(\tau) - \dot{z}(\tau)\|^2$$

with an iterative gradient descent method

$$\theta^{n+1} = \theta^n - \alpha_n(\nabla_\theta V_p(\theta^n)), \; n = 0, 1, 2, \ldots \tag{13}$$

where the iteration maps $\alpha_n : \mathbb{R}^2 \to \mathbb{R}^2$, $n \geq 0$ are defined in accordance with the Adam method of moments for stochastic optimization [14], and the computation of the gradient vectors is implemented using automatic differentiation [17].

The term $g(z)\mathbf{u}$ is not estimated, but, instead, the actual trajectories of the leader particles are used, which incorporate the effect of this term. This requires the knowledge of the leader particles, as well as the followers of each leader. This is provided by the proposed algorithms for leader detection, presented in Sects. 3 and 4. In order to create a scalable learning system, we have focused on the Pytorch [26] deep learning platform that, in addition to automatic differentiation, is endowed with ODE solver capabilities.

6   Experimental Results

6.1   Case of One Leader

We showcase the proposed algorithm in the complex swarm movements shown in Fig. 3 and 5, where the trajectories of the particles are generated by the Cucker-Smale and extended Boids models with one leader, respectively.

We simulated the system of ODEs of the port-Hamiltonian system in (5), with the interaction function as reconstructed by the trained neural network, which resulted in the reconstructed particle trajectories that are depicted in Fig. 4 and 6.

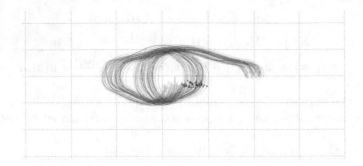

Fig. 3. An example of 2D particle trajectories of a swarm following the dynamics of a Cucker-Smale model with one leader.

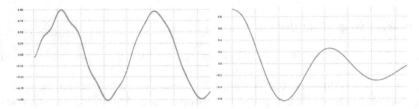

Fig. 4. The actual (blue) and estimated (red) trajectory of the position of a random agent over time for 20s (y-axis in arbitrary units). (left) The x-coordinate. MSE% = 0.0004. (right) The y-coordinate. MSE% = 0.0001. (Color figure online)

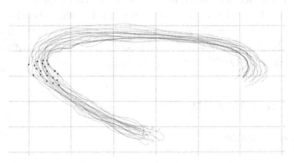

Fig. 5. An example of 2D particle trajectories of a swarm following the dynamics of an extended Boids model with one leader.

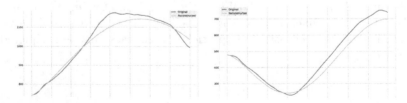

Fig. 6. The actual (blue) and estimated (red) trajectory of the position of a random agent over time for 20s (y-axis in arbitrary units). (left) The x-coordinate. MSE% = 0.1357. (right) The y-coordinate. MSE% = 0.1819. (Color figure online)

We note that the rule-based Boids model generates more jerky trajectories compared with the Cucker-Smale dynamical system and the reconstruction is less than ideal, as expected. This is an indication, however, that the proposed methodology is robust to noisy data generated by a model of unknown form.

6.2   Case of Multiple Leaders

We showcase the proposed algorithm in the complex swarm movement shown in the Fig. 7. where the trajectories of the particles are generated by the CS model with leadership with two leaders.

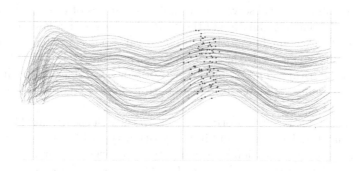

Fig. 7. An example of 2D particle trajectories of a swarm following the dynamics of a Cucker-Smale model with two leaders.

In order to apply our port-Hamiltonian based learning algorithm, we first estimate the sets $\mathcal{L}(i)$, $1 \leq i \leq N$ with our leader detection algorithm presented in Sects. 3 and 4. The results of the reconstruction of the interaction function are shown in Fig. 8.

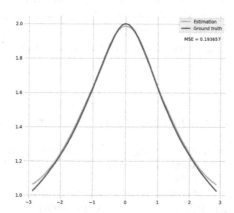

Fig. 8. The actual (blue) and estimated (red) particle interaction function of a swarm following the dynamics of a CS model with two leaders. The x- and y-axes are in arbitrary units. The mean squared error is $MSE = 0.193657$. The x-axis corresponds to the relative distance between a particle and its neighbor. (Color figure online)

7 Conclusion and Discussion

In this work we focus on the problem of defending against adversarial attacks by artificial UAV swarms. The swarms can be driven by multiple dynamically changing leaders and perform highly complex maneuvers. Existing air defense infrastructure is largely inadequate when dealing with the sheer number of agents in the swarm. In this research we propose a method which enables the identification of the leaders of the swarm, as well us the underlying coordination laws. This is the first and most challenging task in the defense strategy against hostile swarm attacks in existing air defense systems.

We develop a leader detection scheme based on the notion of Granger causality, relying on short-time observations of the trajectories of the UAVs. We then proceed with the online estimation of the swarm's coordination laws, modeled by a generalized Cucker-Smale model with non-local repulsive potential functions and dynamically changing leaders, through an appropriately defined iterative optimization algorithm. The proposed methodology is robust to both missing data and noise and is validated using simulation data of complex swarm movements.

While the key focus of this work is related to the defense against hostile UAV swarms, similar problems are found in many other types of large networked systems, including communication and computer networks, sensor networks, networked cyber-physical systems, biological systems, and social networks over the Internet. In such systems there are corresponding notions of leaders, such as initiators of a malicious attack, coordinators of malevolent behavior, initiators of a biological cell-malfunction, or influential sources of miss-information or untrustworthiness. In all these problems fast identification of the leaders and the associated follower groups (or influence groups) is essential for defending and correcting such malevolent actions and functions. Thus the applicability of the ideas and methods proposed in this work is very broad, with the appropriate modeling and semantic changes for the various domains. Important directions of our current and future research include extensions of the framework and algorithms to these broader domains, as well as the utilization of game theoretic methods for their analysis (non-cooperating, cooperating and mean-field games).

References

1. Bajec, I.L., Heppner, F.H.: Organized flight in birds. Anim. Behav. **78**(4), 777–789 (2009)
2. Ballerini, M., et al.: Interaction ruling animal collective behavior depends on topological rather than metric distance: evidence from a field study. Proc. Natl. Acad. Sci. **105**(4), 1232–1237 (2008)
3. Banerjee, A., Merugu, S., Dhillon, I.S., Ghosh, J.: Clustering with Bregman divergences. J. Mach. Learn. Res. **6**(Oct), 1705–1749 (2005)
4. Bongard, J., Lipson, H.: Automated reverse engineering of nonlinear dynamical systems. Proc. Natl. Acad. Sci. **104**(24), 9943–9948 (2007)

5. Brunton, S., Proctor, J., Kutz, J.: Discovering governing equations from data by sparse identification of nonlinear dynamical systems. Proc. Natl. Acad. Sci. **113**(15), 3932–3937 (2016)
6. Carmi, A.Y., Mihaylova, L., Septier, F., Pang, S.K., Gurfil, P., Godsill, S.J.: MCMC-based tracking and identification of leaders in groups. In: 2011 IEEE International Conference on Computer Vision Workshops (ICCV Workshops), pp. 112–119 (2011)
7. Carrillo, J., Fornasier, M., Toscani, G., Vecil, F.: Particle, Kinetic, and Hydrodynamic Models of Swarming. Birkhäuser Boston, Boston (2010)
8. Cucker, F., Smale, S.: Emergent behavior in flocks. IEEE Trans. Autom. Control **52**(5), 852–862 (2007)
9. Giardina, I.: Collective behavior in animal groups: theoretical models and empirical studies. HFSP J. **2**(4), 205–219 (2008)
10. Granger, C.W.J.: Investigating causal relations by econometric models and cross-spectral methods. Econometrica **37**(3), 424–438 (1969). http://www.jstor.org/stable/1912791
11. Ha, S.Y., Liu, J.G., et al.: A simple proof of the Cucker-Smale flocking dynamics and mean-field limit. Commun. Math. Sci. **7**(2), 297–325 (2009)
12. Hamilton, J.: Time Series Analysis. Princeton University Press (1994). https://books.google.com/books?id=B8_1UBmqVUoC
13. Jaynes, E.T.: Information theory and statistical mechanics. Phys. Rev. **106**(4), 620 (1957)
14. Kingma, D.P., Ba, J.: Adam: a method for stochastic optimization. arXiv preprint arXiv:1412.6980 (2014)
15. Kirkpatrick, S., Gelatt, C.D., Vecchi, M.P.: Optimization by simulated annealing. Science **220**(4598), 671–680 (1983)
16. Lu, F., Zhong, M., Tang, S., Maggioni, M.: Nonparametric inference of interaction laws in systems of agents from trajectory data. arXiv preprint arXiv:1812.06003 (2018)
17. Maclaurin, D., Duvenaud, D., Johnson, M., Townsend, J.: Autograd (2018). https://github.com/HIPS/autograd
18. Mao, Z., Li, Z., Karniadakis, G.: Nonlocal flocking dynamics: learning the fractional order of PDEs from particle simulations. arXiv preprint arXiv:1810.11596 (2018)
19. Matei, I., de Kleer, J., Minhas, R.: Learning constitutive equations of physical components with constraints discovery. In: 2018 Annual American Control Conference (ACC), pp. 4819–4824, June 2018. https://doi.org/10.23919/ACC.2018.8431510
20. Matei, I., Mavridis, C., Baras, J.S., Zhenirovskyy, M.: Inferring particle interaction physical models and their dynamical properties. In: 2019 IEEE Conference on Decision and Control (CDC), pp. 4615–4621. IEEE (2019)
21. Mavridis, C.N., Baras, J.S.: Convergence of stochastic vector quantization and learning vector quantization with Bregman divergences. In: 21rst IFAC World Congress. IFAC (2020)
22. Mavridis, C.N., Tirumalai, A., Baras, J.S.: Learning interaction dynamics from particle trajectories and density evolution. In: 2020 59th IEEE Conference on Decision and Control (CDC). IEEE (2020)
23. Mavridis, C.N., Tirumalai, A., Baras, J.S., Matei, I.: Semi-linear Poisson-mediated flocking in a Cucker-Smale model. In: 24th International Symposium on Mathematical Theory of Networks and Systems (MTNS). IFAC (2021)
24. Mavridis, C.N., Vrohidis, C., Baras, J.S., Kyriakopoulos, K.J.: Robot navigation under MITL constraints using time-dependent vector field based control. In: 2019 IEEE 58th Conference on Decision and Control (CDC), pp. 232–237. IEEE (2019)

25. Okubo, A.: Dynamical aspects of animal grouping: swarms, schools, flocks, and herds. Adv. Biophys. **22**, 1–94 (1986)

26. Paszke, A., et al.: Automatic differentiation in PyTorch (2017)

27. Reynolds, C.: Flocks, herds and schools: a distributed behavioral model. In: ACM SIGGRAPH Computer Graphics, vol. 21, pp. 25–34. ACM (1987)

28. Rose, K.: Deterministic annealing for clustering, compression, classification, regression, and related optimization problems. Proc. IEEE **86**(11), 2210–2239 (1998). https://doi.org/10.1109/5.726788

29. van der Schaft, A., Jeltsema, D.: Port-Hamiltonian systems theory: an introductory overview. Foundations Trends® Syst. Control **1**(2–3), 173–378 (2014). https://doi.org/10.1561/2600000002

30. Theodorakopoulos, G., Baras, J.S.: On trust models and trust evaluation metrics for ad hoc networks. IEEE J. Sel. Areas Commun. **24**(2), 318–328 (2006)

31. Will, T.E.: Flock leadership: understanding and influencing emergent collective behavior. Leadersh. Q. **27**(2), 261–279 (2016). https://doi.org/10.1016/j.leaqua.2016.01.002, http://www.sciencedirect.com/science/article/pii/S1048984316000035. Special Issue: Collective and Network Approaches to Leadership

Moving Target Defense for Robust Monitoring of Electric Grid Transformers in Adversarial Environments

Sailik Sengupta, Kaustav Basu[✉], Arunabha Sen,
and Subbarao Kambhampati

Arizona State University, Tempe, USA
{sailiks,kaustav.basu,asen,rao}@asu.edu

Abstract. Electric power grid components, such as high voltage transformers (HVTs), generating stations, substations, etc. are expensive to maintain and, in the event of failure, replace. Thus, regularly monitoring the behavior of such components is of utmost importance. Furthermore, the recent increase in the number of cyberattacks on such systems demands that such monitoring strategies should be robust. In this paper, we draw inspiration from work in Moving Target Defense (MTD) and consider a dynamic monitoring strategy that makes it difficult for an attacker to prevent unique identification of behavioral signals that indicate the status of HVTs. We first formulate the problem of finding a differentially immune configuration set for an MTD in the context of power grids and then propose algorithms to compute it. To find the optimal movement strategy, we model the MTD as a two-player game and consider the Stackelberg strategy. With the help of IEEE test cases, we show the efficacy and scalability of our proposed approaches.

1 Introduction

The electric power grid forms the backbone of all the other critical infrastructures (communication, transportation, water distribution, etc.) of a country, and thus, necessitates the presence of adequate monitoring strategies to quickly detect any anomalous behavior(s) that may have manifested in the system. It is of utmost importance to not only detect such anomalous behavior but also to take appropriate actions quickly to prevent the failures of power grid components which in turn, may lead to a large scale blackout [1]. Components such as High Voltage Transformers (HVTs), generating stations, substations, etc. are essential to the power grid and thus, their operational behaviors are monitored at all times with the help of Phasor Measurement Units (PMUs are devices, which are utilized as sensors, for monitoring the power grid). The problem of placing these sensors has been studied by multiple researchers over the past decade [18, 21]. Recently, in [4,17], the authors proposed a sensor placement approach that can *uniquely identify the source of the anomaly by utilizing the sensor readings generated by PMUs*. With the continuous discovery of real-world attacks such as

© Springer Nature Switzerland AG 2020
Q. Zhu et al. (Eds.): GameSec 2020, LNCS 12513, pp. 241–253, 2020.
https://doi.org/10.1007/978-3-030-64793-3_13

Stuxnet [13], Dragonfly [28] and a wide range of cyberattacks– jamming, Denial of Service, packet dropping, false-data injection and compromise of data integrity [15,16] – robustness of existing sensor placement mechanisms becomes critical. Thus, in this work, we leverage the ideas of Moving Target Defense (MTD) in cybersecurity [12,25] and the Minimum Discriminating Code Set (MDCS) based PMU placement [3,4] to build a defense-in-depth solution.

We continuously move the detection surface to make it challenging for an adversary to impede the unique identification of failure signals of HVTs. While PMUs are difficult to move, as opposed to the movement of physical resources in security games [19], once placed, they can be efficiently activated and deactivated, similar to the dynamic movement in intrusion detection systems [23]. While one may choose to activate all the PMUs placed upfront, the cost of maintaining them can become an impediment. Hence, the periodic use of a smaller subset (that still ensures unique identification) of the sensors placed upfront can be considered. Further, work in MTD has relied solely on heuristic guidance when constructing the configuration set that can result in all defenses being vulnerable to one attack, i.e. it is *not differentially immune* [22]. In this paper, we propose methods that ensure the MTD configuration set is differentially immune.

First, we define a novel variant of the MDCS problem, called the K−differentially Immune MDCS (hereafter K-δMDCS). We find K MDCSs of a graph, in which all K solutions can uniquely identify failing HVTs, with the added constraint that no two MDCSs share a common vertex; thus resulting in a differentially immune configuration set for the MTD. Given that the original MDCS problem is NP-Complete, we show that K-δMDCS is also NP-Complete and provide an optimal Quadratically Constrained Integer Linear Programming (QC-ILP) approach to find the K_{max}-MDCS of a graph. While our approach proves scalable for large power networks (MATPOWER IEEE test cases), we also propose a greedy approach that is computationally faster but trades-off on finding the largest K value. Second, we model the interaction between the power utility company (hereafter, the defender) and the adversary, as a normal-form game. The notion of Strong Stackelberg equilibrium used in this game-theoretic formulation, popular in existing literature [25,26], assumes a strong-threat model and aids in finding a good sensor activation strategy for the defender. Finally, we show the efficacy of our strategy and the scalability of our proposed approach on several IEEE power test cases of varying sizes.

2   Preliminaries

In this section, we first describe an electric power grid scenario and highlight how it can be modeled as a graph. Then, we describe the MDCS problem, showcasing how solutions to it can help with sensor placement, for the unique monitoring of HVTs. Finally, we provide a quick overview of Moving Target Defense (MTD) and the notion of differential immunity.

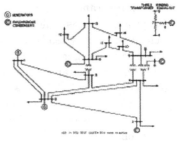

Fig. 1. IEEE 14 Bus Single Line Diagram

$V_1/T =$

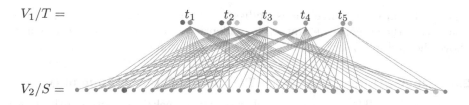

$V_2/S =$

Fig. 2. Bipartite Graph derived from the IEEE 14-bus network with 2-hop signal propagation constraints. (Color figure online)

2.1   The Electric Power Grid as a Graph

In Fig. 1, we show the IEEE 14 Bus single line
diagram of an electrical power grid. In [4], the authors proposed a set of graph construction rules that model the monitoring of HVTs as a bipartite graph $G = (T \cup S, E)$, where T represents the set of High Voltage Transformers (HVTs) that need to be uniquely monitored and S represents the locations where the PMUs (or sensors) can be potentially placed (PMU's cannot be directly placed on HVTs), and E represents the set of edges that exist if the operational behavior signal of an HVT ($t \in T$) reaches a PMU ($s \in S$) within a pre-specified number of hops. As Signal-to-Noise ratio (SNR) is used to measure the operational signal of an HVT in the real-world, and are known to quickly deteriorate over multiple hops, we, similar to prior works [4,17], consider the number of hops to be at most 2 (see Fig. 2).

2.2   Minimum Discriminating Code Set (MDCS)

The MDCS problem is a special case of the Minimum Identifying Code Set (MICS) [14], and was first studied in [6]. Given a graph, the goal of MICS is to identify the smallest set of nodes on which sensors can be placed such that two properties are met (given domain-specific information propagation constraints). First, if an event occurs at an entity represented by a node in the graph, a unique set of sensors is activated leading to easy identification of the node (entity). Second, every node should trigger a non-empty set of sensors if an event occurs at the node. In MDCS, the problem is adapted to a bipartite graph scenario with two (disjoint) sets of nodes– (i) nodes of interest, where an event may occur, which have to be uniquely identified with the sensors, and (ii) nodes on which sensors can be placed. Formally, we can define the MDCS problem in the context of sensor placement in power grid systems as follows [4].

Definition 1. *Given a Bipartite Graph, $G = (T \cup S, E)$, a vertex set $S' \subseteq S$ is defined to be the Discriminating Code Set of G, if $\forall t \in T, N(t) \cap S'$ is unique, where $N(t)$ denotes the neighborhood of t. The* Minimum Discriminating Code Set *(MDCS) problem is to find the Discriminating Code Set of minimum size.*

Figure 2 represents the bipartite graph obtained from Fig. 1, with 5 nodes in T, representing the 5 HVTs, and 40 nodes in S. An MDCS solution $S' \subseteq S$ of this graph consists of three nodes (indicated by the three colored nodes) which ensure that they provide a unique code to identify each of the 5 nodes in T (colors above the nodes of T indicate the unique combination of sensors activated).

2.3 Moving Target Defense (MTD) and Differential Immunity

Conceptually, MTD, popular in cyber-security, seeks to continuously move between a set of system configurations available to a defender, to take away the attacker's advantage of reconnaissance [12]. The key idea is that the attacker may not encounter the expected system configuration at the time of the attack, thereby being rendered ineffective. Formally, an MTD system can be described using the three-tuple $\langle C, T, M \rangle$ where C represents the set of system configurations a defender can move between, T represents a timing function that describes when the defender moves and M represents the movement strategy [24]. The goal of this work is two-fold– (1) to construct a desirable set C (for which we define the K-δMDCS problem in Sect. 3) and (2) an optimal movement strategy M (by modeling the interaction as a game in Sect. 4).

Note that when a single attack can cripple all the defense configurations $\in C$, MTD cannot aid in improving the robustness. In [22], the authors introduce the notion of *differential immunity* that aims at measuring the amount of diversity between configurations $\in C$. In this work, we consider a C that is differentially immune (denoted as δ), i.e. each attack, allowed by the threat model defined later, can only cripple one defense configuration. This ensures maximum diversity of C and implies the highest robustness gains for the formulated MTD.

3 K Differentially Immune MDCS (K-δMDCS)

To design the configuration set C for an MTD system, we first need to find multiple MDCS sets of a bipartite graph. For this purpose, we desire K differentially immune MDCS (K-δMDCS) where no two MDCS solutions share a common sensor placement point. Formally,

Definition 2 *(K-δMDCS). Given a Bipartite Graph, $G = (T \cup S, E)$, K vertex sets $S_i \subseteq S, i \in \{1, \ldots, K\}$ are defined to be K-δMDCS of G, if the following conditions hold– (1) all the sets S_i are MDCSs of graph G and (2) for all possible pairs of sets (S_i, S_j), $S_i \cap S_j = \emptyset$.*

First, we want to activate the minimum number of sensors placed in the network at any point in time. Hence, we use K sets, all of which are MDCS, i.e. have the smallest cardinality. Second, the use of differentially immune MDCS tries to optimize for robustness in adversarial settings. If an attacker were to attack a particular sensor placement point $s \in S$, it can hope to, at best, cripple a singular MDCS $S_i \in C$, from uniquely identifying HVT failure. If the defender selects an MDCS $S_j \in C (j \neq i)$, then the attacker will not succeed in affecting the functionality of the power grid sensors. We will now show that the decision problem corresponding to K-δMDCS is NP-complete.

Lemma 1 *K-δMDCS is NP-Complete, given K is an integer and $K > 0$.*

$V_1/T =$

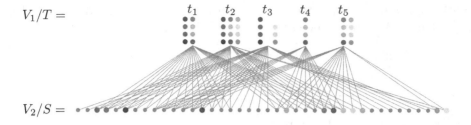

$V_2/S =$

Fig. 3. The IEEE 14-bus power grid graph has $4 - \delta$MCDS solutions.

Proof. We note that the original MDCS problem, which is known to be NP-Complete [6], is a special case (when $K = 1$).   □

Corollary 1 *K-δ Graph Problems such as K-δMinimum Identifying Code Set (MICS), K-δMinimum Set Cover (MSC), K-δMinimum Vertex Cover (MVC) are NP-Complete when K is an integer and $K > 0$.*[1]

Let us denote the size of an MDCS for a bipartite graph G as m. In K-δMDCS, the goal of the defender is to find K MDCSs each of size m. Then, the defender needs to place $K * m$ sensors in the power grid and, at any point in time, activate an MDCS set (of size m) to uniquely identify failures in T. While a large number of defender strategies (i.e. larger values of K) helps to increase their options for sensor activation in turn reducing the success rate for the attacker, it also incurs the cost of placing $K * m$ sensors. Thus, the ideal choice of K should trade-off robustness *vs.* sensor costs (when $K = 1$, robustness using MTD is impossible to achieve).

In cases where the defender has sufficient resources, one might ask *what is the maximum size of K?* Depending on the structure of the underlying graph, this question may have a trivial answer. For example, if the bipartite graph has a $t \in T$ and $N(t) = \{s\}, s \in S$, any MDCS of G needs to place a sensor on s to uniquely detect a fault in t. Hence, there can exist no two MDCSs that do not share a common node since s has to be a part of both. In such cases, the max value of K, denoted as $K_{\max}$, is 1. Beyond such cases, similar to the problem of finding the maximum value of K in the K-clique problem, finding $K_{\max}$ demands a search procedure over the search space of K that we now describe.

3.1   Finding Max K for K-δMDCS

We first propose a Quadratically Constrained Integer Linear Program (QCILP) that given a value of K, finds K Discriminating Code Sets (DCSs). We then showcase the algorithm for searching over possible values of $k \in \{1, \ldots, |S|\}$ to find the largest K. To define the QCILP for $G = (T \cup S, E)$, we first consider $|S| * k$ binary variables where, $x_{sk} = 1$ if a sensor is placed in node $s \in S$ for the

---

[1] Note that in the context of these problems, the distinction between the node sets T and S in MDCS are unnecessary and one can view the graphs as $G = (V, E)$.

kth DCS, and 0 otherwise. We also use a variable l that denotes the size of the DCSs found. We can now describe our QCILP, presented below.

$$\min_{l,x} \quad l$$

$$s.t. \quad l = \sum_s x_{sk} \quad \forall k \quad \text{All } k \text{ DCS has the same size } l.$$

$$\sum_{s \in S} (x_{sk} - x_{sk'})^2 = 2l \quad \forall (k,k') \quad \text{No two DCSs should have a common sensor.}$$

$$\sum_{s \in N(t)} x_{sk} \geq 1 \quad \forall t, \forall k \quad \text{All } t \in T \text{ has a sensor monitoring them for all the } k \text{ solutions.}$$

$$\sum_{s \in N(t) \Delta N(t')} x_{sk} \geq 1 \quad \forall (t,t'), \forall k \quad t \text{ and } t' \text{ trigger unique sensors for the } k\text{-th DCS.}$$

$$x_{sk} \in 0, 1 \forall s, \forall k \tag{1}$$

The last two constraints ensure that each of the K solutions is Discrimination Code Sets where (1) all $t \in T$ trigger at least one sensor $s \in S$ and (2) for all pairs of t and t' (both $\in T$), there exists at least one sensor in the symmetric difference set of t and t' that is a part of the DCS, which in turn uniquely distinguishes between t and t'. The first two constraints ensure that all k DCSs are of equal size and no two DCSs shares a common sensor. We can now ask the question as to whether the DCSs found by Eq. 1 is indeed the Minimum DCSs (MDCSs) for the graph G. In this regard, we now show the following.

Theorem 1 *For all values $K \leq K_{\max}$, the optimization problem in Eq. 1 returns K-δMDCS.*

Proof. We consider proof by contradiction. Given the value of $K(\leq K_{\max})$, let us assume that the solution returned by Eq. 1 is not the K-δMDCS for the graph G. If this is the case, at least one of the two properties in the definition of K-δMDCS is violated. Thus, either (1) the returned solution consists of a DCS that is not the Minimum DCS, or (2) there exists a sub-set (of size greater than one) among the set of DCSs that share a common node.

Owing to the third and fourth constraints, all the solutions constitute a DCS. Now, if (1) is violated, all the DCSs returned by the QCILP, of length l, are not the MDCS for G. Thus, the MDCS must have a DCS of size $l' \leq l$. Given that the minimization objective finds the smallest DCS and $K \leq K_{\max}$, this cannot be possible. Hence, (1) does not hold.

For (2), let us say that there exists a subset of the DCSs returned that share a common node. If this was the case, then at least one solution pair has to share a common node. If this node is denoted as s^* and the two solutions are termed as k and k', then for the second constraint, given $x_{s^*k} = x_{s^*k'} = 1$, the term for s^* is zero. Even if the other $l-1$ nodes in the solutions k and k' are unique, the terms will add up to $2*(l-1)$ thereby violating the second constraint. This is not possible and as a consequence, (2) does not hold.   □

Algorithm 1: Finding $K_{\max} - \delta$MDCS.

1: *In:* $G = (T \cup S, E)$
2: *Out:* $K_{\max} - \delta$MDCS
3: solutions $\leftarrow \emptyset$
4: $K \leftarrow 1$
5: **while** $K \leq |S|$ **do**
6:     solutions$_K$ $\leftarrow$ Solve Eq. 1 with K
7:     **if** solutions$_K$ $== \emptyset$ **then**
8:         break   Infeasible for $K > K_{\max}$
9:     **end if**
10:     **if** solutions $! = \emptyset$ **and** $|$solutions$(l)| < |$solutions$_K(l)|$ **then**
11:         break   DCS returned is not MDCS for $K > K_{\max}$
12:     **end if**
13:     solutions $\leftarrow$ solutions$_K$
14:     $K \leftarrow K + 1$
15: **end while**
16: **return** solutions

Given this, we can now consider cases where $K > K_{\max}$. When $K > K_{\max}$, the optimization problem in Eq. 1 is either infeasible or returns K DCSs that are not MDCS for graph G. This condition holds by the definition of $K_{\max}$ (proof by contradiction ensues if neither of the two cases holds). With these conditions in mind we can design an iterative approach, shown in Algorithm 1, to find the $K_{\max} - \delta$MDCS of a given graph.

Figure 3 showcases the $4 - \delta$MDCS solutions returned by Algorithm 1 for the 14-bus power grid network. The different colors indicate the different MDCSs found for G and the shades of the same color indicate an MDCS set. As shown, each of the four MDCS has a size of $l = 3$ and uniquely identifies all the transformers T. The lack of overlapping colors in the bottom set of nodes indicates that no two MDCS share a common $s \in S$.

While the procedure in Algorithm 1 finds the $K_{\max} - \delta$MDCS, it can be time-consuming for the largest networks (although it works well on large power-grids as shown in the experimental section). Thus, one can consider a greedy approach in which one solves the MDCS problem using [4]. We then solve this ILP with the additional constraints that $x_s = 0$ for all the sensors found in the current solution and keep doing so until (1) the ILP becomes infeasible or (2) results in DCS that does not have minimum cardinality. In the experimental section, we will see that although this approach is faster, it can output K-δMDCS where $K < K_{\max}$. The sub-optimality is a result of the ordering "enforced" by the current optimal MDCSs which in turn, proves to be infeasible constraints for the latter iterations of the problem.

4 Game Theoretic Formulation

The defender's goal is to maintain the unique identifying capability of HVTs at all times. Conversely, the attacker tries to prevent this capability, thereby making it harder for the defender to effectively monitor the HVTs. Here, we seek to find the optimal movement function M for the sensor activation MTD to aid the defender to realize its objective. To do so, we consider a strong threat-model where the attacker $\mathcal{A}$ with recon, is aware of the defender $\mathcal{D}$'s (probabilistic) sensor activation strategy, thereby making the Stackelberg Equilibrium an appropriate solution concept for our setting. We use a polynomial-time approach to find the Strong Stackelberg Equilibrium of the game [8]. We now briefly describe the various parameters of the formulated game (see Fig. 4).

Defense Actions. The defender has $K_{\max}$ pure strategies and the configuration set $C = K_{\max} - \delta$MDCS. If one uses the greedy algorithm instead of the optimal approach (both described in the previous section), the number of pure strategies obtained may be less than $K_{\max}$.

Attack Actions. We assume that an attacker can spend reconnaissance effort in figuring out the sensor placement point. Thus, its action set includes attacking a sensor that may be considered for activation (instead of all nodes in $|S|$). While one can consider attackers with the capability to attack multiple sensor activation points, it is often too expensive a cost model as it demands resource procurement and distribution over a wide geographic area.

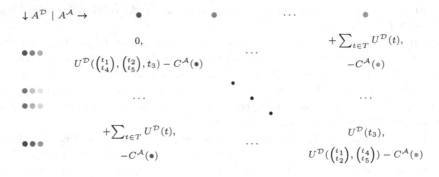

Fig. 4. Game-matrix for the dynamic sensor activation problem.

Player Utilities. The game has two different kinds of utilities that are used to calculate the rewards. First, the defender receives the utility associated with uniquely identifying a transformer $t \in T$ in the case of anomalous spikes indicative of failure (to occur). We assume that a transformer supplying power to an important building (e.g. the White House or the Pentagon) is considered to be more important than one supplying power to a residential area. Second, the attacker's cost for attacking a particular sensor needs to be considered. While some sensors may be placed in high-security areas, others may be easier to access. We conduct randomized trials with both these values $\in [0, 10]$, with 10 indicating the HVT/sensor most important to protect/difficult to attack.

In the bottom right corner of Fig. 4, the defender, owing to the attacker attacking a sensor, is only able to uniquely identify t_3 and thus, only gets reward proportional to it. Contrarily, the attacker, due to attacking a sensor, can make failures of t_1 and t_2 (and t_4 and t_5) indistinguishable and receives the corresponding utilities, minus the cost of attacking the sensor denoted by the light blue node ($\in S$, Fig. 3). Similarly, if the attacker selects the attack represented by the first attack column (sensor denoted by the dark brown node), the defender cannot identify any HVT and thus, gets a utility of zero.

Table 1. Game parameters and defender's reward for playing the different Cs and Ms for the various power-grid networks.

C				Movement function M			
Graph	$|S|+|T|$	$|A^{\mathcal{D}}|$ $(K/K_{\max})$	$|A^{\mathcal{A}}|$ $(K/K_{\max})$	URS (K)	URS $(K_{\max})$	SSE (K)	SSE $(K_{\max})$
14 Bus	45	4/4	12/12	18.5 ± 4.7	18.65 ± 4.7	20.62 ± 4.6	$\mathbf{20.72 \pm 4.6}$
30 Bus	89	4/4	16/16	26.45 ± 5.7	27.25 ± 5.6	29.44 ± 6	$\mathbf{29.9 \pm 5.8}$
39 Bus	96	7/9	28/36	18.7 ± 5	19.24 ± 5.2	$\mathbf{19.8 \pm 5.3}$	19.73 ± 5.3
57 Bus	170	6/6	60/60	70.76 ± 10.8	70.88 ± 11.1	$\mathbf{73.5 \pm 10.6}$	73.07 ± 10.7
89 Bus	422	16/21	96/126	50.67 ± 8.9	51 ± 9	$\mathbf{52.2 \pm 9.2}$	$\mathbf{52.2 \pm 9.2}$
118 Bus	367	2/2	10/10	31.35 ± 6	31.6 ± 6	32.45 ± 6.4	$\mathbf{32.61 \pm 6.1}$
2383 Bus	5927	2/3	212/318	832.7 ± 38.7	836.16 ± 36.7	835.34 ± 39	$\mathbf{842.34 \pm 39.4}$

5   Experimental Simulation

In this section, we conduct simulation studies on seven IEEE test graphs popular in the power domain [29]. Characteristics of these graphs such as the total number of nodes (i.e. $|S| + |T|$) are shown in Table 1. The table further lists the K values for the K-δMDCS found by the greedy and the optimal Algorithm 1, and is denoted by K and K_{max} respectively. The number of attacker strategies is listed in the fourth column. This value can be obtained by multiplying the corresponding K value with the size of an MDCS for graph G, since none of the K-δMDCS share a common node. We now discuss two results – (1) the effectiveness of the game-theoretic equilibrium compared to the Uniform Random Strategy baseline (which chooses to activate a particular MDCS with equal probability) and (2) the time is taken by the greedy and the optimal algorithm and their respective solution quality.

Effectiveness of Game-Theoretic Equilibrium. In Table 1, we show that in all test cases, the optimal movement strategy at the Strong Stackelberg Equilibrium (SSE) gives the defender a higher reward than choosing URS. When using URS or SSE, in most cases we see higher gains when the construction of the MTD configuration set C is optimal ($URS(K_{\max})$ obtained from Algorithm 1) as opposed to using a greedy algorithm ($URS(K)$). We expected this as the higher number of differentially immune options (as $K_{\max} > K$) chosen with equal probability reduces the probability of picking the weakest strategy. When the value of $K_{\max} = K$, such as for 14, 30, 57 and 118 buses, we see that the difference between the two versions of URS (or two versions of SSE) are negligible. A reason for the non-zero difference between the rewards values arises because of the MDCS sets chosen, although the total number of sets chosen are the same. We also see that the difference in defender rewards can be large even when the difference between K and $K_{\max}$ is small in the case of larger networks (e.g. 2383 bus). Thus, without finding the $K_{\max}$ and the SSE for the optimal C, it is hard to establish the loss in rewards. Given that these strategies are pre-computed, the power grid utility operator should not consider the greedy strategy unless the time required becomes prohibitive.

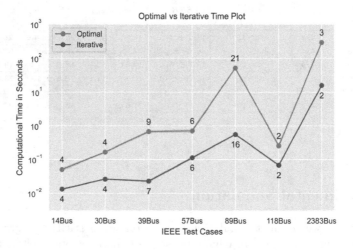

Fig. 5. Time taken by the optimal (Algorithm 1) *vs.* the greedy approach for finding $K_{\max} - \delta$MDCS and K-δMDCS (the K values are shown above the plot points).

Computational Time for Finding. C In Fig. 5, we compare the time taken for finding the configuration set C using the optimal *vs.* the greedy approach. We choose the logarithmic scale for the y-axis because the computational time of the optimal and greedy approaches for the 14, 30, 39, 57, and 118 buses was less than a second, and thus difficult to distinguish between on a linear scale. The largest disparity occurs when the size of the optimal set $K_{\max}$ is greater than the K-sized set found by the greedy approach (39/89/2383 Bus). In other cases, while the optimal approach is slower, it provides the guarantee that no solution with a greater K exists, which is absent in the greedy case. A case where the logarithmic scale, from a visualization perspective, does not do justice is the 2383-Bus. The time taken by the greedy approach is 15 s compared to 291 s taken by the optimal approach. While the K value differs by a factor of one, the resultant gain in defender's game value, as shown in Table 1, is relatively large. Thus, the added time in generating the optimal configuration set needs to be criticized based on the gain obtained in the underlying game.

We also consider the pragmatic scenario when the K value is fixed by the defender up-front owing to budget restrictions of sensors that can be placed in the power network. In this case, the greedy approach has to iteratively find one solution at a time, adding them to the constraint set of future iterations until the desired k is reached. On the other hand, the iterative procedure in Algorithm 1 can be altogether ignored and one can simply return the solution found by the optimization problem in Eq. 1.

6   Related Works

Adversarial attacks on power grids comprise of false-data injection, jamming, DoS and packet-dropping attacks [9,10,15]. While researchers have proposed a multitude of defense mechanisms [27], including Moving Target Defense (MTDs) [7,20], they do not consider the problem of sensor placement to monitor HVTs. On the other hand, works that leverage the formalism of Discriminating Code Sets [6] to optimize sensor placement [4], have focused on scalability issues and provided theoretical bounds in these settings [3]; completely ignore the issue of robustness to adversarial intent. In this work, we attempted to fill in this gap.

While an array of research work has formally investigated the notion of finding an optimal movement function M for MTDs, the configuration set C is pre-decided based on heuristic guidance from security experts [24]. While some works consider the aspect of differential immunity by analyzing code overlap for cyber systems [5] or Jacobians of gradients for deep neural networks [2], these measures have no way of ensuring differential immunity. The notion of k-set diverse solutions in Constraint Satisfaction Programming (CSP) [11], although conceptually similar to our notion of differential immunity, does not have the added constraint of finding a minimum sized solution (as in the case of MDCS). In adversarial scenarios, our work is the first to formalize the notion of diversity in graphs and propose linear programming methods to find them.

7   Conclusion

We considered the problem of monitoring the behavior of HVTs in adversarial settings and proposed an approach based on MTD, formulating it as a game between the power utility company (the defender) and an adversary. We showed that finding the configuration set for the defender is NP-Complete and presented two algorithms– an optimal QC-ILP and a greedy iterative-ILP. Optimal movement strategies at Stackelberg Equilibrium enabled the defender to activate k sensors at a time and uniquely identify failure points in the face of adversarial attacks. Results obtained on several IEEE test cases showed that our method yields the highest expected reward for the defender.

Acknowledgements. The research is supported in part by ONR grants N00014-16-1-2892, N00014-18-1-2442, N00014-18-1-2840, N00014-19-1-2119, AFOSR grant FA9550-18-1-0067, DARPA SAIL-ON grant W911NF-19-2-0006, and DARPA CHASE under Grant W912CG19-C-0003 (via IBM).

References

1. Southwest blackout. https://tinyurl.com/y6xxjsm5. Accessed 30 June 2020
2. Adam, G.A., Smirnov, P., Goldenberg, A., Duvenaud, D., Haibe-Kains, B.: Stochastic combinatorial ensembles for defending against adversarial examples. arXiv:1808.06645 (2018)
3. Basu, K., Dey, S., Nandy, S., Sen, A.: Sensor networks for structural health monitoring of critical infrastructures using identifying codes. In: DRCN. IEEE (2019)
4. Basu, K., et al.: Health monitoring of critical power system equipments using identifying codes. In: Luiijf, E., Žutautaitė, I., Hämmerli, B.M. (eds.) CRITIS 2018. LNCS, vol. 11260, pp. 29–41. Springer, Cham (2019). https://doi.org/10.1007/978-3-030-05849-4_3
5. Carter, K.M., Riordan, J.F., Okhravi, H.: A game theoretic approach to strategy determination for dynamic platform defenses. In: Proceedings of the First ACM Workshop on Moving Target Defense, pp. 21–30 (2014)
6. Charbit, E., Charon, I., Cohen, G., Hudry, O.: Discriminating codes in bipartite graphs. Electronic Notes Discrete Math. **26**, 29–35 (2006)
7. Chatfield, B., Haddad, R.J.: Moving target defense intrusion detection system for IPv6 based smart grid advanced metering infrastructure. In: SoutheastCon 2017
8. Conitzer, V., Sandholm, T.: Computing the optimal strategy to commit to. In: Proceedings of the 7th ACM Conference on Electronic Commerce (2006)
9. Deka, D., Baldick, R., Vishwanath, S.: Optimal data attacks on power grids: leveraging detection & measurement jamming. In: 2015 IEEE International Conference on Smart Grid Communications. IEEE (2015)
10. Deng, R., Xiao, G., Lu, R., Liang, H., Vasilakos, A.V.: False data injection on state estimation in power systems-attacks, impacts, and defense: a survey. IEEE Trans. Ind. Inform. **13**(2), 411–423 (2016)
11. Hebrard, E., Hnich, B., O'Sullivan, B., Walsh, T.: Finding diverse and similar solutions in constraint programming. In: AAAI, vol. 5, pp. 372–377 (2005)
12. Jajodia, S., Ghosh, A.K., Swarup, V., Wang, C., Wang, X.S.: Moving Target Defense: Creating Asymmetric Uncertainty for Cyber Threats, vol. 54. Springer, New York (2011)
13. Karnouskos, S.: Stuxnet worm impact on industrial cyber-physical system security. In: Annual Conference of the IEEE Industrial Electronics Society (2011)
14. Karpovsky, M.G., Chakrabarty, K., Levitin, L.B.: On a new class of codes for identifying vertices in graphs. IEEE Trans. Inf. Theory **44**(2), 599–611 (1998)
15. Nandanoori, S.P., Kundu, S., Pal, S., Agarwal, K., Choudhury, S.: Model-agnostic algorithm for real-time attack identification in power grid using Koopman modes. arxiv:2007.11717 (2020)
16. Niu, L., Clark, A.: A framework for joint attack detection and control under false data injection. In: Alpcan, T., Vorobeychik, Y., Baras, J.S., Dán, G. (eds.) GameSec 2019. LNCS, vol. 11836, pp. 352–363. Springer, Cham (2019). https://doi.org/10.1007/978-3-030-32430-8_21
17. Padhee, M., Biswas, R.S., Pal, A., Basu, K., Sen, A.: Identifying unique power system signatures for determining vulnerability of critical power system assets. ACM SIGMETRICS Perform. Eval. Rev. **47**(4), 8–11 (2020)
18. Pal, A., Vullikanti, A.K.S., Ravi, S.S.: A PMU placement scheme considering realistic costs and modern trends in relaying. IEEE Trans. Power Syst. **32**(1), 552–561 (2016)

19. Paruchuri, P., Pearce, J.P., Marecki, J., Tambe, M., Ordonez, F., Kraus, S.: Playing games for security: an efficient exact algorithm for solving Bayesian stackelberg games. In: AAMAS, vol. 2, pp. 895–902 (2008)
20. Potteiger, B., Cai, F., Dubey, A., Koutsoukos, X., Zhang, Z.: Security in mixed time and event triggered cyber-physical systems using moving target defense. In: IEEE International Symposium on Real-Time Distributed Computing. IEEE (2020)
21. Salehi, V., Mohamed, A., Mazloomzadeh, A., Mohammed, O.A.: Laboratory-based smart power system, part ii: Control, monitoring, and protection. IEEE Trans. Smart Grid 3(3), 1405–1417 (2012)
22. Sengupta, S., Chakraborti, T., Kambhampati, S.: MTDeep: moving target defense to boost the security of deep neural nets against adversarial attacks. In: International Conference on Decision and Game Theory for Security (2019)
23. Sengupta, S., Chowdhary, A., Huang, D., Kambhampati, S.: Moving target defense for the placement of intrusion detection systems in the cloud. In: Bushnell, L., Poovendran, R., Başar, T. (eds.) GameSec 2018. LNCS, vol. 11199, pp. 326–345. Springer, Cham (2018). https://doi.org/10.1007/978-3-030-01554-1_19
24. Sengupta, S., Chowdhary, A., Sabur, A., Alshamrani, A., Huang, D., Kambhampati, S.: A survey of moving target defenses for network security. IEEE Commun. Surv. Tutorials 22(3), 1909–1941 (2020)
25. Sengupta, S., et al.: A game theoretic approach to strategy generation for moving target defense in web applications. In: AAMAS, pp. 178–186 (2017)
26. Sinha, A., Nguyen, T.H., Kar, D., Brown, M., Tambe, M., Jiang, A.X.: From physical security to cybersecurity. J. Cybersecurity 1(1), 19–35 (2015)
27. Tan, S., De, D., Song, W.Z., Yang, J., Das, S.K.: Survey of security advances in smart grid: a data driven approach. IEEE Commun. S&T 19(1), 397–422 (2017)
28. Team, S.: Dragonfly: western energy sector targeted by sophisticated attack group (2017)
29. Zimmerman, R.D., Murillo-Sánchez, C.E., Thomas, R.J.: MATPOWER: steady-state operations, planning, and analysis tools for power systems research and education. IEEE Trans. Power Syst. 26(1), 12–19 (2010)

Security of Network Systems

Blocking Adversarial Influence in Social Networks

Feiran Jia[1]([⊠]), Kai Zhou[1], Charles Kamhoua[2], and Yevgeniy Vorobeychik[1]

[1] Department of Computer Science and Engineering,
Washington University in St. Louis, St. Louis, MO 63130, USA
{feiran.jia,zhoukai,yvorobeychik}@wustl.edu
[2] Army Research Laboratory, 2800 Powder Mill Rd, Adelphi, MD 20783, USA
charles.a.kamhoua.civ@mail.mil

Abstract. While social networks are widely used as a media for information diffusion, attackers can also strategically employ analytical tools, such as influence maximization, to maximize the spread of adversarial content through the networks. We investigate the problem of limiting the diffusion of negative information by blocking nodes and edges in the network. We formulate the interaction between the defender and the attacker as a Stackelberg game where the defender first chooses a set of nodes to block and then the attacker selects a set of seeds to spread negative information from. This yields an extremely complex bilevel optimization problem, particularly since even the standard influence measures are difficult to compute. Our approach is to approximate the attacker's problem as the maximum node domination problem. To solve this problem, we first develop a method based on integer programming combined with constraint generation. Next, to improve scalability, we develop an approximate solution method that represents the attacker's problem as an integer program, and then combines relaxation with duality to yield an upper bound on the defender's objective that can be computed using mixed integer linear programming. Finally, we propose an even more scalable heuristic method that prunes nodes from the consideration set based on their degree. Extensive experiments demonstrate the efficacy of our approaches.

Keywords: Influence maximization · Influence blocking · Stackelberg game

1 Introduction

The problem of diffusion over social networks has received considerable prior attention in the literature, both from the perspective of promoting diffusion (the so-called *influence maximization* problem) as well as in preventing its spread (the *influence blocking* problem). The influence maximization problem aims to select a subset of nodes on a network to maximize the overall spread of influence, such as adoption of a product or an opinion [6,10]. Influence blocking presumes that a

Q. Zhu et al. (Eds.): GameSec 2020, LNCS 12513, pp. 257–276, 2020.
https://doi.org/10.1007/978-3-030-64793-3_14

diffusion process is spreading, typically either from a set of known nodes, or from nodes selected according to some known distribution, with the goal of blocking its path through either a select set of nodes or edges [12–15,30,33].

In many settings, influence maximizers are malicious parties, and our goal is to limit their overall influence. For example, in cybersecurity, influence maximization may correspond to the spread of malware on the network, while in criminology we may be concerned about the spread of criminal influence (such as promoting membership in gangs or terrorist organizations). It is natural in these settings to consider the problem of *adversarial influence blocking (AIB)*, where a defender can first block (inoculate) a set of nodes or edges, and the adversary subsequently unleashes an influence maximization process. In the cybersecurity setting, we may impose use restrictions on a subset of computing devices, or even island these from the internet.

We model the resulting problem as a Stackelberg security game in which the defender first chooses (deterministically) which subset of nodes to block, and the attacker then selects a subset of seed nodes to begin network diffusion. The adversary's goal is to maximize overall influence, whereas the defender aims to minimize it. Note that this problem is significantly more difficult than the traditional influence blocking problem, since we are now allowing the choice of seeds to be adversarial, and to condition on the nodes we choose to block. Despite the extensive prior research on both influence maximization and influence blocking problems and their many variants, however, no general effective solution exists for the adversarial influence blocking problem.

The AIB problem is an extremely challenging bi-level optimization problem for a host of reasons. First, even computing influence for general influence measures is difficult [4,5]. Moreover, influence maximization is hard even if we assume that we can use a black-box (e.g., simulations) to compute expected influence, and it's only a subproblem. To address these technical challenges, we first approximate influence maximization in the lower-level problem by a *maximum node domination problem*. While this problem is still NP-Hard [24], it can be solved using integer linear programming (ILP). We make use of this, together with a constraint generation algorithm, to develop the first practical solution to AIM. To increase scalability, we develop an approximation based on a relaxation of the attacker's ILP combined with duality, which yields a single-level mixed-integer linear program for the defender to solve. We further improve the scalability of the resulting approach by using simple node pruning heuristics (removing a subset of nodes from consideration in the optimization problem). Through extensive experiments, we show that our approach is more effective for computing influence blocking nodes than state of the art alternatives for a variety of influence measures, including domination, independent cascades, and linear threshold models.

Related Work. Influence maximization (IM) is a classical problem in social network analysis, which aims at identifying a set of seeds to maximize the spread of influence under an information diffusion model, such as the independent cascade (IC) and linear threshold (LT) model. It has been shown that identifying such a seed set is NP-hard and proposed a greedy algorithm with provable guarantees [10].

On the contrary, a host of works consider the *influence blocking* problem of limiting the spread of information, typically through blocking the paths of diffusion, or equivalently modifying the underlying network structure. Some of them considered removing the edges, with the goal of minimizing the averaged influence of all nodes by treating each node as a seed independently [13–15], or minimizing the overall influence of a known set of sources [12]. Most of these works proposed heuristic algorithms, and experimentally demonstrated the efficacy under the LT or/add IC models. An exception is that the objective function under the LT model is supermudular, resulting in scalable and effective algorithms [11,12]. There are also other works considering removing nodes from the network and proposed several heuristic approaches based on the node properties, such as out-degrees [1,3,25] and betweenness centrality [33]. However, all these works consider a rather *static* scenario, where the initial set of seeds is known and fixed, which is fundamentally different from ours.

Besides modifying the network structure, an orthogonal line of works [2,9] consider the problem of spreading positive information as the best response to limit the eventual negative influence caused by the static adversary. Other works focus on the game-theoretic version where both the players choose to propagate their influence strategically and simultaneously [26–28]. Several following works model such a setting as games between the two sources in various application scenarios such as the defending against misinformation in elections [32] and protecting assets in an interdependent setting [29].

Our approach relies on approximating the influence of maximization as the *Maximum Node Domination problem*, which we term as *k-MaxVD*. In a graph, the set of dominated nodes of a node i includes i and its neighbors. The Node Domination Set [8] of a node-set U is then the union of all the dominated nodes of every node in U. The *k-MaxVD* problem is then to find the set U of k nodes such that the size of its Node Domination Set is maximized. *k-MaxVD* is proved to be NP-hard, and a simple greedy algorithm achieves an approximation ratio of $(1 - 1/e)$ [24].

2   Problem Formulation

In this section, we formulate the *adversarial influence blocking* problem as a Stackelberg game where the attacker solves the influence maximization problem after observing a network modified by the defender. To make it tractable, we approximate the attacker's problem as the maximum node domination (k-MaxVD) problem.

Stackelberg Game Model. We consider a graph $\mathcal{G} = (V, E)$, with a set of n nodes V and a set of m edges E. A defender selects a set of nodes $S_D \in V$ to block (remove from the graph) aiming at minimizing the negative influence caused by the attacker. We use $\mathcal{G}(S_D)$ to denote the modified graph after nodes in S_D are blocked. After observing $\mathcal{G}(S_D)$, an attacker selects an initial set of seeds S_A to maximize the influence under a given influence diffusion model. Since the attacker's strategy is conditioned on the choice of S_D, we represent it as a function $g(S_D)$. The interaction between the defender and the attacker is formulated as a Stackelberg game with the defender as the leader and the attacker the follower. To formalize, we denote the utilities of the defender and the attacker as $U_D(S_D, S_A)$ and $U_A(S_D, S_A)$, respectively. Our goal is thus to seek the Stackelberg Equilibrium (SE) of the game, which is defined as follows:

Definition 1. *A strategy profile* $(S_D^*, g^*(S_D))$ *forms a Stackelberg Equilibrium of the game if it satisfies two conditions:*

– *The defender plays a best response:*

$$U_D(S_D^*, g^*(S_D^*)) \geq U_D(S_D, g^*(S_D)), \forall S_D.$$

– *The attacker plays a best response to* S_D:

$$U_A(S_D, g^*(S_D)) \geq U_A(S_D, g(S_D)), \forall g, S_D.$$

In particular, we focus on approximating a Strong Stackelberg equilibrium (SSE), in which the attacker breaks ties (if any) in the defender's favor.

Next, we define the utilities for both players in terms of the results of adversarial influence on the network. Specifically, the *influence* of a seed set S_A chosen by the attacker is the total number of influenced nodes resulting from an exogenously specified diffusion model, denoted by $\sigma(S_A|\mathcal{G}(S_D))$. The particular game we consider is a zero-sum game in which the attacker's utility is the influence $\sigma(S_A|\mathcal{G}(S_D))$; formally, $U_D(S_D, S_A) = -\sigma(S_A|\mathcal{G}(S_D))$ and $U_A(S_D, S_A) = \sigma(S_A|\mathcal{G}(S_D))$. A key concept in this model is the *influence maximization problem*, InfluMax($\mathcal{G}$), which takes a graph $\mathcal{G}$ as input and outputs an optimal set of seeds; this is the *attacker's problem*. Consequently, finding the SSE of the game involves solving the following bi-level program:

$$
\begin{aligned}
\min_{S_D} \quad & \sigma(S_A^*|\mathcal{G}(S_D)) \\
\text{s.t.} \quad & |S_D| \leq k_D \\
& S_A^* = \text{InfluMax}(\mathcal{G}(S_D)) \\
\text{s.t.} \quad & |S_A| \leq k_A,
\end{aligned}
\tag{1}
$$

where k_A and k_D are budget constraints on S_A and S_D, the sets of nodes the attacker can influence, and the defender can block (remove from the graph), respectively.

It is evident that the bi-level program (1) is quite intractable, first because common influence measures, such as using the independent cascades model, are intractable to compute, second because influence maximization is itself NP-Hard, and third because both the outer and inner optimization problems are non-convex. Furthermore, given that there are many competing models of diffusion of influence on networks, there is even ambiguity in how to best instantiate the influence function $\sigma(S_A|\mathcal{G}(S_D))$. For these reasons, we next propose an approximation of the influence functions that introduces considerably more structure to the problem, and that can be a proxy for many conventional influence functions in the literature.

Approximating the Influence. Solving the previous bi-level program involves solving $\mathsf{InfluMax}(\mathcal{G}(S_D))$ given any S_D. However, finding the optimal seed set S_A that maximizes $\sigma(S_A|\mathcal{G}(S_D))$ is NP-hard for essentially any common influence measure [10]. In fact, even mathematically formulating $\mathsf{InfluMax}(\mathcal{G}(S_D))$ is not easy – the typical approaches treat $\mathsf{InfluMax}(\mathcal{G}(S_D))$ as a black box and identify the optimal S_A through simulation. To make our problem more tractable, we approximate $\sigma(S_A|\mathcal{G}(S_D))$ as the cardinality of the *dominated node set* with respect to S_A, denoted by $\mathcal{D}(S_A|\mathcal{G}(S_D))$. Specifically, given a node $v \in V$, its dominated node set is defined as the v and its neighbors in the graph, i.e., $\mathcal{D}_v = v \cup N(v)$, where $N(v)$ is the set of neighbors of v. Then the dominated node set of S_A is defined as

$$\mathcal{D}(S_A|\mathcal{G}(S_D)) = \cup_{v \in S_A}\mathcal{D}_v = \{u|\exists v \in S_A, \text{s.t.}(u,v) \in E\},$$

and we approximate the influence function using the cardinality of this set: $\sigma(S_A|\mathcal{G}(S_D)) \approx |\mathcal{D}(S_A|\mathcal{G}(S_D))|$. As a result, the influence maximization problem $\mathsf{InfluMax}(\mathcal{G}(S_D))$ is approximated as the maximum node domination problem, which is to find the node set S_A that maximizes $\mathcal{D}(S_A|\mathcal{G}(S_D))$. The resulting bi-level problem we aim to solve is

$$\begin{aligned}
\min_{S_D} \quad & |\mathcal{D}(S_A^*|\mathcal{G}(S_D))| \\
\text{s.t.} \quad & |S_D| \le k_D \\
& S_A^* = \arg\max_{S_A} \quad |\mathcal{D}(S_A|\mathcal{G}(S_D))| \\
& \text{s.t.} \quad |S_A| \le k_A.
\end{aligned} \tag{2}$$

The solution to problem (2) then becomes the approximate solution to problem (1). We note that approximation here is not formal; rather, we use experiments below to show its effectiveness in comparison with a number of alternatives. Moreover, node domination is itself a natural influence measure (as a generalization of a node's degree centrality).

3   Solution Approach

In this section, we present several approaches for computing the defender's optimal strategy. To begin, we rewrite the bi-level problem as follows. Denote the defender's strategy as a binary vector $\mathbf{x} = \{0,1\}^n$, where $x_i = 1$ means that the defender chooses to block node v_i and $x_i = 0$ otherwise. Similarly, let $\mathbf{y} = \{0,1\}^n$ denote the attacker's strategy, where $y_i = 1$ means that the attacker selects v_i as a seed and $y_i = 0$ otherwise. Then $\mathcal{D}(S_A|\mathcal{G}(S_D))$ can be written as a function of $\mathbf{x}$ and $\mathbf{y}$:

$$F(\mathbf{x}, \mathbf{y}) = \sum_{v_i \in V} (1 - x_i) \cdot \min\{1, \sum_{v_j \in N^I(v_i)} y_j\} \tag{3}$$

where $N^I(v_i) = v_i \cup N(v_i)$. As a result, the defender's problem (2) can be rewritten as

$$\min_{\mathbf{x}} \max_{\mathbf{y}} F(\mathbf{x}, \mathbf{y})$$

$$\text{s.t.} \quad y_i \leq 1 - x_i, \; x_i, y_i \in \{0, 1\}, \; \forall i,$$

$$\sum_{i=1}^{n} x_i \leq k_D, \; \sum_{i=1}^{n} y_i \leq k_A, \tag{4}$$

where the first constraint ensures that the node blocked by the defender cannot be selected as a seed by the attacker.

Next, we begin by developing a mixed-integer linear programming formulation for the attacker's problem, and subsequently make use of it to obtain both optimal and approximately optimal, but more scalable, solutions to the defender's influence blocking problem.

3.1 Computing Attacker's Best Response

We begin with the attacker's problem. Fixing the defender's decision $\mathbf{x}$, the attacker seeks to maximize the objective $F(\mathbf{x}, \mathbf{y})$ in (3). We linearize each nonlinear term $\min\{1, \sum_{v_j \in N^I(v_i)} y_j\}$ by replacing it with one auxiliary continuous variable $t_i \in [0, 1]$ and one extra inequality $t_i \leq \sum_{v_j \in N^I(v_i)} y_j$. Consequently, the attacker's problem can be formulated as a Mixed Integer Linear Program (with fixed $\mathbf{x}$), denoted as BR-MILP:

$$\max_{\mathbf{y}, \mathbf{t}} \sum_{v_i \in V} (1 - x_i) \cdot t_i$$

$$\text{s.t.} \quad y_i \leq 1 - x_i, \; i = 1, 2, \cdots, n$$

$$\sum_{v_i \in V} y_i \leq k_A, \; y_i \in \{0, 1\}$$

$$t_i \leq \sum_{v_j \in N^I(v_i)} y_j, \; 0 \leq t_i \leq 1 \tag{5}$$

The solution $\mathbf{y}^*$ to this MILP corresponds to the optimal strategy of the attacker given the defender's strategy $\mathbf{x}$.

3.2 Optimal Influence Blocking: A Constraint Generation Approach

We now propose a way to compute the exact solution to the bi-level problem (4) by using a constraint generation method. The defender's optimal problem can be alternatively expressed as the following optimization problem:

$$\min_{\mathbf{x},\mathbf{t}} \quad \sum_{i=1}^{n} t_i \tag{6}$$

$$\text{s.t.} \quad \sum_{v_i \in V} x_i \leq k_D, \ x_i \in \{0,1\} \tag{7}$$

$$t_i = \min\{1 - x_i, \sum_{j \in N^I(v_i)} y_j^*(1 - x_j)\}, \forall i, \text{ where} \tag{8}$$

$$y^* = \text{BR-MILP}(x). \tag{9}$$

If we let Y denote the complete set of the attacker's strategies, we can further rewrite this by a very large optimization problem in which we explicitly enumerate all of the attacker's actions. In this problem, the defender aims to find a strategy $\mathbf{x}$ such that the tight upper bound of the attacker's utility is minimized. For each $\mathbf{y} \in Y$, we can introduce the corresponding variables $t_{i,y}$ showing whether node i is influenced given the attacker's strategy $\mathbf{y}$. Constraint (8) given each $\mathbf{y}$ can be linearized to (12)–(14) by introducing binary variables $b_{i,y}$ which indicates whether $1 - x_i < \sum_{j \in N^I(v_i)} y_j(1 - x_j)$. Introducing a sufficiently large constant M allows us to further linearize all of the non-linear terms, yielding the following:

$$\min_{\mathbf{x},\mathbf{t}^{\mathbf{d}}} \quad U_A \tag{10}$$

$$\text{s.t.} \quad \sum_{v_i \in V} x_i \leq k_D, \ x_i \in \{0,1\} \tag{11}$$

$$U_A \geq \sum_{i=1}^{n} t_{i,y}^d, \forall y \in Y \tag{12}$$

$$1 - x_i - M(1 - b_{i,y}) \leq t_{i,y} \leq 1 - x_i, \forall y \in Y, \ \forall i \tag{13}$$

$$\sum_{j \in N^I(v_i)} y_j(1 - x_j) - Mb_{i,y} \leq t_{i,y} \leq \sum_{j \in N^I(v_i)} y_j(1 - x_j), \forall y \in Y, \ \forall i \tag{14}$$

However, the MILP above is clearly intractable since the set Y is combinatorial. To tackle the computational issue, we develop a constraint generation algorithm. The key to this algorithm is to replace Y with a small subset of attacker strategies $\hat{Y} \subset Y$, along with all of the associated constraints, so that the modified MILP above becomes DEF-MASTER($\hat{Y}$), in which we can specify an arbitrary subset of attacks $\hat{Y}$. Now we can start by an arbitrary small set of attacks, and interleave two steps: solve DEF-MASTER($\hat{Y}$) using the set of attacks $\hat{Y}$ generated so far to obtain a provisional solution $\mathbf{x}$ for the defender, and identify a new attack $\mathbf{y}$ that is a best response to $\mathbf{x}$. We can stop this as soon as the best response of the attacker no longer improves their utility compared to the solution obtained by DEF-MASTER($\hat{Y}$). Algorithm 1 fully formalizes the proposed constraint generation procedure, where is the set of optimal BR-MILP is just the mixed-integer linear programming approach for identifying the best response of the attacker presented in formulation (5). Note that we can utilize the returned influence value t_y^a of BR-MILP to prune irrelevant constraints of DEF-MASTER. Specifically, we only generate constraints (13)–(14) for each influenced node ($t_{i,y}^a = 1$). For the node with $t_{i,y}^a = 0$, we add the constraint $t_{i,y}^d = 0$, because given an attacker's strategy $\mathbf{y}$, the uninfluenced node will not be influenced no matter what $\mathbf{x}$ is. Consequently, we denote the refined master problem by DEF-MASTER ($\hat{Y}$, $\hat{T}^a$) in Algorithm 1.

Algorithm 1. Constraint Generation (CG)

1: $\hat{Y} = \emptyset$, $\hat{T}^a = \emptyset$,
2: $U_A^{UB} = \infty$, $U_A^{UB} = 0$
3: $x^*, x_{def} = \mathbf{0}$
4: **while** $U_A^{UB} - U_A^{LB} > gap$ **do**
5:     $(t_y^a, y, U_A) \leftarrow$ BR-MILP(x_{def})
6:     $\hat{Y} = \hat{Y} \cup \{y\}$, $\hat{T}^a = \hat{T}^a \cup \{t_y^a\}$
7:     **if** $U_A < U_A^{UB}$ **then**
8:         Update the upper bound $U_A^{UB} = U_A$
9:         Update the incumbent solution $x^* \leftarrow x_{def}$
10:    $(x_{def}, U_A^{LB}) \leftarrow$ DEF-MASTER$(\hat{Y}, \hat{T}^a)$
11: **return** x^*

3.3 Approximating Optimal Influence

The constraint generation approach enables us to effectively compute optimal influence blocking. However, it fails to scale to networks of even a moderate size. We now propose a principled approximation approach that makes use of a linear programming (LP) relaxation of the attacker's problem combined with LP duality.

Specifically, by relaxing the integer constraint on each y_i, the attacker's problem (5) becomes a linear program (LP) with variables $\mathbf{y}$ and $\mathbf{t}$. Its dual is

$$\min_{\lambda_0, q, \alpha, \beta, \gamma} \quad k_A \lambda_0 + \sum_{i=1}^n (1 - x_i) q_i + \sum_{i=1}^n \beta_i + \sum_{i=1}^n \gamma_i$$

$$\text{s.t.} \quad \lambda_0 + q_i + \beta_i - \sum_{v_j \in N^I(v_i)} \alpha_j \geq 0, \tag{15}$$

$$\alpha_i + \gamma_i \geq 1 - x_i,$$

$$\lambda_0, q_i, \alpha_i, \beta_i, \gamma_i \geq 0, i = 1, 2, \cdots, n$$

where $\lambda_0, q, \alpha, \beta, \gamma$ are the dual variables. By substituting the inner problem with (15), the defender's bi-level program can be reformulated as a minimization problem with the same objective as that in (15), with the difference that $\mathbf{x}$ now are variables. Finally, we can linearize the non-linear terms $\sum_{i=1}^n (1 - x_i) q_i$ as follows. We introduce new variables $w_i \geq 0$ and a large constant M, such that

$w_i = (1 - x_i)q_i$, $i = 1, 2, \cdots, n$. We further introduce linear constraints for each w_i, q_i, and x_i:

$$-M(1 - x_i) \leq w_i \leq M(1 - x_i), \tag{16}$$

$$q_i - Mx_i \leq w_i \leq q_i + Mx_i. \tag{17}$$

The full defender's problem can thus be formulated as a MILP, which we denoted by DEF-MILP:

$$\min_{x, \lambda_0, q, \alpha, \beta, \gamma, \mathbf{w}} \quad k_A \lambda_0 + \sum_{i=1}^{n} w_i + \sum_{i=1}^{n} \beta_i + \sum_{i=1}^{n} \gamma_i$$

$$\text{s.t.} \quad \sum_{i=1}^{n} x_i \leq k_D,$$

$$\lambda_0 + q_i + \beta_i - \sum_{v_j \in N^I(v_i)} \alpha_j \geq 0, \forall\, i \tag{18}$$

$$\alpha_i + \gamma_i \geq 1 - x_i,\ \forall\, i$$

$$\text{constraints}\quad (16-17)$$

$$x_i \in \{1, 0\}, w, \lambda_0, q, \alpha, \beta, \gamma \geq 0.$$

The optimal strategy for the defender is then the solution $\mathbf{x}^*$ to (18).

3.4   Scaling up Through a Pruning Heuristic

Even finding the approximately optimal strategy for the defender above involves solving a MILP (18), of which the number of constraints grows linearly with the number of nodes. This is a computational bottleneck, especially when the network is large. We propose a heuristic approach to deal with very large networks. The basic idea is to limit the strategy space of the defender.

We write the DEF-MILP (18) as a function DEF-MILP ($\mathbb{X}$, k_A, k_D, $\mathcal{G}$), where $\mathbb{X}$ denotes the strategy space of the defender. Our algorithm relies on pruning some *less important* nodes, which significantly reduce the strategy space $\mathbb{X}$. Note that the importance of the nodes can be measured by different metrics, such as the node degree. Our Heuristic Pruning Algorithm is presented in Algorithm 2. The idea is to first sort the nodes according to some importance metric in descending order, and then restrict the defender's strategy space in the top-l_D nodes; that is, setting $x_i = 0$ for the rest. Finally, we solve the MILP with restricted strategy space. The parameter l_D controls the trade-off between the time complexity of solving the MILP and the quality of the solution.

4   Extensions

Weighted Influence Maximization. A natural extension of *influence maximization* allows each node $v_i \in V$ to be associated with non-negative weight μ_i

Algorithm 2. Heuristic Pruning Algorithm

1: **procedure** PRUNED-MILP(k_A, k_D, l_D, $G = (V, E)$)
2: SortedList = SortingAlg(V)
3: $\mathbb{X}_{pruned} \leftarrow \{0, 1\}^n$
4: **for** i in SortedList$[l_d, n]$ **do**
5:   $\forall \mathbf{x} \in \mathbb{X}_{pruned}$, fix $\mathbf{x}[i] = 0$
              ▷ Limit the strategy space to top l_d nodes
6: $x_{def} \leftarrow$ DEF-MILP($\mathbb{X}_{pruned}$, k_A, k_D, G)
7: $lastNum \leftarrow k_d$ - CALBLOCKEDNUM(x_{def})
8: **for** i in SortedList **do**
9:   **if** $lastNum \leq 0$ **then**
10:    **break**
11:   **if** $x_{def}[i] == 0$ **then**
12:    $x_{def}[i] = 1$
13:    $lastNum = lastNum - 1$
14: **return** x_{def}
15: **procedure** CALBLOCKEDNUM(x_{def})
16: $num = 0$
17: **for** i in x_{def} **do**
18:   $num+ = i$
19: **return** num

---

capturing its importance in the final outcome [10]. Here we denote this problem as *weighted influence maximization* (WIM). They defined the weighted influence function $\sigma_\mu(S)$ as the expected value outcomes B of the quantity $\sum_{v_i \in B} \mu_i$, where B denotes the random set activated by the process with initial seed set S.

To incorporate weighted influence maximization, we generalize our model by associating a weight to each node in the objective function (3), i.e., $F(\mathbf{x}, \mathbf{y}) = \sum_{v_i \in V} \mu_i (1 - x_i) \cdot \min\{1, \sum_{v_j \in N^I(v_i)} y_j\}$.

The inner problem of the attacker's best response can be formulated by modifying the objective in (5) to $\sum_{v_i \in V} \mu_i (1 - x_i) \cdot t_i$.

Applying the same procedure of calculating the defense strategy of the non-weighted version, we can formulate the defender's optimization problem. The procedure is briefly described as follows. First, we can directly generalize the MILP formulation of the attacker's best response. Next, we relax the integer constraint on each y_i and take the dual of the resulting LP. The bi-level problem can then be reformulated as a non-linear minimization problem by replacing the inner problem with the relaxed dual. Finally, we introduce the large number M to linearize the non-linear term, we can get the final formulation, denoted as DEF-WMILP, shown as follows.

$$\min_{x, \lambda_0, q, \alpha, \beta, \gamma} k_A \lambda_0 + \sum_{i=1}^{n} w_i + \sum_{i=1}^{n} \beta_i + \sum_{i=1}^{n} \gamma_i \tag{19a}$$

$$s.t. \quad \& w, \lambda_0, q, \alpha, \beta, \gamma \geq 0 \tag{19b}$$

$$\sum_{v_i \in V} x_i \leq k_D \tag{19c}$$

$$\lambda_0 + q_i + \beta_i - \sum_{v_j \in N^I(v_i)} \alpha_j \geq 0, \forall i \tag{19d}$$

$$\alpha_i + \gamma_i \geq \mu_i(1 - x_i), \forall i \tag{19e}$$

$$\text{constraints} \quad (16)-(17) \tag{19f}$$

$$x_i \in \{1, 0\}, \forall i. \tag{19g}$$

For the heuristic pruning algorithm PRUNED-MILP, we can substitute DEF-MILP with DEF-WMILP.

Blocking Both Edges and Nodes. The model can be further generalized by considering blocking both edges and nodes with different costs. Suppose that the cost of blocking an edge is c_e and the cost of blocking a node is c_n, and the defender chooses to block a subset of both edges and nodes given a total budget B_D. Let $z_{ij} = \{0, 1\}$, $\forall (i, j) \in E$ denote the defender's edge strategy, where $z_{ij} = 1$ means that the defender chooses to block edge (i, j) and $z_{ij} = 0$ otherwise. Then the defender's budget constraint becomes:

$$\sum_{v_i \in V} x_i c_n + \sum_{(i,j) \in E} z_{ij} c_e \leq B_D \tag{20}$$

Once blocking a node, it is not necessary to block the edges linked to the node. To demonstrate this node-edge relationship, we introduce an integer variable $k_{ij} \in \{0, 1\}$, $\forall (i, j) \in E$ and the following linear constraints.

$$z_{ij} - 0.5 \leq M k_{ij} \tag{21}$$

$$x_i - 0.5 \leq M(1 - k_{ij}) \tag{22}$$

$$x_j - 0.5 \leq M(1 - k_{ij}) \tag{23}$$

Given the defender's strategy $\mathbf{z}$ and $\mathbf{x}$, the attacker's best response can be modified to

$$\max_{\mathbf{y}, \mathbf{t}} \sum_{v_i \in V} (1 - x_i) \cdot t_i \tag{24}$$

$$s.t. \quad \sum_{v_i \in V} y_i \leq k_A, \; y_i \in \{0, 1\} \tag{25}$$

$$y_i \leq 1 - x_i, \forall i \tag{26}$$

$$t_i \leq y_i + \sum_{v_j \in N(v_i)} y_j(1 - z_{ji}), \; 0 \leq t_i \leq 1, \forall i \tag{27}$$

Finally, taking the dual of the relaxed attacker's problem, the defender's problem can be formulated as a non-linear mixed integer program:

$$\min_{x,Z,\lambda_0,q,\alpha,\beta,\gamma} k_A\lambda_0 + \sum_{i=1}^{n}(1-x_i)q_i + \sum_{i=1}^{n}\beta_i + \sum_{i=1}^{n}\gamma_i$$

$$s.t. \quad w,\lambda_0,q,\alpha,\beta,\gamma \geq 0$$

$$\sum_{v_i \in V} x_i c_n + \sum_{(i,j) \in E} z_{ij}c_e \leq B_D \tag{28}$$

$$\lambda_0 + q_i + \beta_i - \alpha_i - \sum_{v_j \in N(v_i)} \alpha_j(1-z_{ij}) \geq 0, \forall i$$

$$\alpha_i + \gamma_i \geq \mu_i(1-x_i), \forall i$$

$$\text{constraints} \quad (21)-(23)$$

We can linearize the non-linear terms by replacing $(1-x_i)q_i$ by introducing a new variable w_i and replacing $\alpha_j(1-z_{ij})$ with b_{ij}. Then the optimal defense strategy $(\mathbf{x}^*, \mathbf{z}^*)$ can be obtained by solving the large-scale MILP (24).

$$\min_{x,Z,\lambda_0,q,\alpha,\beta,\gamma,\mathbf{b},\mathbf{k},\mathbf{w}} k_A\lambda_0 + \sum_{i=1}^{n}w_i + \sum_{i=1}^{n}\beta_i + \sum_{i=1}^{n}\gamma_i \tag{29a}$$

$$s.t. \quad w,k,b,\lambda_0,q,\alpha,\beta,\gamma \geq 0 \tag{29b}$$

$$\sum_{v_i \in V} x_i c_n + \sum_{(i,j) \in E} z_{ij}c_e \leq B_D \tag{29c}$$

$$\lambda_0 + q_i + \beta_i - \alpha_i - \sum_{v_j \in N(v_i)} b_{ij} \geq 0, \forall i \tag{29d}$$

$$\alpha_i + \gamma_i \geq \mu_i(1-x_i), \forall i \tag{29e}$$

$$M(1-z_{ij}) \geq b_{ij} \geq -M(1-z_{ij}), \forall(i,j) \in E \tag{29f}$$

$$\alpha_j + Mz_{ij} \geq b_{ij} \geq \alpha_j - Mz_{ij}, \forall(i,j) \in E \tag{29g}$$

$$\text{constraints} \quad (16)-(17), \quad (21)-(23)$$

$$z_{ij}, k_{ij} \in \{0,1\}, \forall(i,j) \in E; x_i \in \{0,1\}, \forall i.$$

5   Experiments

In this section, we test our defense approaches against several attacks and also compare them with several defense baselines from previous works. All runtime experiments were performed on a 2.6 6 GHz 8-core Intel Core i7 machine with 16 GB RAM. The MILP instances were solved using CPLEX version 12.10.

Data Sets. We conduct experiments on both synthetic graphs and real-world networks.

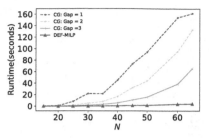 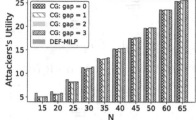

Fig. 1. Comparison between constraint generation and DEF-MILP in terms of runtime (left) and the attacker's utility (right).

- **Synthetic graphs**: We generate synthetic graphs from three graph models: Erdos-Renyi (ER) model [7], Watts-Strogatz (WS) model [31] generates networks with small-world properties., and Barabasi-Albert (BA) model [31]. Specifically, each edge in the ER model is generated with probability $p = 0.1$. In the WS model, each node is initially connected to 5 nodes in a ring topology and we set the rewiring probability as 0.15. In the BA model, at each time we add a new node with $m = 3$ links that attach to existing nodes.
- **Real-world networks**: We consider four real-world networks. The Email-Eu-Core network [20,34] is generated using email data from a large European research institution, which has 1,005 nodes and 25,571 edges. The Hamsterster friendships network [17,18] is an undirected friendship network of the website *hamsterster.com* with 1,858 nodes and 12,534 edges. We also tested on the sub-networks of a Facebook friendship network [23] and the Enron email network [16,22], where the sub-networks are sampled by the Forest Fire sampling method [19].

Methodology. Given a graph $\mathcal{G}$, we employ a defense strategy to block k_D nodes, resulting in a modified graph $\mathcal{G}^M$. The attacker then uses an attack strategy to select k_A seeds to spread the influence. We then measure the utility of the attacker under various combinations of defense and attack strategies. Specifically, we test our proposed defense strategies (CG, DEF-MILP, DEF-WMILP, and the corresponding pruned algorithms) against three attacks (k-MaxVD, IM, WIM). We also compare our defense strategies with several defense baselines. These attack and defense strategies are detailed as follows.

Attacks. We consider three types of attacks: k-MaxVD, IM, and WIM. In the k-MaxVD attack, the attacker solves BR-MILP (5) to find the seeds. In the IM attack, the attacker employs an efficient variation, termed *CELF-greedy* [21], of the classical greedy algorithm [10] to solve the influence maximization problem. Specifically, *CELF-greedy* utilizes the submodularity of the spread function and conduct an early termination heuristic, which achieves up to 700 times efficiency improvement while still providing a $(1 - 1/e)$ approximation guarantee. The WIM attack is a variation of the IM attack adapted to the weighted setting.

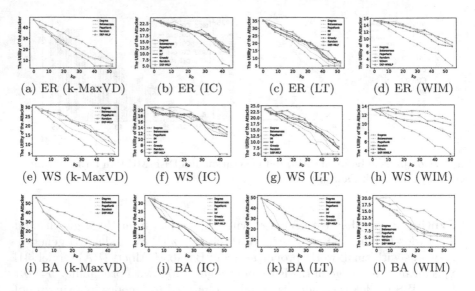

(a) ER (k-MaxVD)   (b) ER (IC)   (c) ER (LT)   (d) ER (WIM)

(e) WS (k-MaxVD)   (f) WS (IC)   (g) WS (LT)   (h) WS (WIM)

(i) BA (k-MaxVD)   (j) BA (IC)   (k) BA (LT)   (l) BA (WIM)

Fig. 2. The performance of DEF-MILP on synthetic networks against several attacks.

Defenses. Our optimal defense strategy is constraint generation(CG), and the primary defense strategy is DEF-MILP, where the defender solves the MILP (18) to find the set of nodes to block. We also consider DEF-WMILP, which is a variation of DEF-MILP in the weighted setting, as well as the corresponding pruning algorithms.

We compare our defense strategies with the following baselines. First, we consider a class of heuristic defense approaches where the defender blocks nodes in descending order of a specific node centrality measurement. The intuition is that node centrality measures the importance of a node in the network and blocking nodes with high centrality is more likely to limit the influence. In the experiment, we use node degree (out-degree in case of directed graphs), betweenness, PageRank, and influence as the centrality measurements and term the corresponding defenses as `Degree`, `Betweenness`, `PageRank`, and `Influence`, respectively. Specifically, the influence of a node is measured by the number of influenced nodes in the network when it is treated as the sole seed. We also consider four other baselines: `Influence Maximization (IM)`, `Greedy`, `WDom`, and `Random`. In `IM`, the defender acts as an influence maximizer and blocks k_D nodes that would cause the maximum influence. `Greedy` is a heuristic approach proposed in [30]. They assume that an attacker chooses some influential nodes at the beginning, and a protector blocks the nodes according to the maximum marginal gain rule. In our experiment, we set the influential nodes as the seeds selected by influence maximization in the original network. In `WDom`, we define a quantity $\text{WDom}_j = \sum_{v_i \in N^I(v_j)} \mu_i$ for a node j, where μ_i is the non-negative weight of the node i, as the sum of weights of node j's dominating nodes. This

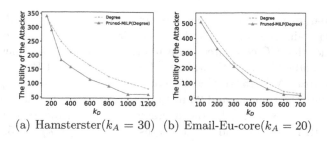

(a) Hamsterster($k_A = 30$) (b) Email-Eu-core($k_A = 20$)

Fig. 3. The performance of PRUNED-MILP on Hamsterster and Email-Eu-core networks against k-MaxVD.

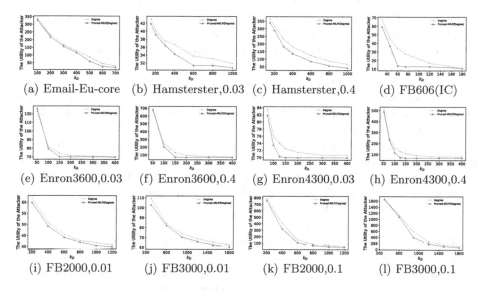

(a) Email-Eu-core (b) Hamsterster,0.03 (c) Hamsterster,0.4 (d) FB606(IC)

(e) Enron3600,0.03 (f) Enron3600,0.4 (g) Enron4300,0.03 (h) Enron4300,0.4

(i) FB2000,0.01 (j) FB3000,0.01 (k) FB2000,0.1 (l) FB3000,0.1

Fig. 4. The performance of PRUNED-MILP on real-world networks against IM attackers.

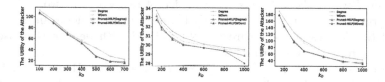

Fig. 5. The performance of PRUNED-MILP on real-world networks against WIM attackers. Left: Email-Eu-core, $k_A = 20$. Middle: Hamsterster, $k_A = 30$, $p = 0.03$. Right: Hamsterster, $k_A = 30$, $p = 0.4$.

heuristic is used to defend WIM attackers by blocking k_D nodes with highest WDom. Finally, Random selects a random set of nodes to block.

Comparison with Constraint Generation. First, we compare DEF-MILP with the constraint generation (CG) algorithm. We consider several variations of CG using a *gap* parameter, which defines the gap between solution quality of newly generated constraint (i.e., attack) and the best previously generated constraint; a gap of 0 implies that CG computes an optimal solution, whereas other gaps trade off optimality and efficiency. We evaluate the algorithms on ER networks whose sizes increase from $N = 15$ to $N = 65$. For each network's size, we generate 50 instances to test the runtime and 25 instances to test the attacker's utility with various random seeds and take the average. The experiments are conducted under DEF-MILP defense and CG defenses with budget $k_D = 5$,against the K-MaxVD attack with $k_A = 5$.

We can see that the results of DEF-MILP are quite close to that of optimal CG solutions, and are in some cases better than CG that uses a small gap. Though the DEF-MILP is not far from the optimal solution, the runtime is significantly reduced. Figure 1 shows that even if we loosen the gap of CG algorithms to 1, 2, and 3, the runtime of DEF-MILP is still considerably lower.

Results on Synthetic Graphs. In our experiments, we generate 64-node graphs for k-MaxVD and IM (including IC and LT) attackers with budgets $k_A = 5$. We generate 80-node networks for WIM attackers with $k_A = 6$. Each node is associated with a value $\mu_i \sim U[0,1]$.

As shown in Fig. 2, our defense strategy DEF-MILP and DEF-WMILP outperform all other baselines under all three attacks. We note that on BA graphs, heuristics based on node importance is comparable to the MILPs, while all these approaches perform significantly better than Random. One possible reason is that in BA graphs, there are a few high-degree nodes that can be effectively identified by centrality based algorithms.

For the defense algorithms, we can see that several heuristics can work effectively. RageRank is a good heuristic under k-MaxVD attack. IM works better than other heuristics under the LT model in our experiments. For the WIM attacker, WDom heuristic can be slightly better than other heuristics.

Results on Real-World Networks. As the size of real-world networks is significantly larger, we only test PRUNED-MILP and prune the nodes in descending order of the degrees. We compare PRUNED-MILP with Degree that uses the same node property to select nodes.

Figure 3 shows the utility of the k-MaxVD attacker on Hamsterster friendships network, with $k_A = 30$, and Email-Eu-core network, with $k_A = 20$. The results show that our proposed approach outperforms the Degree algorithm, even though aggressive pruning is used.

Figure 4 shows the defense of the IM attackers with different diffusion models in three networks. Linear Threshold (LT) model is used in the Email-Eu-core network. Uniform Independent Cascade (UIC) with different propagation probabilities are used in Hamsterster friendship network and the Weighted Independent Cascade (IC), in which each edge from node u to v has the propagation probability $1/deg(v)$ to activate v, is used in a 606-node sampled Facebook network. The budgets of the attacker are set as $k_A = 20$, $k_A = 30$ and $k_A = 10$, respectively.

Table 1. The effect of integrality relaxation of BR-MILP (5) in Hamsterster and Email-Eu-core networks.

k_A	Hamsterster			Email-Eu-core		
	M_{LP}	M_{MILP}	Gap (‰)	M_{LP}	M_{MILP}	Gap (‰)
10	320.500	320.000	1.563	690.380	689.000	2.002
20	443.000	443.000	0.000	784.000	782.000	2.558
30	531.875	531.000	1.648	836.500	836.000	0.598
40	603.750	603.000	1.244	872.090	872.000	0.103
50	660.500	660.000	0.758	895.830	895.000	0.927
60	707.375	707.000	0.530	915.839	915.000	0.917

For the larger two network datasets, we evaluate the performance of PRUNED-MILP in their sub-networks. Enron email network is sampled to Enron3600 containing 3,600 nodes and 11,412 edges and Enron4300 containing 4,300 nodes and 11,968 edges ($k_A = 70$). Facebook network is sampled to sub-networks with 2000 ($k_A = 40$) and 3000 ($k_A = 60$) nodes. The two sets of networks are applying different UIC model in view of small ($p = 0.01$, $p = 0.03$) and large ($p = 0.1$, $p = 0.4$) diffusion probabilities. Figure 4 shows that our algorithm is generally better than the Degree algorithm.

Next, we evaluate our PRUNED-MILP defense of WIM attack. Figure 5 shows the utility of the attacker on the Email-Eu-core network and the Hamsterster friendship network. Each node $v_i \in V$ in the networks is assigned a value μ_i uniformed distributed in [0, 1].

We compare the two pairs of experiments with two kinds of pruning orders, Degree and WDom. Intuitively, WDom considers the value of nodes so that it might be more adaptable to this problem. Figure 5 shows that applying the proposed PRUNED-MILP outperforms the original defense strategies.

The Effect of LP Relaxation. In our approach, we relaxed the integral constraints on the variables **y** of the BR-MILP, through which we are essentially optimizing over an upper bound of the attacker's utility. We demonstrate the quality of this approximation through experiments. Let the relaxed problem be BR-LP. We compare the optimal objective values of BR-MILP and BR-LP, denoted as M_{LP} and M_{MILP}, respectively. We are interested in the integrality gap defined as $IG = M_{LP}/M_{MILP}$. Table 1 shows the gap in percentage, defined as Gap $= (M_{LP} - M_{MILP})/M_{MILP}$, for the Hamsterster network and Email-Eu-core network with the attackers' budget from 10 to 60. The results show that the gaps in various cases are almost negligible, demonstrating a good approximation quality at least from an experimental perspective. The experiments in synthetic networks achieves similar results.

Trade-Off in Heuristic Pruning Algorithm. The parameter l_d in our pruning algorithm trades off the run-time and quality of the algorithm. In Table 2, we

Table 2. The run-time and solution quality in Hamsterster network with $k_D = 400$ and $k_A = 30$

l_d	400.0	500	550.0	600.0	639.0
Run-time (sec)	7.4	12.8	17.4	131.0	589.0
U_{IM}		188.7	153.7	146.8	138.4	133.1
$U_{k-\mathrm{MaxVD}}$		210.0	194	175.0	164.0	155.0

show the run-time and the attacker's utilities with different configurations of l_d in Hamsterster network when $k_D = 400$ and $k_A = 30$. $U_{k-\mathrm{MaxVD}}$ denotes the utility of the k-MaxVD attacker, and U_{IM} denotes the utility of the IM attacker with propagation probability $p = 0.4$. We can observe that when l_d increases, runtime quickly increases, but the solution quality also improves. However, when l_d is larger than one threshold, CPLEX cannot return the solution in reasonable time.

6   Conclusion

In this paper, we investigate the problem of blocking adversarial information in social networks, where a network defender aims to limit the spread of misinformation by blocking nodes in the network. We model the problem as a Stackelberg game and seek the optimal strategy for the defender. The main challenge is to find the best response for the attacker, which involves solving the influence maximization problem. Our approach is to approximate the attacker's influence maximization as the maximum node domination problem, which can be expressed as an integer program. This enables us to develop a constraint generation approach for the defender's problem. Further, by utilizing linear program relaxation and its duality, we reformulate the defender's problem as a mixed-integer linear program, which can be solved efficiently. We further develop a heuristic pruning algorithm to deal with large networks efficiently, as well as a constraint generation algorithm to compute the exact solution iteratively.

We test our defense approaches against several attacks on synthetic graphs and real-world networks and compare them with various state-of-the-art defense baselines. The experiment results show that our proposed defense approaches can effectively limit the spread of misinformation in an adversarial environment, outperforming all other baselines.

Acknowledgment. This research was partially supported by the NSF (IIS-1903207 and CAREER Grant IIS-1905558) and ARO MURI (W911NF1810208).

References

1. Albert, R., Jeong, H., Barabasi, A.: Error and attack tolerance of complex networks. Nature **406**(6794), 378–382 (2000)

2. Budak, C., Agrawal, D., El Abbadi, A.: Limiting the spread of misinformation in social networks. In: International Conference on World Wide Web, pp. 665–674 (2011)
3. Callaway, D.S., Newman, M., Strogatz, S.H., Watts, D.J.: Network robustness and fragility: percolation on random graphs. Phys. Rev. Lett. **85**(25), 5468–5471 (2000)
4. Chen, W., Wang, C., Wang, Y.: Scalable influence maximization for prevalent viral marketing in large-scale social networks. In: ACM SIGKDD International Conference on Knowledge Discovery and Data Mining, pp. 1029–1038 (2010)
5. Chen, W., Yuan, Y., Zhang, L.: Scalable influence maximization in social networks under the linear threshold model. In: IEEE International Conference on Data Mining, pp. 88–97 (2010)
6. Domingos, P., Richardson, M.: Mining the network value of customers. In: ACM SIGKDD International Conference on Knowledge Discovery and Data Mining, pp. 57–66 (2001)
7. Erdös, P., Rényi, A.: On random graphs i. Publicationes Mathematicae Debrecen **6**, 290–297 (1959)
8. Garey, M.R., Johnson, D.S.: Computers and Intractability: A Guide to the Theory of NP-Completeness. W. H. Freeman, New York (1979)
9. He, X., Song, G., Chen, W., Jiang, Q.: Influence blocking maximization in social networks under the competitive linear threshold model. In: SIAM Data Mining Conference, pp. 463–474 (2012)
10. Kempe, D., Kleinberg, J., Tardos, E.: Maximizing the spread of influence through a social network. In: ACM SIGKDD International Conference on Knowledge Discovery and Data Mining, pp. 137–146 (2003)
11. Khalil, E., Dilkina, B., Song, L.: Cuttingedge: Influence minimization in networks (2013)
12. Khalil, E.B., Dilkina, B., Song, L.: Scalable diffusion-aware optimization of network topology. In: ACM SIGKDD International Conference on Knowledge Discovery and Data Mining, pp. 1226–1235 (2014)
13. Kimura, M., Saito, K., Motoda, H.: Minimizing the spread of contamination by blocking links in a network. In: National Conference on Artificial Intelligence, vol. 2, pp. 1175–1180 (2008)
14. Kimura, M., Saito, K., Motoda, H.: Solving the contamination minimization problem on networks for the linear threshold model. In: Ho, T.-B., Zhou, Z.-H. (eds.) PRICAI 2008. LNCS (LNAI), vol. 5351, pp. 977–984. Springer, Heidelberg (2008). https://doi.org/10.1007/978-3-540-89197-0_94
15. Kimura, M., Saito, K., Motoda, H.: Blocking links to minimize contamination spread in a social network. ACM Trans. Knowl. Discov. Data **3**(2), 91–923 (2009)
16. Klimt, B., Yang, Y.: Introducing the enron corpus. In: CEAS (2004)
17. KONECT: Hamsterster friendships network dataset – KONECT, September 2016
18. Kunegis, J.: KONECT - The Koblenz Network Collection. In: International Conference on World Wide Web Companion, pp. 1343–1350 (2013)
19. Leskovec, J., Faloutsos, C.: Sampling from large graphs. In: ACM SIGKDD International Conference on Knowledge Discovery and Data Mining, pp. 631–636 (2006)
20. Leskovec, J., Kleinberg, J., Faloutsos, C.: Graph evolution: Densification and shrinking diameters. ACM Trans. Knowl. Discov. Data **1**(1), 2-es (2007)
21. Leskovec, J., et al.: Cost-effective outbreak detection in networks. In: ACM SIGKDD International Conference on Knowledge Discovery and Data Mining, pp. 420–429 (2007)

22. Leskovec, J., Lang, K.J., Dasgupta, A., Mahoney, M.W.: Community structure in large networks: natural cluster sizes and the absence of large well-defined clusters. Internet Math. **6**, 29–123 (2010)
23. McAuley, J., Leskovec, J.: Learning to discover social circles in ego networks. In: International Conference on Neural Information Processing Systems, pp. 539–547 (2012)
24. Miyano, E., Ono, H.: Maximum domination problem. In: Seventeenth Australasian Symposium on Theory of Computing, pp. 55–62 (2011)
25. Newman, M.E.J., Forrest, S., Balthrop, J.: Email networks and the spread of computer viruses. Phys. Rev. Lett. **66**, 035101 (2002)
26. Tsai, J., Qian, Y., Vorobeychik, Y., Kiekintveld, C., Tambe, M.: Bayesian security games for controlling contagion. In: International Conference on Social Computing, pp. 33–38 (2013)
27. Tsai, J., Nguyen, T.H., Tambe, M.: Security games for controlling contagion. In: AAAI Conference on Artificial Intelligence, pp. 1464–1470 (2012)
28. Tsai, J., Nguyen, T.H., Weller, N., Tambe, M.: Game-theoretic target selection in contagion-based domains. Comput. J. **57**(6), 893–905 (2013)
29. Vorobeychik, Y., Letchford, J.: Securing interdependent assets. Auton. Agents Multi-agent Syst. **29**(2), 305–333 (2014). https://doi.org/10.1007/s10458-014-9258-0
30. Wang, S., Zhao, X., Chen, Y., Li, Z., Zhang, K., Xia, J.: Negative influence minimizing by blocking nodes in social networks. In: AAAI Conference on Artificial Intelligence (2013)
31. Watts, D.J., Strogatz, S.: Collective dynamics of 'small-world' networks. Nature **393**, 440–442 (1998)
32. Wilder, B., Vorobeychik, Y.: Defending elections against malicious spread of misinformation. In: AAAI Conference on Artificial Intelligence, pp. 2213–2220 (2019)
33. Yao, Q., Shi, R., Zhou, C., Wang, P., Guo, L.: Topic-aware social influence minimization. In: International Conference on World Wide Web, pp. 139–140 (2015)
34. Yin, H., Benson, A.R., Leskovec, J., Gleich, D.F.: Local higher-order graph clustering. In: ACM SIGKDD International Conference on Knowledge Discovery and Data Mining, pp. 555–564 (2017)

Normalizing Flow Policies for Multi-agent Systems

Xiaobai Ma[✉][iD], Jayesh K. Gupta[iD], and Mykel J. Kochenderfer[iD]

Stanford University, Stanford, CA 94305, USA
{maxiaoba,jayeshkg,mykel}@stanford.edu

Abstract. Stochastic policy gradient methods using neural representations have had considerable success in single-agent domains with continuous action spaces. These methods typically use networks that output the parameters of a diagonal Gaussian distribution from which the resulting action is sampled. In multi-agent contexts, however, better policies may require complex multimodal action distributions. Based on recent progress in density modeling, we propose an alternative for policy representation in the form of conditional normalizing flows. This approach allows for greater flexibility in action distribution representation beyond mixture models. We demonstrate their advantage over standard methods on a set of tasks including human behavior modeling and reinforcement learning in multi-agent settings.

Keywords: Continuous actions · Stochastic policies · Multi-modality · Density modeling · Continuous security games

1 Introduction

The multi-agent learning literature contains many examples of multiple self-interested agents with imperfect information that are strategically interacting with each other [6]. Imperfect information and strategic interaction conditions require agents that can both model complex strategies of other interacting agents and formulate complex strategies in response. This often requires action distributions that are multi-modal to model the effects of hidden latent variables and to avoid being predictable to other agents. Current success in multi-agent learning is based on representing stochastic policies with categorical distributions over discrete actions [45] and population-based training to maintain a mixture of strategies [31]. Moreover, the recent success with AlphaStar on Starcraft II requires conditioning the agent's policy on hand-crafted features indicating different modes of human play [49].

However, past work in multi-agent contexts has largely focused on discrete action domains where multimodal behaviors are easily represented by categorical distributions. Single agent continuous control tasks are often modeled as either deterministic policies [44] or multivariate Gaussian with diagonal covariances as stochastic policies [41]. Deterministic policies are known to be suboptimal for

© Springer Nature Switzerland AG 2020
Q. Zhu et al. (Eds.): GameSec 2020, LNCS 12513, pp. 277–296, 2020.
https://doi.org/10.1007/978-3-030-64793-3_15

multi-agent scenarios [18]. In our experiments, we find that Gaussian representations of stochastic policies overly restrict the model class to have multimodal behaviors and thus lead to suboptimal performance in multi-agent domains. Consequently, devising methods to learn such complex representations for multi-agent systems is a significant challenge from a practical standpoint and is a key motivation for our work.

Density modeling is a rich field of study. Mixture models are often used to build multi-modal distributions from unimodal ones. This approach can be effective when the degree of multi-modality is known. We show in this work how complex multi-agent interactions can often require more flexible distributions than those achieved by mixture models. Recent advances in generative modeling [8,12,26] have shown promise for modeling complex distributions. Various Normalizing Flow models [8,9,11,25,37] allow learning invertible transformations of distributions that maintain ease of sampling and density evaluation while capturing complex distributions encountered in the real-world [34]. Due to their generality, these models can also allow reasoning about states and actions, making them useful for policy representations.

Our main contributions in this work are:

- Providing several examples of multi-agent problems that require complex action distributions for agent policies.
- Showing how conditional normalizing flow models can be used to represent a continuous stochastic policy, i.e. distributions over actions that are conditioned on the current state of the agent.
- Demonstrating their effectiveness in two multi-agent learning contexts:
  1. Imitation learning in multi-agent multi-modal behavior modeling.
  2. Reinforcement learning in multi-agent imperfect information stochastic games to learn mixed strategies that are difficult to exploit.

We compare against standard multivariate Gaussian policies as well as their mixtures and provide qualitative and quantitative differences in learned agent behavior on a suite of synthetic and real-world tasks.

2   Background and Related Work

This section outlines the components of our approach and discusses relevant prior work.

2.1   Flow Models

Flow models are invertible transformations that map observed data x to a latent variable z from a simpler distribution, such that both computing the probability density $p(x)$ and sampling $x \sim p(x)$ are efficient. Represented as a function f, the key idea is to stack individual simple invertible transformations [8,9] as $z = f(x) = f_1 \circ \cdots \circ f_L(x)$, with each f_i having a tractable inverse and a tractable Jacobian determinant. Sampling is efficient because $x = f^{-1}(z) = f_L^{-1} \circ \cdots \circ$

$f_1^{-1}(z)$, where z is sampled from a simple distribution like the standard normal or logistic, q. To take into account the change in volume due to application of transforming functions, the log density can be written as:

$$\log p(x) = \log q(z) + \sum_{i=1}^{L} \log \left| \det \frac{\partial x^{(i-1)}}{\partial x^{(i)}} \right| \tag{1}$$

where $x^{(i)} = f_i^{-1} \circ \cdots \circ f_1^{-1}(z)$ and $x^{(0)} = z$. Computing the model density and training by maximum likelihood is efficient because Eq. (1) is easy to compute and differentiate with respect to the parameters of the flows f_i.

2.2 Stochastic Games

Multi-agent reinforcement learning problems are typically modeled as stochastic games [30,42]. These comprise of a *state space* $\mathcal{S}$, $\mathcal{I} = \{1, \ldots, n\}$ agents with their *observation* and *action* spaces as $\mathcal{O}^1, \ldots, \mathcal{O}^n$ and $\mathcal{A}^1, \ldots, \mathcal{A}^n$, respectively; (stochastic) *reward* functions $R^i : \mathcal{S} \times \mathcal{A}^1 \times \ldots \times \mathcal{A}^n \to \mathbb{R}$ for each agent; (stochastic) *observation* functions $O^i : \mathcal{S} \to \mathcal{O}^i$ for each agent; a (stochastic) *transition* function $T : \mathcal{S} \times \mathcal{A}^1 \times \ldots \times \mathcal{A}^n \to \mathcal{S}$; and an *initial state distribution* $\rho(s_0)$ on $\mathcal{S}$. The goal of each agent in the game is to maximize the discounted future reward with discount factor γ. A special case of a stochastic game with one agent is a partially observable Markov decision process (POMDP) [27]. A Markov decision process (MDP) in turn is a special case of a POMDP with observation function as identity.

Strategic interactions between agents are studied through the lens of game theory. A repeated *normal-form game* (NFG) is a special case of a stochastic game with only one state. The reward functions R^i can be combined together into a single payoff function $U : \mathcal{S} \times \prod_{k=1}^{n} \mathcal{A}^i \to \mathbb{R}^n$. We can define the strategy profile as $\pi = (\pi^1, \ldots, \pi^n)$ and π^{-i} as the same strategy profile but without the policy π^i of agent i. The expected utility of an agent i is then $u^i(\pi) = \mathbb{E}_\pi[U(\mathbf{a}) \mid \mathbf{a} \sim \pi]$. A best response for agent i given π is $\mathrm{BR}(\pi^{-i}) = \arg\max_{\pi^i} u^i((\pi^i, \pi^{-i}))$. A profile π_* is a Nash equilibrium, if for each agent i, the strategy $\pi^i = \mathrm{BR}(\pi^{-i})$.

Security games between a defender and an attacker are often modeled as a special kind of two-player normal-form games [23]. The attacker may choose to attack any targets from the set $\mathcal{T}$. The defender tries to prevent such attacks by covering targets using resources from the set $\mathcal{D}$. The utilities for each player can be obtained given the game state (i.e. the target locations) and agent actions. These games have been used to model defender-adversary interaction in protecting infrastructure targets such as airports, ports, and flights [7,39,46] with discrete locations. However, this model is increasingly being applied to protecting wildlife [50], fisheries [15], forests [19,21,22], and other domains with continuous spaces.

2.3 Imitation Learning and Agent Modeling

Given a set of observed states and corresponding actions as expert demonstrations, the goal of imitation learning is to learn a policy π_θ that matches the expert's behavior as closely as possible. We focus on the behavior cloning app-roach that treats this task as a supervised learning problem [36], learning a stochastic policy π_θ that maximizes the likelihood of observed expert actions. We leave other imitation learning paradigms [17] for future work. The same principles can be applied to modeling an agent's behavior given sample trajec-tories [38]. Bhattacharyya et al. [3] observe that capturing multi-modality of agent behavior is important in multi-agent contexts such as automated driving. Vinyals et al. [49] show that bootstrapping agent policies via imitation learning is often an important first step for solving complex games.

2.4   Multi-agent Reinforcement Learning

Although there are several approaches for solving zero-sum games, such as linear programming, fictitious play [5], replicator dynamics [48] or regret minimiza-tion [4] for zero-sum games, they often suffer an exponential increase in com-plexity with the size of state-action space. With the recent success of reinforce-ment learning (RL) at solving complex high-dimensional tasks, adapting such methods for multi-agent contexts provides a viable approach for solving high-dimensional multi-agent problems. One can independently apply RL to multiple agents with individual agents treating other agents as parts of stochastic envi-ronments [31]. Other approaches include self-play [16] and policy space response oracles (PSRO) [28]. However, with the exception of Bansal et al. [2] and Liu et al. [31], these have mostly been limited to discrete actions. Liu et al. [31] and Lanctot et al. [28] recognize the importance of training a population of agents to capture the multi-modal behavior. Kamra et al. [21,22] demonstrate the utility of applying deep reinforcement learning methods for continuous space security games but do not explore multi-modality.

Some explored policy architectures for various single-agent continuous control tasks. Haarnoja et al. [13] note that Gaussian mixtures can represent multi-modal policies with the number of modes specified in advance. Recent work shows implicit policies like those based on Normalizing Flows can obtain competitive performance on single agent continuous control tasks but do not explore the context of multi-agent domains [47]. Moreover, the standard choice for policy representation for continuous action spaces continues to be unimodal diagonal Gaussian [29,41], even in the context of multi-agent domains [31]. We show that this choice can limit policy representability for multi-agent contexts.

3   Normalizing Flow Policy Representation

3.1   Conditional Flow as Policy Representation

While a flow model is capable of modeling complex distributions, to use it as a policy representation, we need to condition its output on some state s. We propose to embed such state conditioning in each individual transformation, f_i in Eq. (1), of the flow model while maintaining its invertibility and computational

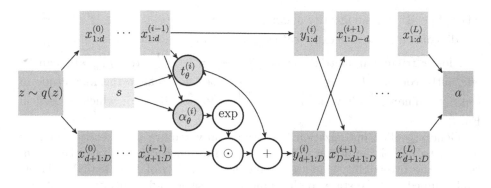

Fig. 1. Computational graph for conditional RealNVP

efficiency. Formally, we want to transform $z \sim q$ to a policy, $a \sim \pi(a \mid s)$ by defining $a = f^{-1}(z, s)$ with $f^{-1}(z, s) = f_L^{-1}(f_{L-1}^{-1}(\cdots f_1^{-1}(z, s) \cdots, s), s)$ and $z \sim q$. The conditional log probability turns into:

$$\log \pi(a \mid s) = \log q(f(a, s)) + \sum_{i=1}^{L} \log \left| \det \frac{\partial x^{(i-1)}}{\partial x^{(i)}} \right| \tag{2}$$

where $x^{(i)} = f_i^{-1}(x^{(i-1)}, s)$ and $x^{(0)} = z$.

Based on RealNVP [9], we propose the following *conditional coupling layer* for f_i^{-1}: Given a D dimensional input $x^{(i-1)}$ and some positive integer $d < D$, the D dimensional output $x^{(i)}$ from the application of f_i^{-1} is defined as:

$$\begin{aligned} y_{1:d}^{(i)} &= x_{1:d}^{(i-1)} \\ y_{d+1:D}^{(i)} &= y_{d+1:D}^{(i-1)} \odot \exp(\alpha^{(i)}(x_{1:d}^{(i-1)}, s)) + t^{(i)}(x_{1:d}^{(i-1)}, s) \end{aligned} \tag{3}$$

where $\alpha^{(i)}$ and $t^{(i)}$ are scale and translation functions from $\mathbb{R}^d \to \mathbb{R}^{D-d}$ and $\odot$ is the Hadamard product. These functions are represented by neural networks. Since $x_{1:d}^{(i-1)}$ is unchanged in $y^{(i)}$, we switch rows in $y^{(i)}$ to get $x^{(i)}$ where $x_{1:D-d}^{(i)} = y_{d+1:D}^{(i)}$ and $x_{D-d+1:D}^{(i)} = y_{1:d}^{(i)}$. Thus, a sequence of two *conditioning coupling layers* modifies all dimensions of x. See Fig. 1 for the computational graph.

The reverse mapping, f_i, is efficient when $x^{(i)}$ is known (and so is $y^{(i)}$) and is performed by:

$$\begin{aligned} x_{1:d}^{(i-1)} &= y_{1:d}^{(i)} \\ x_{d+1:D}^{(i-1)} &= (y_{d+1:D}^{(i)} - t^{(i)}(y_{1:d}^{(i)}, s)) \odot \exp(-\alpha^{(i)}(y_{1:d}^{(i)}, s)) \end{aligned} \tag{4}$$

The Jacobian, $\frac{\partial x^{(i-1)}}{\partial y^{(i)}}$, is of the form:

$$\frac{\partial x^{(i-1)}}{\partial y^{(i)}} = \begin{bmatrix} \mathbf{I}_d & \mathbf{0}_d \\ \frac{\partial x_{d+1:D}^{(i-1)}}{\partial y_{1:d}^{(i)}} & \mathrm{diag}(\exp(-\alpha^{(i)}(y_{1:d}^{(i)}, s))) \end{bmatrix} \tag{5}$$

where $\mathbf{I}_d \in \mathbb{R}^{d \times d}$ is an identity matrix; $\mathrm{diag}(\exp(-\alpha^{(i)}(y_{1:d}^{(i)}, s))) \in \mathbb{R}^{(D-d) \times (D-d)}$ is a diagonal matrix with $\exp(-\alpha^{(i)}(y_{1:d}^{(i)}, s))$ on its diagonal entries. Since $\frac{\partial x^{(i-1)}}{\partial y^{(i)}}$ is a lower triangular matrix, $\log \left| \det \frac{\partial x^{(i-1)}}{\partial y^{(i)}} \right| = -\sum_{i=1}^{D-d} \alpha^{(i)}(y_{1:d}^{(i)}, s))_i$ can be efficiently computed. Since switching rows does not change the magnitude of the determinant, we have $\log \left| \det \frac{\partial x^{(i-1)}}{\partial x^{(i)}} \right| = \log \left| \det \frac{\partial x^{(i-1)}}{\partial y^{(i)}} \right|$, which is used in Eq. (2).

General policy optimization algorithms only require parametrized density models to model the action distributions conditioned on the state. By maintaining the invertibility and the triangular Jacobian of the RealNVP layers while embedding the state conditioning in the scale and translation functions, our flow-based architecture can effectively represent agent policies. At sampling time, we first sample $z \sim p(z)$ and get $a = f_L^{-1}(f_{L-1}^{-1}(\cdots f_1^{-1}(z, s) \cdots, s), s)$ with each $f_i^{-1}(x^{i-1}, s)$ calculated as in Eq. (3). The log probability is calculated by Eq. (2) where $z = f_1(f_2(\cdots f_L(x, s) \cdots, s), s)$ with each $f_i(x^{(i)}, s)$ calculated as in Eq. (4) and $\log \left| \det \frac{\partial x^{(i-1)}}{\partial x^{(i)}} \right|$ as described above.

3.2 Representation Capability

For the internal coupling of different dimensions of the action, at each *conditional coupling layer*, one part of the dimensions of x is coupled with the other part by neural network functions. With the application of row switching, we need at least three coupling layers to have every axis coupled with every other axes [8].

There are multiple possible ways to condition the flow model on the state. Here we discuss the limitations of the two most straightforward modifications and how our proposed structure overcome these limitations.

- Having the state conditioning only at the base distribution q, i.e. $z \sim q(z \mid s)$ and $a = f^{-1}(z)$. In this case, we will have a fixed transformation function f^{-1} for any state s, so $\log \pi(a \mid s) = \log q(f(a) \mid s) + \log \left| \det \frac{\partial z}{\partial a} \right|$. Then for any two states $s_1, s_2 \in \mathcal{S}$, the log probability of the same action a is given by $\log \pi_0(a \mid s_1) - \log \pi_0(a \mid s_2) = \log q(f(a) \mid s_1) - \log q(f(a) \mid s_2)$, i.e., the log probability difference is only in the base distribution. Since the base distribution is often simple (this is the point of using flow models), its representational capability is limited.
- Having the state conditioning only at one of the transformation layer, i.e. $z \sim p(z)$ and $a = f_L^{-1} \circ \cdots \circ f_i^{-1}(f_{i-1}^{-1} \circ \cdots \circ f_1^{-1}(z), s)$. This means that the network needs to embed both the sampling information of z and the state information of s in $x^{(i)} = f_i^{-1}(f_{i-1}^{-1} \circ \cdots \circ f_1^{-1}(z), s)$. In most flow models, the dimension of $x^{(j)} \forall j \in \{1 \ldots L\}$ is equal to the dimension of the action space $|\mathcal{A}|$. In most reinforcement learning tasks, the dimension of the state space $|\mathcal{S}|$ is much larger than $|\mathcal{A}|$. E.g., consider tasks with images as state representations. When $|\mathcal{S}| \gg |\mathcal{A}|$, there could be significant information loss when compressing the state information into $x^{(i)}$. Our experiments also indicate that such a method performs worse than the proposed structure (see results for NFP1 [47] in Sect. 4).

Our method overcomes the above limitations by using the state as side information at each transformation layer. It is able to generate drastically different distributions at different states by changing the transformation at each layer. The network architecture also needs to compress less information. Because the state information is available at each transformation layer, the network does not need to embed all the state information in the latent variables.

4   Experiments

We aim to show that Flow models can be effective policy representations for multi-modal multi-agent scenarios with continuous actions. We first evaluate Flow policies for a synthetic and a real-world agent-modeling task, where multi-modality is important, since often for real world games, agent policies need to be bootstrapped from human demonstrations [43,49]. We then show the importance of multi-modal policy representations for learning difficult-to-exploit strategies in the context of continuous action games.

We compare Flow policies against the standard diagonal multivariate Gaussian policies, as well as the Gaussian policies with full covariance using Cholesky decomposition (noted as CG policy). We also compare against the mixture of multivariate diagonal or full covariance Gaussian policies (noted as GMM and MCG policies). We focus on the conditional RealNVP [9] as described in Sect. 3 as our Flow policy. We also compare against the architecture introduced in Tang and Agrawal [47] (noted as NFP1) which also uses the flow model as the policy representation with state conditioning only at the first transformation layer. Due to the reasons described in Sect. 3.2, we found it suboptimal and more difficult to train compared to our approach. Additional details on the policy and training implementations are in the appendix.

4.1   Agent Modeling

For agent modeling tasks, we use behavior cloning to maximize the likelihood of actions in the training data [36].

Synthetic. To verify that Flow policies can learn to represent multi-modal behavior, we designed a simple environment to model human driving in response to a traffic light at an intersection. As soon as the traffic light turns yellow, the driver either needs to *accelerate* or *decelerate* to avoid coming into conflict with the orthogonal traffic. Figure 2 givens an illustration of the scenario.

Figure 4a shows the sampled expert accelerations along the road ($\ddot{x}$) with noticeable multi-modal behavior. Aggressive drivers decelerate and show negative $\ddot{x}$, while defensive drivers accelerate and display a positive $\ddot{x}$. We randomly split this data into 90% train and 10% test sets. We repeat this experiment 10 times and report the average log-likelihood of the samples from the test partition. Test scores are reported in Table 1.

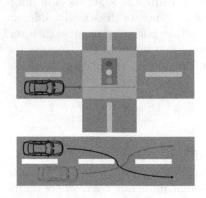

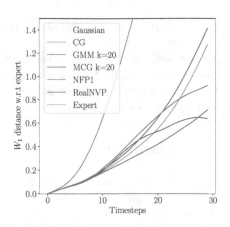

Fig. 2. Agent modeling scenarios: Top: Traffic Light; Bottom: Traffic Weaving

Fig. 3. Traffic Weaving: First Wasserstein distance with respect to the test set expert trajectories.

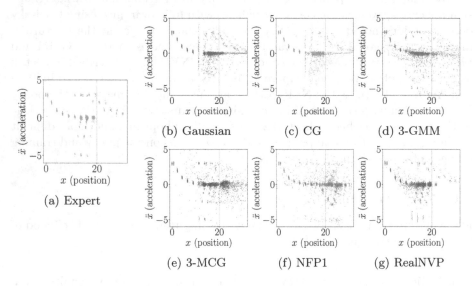

Fig. 4. Traffic Light Intersection: Distribution of agent acceleration along the road for different policy parameterizations. The grey line indicates the intersection location.

Learned policies can be evaluated by sampling their actions for the same batch of initial states. As can be seen in Fig. 4b, the diagonal multivariate Gaussian fails to capture the action distribution as shown by the expert drivers. It tries to cruise along at the same speed even when close to the intersection. Predicting a full covariance matrix (denoted by CG) does not fix the problem as can be seen in Fig. 4c. Figures 4d and e as well as Table 1 suggest that mixture models help a little and have lower spread beyond the intersection.

Table 1. Average best test log-likelihood scores. Best scores for Gaussian mixture models were achieved with $k = 3$ for Traffic Light Intersection, and $k = 20$ for Traffic Weaving. Higher is better.

Policy	Traffic light	Weaving
Gaussian	1.21 ± 0.02	-1.94 ± 0.10
Cholesky Gaussian	1.20 ± 0.02	-1.79 ± 0.21
k-Gaussian mixture	1.40 ± 0.07	0.19 ± 0.14
k-Cholesky Gaussian mixture	1.38 ± 0.07	0.17 ± 0.18
NFP1	1.30 ± 0.08	-0.55 ± 0.11
RealNVP	$\mathbf{1.46 \pm 0.04}$	$\mathbf{0.86 \pm 0.25}$

NFP1 performs significantly worse than mixture models. Figure 4g shows that our conditional RealNVP better models the agents with very little spread of constant speeds beyond the intersection point.

For more complex scenarios, identifying the correct number of Gaussians (k) in a mixture model can be difficult and inference can be quite slow with many modes, especially with full covariance. Flow representations, however, can capture such multi-modality efficiently.

Real World. Schmerling et al. [40] demonstrate the importance of modeling multi-modality in human-robot interaction policies for effective decision making. We use the Flow policy representation to learn a generative model for human driver actions from the dataset associated with the traffic-weaving scenario.[1] Two drivers intend to swap lanes without communication on a straight road with 134 m. Figure 2 illustrates the scenario. The dataset contains 1105 trials recorded from 19 different pairs of human drivers. The state contains the velocity and position of both vehicles, and the action to learn is the acceleration of the vehicles. We divide the trials with 90% for training and 10% for testing. These are then normalized using the mean and the standard deviation of the entire training set.

The test scores are reported in Table 1. On this dataset, the RealNVP policy again obtains the highest score. Gaussian policies, both with a diagonal covariance and a full covariance, behave the worst due to their unimodality. The GMM policies have better performance but are still limited by their representational capability.

To compare the quality of the generated trajectories, we compute their per-timestep first Wasserstein distance [35] to the expert trajectories in the test set. The results are shown in Fig. 3. The RealNVP policy has the lowest distance on almost every time step, indicating that the trajectories sampled from the RealNVP policy distribution are the closest to the demonstration distribution compared to other approaches.

---

[1] https://github.com/StanfordASL/TrafficWeavingCVAE.

4.2   Multi-agent RL

We next test whether our flow policies can be trained using policy optimization in the context of multi-agent reinforcement learning.

Repeated Iterated Games. We first construct a series of simple two player *continuous games* including the polynomial game, the uniform game, and the Bertrand game [32] as didactic examples of the importance of complex action distributions in competitive continuous games.

Table 2. Utility functions for continuous games, where $\overline{a_i}$ is the mean of an agent's 2D action

Game	Player 1 ($u_1(a_1, a_2)$)	Player 2 ($u_2(a_1, a_2)$)
Polynomial	$(\overline{a_1} - \overline{a_2})^2$	$-u_1(a_1, a_2)$
Uniform	$\min(\|\overline{a_1} - \overline{a_2}\|/2, 1 - \|\overline{a_1} - \overline{a_2}\|/2)$	$-u_1(a_1, a_2)$
Bertrand	$\begin{cases} (\overline{a_1} + 1)/3 & \text{if } \overline{a_1} < \overline{a_2} \\ (\overline{a_1} + 1)/6 & \text{if } \overline{a_1} > \overline{a_2} \\ (\overline{a_1} + 1)/4 & \text{if } \overline{a_1} = \overline{a_2} \end{cases}$	$u_1(a_2, a_1)$

Table 3. Continuous games: Average first Wasserstein distance between the sampled distributions and the equilibrium distributions over 5 trials. The GMM and MCG use 10 Gaussian components. Lower is better.

	Gaussian	CG	GMM	MCG	RealNVP
Polynomial					
P1	0.78	0.50	0.09	0.14	**0.04**
P2	0.54	0.42	**0.11**	0.21	**0.11**
Uniform					
P1	0.54	0.19	0.05	**0.04**	0.05
P2	0.36	0.14	0.06	0.05	**0.04**
Bertrand					
P1	0.50	0.57	**0.06**	0.10	**0.06**
P2	0.50	0.66	**0.06**	0.10	0.07

Formally, a continuous game is defined by a tuple $\mathcal{G} \equiv (\mathcal{I}, (\mathcal{A}^i)_{i \in \mathcal{I}}, (u^i)_{i \in \mathcal{I}})$, where $\mathcal{I}$ is a finite set of players, $\mathcal{A}_i$ is the player's action space, $u^i : \prod_i \mathcal{A}^i \to \mathbb{R}$ is the player's associated payoff function. For the games under consideration, agent actions are defined as $a_i \in [-1, 1] \times [-1, 1]$ and the utility functions are defined in Table 2.

Figure 5 shows the equilibrium distribution as well as the histogram of the sampled actions of the learned policies. The figures show that GMM and Real-NVP policies converge more closely to the equilibrium distributions than the standard Gaussian ones. The first Wasserstein distance between the sampled distributions and the equilibrium distributions are shown in Table 3, confirming our observation that RealNVP and mixture policies generate distributions that are closer to the equilibrium.

Farm Security Games. To evaluate the scalability of different policy representation methods with high-dimensional observations, we construct a competitive environment based on the Forest Security game of Kamra et al. [21], called Farm Security, with the defender allocating scarecrows on the farm to save the food from attacker birds. We summarize the farm state, s as a 160×160 matrix

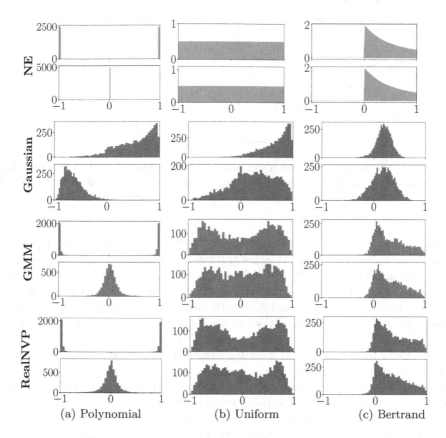

Fig. 5. Repeated iterated game: Nash equilibrium and sampled agent actions. Upper: player 1; Lower: player 2. The horizontal axis is the average action, and the vertical axis is the frequency (probability density function for NE).

containing a grayscale image of the farmland. An example input is shown in color in Fig. 6. The defender chooses the coordinate location of the scarecrow, $a_D \in \mathbb{R}^2$. The attacker crosses the boundary of the farm to move towards the plant locations, stops at any point on their path, eats the food particles in a radius R_a, receives a reward proportional to the food in that radius, and exits back to their starting location. The attacker's action is $a_A \in \mathbb{R}^2$, specifying the coordinate location of its stopping point. The attacker is considered ambushed if its path comes within distance R_g from the scarecrow's location. An ambushed attacker gets a penalty $-r_{\text{pen}}$ and the defender receives a reward r_{pen}.

The farm state represents a 2×2 square area where plants are distributed uniformly in rows with intervals of 0.5. Rows of food are randomly generated with orientations from $-\pi/4$ to $\pi/4$ and widths from $1/12$ to $1/4$. Both agents have an active radius of $1/6$. To avoid expensive image generation during training, we pre-generate 1000 farm states as the training set. We additionally generate 100 farm states as the test set to evaluate generalization.

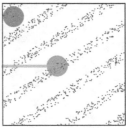

Fig. 6. Left: Example farm. Green dots represent the plants. Right: Farm with the attacker bird (red circle) and the defender scarecrow (blue circle) visualized, the yellow line represents the path from the entering point of the attacker. (Color figure online)

We compare standard multivariate Gaussian and mixture of Gaussian policies against our RealNVP policy. Because the inputs are images, we use a convolutional neural network (CNN) as the feature extractor with structures suggested by Kamra et al. [20]. We show two example trained strategies on environments from the test set in Figs. 7 and 8. For the attacker, the Gaussian policy uniformly spreads the attack and fails to take into account the plant distribution. The GMM policy performs better and is able to cover a large portion of the food particles when the rows of food are flat, as shown in Fig. 7. When the rows of food are more diagonal as in Fig. 8, each Gaussian component in the GMM policy could only cover a small region of food. In both cases, the proposed RealNVP policy is able to adapt its distribution to cover most of the food particles. Since the behavior of the defender is largely affected by the attacker's strategy, its performance is difficult to compare from sample visualizations.

Evaluating complex multi-agent interactions is a challenging problem. Two recent empirical game-theoretic approaches include *Nash Averaging* [1] and *α-Rank* [33]. We focus on the *α-Rank* method based on evolutionary dynamics [33] for comparing different policy representation strategies owing to its applicability to general sum multi-player games. Applying these ranking approaches requires pairwise evaluation of all strategies under consideration to form a payoff matrix for each player. In our case, these strategies correspond to the model used for the player agent's policy representation.

We perform pairwise evaluations with each policy representation for the agent by playing 10^4 games between each individual policy pair. The evaluation matrices for each agent are shown in Fig. 9a and b for train and test sets respectively. Given the α-Rank for the different policy representations shown in Figs. 10 and 11, we find that the RealNVP policy for both attacker and defender form a sink node in the evaluation Markov chain. It is ranked the highest with increasing ranking intensity $α$ (relates to selection pressure in evolutionary dynamics), verifying that conditional flow models lead to more robust policies. Our intuition is that for a given food distribution, the attacker is incentivized to cover a larger area of the food, i.e. to have larger action distribution entropy. This makes it more difficult to be caught by the defender. Similarly, the defender is motivated

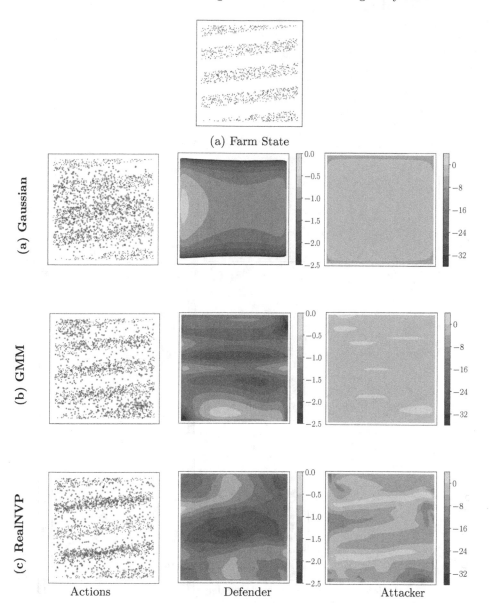

Fig. 7. Farm Security game sample 1: Visualization of agents' policies. Left: Scatter of food particles and agents' actions: Red: attacker, Blue: defender, Green: food; Middle/Right: Log-probability of the agents' action distributions. (Color figure online)

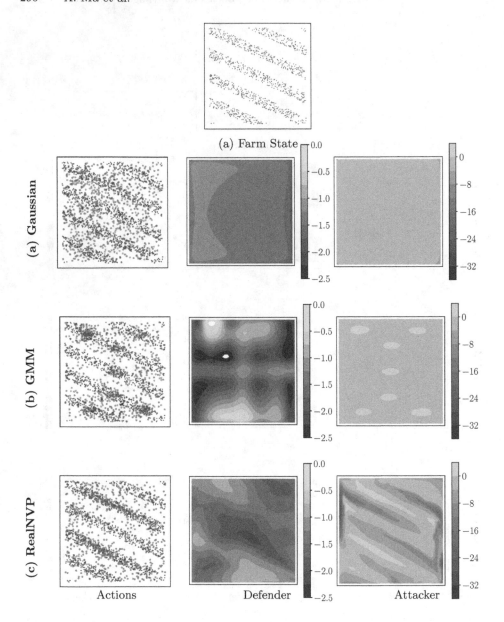

Fig. 8. Farm Security game sample 2: Visualization of agents' policies. Left: Scatter of food particles and agents' actions: Red: attacker, Blue: defender, Green: food; Middle/Right: Log-probability of the agents' action distributions. (Color figure online)

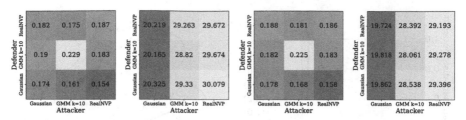

(a) Training set. Left: Defender, Right: Attacker.

(b) Test set. Left: Defender, Right: Attacker.

Fig. 9. Farm Security game: Visualization of agents' average payoff matrix

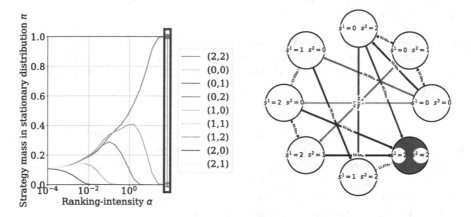

Fig. 10. Farm Security game: Alpha ranking on the training set. Left: Ranking curve, Right: Evaluation Markov chain. The tuple (defender, attacker) follows the order: 0: Gaussian, 1: 10-GMM, 2: RealNVP. The blue node indicates the sink node. (Color figure online)

to cover a larger portion of the farm boundary so that the attacker could not exploit it. However, especially for the attacker, covering an arbitrary food distribution is not easy with Gaussian and GMM policies. For the Gaussian attacker, a small standard deviation would make its attack easily predicted by the defender, while a large standard deviation means that a large portion of its attacks are wasted on no food regions. Due to the high penalty of being ambushed, the policy learns to have a large standard deviation and thus its attacks tend to be uniform. For the GMM attacker, especially in the situations shown in Fig. 8, the covariance between the x and y positions of the food particles is stronger, which is poorly represented by the diagonal Gaussian components in GMM. In this case, each Gaussian component's standard deviation becomes very small to avoid wasted attacks and the entropy of the GMM policy becomes much lower, making it easier to be caught from the defender's perspective. In comparison, the RealNVP attacker is able to show good food coverage on all different food patterns. Although not shown here, using a MCG policy in this environment

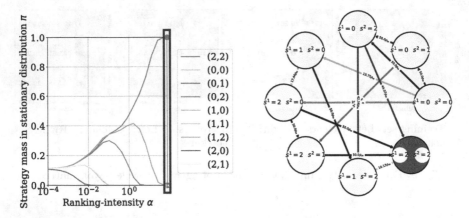

Fig. 11. Farm Security game: Alpha ranking on the test set. Left: Ranking curve, Right: Evaluation Markov chain. The tuple (defender, attacker) follows the order: 0: Gaussian, 1: 10-GMM, 2: RealNVP. The blue node indicates the sink node. (Color figure online)

could converge to similar action distributions as the RealNVP policy. However, the training clock time of MCG is much longer due to its complex structure.

In general, different games may require different form of equilibrium distributions, and some of them might be well fitted by the existing policy representations. However, we often do not know the optimal distribution *a priori* in practice, and thus a flexible representation is needed.

5   Conclusion

We focused on representations for agent policies in multi-agent continuous control contexts. Our experiments showed that even mixture models may not suffice for modeling multi-modal action distributions for optimal behavior. We presented how normalizing flows can be used to represent multi-modal policies and how they can be structured for multi-agent contexts. Their effectiveness was demonstrated on both agent-modeling and reinforcement learning tasks. Conditional normalizing flows significantly improve the learning of complex, multimodal behavior over standard multivariate Gaussian or mixture of Gaussian representations. Our experiments indicate that multi-agent learning requires choosing appropriate policy representations irrespective of learning algorithms. The proposed policy representation does not impose any limitations on the learning algorithms, and thus should be applicable to other domains. The potential applications of this work include, but not limited to, the IT security and commercial competitions where continuous and high dimensional strategies are needed. Combining our model with the recent developments in imitation learning [3] and reinforcement learning [28] for multi-agent systems is important future work.

A   Appendix

Policy Implementation. Our implementation is based on the Garage [10] reinforcement learning library. We use a multi-layer perceptron (MLP) consisting of 3 hidden layers with 64, 64, and 32 hidden units for the Gaussian, Cholesky Gaussian, GMM and MCG policies. The mean and covariance (and weights for mixture models) use the same MLP except the last layer for better knowledge sharing. The NFP1 policy uses the standard RealNVP structure with 5 coupling layers. An additional state conditioning layer is added after the first coupling layer. The state conditioning layer uses an MLP of 2 hidden layers with 64 hidden units [47]. For the proposed conditional flow policy, we use 5 coupling layers and each coupling layer has an MLP of 2 hidden layers with 32 hidden units. The MLP takes the concatenation of the observation and half of the latent variables $(x_{1:d}, d = \lfloor D/2 \rfloor)$ as the input, and output the scale and translation factors α and t as introduced in Sect. 3.1. The output α is then clipped between $[-5, 5]$ for better numerical stability. We additionally add a *tanh* on the final outputs for all policies similar to Haarnoja et al. [14], which helps limit the policy output space as well as bound the entropy term in loss. We make sure that the total number of parameters for different models stay close to 10^4 for a fair comparison. All the hidden layers use ReLU activations. For the farm security game, since the inputs are images, we additionally add a convolutional neural network (CNN) of 2 convolution layers as the feature extractor to all models. The convolution layers have 32 and 16 channels. The filter sizes are 16×16 and 4×4, and the strides are 8×8 and 2×2. This CNN structure is suggested by Kamra et al. [20].

Agent Modeling. We use behavior cloning as our training algorithm in Sect. 4.1 which maximizes the likelihood of actions in the training data [36]. We use a batch size of 1024. The learning rate starts from 0.01 and decays at a rate of 0.8 every 1000 iterations. We train each policy with 5×10^3 and 2×10^4 iterations on the synthetic and real world datasets.

Multi-agent RL. We use *proximal policy optimization (PPO)* [41] as our policy optimization algorithm in Sect. 4.2. We add an extra entropy term to the loss function for better exploration. The entropy of the policies are estimated using the negative log-likelihood of one sampled action for each state. The weight of the entropy loss starts with 1.0 and decays at a rate of 0.999 per iteration. We train all players independently at the same time. We use the Adam optimizer [24] with a fixed learning rate of 10^{-4}. The training lasts 10^4 epochs with a batch size of 512 for the repeated iterated games and 2048 for the farm security game.

References

1. Balduzzi, D., Tuyls, K., Perolat, J., Graepel, T.: Re-evaluating evaluation. In: Advances in Neural Information Processing Systems (NeurIPS), pp. 3268–3279 (2018)

2. Bansal, T., Pachocki, J., Sidor, S., Sutskever, I., Mordatch, I.: Emergent complexity via multi-agent competition. In: International Conference on Learning Representations (ICLR) (2018)
3. Bhattacharyya, R.P., Phillips, D.J., Liu, C., Gupta, J.K., Driggs-Campbell, K., Kochenderfer, M.J.: Simulating emergent properties of human driving behavior using multi-agent reward augmented imitation learning. In: 2019 International Conference on Robotics and Automation (ICRA), pp. 789–795. IEEE (2019)
4. Blum, A., Mansour, Y.: Learning, regret minimization, and equilibria. In: Nisan, N., Roughgarden, T., Tardos, E., Vazirani, V.V. (eds.) Algorithmic Game Theory, chap. 4, pp. 79–102. Cambridge University Press (2007)
5. Brown, G.W.: Iterative solution of games by fictitious play. In: Activity Analysis of Production and Allocation, vol. 13, no. 1, pp. 374–376 (1951)
6. Busoniu, L., Babuska, R., De Schutter, B.: A comprehensive survey of multiagent reinforcement learning. IEEE Trans. Syst. Man Cybern. Part C (Appl. Rev.) **38**(2), 156–172 (2008)
7. Cermák, J., Bošanský, B., Durkota, K., Lisý, V., Kiekintveld, C.: Using correlated strategies for computing Stackelberg equilibria in extensive-form games. In: AAAI Conference on Artificial Intelligence (2016)
8. Dinh, L., Krueger, D., Bengio, Y.: NICE: non-linear independent components estimation. arXiv preprint arXiv:1410.8516 (2014)
9. Dinh, L., Sohl-Dickstein, J., Bengio, S.: Density estimation using Real NVP. arXiv preprint arXiv:1605.08803 (2016)
10. Duan, Y., Chen, X., Houthooft, R., Schulman, J., Abbeel, P.: Benchmarking deep reinforcement learning for continuous control. In: International Conference on Machine Learning (ICML), pp. 1329–1338 (2016)
11. Germain, M., Gregor, K., Murray, I., Larochelle, H.: MADE: masked autoencoder for distribution estimation. In: International Conference on Machine Learning (ICML), pp. 881–889 (2015)
12. Goodfellow, I., et al.: Generative adversarial nets. In: Advances in Neural Information Processing Systems (NeurIPS), pp. 2672–2680 (2014)
13. Haarnoja, T., Tang, H., Abbeel, P., Levine, S.: Reinforcement learning with deep energy-based policies. In: International Conference on Machine Learning (ICML), pp. 1352–1361 (2017)
14. Haarnoja, T., Zhou, A., Abbeel, P., Levine, S.: Soft actor-critic: off-policy maximum entropy deep reinforcement learning with a stochastic actor. arXiv preprint arXiv:1801.01290 (2018)
15. Haskell, W.B., Kar, D., Fang, F., Tambe, M., Cheung, S., Denicola, E.: Robust protection of fisheries with COmPASS. In: AAAI Conference on Artificial Intelligence (2014)
16. Heinrich, J., Silver, D.: Deep reinforcement learning from self-play in imperfect-information games. arXiv preprint arXiv:1603.01121 (2016)
17. Ho, J., Ermon, S.: Generative adversarial imitation learning. In: Advances in Neural Information Processing Systems (NeurIPS), pp. 4565–4573 (2016)
18. Hoen, P.J., Tuyls, K., Panait, L., Luke, S., La Poutré, J.A.: An overview of cooperative and competitive multiagent learning. In: Tuyls, K., Hoen, P.J., Verbeeck, K., Sen, S. (eds.) LAMAS 2005. LNCS (LNAI), vol. 3898, pp. 1–46. Springer, Heidelberg (2006). https://doi.org/10.1007/11691839_1
19. Johnson, M.P., Fang, F., Tambe, M.: Designing patrol strategies to maximize pristine forest area. In: AAAI Conference on Artificial Intelligence (2012)

20. Kamra, N., Fang, F., Kar, D., Liu, Y., Tambe, M.: Handling continuous space security games with neural networks. In: IWAISe: International Workshop on Artificial Intelligence in Security, p. 17 (2017)
21. Kamra, N., Gupta, U., Fang, F., Liu, Y., Tambe, M.: Policy learning for continuous space security games using neural networks. In: AAAI Conference on Artificial Intelligence (2018)
22. Kamra, N., Gupta, U., Wang, K., Fang, F., Liu, Y., Tambe, M.: DeepFP for finding nash equilibrium in continuous action spaces. In: Alpcan, T., Vorobeychik, Y., Baras, J.S., Dán, G. (eds.) GameSec 2019. LNCS, vol. 11836, pp. 238–258. Springer, Cham (2019). https://doi.org/10.1007/978-3-030-32430-8_15
23. Kiekintveld, C., Jain, M., Tsai, J., et al.: Computing optimal randomized resource allocations for massive security games. In: International Conference on Autonomous Agents and Multi-agent Systems, pp. 689–696 (2009)
24. Kingma, D.P., Ba, J.: Adam: a method for stochastic optimization. In: International Conference on Learning Representations (2015)
25. Kingma, D.P., Dhariwal, P.: Glow: generative flow with invertible 1×1 convolutions. In: Advances in Neural Information Processing Systems (NeurIPS), pp. 10215–10224 (2018)
26. Kingma, D.P., Welling, M.: Auto-encoding variational Bayes. In: International Conference on Learning Representations (ICLR) (2013)
27. Kochenderfer, M.J.: Decision Making Under Uncertainty: Theory and Application. MIT Press, Cambridge (2015)
28. Lanctot, M., Zambaldi, V., Gruslys, A., et al.: A unified game-theoretic approach to multiagent reinforcement learning. In: Advances in Neural Information Processing Systems (NeurIPS), pp. 4190–4203 (2017)
29. Lillicrap, T.P., et al.: Continuous control with deep reinforcement learning. arXiv preprint arXiv:1509.02971 (2015)
30. Littman, M.L.: Markov games as a framework for multi-agent reinforcement learning. In: Machine Learning, pp. 157–163. Elsevier (1994)
31. Liu, S., Lever, G., Merel, J., Tunyasuvunakool, S., Heess, N., Graepel, T.: Emergent coordination through competition. In: International Conference on Learning Representations (ICLR) (2018)
32. Muñoz-Garcia, F.: Advanced Microeconomic Theory: An Intuitive Approach with Examples. MIT Press, Cambridge (2017)
33. Omidshafiei, S., et al.: α-rank: multi-agent evaluation by evolution. Sci. Rep. **9**(1), 1–29 (2019)
34. Papamakarios, G., Nalisnick, E., Rezende, D.J., Mohamed, S., Lakshminarayanan, B.: Normalizing flows for probabilistic modeling and inference. arXiv preprint arXiv:1912.02762 (2019)
35. Peyré, G., Cuturi, M., et al.: Computational optimal transport. Found. Trends® Mach. Learn. **11**(5–6), 355–607 (2019)
36. Pomerleau, D.: Efficient training of artificial neural networks for autonomous navigation. Neural Comput. **3**, 88–97 (1991)
37. Rezende, D., Mohamed, S.: Variational inference with normalizing flows. In: International Conference on Machine Learning (ICML), pp. 1530–1538 (2015)
38. Rhinehart, N., Kitani, K.M., Vernaza, P.: R2P2: a ReparameteRized pushforward policy for diverse, precise generative path forecasting. In: Ferrari, V., Hebert, M., Sminchisescu, C., Weiss, Y. (eds.) ECCV 2018. LNCS, vol. 11217, pp. 794–811. Springer, Cham (2018). https://doi.org/10.1007/978-3-030-01261-8_47

39. Rosenfeld, A., Kraus, S.: When security games hit traffic: optimal traffic enforcement under one sided uncertainty. In: International Joint Conferences on Artificial Intelligence (IJCAI), pp. 3814–3822 (2017)

40. Schmerling, E., Leung, K., Vollprecht, W., Pavone, M.: Multimodal probabilistic model-based planning for human-robot interaction. In: IEEE International Conference on Robotics and Automation (ICRA), pp. 1–9 (2017)

41. Schulman, J., Wolski, F., Dhariwal, P., Radford, A., Klimov, O.: Proximal policy optimization algorithms. arXiv preprint arXiv:1707.06347 (2017)

42. Shapley, L.S.: Stochastic games. Proc. Natl. Acad. Sci. **39**(10), 1095–1100 (1953). ISSN 0027–8424

43. Silver, D., et al.: Mastering the game of go with deep neural networks and tree search. Nature **529**(7587), 484 (2016)

44. Silver, D., Lever, G., Heess, N., Degris, T., Wierstra, D., Riedmiller, M.: Deterministic policy gradient algorithms. In: International Conference on Machine Learning (ICML), pp. 387–395 (2014)

45. Silver, D., Schrittwieser, J., Simonyan, K., et al.: Mastering the game of go without human knowledge. Nature **550**(7676), 354 (2017)

46. Tambe, M.: Security and Game Theory: Algorithms, Deployed Systems, Lessons Learned. Cambridge University Press, Cambridge (2011)

47. Tang, Y., Agrawal, S.: Implicit policy for reinforcement learning. arXiv preprint arXiv:1806.06798 (2018)

48. Taylor, P.D., Jonker, L.B.: Evolutionary stable strategies and game dynamics. Math. Biosci. **40**(1–2), 145–156 (1978)

49. Vinyals, O., et al.: Grandmaster level in StarCraft II using multi-agent reinforcement learning. Nature **575**, 350–354 (2019). ISSN 0028–0836

50. Wang, B., Zhang, Y., Zhou, Z.H., Zhong, S.: On repeated Stackelberg security game with the cooperative human behavior model for wildlife protection. Appl. Intell. **49**, 1002–1015 (2017)

A Game Theoretic Framework for Software Diversity for Network Security

Ahmed H. Anwar[1(✉)] (ID), Nandi O. Leslie[1], Charles Kamhoua[1] (ID),
and Christopher Kiekintveld[2] (ID)

[1] US Army Research Laboratory, Adelphi, MD 20783, USA
a.h.anwar@knights.ucf.edu,
{nandi.o.leslie.ctr,charles.a.kamhoua.civ}@mail.mil
[2] University of Texas at El Paso, El Paso, TX 79968, USA
cdkiekintveld@utep.edu

Abstract. Diversity plays a significant role in network security, and we propose a formal model to investigate and optimize the advantages of software diversity in network security. However, diversity is also costly, and network administrators encounter a tradeoff between network security and the cost to deploy and maintain a well-diversified network. We study this tradeoff in a two-player nonzero-sum game-theoretic model of software diversity. We find the Nash equilibrium of the game to give an optimal security strategy for the defender, and implement an algorithm for optimizing software diversity via embedding a graph-coloring approach based on the Nash equilibrium. We show that the opponent (i.e., adversary) spends more effort to compromise an optimally diversified network. We also analyze the complexity of the proposed algorithm and propose a complexity reduction approach to avoid exponential growth in runtime. We present numerical results that validate the effectiveness of the proposed software diversity approach.

Keywords: Software diversity · Game theory · Network security

1 Introduction

Diversity-based defenses to network security have recently emerged as a recognized approach to resilience. In particular, these types of defenses introduce uncertainty and probabilistic protection from attacks and provide a rich framework for diversifying program transformations [2,14,21]. In a few areas of security (e.g.., moving target defense [2]) there has been a wide application of software diversity techniques. For example, methods have been proposed for giving the software a dynamically shifting attack surface for both binary executables and web applications [15]. However, there remain limitations with these defenses depending on the threat. For example, address space layout randomization is ineffective against buffer-overflow attacks, such as the de-randomization attack [23]. Graph theory, and particularly attack graphs, provides a unique formal approach to help quantify the efficiency and effectiveness of temporal and

© Springer Nature Switzerland AG 2020
Q. Zhu et al. (Eds.): GameSec 2020, LNCS 12513, pp. 297–311, 2020.
https://doi.org/10.1007/978-3-030-64793-3_16

spatio-temporal diversity mechanisms. Moreover, security games on graphs [1,3,4] provide mathematical approaches that can offer insights into questions such as what is the tradeoff between network security and software diversity, and what must be diversified and when [14]. To address these questions, we introduce mathematical models that use game theory to examine the connection between the distribution of differing software configurations on a network and the resulting risk to network security against a motivated attacker.

Software diversity involves randomizing transformations that make program implementations diverge between each networked device or between each execution. These proactive defense strategies can increase the attackers' workload [14,16]. There is an analogy to biological ecosystems, where the resiliency of a population to disease or the invasion of a nonnative species depends heavily on biodiversity. Likewise, network resiliency can be increased (especially against novel threats) by using efficient strategies for increasing software diversity. Attack graphs are an important tool that models the network's topology and spatio- temporal vulnerabilities used to validate various defense approaches. Attack graphs can be generated in different ways to represent interactions between the host's vulnerabilities and its neighbors' vulnerabilities. In addition to using the attack graph for understanding how network topology and vulnerabilities impact the effectiveness of diversity-based defenses, a security game on an attack graph captures the connections between diversity, security, and reachability [21]. In this paper, a security game is formulated and played on an attack graph to study the effectiveness of diversity-based defenses. The developed game investigates the tradeoff faced by the defender between diversity cost and security level. Our main contributions in this paper are:

- We propose a general model suitable to study software diversity for the security of networked systems. Our model captures the set of vulnerabilities and the network topology through an attack graph.
- We formulate a novel game model to study the effect of diversity on network security under attack as a two-player nonzero-sum game.
- We present a complete algorithm to solve the game model and obtain the Nash equilibrium diversity strategy.
- We analyze the complexity of the proposed algorithm and introduce a complexity reduction approach that is shown to yield an almost exact reward for the defender in our numerical results.
- Finally, we present numerical results for the developed software diversity approach that show the effectiveness of the obtained diversity strategy at Nash equilibrium.

The rest of the paper is organized as follows. We discuss related work in Sect. 2. In Sect. 3, we present the system model, define the game model, and propose our algorithm for software diversity. Our numerical results is presented in Sect. 4. Finally, we conclude our work and discuss future work in Sect. 5.

2   Related Work

The scope of the problem we consider belongs to three interacting active research fields: network diversity, resilience, and game theory. Diversity has been a design objective to secure networks against various types of attacks including Zero-Day attacks [28]. It has been shown that the intuition behind the ability of diversity to increase the resiliency of systems and networks is effective [10]. Garcia et al. [10] show using a data-driven study that building a system with diverse operating systems is a useful technique to enhance its intrusion tolerance capabilities. Moreover, diversity-by-design has been used to increase a communication network's throughput [6,17]. For security, the authors in [5] proposed an automated approach to diversify network services to enhance the network's resilience against unknown threats and attacks. In their approach, they considered constraints associated with diversity. Software diversification techniques are also used to enhance network security by reducing the attack surface [26,27].

Graph coloring is a well-known problem in dynamic channel assignment to reduce interference between adjacent nodes [4,24]. However, the applications go beyond reducing network interference to include securing medical images [19,25]. Moreover, graph coloring has been used in several computer science applications such as data mining, clustering, image capturing, image segmentation, networking, etc. [11]. Game theory has been used directly to solve graph coloring problems; such research problems are named "coloring games". A coloring game is a two player non-cooperative game played on a finite graph using a set of colors in which players take turns to color the vertices of the graph such that no two adjacent vertices have the same color [13].

Game theory has been used extensively to study security problems and understand the strategic behavior of adversarial users and attackers [1,12,22]. In [1], a game-theoretic framework is developed to investigate jamming attacks on wireless networks and the defender mitigation strategy. Kiekintveld et al. [12] proposed a scalable technique to calculate security resource allocation optimal policy of practical problems like police patrolling schedule for subway and bus stations. A first step to quantify and measure diversity as a security metric appeared in [21] where a game model has been used to investigate the necessary conditions for network defender to diversify and avoid monoculture systems. However, diversity is understudied in the literature of security games. In this paper, we introduce a generalized nonzero-sum game model between the network defender and an attacker. Motivated by the aforementioned benefits of diversity, the defender player selects the best diversity policy in response to the attacker's strategies. The game is played over an attack graph that captures the network topology and the dependencies between the vulnerabilities in the network.

3   System Model

Consider a network of arbitrary size, $|\mathcal{N}|$, where $\mathcal{N}$ is the set of nodes of the network. The network topology is defined by its adjacency matrix. Let $\mathbf{H}$, denote the graph adjacency matrix, where any entry of the network $[\mathbf{H}_{u,v}] = 1$ if node v is connected to node u, and is equal to 0 otherwise, for every $u, v \in \mathcal{N}$.

We assume the network graph is represented using a directed graph denoted by $G(\mathcal{N}, \mathbf{H})$, where $[\mathbf{H}_{u,v}] = 1$, denotes an edge between node u and node v. This assumption fits a hierarchical network with a set of entry nodes that allow users to access the network. Such networks resemble networks with a chain of command. It also represents an interesting scenario where the depth of the network can be captured. Adversaries are interested in reaching targets that are practically installed in deeper layers of the network.

For each node $v \in \mathcal{N}$, there is a certain software type that is running on the node. A software type can abstract several properties, for example, it can model the operating system, honeypot type, or specific application. For simplicity, we assume the set of all used software types to be $\mathcal{S}$, where each node is assigned one software type $s \in \mathcal{S}$. Let NSW denote node-software matrix of size $|\mathcal{N}| \times |\mathcal{S}|$. For instance, the NSW matrix shown in Eq. (1) represents a network of 3 nodes and a set $\mathcal{S} = \{s_1, s_2\}$, where node 1 runs software type s_1 and the remaining two nodes run software type s_2.

$$NSW = \begin{bmatrix} 1 & 0 \\ 0 & 1 \\ 0 & 1 \end{bmatrix} \tag{1}$$

Each software type has one or more vulnerabilities. We let $\mathcal{V}$ be the set of all vulnerabilities. Again we use matrix representation to define the software to vulnerabilities relation. Let SWV be a $|\mathcal{S}| \times |\mathcal{V}|$ be a binary matrix, where each row is a vector associated with each software type that indicates which vulnerability is associated with that software. Specifically, any entry $SWV[i, j] = 1$ if and only if a software $s_i \in \mathcal{S}$ suffers vulnerability $v_j \in \mathcal{V}$, and $SWV[i, j] = 0$ otherwise.

Given NSW and SWV, the set of vulnerabilities that could be exploited by the attacker can be defined for each node. However, to target a node that node should satisfy two conditions. First, it should be *reachable* through a path. Secondly, that node should be *exploitable* through at least one vulnerability. Note that an attacker can *reach* any node if and only if there exists a path between network's entry node and that node subject that the attacker can also compromise all the nodes that belong to this path.

Let $\mathcal{P}_v$ be a set of nodes connecting the network entry node and any node $v \in \mathcal{N}$. Specifically, $\mathcal{P}_v = \{v_0, ..., v\}$, where v_0 is an entry node, and v denotes any node in the network, however v usually denotes the node being targeted by the attacker. Hence, the set of software implemented on each node affects the ability of an adversary to reach v as he is required to exploit all nodes that belong to the path $\mathcal{P}_v$.

We define a two-player nonzero-sum game between the network administrator as the defender and an adversary as the attacker. We consider the defender to be player 1 and the attacker to be player 2. We start by discussing the attacker problem and the possible attack strategies.

3.1   Attacker Problem

The goal of the attacker is to compromise a subset of targeted nodes in the network using an attack toolbox. We assume that the attacker has a set of probes that allow him to compromise a set of vulnerabilities. More specifically, each probe in the toolbox can exploit a subset of vulnerabilities. Let $\mathcal{B}$ denote the set of all probes, i.e, the toolbox available to the attacker. The relation between each probe in $\mathcal{B}$ and the kind of vulnerabilities it exploits is characterized through a probe matrix.

The probe matrix denoted by $\mathbf{P}$ is a $|\mathcal{B}| \times |\mathcal{V}|$ binary matrix. Any entry $\mathbf{P}[i,j] = 1$ if the ith probe is capable of exploiting the jth vulnerability, for every $i \in \mathcal{B}$ and $j \in \mathcal{V}$, and $\mathbf{P}[i,j] = 0$ otherwise. For instance, the matrix in Eq. (2) represents two probes within the attacker action space and three vulnerabilities. If the attacker attacks the network using the first probe, she will only compromise the subset of reachable nodes with software that suffers vulnerability Vul^1. On the other hand, if the attacker attacked the network using the second probe, she will be able to compromise all reachable nodes with software type that suffers Vul^2 and Vul^3.

$$\mathbf{P} = \begin{bmatrix} 1 & 0 & 0 \\ 0 & 1 & 1 \end{bmatrix} \tag{2}$$

The attacker increases his payoff by maximizing the number of compromised nodes in the network. Therefore, the attacker chooses to use a collection of probes instead of using a single probe when attacking the network. We can readily define the attacker action space as the collection set of all elements in the probe set $\mathcal{B}$. Let the attacker action space be denoted by $\mathcal{A}_2$. Specifically, $\mathcal{A}_2 = \{0,1\}^{|\mathcal{B}|}$. Therefore, any attack action $a_2 \in \mathcal{A}_2$ is a binary vector of length $|\mathcal{B}|$, where $a_2(i) = 1$ when the ith probe is used in the attack, and $a_2(i) = 0$ otherwise, for $i = 1, 2, ..., |\mathcal{B}|$. To avoid trivial game scenarios, we assume a cost associated with each probe which can represent (for example) the increased likelihood of detection. Let $C_a(a_2)$ be the cost for each probe. As we discuss in more detail later, the attacker faces an interesting trade-off as he wants to attack the network using a larger number of probes to compromise more nodes, while reducing his attack cost to avoid expensive attacks. Next, we discuss the defender problem before we fully characterize the players' payoff functions in more detail.

3.2   Defender Problem

We focus on a defender who uses diversity to enhance network security. The defender action affects the node software matrix, NSW. Based on the available number of software types and how they are assigned to nodes in the network, the defender can increase the level of diversity in the network. The defender can potentially use all the available software types to achieve the maximum level of security through diversity. However, a highly diversified network is harder to operate and maintain. Therefore, the defender incurs a cost associated with the diversity size, $|\mathcal{S}|$. Let $C_d(a_1)$ denote the cost associated with the defense strategy, for any defender action $a_1 \in \mathcal{A}_1$, where $\mathcal{A}_1$ is the defender action space.

The defender action space contains all the combinations of software types. The defense strategy a_1 selects a subset out of the software set, S. For instance, a defense strategy $a_1 = \{s_1, s_2, s_3\}$ means that the defender is implementing 3 different software types to run on different nodes in the network.

Allocating the selected software types over different nodes is similar to the well-known graph coloring problem. Therefore, we adapt graph-coloring algorithms to implement strategies that ensure that neighboring nodes do not run the same software type whenever possible. Having a larger palette with more colors will directly enhance the effectiveness of the graph coloring algorithm. This in turn reduces the attacker reachability to a smaller set of nodes. In Algorithm 1, we leverage the graph coloring algorithm proposed in [9] to implement such an approach.

The defender trade-off is to minimize the size of the set of software types to be diversified, to reduce nodes' reachability while minimizing the cost associated with such a defense strategy. In other words, the defender aims to secure the maximum number of nodes using the minimum number of different software types. However, the attacker attempts to compromise the maximum number of nodes using the smallest number of probes. Next, we quantify the payoff functions for both players.

3.3   Payoff Functions

The goal of the defender is to secure the network through securing as many nodes as possible using software diversity. Protecting nodes can be achieved through the careful distribution of different software types to neighboring nodes. The subset of secured nodes depends on their topological locations in the network and the vulnerabilities associated with the software type assigned to each of them as defined via the SWV matrix. Given the software vulnerability matrix, SWV, and node software matrix NSW, one can easily define a node vulnerability matrix, NV, that defines the subset of vulnerabilities associated with each node as follows,

$$NV = NSW \times SWV. \tag{3}$$

Recall that the graph is colored according to the action played by the defender, a_1, and hence NSW is defined. However, the attacker action, a_2, defines the set of exploitable vulnerabilities according to probe matrix $\mathbf{P}$. The attacker goal is to maximize the number of compromised nodes, which is denoted by K, and can be expressed as follows:

$$K = mean\left(\sum_{v \in \mathcal{N}}\left(\sum_{u \in \mathcal{P}_v} \mathbb{1}_{\{u \in \mathcal{E}(a_2)\}}\right)\right), \tag{4}$$

where $\mathbb{1}_{\{.\}}$ is an indicator function, which is equal to one when $\{u \in \mathcal{E}(a_2)\}$, where $\mathcal{E}(a_2)$ is the set nodes that can be exploited and compromised by the attacker. The set of exploitable nodes $\mathcal{E}(a_2)$ contains all nodes that are assigned a software type that has any of the vulnerabilities that can be compromised using the probes in a_2. Let $\mathcal{V}^{a_2}$ denote the set of vulnerabilities that the attacking probe(s) can exploit given the attacker action, a_2. Also, let $NV(u)$ be the set of vulnerabilities associated with the software type running on node u. Then, the set of exploitable nodes can be defined as, $\mathcal{E}(a_2) = \{u \in \mathcal{N} | NV(u) \cap \mathcal{V}^{a_2} \neq \Phi\}$. Therefore, K represents the average distances between exploitable nodes (i.e, subgraphs diameter).

The defender encounters a diversity cost $C_d(.)$ that depends on the number of software types (colors) used to color the network graph. For simplicity, we assume a fixed cost per color.

Therefore, the defender payoff function can be written as:

$$R_1(a_1, a_2) = -K - C_d(a_1), \qquad (5)$$

and the attacker payoff function is written as:

$$R_2(a_1, a_2) = K - C_a(a_2). \qquad (6)$$

The K term captures an interesting tradeoff for the defender. If the defender has a large budget and does not care about the defense cost, using a very large number of software types is still a double-edged sword. A higher number of software types (i.e., colors) allows for a better graph coloring outcome and hence limits the attacker's ability to reach a bigger community. However, since each software suffers a subset of vulnerability, this may increase the number of exploitable nodes in the graph. Therefore, using all the available software types to color the graph may not be in favor of the defender. It is worth noting that we do not assume that any of the software types are risk-free, otherwise, the problem is trivial and the defender better off using a complete monoculture of that secured software.

On the attacker side, using the maximum number of available probes is always in favor of the attacker if the cost per probe is zero. Thus, the game is designed to investigate the trade-off between the reward of exploiting nodes using available probes, and the cost associated with each subset of probes.

3.4   Game Problem

We now formulate the game $\Gamma(P, \mathcal{A}, \mathcal{R})$, where:

- $\mathcal{P} = \{Defender, Attacker\}$ is the set of players.
- $\mathcal{A} = \{\mathcal{A}_1 \times \mathcal{A}_2\}$ is the game action space, which is the product of the action space of the defender and the action space of the defender as defined in the previous subsection.
- $\mathcal{R} = \{R_1, R_2\}$ denotes the game reward set.

As shown in Eqs. (5) and (6), Γ is a nonzero-sum game with a finite number of pure actions for every player. Nonzero-sum reflects the fact that the attacker does not benefit from the cost paid by the defender, and vice versa. Let A and B denote payoff matrices for the defender and attacker, respectively.

Both matrices are of size $|\mathcal{A}_1| \times |\mathcal{A}_2|$. The defender maximizes over the rows of A, and the attacker maximizes his reward over the columns of B. Moreover, let $\mathbf{x}$ be a vector of $|\mathcal{A}_1| \times 1$ and $\mathbf{y}$ be a vector of $|\mathcal{A}_2| \times 1$. A mixed strategy, $\mathbf{x}$, is a probability distribution over the action space, $|\mathcal{A}_1|$. Similarly, the attacker mixed strategy, $\mathbf{y}$, is a probability distribution over the action space, $|\mathcal{A}_2|$.

Theorem 1. *For the finite game Γ, there exists at least one point $(\mathbf{x}^*, \mathbf{y}^*)$ of mixed equilibrium.*

Proof. The proof follows Nash's theory in [20] directly. The theory states that for every pair of payoff matrices A, B there is a nonzero number of mixed equilibria.

$\square$

For any mixed strategy, $\mathbf{y}$, played by the attacker, the defender maximizes his expected reward by solving the following optimization problem to find his best response strategy $\mathbf{x}^*$,

$$\underset{\mathbf{x}}{\text{maximize}} \qquad \mathbf{x}^T A \mathbf{y}$$

$$\text{subject to} \qquad \sum_{i=1}^{|\mathcal{A}_1|} x(a_1^i) = 1, \qquad (7)$$

$$\mathbf{x} \geq 0.$$

On the other side, for any mixed strategy, $\mathbf{x}$, played by the defender, the attacker finds the optimal attacking strategy $\mathbf{y}^*$ by solving the following optimization problem,

$$\underset{\mathbf{y}}{\text{maximize}} \qquad \mathbf{x}^T B \mathbf{y}$$

$$\text{subject to} \qquad \sum_{j=1}^{|\mathcal{A}_2|} y(a_2^j) = 1, \qquad (8)$$

$$\mathbf{y} \geq 0.$$

It has been shown by Chen et al. [8] that for the general n-person nonzero-sum non-cooperative games, computing Nash equilibria is PPAD-complete. However, for the two-player case of a nonzero-sum game with a finite number of pure strategies as Γ, a necessary and sufficient condition for a point to be a point of equilibrium is that it is a solution of a single programming problem of a quadratic objective function and a set of linear constraints and the objective function has a global maximum of zero as shown in [18]. Based on the work in [18], MATLAB code has been developed in [7] that computes at least one point of Nash equilibrium using sequential quadratic programming based quasi-Newton technique which is used to solve the above optimization problems in (7) and (8). We apply the procedure shown in Algorithm 1 to obtain a software diversity strategy based on the formulated game.

Algorithm 1. Diversify

1: **procedure** DIVERSIFY($G, \mathcal{S}, \mathcal{B}, SWV, P, C_d, C_a$)   ▷ Input parameters
2:    System Initialization
3:    Define: $\mathcal{A}_1, \mathcal{A}_2$
4:    **for** $a_1 \in \mathcal{A}_1$ **do**
5:        Graph Color (G, a_1) ▷ Graph coloring algorithm
6:        Update NSW ▷ Build node-software matrix
7:        Compute $NV = NSW \times SWV$ ▷ node-vulnerability matrix
8:        **for** $a_2 \in \mathcal{A}_2$ **do**
9:            Compute $R_1(a_1, a_2) \rightarrow$ update A
10:           Compute $R_2(a_1, a_2) \rightarrow$ update B
11:   GameSolver$(A, B) \rightarrow \mathbf{x}^*, \mathbf{y}^*$ ▷ Mixed strategies equilibrium for (7), (8)

3.5   Game Complexity

The computational time for solving the game programs depends on the dimensions of the action space $\mathcal{A}$, or the number of pure actions for each player. Unfortunately, the time grows exponentially in the number of strategies of both players.

For our game model, the number of pure actions does not grow with the number of nodes of the network. Instead, it grows with the number of software types available to the defender, and with the number of probes used by the attacker. However, this rate of growth is exponentially increasing with the number of software types (colors). For instance, if the number of available software $|\mathcal{S}|$, then the number of pure strategies for the defender, $|\mathcal{A}_1| = 2^{|\mathcal{S}|}$. Similarly, if the number of available probes to the attacker is $|\mathcal{B}|$, the number of pure attacker's pure actions is $|\mathcal{A}_2| = 2^{|\mathcal{B}|}$.

3.6   Complexity Reduction

Since the set of vulnerabilities associated with each software type is known to the defender, the defender can prioritize the use of available software types accordingly. More specifically, let $\mathbf{w}$ be weight vector of size $|S|$, such that,

$$\mathbf{w} = SWV \times e, \qquad (9)$$

where e, is a column vector of all ones of size $|\mathcal{V}| \times 1$. Hence, $\mathbf{w}$ represents the weight of each software type $s \in \mathcal{S}$, in terms of the number of vulnerabilities it introduces into the network when used by the defender.

Therefore, the defender does not need to consider all the possible combinations of the available software types. Instead, the defender optimizes over the number of software types (i.e, number of colors) to implement, and sorts the software set according to their weights in ascending order. For instance, if the defender decided to use three software types, she can immediately pick the three colors with the smallest weights according to $\mathbf{w}$ as defined in (9).

This approach leads to a significant reduction in the complexity of the game as the size of the action space $|\mathcal{A}_1|$ will not grow exponentially with the number of the available software types $|\mathcal{S}|$, it will grow linearly, instead.

Moreover, in the case of a perfect information game, the defender is assumed to know the probe matrix $\mathbf{P}$ as defined in Eq. (2). Therefore, the defender may sort the attacker's probes according to their potential damage. Along the same lines as $\mathbf{w}$, let $\mathbf{d} = \mathbf{P} \times e$ denote the damage vector of size $|\mathcal{B}| \times 1$, the defender can sort the probes available to her opponent in descending order according to damage vector $\mathbf{d}$ assuming a worst-case scenario in which the attacker always uses the most powerful probe first. The attacker is now optimi- zing the number of probes to use when launching an attack. With this reduction, we can redefine the action space for both players as follows, $\bar{\mathcal{A}}_1 = \{1, 2, ..., |\mathcal{S}|\}$ and $\bar{\mathcal{A}}_2 = \{1, 2, ..., |\mathcal{B}|\}$.

Using these heuristics we can significantly enhance the runtime of Algorithm 1 and present a Fast-Diversify as shown in Algorithm 2.

Algorithm 2. Fast-Diversify

1: **procedure** DIVERSIFY$(G, \mathcal{S}, \mathcal{B}, SWV, P, C_d, C_a)$ ▷ Input parameters
2:     System Initialization
3:     Compute $\mathbf{w}, \mathbf{d}$
4:     Sort $\mathbf{w}$ "Ascend"
5:     Sort $\mathbf{d}$ "Descend"
6:     Define: $\bar{A}_1, \bar{A}_2$
7:     **for** $a_1 \in \mathcal{A}_1$ **do**
8:         Graph Color (G, a_1) ▷ Graph coloring algorithm
9:         Update NSW ▷ Build node-software matrix
10:        Compute $NV = NSW \times SWV$ ▷ node-vulnerability matrix
11:        **for** $a_2 \in \mathcal{A}_2$ **do**
12:            Compute $R_1(a_1, a_2) \rightarrow$ update A
13:            Compute $R_2(a_1, a_2) \rightarrow$ update B
14:     GameSolver$(A, B) \rightarrow \mathbf{x}^*, \mathbf{y}^*$ ▷ Mixed strategies equilibrium for (7), (8)

In the following section, we present numerical results to validate the developed algorithms.

4   Numerical Results

We now present numerical results that validate the proposed game model. First, we consider a 20-node network that we generated such that any two nodes are connected directly with an edge with probability 0.5, as illustrated in Fig. 1a. We investigate the behavior of the players based on the Nash equilibrium strategies computed for the proposed game model with different values of the game model parameters.

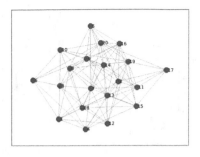

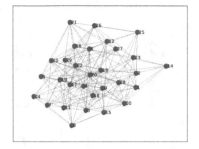

(a) A 20-node network topology.   (b) A 30-node network topology

Fig. 1. The two generated network topologies with randomly generated edges.

For the network topology shown in Fig. 1a, we plot the attacker's reward in Fig. 2a for different numbers of software types. It is clear that as the number of available software types increases, the defender can color the graph more efficiently, and hence software diversity will significantly reduce the attacker reward. However, increasing the number of available software types does not imply that the reward of the defender increases steadily since the defender plays his Nash equilibrium strategy. The Nash equilibrium strategy may lead the defender not to use all the available colors, since the use of a larger set of software types may introduce new vulnerabilities to the network. Therefore, in Fig. 2a, the attacker reward when the defender unilaterally deviated from his Nash strategy was higher than the attacker reward even when the defender used only a single software type (i.e., mono-culture case). In Fig. 2b, the defender reward is plotted at a different number of software types for the Nash equilibrium defense strategy from both sides. The defender reward is non-decreasing as the number of available software types increases.

To understand the effect of the cost parameter for both players, we plot the defender and attacker rewards at different cost values when the game played on a 30-node network, as shown in Fig. 1b.

As shown in Fig. 3a, the defender and the attacker rewards are plotted for different cost values per each software used by the defender at Nash equilibrium. The defender reward decreases as the cost increases since the defender tends to exclude more software types to avoid the defender cost C_d. On the other side, the attacker reward increases as the defender diversity capabilities are limited by the increasing cost while the cost per probe is fixed at 1. For the considered network, the vulnerability set contains 3 vulnerabilities, and the attacker has four probe types. To illustrate the role of the cost per probe, we plotted the reward of both players versus the cost per probe in Fig. 3b. At a low cost per probe, the defender reward is stably low as the attacker can afford the cost to use all his probes in the attack. As the cost per probe increases beyond 1, the defender reward starts to increase. However, since the defender cost is fixed at

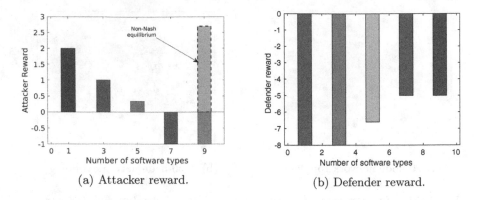

Fig. 2. Players' reward vs. the number of software types at Nash equilibrium.

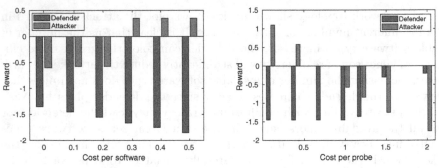

(a) Varying the cost per each software type, the cost per probe is 1

(b) Varying the cost per probe, the cost per software is 0.1.

Fig. 3. Comparing players' reward versus their action cost values

a low value of 0.1, the attacker is being punished more and hence the attacker cost starts to decrease significantly.

Finally, we compare the efficiency of the proposed algorithm versus the cost per software and cost per probe in Fig. 4a. We made the cost per software equal to the cost per probe for simplicity. As shown in Fig. 4a, the Fast-Diverisfy algorithm yields the exact reward for the defender and very comparable to the attacker as Algorithm 2 assumes a worst-case scenario for the attacker to reduce complexity. Moreover, in Fig. 4b we compare the runtime of both algorithms to show the significant reduction in complexity achieved via Algorithm 2.

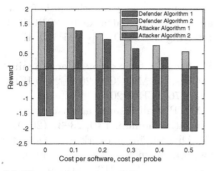

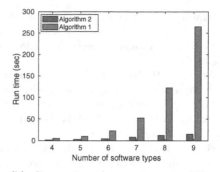

(a) Players reward at different cost values.

(b) Comparing the runtime at different numbers of software type.

Fig. 4. Comparison between the performance of the two proposed algorithms.

5 Conclusion and Future Work

We studied a software diversity approach for network security via a formulated game-theoretic model over an attack graph. In this context, we developed a novel game model to study the interactions between network defender and an adversary when software diversity is the main defensive strategy for the defender. We adapted a graph-coloring algorithm for computing Nash equilibrium diversifying strategy and developed a complexity reduction approach to obtain Nash equilibrium more efficiently making the proposed diversifying algorithm applicable in large-scale networks with a larger number of colors. Numerical results computed using our model show both the benefits of software diversity as well as the detailed tradeoffs that are necessary for both attackers and defenders in this scenario. We also validate the computational effectiveness of our algorithms for practical applications. Our ongoing research is focused on extending the formulated game model to account for cases of incomplete information. In this case, the software vulnerability matrix and the probe matrix are unknown beforehand by the defender.

Acknowledgment. Research was sponsored by the Army Research Laboratory and was accomplished under Cooperative Agreement Number W911NF-19-2-0150. The views and conclusions contained in this document are those of the authors and should not be interpreted as representing the official policies, either expressed or implied, of the Army Research Laboratory or the U.S. Government. The U.S. Government is authorized to reproduce and distribute reprints for Government purposes notwithstanding any copyright notation herein.

References

1. Anwar, A.H., Atia, G., Guirguis, M.: Game theoretic defense approach to wireless networks against stealthy decoy attacks. In: 2016 54th Annual Allerton Conference on Communication, Control, and Computing (Allerton), pp. 816–821. IEEE (2016)

2. Anwar, A.H., Atia, G., Guirguis, M.: It's time to migrate! a game-theoretic framework for protecting a multi-tenant cloud against collocation attacks. In: 2018 IEEE 11th International Conference on Cloud Computing (CLOUD), pp. 725–731. IEEE (2018)

3. Anwar, A.H., Kelly, J., Atia, G., Guirguis, M.: Stealthy edge decoy attacks against dynamic channel assignment in wireless networks. In: MILCOM 2015–2015 IEEE Military Communications Conference, pp. 671–676. IEEE (2015)

4. Anwar, A.H., Kelly, J., Atia, G., Guirguis, M.: Pinball attacks against dynamic channel assignment in wireless networks. Comput. Commun. **140**, 23–37 (2019)

5. Borbor, D., Wang, L., Jajodia, S., Singhal, A.: Diversifying network services under cost constraints for better resilience against unknown attacks. In: Ranise, S., Swarup, V. (eds.) DBSec 2016. LNCS, vol. 9766, pp. 295–312. Springer, Cham (2016). https://doi.org/10.1007/978-3-319-41483-6_21

6. Casini, E., De Gaudenzi, R., Herrero, O.D.R.: Contention resolution diversity slotted aloha (CRDSA): an enhanced random access schemefor satellite access packet networks. IEEE Trans. Wireless Commun. **6**(4), 1408–1419 (2007)

7. Chatterjee, B.: An optimization formulation to compute nash equilibrium in finite games. In: 2009 Proceeding of International Conference on Methods and Models in Computer Science (ICM2CS), pp. 1–5. IEEE (2009)

8. Chen, X., Deng, X.: Settling the complexity of two-player nash equilibrium. In: 2006 47th Annual IEEE Symposium on Foundations of Computer Science (FOCS 2006), pp. 261–272. IEEE (2006)

9. Farzaneh, M.: Graph Coloring by Genetic Algorithm. https://www.mathworks.com/matlabcentral/fileexchange/74118-graph-coloring-by-genetic-algorithm (2020), [MATLAB Central File Exchange. Accessed 12 July 2020]

10. Garcia, M., Bessani, A., Gashi, I., Neves, N., Obelheiro, R.: Os diversity for intrusion tolerance: myth or reality? In: 2011 IEEE/IFIP 41st International Conference on Dependable Systems & Networks (DSN), pp. 383–394. IEEE (2011)

11. Jensen, T.R., Toft, B.: Graph Coloring Problems, vol. 39. Wiley, New York (2011)

12. Kiekintveld, C., Jain, M., Tsai, J., Pita, J., Ordóñez, F., Tambe, M.: Computing optimal randomized resource allocations for massive security games. In: Proceedings of the 8th International Conference on Autonomous Agents and Multiagent Systems, vol. 1, pp. 689–696 (2009)

13. Kierstead, H.A.: Asymmetric graph coloring games. J. Graph Theory **48**(3), 169–185 (2005)

14. Larsen, P., Homescu, A., Brunthaler, S., Franz, M.: SOK: automated software diversity. In: 2014 IEEE Symposium on Security and Privacy, pp. 276–291. IEEE (2014)

15. Le Goues, C., Forrest, S., Weimer, W.: Current challenges in automatic software repair. Softw. Qual. J. **21**(3), 421–443 (2013)

16. Le Goues, C., Nguyen-Tuong, A., Chen, H., Davidson, J.W., Forrest, S., Hiser, J.D., Knight, J.C., Van Gundy, M.: Moving target defenses in the helix self-regenerative architecture. In: Jajodia, S., Ghosh, A., Subrahmanian, V., Swarup, V., Wang, C., Wang, X. (eds.) Moving Target Defense II, pp. 117–149. Springer, New York (2013). https://doi.org/10.1007/978-1-4614-5416-8_7

17. Liva, G.: Graph-based analysis and optimization of contention resolution diversity slotted aloha. IEEE Trans. Commun. **59**(2), 477–487 (2010)

18. Mangasarian, O.L., Stone, H.: Two-person nonzero-sum games and quadratic programming. J. Math. Anal. Appl. **9**(3), 348–355 (1964)

19. Moumen, A., Bouye, M., Sissaoui, H.: New secure partial encryption method for medical images using graph coloring problem. Nonlinear Dyn. **82**(3), 1475–1482 (2015). https://doi.org/10.1007/s11071-015-2253-4
20. Nash, J.F., et al.: Equilibrium points in n-person games. Proc. Natl. Acad. Sci. **36**(1), 48–49 (1950)
21. Neti, S., Somayaji, A., Locasto, M.E.: Software diversity: Security, entropy and game theory. In: HotSec (2012)
22. Roy, S., Ellis, C., Shiva, S., Dasgupta, D., Shandilya, V., Wu, Q.: A survey of game theory as applied to network security. In: 2010 43rd Hawaii International Conference on System Sciences, pp. 1–10. IEEE (2010)
23. Shacham, H., Page, M., Pfaff, B., Goh, E.J., Modadugu, N., Boneh, D.: On the effectiveness of address-space randomization. In: Proceedings of the 11th ACM Conference on Computer and Communications Security, pp. 298–307 (2004)
24. Sohn, S.: Graph coloring algorithms and applications to the channel assignment problems. In: Kim, K.J., Chung, K.-Y. (eds.) IT Convergence and Security 2012. LNEE, vol. 215, pp. 363–370. Springer, Dordrecht (2013). https://doi.org/10.1007/978-94-007-5860-5_44
25. Thiyagarajan, P., Aghila, G.: Reversible dynamic secure steganography for medical image using graph coloring. Health Policy Technol. **2**(3), 151–161 (2013)
26. Wang, S., Wang, P., Wu, D.: Composite software diversification. In: 2017 IEEE International Conference on Software Maintenance and Evolution (ICSME), pp. 284–294. IEEE (2017)
27. Wartell, R., Mohan, V., Hamlen, K.W., Lin, Z.: Binary stirring: self-randomizing instruction addresses of legacy x86 binary code. In: Proceedings of the 2012 ACM Conference on Computer and Communications Security, pp. 157–168 (2012)
28. Zhang, M., Wang, L., Jajodia, S., Singhal, A., Albanese, M.: Network diversity: a security metric for evaluating the resilience of networks against zero-day attacks. IEEE Trans. Inf. Forensics Secur. **11**(5), 1071–1086 (2016)

Partially Observable Stochastic Games for Cyber Deception Against Network Epidemic

Olivier Tsemogne[1,2], Yezekael Hayel[2(✉)], Charles Kamhoua[3],
and Gabriel Deugoue[1]

[1] University of Dschang, Dschang, Cameroon
[2] CERI/LIA, Avignon Université, Avignon, France
`yezekael.hayel@univ-avignon.fr`
[3] US Army Research Laboratory, Adelphi, USA

Abstract. A Decentralized Denial of Service is an attack done by an agent capable to control the spread of a malware. This is a combination of epidemiological and conflictual aspects between several decision makers. There exists in the literature papers that study (non oriented) epidemics and papers that study network attacks regardless the epidemiological aspect. We put together the two aspects and provide a new game theoretical model which is part of the family of partially observable stochastic games (POSG) but with particular features. We prove the consistency of heuristic search value iteration (HSVI) based algorithms. Our framework is applied to optimally design a cyber deception technique based on honeypots in order to control an epidemic cyber-attack of a network by a strategic attacker. Some basic simulations are proposed to illustrate the framework described in this work-in-progress paper.

Keywords: Epidemic models · Partially observable stochastic game · Heuristic search value iteration

1 Introduction

Cyber security is becoming an important research area in global security world. First, with the high level of usage of connected devices and equipments, understanding cyber attacks is the most important stage in order to build efficient cyber defense. Second, we are living in a word that is more and more connected, and the effect of networks is no more to prove its impact on our everyday life, particularly in cyber security. For example, despite most internet of things (IoT) providers have improved the security of their devices, the number of IoT devices attacked by distributed denial of service (DDoS) is still increasing [1]. Recently, the combination of tools from game theory (understanding strategic situations with several decision makers), mathematical modelling of infectious disease and network science (understanding interaction structure between decision makers)

© Springer Nature Switzerland AG 2020
Q. Zhu et al. (Eds.): GameSec 2020, LNCS 12513, pp. 312–325, 2020.
https://doi.org/10.1007/978-3-030-64793-3_17

have demonstrated their strength to build new models that bring interesting cyber defense mechanisms [8] and [9]. An important cyber deception technique in order to mitigate cyber attacks is the use of honeypots. A honeypot is a token that a player can place on an edge of the network to create fake information. Honeypot strategies have been recently theoretically and practically optimized in lateral movement [3] through the heuristic search value iteration (HSVI) [10] discussed in the field of partially observable Markov decision processes (POMDPs). However, the definition of HSVI in game theory applies to the more general concept of one-sided partially observable stochastic games (OS-POSGs). Furthermore, in a context of attack by epidemics, (1) the aim of the network attacker is to make on every node a transition from his desire, non infected to infected for example, (2) attacker has the true information over the network state. One of such epidemics is Mirai botnet, an epidemic that compromises a maximum number of IoT devices before launching a DDoS using the compromised IoT devices. Consequently, the fight against botnet epidemics can be studied as a zero-sum OS-POSG like in [11]. To the best of our knowledge, there is no work that addresses the stopping of epidemic from the perspective of POSGs. This work-in-progress paper illustrates how to deal with this scientific gap.

We define a game model based on the actions of an attacker trying to compromise and take control of vulnerable nodes in a network, and the actions of a defender trying to mitigate attacker's actions while offering patches to vulnerable nodes. Moreover, each node reacts to both players actions and therefore the global state of the system evolves accordingly. This model associates epidemics and POSG models. The definition of an epidemic model corresponds to the compartmentalisation of the individual states and the possible transitions of an individual from one compartment to another. The Susceptible-Infected-Recovered (SIR) model [2] for instance involves infectious (or infected) nodes (compartment I), who carry the virus, susceptible nodes (compartment S), which are vulnerable but not infected and recovered (or resistant, non vulnerable) nodes (compartment R). Botnet epidemics are SIR epidemics type like in [5], in which, without loss of generality, we consider only $S \to I$ (S to I), $S \to R$ and $I \to S$ transitions. The attacker does not observe defender's actions, which induces a general POSG with partial observations for both sides. Indeed, even-though she knows the game state (perfect information on one side), no player observes the opponent's moves (incomplete information on both sides). Our model considers the vulnerability of nodes and the defender placing honeypots on edges to detect some propagation and cure relevant nodes. The contributions of the paper are threefold:

- a zero-sum stochastic game model is proposed to study optimal deception strategies against virus propagation,
- we study a two-player zero-sum stochastic game in which no player observes the opponent's actions and prove that the heuristic search value iterated can be applied in this model,
- our model involves two players acting strategically on the system composed of actors acting in a probabilistic way.

The rest of the paper is organized as follows. In the next section, we describe our model and the problem. Then, in Sect. 3, the solution of the problem is given and in Sect. 4, we prove several properties of the dynamic programming operator. After this, we provide some numerical illustrations in Sect. 5 and finally we present a short discussion on further works and a conclusion in Sect. 6. Note that all proofs and a complete related work section are fully described in the long version of this paper [7].

2   Model Description

We present the model that describes interactions between the botnet (controlled by an attacker), the devices and the agent (the defender) who intends to prevent the botnet from controlling the network throughout the infected nodes.

2.1   Problem Description

An attacker is trying to take control of a large number of devices of a network and make it a foothold to lunch a fatal attack. This attack may be for example to overload a server with a very large number of requests. Her strategy consists in silently spreading over the network a worm that ensures her the control of any device. She will propagate the worm until she has taken control of the desired number of devices. Fortunately for attacker, as observed in the Mirai attack [1], many devices do not have customized passwords and are therefore vulnerable, so attacker just has to select these vulnerable devices to spread the worm up to the targeted number. She frequently makes a probe over the network and then knows which nodes are vulnerable, which nodes are infected (and which nodes are resistent). To mitigate this spread, a defender combines two solutions:

1. He offers patches for infected devices and incites them to accept it. He also incites vulnerable, non-infected devices to customize their passwords and therefore become resistant against any attack. However, the result of this incitement is not predictable. Nevertheless, defender knows the decision of any device, i.e. knows if a device has been patched or not.
2. Defender has at his disposal a fixed number of honeypots that he can deploy on edges. The validity of each honeypot is one time-slot. Note the attacker does not have the honeypots localization knowledge. A honeypot detects any virus propagation that traverses the edge and then the defender strongly incites the device and the newly infected nodes to patch.

This scenario is repeated until attacker has reached the targeted number of infected devices or there is no infected device left in the network (the latter is an absorbing state of the system as the virus has totally disappeared). Defender's action consists in reallocating a limited number of honeypots (not necessarily all) on edges of the network at any new time-slot of the game. Attacker's action at any time-slot consists in choosing neighbours of infected devices to propagate the worm from, i.e. choosing an edge to propagate the virus from an infected node to a non-infected one. We assume that from each infected device she can chose at most one adjacent node to contaminate. Also, at each time-slot of the game, each node may decide to change his state by applying the patch if the node is infected, or changing his password if the node is susceptible to be infected by the virus. This node decision is made randomly and known by defender. The nodes behavior given by the probability distribution of their choice is known by the attacker and the defender.

2.2   Model

Because of an epidemic spreading over the network and users' actions, there are 3 classes of devices: *infected* devices (I), *susceptible* devices (S), that are vulnerable and non infected, and *resistant* devices (R), that cannot be successfully attacked.[1] For instance, a resistant device has a customized password and we assume that he will be resistant forever. In other words, R is an absorbing state, or there is no transition from R to any other state. For an infected device to become resistant, two transitions are necessary: $I \rightarrow S$ then $S \rightarrow R$. This is because an infected device must be patched first (transition from state I to state S) to be restored with basic features including default password, and then to change the default password to a customized password (transition from state S to state R). These two transitions cannot be done during a single stage. Indeed, changing the default password is useless while the node is under the control of the botnet. So we consider transition $I \rightarrow R$ is not possible at one stage. Consequently, only 3 transitions are possible for any device state dynamic in our framework: $S \rightarrow I$, $S \rightarrow R$ and $I \rightarrow S$ as depicted in Fig. 1.

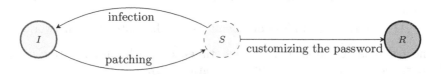

Fig. 1. Possible effective state transitions for each device.

There is a clear conflict between the attacker and the defender, but the information knowledge is not the same for these two decision makers. Attacker knows the global state of network (i.e. the state of each device at any time-slot of the game) but cannot observe defenders' actions while defender, who only knows the decision taken by devices about patching and password changing, has a partial observation of the global state. At the beginning of each time-slot, he only knows nodes who became susceptible or resistant in the past time-slot, but not the ones that are infected.

---

[1] Unlike in [6], we consider the use of the world "resistant": (1) instead of "recovered" to keep in thought the non-vulnerability of the device; (2) instead of "removed" to keep in thought that the device is still in the game scenario.

The problem can be modeled with a *two-player zero-sum OS-POSG* concept with private observation in which attacker does not know the actions defender has taken. Such a model is neither a classical POSG ([3]), in which attacker observes defender's actions, nor POSG with private information, in which no player can observe another player's private state [4]. Furthermore, the epidemic aspect brings forward two additional parameters: the endogenous probabilities of transitions $S \to R$ and $I \to S$. Our model is a stochastic game represented by the tuple:

$$\mathcal{G} = \left(G,\, Z,\, A_1,\, A_2,\, O,\, \varrho,\, \alpha,\, T,\, r,\, b^0\right),$$

where:

- $G = (V, E)$ is the network (a finite and non directed graph) with V set of nodes (devices) and E set of edges;
- Z is the set of possible states of the devices, $\Delta(Z)$ is the set of probability distributions over Z. The global state is given by the class (S, I or R) of each node and the total number of states is $3^{|V|}$.
- A_1 and A_2 respectively denote the sets of possible actions for defender and attacker, $A = A_1 \times A_2$ is the set of possible joint actions;
- O is the observation space (of the defender);
- ϱ and α are respectively the probability for a susceptible node to become resistant at the next time step and the probability for an infected node to become susceptible at the next time step (see Fig. 1);
- $T : Z \times O \times Z \times A \longrightarrow [0, 1]$ is an application such that $T(\cdot \mid z, a) \in \Delta(Z \times O)$ (i.e. $T(\cdot \mid z, a)$ is a probability distribution over $\Delta(Z \times O)$) for any $(z, a) \in Z \times A$. T is called the *transition function*;
- $r : Z \times Z \longrightarrow \mathbb{R}$ is the *reward function* induced from a transition of a node state. $r(z_i, z_i')$ is the reward of defender when state of node i changes from z_i to state z_i';
- $b^0 \in \Delta(Z)$ is the initial belief of defender over the state of the network.

The game is repeated and at each time-slot, each player (attacker and defender) chooses an action as illustrated on Fig. (2).

2.3 Model Description

For a better understanding of the proposed framework, we bring up the following mathematical notations.

The system. To simplify, we say that nodes are indiced by 1, 2, ..., i, ..., $|V|$. An edge is any pair $\{i, j\}$ of connected nodes, i.e. a subset of V of 2 elements. So, $E \subseteq \{e \in 2^V \mid |e| = 2\}$. 3 different objects ($S$, I and R) define the possible states of any node at each time-slot of the repeated game. The state of each node defines the global state $z = (z_i)_{i=1}^{|V|}$ of the network with

$$z_i = \begin{cases} S \text{ if node } i \text{ is susceptible} \\ I \text{ if node } i \text{ is infected} \\ R \text{ if node } i \text{ is resistant} \end{cases}.$$

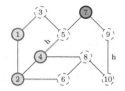 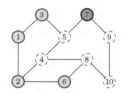 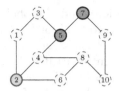

Beginning of the time-slot (and of the first stage). Defender places 2 honeypots, on edges 4 ↔ 5 and 9 ↔ 10; attacker lunches the propagation 1 → 3, 2 → 6 and 4 → 5; the first two ones are undetected but the last one is detected.

End of the first stage (and beginning of the second stage). The propagation on nodes 3 and 6 is not detected and therefore result in two new hosts, whereas defender has intercepted an infection traversing the edge 4 ↔ 5. Nodes 4 and 5 therefore accept to patch.

End of the time-slot (and of the second stage). With respect to probabilities α and ϱ, nodes 1, 3 and 6 transition I → S, node 5 transitions S → R and the other nodes do not effectively change their state.

⟨i⟩ = susceptible node; (i) = infected node; ● = resistant node; ____ = edge; ____ = edge chosen by attacker; h = honeypot edge.

Fig. 2. One time-slot of the game: a possible scenario with 10 nodes

The actions

- Defender's action consists in deploying honeypots on edges. The maximum number h of honeypots is fixed and a honeypot remains on an edge only for one time-slot. Since he knows resistant nodes and also knows that there is no interest for the attacker to attack a resistant node, the defender will place a honeypot only on an edge between non-resistant ends. Hence, a defender's action is any set a_1 of at most h edges that are disjoint from R and has the following properties:

$$\begin{cases} a_1 \subseteq E \\ |a_1| \leq h \\ \forall u \in a_1, \quad u \cap R = \emptyset \end{cases} . \tag{1}$$

- Attacker's action consists in propagating the worm from each infected node through one edge of her choice linking this node to an adjacent, susceptible node if such a node exists. To model this action, we say that any attacker's action is an edge, keeping in mind that : attack is lunched from an infected node; attacker will infect only susceptible nodes; from every infected node, infection will propagate to at most one node. Finally, an attacker's action is a set a_2 of edges such that: each edge contains an infected node and a susceptible node; for all infected node i there exists at most one edge through which an infection is lunched. i.e.:

$$\begin{cases} a_2 \subseteq E \\ \forall u \in a_2, \quad \begin{cases} u \cap I \neq \emptyset \\ u \cap S \neq \emptyset \end{cases} \\ \forall i \in I, \quad |\{u \in a_2 : i \in u\}| \leq 1 \end{cases} . \tag{2}$$

The transition happens in two steps: the joint action $a = (a_1, a_2)$ in the state z makes the network transition to an intermediate state $a(z)$ (Players' action); nodes' probabilistic moves in the state $a(z)$ causes another transition to a state z' for the following time-slot (nodes' actions).

– *Players' action.* In case node i is susceptible, his state changes (to infected) if and only if attacker lunches an attack from an infected node to him. In case node i is infected, his state changes (to susceptible) if and only if defender detects an attack lunched from its position through a honeypot to a susceptible node. Remember that resistant nodes remain resistant.

We introduce for any collection X of sets, the set $\mathcal{U}(X) = \bigcup_{w \in X} w$. Note that: a node i is a side of an infection (either the side propagating or receiving) if and only if $i \in \mathcal{U}(a_2)$; node i is a side of an undetected infection if and only if $i \in \mathcal{U}(a_2) \setminus \mathcal{U}(a_1 \cap a_2)$. The transitions due to player's action can be explained as follows: the state of a susceptible node transitions if and only if the node is a side an infection and is not a side of a detected infection; the state of an infected node transitions if and only if the node is a side of a detected infection. We denote by $a(z)_i$ the intermediate state of node i induced by player's actions a when the state of the system is z. Then, for all node i:

$$z_i = S \implies \begin{cases} a(z)_i = I & \Longleftrightarrow & i \in \mathcal{U}(a_2) \setminus \mathcal{U}(a_1 \cap a_2) \\ a(z)_i = S & \Longleftrightarrow & i \notin \mathcal{U}(a_2) \setminus \mathcal{U}(a_1 \cap a_2) \end{cases},$$

$$z_i = I \implies \begin{cases} a(z)_i = I & \Longleftrightarrow & i \notin \mathcal{U}(a_1 \cap a_2) \\ a(z)_i = S & \Longleftrightarrow & i \in \mathcal{U}(a_1 \cap a_2) \end{cases},$$

$$z_i = R \implies a(z)_i = R.$$

– *nodes' actions.* After this first intermediate transition, each node who is still susceptible after player's actions becomes resistant with probability ϱ or remains susceptible; each node who is still infected after player's actions becomes susceptible with probability α or remains infected. The relying probabilities $\mathbb{P}(z_i' \mid a(z)_i, z_i)$ are given in the following table:

			z_i'	
		S	I	R
z_i	$a(z)_i$			
S	S	$1-\varrho$	0	ϱ
	I	0	1	0
I	S	1	0	0
	I	α	$1-\alpha$	0
R	R	0	0	1

The observations. Defender information concerns the nodes who decide to change their states, possibly under the incitement of defender. Formally, if we consider observation to be the result of such a transition, an observation is a set o such that:

$$\begin{cases} o \subseteq S \cup R \\ i \in o \end{cases} \iff \left(\begin{cases} a(z)_i = S \\ z'_i = R \end{cases} \text{ or } \begin{cases} a(z)_i = I \\ z'_i = S \end{cases} \right). \tag{3}$$

The transition function. The calculation of the probability $T(z',o \,|\, z,a)$ for a transition from a state z to a state z' is worth done only for the subsequent observation, i.e. for the unique observation $o = o(z,z')$ such that:

$$i \in o(z,z') \iff \left(\begin{cases} z_i = S \\ z'_i = R \end{cases} \text{ or } \begin{cases} z_i = I \\ z'_i = S \end{cases} \right).$$

More explicitly, $T(z',o \,|\, z,a) = \begin{cases} \mathbb{P}(z'_i \,|\, a(z)_i, z_i) & \text{if } o = o(z,z') \\ 0 & \text{otherwise} \end{cases}$, where

$a(z)_i$ is the intermediate state from the state z to the state z' when the joint action $a = (a_1, a_2)$ is taken.

The rewards. The transition of any node's state results in a payoff to defender and exactly the opposite value to attacker. This payoff function of the node states at current and next time-slots and we define it by tree non-negative constants r_1, r_2 and r_3 as shown in Fig. 3.

		Next state z'_i		
		S	I	R
	S	0	$-r_2$	r_3
Current state z_i	I	r_2	$-r_1$	$--$
	R	$--$	$--$	0

Fig. 3. Defender's payoff for any node i state transition.

Defender's total payoff is defined by:

$$R(z,z') = \sum_{i \in V} r(z_i, z'_i), \tag{4}$$

while his reward is the expected total payoff:

$$\bar{R}(z,a) = \sum_{z' \in Z} \mathbb{P}(z' \,|\, a(z), z) \times R(z,z') = \sum_{z' \in Z} \sum_{i \in V} \mathbb{P}(z' \,|\, a(z), z) \times r(z_i, z'_i). \tag{5}$$

3   Solution Description

Defender does not know the targeted number of nodes attacker wishes to infect, but attacker's payoff measures how much she is coming close or far to her objective. So we solve the game where defender's objective is to maximize her total (or expected total) reward at infinite horizon. We precise some notion of game theory for a better understanding of the strategy in our particular context.

3.1   Strategies

Attacker may be playing a mixed strategy. Henceforth, any defender's strategy that is optimal in pure strategy is also optimal in mixed strategy. So we are interested only in mixed strategies. At each time-slot of the repeated game, players strategies are called *one-stage strategies*. For defender who does not know the network's state, the strategy π_1 is a probability distribution over the set A_1 of his possible actions. i.e. $\pi_1 \in \Delta(A_1)$. The set of defender one-stage strategies is $\Delta(A_1)$. Attacker's strategy depends on the state z of the network and, for any state z, she plays conditional strategy $\pi_2(\cdot \mid z) \in \Delta(A_2)$. i.e. she plays action a_2 with probability $\pi_2(a_2 \mid z)$. So, attacker's one-stage strategy is a probability vector $\pi_2 : Z \longrightarrow \Delta(A_2)$ that maps a probability distribution $\pi_2(\cdot \mid z)$ to any state z. The set of attacker's one-stage strategies is $\Delta(A_2)^Z$.

Defender updates his belief time-slot after time-slot according to the one-stage strategies. If he has the belief b at current time-slot, plays action a_1, makes observation o while he knows that attacker has played strategy π_2, then he updates his belief to a value b' such that:

$$b_{\pi_2}^{a_1, o}\left(z'\right) = \frac{1}{\mathbb{P}_{b, \pi_2}\left(o \mid a_1\right)} \sum_{z \in Z} \sum_{a_2 \in A_2} T\left(z', o \,\middle|\, z, a_1, a_2\right) b(z) \pi_2\left(a_2 \mid z\right), \quad (6)$$

where

$$\mathbb{P}_{b, \pi_2}\left(o \mid a_1\right) = \sum_{z', z \in Z} \sum_{a_2 \in A_2} T\left(z', o \,\middle|\, z, a_1, a_2\right) b(z) \pi_2\left(a_2 \mid z\right). \quad (7)$$

Yet, each one-stage strategy may follow player's information up to the moment he/she is going to take his/her action. This information is called *history*. The history of defender at time-slot $t \geq 2$ is the sequence $h_1 = \left(a_1^1, o^1, a_1^2, o^2, \ldots, a_1^{t-1}, o^{t-1}\right)$ of observations and defender's actions up to time-slot $t-1$; the history of attacker at time-slot $t \geq 2$ is the sequence $h_2 = \left(z^1, a_2^1, z^2, a_2^2, \ldots, z^{t-1}, a_2^{t-1}, z^t\right)$ of network's states and attacker's actions up to time-slot $t-1$, added to the current state; at time-slot 1 attacker's history is reduced to state of the network and defender has an empty history.

3.2   Utility

Discounting the reward with a factor $\gamma \in [0, 1]$, we consider the total expected reward, denoted utility, at infinite horizon.[2] At any time-slot at which each player i plays strategy π_i in state z, the expected reward (of defender) is given by:

$$\mathbb{E}_{\pi_1, \pi_2}^z[\bar{R}] = \sum_{a_1 \in A_1} \sum_{a_2 \in A_2} \pi_1(a_1) \pi_2(a_2 \mid z) \bar{R}(z, a_1, a_2) = \sum_{a \in A} \pi(a \mid z) \bar{R}(z, a), \quad (8)$$

---

[2] Since the number of infected node cannot exceed $|V|$, the probability at each time-slot that all infected nodes become susceptible is greater or equal to $(1 - \alpha)^{|V|}$. So, at a certain time-slot, there will be no infected node and later all node will be resistant. There is no payoff from this time-slot and consequently the total expected reward converges even with discount factor $\gamma = 1$.

where $\pi\left(a\,|\,z\right) = \pi_1\left(a_1\right)\pi_2\left(a_2\,|\,z\right)$ is the probability that players play the joint action a. The expected reward (of defender) who plays with belief b over the network state is:

$$\mathbb{E}^b_{\pi_1,\pi_2}\left[\bar{R}\right] = \sum_{z\in Z} b\left(z\right)\mathbb{E}^z_{\pi_1,\pi_2}\left[\bar{R}\right]. \tag{9}$$

So, if both players are playing a joint strategy $\pi = \left(\pi_1,\pi_2\right)$, then, given initial belief b^0, the *utility* (of defender) is given by:

$$
\begin{aligned}
U_{\pi_1,\pi_2}\left(b^0\right) &= \sum_{z\in Z} b^0\left(z\right)\mathbb{E}^z_{\pi z}\left[\bar{R}\right] + \sum_{t=2}^{\infty}\gamma^{t-1}\\
&\quad \times \sum_{z\in Z}\sum_{\substack{z_2,\cdots,z_t\in Z\\ a_1,\cdots,a_{t-1}\in A\\ o_1,\cdots,o_{t-1}\in O}}\left[b^0\left(z\right)\left(\prod_{\tau=2}^{t}\left[T\left(z^\tau,o^{\tau-1}\big|z^{\tau-1},a^{\tau-1}\right)\pi\left(a^{\tau-1}\big|z^{\tau-1}\right)\right]\right)\mathbb{E}^{z_t}_{\pi_h}\left[\bar{R}\right]\right]\\
&= \sum_{z\in Z} b^0\left(z\right)\varphi\left(z\right), \tag{10}
\end{aligned}
$$

where

$$
\begin{aligned}
\varphi\left(z\right) &= \mathbb{E}^z_{\pi z}\left[\bar{R}\right]\\
&\quad + \sum_{t=2}^{\infty}\gamma^{t-1}\sum_{\substack{z_2,\cdots,z_t\in Z\\ a_1,\cdots,a_{t-1}\in A\\ o_1,\cdots,o_{t-1}\in O}}\left[\left(\prod_{\tau=2}^{t}\left[T\left(z^\tau,o^{\tau-1}\big|z^{\tau-1},a^{\tau-1}\right)\pi\left(a^{\tau-1}\big|z^{\tau-1}\right)\right]\right)\mathbb{E}^{z_t}_{\pi_h}\left[\bar{R}\right]\right] \tag{11}
\end{aligned}
$$

3.3 Objectives

Defender's objective is to maximize his utility, which is the opposite for attacker's objective. The solution is then a strategy π_1 which is defender's a best response to some strategy π_2 which is also a best response to π_1. When defender plays a strategy π_1, we should suppose that attacker is best responding to π_1 and consider the utility in this case, referred to as the *value function* v_{π_1} *of strategy* π_1 with initial belief b^0, defined by:

$$
\begin{aligned}
v_{\pi_1} &: \Delta\left(A_1\right) \longrightarrow \mathbb{R}\\
b^0 &\longmapsto \min_{\pi_2} U_{\pi_1,\pi_2}\left(b^0\right). \tag{12}
\end{aligned}
$$

Denote

$$U = \sum_{t=0}^{\infty}\gamma^t\left(\min_{z,a_1,a_2}\bar{R}\left(z,a_1,a_2\right)\right) = \frac{\min\limits_{z,a_1,a_2}\bar{R}\left(z,a_1,a_2\right)}{1-\gamma} = \frac{r}{1-\gamma} \tag{13}$$

and

$$L = \sum_{t=0}^{\infty}\gamma^t\left(\max_{z,a_1,a_2}\bar{R}\left(z,a_1,a_2\right)\right) = \frac{\max\limits_{z,a_1,a_2}\bar{R}\left(z,a_1,a_2\right)}{1-\gamma} = \frac{\bar{r}}{1-\gamma}, \tag{14}$$

where $\underline{r} = \min\limits_{z,a_1,a_2} \bar{R}\left(z,a_1,a_2\right)$ and $\bar{r} = \max\limits_{z,a_1,a_2} \bar{R}\left(z,a_1,a_2\right)$. It is clear each reward is bounded between $\min\limits_{z,a_1,a_2} \bar{R}\left(z,a_1,a_2\right)$ and $\max\limits_{z,a_1,a_2} \bar{R}\left(z,a_1,a_2\right)$. Consequently, each utility is bounded between L and U and Eq. (12) is consistent. The goal of defender who has the belief b^0 is to maximize the value of the game. The *optimal value v^* of the game* when defender has initial belief b^0 is the application:

$$
\begin{aligned}
v^* : \Delta\left(A_1\right) &\longrightarrow \mathbb{R} \\
b^0 &\longmapsto \max_{\pi_1} v_{\pi_1}\left(b^0\right).
\end{aligned}
\tag{15}
$$

This notation is consistent for the aforementioned reason.

The following theorem gives the main result of important properties over the optimal value function v^*.

Theorem 1. *The optimal value function v^* of the game is convex and δ-Lipschitz continuous.*

Following this theorem, we can prove that the heuristic search with the value iteration (HSVI) procedure holds and can be used to determine solutions of the game.

4   Value Backup Operator

In this section, we prove that the heuristic search with the value iteration (HSVI) procedure holds under our assumptions as well as in the general concept of two-player zero-sum OS-POSG where one player knows everything but not the current action of his opponent. To this end, we review the proof of all relevant properties in the following section. Let us first introduce the value backup operator for stochastic games in which attacker has a complete information and we prove that important results for this operator still hold for our particular stochastic game with partial information. The defender's reward in this time-slot game when strategies π_1 and π_2 are played is

$$
U^V_{\pi_1,\pi_2}\left(b\right) = \bar{R}^{\text{imm}}_{\pi_1,\pi_2}\left(b\right) + \gamma \bar{R}^{b,\text{subs}}_{\pi_1,\pi_2}\left(V\right),
\tag{16}
$$

where

$$
\begin{aligned}
\bar{R}^{\text{imm}}_{\pi_1,\pi_2}\left(b\right) &= \sum_{z\in Z}\sum_{a_1\in A_1}\sum_{a_2\in A_2} b\left(z\right)\pi_1\left(a_1\right)\pi_2\left(a_2\mid z\right)\bar{R}\left(z,a_1,a_2\right) \\
&= \sum_{z\in Z}\sum_{a\in A} b\left(z\right)\pi\left(a\mid z\right)\bar{R}\left(z,a\right)
\end{aligned}
\tag{17}
$$

is the reward in the one-stage game and

$$
\bar{R}^{\text{subs}}_{\pi_1,\pi_2}\left(b,V\right) = \sum_{a_1\in A_1}\sum_{o\in O} \pi_1\left(a_1\right)\mathbb{P}_{b,\pi_2}\left(o\mid a_1\right) V\left(b^{a_1,o}_{\pi_2}\right)
\tag{18}
$$

is the reward in the subsequent game. Denote by HV the optimal value function of the stage game, called *value backup* operator, i.e.:

$$[HV](b) = U^V_{\pi_1,\pi_2}(b) = \max_{\pi_1} \min_{\pi_2} \left[\bar{R}^{\text{imm}}_{\pi_1,\pi_2}(b) + \gamma \bar{R}^{\text{subs}}_{\pi_1,\pi_2}(b,V) \right]. \qquad (19)$$

After several lemmas and properties described in the full version of the paper in [7], we have the following main theorem which induces that the optimal value v^* of the game is the fix point of the value backup operator H.

Theorem 2. *The operator H is γ-contracting in the space of convex continuous functions $V : \Delta(Z) \longrightarrow \mathbb{R}$ under the max-norm:* $\|V\|_\infty = \max\limits_{b \in \Delta(Z)} \|V(b)\|$.

Henceforth from Banach fix point theorem, operator H admits a fix point V^* to which converges any sequence $(V_n)_{n \in \mathbb{N}^*}$ of convex continuous functions such that $V_{n+1} = HV_n$ for every n. The following theorem states that this fix point is the value v^* of the game, which means that any algorithm that iteratively corrects the value converges to v^*.

Theorem 3. *The value v^* of the game is the fix point of the backup operator H.*

Following this important property and based on dual linear programs, two algorithms are proposed in the longer version of this work-in-progress paper [7] in order to compute the lower bound V^Υ_{UB} and the upper bound V^Γ_{LB} of the optimal value v^* of the game. Since V^Υ_{UB} and V^Γ_{LB} are iteratively refined upper and lower bounds of the optimal value function at any belief b, it is possible to get a ε-optimal value at any belief b with any precision ε, i.e: $V^\Upsilon_{\text{UB}}(b) - V^\Gamma_{\text{LB}}(b) \leq \varepsilon$.

5   Numerical Illustrations

Some simulations of simple strategies for both players are presented in this section. We consider an Erdos-Reyni random graph with 50 nodes and a parameter 0.3 (probability to active each edge). Both players strategy is a fully random strategy without history. Meaning that the attacker chooses randomly a susceptible device from an infected device uniformly, and the defender chooses randomly the edges to allocate honeypots uniformly over the possible edges (edges that connect two not resistant nodes). A single node, chosen randomly, is infected at time-slot 1 and all the other nodes are susceptible. Examples of simulations are depicted on Fig. (4). Note that on Fig. (4b) we observe the impact of the probability to change the default password on the defender's utility and also on the extinction time of the virus. The number of honeypots h has also an important impact on these two performance measures. Other simulations run 100 times with $\rho = 0.1$, show that the average utility goes from 83.03 with a 99% confidence interval $[23.38 - 142.68]$ to 385.40 with a 99% confidence interval $[355.23 - 415.58]$, when h goes from 3 to 10.

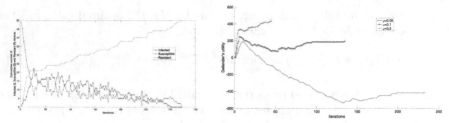

(a) Evolution of each state categories when $\rho = 0.1$.

(b) Impact of the reaction of devices to become resistant.

Fig. 4. Output of simulations with $\gamma = 0.99$, $h = 3$, $r_1 = 0.1$, $r_2 = 1$, $r_3 = 10$ and $\alpha = 0.5$.

6   Conclusions and Further Work

This work is related to possible transitions of node states in a network prone to malware attack. Each transition makes attacker loose what defender gains and may be probabilistic or caused by actions of both decision makers. This security problem is part of the large family of cyber security and the solution concept studied here is cyber deception. Particularly, we are interested in honeypots techniques which help to discover infected nodes into a network through observing cyber contamination. Our framework is much more complicated than traditional zero-sum OS-POSG model, because information about player's actions is not fully observable. Even in this complex system, we have been able to prove that the heuristic search value iteration can be applied in order to find lower and upper bound on the optimal value of the game.

This work is still in progress and implementation of the algorithms are on going. The epidemiological aspect of this model further makes intricate the non-scalability of algorithms designed for the general model. So we wish to outline efficient algorithm specially designed for this model.

References

1. Antonakakis, M., et al.: Understanding the mirai botnet. In: 26th USENIX Security Symposium (USENIX Security 17), pp. 1093–1110. USENIX Association, Vancouver (2017). https://www.usenix.org/conference/usenixsecurity17/technical-sessions/presentation/antonakakis
2. Colizza, V., Vespignani, A.: Invasion threshold in heterogeneous meta population networks. Phys. Rev. Lett. **99**, 148701 (2007)
3. Horák, K., Bošanský, B., Pěchouček, M.: Heuristic search value iteration for one-sided partially observable stochastic games. In: Proceedings of the 1st International Joint Conference on Artificial Intelligence, vol. 31, pp. 558–564 (2017). 978-1-57735-780-3
4. Kartir, D., Nayyar, A.: Stochastic zero-sum games with asymmetric information (2019)

5. Kim, J., Radhakrishnan, S., Dhall, S.K.: Measurement and analysis of worm propagation on internet network topology (2004)
6. Kiss, I.Z., Miller, J.C., Simon, P.L.: Mathematics of Epidemics on Networks. IAM, vol. 46. Springer, Cham (2017). https://doi.org/10.1007/978-3-319-50806-1
7. Tsemogne, O., Hayel, Y., Kamhoua, C., Degoue, G.: Epidemic model and partially observable stochastic games for cyber deception. draft full version (2020). https://drive.google.com/file/d/1k4Qs0d38cmYXfxV5YE6D1SJqDjqqukE6/ view?usp=sharing
8. Pawlick, J., Colbert, E., Zhu, Q.: A game-theoretic taxonomy and survey of defensive deception for cybersecurity and privacy. ACM Comput. Surv. **52**, 1–28 (2019)
9. Roy, S., Ellis, C., Shiva, S., Dasgupta, D., V. Shandilya, C.W.: A survey of game theory as applied to network security, pp. 1–10 (2010)
10. Smith, T., Simmons, R.: Heuristic search value iteration for pomdps. In: Proceedings of UAI (2012)
11. Wiggers, A., Oliehoek, F., Roijers, D.: Structure in the value function of zero-sum games of incomplete information (2015)

Combating Online Counterfeits: A Game-Theoretic Analysis of Cyber Supply Chain Ecosystem

Yuhan Zhao[✉] and Quanyan Zhu

New York University, Brooklyn, NY 11201, USA
{yhzhao,qz494}@nyu.edu

Abstract. Counterfeiting has been a pervasive threat to the security of supply chains. With the development of cyber technologies, traditional supply chains move their logistics to the cyberspace for better efficiency. However, counterfeiting threats still exist and may even cause worse consequences. It is imperative to find mitigating strategies to combat counterfeiting in the cyber supply chain. In this paper, we establish a games-in-games framework to capture the interactions of counterfeiting activities in the cyber supply chain. Specifically, the sellers in the cyber supply chain play a Stackelberg game with consumers, while sellers compete with each other by playing a Nash game. All sellers and consumers aim to maximize their utilities. We design algorithms to find the best response of all participants and analyze the equilibrium of the supply chain system. Finally, we use case studies to demonstrate the equilibrium behavior and propose effective anti-counterfeit strategies.

Keywords: Game theory · Cyber supply chain · Supply chain security · Games-in-games framework · Anti-counterfeit strategy

1 Introduction

A supply chain is a network that integrates business entities, information, and resources to produce and distribute a specific product to final consumers [2,13,15]. One of the significant threats to supply chain security is counterfeiting. Counterfeits can be roughly categorized into *deceptive* and *non-deceptive* counterfeits. Deceptive counterfeits can penetrate the licit supply chain in intermediate processes such as manufacturing and distribution, directly disrupting the market order and damaging the market regulations. Non-deceptive counterfeits, on the other hand, influence the market through the illicit supply chain, which opens a way for counterfeit trafficking. The non-deceptive counterfeits

This research is partially supported by award 2015-ST-061-CIRC01, U. S. Department of Homeland Security, awards ECCS-1847056, CNS-1544782, CNS-2027884, and SES-1541164 from National Science of Foundation (NSF), and grant W911NF-19-1-0041 from Army Research Office (ARO).

Q. Zhu et al. (Eds.): GameSec 2020, LNCS 12513, pp. 326–345, 2020.
https://doi.org/10.1007/978-3-030-64793-3_18

circulate to consumers via the illicit market and produce an indirect negative impact on the licit market by occupying the market share that belongs to the genuine goods. To summarize, counterfeiting can pose security threats to the supply chain both *explicitly* and *implicitly* by deceptive and non-deceptive counterfeits.

With the development of cyber technologies, many corporations have moved the operation of their supply chains to the cyberspace by developing online markets. Despite the merits of convenience and efficiency, such a paradigm shift does not address counterfeiting issues in the cyber supply chain. It can even exacerbate counterfeiting threats due to the new features of the cyber supply chain.

One notable feature of the cyber supply chains is its simplicity. While the traditional supply chain contains sophisticated intermediate processes such as inventory and transportation to ensure the completeness, the structure of the cyber supply chain is more straightforward. The postal services replace the distribution process, and the retail takes place online instead of in physical stores. Therefore, sellers and buyers can make direct contact through online markets. The lack of intermediate processes in the cyber supply chain makes it even harder for inspections. For example, the massive amount of packages in postal services challenge the authority to trace counterfeits. The inspection deficiency may result in more severe counterfeiting in supply chains.

Another feature of the cyber supply chain is its accessibility. Cyber technologies enable a large population to conveniently access the cyber supply chain, resulting in a large potential market scale. However, easy accessibility may worsen the counterfeiting issues. First, the identity of participants in the cyber supply chain can be anonymous. The anonymity and indifference facilitate the vending of counterfeits. Second, the illicit market scale becomes non-negligible. The traditional illicit market highly depends on geographical locations. Nevertheless, the advent of online markets and cyber supply chains break geographical location limitations. People can buy counterfeits online, which results in a significant expansion of the illicit market scale.

Due to these new features, counterfeiting in the cyber supply chain has created a series of losses in various industries [7,14]. Effective policies are imperative to reduce counterfeiting losses. However, some seemingly reasonable and direct strategies may not be sufficient and, at times, counter-productive. An example is the opioid supply chain [17]. The misuse of opioids has caused a growing number of overdose deaths, forcing medical and public health to reduce prescription opioids from 2010 to 2016. However, the reduced supply increased demand for illicit opioids and resulted in the prosperity of the opioid illicit market, especially the illicit online market, causing even more overdose deaths. The failure of such a seemingly reasonable policy is because of the lack of understanding of the ecosystem of the coexisting illicit and licit supply chains.

The concept of equilibrium from game theory can be used to understand the interaction and balanced behaviors of multiple players. Therefore, we propose a games-in-games framework to capture the features of the coexisting cyber supply chains and model the interaction of counterfeiting activities. The proposed framework enables a holistic understanding of how counterfeiting in the cyber supply chain works and the development of effective anti-counterfeit policies. In our model, we aggregate the large population of sellers and consumers into single players to focus on the population level interaction. To characterize the consumers' diversity, we adopt a random variable to represent the consumers' attitude towards the counterfeits. The sellers are abstracted into three individual players: one licit seller and two illicit sellers, who only sell deceptive and non-deceptive counterfeits, respectively. All of them seek to occupy the market share and maximize their utilities. The consumers decide which market to buy the product to maximize their utility. The interactions between the sellers and the consumers can be modeled by a Stackelberg game, and all the sellers' interactions can be represented by a Nash game. We integrate the Nash game and the Stackelberg game into a games-in-games framework. The proposed framework provides an approach for understanding the interactions of counterfeiting activities in the cyber supply chain. It also enables us to simultaneously capture the explicit and implicit impacts of counterfeiting on the cyber supply chain. Through the analysis, we discover the key factors that affect the equilibrium of the counterfeit ecosystem and propose effect population-level anti-counterfeit strategies to overcome counterfeiting in the cyber supply chain.

The contributions of this paper are summarized as follows:

(i) We identify the unique features of the cyber supply chain and propose a games-in-games framework to characterize counterfeiting activities in the cyber supply chains.

(ii) We formulate the counterfeiting problem as a game with piece-wise continuous utilities and develop computational algorithms for this class of games.

(iii) We analyze the impact of different factors on the equilibrium of the counterfeiting problem and propose effective anti-counterfeit strategies to suppress counterfeiting in the cyber supply chain.

1.1 Related Work

Counterfeiting has posed security threats to the supply chain infrastructure. Many recent works have focused on the modeling of the counterfeit supply chains to provide a fundamental understanding of the impact of counterfeiting. Li and Yi [12] have reviewed counterfeiting in supply chains, identifying the impact of counterfeiting, possible producers' reactions, and supply chain structure under counterfeiting issues. Works such as [1,8,11] have provided a general analysis of the counterfeiting in supply chains and their impact on the producers and consumers. Studies also examined possible anti-counterfeit methods to mitigate counterfeiting activities. Anti-counterfeit detection and mitigation strategies have been studied in [3,10]. In particular, Grossman et al. in [9] have categorized counterfeit products into deceptive and non-deceptive ones, and analyzed the impact of foreign non-deceptive counterfeits to the domestic welfare. They have also discussed the enforcement and confiscation policies to fight counterfeits. In the more recent work [18], Zhang et al. have analyzed the strategies to fight counterfeiting when there are one brand name product and a non-deceptive counterfeit in the market. The authors have also studied the fighting strategies equilibrium in the market with two competing brand name product and one counterfeit.

Game-theoretic approaches have been extensively used in supply chain studies to develop strategic solutions to combat counterfeits. The strategic pricing mechanism in the supply chain with counterfeiter and defective items have been studied in [4,16]. In particular, Cho et al. in [5] have studied the strategic deceptive and non-deceptive counterfeiters' behaviors in licit and illicit supply chain separately. The authors have also analyzed the impact of counterfeiting on the brand-name company and consumers' welfare, and have provided viable strategies to combat counterfeiting. In this work, we adopt a similar consumer model that views consumers as a continuum. The proposed game-theoretic framework focuses on the analysis of the ecosystem consisting of a licit supplier, an illicit online supplier, and consumers, and studies the outcomes of the games between licit and illicit suppliers who anticipate the consumer demands. We observe a phenomenon of oversupply in the market when the licit supplier competes with the illicit supplier in the markets. The analysis of the ecosystem leads to a design of mitigation strategies to mitigate the impact of the illicit products.

1.2 Organization of the Paper

The rest of the paper is organized as follows. Section 2 models all the participants in the licit and illicit supply chains. Section 3 formulates the counterfeiting problem using the games-in-games framework. We analyze the problem and present algorithms to find the best response of each player and the equilibrium solution in Sect. 4. Case studies are used in Sect. 5 to demonstrate the algorithms and the equilibrium solution. Several practical anti-counterfeit strategies based on the interaction model are also proposed. Section 6 concludes the paper.

2 Model of Cyber Supply Chain

We focus on the counterfeits of substitute products in the cyber supply chain. These products are more prone to counterfeiting, and the cyber supply chain related to these products suffers both explicit and implicit influence from counterfeiting simultaneously. Regarding the straightforward structure and accessibility features, we aggregate the massive participants in the cyber supply chain into four players, and abstract the interaction of counterfeiting activities in Fig. 1.

The licit seller S_1 manufactures and vends genuine goods with quantity q_1 to the licit market[1]. The illicit seller S_2 (S_3) fabricates deceptive (non-deceptive) counterfeits with quantity q_2 (q_3) and sells them to the licit (illicit) market. The notation in the paper is summarized in Table 1.

---

[1] We will use licit and illicit markets to refer to the licit and illicit online markets for simplicity. The same applies to the licit and illicit cyber supply chains.

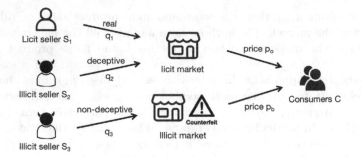

Fig. 1. Sketch of the interaction of counterfeiting activities. We use S_1, S_2, and S_3 to denote the licit seller and two illicit sellers, and C to denote consumers.

Table 1. Summary of notations.

q_i:	the production size of the seller S_i (units);
u_i:	the utility of the seller S_i (\$);
p_o, p_b:	the licit and illicit market sale price per unit (\$/unit);
D_o, D_b:	the licit and illicit market share (or demand) (units);
ϕ_g, ϕ_f:	the consumers' valuation for the real and fake product per unit (\$/unit);
u_c:	the consumers' utility (\$);
a_o, a_b:	the sale price elasticity in the licit and illicit market (\$/unit);
b_o, b_b:	the maximum price in the licit and illicit market (\$);
c_i:	the marginal cost for the seller S_i (\$/unit);
θ:	the type of each consumer;
k:	the scaling factor in consumers' valuation (\$/unit);
a:	the consumers' valuation elasticity;
α:	the weight of price-taking strategy in the illicit market;
η:	the portion of the non-vigilant consumers in the licit market;
γ:	the confiscation probability of the illicit seller in the licit market;
s:	the confiscation penalty of the illicit seller (\$)

2.1 Consumers' Model

Each consumer is characterized by her type θ, a random variable representing her interest in the real and fake product. Consumers with small θ care less about product authenticity because counterfeits may be acceptable substitutes for them. The consumer with $\theta = 0$ has the same interest in the real and fake products. As θ increases, the consumer cares more about product authenticity and gives less valuation to counterfeits. We assume that θ has a uniform distribution over $[0, 1]$, and that the total market scale is 1. A consumer's valuations on a genuine product ϕ_g and a counterfeit ϕ_f are

$$\phi_g = k \cdot 1, \quad \phi_f = k(1 - a\theta), \tag{1}$$

where $k > 0$ is the scaling factor, and $a > 0$ is the valuation elasticity. A consumer has three available actions to maximize her utility: going to the licit market (L), or going to the illicit market (I), or buying nothing (N), denoted as $\mathcal{A}_c = \{L, I, N\}$. When a consumer decides to buy nothing, her utility is trivially zero, $i.e.$, $u_{\theta n} = 0$. The utility for going to the illicit market is

$$u_{\theta b} = \phi_f - p_b. \tag{2}$$

We assume that some of the consumers who choose the licit market are vigilant and skeptical. They prefer to suspect the product is counterfeit. Let η denote the portion of the ordinary consumers, and hence $1 - \eta$ is the portion of the vigilant consumers. The average utility of a consumer for choosing the licit market is

$$u_{\theta o} = \eta\phi_g + (1 - \eta)\phi_f - p_o. \tag{3}$$

Let $a_\theta \in \mathcal{A}_c$ denote the consumer's action with type θ. The individual consumer's utility with type θ is

$$u_\theta = u_{\theta o}\mathbf{1}_{\{a_\theta = L\}} + u_{\theta b}\mathbf{1}_{\{a_\theta = I\}} + u_{\theta n}\mathbf{1}_{\{a_\theta = N\}}, \tag{4}$$

where $\mathbf{1}_{\{\bullet\}}$ is the indicator function. Since the population of all consumers is normalized to 1, and θ is uniformly distributed over $[0, 1]$, the net utility u_c of total consumers is the accumulative result of all u_θ:

$$u_c = \int_0^1 u_\theta d\theta, \tag{5}$$

which is independent of consumers' type θ.

2.2   Pricing Mechanisms in Licit and Illicit Market

The sale price is related to the amount of products in the market. We assume that the licit market's sale price has a linear relationship with the total amount of products in the licit market:

$$p_o = b_o - a_o(q_1 + q_2), \tag{6}$$

where b_o is the maximum price that may come from price controls, and a_o is the sale price elasticity. Illicit sellers may set the price for counterfeits based on their intentions. We assume that the illicit market's sale price comprises two terms:

$$p_b = \alpha p_o + (1 - \alpha)(b_b - a_b q_3). \tag{7}$$

The first term explains the price-taking strategy. The second term illustrates the price-setting strategy, in which illicit sellers have more control to set the price. We assume such control is linear in the production size q_3. b_b is the maximum price, and a_b is the price elasticity. $\alpha \in [0, 1]$ emphasizes the relative weight of two pricing strategies in the illicit market.

Since the market scale is 1, we can rescale the production size of each seller to the unit interval $[0, 1]$, as producing products more than one unit is not necessary. Therefore, the sale prices p_o and p_b vary in a range.

2.3   Sellers' Utility

Let D_o and D_b denote the licit and illicit market share, respectively. Note that D_o may contain deceptive counterfeits due to the counterfeit penetration. The real licit market share for the licit seller S_1 is $\frac{q_1}{q_1+q_2}D_o$. Likewise, the real licit market share for the illicit seller S_2 is $\frac{q_2}{q_1+q_2}D_o$. Thus, S_1's utility is given by

$$u_1 = \frac{q_1}{q_1 + q_2}D_o p_o - c_1 q_1. \tag{8}$$

S_2's utility is similar, but he will face confiscation risks in the licit market. Let γ denote the seizure probability from authorities and s denote the confiscation penalty, then the utility of the seller S_2 is

$$u_2 = (1 - \gamma)\frac{q_2}{q_1 + q_2}D_o p_o - c_2 q_2 - \gamma s. \tag{9}$$

Due to the virtuality of the online market, illicit trades are hard to detect. Even when the authority discovers several illicit trades, illicit sellers can quickly close their virtual trade portals and start a new one elsewhere. Therefore, we set the confiscation probability for illicit sellers in the illicit market as 0. The utility of the illicit seller S_3 is

$$u_3 = D_b p_b - c_3 q_3. \tag{10}$$

3   Problem Formulation and Game Structure

In this section, we propose a games-in-games framework to formulate the counterfeiting problem. The action space of the seller S_i is $\mathcal{A}_i = \{q_i \mid 0 \leq q_i \leq 1\}$ for $i = 1, 2, 3$. A Nash game can capture the competition among three sellers. Each seller seeks to maximize his utility by choosing the optimal production size. Also, all sellers play a Stackelberg game with consumers. All consumers form the follower to make the purchase decisions and maximize their utility. The games-in-games framework is presented in Fig. 2.

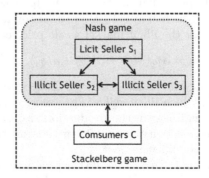

Fig. 2. The structure of the games-in-games framework.

3.1   Stackelberg Game

In the Stackelberg game, three sellers are the leader, and consumers are the follower. After observing the sale price p_o and p_b, every consumer decides her action to maximize her utility so that the consumers' net utility is maximized:

$$\mathcal{P}_c: \quad \max_{a_\theta \in \mathcal{A}_c} \int_0^1 u_\theta d\theta. \tag{11}$$

The leader's problem in the Stackelberg game is defined by another Nash game because three sellers compete with each other. The Stackelberg game can be represented by $\mathcal{G}_s := \{C, S_i, \mathcal{A}_c, \mathcal{A}_i, u_c, u_i\}$ for $i = 1, 2, 3$.

3.2   Nash Game

The interaction among thee sellers can be characterized as a Nash game, where each player aims to maximize his profit. We denote this strategic game by $\mathcal{G}_n := \{S_i, \mathcal{A}_i, u_i\}$, $i = 1, 2, 3$. The utility u_i, $i = 1, 2, 3$, are defined in (8)–(10). We denote the aggregated action space as $\mathcal{A} = \{(q_1, q_2, q_3) \mid 0 \le q_1, q_2, q_3 \le 1\}$. Therefore, $\mathcal{G}_n$ is a continuous game defined on the unit cube.

4   Analysis of Counterfeiting in Cyber Supply Chain

In this section, we present the equilibrium analysis of the counterfeiting problem. We first analyze the market share and derive its piecewise linear expression, which leads to a game with piecewise continuous utilities. Then we study algorithms to find the equilibrium solution by solving each seller's best response.

4.1   Market Share Analysis

The market share is a function of the solution to the consumers' problem (11). When solving for (11), we fix the production size q_1, q_2, q_3, and the sale price p_o, p_b. As u_c in (5) contains indicator functions, the consumers' problem (11) is equivalent to

$$\tilde{\mathcal{P}}_c: \quad \int_0^1 \max\{u_{\theta o}(\theta), u_{\theta b}(\theta), u_{\theta n}(\theta)\} d\theta, \tag{12}$$

The solution to (12) generates a series of critical points θ^*'s, which partitions the interval $[0, 1]$ into several subintervals. In each subinterval, $u_{\theta o}, u_{\theta b}$, or $u_{\theta n}$ is greater than the other two. Since the total market scale is 1, each subinterval length can be interpreted as the corresponding market share. Suppose that critical points yield an interval $[a, b]$ where $u_{\theta o}$ is greater than $u_{\theta b}$ and u_{θ_n}. This means that the licit market share $D_o = |b - a|$. Therefore, the market shares D_o and D_b refer to the subintervals where $u_{\theta o}$ and $u_{\theta b}$ is the largest element among $\{u_{\theta o}, u_{\theta b}, u_{\theta n}\}$, respectively.

Since $u_{\theta o}, u_{\theta b}$, and $u_{\theta n}$ are linear in θ, we can find the critical points θ_{on}, θ_{bn}, and θ_{ob} by solving three equations: $u_{\theta o} = u_{\theta n}$ gives $\theta_{on} = \frac{k - p_o}{ka(1 - \eta)}$; $u_{\theta b} = u_{\theta n}$

gives $\theta_{bn} = \frac{k-p_b}{ka}$; $u_{\theta o} = u_{\theta b}$ gives $\theta_{ob} = \frac{p_o-p_b}{\eta ka}$. These critical points form intervals that represent the market shares. Note that the market share can vary quite often due to the change of the production size q_i. We make two assumptions to simplify our analysis.

First, we assume that the illicit market sale price is always less than the licit market sale price, *i.e.*, $p_b \leq p_o$. There is no reason for a consumer to purchase a counterfeit if she knows it is more expensive than a genuine product.

Second, we assume that the illicit market is always attractive to some portion of the consumers, but it will never attract the entire consumer body to purchase counterfeits. The former part of the assumption indicates that the illicit market is preferable for the consumers with small θ (near 0). It can happen because the first assumption suggests that the counterfeit price is always less than the real goods. Mathematically, it means that $k - p_{b,\max} \geq 0$. The latter part of the assumption is natural as we never expect all consumers to go to the illicit market to buy counterfeits. Mathematically, it is equivalent to the critical point $\theta_{bn} < 1$, which is illustrated in the following proposition.

Proposition 1. *If $k - ka \leq p_{b,\min}$, then θ_{bn} is guaranteed to be within $[0, 1]$.*

With the assumptions above, there are three cases to discuss to find the market shares. Each case corresponds to a sub-region in the aggregated action space $\mathcal{A}$.

- Region I ($\mathcal{R}_1$), *the illicit market monopoly region*, where only the illicit market share is positive. We have $\theta_{on} \leq \theta_{bn}$; $D_o = 0$ and $D_b = \theta_{bn}$.
- Region II ($\mathcal{R}_2$), *the partial competition region*, where consumers have three actions to take. We have $\theta_{on} > \theta_{bn}$ and $\theta_{on} < 1$; $D_o = \theta_{on} - \theta_{ob}$ and $D_b = \theta_{ob}$.
- Region III ($\mathcal{R}_3$), *the pure competition region*, where consumers only have two available actions (I and L), because buying nothing yields the least utility. We have $\theta_{on} > \theta_{bn}$ and $\theta_{on} \geq 1$; $D_o = 1 - \theta_{ob}$ and $D_b = \theta_{ob}$.

Therefore, the aggregated action space $\mathcal{A}$ is partitioned into three sub-regions by $\theta_{on} = \theta_{bn}$ and $\theta_{on} = 1$. Let $q := \begin{bmatrix} q_1 & q_2 & q_3 \end{bmatrix}^T \in \mathbb{R}^3$. We write

$$\theta_{on} = \theta_{bn} \ \Rightarrow \ A_1 q + b_1 = 0, \quad \theta_{on} = 1 \ \Rightarrow \ A_2 q + b_2 = 0.$$

where $A_1 = \begin{bmatrix} -a_o(1 - \alpha(1 - \eta)) & -a_o(1 - \alpha(1 - \eta)) & (1 - \alpha)(1 - \eta)a_b \end{bmatrix}$ and $b_1 = -(\alpha(1 - \eta) - 1)b_o - (1 - \alpha)(1 - \eta)b_b - \eta k$; $A_2 = \begin{bmatrix} -a_o & -a_o & 0 \end{bmatrix}$ and $b_2 = b_o - k + (1 - \eta)ka$. Therefore, three sub-regions can be characterized as

$$\begin{aligned} \mathcal{R}_1 &= \{q \mid A_1 q + b_1 \geq 0, 0 \leq q \leq 1\}, \\ \mathcal{R}_2 &= \{q \mid A_1 q + b_1 \leq 0, A_2 q + b_2 \geq 0, 0 \leq q \leq 1\}, \\ \mathcal{R}_3 &= \{q \mid A_2 q + b_2 \leq 0, 0 \leq q \leq 1\}. \end{aligned} \tag{13}$$

Figure 3 shows an example of the partition of $\mathcal{A}$.

Remark 1. We denote $\mathcal{C}_{ij}$ as the plane that separates $\mathcal{R}_i$ and $\mathcal{R}_j$. $\mathcal{C}_{12} = \{q \mid A_1 q + b_1 = 0, 0 \leq q \leq 1\}$ is called the *profit plane* as $\mathcal{C}_{12}$ determines whether D_o is zero or not. $\mathcal{C}_{23} = \{q \mid A_2 q + b_2 = 0, 0 \leq q \leq 1\}$ is called the *growth rate switch plane* as the growth rate of D_o changes when crossing $\mathcal{C}_{23}$.

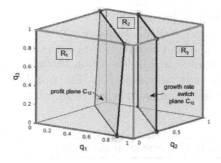

Fig. 3. Partition sketch of the aggregated action space $\mathcal{A}$.

Based on (13), we obtain the expression of the market shares D_o and D_b:

$$
D_o = \begin{cases} 0 & q \in \mathcal{R}_1 \\ \frac{k-p_o}{ka(1-\eta)} - \frac{p_o - p_b}{\eta ka} & q \in \mathcal{R}_2 \\ 1 - \frac{p_o - p_b}{\eta ka} & q \in \mathcal{R}_3 \end{cases}, \quad D_b = \begin{cases} \frac{k-p_b}{ka} & q \in \mathcal{R}_1 \\ \frac{p_o - p_b}{\eta ka} & q \in \mathcal{R}_2 \cup \mathcal{R}_3 \end{cases}, \quad (14)
$$

where p_o and p_b are defined in (6) and (7), respectively. Therefore, D_o and D_b are piecewise continuous, which results in piecewise continuous utility u_i, $i = 1, 2, 3$. The game $\mathcal{G}_n$ is a three-player Nash game with piecewise continuous utility functions.

4.2   Best Response Functions

The definition of seller S_i's best response is as follows.

Definition 1 (Best response). *For the seller S_i with action q_i, his best response is defined by $BR_i(q_{-i}) := \{v \in \mathcal{A}_i \mid u_i(v, q_{-i}) \geq u_i(w, q_{-i}) \; \forall w \in \mathcal{A}_i\}$, where $i \in \{1, 2, 3\}$ and $-i := \{1, 2, 3\} \setminus \{i\}$.*

Best Response of Seller S_3. Since D_b varies differently in $\mathcal{R}_1$ and $\mathcal{R}_2 \cup \mathcal{R}_3$ from (14), the utility u_3 has two distinct expressions in the corresponding regions. We first find the unconstrained maximizers of u_3 in $\mathcal{R}_1$ and $\mathcal{R}_2 \cup \mathcal{R}_3$, respectively, and then compute the best response of S_3 by comparing the utility values at the boundary points and at the unconstrained maximizers.

In $\mathcal{R}_1$, we have $u_3 = \frac{k-p_b}{ka}p_b - c_3 q_3$, which is quadratic and concave in q_3. The unconstrained maximizer in $\mathcal{R}_1$ is:

$$
q^*_{3,R1}(q_1, q_2) = \arg\max_{q_3} u_3 = \frac{b_b}{a_b} + \frac{\alpha p_o}{(1-\alpha)a_b} - \frac{k}{2(1-\alpha)a_b} - \frac{c_3 ka}{2(1-\alpha)^2 a_b^2}. \quad (15)
$$

Likewise, in $\mathcal{R}_2 \cup \mathcal{R}_3$, we have $u_3 = \frac{p_o - p_b}{\eta ka}p_b - c_3 q_3$. The unconstrained maximizer in this region is

$$
q^*_{3,R23}(q_1, q_2) = \frac{b_b}{a_b} + \frac{\alpha p_o}{(1-\alpha)a_b} - \frac{p_o}{2(1-\alpha)a_b} - \frac{c_3 \eta ka}{2(1-\alpha)^2 a_b^2}. \quad (16)
$$

Note that the given pair (q_1, q_2) affects which sub-region the seller S_3 will stay. For example, if $(q_1, q_2) = (0, 0)$, S_3 must stay in $\mathcal{R}_1$. If $(q_1, q_2) = (1, 1)$, S_3 can only stay in $\mathcal{R}_2 \cup \mathcal{R}_3$. Also, the separating plane $\mathcal{C}_{12}$ and the box constraints are also critical to determine which sub-region the seller S_3 is in. We propose Algorithm 1 to find the best response of S_3. For simplicity we write $u_3(q_3) := u_3(q_1, q_2, q_3)$ as (q_1, q_2) are parameters when computing best response.

Algorithm 1: Calculate the best response $BR_3(q_1, q_2)$ of the seller S_3.

---

input: q_1, q_2
$q_t \leftarrow (-b_1 - A_{1,1}q_1 - A_{1,2}q_2)/A_{1,3}$; // compute crossing point on $\mathcal{C}_{12}$
if $q_t \leq 0$ **then**
$\quad \mid \quad BR_3(q_1, q_2) \leftarrow \arg\max\{u_3(0), u_3(1), u_3(q^*_{3, R1})\}$; // S_3 is in $\mathcal{R}_1$
else if $q_t \geq 1$ **then**
$\quad \mid \quad BR_3(q_1, q_2) \leftarrow \arg\max\{u_3(0), u_3(1), u_3(q^*_{3, R23})\}$; // S_3 is in $\mathcal{R}_2 \cup \mathcal{R}_3$
else
$\quad \mid \quad \tilde{q}^*_{3, R1} \leftarrow \arg\max\{u_3(0), u_3(q_t), u_3(q^*_{3, R1})\}$; // maximizer in $\mathcal{R}_1$
$\quad \mid \quad \tilde{q}^*_{3, R23} \leftarrow \arg\max\{u_3(q_t), u_3(1), u_3(q^*_{3, R23})\}$; // maximizer in $\mathcal{R}_2 \cup \mathcal{R}_3$
$\quad \mid \quad BR_3(q_1, q_2) \leftarrow \arg\max\{u_3(\tilde{q}^*_{3, R1}), u_3(\tilde{q}^*_{3, R23})\}$
end

Note that $\arg\max\{\cdot\}$ is the argument of the maximum element. For example, if $f(a) > f(b)$, then $a = \arg\max\{f(a), f(b)\}$.

Best Response of Seller S_1. For the seller S_1, as D_o has distinct definitions in $\mathcal{R}_1, \mathcal{R}_2$ and $\mathcal{R}_3$, we have three different cases for the utility u_1. Since $D_o = 0$ in $\mathcal{R}_1$, the utility becomes $u_1 = -c_1 q_1$. Thus, the maximizer of u_1 in $\mathcal{R}_1$ is $q^*_{1, R1} = 0$. When entering $\mathcal{R}_2$, D_o becomes positive, and the utility is

$$u_1 = \frac{q_1}{q_1 + q_2} \left(\frac{k - p_o}{ka(1 - \eta)} - \frac{p_o - p_b}{\eta ka} \right) p_o - c_1 q_1.$$

To find the maximizer of u_1 in $\mathcal{R}_2$, we note that both the sale price p_o and the market share D_o are positive in $\mathcal{R}_2$. Although the concavity of u_1 is not guaranteed, the positivity of the two quantities allows us to use the gradient accent method to find the maximizer. We arrive at the following theorem.

Theorem 1 *Suppose $f(x)$ is a concave and quadratic function and let $g(x) = \frac{x}{x+a}$ where $a > 0$. Suppose that $f(x)$ is positive on $[b, c]$ where $b > 0$, then the maximizer of $f(x)g(x)$ on $[b, c]$ is either at the boundary or a stationary point that satisfies the first-order condition, and the maximizer is unique.*

Proof See Appendix A. □

From (6) and (14), we know that in $\mathcal{R}_2$ and $\mathcal{R}_3$, D_o and p_o are both positive and linear in q_1. D_o has a positive coefficient for q_1 while p_o has a negative one.

Algorithm 2: Calculate the best response $BR_1(q_2, q_3)$ of the seller S_1.

---

input: q_2, q_3

Compute crossing points for each sub-region ;

// $\mathcal{I}_1 = [0, a], \mathcal{I}_2 = [a, b], \mathcal{I}_3 = [b, 1]$

for $i \leftarrow 1$ **to** 3 **do**

$\quad$ $u_1 \leftarrow \lambda D_{o,i} p_o - c_1 q_1$; // $D_{o,i}$ refers to D_o in $\mathcal{R}_i$

$\quad$ **if** $i = 1$ **then**

$\quad\quad$ $\mid$ $q^*_{1,Ri} \leftarrow 0$

$\quad$ **else**

$\quad\quad$ $\mid$ Gradient ascent: $q^*_{1,Ri} \leftarrow \arg\max_{q_1 \in \mathcal{I}_i} u_1(q_1)$;

$\quad$ **end**

end

$BR_1(q_2, q_3) \leftarrow \arg\max\{u_1(q^*_{1,R1}), u_1(q^*_{1,R2}), u_1(q^*_{1,R3})\}$;

So $D_o p_o$ is positive, quadratic, and concave in q_1. Using Theorem 1, we can get the unique maximizer of u_1 in $\mathcal{R}_2$ and $\mathcal{R}_3$ using the gradient ascent method.

Figure 3 helps visualize how to compute the crossing points of each sub-region. When fixing (q_2, q_3) and varying q_1 from 0 to 1, S_1 will pass $\mathcal{R}_1$, $\mathcal{R}_2$ and $\mathcal{R}_3$ in turn, leaving two crossing points denoted as a and b. The crossing points generate three intervals $\mathcal{I}_1 = [0, a]$, $\mathcal{I}_2 = [a, b]$, and $\mathcal{I}_3 = [b, 1]$. $q_1 \in \mathcal{I}_i$ indicates that S_1 is in the sub-region $\mathcal{R}_i$, $i = 1, 2, 3$. Note that when q_2 is close to 0 (or 1), we have $b = 1$ (or $a = 0$), which means S_1 will not appear in $\mathcal{R}_3$ (or $\mathcal{R}_1$).

Best Response of Seller S_2. The seller S_2's utility u_2 has almost the same structure as u_1. Therefore, Algorithm 2 can be applied to find the best response of S_2 by substituting u_1 with u_2. The computation of crossing points of each sub-region for S_2 is also similar. We fix (q_1, q_3) and vary q_2 from 0 to 1, and then compute the crossing point a, b and the related intervals $\mathcal{I}_1, \mathcal{I}_2$, and $\mathcal{I}_3$.

4.3   Iterative Algorithm

The definition of the Nash equilibrium of three sellers is as follows.

Definition 2 (Nash equilibrium). *The Nash equilibrium solution to the game* $\mathcal{G}_n$ *is a set of strategies* $(q^*_1, q^*_2, q^*_3) \in \mathcal{A}$ *such that for all* $q_i \in \mathcal{A}_i$, $i \in \{1, 2, 3\}$,

$$u_i(q^*_i, q^*_{-i}) \geq u_i(q_i, q^*_{-i}).$$

The equilibrium of a Nash game can be found by the intersection of all players' best responses. We propose Algorithm 3 based on iterative methods to find the equilibrium of the game $\mathcal{G}_n$. The existence of the equilibrium can be demonstrated by simulations. A notable result in our problem is that the best response of the seller S_3 is a point-to-point mapping provided that some conditions are satisfied. We arrive at the following results.

Theorem 2 *The seller S_3 in the Nash game $\mathcal{G}_n$ has a point-to-point best response provided that the inequalities (17)–(18) hold:*

$$\frac{\eta k + (1-\eta)(1-\alpha)b_b}{1-\alpha(1-\eta)} \leq \frac{3-\eta}{2}k + \frac{(1-\eta)c_3 ka}{2(1-\alpha)a_b}, \tag{17}$$

$$\frac{\eta k + (1-\eta)(1-\alpha)(b_b - a_b)}{1-\alpha(1-\eta)} \geq \frac{2\eta k}{1+\eta} - \frac{\eta(1-\eta)c_3 ka}{(1+\eta)(1-\alpha)a_b}. \tag{18}$$

Besides, the best response is continuous.

Proof See Appendix B.   □

Numerical results corroborate that the best responses of the players S_1 and S_2 are point-to-point mappings under suitable parameters. The fixed point iterative method can be used to find the pure strategy equilibrium of the problem given an initial point $q_0 := (q_{1,0}, q_{2,0}, q_{3,0})$.

Algorithm 3: Iterative method to find Nash equilibrium.

---

input: $q_0 = (q_{1,0}, q_{2,0}, q_{3,0})$, ϵ, $k_{\max}$
$k \leftarrow 0$; // iteration counter
while $k < k_{\max}$ **do**

> /* we denote $br_k(q)$ as best responses of player S_i */
> $BR_k(q_k) \leftarrow [br_1(q_k) \quad br_2(q_k) \quad br_3(q_k)]^T$; // form aggregated best response
> $q_{k+1} \leftarrow BR_k(q_k)$;
> **if** $\|q_{k+1} - q_k\| \leq \epsilon$ **then**
> > | break ;
> **end**
> $q_k \leftarrow q_{k+1}$;
> $k \leftarrow k + 1$;

end
$q_{nash} \leftarrow q_{k+1}$.

---

5   Case Studies and Simulations

In this section, we use case studies to quantify the equilibrium strategy using the designed algorithms. Consider a licit and an illicit market characterized by $b_o = 10, a_o = 2$ and $b_b = 7.5, a_b = 1.5$. The parameter $\alpha = 0.6$ indicates the weight of the illicit seller's price-taking strategy. The consumers are parameterized by $a = \frac{1}{3}$ and $k = 9.5$. The production costs for three sellers are set to $c_1 = 4$ and $c_2 = c_3 = 2$. The cheap production cost differentiates the counterfeits with the genuine product and indicates the counterfeit's low quality. The confiscation probability and the penalty are $\gamma = 0.2$ and $s = 3$. The portion of non-vigilant consumers in the licit market is $\eta = 0.7$.

5.1   Best Response and Equilibrium Strategy

The best responses of S_1, S_2, and S_3 are presented in Fig. 4. The best response of S_3 is continuous, as proved before. Simulations also show that the other two players' best responses are point-to-point mappings. The equilibrium in this case is $(q_1, q_2, q_3) = (0.44, 0.82, 0.09)$. We notice that S_1's best response production increases with q_3 when there are few deceptive counterfeits. This shows that in the competition with S_3, S_1 can always keep a low sale price to attract more consumers from the illicit market. The best response of S_3 corroborates the claim. It decreases when q_1 increases (for large q_1), which indicates that non-deceptive counterfeits are no longer attractive to consumers as the licit market price goes down. This is common in the cyber supply chain because sellers' anonymity provides less useful information to products and makes consumers more price sensitive. However, deceptive counterfeits can significantly erode the licit market share and affect S_1's best production strategies. We see that S_1's best response decreases with q_2, and whatever the condition is, the best-response production of S_2 is large. This is because S_2 takes advantage of consumers' trust in the licit market and the low counterfeit production cost to steal the licit market share. The anonymity and the reduced structure in the cyber supply chain make the situation even worse, accounting for the considerable value of q_2 in the equilibrium. The fact indicates the deceptive counterfeits can pose more severe threats to the cyber supply chain security than non-deceptive counterfeits.

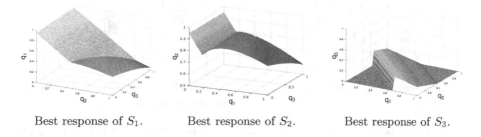

Best response of S_1.   Best response of S_2.   Best response of S_3.

Fig. 4. All sellers' best responses are continuous and point-to-point mappings.

Remark 2 We notice that the simulation shows the total production size ($q_1 + q_2 + q_3$) not equal to the total demand (1) at the equilibrium. This result can be viewed as the outcome of the competitive production planning process. The competition in production planning can lead to oversupply and thus the inefficiency of the equilibrium. The phenomenon of oversupply aligns with several observations made by works in management operations. Christensen in [6] has discussed the oversupply issues of rigid disk drivers due to competitions. The oversupply can also be interpreted by the asymmetric position of sellers and buyers. In economics, the perfect market equilibrium is characterized by the best response of sellers and buyers; *i.e.*, they are in the symmetric position.

The impact on each other eventually leads to the market equilibrium with supply equal to demand. In our framework, the consumers are the follower of a
Stackelberg game instead of a Nash game player. The sellers can anticipate
the consumers' demand, but the consumers follow the price determined by the
sellers' production decision-making. Three sellers plan their optimal production
volumes by mainly considering the competition among each other.

5.2 Discussion on Parameter Sensitivity

Some parameters are critical for the player's performance and the equilibrium.
We discuss and visualize their impact on the equilibrium using simulations.

Valuation Elasticity a. Consumers' tolerance on counterfeits is reflected by
a. The larger a is, the fewer consumers are willing to tolerate counterfeits,
leading to a decreasing profit and production size to the illicit sellers. We
let $a = 0.25, 0.3, 0.33$, respectively, leaving other parameters unchanged. The
equilibria when $a = 0.3$ and $a = 0.33$ are $(q_1, q_2, q_3) = (0.31, 0.85, 0.73)$ and
$(0.44, 0.82, 0.09)$, respectively. As a progresses, counterfeits become less attractive. The production volumes of S_1 and S_2 are suppressed as shown in Fig. 5.

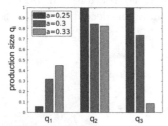 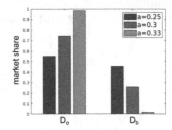

(a) Production size q_i in different valuation (b) Market shares D_o and D_b in different
elasticity a.   valuation elasticity a.

Fig. 5. Increasing a can diminish the production size of illicit sellers and the illicit
market share.

Weight of Price-Taking Strategy α. Large α means that the illicit seller is
more willing to follow the licit market sale price than set the price. As Fig. 6
indicates, large α corresponds to a small best-response production of S_3. S_3
gradually loses his price advantage as α increases. The consequence of large
α is that the licit and illicit markets have comparable sale prices. Consumers
naturally prefer the licit market when the prices are similar. Although there may
be deceptive counterfeits in the licit market, the average utility of purchasing in
the licit market can be higher than that in the illicit market, depending on the
consumers' belief η. This explains why S_3 loses the market share under large α.

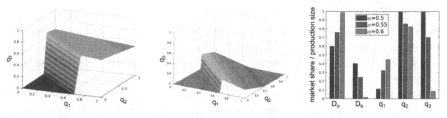

(a) Best response of S_3 when $\alpha = 0.55$.   (b) Best response of S_3 when $\alpha = 0.6$.   (c) Market shares and equilibrium under different α.

Fig. 6. Large α can effectively diminish the illicit seller S_3's production, and free more market share to the licit market.

Consumers' Belief in Licit Market η. We see that $\eta < 1$ tilts the profit plane $\mathcal{C}_{12}$, which amplifies the illicit market's impact on the licit market by reducing the consumers' average utility in the licit market. The licit market has to attract more consumers to maintain the same consumers' utility than $\eta = 1$. Also, increasing η helps reduce the size of $\mathcal{R}_1$ as Fig. 7 shows. Smaller $\mathcal{R}_1$ allows S_1 to establish a positive market share D_o more easily. As the total market share is fixed, larger η decreases illicit sellers' profit and crushes counterfeits production. The simulation corroborates the conclusion. The market equilibrium is $(q_1, q_2, q_3) = (0.05, 1.0, 1.0)$ when $\eta = 0.5$, which yields $D_o = 0.51$ and $D_b = 0.49$. When η increases to 0.7, the equilibrium becomes $(0.44, 0.82, 0.09)$, which gives a market share $D_o = 0.98$ and $D_b = 0.02$. Two illicit sellers' production capacities are reduced, and the illicit market share is also suppressed. The utility of the licit seller S_1 increases from $u_1 = 0$ to $u_1 = 0.8$.

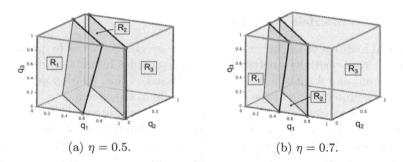

(a) $\eta = 0.5$.   (b) $\eta = 0.7$.

Fig. 7. The partition of the aggregated action space $\mathcal{A}$. Larger η yields smaller $\mathcal{R}_1$, which helps S_1 take positive market share more easily.

Confiscation Probability γ. We discuss the impact of γ because the penalty s is a constant term in S_2's utility. As Fig. 8 shows, a large γ reduces the illicit seller S_2's production size and profit. S_1's production size and profit are increasing with γ as expected. However, S_1 does not entirely absorb the market share freed by S_2.

S_3 also takes some of it, which is because of the *price advantage*: the illicit market sale price is less than the licit price, so counterfeits are always attractive to some portion of consumers. Notably, deceptive counterfeit penetration is more severe than expected. When $\gamma = 0.2$, the amount of deceptive counterfeits reaches $q_2 = 0.82$. Counterfeiting is rampant when the inspection is loose, and the deceptive counterfeit penetration scale is much larger than the non-deceptive counterfeit trafficking in the illicit market. This is particularly true in the cyber supply chain because the wide availability and online sellers' anonymity make inspections much difficult. Note that S_2's utility is negative when $\gamma = 0.4$. It means the confiscation risk is greater than the revenue of selling deceptive counterfeits, providing an effective anti-counterfeit strategy.

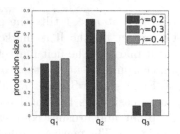

(a) Production size q_i under different γ.

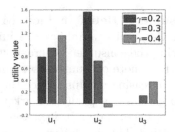

(b) Utility u_i under different γ.

Fig. 8. Large γ can restrain the illicit seller S_2's production and free more market share. However, the freed market share is taken by both sellers S_1 and S_3.

5.3   Anti-Counterfeit Strategies

The special features of the cyber supply chain are characterized by parameters. The parameter sensitivity analysis in Sect. 5.2 provides insights on how to suppress the profit and illicit sellers' production. Based on this, we propose strategies to mitigate counterfeiting in the cyber supply chain ecosystem.

First, the strategies that improve the consumers' faith in the licit market (increasing η) and reduce their tolerance on counterfeits (increasing a) can weaken counterfeiting problems in the cyber supply chain. Based on the cyber platform, actions such as third-party cyber insurance for products and digital authentications from the market organizer will help.

Second, the strategies that increase α can help diminish counterfeit production size. Large α indicates less power of illicit sellers in setting the illicit market sale price. One way to enlarge α is to attract more licit sellers to participate in the cyber supply chain. In this way, the illicit sellers' autonomy on price-making will be weakened, and they are forced to follow the licit market sale price. Optimizing the cyber supply chain process for licit sellers also contributes to improving α. For example, more efficient delivery and economical production processes can make genuine products more competitive, so that licit sellers seize more initiative in the price-making stage.

Third, improving confiscation probability γ can suppress the deceptive counterfeits. Deceptive counterfeits can jeopardize the licit market and licit supply chain by taking more market share and disrupting the market order. Although it is potentially hard to trace the deceptive counterfeits in the cyber supply chain, advanced techniques can be considered, such as using RFID chip nad QR code for verification, adopting blockchain technologies to track product life cycle.

6 Conclusion

In this work, we have investigated the equilibrium and anti-counterfeit strategies on counterfeiting activities in the cyber supply chain ecosystem by establishing a games-in-games framework. We first analyze the features of the cyber supply chain and use the game-theoretic approach to capture the interactions in counterfeiting activities. A Nash game and a Stackelberg game are then formulated to yield a games-in-games framework. The developed algorithms are used to calculate the best responses of the sellers and the market equilibrium. Case studies investigate different sellers' behaviors under different scenarios. Based on the analysis and numerical experiments, three anti-counterfeit strategies are proposed to restrain counterfeiting activities. The framework also opens a way to understand the complex interactions of counterfeiting in the cyber supply chain. Future work will explore the equilibrium in incomplete information scenarios. Information asymmetry may affect the market equilibrium, which is crucial to combat counterfeiting in the cyber supply chain ecosystem. Limited information will also impact the available anti-counterfeit strategies for both authorities and licit suppliers.

A Proof of Theorem 1

Let $f(x) = px^2 + qx + r$. The concavity of f indicates that $p < 0$, and let $h(x) = f(x)g(x)$. Then

$$h''(x) = 2pg(x) + f(x)\frac{-2a}{(x+a)^3} + \frac{2a}{(x+a)^2}(2px + q).$$

Note that $g(x)$ is concave and increasing on $[b, c]$. We discuss three possibilities.

- $f(x)$ is increasing on $[b, c]$, i.e., $-\frac{q}{2p} \geq c$. Since $f(x)$ and $g(x)$ are both increasing and positive on $[b, c]$, thus $x^* = \arg\max h(x) = c$.
- $f(x)$ is decreasing on $[b, c]$, i.e., $-\frac{q}{2p} \leq b$. We check the Hessian of $h(x)$. The first two term are clearly negative. As $f(x)$ is decreasing, we have $f'(x) = 2px + q < 0$ on $[b, c]$. Therefore, the Hessian $h''(x) < 0$ and $h(x)$ is concave on $[b, c]$. The maximizer of $h(x)$ can characterized by the first-order condition $h'(x_{foc}) = 0$. Thus x^* is the argument of $\max\{h(b), h(c), h(x_{foc})\}$.

– $f(x)$ is both increasing and decreasing on $[b, c]$, *i.e.*, $b < -\frac{q}{2p} < c$. We split $[b, c]$ into two subintervals $[b, -\frac{q}{2p}]$ and $(-\frac{q}{2p}, c]$. In the first interval, $h(x)$ is increasing. In the second interval, $h(x)$ is concave. Note that $h(x)$ is continuously differentiable on $[b, c]$, which means $h'(x)$ is continuous. Since

$$h'(-\frac{q}{2p}) = f(-\frac{q}{2p})g'(-\frac{q}{2p}) > 0,$$

$h'(x)$ is positive in a small neighborhood of $x = -\frac{q}{2p}$, which means $h(x)$ is still increasing in that small neighborhood. Therefore, we obtain that the maximizer is either $x = c$ or the point which satisfies the first-order condition, *i.e.*, x^* is the argument of $\max\{h(c), h(x_{foc})\}$.

Since $h'(x)$ is continuous and is nonzero constant on any subintervals of $[b, c]$, the uniqueness of the maximizer is guaranteed.

B   Proof of Theorem 2

From (14), The nonsmoothness of D_b occurs when q_3 crosses C_{12}. Let $\mathcal{I}_1$ and $\mathcal{I}_{23}$ denote the interval such that $D_b = \frac{k-p_b}{ka}$ when $q_3 \in \mathcal{I}_1$ and $D_b = \frac{p_o-p_b}{\eta ka}$ when $q_3 \in \mathcal{I}_{23}$. Note that $\mathcal{I}_1$ and $\mathcal{I}_{23}$ are parameterized by q_1 and q_2. We write $\mathcal{I}_{23} = [0, q_{3,s}]$ and $\mathcal{I}_1 = [q_{3,s}, 1]$. When $q_{3,s} = 0$ or 1, $\mathcal{I}_{23}$ or $\mathcal{I}_1$ is empty; when $q_{3,s} \in (0, 1)$, both $\mathcal{I}_1$ and $\mathcal{I}_{23}$ are nonempty. We call $q_{3,s}$ the *crossing point*.

When one of $\mathcal{I}_1$ and $\mathcal{I}_{23}$ is empty, D_b is smooth on the entire $[0, 1]$. As the utility function u_3 is concave, the maximizer is unique. When $\mathcal{I}_1$ and $\mathcal{I}_{23}$ are both nonempty, u_3 comprises two concave and quadratic functions $u_{3,1}, u_{3,23}$ on $\mathcal{I}_1$ and $\mathcal{I}_{23}$. Clearly, the concavity of u_3 is not guaranteed.

Let $\mathcal{W} = \{(q_1, q_2, q_3) \mid 0 \leq q_1, q_2 \leq 1, q_3 = 0\}$, and $\text{proj}_{\mathcal{W}} C_{12}$ be the projection of C_{12} onto $\mathcal{W}$. Note that if $\eta < 1$, the profit plane C_{12} is not parallel to the q_3 axis, and hence the projection forms a closed polytope: $\text{proj}_{\mathcal{W}} C_{12} = \{(q_1, q_2) \mid (q_1, q_2, q_3) \in C_{12}, \forall q_3 \in [0, 1]\}$. When $(q_1, q_2) \in \text{proj}_{\mathcal{W}} C_{12}$, $\mathcal{I}_1$ and $\mathcal{I}_{23}$ are both nonempty. When $(q_1, q_2) \notin \text{proj}_{\mathcal{W}} C_{12}$, either $\mathcal{I}_1$ or $\mathcal{I}_{23}$ is empty. Next, we let $q_{3,u}^*$ and $q_{3,u}^{**}$ be the unconstrained maximizers of $u_{3,1}$ and $u_{3,23}$, respectively. Let q_3^* be the maximizer of u_3 in $[0, 1]$. To guarantee the uniqueness of q_3^*, we set q_3^* as the crossing point $q_{3,s}$. The following inequalities must hold:

$$q_{3,u}^* \leq q_{3,s}, \quad q_{3,u}^{**} \geq q_{3,s} \quad \forall(q_1, q_2) \in \text{proj}_{\mathcal{W}} C_{12}$$

Further simplification tells for all $(q_1, q_2) \in \text{proj}_{\mathcal{W}} C_{12}$, we have

$$p_o \leq \frac{3-\eta}{2}k + \frac{(1-\eta)c_3 ka}{2(1-\alpha)a_b}, \quad p_o \geq \frac{2\eta k}{1+\eta} - \frac{\eta(1-\eta)c_3 ka}{(1+\eta)(1-\alpha)a_b}$$

Since $\text{proj}_{\mathcal{W}} C_{12}$ is closed, $p_{o,\min}$ and $p_{o,\max}$ exist. By taking these two values into the inequalities above, we obtain the inequalities (17)-(18).

To prove the continuity, it is clear that $\text{proj}_{\mathcal{W}} C_{12} \subset \mathcal{W}$. For the region $\{(q_1, q_2, q_3) \mid (q_1, q_2) \in \text{proj}_{\mathcal{W}} C_{12}, q_3 \in [0, 1]\}$, the best response is the crossing point $q_{3,s}$. All the crossing points form the plane C_{12}, which is continuous in (q_1, q_2). For the region $\{(q_1, q_2, q_3) \mid (q_1, q_2) \in \mathcal{W} \backslash \text{proj}_{\mathcal{W}} C_{12}, q_3 \in [0, 1]\}$, the best response is either 0 or 1 or the unconstrained minimizer calculated by (15) or (16). All of them are continuous in (q_1, q_2). This proves the continuity of the best response of the seller S_3.

References

1. Association, I.T., et al.: Addressing the sale of counterfeits on the internet (2013)
2. Beamon, B.M.: Supply chain design and analysis: models and methods. Int. J. Prod. Econ. **55**(3), 281–294 (1998)
3. Berman, B.: Strategies to detect and reduce counterfeiting activity. Bus. Horiz. **51**(3), 191–199 (2008)
4. Buratto, A., Grosset, L., Zaccour, G.: Strategic pricing and advertising in the presence of a counterfeiter. IMA J. Manage. Math. **27**(3), 397–418 (2016)
5. Cho, S.H., Fang, X., Tayur, S.: Combating strategic counterfeiters in licit and illicit supply chains. Manuf. Serv. Oper. Manage. **17**(3), 273–289 (2015)
6. Christensen, C.: Patterns in the evolution of product competition. Eur. Manage. J. **15**(2), 117–127 (1997)
7. deKieffer, D.E.: The internet and the globalization of counterfeit drugs. J. Pharm. Pract. **19**(3), 171–177 (2006)
8. Eser, Z., Kurtulmusoglu, B., Bicaksiz, A., Sumer, S.I.: Counterfeit supply chains. Procedia Econ. Finance **23**, 412–421 (2015)
9. Grossman, G.M., Shapiro, C.: Foreign counterfeiting of status goods. Q. J. Econ. **103**(1), 79–100 (1988)
10. Guin, U., Forte, D., Tehranipoor, M.: Anti-counterfeit techniques: from design to resign. In: 2013 14th International Workshop on Microprocessor Test and Verification, pp. 89–94. IEEE (2013)
11. Guin, U., Huang, K., DiMase, D., Carulli, J.M., Tehranipoor, M., Makris, Y.: Counterfeit integrated circuits: a rising threat in the global semiconductor supply chain. Proc. IEEE **102**(8), 1207–1228 (2014)
12. Li, F., Yi, Z.: Counterfeiting and piracy in supply chain management: theoretical studies. J. Bus. Ind. Mark. **32**(1), 98–108 (2017)
13. Min, H., Zhou, G.: Supply chain modeling: past, present and future. Comput. Ind. Eng. **43**(1–2), 231–249 (2002)
14. Radón, A.: Counterfeit luxury goods online: an investigation of consumer perceptions. Int. J. Mark. Stud. **4**(2), 74 (2012)
15. Shen, Z.: Integrated supply chain design models: a survey and future research directions. J. Ind. Manage. Optim. **3**(1), 1 (2007)
16. Taleizadeh, A.A., Noori-daryan, M., Tavakkoli-Moghaddam, R.: Pricing and ordering decisions in a supply chain with imperfect quality items and inspection under buyback of defective items. Int. J. Prod. Res. **53**(15), 4553–4582 (2015)
17. The Council of Economic Advisers: The role of opioid prices in the evolving opioid crisis (2019). https://www.whitehouse.gov/cea/research/. Accessed 10 Aug 2020
18. Zhang, J., Hong, L.J., Zhang, R.Q.: Fighting strategies in a market with counterfeits. Ann. Oper. Res. **192**(1), 49–66 (2012)

Theoretic Foundations of Security Games

On the Characterization of Saddle Point Equilibrium for Security Games with Additive Utility

Hamid Emadi[✉][iD] and Sourabh Bhattacharya[iD]

Iowa State University, Ames, IA 50011, USA
{emadi,sbhattac}@iastate.edu

Abstract. In this work, we investigate a security game between an attacker and a defender, originally proposed in [6]. As is well known, the combinatorial nature of security games leads to a large cost matrix. Therefore, computing the value and optimal strategy for the players becomes computationally expensive. In this work, we analyze a special class of zero-sum games in which the payoff matrix has a special structure which results from the *additive property* of the utility function. Based on variational principles, we present structural properties of optimal attacker as well as defender's strategy. We propose a linear-time algorithm to compute the value based on the structural properties, which is an improvement from our previous result in [6], especially in the context of large-scale zero-sum games.

Keywords: Security game · Zero-sum game · Nash equilibrium · Computational complexity

1 Introduction

Game theory [2] is a useful tool to model adversarial scenarios. *Security games* model attack scenarios wherein an attacker attacks a number of targets while the defender allocates its resources to protect them to minimize the impact. One of the main questions in the area of security is how to allocate resources efficiently due to the limited available resources for the defender. The payoff for the attacker and the defender is based on the successfully attacked and protected targets, respectively. Traditionally, due to the adversarial nature of the problem, attacker-defender games have been modeled as zero-sum games, and the resulting saddle-point strategies are assumed to be optimal for both players. In general, two-player zero-sum game can be formulated as an linear programming (LP) problem [2], and therefore saddle-point equilibrium can be computed in polynomial time. The most efficient running time of solver for a general LP problem is $\mathcal{O}(n^{2.055})$ [9]. However, solving security games with more than 2 resources for

This work was supported in part by NSF CPS grant ECCS 1739969.

© Springer Nature Switzerland AG 2020
Q. Zhu et al. (Eds.): GameSec 2020, LNCS 12513, pp. 349–364, 2020.
https://doi.org/10.1007/978-3-030-64793-3_19

attacker and defender with a general LP solver is computationally expensive due to the combinatorial nature of the problem.

In the past two decades, game theory has played an important role in quantifying and analyzing security in large-scale networked systems. Here, we mention some of these efforts across several applications. For example, a game theoretic framework is proposed for security of smart grids in [4,17,18,21]. In these models, players can distribute the limited budget over the entire set of nodes of the network, and consequently the combinatorial nature of the game is relaxed. Authors in [4] propose an evolutionary game framework that models integrity attacks and defenses in an Advanced Metering Infrastructure (AMI), modeled as a tree, in a smart grid. In [18], a game-theoretic defense strategy is developed to protect sensor nodes from attacks and to guarantee a high level of trustworthiness for sensed data. Authors in [5,8,10,16] and [22] consider the notion of information security in a networked system from game theoretic perspective. [10] introduces a method for resolving uncertainty in interdependent security scenarios in computer network and information security. In [22], authors examine security game in which each player collectively minimizes the cost of virus spread while assuring connectivity. In [5,8], authors propose a game-theoretic model for adaptive security policy and power consumption in the Internet of Things. In [16], authors introduce a game-theoretic framework for optimal stochastic message authentication, and they provide guarantees for resource-bounded systems. In [7], authors focus on notions of self-protection (e.g., patching system vulnerabilities) and self insurance (e.g., having good backups) rather than only security investments in information security games. In [11], authors propose a game theoretic framework for picking vs guessing attacks in the presence of preferences over the secret space, and they analyze the trade-off between usability and security. For a comprehensive survey of game-theoretic approaches in security and privacy in computer and communication, a reader could refer to [19].

Security games pose computational challenges in analysis and synthesis of optimal strategies due to exponential increase in the size of the strategy set for each player. A class of security games which renders tractable computational analysis is that of Stackelberg games [1]. In Stackelberg models, the leader moves first, and the follower observes the leader's strategy before acting. Efforts involving randomized strategies [12] and approximation algorithms [3] for Stackelberg game formulation of security games have been proposed to efficiently allocate multiple resources across multiple assets/targets. In order to extend the efficient computational techniques for simultaneous move games, efforts have been made to characterize conditions under which any Stackelberg strategy is also a NE strategy [15]. An extensive review of various efforts to characterize and reduce the computational complexity of Stackelberg games with application in security can be found in [6], and references therein. Here, we mention a few that are relevant to the problem under consideration. [13] shows that computing the optimal Stackelberg strategy in security resource allocation game, when attacker attacks one target, is NP-hard in general. However, when resources are homogeneous and cardinality of protection set is at most 2, polynomial-time algorithms have been proposed by the authors. [13] propose an LP formulation similar to Kiek-intveld's formulation, and presents a technique to compute the mixed strategies in polynomial time.

In [14], a security game between an attacker and a defender is modeled as a non-zero-sum game with multiple attacker resources. The authors analyze the scenario in which the payoff matrix has an *additive structure*. They propose an $\mathcal{O}(m^2)$ iterative algorithm for computing the mixed-strategy Nash Equilibrium where m is the size of the parameter set. Motivated from [14], in [6], we ana-lyzed a zero-sum security game with multiple resources for attacker and defender in which the payoff matrix has an additive structure. Based on combinatorial arguments, we presented structural properties of the saddle-point strategy of the attacker, and proposed an $\mathcal{O}(m^2)$ algorithm to compute the saddle-point equilibrium and the value of the game, and provided closed-form expressions for both. In this paper, we show that a zero-sum security game can be reduced to the problem of minimizing the sum of the k-largest functions over a polyhedral set which can be computed in linear time [20]. Based on this insight, we use a variational approach to propose an $\mathcal{O}(m)$ algorithm which is the best possible in terms of the complexity. Moreover, we present structural properties of the saddle-point strategy of both players, and an explicit expression for the value of the game.

The rest of the paper is organized as follows. In Sect. 2, we present the problem formulation. In Sect. 3, we present structural properties of the opti-mal attacker strategy. In Sect. 4, we present a linear time algorithm to compute the value of a large-scale zero-sum game. In Sect. 5, we present structural prop-erties of the defender's optimal strategy, and a dual algorithm to compute the value and equilibrium. In Sect. 6, we present our conclusions along with some future work.

2   Problem Formulation: Security Game

Consider a two-person zero-sum game, and let $\mathcal{I} = \{1, \ldots, m\}$ denote a set of targets. We assume an attacker (player 1) chooses k_a-targets to attack. So, there are $n_a = \binom{m}{k_a}$ actions for player 1. On the other hand, protection budget of targets is limited, and we assume that only k_d targets will be protected by the defender (player 2). So, there are $n_d = \binom{m}{k_d}$ actions for player 2. The defender has no knowledge about the targets chosen by player 1. In order to find the optimal strategy for the players, we formulate a strategic security game $(\mathcal{X}, \mathcal{Y}, A)$, where $\mathcal{X}$ and $\mathcal{Y}$ denote the action sets for attacker and defender, respectively, and $\operatorname{card}(\mathcal{X}) = n_a, \operatorname{card}(\mathcal{Y}) = n_d$. Every element $x_i \in \mathcal{X}$ represents a set of targets that are attacked. Similarly, $y_i \in \mathcal{Y}$ represents a protected targets. Each $x_i \in \mathcal{X}$ and $y_i \in \mathcal{Y}$ is a k_a-tuple, and k_d-tuple subset of $\mathcal{I}$, respectively.

The attacker has no information about the targets that are protected by the defender. Let ϕ_i denote the cost associated to target i. Moreover, without loss of generality, we assume that targets are labeled such that $\phi_i \geq \phi_j \geq 0$ for $i > j$.

We consider an additive property for the utility function i.e., entries of the cost matrix A are defined as follows:

$$A_{ij} = \sum_{\{l | l \in x_i \cap y_j^c\}} \phi_l. \tag{1}$$

A represents the game matrix or payoff matrix for player 1. Since we consider a zero-sum game, the payoff matrix for player 2 is $-A$. Note that we assume both players have the complete information of the target costs.

Let p, q be the probability vectors representing the mixed strategies for player 1 and player 2, respectively. The expected utility function is

$$v = p^T A q.$$

According to the minimax theorem, every finite two-person zero-sum game has a saddle point with the value, v^*, in mixed strategy $p^* = \begin{bmatrix} p_1^*, \ldots, p_{n_a}^* \end{bmatrix}^T$ for player 1, and mixed strategy $q^* = \begin{bmatrix} q_1^*, \ldots, q_{n_d}^* \end{bmatrix}^T$ for player 2, such that player 1's average gain is at least v^* no matter what player 2 does. And player 2's average loss is at most v^* regardless of player 1's strategy, that is

$$p^T A q^* \le p^{*T} A q^* \le p^{*T} A q.$$

In order to solve every finite matrix game, we can reduce the game to the following LP problem,

$$
\begin{aligned}
\underset{p}{\text{maximize}} \quad & v \\
\text{subject to} \quad & v \le \sum_{i=1}^{n_a} p_i A_{ij}, \quad j = 1, \ldots, n_d \\
& p_1 + \cdots + p_{n_a} = 1 \\
& p_i \ge 0 \quad \text{for} \quad i = 1, \ldots, n_a.
\end{aligned}
\tag{2}
$$

However, the dimension of the decision variables in the above formulation is $(n_a + 1)$ which is exponential in terms of m. In the next section, we present an equivalent LP formulation with dimension m to compute v^*.

3 Structural Properties of the Attacker's Strategy

In this section, we investigate the structural properties of the optimal attacker's strategy. The value of the game (v^*) can be defined as follows based on the attacker's mixed strategy p:

$$v^* = \max_{p} \min_{1 \le i \le n_d} (p^T A)_i,$$

where $(p^T A)_i$ denote the ith element of $p^T A$. From (1), $(p^T A)_i$ can be written in the following form,

$$(p^T A)_i = \sum_{j=1}^{n_a} p_j a_{ji} = \sum_{j=1}^{n_a} p_j \sum_{l \in x_j \cap y_i{}^c} \phi_l = \sum_{l \in y_i^c} \alpha_l \phi_l,$$

where,

$$\alpha_j = \sum_{\{i \mid j \in x_i\}} p_i \implies M_{[m,k_a]} p = \alpha, \tag{3}$$

where $\alpha = [\alpha_1, \ldots, \alpha_m]^T$, and $M_{[m,k_a]} \in \mathbb{R}^{m \times n_a}$ is a *combinatorial matrix*[1].

Since $M_{[m,k_a]}$ is a combinatorial matrix, $\sum_{i=1}^m \alpha_i = k_a$. Moreover, in the following lemma we show that for any feasible α there exists a feasible p. Hence, the problem reduces to computing α^*.

In the following, let e_i denote the unit vector of dimension m with i^{th} element equal to one, and $\nabla_\alpha v$ represents the gradient of v respect to α.

Lemma 1. $M_{[m,k_a]}$ *is a surjective mapping.*

Proof. Please refer to [6] for the proof. □

Based on the above lemma, the problem reduces to computing α^*.

Lemma 2. α^* *satisfies the following property:*

$$\alpha_i^* \phi_i \geq \alpha_j^* \phi_j \quad for \quad i > j \tag{4}$$

where α_j^* is defined in (3) for p^*.

Proof. Assume the following holds for α^*:

$$\alpha_{i_m}^* \phi_{i_m} \geq \cdots \geq \alpha_{i_1}^* \phi_{i_1}. \tag{5}$$

Note that v^* is $(m - k_d)$-sum of smallest $\alpha_l \phi_l$, that is $v^* = \sum_{l=i_1}^{i_{m-k_d}} \alpha_l^* \phi_l$. Assume that there exist i and j such that $\alpha_i^* \phi_i < \alpha_j^* \phi_j$ for $i > j$. $\phi_i \geq \phi_j \Rightarrow \alpha_j^* > \alpha_i^*$. $\alpha_i^* < 1, \alpha_j^* > 0 \Rightarrow (e_i - e_j)^T \nabla_\alpha v|_{v^*} \leq 0$. Since v^* is the maximum value of the $(m - k_d)$-sum of smallest $\alpha_l \phi_l$, we arrive at a contradiction. Therefore, $\alpha_i^* \phi_i \geq \alpha_j^* \phi_j$ for $i > j$. □

Corollary 1. α^* *and v^* satisfy the following property:*

(a) $v^* = \sum_{l=1}^{m-k_d} \alpha_l^* \phi_l$,
(b) $\alpha_m^* \phi_m = \cdots = \alpha_s^* \phi_s > \alpha_{s-1}^* \phi_{s-1} \geq \cdots \geq \alpha_{s-r}^* \phi_{s-r}$, $\alpha_{s-r-1}^* = \cdots = \alpha_1^* = 0$
   for $1 \leq s \leq \max(k_a, m - k_d)$ and $0 \leq r \leq s - 1$.

---

[1] A combinatorial matrix $M_{[m,k]} \in \mathbb{R}^{m \times \binom{m}{k}}$ is a boolean matrix containing all combinations of k 1's. Each column of M has k entries equal to 1 and rest of the entries equal to 0. In other words, M is a matrix constructed from $\binom{m}{k}$ combinations of k one in an m dimensional vector.

Proof. (a) Since v^* is $(m - k_d)$-sum of smallest $\alpha_l \phi_l$, This property can be concluded directly from Lemma 2.

(b) Let k denote $\max(k_a, m - k_d)$. First, we show that there is an optimal solution such that $\alpha_m^* \phi_m = \cdots = \alpha_k^* \phi_k$. We proceed the proof by contradiction. We assume that $\exists i \in \{k+1, \ldots, m\}$ such that $\alpha_i^* \phi_i > \alpha_{i-1}^* \phi_{i-1}$. Since $\sum_{l=1}^{m} \alpha_l = k_a$, there is $j \in \{1, \ldots k\}$ such that $\alpha_j^* < 1$. Therefore, $(e_j - e_i)^T \nabla_\alpha v|_{v^*} \leq 0$. Note that if $(e_i - e_j)^T \nabla_\alpha v|_{v^*} < 0$ is a contradiction with the fact that v^* is the optimal value, and if $(e_i - e_j)^T \nabla_\alpha v|_{v^*} = 0$ then it means there are multiple solutions which at least one satisfy the property. Moreover, from Lemma 2, if $\alpha_m^* \phi_m = \alpha_s^* \phi_s$ then $\alpha_m^* \phi_m = \cdots = \alpha_s^* \phi_s$, which completes the proof. □

Let s^*, r^* denote the indices for optimal structure expressed in Corollary 1. Let $\mathcal{U}_a$ and $\mathcal{U}_d$, called active sets of attacker and defender, denote the union of x_i's and y_i's corresponding to the support sets of p^* and q^*, respectively.

Corollary 2. *In a security game* $(\mathcal{X}, \mathcal{Y}, A)$, $\mathcal{U}_a = \{s^* - r^*, \ldots, m\}$. *When* $s^* > m - k_d$, *the defender has a pure strategy with* $\mathcal{U}_d = \{m - k_d + 1, \ldots, m\}$, *else* $\mathcal{U}_d = \{s^*, \ldots, m\}$ *(for* $s^* \leq m - k_d$).

Proof. The proof of first part directly follows from the fact that $\alpha_m, \ldots, \alpha_{s^* - r^*} > 0$ and $\alpha_{s^* - r^* - 1} = \cdots = \alpha_1 = 0$.

For second part, consider $(p^{*T} A)_j$. The following condition holds for $U_{i^*, i^* + r^*}$:

$$\alpha_m \phi_m = \cdots = \alpha_{s^*} \phi_{s^*} > \alpha_{s^* - 1} \phi_{s^* - 1} \geq \cdots \geq \alpha_{s^* - r^*} \phi_{s^* - r^*}$$

$$\alpha_{s^* - r^* - 1} = \cdots = \alpha_1 = 0.$$

When $k_a + k_d \leq m$, $(p^{*T} A)_j > v^*$ for all j such that $\{1, \ldots, s - 1\} \nsubseteq y_j^c$. Consequently,

$$q_j^* = 0 \quad \forall j \quad \text{s.t.} \quad \{1, \ldots, s - 1\} \nsubseteq y_j^c,$$

else $p^{*T} A q^* > v^*$, which is a contradiction. Therefore, any q_j^* corresponding to y_j such that $y_j \cap \{1, \ldots, s - 1\} \neq \emptyset$ is zero. In other words, $\mathcal{U}_d = \{s^*, \ldots, m\}$.

Based on similar arguments, we can conclude that $\mathcal{U}_d = \{s^*, \ldots, m\}$ for $k_a + k_d > m$ and $s^* \leq m - k_d$. When $k_a + k_d > m$ and $s^* > m - k_d$, $(p^{*T} A)_j > v^*$ for all j such that $\{s, \ldots, m\} \cap y_j^c \neq \emptyset$, and consequently $q_j^* = 0$. Therefore,

$$q_j^* = 0 \quad \forall j \quad \text{s.t.} \quad \{s, \ldots, m\} \nsubseteq y_j$$

Since the defender has k_d resources, it has a pure strategy to allocate it to targets $\{m - k_d + 1, \ldots, m\}$. □

Remark 1. According to Corollary 2, both players choose mixed strategies that involve targets with highest impacts (ϕ_i).

4 Computation of v^*

Based on Lemma 2, we can solve the following LP to compute v^*:

$$\underset{\alpha_1,\ldots,\alpha_m}{\text{maximize}} \quad \sum_{l=1}^{m-k_d} \alpha_l \phi_l$$

$$\text{subject to} \quad \alpha_i \phi_i \geq \alpha_j \phi_j \quad \text{for all} \quad i > j \tag{6}$$

$$\sum_{i=1}^{m} \alpha_i = k_a$$

$$\alpha_i \leq 1 \quad i = 1, \ldots, m.$$

Note that from Lemma 1, we show that for any α which satisfies the conditions in (6), there exists a p on a simplex such that $Mp = \alpha$, which satisfy the feasibility condition of (6).

From Corollary 1, v^* and α^* can be computed by examining all feasible solutions for $1 \leq s \leq k$ ($k = \max(k_a, m - k_d)$), and $0 \leq r \leq s - 1$ which satisfy the condition in Corollary 1 (b). Let U denote a square matrix of dimension k. The $(i, i+r)^{\text{th}}$ entry of U (denoted by $U_{i,i+r}$) is the solution to the following problem:

$$\underset{\alpha_1,\ldots,\alpha_m}{\text{maximize}} \quad \sum_{l=1}^{m-k_d} \alpha_l \phi_l$$

$$\text{subject to} \quad \alpha_m \phi_m = \cdots = \alpha_s \phi_s > \alpha_{s-1} \phi_{s-1} \geq \cdots \geq \alpha_{s-r} \phi_{s-r}$$

$$\alpha_{s-r-1} = \cdots = \alpha_1 = 0, \qquad s = k - i + 1$$

$$0 \leq \alpha_l \leq 1, \forall l \in \mathcal{I}.$$

The following theorem relates v^* to the elements of U.

Theorem 1. $v^* = \underset{i,j}{\max}\{U_{i,j}\}$, and the entries of U are as follows:

For $i \leq k_a + k_d - m$:

$$\begin{cases} U_{i,i} = 0, \\ U_{i,i+r} = \sum_{l=s-r}^{m-k_d} \phi_l \quad \text{when} \quad c_i \phi_s \geq k_a - r > c_i \phi_{s-1} \end{cases}$$

For $i > k_a + k_d - m$:

$$\begin{cases} U_{i,i} = \dfrac{k_a(i-k-k_d+m)}{c_i} \quad \text{when} \quad c_i \phi_s \geq k_a \\ U_{i,i+r} = \sum_{l=s-r}^{s-1} \phi_l + \dfrac{(k_a-r)(i-k-k_d+m)}{c_i}, \\ \qquad \text{when} \quad c_i \phi_{s-r} > (i-k-k_d+m), \quad \text{and} \quad c_i \phi_s \geq k_a - r > c_i \phi_{s-1}, \\ U_{i,i+r} = (k_a - r - c_{i-1}\phi_s)\phi_{s-r} + \sum_{l=s-r+1}^{s-1} \phi_l + (i-k-k_d+m)\phi_s \\ \qquad \text{when} \quad c_i \phi_{s-r} \leq (i-k-k_d+m) \quad \text{and} \quad c_i \phi_s \geq k_a - r > c_i \phi_s - 1 \\ U_{i,i+r} = 0 \quad \text{otherwise} \end{cases}$$

where $c_i = \sum_{j=s}^{m} \frac{1}{\phi_j}$.

Proof. First, we consider the case $s \leq m - k_d$. Let the optimal solution be $\alpha^* = (\alpha_1^*, \ldots, \alpha_m^*)$. Since $\alpha_i = \alpha_s(\phi_s/\phi_i)$ for $i \geq s$, $\delta\alpha_i = \delta\alpha_s(\phi_s/\phi_i)$ for any perturbation $\delta\alpha_s$. Since $\sum \alpha_i = k_a$, any allowable perturbation around α^* satisfies the following condition:

$$\sum_{j=1}^{m} \delta\alpha_j = 0 \implies \sum_{j=1}^{s-1} \delta\alpha_j + c_i\phi_s\delta\alpha_s = 0, \tag{7}$$

where $c_i = \sum_{j=s}^{m} \frac{1}{\phi_j}$. Consider a perturbation that involves perturbing α_l for $l < s$ and $\alpha_s, \ldots, \alpha_m$. From (7), we obtain the following:

$$\delta\alpha_l = -c_i\phi_s\delta\alpha_s \tag{8}$$

Based on the first order necessary conditions for maxima, we obtain the following:

$$\delta v|_{v^*} < 0 \implies \phi_l\delta\alpha_l + \sum_{j=s}^{m-k_d} \phi_s\delta\alpha_s = \phi_l\delta\alpha_l + \phi_s(m - k_d - s + 1)\delta\alpha_s < 0 \tag{9}$$

Let $g(\phi) = -c_i\phi + (m - k_d - s + 1)$. Substituting (8) in (9) leads to the condition $g(\phi_l)\delta\alpha_s < 0$. $g(\phi_l) > 0 \Rightarrow \delta\alpha_s < 0 \Rightarrow \forall j < s, \alpha_j^* = 1$. If for any $l < s$, $g(\phi_l) < 0 \Rightarrow \delta\alpha_s > 0 \Rightarrow \alpha_s^* = 1$.

As a result, we obtain the following conditions:

$$\begin{aligned} \alpha_j^* = 1 \quad &\text{if} \quad g(\phi_j) > 0 \\ \alpha_s^* = 1 \quad &\text{if} \quad \exists j \quad \text{such that} \quad \alpha_j g(\phi_j) < 0, \end{aligned} \tag{10}$$

From (10), we conclude that α^* and v^* can have the following forms:

1.

$$\alpha_j = \begin{cases} 0 & j = 1, \ldots, s - r - 1 \\ 1 & j = s - r, \ldots, s - 1 \\ \frac{k_a - r}{c_i\phi_j} & j = s, \ldots, m \end{cases} \tag{11}$$

From feasibility conditions in (6) (i.e. $\sum_{l=1}^{m} \alpha_l = k_a, \alpha_j \leq 1$ and $\alpha_s\phi_s > \alpha_{s-1}\phi_{s-1}$), we conclude that at $(i, i+r)^{th}$ entry of U, feasibility conditions are satisfied if $c_i\phi_s \geq k_a - r > c_i\phi_{s-1}$. Substituting (11) in $U_{i,i+r} = \sum_{j=1}^{m-k_d} \alpha_j\phi_j$ leads to the following expression for $U_{i,i+r}$:

$$U_{i,i+r} = \sum_{l=s-r}^{s-1} \phi_l + \frac{(k_a - r)(i - k - k_d + m)}{c_i} \tag{12}$$

2.

$$\alpha_j = \begin{cases} 0 & j = 1, \ldots, s - r - 1 \\ \delta & j = s - r \\ 1 & j = s - r + 1, \ldots, s \\ \frac{\phi_s}{\phi_j} & j = s + 1, \ldots, m, \end{cases} \tag{13}$$

where $\delta = (k_a - r - c_{i-1}\phi_s)$, which results from $\sum_{j=1}^{m} \alpha_j = k_a$. Since $0 < \delta \leq 1$, $0 < k_a - r - c_{i-1}\phi_s \leq 1$, which is equivalent to $c_i\phi_s \geq k_a - r > c_i\phi_s - 1$. Moreover, substituting (13) in $U_{i,i+r} = \sum_{l=1}^{m-k_d} \alpha_l \phi_l$ leads to the following expression for v:

$$U_{i,i+r} = \delta\phi_{s-r} + (i - k - k_d + m)\phi_s + \sum_{l=s-r+1}^{s-1} \phi_l. \tag{14}$$

3.

$$\alpha_m \phi_m = \cdots = \alpha_s \phi_s, \quad \alpha_s \neq 0, \quad \alpha_j = 0 \quad \text{for} \quad j \in \{1, \ldots, s-1\}$$

Substituting the above condition in $U_{i,i+r} = \sum_{l=1}^{m-k_d} \alpha_l \phi_l$, we obtain the following:

$$U_{i,i+r} = \sum_{l=s}^{m-k_d} \alpha_l \phi_l = (i - k - k_d + m)\alpha_j \phi_j \tag{15}$$

$$\implies \alpha_j = \frac{U_{i,i+r}}{(i - k - k_d + m)\phi_j}, \quad j \in \{s, \ldots, m\} \tag{16}$$

By substituting (16) into $U_{i,i+r} = \sum_{l=1}^{m-k_d} \alpha_l v_l$, we obtain the following:

$$\sum_{j=s}^{m} \frac{U_{i,i+r}}{(i - k - k_d + m)\phi_j} = k_a \implies U_{i,i+r} = \frac{k_a(i - k - k_d + m)}{\sum_{j=s}^{m} \frac{1}{\phi_j}} \tag{17}$$

Let $c_i = \sum_{j=s}^{m} \frac{1}{\phi_j}$. Next, we have to check whether α satisfies the feasibility conditions of (6). Substituting $U_{i,i+r}$ in (16) leads to the following:

$$\alpha_j = \begin{cases} \frac{k_a}{\phi_j c_i} & j \in \{s, \ldots, m\} \\ 0 & j \in \{1, \ldots, s-1\} \end{cases}$$

Finally, we consider the case when $k_a + k_d > m$. Since $U_{i,i+r} = \sum_{l=s-r}^{m-k_d} \alpha_l \phi_l$ and $\alpha_j = 0$ for $j = 1, \ldots, m - k_d$, for $i = 1, \ldots, k_a + k_d - m$, $U_{i,i} = 0$. Moreover, $U_{i,i+r}$ can be written as $U_{i,i+r} = \sum_{l=s-r}^{m-k_d} \alpha_l \phi_l$, and the feasible α's are given as follows:

$$\alpha_j = \begin{cases} 0 & j = 1, \ldots, s - r - 1 \\ 1 & j = s - r, \ldots, s - 1 \\ \frac{k_a - r}{c_i \phi_j} & j = s, \ldots, m \end{cases} \tag{18}$$

If $c_i\phi_s \geq k_a - r > c_i\phi_{s-1}$, then $(i, i+r)^{\text{th}}$ entry of U is feasible. For all $i > k_a + k_d - m$, the arguments are same as for the case $k_a \leq m - k_d$.

Since v^* is the maximum value which satisfies all feasibility conditions, v^* is the maximum entry of U. $\qquad\square$

Next, we show that U is a sparse matrix, which leads to a linear time algorithm for computing v^*. Let U^I and U^{II} be square matrices of dimension k defined as follows:

$$U^I_{i,i+r} = \begin{cases} U_{i,i+r} & c_i\phi_{s-r} > (i-k-k_d+m), c_i\phi_s \geq k_a - r > c_i\phi_{s-1}, \\ 0 & \text{otherwise} \end{cases} \quad (19)$$

$$U^{II}_{i,i+r} = \begin{cases} U_{i,i+r} & c_i\phi_{s-r} \leq (i-k-k_d+m), c_i\phi_s \geq k_a - r > c_i\phi_s - 1 \\ 0 & \text{otherwise} \end{cases} \quad (20)$$

Lemma 3. *Given an infeasible cell in U^I, either all the cells to the right (in the same row) or all the cells below (in the same column) are infeasible.*

Proof. Consider an infeasible cell $(i, i + r)$ in U^I. For a cell to be infeasible, at least one of the three inequalities in (19) needs to be violated.

(a) First, consider the case $c_i\phi_{s-1} \geq k_a - r \Rightarrow c_i\phi_{s-1} \geq k_a - r', \quad \forall r' \geq r$. In other words, if $c_i\phi_{s-1} \geq k_a - r$, there is no feasible solution in $(i, i + r')^{\text{th}}$ entry of U^I for all $r' \geq r$.

(b) Next, consider the case, $k_a - r > c_i\phi_s$. Since $c_{i+1}\phi_{s-1} = c_i\phi_{s-1} + 1$, $k_a - r + 1 > c_{i+1}\phi_{s-1} \Rightarrow (i+1, i+r)^{\text{th}}$ entry of U^I cannot be feasible. Since i is arbitrary, we can conclude that $(i+j, i+r)^{\text{th}}$ entry of U^I cannot be feasible for all $j \geq 1$.

(c) Finally, consider the case in which the inequality $c_i\phi_{s-r} > (i - k - k_d + m)$ is the only one that is violated at $(i, i+r)^{\text{th}}$ entry of U^I. Therefore, $c_i\phi_s \geq k_a - r > c_i\phi_{s-1} \Rightarrow k_a - r + 1 > c_{i+1}\phi_{s-1}$, and consequently, there is no feasible solution in $(i+j, i+r)^{\text{th}}$ entry of U^I for all $j \geq 1$. Therefore, any column of U^I contains at most one feasible (non-zero) entry.

Corollary 3. *At most one cell in a column of U^I is feasible.*

Proof. The proof follows directly Lemma 3(c).

Theorem 2. *v^*, α^* can be computed in $\mathcal{O}(k)$ time.*

Proof. From Lemma 3 and Corollary 3, we can conclude that from a current cell (i, j) in U^I, one needs to search either in cell $(i+1, j)$ or cell $(i, j+1)$ to find the next feasible element. Therefore, a linear search $(\mathcal{O}(k))$ that alternates between rows and columns leads to the cell containing the maximum element.

Next, we show that all feasible entries in U^{II} can be computed in $\mathcal{O}(k)$ time. For each row i, there is at most one r which satisfies $c_i\phi_s \geq k_a - r > c_i\phi_s - 1$ in (20). Therefore, for each row in U^{II}, we can find the feasible cell in constant time. This implies that all feasible entries in U^{II} can be computed in $\mathcal{O}(k)$ time, and a linear or a logarithmic search among the feasible entries provides the maximum element. □

Algorithm 1 gives v^*, α^* and active targets for the attacker and the defender in linear time.

Algorithm 1. Computation of the value, and active targets

1: **Input:** $\phi_1, \ldots, \phi_m$ and k_a, k_d
2: **Output:** $v^*, \alpha^*, \mathcal{U}_a, \mathcal{U}_d$
3: Construct U based on Theorem 1 and Theorem 2.
4: $i_1 \leftarrow 1$
5: **for** $j = 1 : m - k_d$ **do**
6:     **for** $i = i_1 : j$ **do**
7:         **if** $c_i \phi_s \geq k_a - r > c_i \phi_{s-1}$ **then**
8:             **if** $c_i \phi - s - r > i - k - k_d + m$ **then**
9:                 $U_{i,i+r} = \sum_{l=s-r}^{s-1} \phi_l + \frac{(k_a - r)i - k - k_d + m}{c_i},$
10:             **end if**
11:             $i_1 \leftarrow i$
12:             **return** i
13:         **else if** $k_a - r > c_i \phi_s$ **then**
14:             $i_1 \leftarrow i$
15:             **return** i
16:         **else**
17:             $U_{i,i+r} = 0$
18:             $i_1 \leftarrow i$
19:         **end if**
20:     **end for**
21: **end for**
22: **for** $i = 1 : k$ **do**
23:     find r such that $c_i \phi_s \geq k_a - r > c_i \phi_s - 1$
24:     **if** $c_i \phi_{s-r} \leq i - k - k_d + m$, and $c_i \phi_s \geq k_a - r > c_i \phi_s - 1$ **then**
25:         $U_{i,i+r} = (k_a - r - c_{i-1}\phi_s)\phi_{s-r} + \sum_{l=s-r+1}^{s-1} \phi_l + (i - k - k_d + m)\phi_s$
26:     **else**
27:         $U_{i,i+r} = 0$
28:     **end if**
29: **end for**
30: $v^* \leftarrow \max U_{i,j}$
31: $(i^*, j^*) \leftarrow \arg \max U_{i,j}$
32: $\mathcal{U}_a \leftarrow \{k - j^* + 1, \ldots, m\}$
33: $\mathcal{U}_d \leftarrow \{k - i^* + 1, \ldots, m\}$

5 Dual Analysis: Structural Properties of the Defender's Strategy and Algorithms

In this section, we present structural results for the optimal strategy of the defender, and present an $\mathcal{O}(m)$ algorithm to compute v^* and its corresponding optimal strategy. From the definition of v^*, we obtain the following:

$$v^* = \min_q \max_{1 \leq j \leq n_a} (Aq)_j.$$

where $(Aq)_j$ denote the jth element of Aq. From (1), $(Aq)_j$ can be written in the following form,

$$(Aq)_j = \sum_{i=1}^{n_d} q_i a_{ji} = \sum_{i=1}^{n_d} q_i \sum_{l \in x_j \cap y_i{}^c} \phi_l = \sum_{l \in x_j} \beta_l \phi_l,$$

where,

$$\beta_j = \sum_{\{i | j \in y_i{}^c\}} q_i \implies \beta = M_{[m, m-k_d]} q, \tag{21}$$

where $\beta = [\beta_1, \ldots, \beta_m]^T$, and $M_{[m,(m-k_d)]} \in \mathbb{R}^{m \times n_d}$ is a *combinatorial matrix*. Since $M_{[m, m-k_d]}$ is a combinatorial matrix, $\sum_{i=1}^{n_d} \beta_i = m - k_d$. Moreover, from Lemma 1, for any feasible β there exists a feasible q.

The following lemma provides the structure of β^*.

Lemma 4. β^* *satisfies one of the following conditions:*

(a) $\phi_{s-r} \geq \beta_s^* \phi_s = \cdots = \beta_m^* \phi_m \geq \phi_{s-r-1}$, *and* $\beta_1^* = \cdots = \beta_{s-1}^* = 1$,
(b) $\phi_{s-r} \geq \beta_s^* \phi_s = \cdots = \beta_m^* \phi_m = \phi_{s-r-1}$,
   and $\beta_{s-1}^* \phi_{s-1} \geq \beta_s^* \phi_s$, *and* $\beta_1^* = \cdots = \beta_{s-2}^* = 1$,
   where $1 \leq s \leq m$, $0 \leq r \leq s - 1$, $r + 1 \leq k_a \leq r + m - s$.

Proof. Let the sequence $\{i_1, \ldots, i_m\}$ of indices satisfy the following condition:

$$\beta_{i_1}^* \phi_{i_1} \geq \cdots \geq \beta_{i_m}^* \phi_{i_m} \tag{22}$$

Note that $v^* = \sum_{l=i_1}^{i_{k_a}} \beta_l^* \phi_l$.

First, we show that $\beta_{i_{k_a}}^* \phi_{i_{k_a}} = \beta_{i_{k_a+1}}^* \phi_{i_{k_a+1}}$. Assume 1) $\beta_{i_{k_a}}^* \phi_{i_{k_a}} > \beta_{i_{k_a+1}}^* \phi_{i_{k_a+1}}$ 2) there exists an $i \in \{i_{k_a}, \ldots, i_m\}$ such that $\beta_i^* < 1$. Since $(e_i - e_{i_{k_a}})^T \nabla_\beta v|_{v^*} < 0$ at v^*, we arrive at a contradiction. Now, assume $\beta_{i_{k_a+1}}^* = \cdots = \beta_{i_m}^* = 1$. Since $\sum_{l=1}^m \beta_l = m - k_d$ and $k_d \geq 1$, there exist $i, j \in \{i_1, \ldots, i_{k_a}\}, i > j$ such that $\beta_i^*, \beta_j^* < 1$. Therefore, $(e_j - e_i)^T \nabla_\beta v|_{v^*} < 0$, and we arrive at a contradiction. Therefore, $\beta_{i_{k_a}}^* \phi_{i_{k_a}} = \beta_{i_{k_a+1}}^* \phi_{i_{k_a+1}}$. In a similar manner, we can show that $\beta_m^* \phi_m = \beta_{i_{k_a}}^* \phi_{i_{k_a}}$.

Next, we prove that $\forall i$ such that $\beta_i^* \phi_i \neq \beta_m^* \phi_m$, there is at most one $\beta_j^* < 1$ and $\beta_j^* \phi_j > \beta_m^* \phi_m$, and the rest of β_i^*'s are 1. Assume that there are $\beta_j^* < 1, \beta_k^* < 1$ such that $\beta_j^* \phi_j \neq \beta_m^* \phi_m$ and $\beta_k^* \phi_k \neq \beta_m^* \phi_m$. If $\beta_k^* \phi_k, \beta_j^* \phi_j > \beta_m^* \phi_m$, and $j > k$, then $(e_k - e_j)^T \nabla_\beta v|_{v^*} < 0$, and we arrive at a contradiction. Now, assume that $\beta_j^* \phi_j < \beta_m^* \phi_m$, and $\beta_j^* < 1$, therefore $(e_j - e_i)^T \nabla_\beta v|_{v^*} < 0$ for all i such that $\beta_i^* \phi_i > \beta_j^* \phi_j$, which leads to a contradiction.

Next, we prove that β^* always satisfies one of the conditions in the Lemma. Let $\Gamma = \{i | \beta_i^* \phi_i = \beta_m^* \phi_m\}$. First, we prove that $\forall j \in \Gamma$ if $\beta_j^* < 1$ then $j + 1 \in \Gamma$. To begin with, we assume that $\beta_j^* < 1, \beta_j^* \phi_j = \beta_m^* \phi_m$ and $j + 1 \notin \Gamma$. If $\beta_{j+1}^* \phi_{j+1} > \beta_j^* \phi_j$, $(e_j - e_{j+1})^T \nabla_\beta v|_{v^*} < 0$, which leads to a contradiction. Moreover, if $\beta_{j+1}^* \phi_{j+1} < \beta_j^* \phi_j$ then $\beta_{j+1}^* < 1$ and $(e_{j+1} - e_i)^T \nabla_\beta v|_{v^*} < 0$ for all i such that $\beta_{j+1}^*\phi_{j+1} < \beta_i^*\phi_i$. This completes the proof for the first structure in the Lemma. Let $j = \min(\Gamma)$ and $\beta_{j*} = 1$. Therefore, for any $i \in \Gamma$, either $\beta_i^* < 1 \Rightarrow i+1 \in \Gamma$ or $\beta_i^* = 1, \phi_j = \phi_i$. The last condition leads to the second structure in the Lemma. □

Similar to the analysis for the attacker, from the above Lemma, we can compute v^* and β^* by examining all possible solutions which satisfy conditions (a) or (b) in Lemma 4. Let W be a square matrix of dimension m.

Theorem 3. $v^* = \min_{i,j}\{W_{i,j}\}$, where entries of W are defined as follows:

$$
\begin{cases}
W_{i,i+r} = \frac{(k_a-r)(i-k_d)}{c_i} + \sum_{l=s-r}^{s-1}\phi_l, \\
\quad for \quad s-1 \geq r \geq 0, r+m-s \geq k_a \geq r+1, c_i\phi_{s-r} \geq i-k_d \geq c_i\phi_{s-r-1}, \\
W_{i,i+r} = (i-k_d+1-c_i\phi_{s-r-1})\phi_{s-1} + (k_a-r)\phi_{s-r-1} + \sum_{l=s-r}^{s-2}\phi_l, \\
\quad for \quad s-1 \geq r \geq 0, r+m-s \geq k_a \geq r+1, \\
\quad c_i\phi_{s-r-1}+1 > i-k_d+1 \geq c_{i+1}\phi_{s-r-1} \\
W_{i,i+r} = +\infty, \quad otherwise
\end{cases}
$$

where, $c_i = \sum_{j=s}^m \frac{1}{\phi_j}$.

Proof. First case corresponds to the structure (a) in Lemma 4. In this case, $\beta_1 = \cdots = \beta_{s-1} = 1$. Since $\sum_{l=1}^m \beta_l = m - k_d$, and $\beta_s\phi_s = \cdots = \beta_m\phi_m$, we obtain the following expression for β_j

$$
\beta_j = \frac{i-k_d}{c_i\phi_j}, \quad j = s,\ldots,m, \tag{23}
$$

where $i = m-s+1$ and $c_i = \sum_{j=s}^m \frac{1}{\phi_j}$. Next, we provide the feasibility conditions for structure (a). Since $0 \leq \beta_j \leq 1$, $c_i\phi_s \geq i-k_d$. Moreover, $\phi_{s-r} \geq \beta_s\phi_s \Rightarrow c_i\phi_{s-r} \geq i-k_d$. Additionally, $\beta_s\phi_s \geq \phi_{s-r-1} \Rightarrow i-k_d \geq c_i\phi_{s-r-1}$. Note that k_a-largest terms of $\beta_l\phi_l$ contain at least one term in the set $\{\beta_s\phi_s,\ldots,\beta_m\phi_m\}$. Therefore, $r+m-s \geq k_a \geq r+1$. By substituting (23) into $W_{i,i+r} = \sum_{l=i_1}^{i_{k_a}}\beta_l\phi_l$,

$$
W_{i,i+r} = \frac{(k_a-r)(i-k_d)}{c_i} + \sum_{l=s-r}^{s-1}\phi_l. \tag{24}
$$

The second case corresponds to the structure (b) in Lemma 4. In this case, $\beta_1 = \cdots = \beta_{s-2} = 1$. Since $\sum_{l=1}^m \beta_l = m-k_d$ and $\beta_s\phi_s = \cdots = \beta_m\phi_m = \phi_{s-r-1}$, we obtain the following:

$$
\beta_j = \frac{\phi_{s-r-1}}{\phi_j}, \quad j = s,\ldots,m, \tag{25}
$$

$$
\beta_{s-1} = i-k_d+1-c_i\phi_{s-r-1}, \tag{26}
$$

where $i = m-s+1$ and $c_i = \sum_{j=s}^m \frac{1}{\phi_j}$. Next, we provide the feasibility conditions for structure (b). Since $\beta_{s-1}\phi_{s-1} \geq \phi_{s-r-1}$, and $0 \leq \beta_{s-1} < 1$, $c_i\phi_{s-r-1}+1 >$

$i - k_d + 1 \geq c_{i+1}\phi_{s-r-1}$. Note that k_a-largest terms of $\beta_l\phi_l$ contain at least one term in the set $\{\beta_s\phi_s, \ldots, \beta_m\phi_m\}$. Therefore, $r + m - s \geq k_a \geq r + 1$. By substituting (25), (26) into $W_{i,i+r} = \sum_{l=i_1}^{i_{k_a}} \beta_l\phi_l$,

$$W_{i,i+r} = (i - k_d + 1 - c_i\phi_{s-r-1})\phi_{s-1} + (k_a - r)\phi_{s-r-1} + \sum_{l=s-r}^{s-2} \phi_l. \quad (27)$$

□

Since W is a square matrix of dimension m, v^* can be computed in $\mathcal{O}(m^2)$. As in the case of the defender, we can show that W can be computed in $\mathcal{O}(m)$ due to sparsity of W (the feasibility conditions).

Theorem 4. v^* *can be computed in* $\mathcal{O}(m)$.

Proof. Let W^a and W^b denote matrices of the following form:

$$W^a_{i,i+r} = \begin{cases} W_{i,i+r} & \text{satisfying structure (a) in Lemma 4} \\ 0 & \text{otherwise} \end{cases}, \quad (28)$$

$$W^b_{i,i+r} = \begin{cases} W_{i,i+r} & \text{satisfying structure (b) in Lemma 4} \\ 0 & \text{otherwise} \end{cases}. \quad (29)$$

First, note that all feasible entries of W^a and feasible entries of W^b are disjoint due to complimentary feasibility conditions ($i - k_d \geq c_i\phi_{s-r-1}$ in W^a, and $i - k_d < c_i\phi_{s-r-1}$ in W^b). Moreover, since $c_i\phi_{s-r} \geq i - k_d \geq c_i\phi_{s-r-1}$, for any s there is at most one specific r which satisfies conditions of W^a. This implies that computation of all feasible entries of W^a is in $\mathcal{O}(m)$. Therefore, any row of W has at most one feasible entry of W^a.

Next, we show that computing all feasible entries of W^b is in $\mathcal{O}(m)$. From the second structure of Lemma 4, for any $\hat{s}, \hat{r}$ and $\hat{i} = m - \hat{s} + 1$, if $\beta_{\hat{s}-1} > 1$ ($\beta_{\hat{s}-1} < 0$), $(i, \hat{i} + r)^{\text{th}}$ entry of W is infeasible for all $i > \hat{i}, r > \hat{r}$ ($i < \hat{i}, r < \hat{r}$) since it implies $\beta_{s-1} > 1$ ($\beta_{s-1} < 0$). Therefore, at every entry of W, β_{s-1} provides a criteria for which the rest of entries, in the same row and in the same column are entirely infeasible, and consequently it is not required to check the feasibility of those entries. In other words, value of β_{s-1} provides a criteria for direction of searching for feasible entries of W^b. Thus, computing feasible entries of W^b is in $\mathcal{O}(m)$. □

6   Conclusion

In this work, we address a security game as a zero-sum game in which the utility function has additive property. We analyzed the problem from attacker and defender's perspective, and we provided necessary conditions for the optimal solutions. Consequently, the structural properties of the saddle-point strategy for both players are given. Using the structural properties, we reach to the linear time algorithm, and semi-closed form solutions for computing the saddle points and value of the game.

There are several directions of future research. One direction is to use the proposed structural properties to formulate a network design problem to minimize the impact of attacks, which leads to design of resilient networks from security perspective. Another direction of future research is to generalize the results of this work to nonzero-sum games with different utility functions for attacker and defender. Finally, we plan to extend our analysis to security games with non-additive utility functions.

References

1. Başar, T.: On the relative leadership property of stackelberg strategies. J. Optim. Theory Appl. **11**(6), 655–661 (1973)
2. Başar, T., Olsder, G.J.: Dynamic noncooperative game theory, vol. 23. Siam (1999)
3. Bhattacharya, S., Conitzer, V., Munagala, K.: Approximation algorithm for security games with costly resources. In: Chen, N., Elkind, E., Koutsoupias, E. (eds.) WINE 2011. LNCS, vol. 7090, pp. 13–24. Springer, Heidelberg (2011). https://doi.org/10.1007/978-3-642-25510-6_2
4. Boudko, S., Abie, H.: An evolutionary game for integrity attacks and defences for advanced metering infrastructure. In: Proceedings of the 12th European Conference on Software Architecture: Companion Proceedings, pp. 1–7 (2018)
5. Boudko, S., Abie, H.: Adaptive cybersecurity framework for healthcare internet of things. In: 2019 13th International Symposium on Medical Information and Communication Technology (ISMICT), pp. 1–6. IEEE (2019)
6. Emadi, H., Bhattacharya, S.: On security games with additive utility. IFAC-PapersOnLine **52**(20), 351–356 (2019)
7. Grossklags, J., Christin, N., Chuang, J.: Secure or insure? A game-theoretic analysis of information security games. In: Proceedings of the 17th international conference on World Wide Web, pp. 209–218 (2008)
8. Hamdi, M., Abie, H.: Game-based adaptive security in the internet of things for ehealth. In: 2014 IEEE International Conference on Communications (ICC), pp. 920–925. IEEE (2014)
9. Jiang, S., Song, Z., Weinstein, O., Zhang, H.: Faster dynamic matrix inverse for faster LPs. arXiv preprint arXiv:2004.07470 (2020)
10. Johnson, B., Grossklags, J., Christin, N., Chuang, J.: Uncertainty in interdependent security games. In: Alpcan, T., Buttyán, L., Baras, J.S. (eds.) GameSec 2010. LNCS, vol. 6442, pp. 234–244. Springer, Heidelberg (2010). https://doi.org/10.1007/978-3-642-17197-0_16
11. Khouzani, M., Mardziel, P., Cid, C., Srivatsa, M.: Picking vs. guessing secrets: a game-theoretic analysis. In: 2015 IEEE 28th Computer Security Foundations Symposium, pp. 243–257. IEEE (2015)
12. Kiekintveld, C., Jain, M., Tsai, J., Pita, J., Ordóñez, F., Tambe, M.: Computing optimal randomized resource allocations for massive security games. In: Proceedings of The 8th International Conference on Autonomous Agents and Multiagent Systems-Volume 1, pp. 689–696. International Foundation for Autonomous Agents and Multiagent Systems (2009)

13. Korzhyk, D., Conitzer, V., Parr, R.: Complexity of computing optimal stackelberg strategies in security resource allocation games. In: Twenty-Fourth AAAI Conference on Artificial Intelligence (2010)
14. Korzhyk, D., Conitzer, V., Parr, R.: Security games with multiple attacker resources. In: Twenty-Second International Joint Conference on Artificial Intelligence (2011)
15. Korzhyk, D., Yin, Z., Kiekintveld, C., Conitzer, V., Tambe, M.: Stackelberg vs. nash in security games: an extended investigation of interchangeability, equivalence, and uniqueness. J. Artif. Intell. Res. **41**, 297–327 (2011)
16. Laszka, A., Vorobeychik, Y., Koutsoukos, X.: A game-theoretic approach for integrity assurance in resource-bounded systems. Int. J. Inf. Secur. **17**(2), 221–242 (2017). https://doi.org/10.1007/s10207-017-0364-2
17. Law, Y.W., Alpcan, T., Palaniswami, M.: Security games for risk minimization in automatic generation control. IEEE Trans. Power Syst. **30**(1), 223–232 (2014)
18. Lim, H.S., Ghinita, G., Bertino, E., Kantarcioglu, M.: A game-theoretic approach for high-assurance of data trustworthiness in sensor networks. In: 2012 IEEE 28th International Conference on Data Engineering, pp. 1192–1203. IEEE (2012)
19. Manshaei, M.H., Zhu, Q., Alpcan, T., Başar, T., Hubaux, J.P.: Game theory meets network security and privacy. ACM Comput. Surv. (CSUR) **45**(3), 25 (2013)
20. Ogryczak, W., Tamir, A.: Minimizing the sum of the k largest functions in linear time. Inf. Process. Lett. **85**(3), 117–122 (2003)
21. Shan, X.G., Zhuang, J.: A game-theoretic approach to modeling attacks and defenses of smart grids at three levels. Reliab. Eng. Syst. Saf. **195**, 106683 (2020)
22. Trajanovski, S., Kuipers, F.A., Hayel, Y., Altman, E., Van Mieghem, P.: Designing virus-resistant networks: a game-formation approach. In: 2015 54th IEEE Conference on Decision and Control (CDC), pp. 294–299. IEEE (2015)

MASAGE: Model-Agnostic Sequential and Adaptive Game Estimation

Yunian Pan[1]([✉]) [iD], Guanze Peng[1] [iD], Juntao Chen[2] [iD], and Quanyan Zhu[1] [iD]

[1] New York University, Brooklyn, NY, USA
{yp1170,gp1363,qz494}@nyu.edu
[2] Fordham University, The Bronx, NY, USA
jchen504@forham.edu

Abstract. Zero-sum games have been used to model cybersecurity scenarios between an attacker and a defender. However, unknown and uncertain environments have made it difficult to rely on a prescribed zero-sum game to capture the interactions between the players. In this work, we aim to estimate and recover an unknown matrix game that encodes the uncertainties of nature and opponent based on the knowledge of historical games and the current observations of game outcomes. The proposed approach effectively transfers the past experiences that are encoded as expert games to estimate and inform future game plays. We formulate the game knowledge transfer and estimation problem as a sequential least-square problem. We characterize the structural properties of the problem and show that the non-convex problem has well-behaved gradient and Hessian under mild assumptions. We propose gradient-based methods to enable dynamic and adaptive estimation of the unknown game. A case study is used to corroborate the results and illustrate the behavior of the proposed algorithm.

Keywords: Zero-sum games · Security games · Neural networks · Least-square estimation · Sensitivity analysis · Gradient-based methods

1 Introduction

In many adversarial scenarios, such as a battlefield and cyber threats, a defender plays against unknown opponents in uncertain environments. The prior knowledge or experience of the game may provide the defender a way to estimate the game by leveraging his past experience with the environment, or transfering other experiences of his own or from someone else. These experiences are encoded or represented by games that capture critical characteristics of an adversarial entity, including the incentives, the capabilities, and the information structures. The direct estimation of the game provides the defender a sufficient situational awareness of the unknown environment and enables dependable reasoning for making decisions.

This research is partially supported by awards ECCS-1847056, CNS-1544782, CNS-2027884, and SES-1541164 from National Science of Foundation (NSF), and grant W911NF-19-1-0041 from Army Research Office (ARO).

© Springer Nature Switzerland AG 2020
Q. Zhu et al. (Eds.): GameSec 2020, LNCS 12513, pp. 365–384, 2020.
https://doi.org/10.1007/978-3-030-64793-3_20

Dealing with uncertainties in games has a long history. Harsanyi in 1967 [9] introduced Bayesian games and the notion of "type", encapsulating all uncertainties in payoffs, actions, and psychological attributes of a player into the "type" space to overcome the technical difficulty created by the reasoning using infinite hierarchies of beliefs [15]. Built on Harsanyi's Bayesian game framework, many recent efforts have been on identifying and estimating structures of the game model, given the data of multiple equilibria [12, 23] or the observed frequency of choices [10, 19].

The estimation of games within Bayesian frameworks often requires the structural knowledge of baseline game models. However, in many security applications, this knowledge may not be directly available. It is difficult, if not impossible, to specify the set of uncertain parameters and the unknowns in security games, since mapping out the structural unknowns can be a challenging task, let alone the unknown unknowns. Hence, there is a need to shift the paradigm from a Bayesian-based approach to a completely data-driven and model-agnostic one. To this end, this work presents an estimation framework that is purely based on the past experiences and the real-time observations. We focus on the estimation of finite zero-sum static games, which are central to security applications, such as in network configurations [24], network provisioning [20], and jamming attacks [25].

We formulate MASAGE, a sequential least-square estimation problem over the game space, which is formed by the past transferable experiences. This approach dispenses with the knowledge of parametric uncertainties and the payoff structure of the game but takes the game as an object for estimation instead. In this work, we focus on a class of linear game estimators. Under mild assumptions, the static least-square game estimation problem is probably solvable by gradient-based algorithms. We extend the static framework to its sequential counterpart, in which the security game is estimated dynamically based on sequential observations. We characterize the structural properties of the estimation problem and show the convergence properties of the gradient-based data-driven adaptive algorithm.

2   Related Work

Game identification and estimation [2, 10, 12, 18, 19] have been investigated in economics literature. Hotz et al. in [10] have first considered a conditional choice probability estimator of the structural parameters in dynamic programming models. Following this work, [18, 19] have proposed an identification and estimation framework based on time-series data using observed choices. They have considered a class of asymptotic least-square estimators defined by the equilibrium conditions. For discrete games and normal-form games, Bajari et al. in [1] and [2] have proposed simulation-based estimators for parametric games using algorithms that compute all the game equilibria. With a focus on the multiplicity of equilibira, Jovanovic in [12] has highlighted that the information of multiple solutions affects the statistical inference strategy. These works share a common structure that uses equilibria data from firms or companies to estimate the structural parameters of static or dynamic models. Our work studies this problem from a model-agnostic perspective by formulating the estimation directly on the game space. This work focuses on the class of zero-sum matrix games, which plays an important role in cybersecurity.

The analysis of the least-square game estimation problem relies on the perturbation theory of matrix games. Two closely related works are [8] and [6]. Gross in [8] has considered a general case of real matrices and computed the left and right value derivative with respect to arbitrary matrix entries. The author has observed that when the matrix has only one Nash equilibrium pair, the derivative exists, and the right and left derivatives are equal. Cohen et al. in [6] and [7] have studied the completely mixed matrix games and bi-matrix games, and have given the value derivatives with respect to the matrix entries. The authors have provided useful results of strategy derivative and higher-order derivatives of saddle-point values.

3   Problem Formulation

3.1   Preliminary

Game Description. Consider a two-player zero-sum finite game G represented by a triplet $\langle \mathcal{N}, \{\mathscr{A}_1, \mathscr{A}_2\}, \{u_1, u_2\} \rangle$. Here, $\mathcal{N} = \{P_1, P_2\}$ is the player set containing a defender P_1 and an attacker P_2; $\mathscr{A}_1 = \{1, 2, \dots, N_1\}$ and $\mathscr{A}_2 = \{1, 2, \dots, N_1\}$ are action sets for P_1 and P_2, respectively, with $N_1 = |\mathscr{A}_1|$ and $N_2 = |\mathscr{A}_2|$; $u_1 : \mathscr{A}_1 \times \mathscr{A}_2 \to \mathbb{R}$ and $u_2 : \mathscr{A}_1 \times \mathscr{A}_2 \to \mathbb{R}$ are the utility functions of P_1 and P_2, respectively. Since the game is zero-sum, $u_1 + u_2 = 0$. The zero-sum game can be fully characterized by a single matrix of the size $N_1 \times N_2$. P_1 is the row player. P_2 is the column player. Each row and column is indexed by the corresponding actions of the player. Each entry of the matrix is associated with a payoff value that is viewed as cost to P_1 but utility to P_2.

We consider the scenario where the payoffs of the games are uncertain. To capture the uncertainties, we define a random matrix $\mathbf{M} : \Omega \to \mathbb{R}^{N_1 \times N_2}$ over an underlying probability space $(\Omega, \mathscr{F}, \mathbb{P})$. Each entry of matrix $\mathbf{M}$ is a random variable defined on the probability space. The underlying distributions of the random variables are unknown to the players. Let $\mathrm{val}(\cdot)$ be the saddle-point value of a matrix game. Random matrix game $\mathbf{M}$ gives rise to its associated game value $\mathbf{z} = \mathrm{val}(\mathbf{M})$.

Expert Games and Game Estimation. We consider the following scenario. The players do not know their game prior to the play. However, they are given a set of expert games that they have played before and know that their game will be similar and related to the set of expert games. The game is determined by nature, i.e., $\omega \in \Omega$ is realized when the game starts. Let $\bar{M} \in \mathbb{R}^{N_1 \times N_2}$ denote this game. The players cannot observe ω but can observe the outcome of the play of the game, i.e., the value of the sampled game $\bar{M}$, denoted by $\bar{z}$. $\bar{M}$ is also called the target game as the goal of the sequential play of the game is to estimate its value based on the prior information of the expert games and the sequential observations of $\bar{z}$. The formulation of this problem will be made clear later in Subsect. 3.2.

A Nonlinear Least-Square Estimator. To provide a formal framework of the estimation problem, we first consider the following non-sequential estimation problem. At the start of the game, the defender has a set of S expert games $\mathcal{M} = \{M_1, \dots, M_S\}$ that is non-random and observable, where $S \in \mathbb{N}$ is the number of expert games; Let $\mathscr{S} := \{1, \dots, S\}$, $M_i, i \in \mathscr{S}$ are informed to the player from past interactions or experiences that satisfy following properties:

(i) All expert games have nonzero saddle-point values, i.e., for all $i \in \mathscr{S}$,

$$\text{val}(M_i) \neq 0; \tag{1}$$

(ii) each pair of expert games are not strategically equivalent, i.e., for all $i, j \in \mathscr{S}$,

$$\forall c \in \mathbb{R}, \qquad M_i \neq cM_j; \tag{2}$$

(iii) entries of expert games are bounded, i.e., for all $i \in \mathscr{S}$, $a \in \mathscr{A}_1$, $b \in \mathscr{A}_2$,

$$\exists B \in \mathbb{R}, \qquad (M_i)_{ab} \leq B. \tag{3}$$

The defender can observe the value of the game of the unknown game $\bar{M}$, $\bar{z}$ before the play of the game. The information that is available to the defender is $I = \{\mathcal{M}, \bar{z}\}$. The goal of the defender is to find an estimator $\mu : \mathscr{I} \to \mathbb{R}^{N_1 \times N_2}$ that maps the information set of the defender to find an estimate $\hat{M} = \mu(I)$. Here, $\mathscr{I}$ denotes the set of all possible information to the defender.

We consider a class of linear estimators $L(\mathcal{M}; \alpha)$ that are parameterized by a weight vector $\alpha \in \mathscr{X}$, where $\mathscr{X} \subseteq \mathbb{R}^S$ is the parameter space, $\alpha = [\alpha_1, \alpha_2, \ldots, \alpha_S]^\mathsf{T}$. The estimators take the following form:

$$\hat{M} = L(\mathcal{M}; \alpha) = \sum_{i=1}^{S} \alpha_i M_i \tag{4}$$

From (4), we can see that the linear estimator is taken as the linear combination of expert games. A natural criterion of an optimal estimator is the one that minimizes the error between the outcomes of the estimated game and the target game. The outcome of the estimated game is given by $\text{val}(L(\mathcal{M}; \alpha))$, while the outcome of the target game is assumed to be observable by the defender, which takes the value of $\bar{z}$. Hence, the residue error of the estimation is

$$\varepsilon = \bar{z} - \text{val}(L(\mathcal{M}; \alpha)) \tag{5}$$

An optimal linear estimator $\mu^* = L(\mathcal{M}; \alpha^*)$ with the optimal parameters α^* is the one that minimizes the residue error (5) using the following squared error criterion $J(\alpha)$:

$$J(\alpha) := |\text{val}(L(\mathcal{M}; \alpha)) - \bar{z}|^2. \tag{6}$$

To sum up, finding an optimal linear estimator is equivalent to solve the following finite-dimensional unconstrained problem (**SP**):

$$\textbf{(SP)} \qquad \min_{\alpha} J(\alpha) \tag{7}$$

The solutions to optimization problem (SP) provide a foundation for sequential estimation of the game. One trivial solution to the problem is to let α^* such that $J(\alpha^*) = 0$. Consider ratio $\kappa_i := z/\text{val}(M_i)$, $i \in \mathscr{S}$. A subset of optimal points α^* would be $\{\kappa_i e_i\}_{i=1}^{S}$, where $\{e_i\}_{i=1}^{S}$ represents the standard basis of $\mathbb{R}^S$. These vectors are trivial solutions obtained by degenerating the set of multiple expert games into a singleton. The resulting estimation is a scaling of a chosen expert game. It is apparent that they are strategically equivalent games. However, these trivial solutions are arguably biased in terms of combining the information given by the experts and we need optimal points that take multiple expert games into consideration. In Sect. 4, we study $J(\alpha)$ further to develop iterative algorithmic solutions.

3.2   Dynamic Linear Estimation Problem

Building on the estimation problem above, we formulate a dynamic linear estimation problem. Consider that the game is played sequentially. At the beginning of each time step t, the player has cumulated t expert-game sets $\{\mathcal{M}^{(t')}\}_{t'=1}^{t}$. At step t, an unknown game $\bar{M}^{(t)}$ is sampled from the underlying probability space $(\Omega, \mathscr{F}, \mathbb{P})$. The defender can observe the outcome of the play $\bar{z}^{(t)}$, which is the saddle-point value of the unknown game, i.e., $\bar{z}^{(t)} = \mathrm{val}(\bar{M}^{(t)})$. By the end of the play, the defender has accumulated information $I^{(t)} = \{ \{\mathcal{M}^{(t')}\}_{t'=1}^{t}, \{\bar{z}^{(t')}\}_{t'=1}^{t} \}$.

The goal of the defender is to find a sequential estimator $\mu_t(I^{(t)})$ to estimate a sequence of unknown games $\bar{M}^{(t)}$ based on his accumulated information.

At each step t, we consider a linear estimator $\mu_t(I^{(t)})$ taking the form of

$$\mu_t(I^{(t)}) := L(\mathcal{M}^{(t)}; \alpha) := \alpha_1 M_1^{(t)} + \alpha_2 M_2^{(t)} + \ldots + \alpha_S M_S^{(t)}.$$

Here, the linear mapping $L : \mathbb{R}^S \to \mathbb{R}^{N_1 \times N_2}$ is parameterized by a fixed vector α. At time t, the optimal parameters $\alpha^*(t)$ minimize the time-average accumulated residue error as follows:

$$J^{(t)}(\alpha) = \frac{1}{t} \sum_{t'=1}^{t} |\bar{z}^{(t')} - \mathrm{val}(L(\mathcal{M}^{(t')}; \alpha))|^2. \tag{8}$$

It is clear that $J^{(t)}$ depends on the samples of the game at each step t. We formulate the nonlinear regression problem at time t called **DP**-t.

$$(\mathbf{DP} - t) \qquad\qquad \min_\alpha J^{(t)}(\alpha) \tag{9}$$

Discussion on Asymptotic Behavior. The formulated problem coincides with the standard form of nonlinear regression with a linearly parameterized function class, in which the following presumption holds:

$$\bar{z}^{t'} = \mathrm{val}(L(\mathcal{M}^{(t')}; \alpha_0)) + \varepsilon^{(t')} \qquad t' = 1, \ldots, t \tag{10}$$

where $\varepsilon^{(t')}$ are i.i.d. errors with zero mean and bounded variance, and α_0 is the true parameter. The least-square estimator $\alpha^*(t)$ is said to be strongly (weakly) consistent if $\alpha^*(t) \to \alpha_0$ a.s. (in prob.) as $t \to \infty$ [22].

The strong or weak consistency of $\alpha^*(t)$ depends on a series of conditions rigorously proved in [11,14,22]. Under the assumption of consistency, $\alpha^*(t)$ is asymptotically unbiased and induces minimum variance. In such case, while the estimation of game matrix is not necessarily unbiased, it still provides valuable information, since the value of estimated game enjoys asymptotic optimality.

4   Objective Function Analysis

In this section, we provide analytical results to give theoretical insights on the problem. We first characterize several properties of the objective functions including their continuity, differentiability, and convexity. In the second part of this section, we study parameter perturbations on the objective function.

4.1 Basic Properties

Let $v^{(t)}(\alpha)$ be the error between observations and value of output game at step t for a linear estimator with parameter α, given by

$$v^{(t)}(\alpha) := \mathrm{val}(L(\mathcal{M}^{(t)}; \alpha)) - \bar{z}^{(t)} = \mathrm{val}(L(\mathcal{M}^{(t)}; \alpha) - z^{(t)}E) \qquad (11)$$

Let $f^{(t)}(\alpha)$, and $g^{(t)}(\alpha)$ be the saddle-point strategies of estimated game M for a given α. The error (11) can be rewritten as

$$v^{(t)}(\alpha) = f^{(t)\mathrm{T}}(\alpha)(L(\mathcal{M}^{(t)}; \alpha) - z^{(t)}E)g^{(t)}(\alpha)$$

where $E \in \mathbb{R}^{N_1 \times N_2}$ is a matrix with all entries being 1. In dynamic estimation problems, the accumulated squared error up to time t is $J^{(t)}(\alpha) = \sum_{t'=1}^{t} \left(v^{(t')}(\alpha)\right)^2$.

Lemma 1. $v^{(t)}(\alpha)$ *is continuous differentiable in domain* $\mathbb{R}^S$, *so is* $J^{(t)}(\alpha)$.

Proof. From [21], $|\mathrm{val}(A) - \mathrm{val}(B)| \le d(A, B)$ for any real matrices $A, B \in \mathbb{R}^{N_1 \times N_2}$ with metric $d(A, B) = \max_{i \in \mathscr{A}_1, j \in \mathscr{A}_2} |A_{ij} - B_{ij}|$. For sufficiently small ε and all-one S dimension vector $\mathbf{1}_S$,

$$|v^{(t)}(L(\mathcal{M}; \alpha + \varepsilon \mathbf{1}_S)) - v^{(t)}(L(\mathcal{M}; \alpha))| \le \varepsilon \max_{i \in \mathscr{A}_1, j \in \mathscr{A}_2} |\sum_{s \in \mathscr{S}} (M_s)_{ij}|.$$

$v^{(t)}(\alpha)$ is continuous as the term $\max_{i \in \mathscr{A}_1, j \in \mathscr{A}_2} |\sum_{s \in \mathscr{S}} (M_s)_{ij}|$ is bounded. Picking the $\| \cdot \|_2$ norm, we arrive at

$$\lim_{\varepsilon \to 0} \frac{|v^{(t)}(L(\mathcal{M}; \alpha + \varepsilon \mathbf{1}_S)) - v^{(t)}(L(\mathcal{M}; \alpha))|}{\|\alpha + \varepsilon \mathbf{1}_S - \alpha\|_2} \le \frac{1}{\|\mathbf{1}_S\|_2} \max_{i \in \mathscr{A}_1, j \in \mathscr{A}_2} |\sum_{s \in \mathscr{S}} (M_s)_{ij}|.$$

Thus, given bounded expert game matrices, $v^{(t)}(\alpha)$ is continuous differentiable in $\mathbb{R}^S$, and so is $J^{(t)}(\alpha)$ since it is a sum of squares of $v^{(t')}(\alpha)$. $\qquad \square$

Lemma 2. $J(\alpha)$ *is non-convex in domain* $\mathbb{R}^S$.

Proof. We prove the result by contradiction. Suppose that $J(\alpha)$ is convex in the convex domain $\mathbb{R}^S$, then it must satisfy that $\forall \lambda \in [0, 1]$ and $\forall \alpha_1, \alpha_2 \in \mathbb{R}^S$,

$$J(\lambda \alpha_1 + (1 - \lambda)\alpha_2) \le \lambda J(\alpha_1) + (1 - \lambda)J(\alpha_2). \qquad (12)$$

Pick arbitrary $\lambda \in (0, 1)$ and two fundamental solutions: $\alpha_1 = \kappa_1 e_1, \alpha_2 = \kappa_2 e_2$ in (12) and yield

$$|\mathrm{val}(L(\mathcal{M}^{(t)}; \lambda \alpha_1 + (1 - \lambda)\alpha_2)) - \bar{z}|^2 \le 0$$

$$\Rightarrow \qquad \mathrm{val}\left(\frac{M_2}{\mathrm{val}(M_2)} + \lambda \left(\frac{M_1}{\mathrm{val}(M_1)} - \frac{M_2}{\mathrm{val}(M_2)}\right)\right) = 1$$

Thus, for bounded matrix M_1 and M_2 which has nonzero saddle-point values, it must hold that

$$M_1 = \frac{\mathrm{val}(M_1)}{\mathrm{val}(M_2)} M_2,$$

which contradicts to property (2). This contradiction indicates that $J(\alpha)$ is not convex. $\qquad \square$

4.2 Perturbation Theory of Parameterized Matrix Game

In this subsection, we determine the first-order and second-order derivatives of the game value with respect to entries of the payoff matrix. We first introduce the concept of completely mixed games.

Definition 1. *A matrix game M is said to be completely mixed if, for every saddle-point solution (f, g), no element of f or g is zero. If M is completely mixed, then $N_1 = N_2$ and the saddle-point solution of M is unique.*

Let $\hat{M}^{(t)} := L(\mathcal{M}^{(t)}; \alpha)$ denote the estimation of the game at time t. We make the following assumptions on the parameter space and estimated game.

Assumption 1. *The parameter space $\mathcal{X}$ is a subset of Euclidean space $\mathbb{R}^S$ where for all $\alpha \in \mathcal{X}$, $c(\alpha) \leq \|\alpha\| \leq C(\alpha)$.*

Assumption 1 restricts the parameter to a compact space. It prevents the output estimation from approaching infinity or $\mathbf{0}$.

Assumption 2. *$\hat{M}^{(t)}$ is completely mixed for all t.*

Assumption 2 implies that the estimated game matrix is square and nonsingular. It enables the computation of first-order and second-order derivatives of the objective functions.

For games that are not completely mixed, their computations remain an open problem. Lloyd Shapley [6] has observed that the nonexistence of any derivatives as a function of a given matrix element correspond to degeneracies in the linear-programming solution of the game. Assumption 2 coincides with the facts in [5] that the set of $N_1 \times N_2$ matrices which have unique saddle-point points is open and everywhere dense in $N_1 \times N_2$-space; i.e., solutions are unique for most of the $N_1 \times N_2$ matrices. With Assumption 2, we avoid equilibrium selection by degenerating saddle-point solution sets into singletons and ensure the uniqueness of $f^{(t)}(\alpha)$ and $g^{(t)}(\alpha)$. The explicit expression of saddle-point solutions are feasible under Assumption 2, as shown in Lemma 3 following [21].

Lemma 3. *Assume that $\mathbf{1}^T[\hat{M}^{(t)}]^{-1}\mathbf{1}$ is nonzero. For every t and given α, under Assumption 2 and we have:*

(i) $v^{(t)}(\alpha) = 1/\mathbf{1}^T[\hat{M}^{(t)}]^{-1}\mathbf{1} - z^{(t)}$.
(ii) $f^{(t)T}(\alpha) = \mathbf{1}^T[\hat{M}^{(t)}]^{-1}\mathrm{val}(\hat{M}^{(t)})$.
(iii) $g^{(t)}(\alpha) = [\hat{M}^{(t)}]^{-1}\mathbf{1}\mathrm{val}(\hat{M}^{(t)})$.

Here, vector $\mathbf{1}$ is a vector of appropriate dimension with all entries being 1. The assumption of $\mathbf{1}^T[\hat{M}^{(t)}]^{-1}\mathbf{1}$ being nonzero is without loss of generality. Lemma 3 enables the following direct computation of the gradient of the error (11).

Theorem 1. *For every t, under Assumption 2, the gradient vector of the error (11) is given by*

$$\nabla v^{(t)}(\alpha) = (\delta_1^{(t)}(\alpha), \ldots, \delta_S^{(t)}(\alpha))^T, \tag{13}$$

where $\delta_i(\alpha) = f^{(t)T}(\alpha)M_i^{(t)}g^{(t)}(\alpha)$, $i \in \mathcal{S}$. Furthermore, $\|\nabla v^{(t)}(\alpha)\|$ is bounded by some positive constant.

Proof. Given that $\hat{M}^{(t)}$ is completely mixed, the results in Lemma 3 hold. According to the product rule of derivatives, we have $\forall i \in \mathscr{S}$:

$$\frac{\partial v^{(t)}(\alpha)}{\partial \alpha_i} = f^{(t)\mathrm{T}}(\alpha)M_i^{(t)}g^{(t)}(\alpha) + \frac{\partial f^{(t)\mathrm{T}}(\alpha)}{\partial \alpha_i}\hat{M}^{(t)}g^{(t)}(\alpha) + f^{(t)\mathrm{T}}(\alpha)\hat{M}^{(t)}\frac{\partial g^{(t)}(\alpha)}{\partial \alpha}$$

$$= f^{(t)\mathrm{T}}(\alpha)M_i^{(t)}g^{(t)}(\alpha) + \frac{\partial f^{(t)\mathrm{T}}(\alpha)}{\partial \alpha_i}\hat{M}^{(t)}[\hat{M}^{(t)}]^{-1}\mathbf{1}v^{(t)}(\alpha)$$

$$+ v^{(t)}(\alpha)\mathbf{1}^{\mathrm{T}}[\hat{M}^{(t)}]^{-1}\hat{M}^{(t)}\frac{\partial g^{(t)}(\alpha)}{\partial \alpha_i}$$

$$= f^{(t)\mathrm{T}}(\alpha)M_i^{(t)}g^{(t)}(\alpha) + v^{(t)}(\alpha)\left(\frac{\partial f^{(t)\mathrm{T}}(\alpha)\mathbf{1}}{\partial \alpha_i} + \frac{\partial \mathbf{1}^{\mathrm{T}}g^{(t)}(\alpha)}{\partial \alpha_i}\right)$$

$$= f^{(t)\mathrm{T}}(\alpha)M_i^{(t)}g^{(t)}(\alpha).$$

Stacking all the partial derivatives of i's gives the gradient. For any $\alpha \in \mathscr{X}$ that satisfies Assumption 2, we have

$$\|\nabla v^{(t)}(\alpha)\| \leq \|(\max_{i\in\mathscr{A}_1, j\in\mathscr{A}_2}|(M_1^{(t)})_{ij}|, \ldots, \max_{i\in\mathscr{A}_1, j\in\mathscr{A}_2}|(M_S^{(t)})_{ij}|)^{\mathrm{T}}\|$$

$$\|\nabla v^{(t)}(\alpha)\| \leq \|(\min_{i\in\mathscr{A}_1, j\in\mathscr{A}_2}|(M_1^{(t)})_{ij}|, \ldots, \min_{i\in\mathscr{A}_1, j\in\mathscr{A}_2}|(M_S^{(t)})_{ij}|)^{\mathrm{T}}\|.$$

Thus, for bounded expert matrices, $\|\nabla v^{(t)}(\alpha)\|$ is bounded too, which can be viewed as a corollary of Lemma 1. □

Corollary 1. *Under Assumption 2, the gradient of* $J^{(t)}(\alpha)$ *is given by*

$$\nabla J^{(t)}(\alpha) = \frac{2}{t}\sum_{t'=1}^{t'}((\delta_1^{(t)}(\alpha), \ldots, \delta_S^{(t')}(\alpha))^{\mathrm{T}}v^{(t')}(\alpha). \tag{14}$$

Remark 1. The entry $\delta_i^{(t)}(\alpha)$ indicates the sensitivity or the change in the accumulated square error with respect to a perturbation of α_i. It can be interpreted as the partial contribution by expert i to the reduction of the error. Note that $f^{(t)\mathrm{T}}(\alpha)M_i^{(t)}g^{(t)}(\alpha)$ is the expected outcome of the expert game i, $M_i^{(t)}$, achieved with the saddle-point strategies of $\hat{M}^{(t)}$.

We are also interested in the sensitivity of $\nabla J^{(t)}(\alpha)$ with respect to the changes in variable α.

Theorem 2. *For every t, under Assumptions 1 and 2, $v^{(t)}(\alpha)$ is twice continuously differentiable, and so is $J^{(t)}(\alpha)$. The Hessian of* $v^{(t)}(\alpha) := \left[\dfrac{\partial^2 v^{(t)}(\alpha)}{\partial \alpha_i \partial \alpha_j}\right]_{i,j\in\mathscr{S}}$ *is given by*

$$\frac{\partial^2 v^{(t)}(\alpha)}{\partial \alpha_i \partial \alpha_j} = \phi_{ij}^{(t)}M_i^{(t)}g^{(t)}(\alpha) + f^{(t)\mathrm{T}}(\alpha)M_i^{(t)}\varphi_{ij}^{(t)}, \quad i,j \in \mathscr{S}, \tag{15}$$

where

$$\phi_{ij}^{(t)} = \left(\mathbf{1}^\mathrm{T} f^{(t)\mathrm{T}}(\alpha) M_j^{(t)} g^{(t)}(\alpha) - f^{(t)\mathrm{T}}(\alpha) M_i^{(t)}\right) [\hat{M}^{(t)}]^{-1}$$

$$\varphi_{ij}^{(t)} = [\hat{M}^{(t)}]^{-1} \left(f^{(t)\mathrm{T}}(\alpha) M_j^{(t)} g^{(t)}(\alpha) \mathbf{1} - M_i^{(t)} g^{(t)}(\alpha)\right).$$

Furthermore, the Hessian $\nabla^2 J^{(t)}(\alpha)$ is bounded; i.e., there exists a positive constant, such that $\|\nabla^2 J^{(t)}(\alpha)\| \le \frac{1}{2}\beta$, where $\|\nabla^2 J^{(t)}(\alpha)\|$ is the maximum (real) eigenvalue.

Proof. Under Assumption 2, the derivative of (13) exists, for $i, j \in \mathscr{S}$:

$$\frac{\partial^2 v^{(t)}(\alpha)}{\partial \alpha_i \partial \alpha_j} = \frac{\partial f^{(t)}(\alpha)}{\partial \alpha_j} M_i^{(t)} g^{(t)}(\alpha) + f^{(t)\mathrm{T}}(\alpha) M_i^{(t)} \frac{\partial g^{(t)}(\alpha)}{\partial \alpha_j}$$

From Lemma 3, we have

$$f^{(t)\mathrm{T}}(\alpha)\hat{M}^{(t)} = \mathbf{1}^\mathrm{T} \mathrm{val}(\hat{M}^{(t)})$$

$$\hat{M}^{(t)} g^{(t)}(\alpha) = \mathrm{val}(\hat{M}^{(t)})\mathbf{1}.$$

Take derivative w.r.t α_j on both sides and we arrive at the derivative of the saddle-point strategies:

$$\phi_{ij}^{(t)} = \frac{\partial f^{(t)}(\alpha)}{\partial \alpha_j} = \left(\mathbf{1}^\mathrm{T} f^{(t)\mathrm{T}}(\alpha) M_j^{(t)} g^{(t)}(\alpha) - f^{(t)\mathrm{T}}(\alpha) M_i^{(t)}\right) [\hat{M}^{(t)}]^{-1}$$

$$\varphi_{ij}^{(t)} = \frac{\partial g^{(t)}(\alpha)}{\partial \alpha_j} = [\hat{M}^{(t)}]^{-1} \left(f^{(t)\mathrm{T}}(\alpha) M_j^{(t)} g^{(t)}(\alpha)\mathbf{1} - M_i^{(t)} g^{(t)}(\alpha)\right)$$

The Hessian $\nabla^2 J^{(t)}(\alpha)$ can be constructed using the first and second-order derivatives of $v^{(t)}(\alpha)$. Its entry takes the following form:

$$[\nabla^2 J^{(t)}(\alpha)]_{ij} = \sum_{t'=1}^{t} \frac{\partial v^{(t')}(\alpha)}{\partial \alpha_i} \frac{\partial v^{(t')}(\alpha)}{\partial \alpha_j} + \frac{\partial^2 v^{(t')}(\alpha)}{\partial \alpha_i \partial \alpha_j} v^{(t')}(\alpha).$$

Using triangular inequality, we obtain

$$\|[\nabla^2 J^{(t)}(\alpha)]_{ij}\| \le \sum_{t'=1}^{t} \|\frac{\partial v^{(t')}(\alpha)}{\partial \alpha_i} \frac{\partial v^{(t')}(\alpha)}{\partial \alpha_j} + \frac{\partial^2 v^{(t')}(\alpha)}{\partial \alpha_i \partial \alpha_j} v^{(t')}(\alpha)\|$$

$$\le \sum_{t'=1}^{t} \underbrace{\|\frac{\partial v^{(t')}(\alpha)}{\partial \alpha_i} \frac{\partial v^{(t')}(\alpha)}{\partial \alpha_j}\|}_{\text{first term}} + \underbrace{\|\frac{\partial^2 v^{(t')}(\alpha)}{\partial \alpha_i \partial \alpha_j} v^{(t')}(\alpha)\|}_{\text{second term}}.$$

The boundedness of Hessian entry is determined by the first term and the second term. We have for any $t' \in \{1, \dots, t\}$, the first term is bounded according to Theorem 1:

$$\|\frac{\partial v^{(t')}(\alpha)}{\partial \alpha_i} \frac{\partial v^{(t')}(\alpha)}{\partial \alpha_j}\| \le \|\max_{a,b}[M_i^{(t')}]_{ab}\| \cdot \|\max_{a,b}[M_j^{(t')}]_{ab}\|.$$

For the second term,

$$\left\|\frac{\partial^2 v^{(t')}(\alpha)}{\partial \alpha_i \partial \alpha_j} v^{(t')}(\alpha)\right\| \leq \|v^{(t')}(\alpha)\phi_{ij}^{(t')} M_i^{(t')} g^{(t')}(\alpha)\| + \|f^{(t')\mathrm{T}}(\alpha)M_i^{(t')}\varphi_{ij}^{(t')} v^{(t')}(\alpha)\|$$

$$\leq (Q+P)\|\mathrm{val}(\hat{M}) - \bar{z}^{(t')}\|\|[\hat{M}^{(t')}]^{-1}\|$$

$$\leq (Q+P)(\|\mathrm{val}(\hat{M})\|\|[\hat{M}^{(t')}]^{-1}\| + \|\bar{z}^{(t')}\|\|[\hat{M}^{(t')}]^{-1}\|),$$

where Q and P are positive constants such that

$$\|\mathbf{1}^{\mathrm{T}} f^{(t)\mathrm{T}}(\alpha)M_j^{(t)} g^{(t)}(\alpha) - f^{(t)\mathrm{T}}(\alpha)M_i^{(t)}\| \cdot \|M_i^{(t)} g^{(t)}(\alpha)\| \leq Q$$

$$\|f^{(t)\mathrm{T}}(\alpha)M_j^{(t)} g^{(t)}(\alpha)\mathbf{1} - M_i^{(t)} g^{(t)}(\alpha)\| \cdot \|f^{(t)\mathrm{T}}(\alpha)M_i^{(t)}\| \leq P.$$

The parameterized $\|[\hat{M}^{(t')}]\|^{-1}$ is bounded since α is lower bounded by positive constant according to Assumption 1. Since the eigenvalue of a square matrix is bounded by its maximum entry multiplied by its order, $\|[\hat{M}^{(t)}]^{-1}\|\|\mathrm{val}(\hat{M}^{(t)})\|$ is also bounded, according to Lemma 3:

$$\|[\hat{M}^{(t)}]^{-1}\|\|\mathrm{val}(\hat{M}^{(t)})\| = \|[\hat{M}^{(t)}]^{-1}\|/\|\mathbf{1}^{\mathrm{T}}[\hat{M}^{(t)}]^{-1}\mathbf{1}\|$$

$$\leq \frac{N_1 \max_{i,j} \left([\hat{M}^{(t')}]^{-1}\right)_{ij}}{\sum_{i,j} \left([\hat{M}^{(t')}]^{-1}\right)_{ij}}$$

Similarly, boundedness of Hessian entries implies that its eigenvalues are bounded by some constant, and thus we arrive at a bound β.   □

In the following, we provide a lemma that establishes the relation between bounded Hessian and Lipschitz continuity, and then give the main theorem that ensures the convergence of gradient-based algorithms.

Lemma 4. *Let $f : \mathbb{R}^S \to \mathbb{R}$ be a twice continuously differentiable function. If there exists a positive constant β such that $\|\nabla^2 f\| \leq \beta$, where $\|\nabla^2 f\|$ is the matrix norm, then*

$$\forall \alpha, \tilde{\alpha} \in \mathbb{R}^S : \quad \|\nabla f(\alpha) - \nabla f(\tilde{\alpha})\| \leq \beta \|\alpha - \tilde{\alpha}\|.$$

Proof. The result can be proved by using a second-order Taylor expansion around α and $\tilde{\alpha}$, i.e.,

$$f(\alpha) - f(\tilde{\alpha}) = \nabla f(\tilde{\alpha})^{\mathrm{T}}(\alpha - \tilde{\alpha}) + \frac{1}{2}(\tilde{\alpha} - \alpha)^{\mathrm{T}}\nabla^2 f(\xi_1)(\tilde{\alpha} - \alpha)$$

$$= -\nabla f(\alpha)^{\mathrm{T}}(\tilde{\alpha} - \alpha) - \frac{1}{2}(\alpha - \tilde{\alpha})^{\mathrm{T}}\nabla^2 f(\xi_2)(\alpha - \tilde{\alpha}),$$

where $\xi_1 = \alpha + t_1(\tilde{\alpha} - \alpha)$ and $\xi_2 = \tilde{\alpha} + t_2(\alpha - \tilde{\alpha})$ and $t_1, t_2 \in (0,1)$. We combine the two relations and obtain

$$\|\nabla f(\alpha) - \nabla f(\tilde{\alpha})\| \leq \frac{1}{2}\|\nabla^2 f(\xi_2)\|\|\tilde{\alpha} - \alpha\| + \frac{1}{2}\|\nabla^2 f(\xi_2)\|\|\alpha - \tilde{\alpha}\|$$

$$\leq \beta\|\tilde{\alpha} - \alpha\|.$$

□

Theorem 3. *For every t, under Assumption 2, the vector functions $|v^{(t)}(\alpha)|^2$ are Lipschitz continuous; i.e., there exists a Lipschitz constant $\beta > 0$, such that for all $\alpha, \tilde{\alpha} \in \mathscr{X}$ that satisfies*

$$\|\nabla v^{(t')}(\alpha)v^{(t')}(\alpha) - \nabla v^{(t')}(\tilde{\alpha})v^{(t')}(\tilde{\alpha})\| \le \beta \|\alpha - \tilde{\alpha}\|; \tag{16}$$

and

$$\|\nabla J^{(t)}(\alpha) - \nabla J^{(t)}(\tilde{\alpha})\| \le 2\beta \|\alpha - \tilde{\alpha}\|. \tag{17}$$

Furthermore, the following holds:

$$J^{(t)}(\alpha) - J^{(t)}(\tilde{\alpha}) \le (\nabla J^{(t)}(\tilde{\alpha}))^{\mathrm{T}}(\alpha - \tilde{\alpha}) + \beta \|\alpha - \tilde{\alpha}\|^2. \tag{18}$$

Proof. Inequality (16) immediately follows Lemma 4 and the analysis in Theorem 2. To obtain (17), we add up (16) for all t' and use the triangular inequality.

$$\|\nabla J^{(t)}(\alpha) - \nabla J^{(t)}(\tilde{\alpha})\| \le 2 \sum_{t'=1}^{t} \|\nabla v^{(t')}(\alpha)v^{(t')}(\alpha) - \nabla v^{(t')}(\tilde{\alpha})v^{(t')}(\tilde{\alpha})\|$$
$$\le 2\beta \|\alpha - \tilde{\alpha}\|.$$

Inequality (18) is a basic result following (17):

$$J^{(t)}(\alpha) - J^{(t)}(\tilde{\alpha}) = \int_0^1 (\alpha - \tilde{\alpha})^{\mathrm{T}} \nabla J^{(t)}(\tilde{\alpha} + \xi(\alpha - \tilde{\alpha}))d\xi$$
$$\le \int_0^1 (\alpha - \tilde{\alpha})^{\mathrm{T}} \nabla J^{(t)}(\tilde{\alpha})d\xi$$
$$+ \int_0^1 \|\alpha - \tilde{\alpha}\| \|\nabla J^{(t)}(\tilde{\alpha} + \xi(\alpha - \tilde{\alpha})) - \nabla J^{(t)}(\tilde{\alpha})\|d\xi$$
$$\le (\nabla J^{(t)}(\tilde{\alpha}))^{\mathrm{T}}(\alpha - \tilde{\alpha}) + \beta \|\alpha - \tilde{\alpha}\|^2.$$

$\square$

The gradient and the Hessian of the errors, together with the property of Lipschitz continuity, provides a theoretical foundation for developing gradient-based algorithms, which will be discussed in Sect. 5.

5 Algorithmic Analysis

In this section, we develop gradient-based algorithms to find the linear optimal estimator, and study their convergence properties. We first formally present the optimality conditions that characterize the solutions to the dynamic problem 8.

Proposition 1 *(Stationary Points). For every t, due to non-convexity, we are satisfied at finding a solution $\alpha^*(t)$ for $J^{(t)}(\alpha)$ in DP-t that satisfies the first-order conditions,*

$$\nabla J^{(t)}(\alpha^*) = 0$$

which we refer to as stationary points.

A descent algorithm starts from initial point α^0, proceeding iteratively as follows:

$$\alpha^{k+1} = \alpha^k + \gamma^k s^k, \qquad k = 0, 1, 2, \ldots,$$

where $\gamma^k \in \mathbb{R}_+$ is the stepsize and $s_k \in \mathbb{R}^S$ represents the descent direction. Many choices are plausible for the descent direction, resulting in different algorithmic implementations; e.g., *steepest gradient* (i.e., $s^k = -\nabla J^{(t)}(\alpha^k)$), *Newton's method* (i.e., $s^k = -(\nabla^2 J^{(t)}(\alpha^k))^{-1}\nabla J^{(t)}(\alpha^k)$), and other variants (e.g., quasi-Newton methods). Algorithm 1 gives a steepest gradient descent algorithm, which is well known to achieve a linear convergence rate. The tolerance ε denotes the stopping criteria.

Algorithm 1: Optimal Linear Estimation Using Steepest Gradient

---

Data: $\{\mathscr{M}^{(t')}\}_{t'=1}^t$, $\{z^{(t')}\}_{t'=1}^t$;
Input: α^0, $\{\gamma^k\}$, ε;
for $k \leftarrow 1, 2, \ldots$ **do**
    foreach $i \leftarrow 1$ **to** t **do**
       | $(f^{(i)}, g^{(i)}) \leftarrow$ saddle-point$(L(\mathscr{M}^{(i)}, \alpha) - z^{(i)} E)$
    end
    $\nabla J^{(t)}(\alpha^k) \leftarrow \frac{1}{t} \sum_{i=1}^t \left(\nabla v^{(i)}(\alpha) \right) v^{(i)}(\alpha)$;
    if $\|\nabla J^{(t)}(\alpha^k)\| \leq \varepsilon$;
    then
       | Break
    end
    $\alpha^{k+1} \leftarrow \alpha^k - \gamma^k \nabla J^{(t)}(\alpha^k)$;
end
Result: α^*

Pseudo-Gradient Approximation. As saddle-point strategies are computationally costly to obtain, determining a steepest direction is relatively inefficient. In fact, the descent direction can be approximated once the approximation error is sufficiently small. We hereby provide a pseudo gradient method that uses a surrogate descent direction $\bar{s}^k$, where for all $i \in \mathscr{S}$

$$\bar{s}_i^k = \sum_{t'=1}^t \frac{1}{N_1 N_2} \sum_{i,j} (M_i^{(t')})_{ij} \left(\frac{1}{N_1 N_2} \sum_{i,j} (\hat{M}^{(t')})_{ij} - \bar{z}^{(t')} \right). \tag{19}$$

In short, the pseudo-gradient approximates the gradient by replacing $\delta_i^{(t')}$ with the mean value of $M_i^{(t')}$ and replacing val$(\hat{M}^{(t')})$ with average entry value of $\hat{M}^{(t')}$. By doing so, we eliminate the problem for computing the saddle-point strategies and game values, significantly reducing the computational complexity.

5.1 Sequential Observation and Adaptation

When t becomes large, steepest gradient methods are inefficient as it needs to sweep through the entire dataset. It is more attractive to use an incremental method that can sequentially update the gradient. The incremental gradient method is described as follows:

$$\alpha^{k+1} = \alpha^k - \gamma^k \left(\sum_{i=1}^{t} \nabla v^{(i)}(\psi^{i-1}) v^{(i)}(\psi^{i-1}) \right), \tag{20}$$

where at iteration k:

$$\psi^i = \psi^{i-1} - \gamma^k \nabla v^{(i)}(\psi^{i-1}) v^{(i)}(\psi^{i-1}) \qquad i = 1,\ldots,t.$$

The stepsize selection is essential to ensure the convergence of the iterations. Usually when γ^k does not diminish to 0, there will be an oscillation within ψ^i.

Assumption 3. *The following conditions are satisfied:*

(a) *The product of every error (11) and its gradient is bounded for all $\alpha \in \mathscr{X}$ and every t', t; i.e.,*

$$\|\nabla v^{(t')}(\alpha) v^{(t')}(\alpha)\| \le c_1 + c_2 \|\nabla J^{(t)}(\alpha)\| \tag{21}$$

for positive constants c_1 and c_2;

(b) *Diminishing stepsize, i.e., $\sum_{k=0}^{\infty} \gamma^k = \infty$ and $\sum_{k=0}^{\infty} (\gamma^k)^2 < \infty$.*

Corollary 2. *Under Assumption 3, for all $\alpha \in \mathscr{X}$, we have*

$$(1 - 2c_2)\|\nabla J^{(t)}(\alpha)\| \le 2c_1. \tag{22}$$

Particularly, when $0 < c_2 < \frac{1}{2}$, $\|\nabla J^{(t)}(\alpha)\|$ is bounded by $\dfrac{2c_1}{1 - 2c_2}$.

This bound can be obtained through triangular inequality:

$$\|\nabla J^{(t)}(\alpha)\| = \frac{2}{t} \| \sum_{t'=1}^{t} \nabla v^{(t')}(\alpha) v^{(t')}(\alpha)\|$$

$$\le \frac{2}{t} \sum_{t'=1}^{t} \|\nabla v^{(t')}(\alpha) v^{(t')}(\alpha)\|$$

$$\le 2c_1 + 2c_2 \|\nabla J^{(t)}(\alpha)\|$$

Proposition 2. *Under Assumption 3, the incremental gradient method 20 applied to 8 generates a sequence $\{\alpha^k\}$. $J^{(t)}(\alpha^k)$ converges to a finite value and $\lim_{k\to\infty} \nabla J^{(t)}(\alpha^k) = 0$. Every limit point of α^k is a stationary point of problem 8.*

Proof. We provide a sketch of the proof here. At iteration k, we have

$$\psi^1 = \alpha^k - \gamma^k \nabla v^{(1)}(\alpha^k) v^{(1)}(\alpha^k)$$

$$\psi^2 = \alpha^k - \gamma^k \nabla v^{(2)}(\psi^1) v^{(2)}(\psi^1)$$

$$\vdots \qquad \vdots$$

$$\psi^t = \alpha^k - \gamma^k \nabla v^{(t)}(\psi^{t-1}) v^{(t)}(\psi^{t-1})$$

Adding them up, we obtain

$$\alpha^{k+1} = \alpha^k - \gamma^k \left(\nabla J^{(t)}(\alpha^k) - \sum_{t'=2}^{t} (\nabla v^{(t')}(\alpha^k) v^{(t')}(\alpha^k) - \nabla v^{(t')}(\psi^{t'-1}) v^{(t')}(\psi^{t'-1})) \right)$$

$$= \alpha^k - \gamma^k \left(\nabla J^{(t)}(\alpha^k) - w^k \right)$$

Using Theorem 3, we see that the error term $w^k = \sum_{t'=2}^{t} \nabla v^{(t')} v^{(t')}(\alpha^k) - \nabla v^{(t')} v^{(t')}(\psi^{t'-1}) = \sum_{t'=2}^{t} w_{t'}^k$ is bounded, for every t':

$$w_{t'}^k \leq \sum_{i=2}^{t-1} \|\nabla v^{(t')} v^{(t')}(\psi^i) - \nabla v^{(t')} v^{(t')}(\psi^{i-1})\|$$

$$+ \|\nabla v^{(t')} v^{(t')}(\alpha^k) - \nabla v^{(t')} v^{(t')}(\psi^1)\|$$

$$\leq \beta \left(\|\alpha^k - \psi^1\| + \sum_{i=2}^{t-1} \|\psi^i - \psi^{i-1}\| \right)$$

$$= \beta \gamma^k \left(\|\nabla v^{(t')} v^{(t')}(\alpha^k)\| + \sum_{i=1}^{t-2} \|\nabla v^{(t')} v^{(t')}(\psi^i)\| \right).$$

According to Assumption 3 (21),

$$w_{t'}^k \leq \beta \gamma^k \left((t-1)(c_1 + c_2 \|\nabla J^{(t')}(\alpha^k))\| + \sum_{i=1}^{t-2} \|\nabla J^{(t')}(\alpha^k) - \nabla J^{(t')}(\psi^i)\| \right)$$

Leveraging Corollary 2, we recursively eliminate $\nabla J^{(t')}(\psi^i)$ and see that the error term w_t is bounded; i.e., there exist positive constants C_1 and C_2 such that

$$w^k \leq \gamma^k (C_1 + C_2 \|\nabla J^{(t)}(\alpha^k)\|) \tag{23}$$

Here, we omit the algebraic calculation of constants C_1 and C_2. Note that the elimination procedures are similar. Using (18), we obtain

$$J^{(t)}(\alpha^{k+1}) - J^{(t)}(\alpha^k) \leq \gamma^k (-\|\nabla J^{(t)}(\alpha^k)\|^2 + \|\nabla J^{(t)}(\alpha^k)\| \|w^k\|)$$

$$+ \gamma^2 \beta \|\nabla J^{(t)}(\alpha) + w^k\|^2$$

$$\leq \gamma^k (-1 + \gamma^k (C_2 + 2\beta) + 2(\gamma^k)^3 C_2^2 \beta) \|\nabla J^{(t)}(\alpha)\|^2$$

$$+ (\gamma^k)^2 (C_1 + 4\gamma^2 C_1 C_2 \beta) \|\nabla J^{(t)}(\alpha)\| + 2(\gamma^k)^4 C_1^2 \beta$$

As Assumption 3 states that $(\gamma^k)^2$ diminishes to 0, the terms multiplying γ^k with order 2 or higher will go to 0. For k sufficiently large, $\gamma^k \to 0$, for some positive constants c_1' and c_2',

$$J^{(t)}(\alpha^{k+1}) - J^{(t)}(\alpha^k) \leq -\gamma^k c_1' \|\nabla J^{(t)}(\alpha)\|^2 + (\gamma^k)^2 c_2' \|\nabla J^{(t)}(\alpha)\| + 2(\gamma^k)^4 C_1^2 \beta.$$

Observe that if $\|\nabla J^{(t)}(\alpha)\| \geq 1$, then $\|\nabla J^{(t)}(\alpha)\| < \|\nabla J^{(t)}(\alpha)\|^2$, or else $\|\nabla J^{(t)}(\alpha)\|^2 \leq \|\nabla J^{(t)}(\alpha)\| \leq 1$, and thus $\|\nabla J^{(t)}(\alpha)\| \leq 1 + \|\nabla J^{(t)}(\alpha)\|^2$. Then,

$$J^{(t)}(\alpha^{k+1}) - J^{(t)}(\alpha^k) \leq -\gamma^k (c_1' - \gamma^k c_2') \|\nabla J^{(t)}(\alpha)\|^2 + o((\gamma^k)^2). \tag{24}$$

For k sufficiently large, $c_1' - \gamma^k c_2' \leq 0$, so that $J^{(t)}(\alpha^{k+1}) \leq J^{(t)}(\alpha^k)$ and $J^{(t)}(\alpha^{k+1}) \geq 0$. (24) satisfies the deterministic form of supermartingale theorem. Hence $J(\alpha)$ converges to some finite value and it must have $\sum_{k=0}^{\infty} \gamma^k \|\nabla J^{(t)}(\alpha^k)\|^2 \leq \infty$. Since we assume $\sum_{k=0}^{\infty} \gamma^k = \infty$, it also has to satisfy $\liminf_{k \to \infty} \|\nabla J^{(t)}(\alpha^k)\| = 0$. Due to Lipschitz continuity, $\limsup_{k \to \infty} \nabla J^{(t)}(\alpha^k)$ is also 0 (the proof is omitted here), and hence the limit points are stationary points. $\qquad\square$

Stochastic Gradient Descent (SGD). The surrogate estimated gradient is:

$$\alpha^{k+1} = \alpha^k - \gamma^k \nabla \hat{J}^{(t)}(\alpha^k) \tag{25}$$

$$= \alpha^k - \gamma^k \frac{1}{|B|} \sum_{b \in B} \nabla v^{(b)}(\alpha^k) v^{(b)}(\alpha^k), \tag{26}$$

where the indices b is chosen from batch set B. SGD is a stochastic version of incremental method, exhibiting a lower computational cost in one single iteration with less gradient memory storage. SGD guarantees weak convergence in non-convex systems under Lipschitz-smoothness, pseudo-gradient property, and bounded variance of the descent direction [4]. In our problem where there may exist multiple minimum, SGD potentially admits global optimum.

5.2 Extended Kalman Filter

We consider a commonly used iterative method for nonlinear least-square estimation, *Gauss-Newton* method, which is given as follows:

$$\alpha^{k+1} = \alpha^k - \gamma^k (\mathbf{J}_v \mathbf{J}_v^{\mathrm{T}} + \lambda I)^{-1} \mathbf{J}_v \mathbf{v}(\alpha^k), \tag{27}$$

where $\mathbf{J}_v = \left(\nabla v^{(1)}(\alpha^k), \ldots, \nabla v^{(t)}(\alpha^k) \right)$ is the Jacobian of the vector $\mathbf{v}(\alpha^k) = \left(v^{(1)}(\alpha^k), \ldots, v^{(t)}(\alpha^k) \right)^{\mathrm{T}}$ and λI stands for a possitive multiple of the identity matrix as proposed in *Levenberg-Marquardt* method [17] to ensure nonsingularity caused by the rank deficiency of $\mathbf{J}_v$.

Gauss-Newton iteration (27) is obtained by approximating Hessian with $(\mathbf{J}_v \mathbf{J}_v^{\mathrm{T}} + \Delta_t)$ as result of solving quadratic subproblems iteratively using linearized objective function around every α^k. This approximation avoids computing the individual residue Hessian $\nabla^2 v^{(t')}(\alpha), t' = 1, \ldots, t$, in Theorem 2.

Extended Kalman Filter (EKF) [3,4,16] is an incremental version of the Gauss-Newton method. Starting with some point α^0, a single cycle of the method updates the α via iterations that aims to minimize the partial sums $\sum_{t'=1}^{j} |v^{(t')}(\alpha)|^2 \ j = 1, \ldots, t$ successively. Thus, it sequentially generates the vectors:

$$\psi^{t'} = \arg\min_{\alpha} \sum_{i=1}^{t'} |v^{(i)}(\psi^{i-1}) + \left(\nabla v^{(i)}(\psi^{i-1}) \right)^{\mathrm{T}} (\alpha - \psi^{i-1})|^2 \qquad t' = 1, \ldots, t$$

We consider the algorithm where $\psi^{t'}$ are obtained through increments:

$$\psi^i = \psi^{i-1} - (H^i)^{-1} \nabla v^{(i)}(\psi^{i-1}) v^{(i)}(\psi^{i-1}), \qquad i = 1, \ldots, t, \tag{28}$$

with $\psi^0 = \alpha^k$ at step k, where matrices H^i are generated by:

$$H^i = \lambda H^{i-1} + \nabla v^{(i)}\left(\psi^{i-1}\right) \nabla v^{(i)}\left(\psi^{i-1}\right)^{\mathrm{T}}, \qquad i = 1,\ldots,t, \qquad (29)$$

with λ being a positive constant and $H^0 = \lambda I$ at iteration $k = 0$. The algorithm uses ψ^t at the end of an iteration to update α^k:

$$\alpha^{k+1} = \alpha^k - (H^{t(k+1)})^{-1}\Big(\sum_{i=1}^{t} \nabla v^{(i)}(\psi^{kt+i-1}) v^{(i)}(\psi^{kt+i-1})\Big), \qquad (30)$$

where

$$H^{t(k+1)} = \lambda I + \sum_{j=0}^{k}\sum_{i=1}^{t} \nabla v^{(i)}\left(\psi^{kt+i-1}\right) \nabla v^{(i)}\left(\psi^{kt+i-1}\right)^{\mathrm{T}}. \qquad (31)$$

Proposition 3 *(Extended Kalman Filter (EKF) [3]). Assuming that there is a constant $c > 0$ such that scalar λ_k used in the EKF algorithm at iteration k satisfies:*

$$0 \le 1 - \lambda_k^t \le \frac{c}{k}, \qquad k = 1, 2,\ldots.$$

Then, the EKF algorithm generates a bounded sequence of vectors ψ^i. Each of the limit points of $\{\alpha^k\}$ is a stationary point of the least-square problem 8.

Proof. One can follow the argument in Proposition 2 of [3] to show the convergence of EKF, when a series of conditions are satisfied, among which the Lipschitz condition has been verified.   □

Remark 2. λ represents the discount factor that discounts the effects of old information. An interpretation of this algorithm is that, as the defender proceeds to estimate, the previous experience tends to be gradually out-of-date, while newly encountered ones should be highly valued in the estimation.

6   Case Study

In this section, we study a network configuration game to corroborate the results and investigate the numerical properties of the algorithms. Consider a game with an attacker and a defender in a network of server group. The defender chooses a subset of servers to monitor and protect, while the attacker selects a subset of them to attack. The interactions induce some value for both players.

Assuming that each player has four strategies and the defender does not know the game, we can use a $N_1 \times N_2$ matrix game with random entries to capture this scenario. The defender sequentially estimates the game based on past experiences (i.e., expert games) and value observation. This situation is illustrated in Fig. 1.

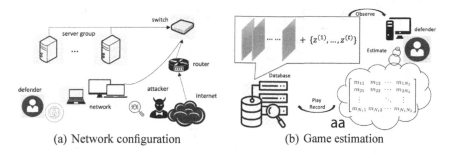

(a) Network configuration   (b) Game estimation

Fig. 1. Illustration of adversarial interaction and estimation process.

6.1 Experimental Setting and Results

Here, we conduct the experiment by fixing configuration parameters shown in Table 1. We generate the matrices $M^{(t')}$ and values of $\bar{z}^{(t')}$ from i.i.d. distributions $\mathcal{N}(\mu \mathbf{1}_4, \sigma^2 I_{4\times4})$ and $\mathcal{N}(\mu_z, \sigma_z^2)$, with a fixed random seed. As a result, the differences between values of expert games and target games scale well. We compare the performances of different methods for both **SP** and **DP**-t, and show their convergences in Fig. 2.

Table 1. Configurations

Variables	Values	Variables	Values
Data horizon t	30	$\mathcal{M}^{(t')}$ entry distribution (μ, σ)	$(1,1)$
Vector α Size S	5	$\bar{z}^{(t')}$ value distribution (μ_z, σ_z)	$(1,1)$
Stepsize γ^k	$0.98^k \times 0.01$	Parameter α initialization	$\mathbf{1}_S$
Tolerance ε	$1e-5$	Batch size $|B|$	1
Game size	4×4	Fading factor λ for EKF	0.9

The well-known Lemke-Howson algorithm [13] is implemented to find the saddle-point strategies and values of matrix games.

6.2 Discussions

From Fig. 2, one shall see Gauss-Newton method as well as EKF exhibit convergence faster than others as they naturally tune the stepsize. Meanwhile, the pseudo-gradient method displays promising convergence behavior. It can be seen in (a) that the partial contribution by expert 2 dominates the learning process, indicating greater similarity between expert game $M_2^{(1)}$ and $\hat{M}$.

We notice that the output square matrix $\hat{M}$ usually does not satisfy Assumption 2 as the estimated saddle-point mixed strategies have 0 elements in the iterative process. However, despite this, the algorithms still converge, indicating that Assumption 2 is a conservative assumption for practice.

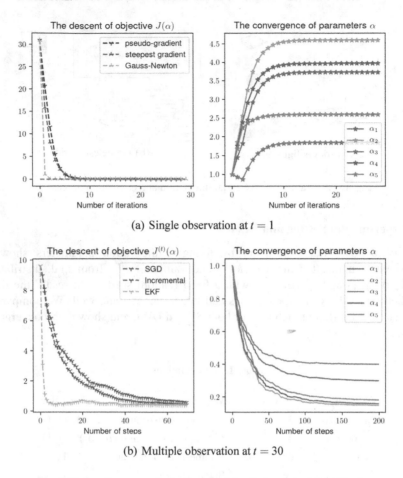

(a) Single observation at $t = 1$

(b) Multiple observation at $t = 30$

Fig. 2. Estimation curve for both static (a) and dynamic (b) problems

7   Conclusions and Future Research

This work has formulated and analyzed static and dynamic least-square game estimation problems for a class of finite zero-sum security games. The formulation captures the scenario where the players do not know the adversarial environments they interact with. We have studied the basic properties of least-square errors and developed iterative algorithms to solve the game estimation problem. The proposed approach effectively transfers the past experiences that are encoded as expert games to estimate the unknown game and inform future game plays. We have seen that the algorithms work over randomly generated datasets despite certain assumptions are not strictly satisfied.

There are many open research problems that could be addressed as future work. First, it has been observed that the assumption for completely mixed game is conservative. The future work would investigate the properties of the error functions when the assumption does not hold. Second, it would be possible to extend this framework for stochastic games. We would capture the dynamic adversarial environment using a stochastic game representation, and estimate the environment using multi-time scale observations.

References

1. Bajari, P., Hong, H., Ryan, S.: Identification and estimation of a normal form game. manuscript, Duke University (2004)
2. Bajari, P., Hong, H., Ryan, S.P.: Identification and estimation of a discrete game of complete information. Econometrica **78**(5), 1529–1568 (2010)
3. Bertsekas, D.P.: Incremental least squares methods and the extended kalman filter. SIAM J. Optim. **6**(3), 807 (1996)
4. Bertsekas, D.P., Tsitsiklis, J.N.: Neuro-dynamic programming. Athena Scientific (1996)
5. Bohnenblust, H., Karlin, S., Shapley, L.: Solutions of discrete, two-person games. Contrib. Theory Games **1**, 51–72 (1950)
6. Cohen, J.E.: Perturbation theory of completely mixed matrix games. Linear Algebra Appl. **79**, 153–162 (1986). https://doi.org/10.1016/0024-3795(86)90297-1, http://www.sciencedirect.com/science/article/pii/0024379586902971
7. Cohen, J.E., Marchi, E., Oviedo, J.A.: Perturbation theory of completely mixed bimatrix games. Linear Algebra Appl. **114**, 169–180 (1989)
8. Gross, O.A.: The derivatives of the value of a game (1954)
9. Harsanyi, J.C.: Games with incomplete information played by "bayesian" players, i–iii part i. the basic model. Manage. Sci. **14**(3), 159–182 (1967)
10. Hotz, V.J., Miller, R.A.: Conditional choice probabilities and the estimation of dynamic models. Rev. Econ. Stud. **60**(3), 497–529 (1993)
11. Jennrich, R.I.: Asymptotic properties of non-linear least squares estimators. Ann. Math. Stat. **40**(2), 633–643 (1969)
12. Jovanovic, B.: Observable implications of models with multiple equilibria. Econometrica: J. Econometric Soc., 1431–1437 (1989)
13. Lemke, C.E., Howson Jr., J.T.: Equilibrium points of bimatrix games. J. Soc. Ind. Appl. Math. **12**(2), 413–423 (1964)
14. Malinvaud, E.: The consistency of nonlinear regressions. Ann. Math. Stat. **41**(3), 956–969 (1970)
15. Mertens, J.F., Zamir, S.: Formulation of bayesian analysis for games with incomplete information. Int. J. Game Theory **14**(1), 1–29 (1985)
16. Moriyama, H., Yamashita, N., Fukushima, M.: The incremental gauss-newton algorithm with adaptive stepsize rule. Comput. Optim. Appl. **26**(2), 107–141 (2003)
17. Nocedal, J., Wright, S.: Numerical Optimization. Springer Science & Business Media, New York (2006). https://doi.org/10.1007/978-0-387-40065-5
18. Pesendorfer, M., Schmidt-Dengler, P.: Identification and estimation of dynamic games. Technical report, National Bureau of Economic Research (2003)
19. Pesendorfer, M., Schmidt-Dengler, P.: Asymptotic least squares estimators for dynamic games. Rev. Econ. Stud. **75**(3), 901–928 (2008)
20. Rass, S.: On game-theoretic network security provisioning. J. Netw. Syst. Manage. **21**(1), 47–64 (2013)
21. Shapley, L.S., Snow, R.: Basic solutions of discrete games. Contrib. Theory Games **1**, 27–35 (1952)
22. Wu, C.F.: Asymptotic theory of nonlinear least squares estimation. Ann. Stat. **9**, 501–513 (1981)

23. Xiao, R.: Identification and estimation of incomplete information games with multiple equilibria. J. Econ. **203**(2), 328–343 (2018)
24. Zhu, Q., Başar, T.: Dynamic policy-based ids configuration. In: Proceedings of the 48h IEEE Conference on Decision and Control (CDC) held jointly with 2009 28th Chinese Control Conference, pp. 8600–8605. IEEE (2009)
25. Zhu, Q., Li, H., Han, Z., Başar, T.: A stochastic game model for jamming in multi-channel cognitive radio systems. In: 2010 IEEE International Conference on Communications, pp. 1–6. IEEE (2010)

Using One-Sided Partially Observable Stochastic Games for Solving Zero-Sum Security Games with Sequential Attacks

Petr Tomášek[1]([✉]), Branislav Bošanský[1], and Thanh H. Nguyen[2]

[1] Artificial Intelligence Center, Department of Computer Science, Faculty of Electrical Engineering, Czech Technical University in Prague, Prague, Czechia
{petr.tomasek,branislav.bosansky}@fel.cvut.cz
[2] Department of Computer and Information Science, University of Oregon, Eugene, USA
tnguyen11@uoregon.edu

Abstract. Security games are a defender-attacker game-theoretic model where the defender determines how to allocate scarce resources to protect valuable targets against the attacker. A majority of existing work has focused on the one-shot game setting in which the attacker only attacks once. However, in many real-world scenarios, the attacker can perform multiple attacks in a sequential manner and leverage observable effects of these attacks for better attack decisions in the future. Recent work shows that in order to provide effective protection over targets, the defender has to take the prospect of sequential attacks into consideration. The algorithm proposed by existing work to handle sequential attacks, however, can only scale up to two attacks at most. We extend this line of work and focus on developing new *scalable* algorithms for solving the zero-sum variant of security games. We formulate security games with sequential attacks as a one-sided partially observable stochastic games. We show that the uncertainty about the state in the game can be modeled compactly and we can use variants of heuristic search value iteration algorithm for solving these games. We give two variants of the algorithm – an exact one and a heuristic formulation where the resource reallocation possibilities of the defender are simplified. We experimentally compare these two variants of the algorithm and show that the heuristic variant is typically capable of finding high-quality strategies while scaling to larger scenarios compared to the exact variant.

Keywords: Security games · Sequential attacks · Partially observable stochastic games · Zero-sum games

This research was supported by the Czech Science Foundation (no. 19-24384Y) and by the OP VVV MEYS funded project CZ.02.1.01/0.0/0.0/16 019/0000765 "Research Center for Informatics".

© Springer Nature Switzerland AG 2020
Q. Zhu et al. (Eds.): GameSec 2020, LNCS 12513, pp. 385–404, 2020.
https://doi.org/10.1007/978-3-030-64793-3_21

1   Introduction

Defender-attacker security games are a well-known class of resource allocation games where a defender has to protect a set of targets against an attacker. The defender chooses how to allocate his limited resources to these targets while the attacker chooses which target(s) to attack. In practice, the *one-shot* security game setting was used in several successful applications, in which the attacker is assumed to attack only *once* [1,5,6,8,9,13]. However, in many real-world security domains, the attacks might occur *sequentially* – the attacker can choose to attack targets in a sequence while observing the results of executed attacks. Performing a sequential attack is beneficial for the attacker due to discovered knowledge (by attacking a target, the attacker can partially discover the current allocation of the defending units). Only recently, a new model of *security games with sequential attacks* (SGSA) has been introduced [7] showing that it is indeed necessary for the defender to be prepared for the sequential attacks.

In SGSA, both players choose their actions *simultaneously* over several rounds—each round corresponds to a simple security game (in which the defender allocates the resources to the targets and the attacker chooses one target to attack). Afterwards, the outcome of the actions is determined—if the attacked target has been unprotected (protected, respectively), the attack is successful (unsuccessful). The game then enters into the next round while assuming that the attacked target is no longer available for protection/attack. Moreover, if the attack was unsuccessful, the defending unit that was present at the target cannot be reallocated to protect other targets. The initial work [7] introduced several variants of SGSA and showed that it is indeed better for the attacker to attack in sequence. Therefore, the defender must take the possibility of sequential attacks into consideration and provided an algorithm for computing Strong Stackelberg equilibrium for selected variants. However, the general algorithms for solving SGSA are missing. The existing algorithms for computing a Strong Stackelberg equilibrium for SGSA are restricted to two rounds only (the attacker can perform two attacks) if the defender is able to reallocate the units and it is not clear whether a generalization to multiple rounds is possible.

In this work, we attempt to address this computation limitation of the previous work, with the following main contributions. First, we leverage recent advancement in solving sub-classes of zero-sum *partially observable stochastic games (POSGs)* in which one player has perfect information and the other player has partial information, termed *one-sided POSGs (OS-POSGs)* [3,4]. Algorithms for solving OS-POSGs are based on a heuristic search value iteration (HSVI) algorithm and are capable of handling very long horizons. We show that zero-sum SGSA can be formulated as a OS-POSGs, thus allowing us to use the existing algorithms of solving OS-POSGs. Second, we develop a new compact representation for SGSA to avoid the exploration of an exponential number of states (due to exponentially many possible subsets of protected targets) involved in the computation of the original HSVI algorithm. While the idea behind using the compact representation in HSVI has been introduced for a lateral-movement game in computer networks [2,3], the technical realization of this idea in the domain of security games is non-trivial and novel. Third, in order to further improve the scalability, we introduce a heuristic variant of the game where we introduce a mild restriction for the defending units—each target can be in one stage protected only by one unit, and this allocation of units is determined heuristically. While this heuristic partitioning of targets among the defending units can negatively affect the quality of defending strategies, our experimental evaluation shows that with an increasing number of targets, the quality of strategies is very close to the exact formulation. Moreover, the heuristic variant scales to larger scenarios. Finally, we conduct extensive experiments to evaluate proposed methods. We show that (1) ignoring the sequential aspect and solving each round separately results in strategies with poor quality and that (2) our methods can solve larger SGSA with multiple rounds (which the existing algorithm cannot handle) while maintaining high-quality strategies for the players in the game.

2   Technical Background

In this section, we first provide the basic definitions for one-sided partially observable stochastic games (OS-POSGs) and describe the ideas behind the heuristic search value iteration (HSVI) algorithm. We then formally define security games with sequential attacks (SGSAs).

2.1   One-Sided Partially Observable Stochastic Games (OS-POSG)

OS-POSG [4] is an imperfect-information two-player zero-sum infinite-horizon game with perfect recall, formally defined as a tuple $G = \langle S, A_1, A_2, O, \tau, \rho \rangle$. The game evolves in rounds, where in each round a *stage game* is played. At each stage, the game is in one of the states $s \in S$ and players simultaneously pick their actions $a_1 \in A_1$ and $a_2 \in A_2$. The initial state of the game is drawn from a probability distribution $b^0 \in \Delta(S)$ over the set of states S, which is treated as a parameter of the game and termed *the initial belief*. The one-sided nature of the game results in the fact that while player 2 can observe the game perfectly (i.e., his only uncertainty is the action a_1 player 1 decided to take in the current stage), player 1 lacks detailed information about the course of the game (i.e., he is uncertain not only about the action a_2 for the current stage but also about the current state of the game).

The choice of actions determines the outcomes for the current stage: player 1 gets an observation $o \in O$ and the game transitions to a state $s' \in S$ with transition probability $\tau(o, s' \mid s, a_1, a_2)$, where s is the current state of the game. Furthermore, player 1 gets a reward $\rho(s, a_1, a_2)$ for this transition, and player 2 receives $-\rho(s, a_1, a_2)$ (the rewards are not directly observable by player 1). Note that the next stage of the game s' is a result of joint action (a_1, a_2) and actions of player 2 (who has perfect information) directly affects the observations received by player 1 and thus his belief as well. The rewards are discounted over time with discount factor γ, $0 < \gamma < 1$.

2.2   Heuristic Search Value Iteration (HSVI)

State of the art method for solving OS-POSGs [4] is a modification of the HSVI
algorithm for Partially Observable Markov Decision Processes [10,12] that combines heuristic search techniques with piecewise linear convex value function
representations. The goal of HSVI is to approximate the optimal value function
$V^* : \Delta(S) \to \mathbb{R}$ that maps each belief point to a value of the game (should the
players follow optimal strategies) using a pair of value functions $\underline{V}$ (lower bound
on V^*) and $\overline{V}$ (upper bound on V^*) – see Fig. 1. HSVI refines these bounds by
solving a sequence of stage games. In each of these stage games, the algorithm
searches for the optimal strategies of both players (i.e., $\pi_1 \in \Delta(A_1)$ for player 1
and $\pi_2(s) \in \Delta(A_2)$ for player 2) while assuming that the play in the subsequent
stages yields values represented by value functions $\underline{V}$ or $\overline{V}$, respectively. When
moving to the next stage in sequence, the stage with maximum excess approxi-
mation error between corresponding upper and lower bound weighted by reach
probability is selected. The key advantage of this approach is that in practice,
we do not need to solve the whole game tree but only a smaller portion of it.
Furthermore, the algorithm uses two approximations on the optimal value func-
tion V^* ($\underline{V}$ and $\overline{V}$). By further refining, these approximations are converging to
the optimal value and the margin by which the approximated solution is worse
than the optimal one has guaranteed bounds (unlike in other value iteration
methods).[1]

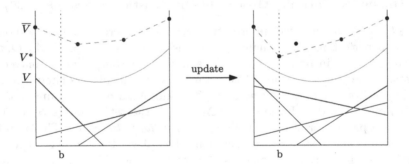

Fig. 1. HSVI local update in the belief b [11] (Color figure online)

The lower bound $\underline{V}$ (blue line in Fig. 1) on V^* is represented by commonly
used vector representation as a finite set Γ of linear functions $\alpha_i : \Delta(S) \to \mathbb{R}$.
Where the value at a belief state b is the maximum projection of b onto the set
Γ. The value of $\underline{V}(b)$ is point-wise maximum over this set

$$\underline{V}(b) = \max_{\alpha \in \Gamma}(\alpha \cdot b)$$

These linear functions are termed *alpha vectors* and represent expected outcomes
of strategies found by the algorithm (black lines in the bottom part of Fig. 1).

---

[1] For theoretical results and proofs refer to [11].

Since the HSVI algorithm relies on the local updates (i.e., updating bounds for specific belief point) and improving bounds in the neighborhood of the local update (as shown in Fig. 1 local update results not only in improving bounds in particular belief point but also in its neighborhood), the upper bound cannot be represented by a vector set. Therefore, the upper bound $\overline{V}$ on V^* is expressed using a set $\Upsilon = \{(b^{(i)}, y^{(i)}) \mid 1 \leq i \leq |\Upsilon|\}$ of belief/value points $(b^{(i)}, y^{(i)})$ (dots in the upper part of Fig. 1). The lower convex hull of this set of points is then used to obtain the value of $\overline{V}(b)$ (red dashed line in Fig. 1).

$$\overline{V}(b) = \min_{\lambda \in \mathbb{R}_{\geq 0}^{|\Upsilon|}} \left\{ \sum_{1 \leq i \leq |\Upsilon|} \lambda_i y^{(i)} \mid \mathbf{1}^T \lambda = 1, \sum_{1 \leq i \leq |\Upsilon|} \lambda_i b^{(i)} = b \right\}$$

Finally, HSVI local updates are performed by adding a new vector (for the lower bound) or a point (for the upper bound) to the current sets Γ and Υ, respectively.

Compact Representation HSVI. The dimension of the value function V^* depends on the number of states, which can be potentially very large. Therefore an abstraction scheme was proposed [3]. This abstraction scheme reduces the dimensionality of the problem by creating a simplified representation of the beliefs over the state space. This means that each belief $b \in \Delta(S)$ in the game is associated with a *characteristic vector* $\chi^{(b)} = \mathbf{A} \cdot b$ (for some matrix $\mathbf{A} \in \mathbb{R}^{k \times |S|}$ where $k \ll |S|$). The characteristic vector corresponding to the initial belief b^0 is denoted as χ^0. It was proved that value function V^s computed using compact representation is valid lower bound on the solution of the original game (value function V^*) – [3, Theorem 1]. And also that the value function V^s is convex – [3, Theorem 2]. Compact representation HSVI was shown to outperform the current state of the art algorithms for solving large OS-POSGs [2,3] in terms of scalability with only negligible loss in quality. In this work, we aim to modify this method for a different domain of games and achieve similar results.

2.3 Security Games with Sequential Attacks

Security games with sequential attacks (SGSA) [7] are an extension to the classical Stackelberg security games (SSG) model. The defender has to perpetually defend a set of targets T using a limited number of resources R. The attacker is able to surveil the defender's strategy and adjust his attack based on the surveillance. An action of the defender is deploying his limited set of resources R^s to protect targets from T^s in each game state $s \in S$. Similarly, an action of an attacker represents attacking one of the targets from T^s in each game state $s \in S$. The mixed strategy of the defender in each state $s \in S$ then corresponds to a probability distribution over pure strategies in that state. Finally, each target has associated a set of payoff values that define the utilities for both players. Since we restrict to the zero-sum case, we assume that the payoff values correspond to the perspective of the attacker receiving in case of a successful or failed attack, respectively. SGSAs further extend this model by incorporating sequential attacks allowing an attacker to attack multiple times during one game.

The SGSA dynamic works as follows. Initially, the resources of the defender are randomly allocated to targets according to a mixed strategy of the defender in the initial stage. During the execution time, the defender samples a specific allocation of resources from his mixed strategy. The attacker is aware of defender's mixed strategy, but he lacks the information which targets are protected at the execution time. By attacking targets sequentially, the attacker is able to obtain additional information about a state of the game through observations from previous attacks. Based on the observation, the attacker can update his belief about the strategy of the defender and decide on targets to attack next that would benefit the attacker the most. After each attack, the game moves to the next stage and the defender decides whether to move security resources to any other target or not (by sampling from his mixed strategy for that particular stage of the game).

This paper focuses on solving SGSAs in the resource-movement setting under the following assumptions. First, we assume that the attacker can carry out $K > 1$ rounds of attacks and attack one target per round. Furthermore, the attacker can discover whether target t_i was protected after attacking that particular target. Note that this observation reveals only protection status for target t_i and the attacker is still unaware of the current protection status of remaining targets. The defender has to move security resources among targets in response to each attack, and there is a constant reallocation cost $c \geq 0$ for moving a resource from one target to another one[2]. Further, we assume that when a target t_i is attacked, the damage caused by the attack (if any) to t_i is already done. Therefore, that target will not be considered in future rounds. In addition, if there is a security resource protecting the attacked target, the resource has to resolve that attack. Thus the defender can no longer use that resource for future defense.

3   Using OS-POSGs for Sequential Attacks

In this section, we first represent our SGSA modeled game as OS-POSG. Then we present an HSVI-inspired algorithm for solving such games and discuss two variants of it—an exact one and a simplified heuristic formulation.

3.1   Representing SGSA as OS-POSG

Since the attacker can attack multiple times in SGSA, the game itself is divided into several rounds (stage games). Each of these stage games is equivalent to a state of the game we are trying to solve forming a set of states S. These states are described by a set of remaining security resources R, set of remaining targets T, the number of remaining attacks K and initial allocation of security resources χ (based on the final allocation in the previous state). As mentioned above, in

---

[2] Note that this can be generalized even further so that costs correspond to, for example, distances between the targets in a graph.

SGSA the defender has perfect information about the current situation in the game (current state of the game) and is only uncertain about the attack that will be performed. On the other hand, the attacker has only partial information since he knows only the set of remaining targets and the number of remaining resources. Therefore we can easily represent SGSA as OS-POSG. The defender from SGSA corresponds to the perfect-info player in OS-POSG (player 2 in the definition) and the attacker corresponds to the imperfect-info player (player 1 in the definition). Observation sent to the attacker contains information about whether there was a security resource on the attacked target or not. Reward function ρ returns utility of attack based on whether it succeeded or not plus the cost for reallocating security resources (if the reallocation cost $c > 0$). Finally, transition function τ determines the set of remaining resources R' and targets T' and initial allocation χ' for state s' based on taken actions. Each state $s \in S$ has its own specific value function V^s (note that this value function is equal to the value function of a subgame rooted in the state s) with corresponding upper $(\overline{V}^s)$ and lower $(\underline{V}^s)$ bound.

The initial allocation χ consists of a set of marginal distributions over targets—one for each resource $r \in R$—stating what is the probability that resource r is protecting target i. As the following example demonstrates, we cannot use aggregated marginal coverage ignoring the resources. In this case, the transition function τ could not uniquely define the next state of the game – the rules of SGSA require that we can identify which resource was protecting a target in case of an unsuccessful attack (that resource is removed for next stages and the allocation of other resources has to be rescaled appropriately).

Example: Let's consider instance of SGSA presented in Fig. 2. This instance corresponds to stage game with 2 security resources and 4 targets and possible transitions to future stage games after target t_1 is attacked. Note that the final allocations in the root game are represented by marginal probabilities x^r per resource r. In this representation, we can easily determine the initial allocation in future stage after attacker being caught either by resource r_1 or r_2 (the initial allocation is normalized distribution consisting of probabilities $x^r[i]$ that are not crossed out). Let's assume that we will use marginal probabilities over targets $(x[i] = \sum_{r \in R} x^r[i]; \forall i \in T)$ instead. In such a case, we will be still able to compute coverage of targets that will ensure the same immediate reward in first stage game as marginal probabilities per resource representation. After successful defense of a target i, security resource r protecting i is removed from the game and all contributions of r to marginal probabilities over targets must be deleted. However, when representing initial allocations by marginal probabilities over targets, we do not know the exact contributions of individual resources. Therefore, we cannot compute the exact initial allocation for sub-games after catching the attacker. To handle this issue, we have to use marginal probabilities per resource.

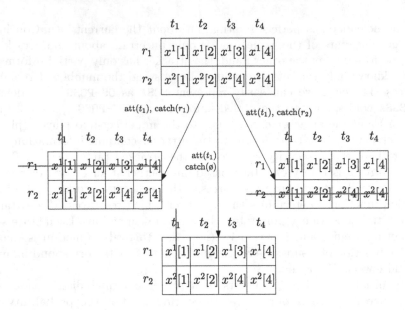

Fig. 2. Example of SGSA

3.2 HSVI-Inspired Algorithm

Our definition of SGSA uses a compact representation of states and uncertainty. Our algorithm (the pseudocode is shown in Algorithm 1) is based on the HSVI algorithm for compactly-represented lateral-movement game in computer networks [2,3]. While the overall schema of the algorithm is similar and follows the steps of the original HSVI as described in Sect. 2.2, the main technical difference is in the algorithms for solving stage games and thus updating the lower and upper bound functions (described in Sects. 3.3 and 3.4).

Besides this, there are two minor changes to the structure of the algorithm itself. One of the differences is that SGSA is finite horizon game (the number of rounds is limited by the number of attacks K) while the OS-POSG is infinite horizon thus we can omit discount factor γ. Another difference between Algorithm 1 and HSVI for abstracted OS-POSGs is that we do not explore only state s'_{max} with maximum weighted gap $p(s'_{max}) * (\overline{V}^{s'_{max}}(\chi') - \underline{V}^{s'_{max}}(\chi')$ but instead we explore each possible state s' for which holds $p(s') * (\overline{V}^{s'}(\chi') - \underline{V}^{s'}(\chi') > 0$. This decision is based on the experimental evaluation, where we achieved significantly better runtime when exploring all possible states with a non-zero weighted gap.

The algorithm (Algorithm 1) works as follows. First, for each state $s \in S$ we initialize bounds $\overline{V}^s$ and $\underline{V}^s$ (line 1) to valid piecewise linear and convex lower and upper bound on V^s. During the initialization phase, we initialize sets Γ and Υ for each state of the game. Every set Γ is initialized by one linear function representing the value of corresponding game state assuming that reallocation cost $c = 0$ and in the future states the defender will always catch the attacker on such a target from the remaining ones where the attacker has the highest penalty for being caught. Similarly, every set Υ is initialized by points representing all possible pure strategies of the defender in that particular state and value achieved when playing according to that strategy assuming that all resources have to be reallocated, and in the future states, the defender will never catch the attacker while the attacker always attacks the most valuable target from the set of remaining targets. After the initialization, we perform a sequence of trials (lines 3–5) from initial characteristic vector χ^0 until the desired precision $\epsilon > 0$ (determined on line 2) is reached.

In each of the trials, we first compute the optimal *optimistic* strategy of player 2 (line 7) and update sets Γ and Υ based on the solutions of $\underline{V}^s(\chi)$ and $\overline{V}^s(\chi)$ (line 8). Next, we iterate over each pair of action a_1 of player 1 and observation o leading to next state s' with a non-zero weighted gap (lines 9–12). For each of these states we update Γ' and Υ' based on the solutions of $\underline{V}^{s'}(\chi')$ and $\overline{V}^{s'}(\chi')$ (line 13). If the gap $\overline{V}^{s'}(\chi') - \underline{V}^{s'}(\chi')$ is greater than desired ϵ, we recurse to the characteristic vector χ' (lines 14–15). Finally, the update of sets Γ and Υ is done by adding a new alpha vector or point to the corresponding set.

---

1   Initialization

2   Set $\epsilon = (\overline{V}^{s^0}(\chi^0) - \underline{V}^{s^0}(\chi^0)) * 10^{-2}$

3   **while** $\overline{V}^{s^0}(\chi^0) - \underline{V}^{s^0}(\chi^0) > \epsilon$ **do**

4   Explore(s^0, χ^0, ϵ)

5   Update Γ and Υ based on the solutions of $\underline{V}^{s^0}(\chi^0)$ and $\overline{V}^{s^0}(\chi^0)$

6   **procedure** Explore(s, χ, ϵ)

7      $(b, \pi_2) \leftarrow$ optimal belief and strategy of defender in $\underline{V}^s(\chi)$

8   Update Γ and Υ based on the solutions of $\underline{V}^s(\chi)$ and $\overline{V}^s(\chi)$

9   **for** $(a_1, o) \in A_1 \times O$ **do**

10        $s', \chi' \leftarrow \tau(\chi, a_1, \pi_2, o)$

11   Determine reach probability $p(s')$ of state s'

12   **if** $p(s') * (\overline{V}^{s'}(, \chi') - \underline{V}^{s'}(\chi') > 0$ **then**

13   Update Γ' and Υ' based on the solutions of $\underline{V}^{s'}(\chi')$ and $\overline{V}^{s'}(\chi')$

14   **if** $\overline{V}^{s'}(\chi') - \underline{V}^{s'}(\chi') > \epsilon$ **then**

15   Explore(s', χ', ϵ)

Algorithm 1: HSVI inspired algorithm for SGSA

As mentioned previously, one of the key differences in our HSVI-inspired algorithm for solving SGSAs compared with the original HSVI is in the computation of lower bound $\underline{V}$ and upper bound $\overline{V}$, which is domain dependent. We propose two variants of HSVI inspired algorithm for solving our SGSAs. The difference between them is in the way how they approach solution (i.e., estimation of $\underline{V}$ and $\overline{V}$) of stage games (i.e., the assumed set of available actions of the defender in each stage game). The first one is exact and assumes the whole action space consisting of all possible joint actions. The second one is a simplified heuristic formulation and reduces the size of the action space by assuming that each

resource has its own set of assigned targets that can be covered by that particular resource and these sets are mutually disjoint. Therefore, it is ensured that no
target can be covered by more than one resource and we do not need to use joint
actions and can use separate reallocation actions for each individual resource.
The different action sets used by these variants result in a different construction
of linear programs used for solving stage games as well. We describe these two
variants in the following.

3.3 Exact Variant of the Algorithm

As we mentioned above, the marginal probabilities of covering targets are not
enough and we need probability for each target being covered by particular
resource. Therefore we have to consider all possible joint reallocation actions
(i.e., all possible combinations of reallocating each resource from all possible
starting positions to every possible end position[3]). This means that we have to
deal with extremely large action space with size exponential in the number of
resources R (the size of the action space is T^{2*R}). The huge action spaces result
in extremely large linear programs for computing game values.

Initializing Lower Bound and Upper Bound. The presented linear program
is general for an arbitrary number of resources R. For the sake of simplicity, we
show the linear program for lower bound initialization of a game with $R = 2$:

$$\min V^s \tag{1a}$$

$$\text{s.t.} \sum_{i \in N} x^r[i] = 1 \qquad\qquad \forall r \in R \tag{1b}$$

$$\sum_{i,j} m[i,k,j,k] = 0 \qquad\qquad \forall k \in T \tag{1c}$$

$$\sum_{j,k,l} m[i,k,j,l] = \chi^1[i] \qquad\qquad \forall i \in T \tag{1d}$$

$$\sum_{i,k,l} m[i,k,j,l] = \chi^2[j] \qquad\qquad \forall j \in T \tag{1e}$$

$$\sum_{i,j,l} m[i,k,j,l] = x^1[k] \qquad\qquad \forall k \in T \tag{1f}$$

$$\sum_{i,j,k} m[i,k,j,l] = x^2[l] \qquad\qquad \forall l \in T \tag{1g}$$

$$x_-[i] = \sum_{j,k \in T} \sum_{l,n \in N \setminus i} m[j,l,k,n] \qquad\qquad \forall i \in T \tag{1h}$$

$$x_-[i] * u[i] + \sum_{r \in R} x^r[i] * p[i] \le V^s \qquad\qquad \forall i \in T \tag{1i}$$

$$m[i,j,k,l] \ge 0 \qquad\qquad \forall i,j,k,l \in T \tag{1j}$$

---

[3] Note that only reallocation actions resulting in situations where no target is covered
by more than one resource are assumed.

In the above linear program, the defender is looking for a new allocation of 2 security resources in stage game without considering future stages and realloca- tion. The probability of executing a joint reallocation action is expressed using the variable m, where the value of $m[i, k, j, l]$ corresponds to the probability of the first resource moving from target i to target k AND the second resource moving from target j to target l. We have to ensure that probabilities m of joint actions cannot exceed the initial allocation χ^r of each resource r (constraints (1d), (1e)) and sums to the final marginal probabilities x^r per resource $r \in R$ (constraints (1f), (1g)). The final marginal probabilities x^r over targets T per resource $r \in R$ must sum to 1 (constraint (1b)). We also need to ensure that one target cannot be covered by more than 1 resource at a time (constraint (1c)). Now, in order to correctly identify the initial allocation in possibly subse- quent stages of the game, we need conditional probabilities in case the attacker attacks a target i that would be protected by some resource or unprotected, respectively. The probability that no resource protects target i is represented by variable $x_-[i]$. Finally, constraints (1i) represent the best response of the attacker to the defender's strategy and ensure that the defender will minimize the reward received by the attacker.

Updating Lower Bound and Upper Bound. During HSVI inspired compu- tation, we need to solve linear programs for lower and upper bound and based on the solutions of these programs update set of alpha vectors Γ and set of points Υ respectively. The linear programs for computing value of lower and upper bound look almost the same as for the initialization. The only difference is that these linear programs will take into account future stages and reallocation cost.

First, we add constraints defining the reallocation costs for all actions:

$$C[k, l, m, n] = 2 * c \qquad \forall k, m \in R, \forall l \in R \setminus k, \forall n \in R \setminus m \quad (2a)$$

$$C[k, l, m, m] = c \qquad \forall k, m \in R, \forall l \in R \setminus k \quad (2b)$$

$$C[k, k, m, n] = c \qquad \forall k, m \in R, \forall n \in R \setminus m \quad (2c)$$

$$C[k, k, m, n] = 0 \qquad \forall k, m \in R \quad (2d)$$

$$\mathbb{C} = \sum_{i,j,k,l \in T} m[i, j, k, l] * C[i, j, k, l] \quad (2e)$$

Where constraints (2a)–(2d) ensure that the reallocation cost C for each joint action corresponds to the number of resources reallocated by that joint action. Variable $\mathbb{C}$ represents a reallocation cost of defenders mixed strategy.

Second, we must add constraints for values propagating from future stage games. In the stage game with 2 resources, there are three possible next stages reachable after an attack on target i is performed. The defender either did not catch the attacker or the attacker was caught by either resource r_1 or r_2.

We need two components to correctly compute the values of future stage games: (1) alpha vectors representing the value function of each particular sub- game and (2) initial allocation of security resources in those sub-games. Note that the future initial allocations must correspond to the final allocation in the current stage game and that the future initial allocations are already weighted by probabilities of reaching corresponding sub-games (initial allocation of individual resources in a sub-game sums to the reach probability of that sub-game). For the sub-game reachable when the attacker was not caught on target i, we will use set of alpha vectors $\mathbb{A}_-[i]$ (stands for set Γ in lower bound linear program and for the lower convex hull of set Υ in upper bound linear program) and initial allocation $b_-[i]$ which consist of initial allocation $b_-^1[i]$ of resource r_1 and initial allocation $b_-^2[i]$ of resource r_2—constraints (3a) and (3b). When the attacker was caught on target i we will use set of alpha vector $\mathbb{A}_+[i]$ (corresponding to set Γ or lower convex hull of set Υ respectively). As initial allocation we will either use $b_+^1[i]$ (when caught by r_1) or $b_+^2[i]$ (when caught by r_2)—constraints (3e) and (3f).

$$b_-^1[att] = [\sum_{j,k \in T, l \in T \setminus att} m[j,i,k,l]; \forall i \in R \setminus att] \qquad \forall att \in T \qquad (3a)$$

$$b_-^2[att] = [\sum_{j,k \in T, l \in T \setminus att} m[j,l,k,i]; \forall i \in R \setminus att] \qquad \forall att \in T \qquad (3b)$$

$$b_-[i] = [b_-^1[i], b_-^2[i]] \qquad \forall i \in T \qquad (3c)$$

$$\sum_{\alpha \in \mathbb{A}_-[i]} \alpha * b_-[i] \leq V^-[i] \qquad \forall i \in T \qquad (3d)$$

$$b_+^1[i] = [\sum_{j,k \in T} m[j,i,k,l]; \forall l \in T \setminus i] \qquad \forall i \in T; \qquad (3e)$$

$$b_+^2[i] = [\sum_{j,k \in T} m[j,l,k,i]; \forall l \in T \setminus i] \qquad \forall i \in T \qquad (3f)$$

$$\sum_{\alpha \in \mathbb{A}_+[i]} \alpha * b_+^1[i] \leq V_{+,1}[i] \qquad \forall i \in T \qquad (3g)$$

$$\sum_{\alpha \in \mathbb{A}_+[i]} \alpha * b_+^2[i] \leq V_{+,2}[i] \qquad \forall i \in T \qquad (3h)$$

Constraint (3d) stands for expected future value if no resource is present at target i. Constraints (3g) and (3h) represent expected future values if resource r_1 or r_2 is protecting target i.

Finally, we need to modify constraints (1i) to take into account reallocation cost and values of future states

$$x_-[i] * u[i] + V_-[i] + \sum_{r \in R} (x^r[i] * p[i] + V_{+,r}[i]) + \mathbb{C} \leq V^s \qquad (4)$$

3.4   Heuristic Variant of the Algorithm

To tackle the issue with large action space needed for the exact variant of our algorithm, we devised a simplified heuristic formulation of stage games we need to solve. The heuristic formulation assumes that each resource has its own set of

assigned targets that can be covered by that particular resource and these sets
are mutually disjoint. Such distribution ensures that every target can be covered
by only one resource and therefore we can have separate reallocation actions
for each resource r. This means that the size of the action space is significantly
reduced since it is no longer exponential but linear.

Initializing Lower Bound and Upper Bound. The smaller number of
actions in the game results in less variables in the linear program and easier
construction of the linear program as well. In general, the linear program for
initialization of lower bound looks as follows:

$$\min V^s \tag{5a}$$

$$\text{s.t.} \sum_{i,j \in T} m^r[i,j] = 1 \qquad\qquad\qquad \forall r \in R \tag{5b}$$

$$\sum_{j \in T} m^r[j,i] = x^r[i] \qquad\qquad\qquad \forall r \in R, \forall i \in T \tag{5c}$$

$$\sum_{j \in T_r} m^r[i,j] = \chi^r[i] \qquad\qquad\qquad \forall i \in T \tag{5d}$$

$$\sum_{j \in T_r \setminus i} x^r[j] * u[i] + x^r[i] * p[i] \leq V^s \qquad \forall i \in T, r \in R; T_r \ni i \tag{5e}$$

$$m^r[i,j] \geq 0 \qquad\qquad\qquad \forall i,j \in T \tag{5f}$$

Where $m^r[i,j]$ stands for the probability of executing a reallocation action of
resource r from target i to target j. As in the linear program in the exact variant
of algorithm, we have to ensure that the probabilities of reallocation actions m^r
of resource r sums to 1 (constraints (5b)) and do not exceed the initial allocation
χ^r (constraints (5d)) and sums to final marginal probabilities x^r per resource
r (constraints (5c)). Finally, we represent best response of the attacker by the
constraints (5e).

Updating Lower Bound and Upper Bound. The modifications needed to
obtain linear programs for computing lower and upper bound are similar to the
ones used for the exact variant. Since actions in the heuristic variant correspond
to the reallocation of only one resource (unlike the joint actions in the exact
variant that correspond to the reallocation of multiple resources), we do not
need to specifically define reallocation costs for actions. Thus first step is to add
constraints for values of future states, which can be represented as follows:

$$b_-^r[i] = [\sum_{k\in T} m^r[k,j] - \lambda_-^r[i,j]; \forall j \in T_r] \qquad\qquad \forall i \in T, \forall r \in R \qquad (6a)$$

$$\sum_{j\in T} \lambda_-^r[i,j] = \sum_{r'\in R} x^r[i] \qquad\qquad\qquad \forall i \in T, \forall r \in R \qquad (6b)$$

$$b_-[i] = [b_-^r[i]; \forall r \in R] \qquad\qquad\qquad\qquad \forall i \in T \qquad (6c)$$

$$\sum_{\alpha\in \mathbb{A}_-[i]} \alpha * b_-[i] \leq V^-[i] \qquad\qquad\qquad\qquad \forall i \in T \qquad (6d)$$

$$b_+^r[i] = [\sum_{k\in T} m^r[k,j] - \lambda_+^r[i,j]; \forall j \in T_r] \qquad\qquad \forall i \in T, \forall r \in R \qquad (6e)$$

$$\sum_{j\in T} \lambda_+^r[i,j] = \sum_{j\in T_r\setminus i} x^r[j] \qquad\qquad \forall i \in T, \forall r \in R \qquad (6f)$$

$$b_+[i] = [b_+^r[i]; \forall r \in R \wedge i \notin T_r] \qquad\qquad\qquad \forall i \in T \qquad (6g)$$

$$\sum_{\alpha\in \mathbb{A}_+[i]} \alpha * b_+[i] \leq V_{+,r}[i] \qquad\qquad \forall i \in T, r \in R; T_r \ni i \qquad (6h)$$

$$\lambda_-^r[i,j] >= 0 \qquad\qquad\qquad\qquad \forall r \in R, \forall i,j \in T \qquad (6i)$$

$$\lambda_+^r[i,j] >= 0 \qquad\qquad\qquad\qquad \forall r \in R, \forall i,j \in T \qquad (6j)$$

Since we are not using joint actions anymore, the initial allocation for reached sub-game conditioned by final allocation in the current game can be easily obtained. However, it will not be automatically weighted by reach probability (initial allocation of individual resources will not sum to the reach probability of that stage game) like in the exact variant. To achieve that we allow the defender to modify the initial allocation of the followup stage game. Therefore we introduce slack variables λ_- and λ_+ that are used by the defender to decrease initial allocations of individual resources and make it sum to reach probability of that stage game. Value of slack variable $\lambda_-^r[i,j]$ represents how much the defender reduced initial allocation of resource r on target j if target i was attacked and the attacker was not caught. Similarly, the value of slack variable $\lambda_+^r[i,j]$ represent how much the defender reduced initial allocation of resource r on target j if target i was attacked and the attacker was caught. Constraints (6a) (equivalent to constraints (3a) and (3b)) and (6e) (equivalent to constraints (3e) and (3f)) select the initial allocations of individual resources for sub-games while constraints (6b) and (6f) ensure that selected initial allocations will remain non-negative. Constraints (6d) and (6h) represent expected future values after successful attack and after attacker being caught, respectively (equivalent to constraints (3d) and constraints (3g) and (3h), respectively).

Finally, just like in the case of exact variant, we need to modify (5e) in similar way as (1i), resulting in the following constraint:

$$\sum_{j\in T_r\setminus i} x^r[j] * u[i] + V_-[i] + x^r[i] * p[i] + V_{+,r}[i] + \sum_{l\in R, m,n\in T} m^l[m,n] * c \leq V^s \qquad (7)$$

4   Experimental Evaluation

In this section we present experimental evaluation of proposed variants of our algorithm introduced in Sects. 3.3 and 3.4. We compare these variants based on their runtime and solution quality.

4.1   Experiments Setting

The evaluation has been performed on sets of randomly generated games with varying parameters – the number of targets T, number of resources R and number of attacks K. Each of these games has randomly generated rewards of the attacker for successful attacks on targets (uniformly taken from interval $[0, 6]$), attacker's penalties from being caught on individual targets (uniformly taken from interval $[-6, 0]$), reallocation cost (uniformly taken from interval $[0, 1]$) and initial allocation (i.e., χ^0). In the heuristic variant of our algorithm, targets were uniformly distributed to individual resources in descending order of attacker's utility for a successful attack.

All computational results have been obtained on computers equipped with *Intel Xeon Scalable Gold 6146* processors and 32 GB of available RAM while limiting the runtime to 2 h. We used CPLEX 12.9 to solve linear programs. The solution approaches were required to find an ϵ-optimal solution where ϵ is set to 1% of the error $(\overline{V}^{s^0}(\chi^0) - \underline{V}^{s^0}(\chi^0))$ after the initialization phase described in Sect. 3.2 is completed. If the algorithm failed to reach this level of precision within 2 h, we report such instance as unsolved. The results are based on 50 randomly generated games for each parameter set.

In order to compare the quality of computed defense strategies across multiple instances of generated games, we (1) evaluate the exploitability of the strategies of the defender by computing a best response for the attacker (since we are restricted to zero-sum games) and we (2) normalize the differences between the expected outcomes against the best-responding attacker to obtain comparable relative differences across various instances of generated games. Similarly to setting the target error ϵ, we use the initial size of the interval between the upper and the lower bound for the initial belief as the normalization factor.

4.2   Comparison with State of the Art

To the best of our knowledge, right now there is no clear state of the art solution approach to compare with. Comparing to the methods proposed in [7] is not possible due to the different assumed setting. We focus on solving zero-sum SGSAs with reallocations costs without limiting the number of attacks. On the other hand, previous work focused on solution of general-sum SGSAs without reallocation cost with limiting the number of attacks $K = 2$ [7].

The solution approach closest to the state of the art is solving the game as separate SSGs. This method scales much better than other proposed methods; however, it significantly falls behind in the quality of the solution. As we can

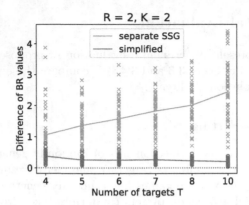

Fig. 3. Difference of best response values produced by heuristic algorithm and separate SSG approach compared to non-heuristic algorithm.

observe in Fig. 3, solution quality of separate SSGs approach (compared to the solution found by the exact variant of our algorithm) becomes significantly worse with an increased size of the game. This is due to the fact that each stage game is solved separately without taking into account future stages. This means that we can solve each stage optimally in the sense of separate games. However, since solution in previous time step directly affects solution in the current one, these solutions are not optimal from the global point of view (e.g., the defender cannot control reach probabilities of individual stage games).

On the other hand, for the simplified version of our algorithm holds the opposite, the difference in solution quality (compared to the solution found by the exact variant of our algorithm) decreases with an increased size of the game. Therefore we focus solely on analysis of HSVI solution approach.

4.3   Algorithm Scalability

First we focused on the scalability of proposed variants in the size of the game - number of targets T, number of resources R and number of attacks K (Fig. 4). In Fig. 4, we use two y-axes. The left y-axis represents the runtime (seconds) in a logarithm scale (upper part of the figure). The right y-axis presents the percentage of unsolved games (bottom part of the figure).

Figure 4a depicts the scalability in the number of targets T. We can observe that with a fixed small number of resources R and attacks K both variants scale quite well up to the $T = 10$ solving nearly 100% of instances for each game size. With further increasing number of targets, the percentage of unsolved instances becomes higher, especially for the exact variant.

In Fig. 4b, we present the scalability in the number of resources R. The exact approach was able to solve only the smallest game instances with $R = 2$. On the other hand, the heuristic variant was capable of finishing all computations within 2 h and achieved reasonable runtime across all sizes of game instances.

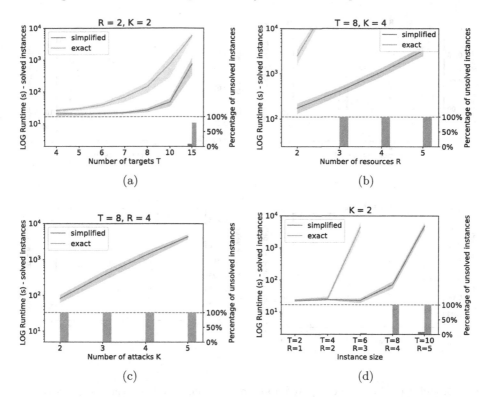

Fig. 4. Scalability in different parameters affecting the size of the game (a) number of targets T, (b) number of resources R, (c) number of attacks K and (d) number of targets T and resources R with a fixed number of attacks K. Averages based on 50 instances for each parameter set. Confidence intervals mark the standard error. The reported runtimes include only instances solved by the algorithm variants. The percentage of instances where the algorithm variants failed to terminate within 2 h are reported separately.

Figure 4c shows the scalability in number of attacks K. Again, we can observe that the exact variant struggles when it comes to solving larger games resulting this time in no instances solved. The heuristic approach keeps its performance and solves all instances in the given time limit.

Finally, in Fig. 4d, we present scalability for fixed number of attacks $K = 2$ and increasing number of targets T and resources R with fixed ratio $T : R$. These results support what we were able to observe in all previous scalability experiments. The exact variant can easily solve smaller games with runtimes not very different from those achieved by the simplified one. However, with the increasing game size, the solution speed rapidly degrades. This behaviour is closely connected to the number of actions considered by these variants. The exact one has to use joint-actions which results in T^{2*R} actions in the problem. On the other hand, the simplified heuristic variant assumes that targets are exclusively

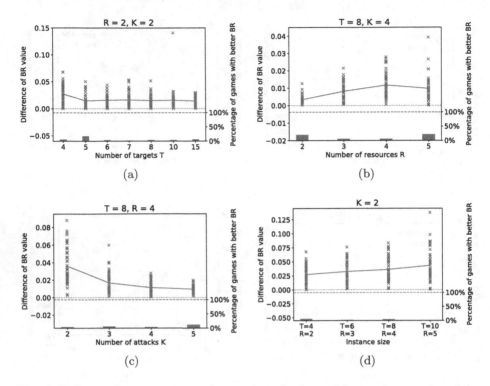

Fig. 5. Difference between computed upper bound value and best response value of the corresponding strategy depending on different parameters affecting size of the game (a) number of targets T, (b) number of resources R, (c) number of attacks K and (d) number of targets T and resources R with a fixed number of attacks K. Averages based on 50 instances for each parameter set. The reported differences include only instances where best response value was worse than upper bound value. The percentage of instances where the best response value was better than upper bound value is reported separately.

assigned to individual resources for cover (i.e. each resource has assigned a list of targets that can be covered by this resource and these sets are mutually disjoint). Thus the heuristic approach can work with separate reallocation actions for each resource, resulting in $T^2 * R$ actions. The number of actions directly affects the size of a linear program and therefore the memory and time requirements for solving it.

4.4   Solution Quality

In this section, we focus on the solution quality of our proposed approaches. First, we compare the exact version of our algorithm with its heuristic variant. We observe that the solution quality of the simplified heuristic approach highly depends on the size of the game, and the bigger the game is the closer the heuristic best response gets to the exact one (Fig. 3). The worse values achieved by the heuristic approach are due to the exclusive target assignment used in the heuristic.

The following example demonstrates the key limitation of the heuristic approach and the reason for not good quality of the strategies found by the heuristic variant in games with small number of targets (see the difference for $T = 4$ in Fig. 3 that is 0.373 on average). Without loss of generality, let's assume we want to solve a game with $T = 3$, $R = 2$, attacker's rewards for attacking non-covered target $u = [3, 3, 3]$ and no penalties for the attacker when being caught or reallocation cost. In the exact variant, we are able to achieve the game value of 1 since it is possible to cover all three targets with uniform probability $\frac{2}{3}$. On the other hand, in the heuristic approach two targets will be assigned to one resource and one target to the other resource. Because of this, we are no longer able to achieve the same coverage as in the exact approach and the best we can do is to cover that single-assigned target with probability 1 and the remaining two targets (those assigned to the same resource) with uniform probability $\frac{1}{2}$ resulting in the game value of 1.5. The actual difference in expected outcomes between the optimal strategy and the heuristic strategy can be even higher if the rewards of the attacker for a successful attack are higher or if the reallocation costs are considered. However, with the increasing number of targets T (or the number of resources R), the impact of this limitation decreases (to 0.201 for $T = 10$).

Since we cannot compute optimal strategies using the exact variant for larger instances, we evaluate the robustness of strategies computed by the heuristic variant of our algorithm as the difference between the computed upper bound value and the best response value of the corresponding strategy (normalized by initial gaps – Fig. 5). In this figure, we use two y-axes. The left one represents the difference between the upper bound and best response values (upper part of the figure) and the right one presents the percentage of games in which the best response value was strictly better than the computed upper bound value (bottom part of the figure). As Fig. 5 shows, the heuristic algorithm was capable of retaining its properties across all instances and keep the average exploitability of computed strategies below 5%.

5   Conclusion

In this work, we study the problem of sequential attacks in security games. We introduce a new formulation of zero-sum security games that consider such sequential attacks, and we use the formalism of one-sided partially observable stochastic games. This allows us to use existing algorithms developed for this class of games. We exploit compact representation of uncertainty and design a heuristic variant of the problem that, for larger games, achieves very similar quality of strategies compared to the exact formulation, while scaling to greater depths and the number of resources. Our paper opens a new possible direction for studying security games with sequential attacks. Key components of the algorithm can be improved to achieve even better scalability. The second important direction is a modification of the algorithm to support also general-sum security games and computation of Strong Stackelberg equilibria.

References

1. Fang, F., et al.: Deploying PAWS: Field optimization of the protection assistant for wildlife security. In: IAAI (2016)
2. Horák, K., Bošanský, B., Kiekintveld, C., Kamhoua, C.: Compact representation of value function in partially observable stochastic games. IJCAI (2019)
3. Horák, K., Bošanský, B., Tomášek, P., Kiekintveld, C., Kamhoua, C.: Optimizing honeypot strategies against dynamic lateral movement using partially observable stochastic games. Comput. Secur. **87**, 101579 (2019). https://doi.org/10.1016/j. cose.2019.101579
4. Horák, K., Bošanský, B., Pěchouček, M.: Heuristic search value iteration for one-sided partially observable stochastic games. In: 31st AAAI Conference on Artificial Intelligence, pp. 558–564 (2017)
5. Kiekintveld, C., Jain, M., Tsai, J., Pita, J., Ordóñez, F., Tambe, M.: Computing optimal randomized resource allocations for massive security games. In: Proceedings of the 8th International Conference on Autonomous Agents and Multiagent Systems, pp. 689–696 (2009). http://portal.acm.org/citation.cfm? id=1558013.1558108
6. Nguyen, T.H., et al.: CAPTURE: A new predictive anti-poaching tool for wildlife protection. In: Proceedings of the 2016 International Conference on Autonomous Agents and Multiagent Systems, pp. 767–775. AAMAS, Richland, SC (2016). http://dl.acm.org/citation.cfm?id=2937029.2937037
7. Nguyen, T.H., Yadav, A., Bošanský, B., Liang, Yu.: Tackling sequential attacks in security games. In: Alpcan, T., Vorobeychik, Y., Baras, J.S., Dán, G. (eds.) GameSec 2019. LNCS, vol. 11836, pp. 331–351. Springer, Cham (2019). https:// doi.org/10.1007/978-3-030-32430-8_20
8. Shieh, E., et al.: PROTECT: A deployed game theoretic system to protect the ports of the United States. In: AAMAS (2012)
9. Sinha, A., Fang, F., An, B., Kiekintveld, C., Tambe, M.: Stackelberg security games: Looking beyond a decade of success. In: IJCAI, pp. 5494–5501 (2018)
10. Smith, T., Simmons, R.: Heuristic search value iteration for POMDPs. In: 20th Conference on Uncertainty in Artificial Intelligence (UAI), pp. 520–527 (2004)
11. Smith, T., Simmons, R.: Heuristic search value iteration for POMDPs: Detailed theory and results. Technical report, Robotics Institute, Carnegie Mellon University (2004)
12. Smith, T., Simmons, R.: Point-based POMDP algorithms: Improved analysis and implementation. In: 21st Conference on Uncertainty in Artificial Intelligence (UAI), pp. 542–549 (2005)
13. Tambe, M. (ed.): Security and Game Theory: Algorithms, Deployed Systems, Lessons Learned. Cambridge University Press, Cambridge (2011)

A Data-Driven Distributionally Robust Game Using Wasserstein Distance

Guanze Peng$^{(\boxtimes)}$, Tao Zhang , and Quanyan Zhu

Department of Electrical and Computer Engineering, Tandon School of Engineering,
New York University, Brooklyn, NY 11201, USA
{guanze.peng,tz636,quanyan.zhu}@nyu.edu

Abstract. This paper studies a special class of games, which enables
the players to leverage the information from a dataset to play the game.
However, in an adversarial scenario, the dataset may not be trustworthy.
We propose a distributionally robust formulation to introduce robustness
against the worst-case scenario and tackle the curse of the optimizer. By
applying Wasserstein distance as the distribution metric, we show that
the game considered in this work is a generalization of the robust game
and data-driven empirical game. We also show that as the number of data
points in the dataset goes to infinity, the game considered in this work
boils down to a Nash game. Moreover, we present the proof of the existence of distributionally robust equilibria and a tractable mathematical
programming approach to solve for such equilibria.

Keywords: Data-driven optimization · Distributionally robust game ·
Mathematical programming

1 Introduction

In the past decade, game theory as a powerful mathematical tool has been used
by researchers to analyze security issues in Cyber-physical systems (CPS) [14],
Internet-of-Things [5], cloud computing [20], etc. As the advancements in data
analysis, attackers can deploy more sophisticated attacks using information from
the dataset [4,15,16]. The dataset can be log files, connection histories, or server
deployment diagrams. The defender can also use statistical methods to defend
herself from these attacks. The classical game theory approach does not capture
this data-driven feature of modern security concerns. Thus, there are potentials
in combining data science and game theory to further the analysis of the case
where the players extract information from data to play the game.

With reference to Fig. 1, consider the following cyber security scenario: both
the attacker and the defender have the access to an open-source dataset. Both of

This research is partially supported by awards ECCS-1847056, CNS-1544782, CNS-
2027884, and SES-1541164 from National Science of Foundation (NSF), and grant
W911NF-19-1-0041 from Army Research Office (ARO).

© Springer Nature Switzerland AG 2020
Q. Zhu et al. (Eds.): GameSec 2020, LNCS 12513, pp. 405–421, 2020.
https://doi.org/10.1007/978-3-030-64793-3_22

them aim to improve their performance by using this dataset. Nevertheless, fully trusting this dataset is not plausible as the dataset can be either incomplete or sometimes intentionally poisoned. Mathematically speaking, blindly extracting information from a dataset in an empirical fashion oftentimes will result in an overoptimistic result. We propose a distributionally robust game framework capture the balance between optimism and conservativeness. In this work, we assume that all the players have the same uncertainty of the game, i.e., there is no information privately possessed by any players. We also assume that the uncertainty can be characterized by a random variable. Each player faces a distributionally robust optimization problem and is robust to the worst-case distribution of the uncertainty parameter in the system model.

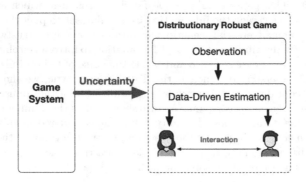

Fig. 1. A block diagram of the interaction between the attacker and the defender.

Our contributions are summarized as follows: we first define a data-driven empirical game (EG). A data-driven EG involves players estimating the distribution of the uncertainty parameter in an empirical way, and the players are able to learn the true distribution asymptotically. The empirical players suffer from the curse of the optimizer and oftentimes are too optimistic. Therefore, we propose a data-driven distributionally robust game framework to combat the overoptimism, while making sure that players are too not conservative as in robust games. We identify the relations between the proposed game with existing games. We define a special class of equilibria, which is termed *distributionally robust equilibrium (DRE)*. As the ambiguity in distribution can be characterized by a robustness parameter, this DRE can potentially simplify the distributionally robust mechanism design problem. Besides, as the ambiguity is generated by a dataset, the DRE considered in this work is endowed with the data-driven feature, which allows the possibility of sequential mechanism design. We show that when the robustness parameter goes to zero, the game boils down to an *empirical game* which is a Nash game. And when the robustness parameter goes to infinity, the game becomes a classical robust game. Then, we prove the existence of the DRE using Kakutani's fixed point theorem. Finally, we present a mathematical programming to solve for DRE.

Our work is closely related to [4,11], in which the authors provide the performance guarantees and tractable formulations for a data-driven distributionally robust optimization problem using the Wasserstein metric. Moreover, as the equilibrium concept considered here falls in the category of *Knightian equilibrium*, our work is related to [9] as well. There are also numerous papers on distributionally robust game theory [3,12,17], in which the ambiguity sets are not data-driven. Our work can be considered as a generalization of robust game [1], where the authors focus on the distribution-free setting.

Section 3 reviews the robust game theory. Section 4 develops a data-driven game model in which players utilize the information from data empirically. In Sect. 5, we first motive the formulation of the data-driven distributionally robust game. Then, we formally define such games, prove the existence of the equilibrium, and provide a tractable mathematical programming approach to solve for such equilibria. In Sect. 6, we use a bimatrix game as a toy example to validate the convergence result. Finally, Sect. 7 concludes the paper and points out the possible directions for future work.

2   Preliminaries

Let $\xi \in \Xi \subseteq \mathbb{R}^m$ be a random variable, where $m \in \mathbb{Z}_+$. Let $\mathcal{M}(\Xi)$ be the space of all probability distributions $\mathbb{Q}$ supported on Ξ with $\mathbb{E}_\mathbb{Q}[\|\xi\|] = \int_\Xi \|\xi\| \mathbb{Q}(d\xi) < \infty$. Here, $\|\cdot\|$ represents an arbitrary norm on $\mathbb{R}^m$.

Definition 1. *(**Wasserstein Distance**) [19] The Wasserstein metric d : $\mathcal{M}(\Xi) \times \mathcal{M}(\Xi) \to \mathbb{R}_+$ is defined via*

$$d(\mathbb{Q}_1, \mathbb{Q}_2) = \inf_{\pi \in \Pi} \left\{ \int_{(\xi_1;\xi_2) \in \Xi \times \Xi} \|\xi_1 - \xi_2\| \pi(d\xi_1, d\xi_2) \right\}$$

for all measures $\mathbb{Q}_1, \mathbb{Q}_2 \in \mathcal{M}(\Xi)$, where Π the space of all the joint distributions of ξ_1 and ξ_2 with marginals $\mathbb{Q}_1$ and $\mathbb{Q}_2$, respectively.

Theorem 1. *(**Kakutani's Fixed-Point Theorem**) [8] If $x \to \phi(x)$ has an upper semicontinuous point-to-set mapping of an r-dimensional closed simplex S in to $\omega_i(S)$, then $\exists\, x_0 \in S$, such that $x_0 \in \phi(x_0)$.*

3   Robust Game

Consider an incomplete-information game (I-game) with a finite set of players $\mathcal{I} = \{1, 2, ..., N\}$ and a finite set of actions $\mathcal{A}_i \in \mathbb{R}^{A_i}$ for each player i, where $A_i \in \mathbb{Z}_+$. As mention by Harsanyi in [6], the incompetence of information induced by uncertainty can be summarized and embedded in the cost functions (objective functions, cost matrix). We denote the uncertain parameter by $\xi \in \Xi$. For player i, we define his cost functions as $C_i(a_i, a_{-i}; \xi) : \prod_{i \in \mathcal{I}} \mathcal{A}_i \times \Xi \to \mathbb{R}$, where $a_{-i} := (a_1, ..., a_{i-1}, a_{i+1}, ..., a_N)$ is the collection of other players' actions. Note that all the players considered in this work are minimizers. Moreover, we assume that the uncertainty set Ξ is finite.

In [2,6], with the assumptions common prior and common knowledge of rationality, we can transform an I-game to a complete-information game (C-game), which is commonly known as a Bayesian game. However, the Bayesian game fails to characterize the case where common prior or stochastic information of the uncertainty is unavailable.

In [1], the authors have proposed a distribution-free game framework to study incomplete-information games. In their proposed game, *robust game*, players are assumed to be robust to the uncertainty. Formally, a robust game can be defined as a tuple,

$$\mathcal{G} := (\mathcal{I}, \mathcal{S}), \tag{1}$$

where $\mathcal{S}$ is the state of nature. Every state of nature $s \in \mathcal{S}$ is a vector

$$s = (\mathcal{I}, (\mathcal{A}_i)_{i \in \mathcal{I}}, (c_i)_{i \in \mathcal{I}}),$$

where $\mathcal{A}_i$ is a nonempty finite set of actions of Player i. $c_i : \mathcal{A}_i \times \Xi \to \mathbb{R}$ the cost function of Player i where $\mathcal{A} = \times_{i \in \mathcal{I}} \mathcal{A}_i$. In this work, we assume that the players do not have private information and this allows us to transform the I-game $\mathcal{G}$ to a C-game.

For every $i \in \mathcal{I}$, let $\mathbf{x}_i$ be the mixed strategy of Player i, which is defined to be a probability over the action space, i.e., $\mathbf{x}_i = (x_i(a_i))_{a_i \in \mathcal{A}_i} \in \Delta_i := \Delta(\mathcal{A}_i)$ and $\Delta(\cdot)$ is the simplex of a finite set. For the ease of notation, define the expected cost induced by the mixed strategy profile $\mathbf{x} = (\mathbf{x}_i, \mathbf{x}_{-i})$ as the following

$$c_i(\mathbf{x}_i, \mathbf{x}_{-i}; \xi) = \sum_{a_i \in \mathcal{A}_i} \sum_{a_{-i} \in \mathcal{A}_{-i}} C_i(a_i, a_{-i}; \xi) x_i(a_i) \prod_{j \neq i, j \in \mathcal{I}} x_j(a_j),$$

where $\mathcal{A}_{-i} = \times_{j \neq i, j \in \mathcal{I}} \mathcal{A}_i$. The equilibrium concept used in robust game $\mathcal{G}$ is given by the following:

Definition 2. *A mixed strategy profile* $\mathbf{x}^* = (\mathbf{x}_i^*, \mathbf{x}_{-i}^*)$ *is robust-optimization equilibrium solution in* $\mathcal{G}$ *if for* $i \in \mathcal{I}$,

$$\max_{\xi \in \Xi} c_i(\mathbf{x}_i^*, \mathbf{x}_{-i}^*; \xi) \leqslant \max_{\xi \in \Xi} c_i(\mathbf{x}_i, \mathbf{x}_{-i}^*; \xi), \tag{2}$$

where $\mathbf{x}_{-i} \in \Delta_{-i} := \times_{j \neq i, j \in \mathcal{I}} \Delta(\mathcal{A}_j)$.

The following theorem guarantees the existence of the robust-optimization equilibrium in $\mathcal{G}$.

Theorem 2. *(Existence of Equilibria in Robust Finite Games) [1] In the game defined by* $\mathcal{G}$, *if* $C_i(a_i, a_{-i}; \xi)$ *is bounded for all* $i \in \mathcal{I}$, $(a_i, a_{-i}) \in \mathcal{A}$ *and* $\xi \in \Xi$, *then there exists an ex post equilibrium.*

4   Data-Driven Empirical Game

In a data-driven empirical game (EG), we assume that the uncertainty parameter is a random variable, and is selected according to some unknown distribution by a chance move at the beginning of the game. Let $\mathbb{P}$ be the measure induced by the random variable ξ. The players can observe N such games played independently and the realizations of the uncertainty parameter. Then every player makes the estimation from the same set

$$\hat{\Xi}^{(N)} = \left\{ \hat{\xi}^{(1)}, \hat{\xi}^{(2)}, \ldots, \hat{\xi}^{(N)} \right\} \subseteq \Xi^N, \tag{3}$$

which consists of N independent realizations of the random variable ξ. We call $\hat{\Xi}^{(N)}$ *dataset*, and each element in it *data point*. In [10], the author formalizes a framework which enables the players to learn as *statisticians*. Formally, define the learning rule as a mapping from the dataset (3) to the belief space:

$$\ell \; : \; \Xi^N \; \rightarrow \; \Delta(\Xi).$$

In particular, we are interested in *empirical players* in this work, who estimate $\mathbb{P}$ using an empirical approach as follows

$$\hat{\mathbb{Q}}^{(N)} := \ell \left(\hat{\Xi}^{(N)} \right) = \frac{1}{N} \sum_{n=1}^{N} \delta_{\hat{\xi}^{(n)}},$$

where δ is the Dirac delta function. We term $\hat{\mathbb{Q}}^{(N)}$ as *common empirical prior* in this work. The empirical learning rule not only is appealing for its neat and simple form, but also enjoys the following property:

Lemma 1. *Let the dataset $\hat{\Xi}^{(N)}$ be defined as (3) which contains N independent realizations of ξ. When the number of realizations (data points) N goes to infinity,*

$$\ell \left(\hat{\Xi}^{(N)} \right) \; \rightarrow \; \mathbb{P}, \quad a.s.$$

Proof. The proof of this lemma is an immediate result of law of large numbers. $\square$

The lemma above says that as the number of samples goes to infinity, the empirical players can learn the *true distribution* of ξ, $\mathbb{P}$.

The empirical players can benefit from the information obtained from the dataset. Indeed, it is not hard to show that given $\mathbf{x}_{-i} \in \Delta_{-i}$, for every possible empirical measure $\hat{\mathbb{Q}}^{(N)}$ induced by the dataset $\hat{\Xi}^{(N)}$

$$\mathbf{E}_{\hat{\mathbb{Q}}^{(N)}} \left[c_i(\mathbf{x}_i, \mathbf{x}_{-i}; \xi) \right] \leqslant \max_{\xi \in \Xi} c_i(\mathbf{x}_i, \mathbf{x}_{-i}; \xi).$$

By letting

$$\zeta_i^*(\mathbf{x}_{-i}) \in \arg \min_{\mathbf{x}_i \in \Delta_i} \mathbf{E}_{\hat{\mathbb{Q}}^{(N)}} \left[c_i(\mathbf{x}_i, \mathbf{x}_{-i}; \xi) \right],$$

we have that

$$\mathbf{E}_{\hat{\mathbb{Q}}^{(N)}} \left[c_i(\zeta_i^*(\mathbf{x}_{-i}), \mathbf{x}_{-i}; \xi) \right] \leqslant \min_{\mathbf{x}_i \in \Delta_i} \max_{\xi \in \Xi} \ c_i(\mathbf{x}_i, \mathbf{x}_{-i}; \xi).$$

This inequality says that by leveraging the stochastic information from the dataset, the players behave *less conservatively*.

It is worth noting that as all the players make use of the same dataset to estimate in the same empirical fashion, they share the same empirical distribution. Thus, this distribution is also common knowledge. We further assume that the fact that all the players being empirical is common knowledge. We proceed by defining the data-driven EG, which falls into the category of I-game. A data-driven EG is given by a tuple

$$\mathcal{G}^{(N)} := \left(\mathcal{I}, \mathcal{S}, \mathbb{P}, \hat{\Xi}^{(N)} \right),$$

where $\mathbb{P}$ is the true measure of ξ. Now, we are ready to show that data-driven EBG as an I-game is equivalent to a C-game. As mentioned earlier, the players acknowledge that all of them are empirical and they share the empirical distribution, the data-driven EG is equivalent to a Nash game by replacing the cost matrix $C_i(a_i, a_i; \xi)$ with

$$\tilde{C}_i(a_i, a_{-i}) := \mathbb{E}_{\hat{\mathbb{Q}}^{(N)}} \left[C_i(a_i, a_i; \xi) \right],$$

where the expectation is taken over ξ with respect to $\hat{\mathbb{Q}}^{(N)}$. Thus, data-driven EG is also equivalent to a C-game. Moreover, as it is equivalent to a Nash game, the existence of the Nash equilibrium is also guaranteed.

5 Data-Driven Distributionally Robust Game

In this section, we propose a new class of games which is termed data-driven Distributionally Robust Game (DRG) in which we use Wasserstein distance as the distribution metric. To motive this framework, we first answer a few essential questions.

5.1 Motivation

Why Distributionally Robust Formulation? The direct application of empirical distribution as estimated distribution suffers from *optimizer's curse* [18]. It is well known that the empirical estimator $\hat{\mathbb{Q}}^{(N)}$ is be an unbiased estimator of $\mathbb{P}$, i.e.,

$$\mathbb{E}_{\mathbb{Q}^{(N)}} \left[\hat{\mathbb{Q}}^{(N)} \right] = \mathbb{P}.$$

where $\mathbb{Q}^{(N)}$ is the measure induced by the N data points. With fixed $\mathbf{x}_{-i}$,

$$\mathbb{E}_{\mathbb{Q}^{(N)}} \left[\mathbb{E}_{\hat{\mathbb{Q}}^{(N)}} \left[c_i(\mathbf{x}_i, \mathbf{x}_{-i}; \xi) \right] \right] = \mathbb{E}_{\mathbb{P}} \left[c_i(\mathbf{x}_i, \mathbf{x}_{-i}; \xi) \right].$$

By Jensen's inequality,

$$\mathbb{E}_{\mathbb{Q}^{(N)}} \left[\min_{\mathbf{x}_i \in \Delta_i} \mathbb{E}_{\hat{\mathbb{Q}}^{(N)}} \left[c_i(\mathbf{x}_i, \mathbf{x}_{-i}; \xi) \right] \right] \leqslant \min_{\mathbf{x}_i \in \Delta_i} \mathbb{E}_{\mathbb{Q}^{(N)}} \left[\mathbb{E}_{\hat{\mathbb{Q}}^{(N)}} \left[c_i(\mathbf{x}_i, \mathbf{x}_{-i}; \xi) \right] \right]$$

$$= \min_{\mathbf{x}_i \in \Delta_i} \mathbb{E}_{\mathbb{P}} \left[c_i(\mathbf{x}_i, \mathbf{x}_{-i}; \xi) \right].$$

Let

$$\zeta_i^*(\mathbf{x}_{-i}) \in \arg \min_{\mathbf{x}_i \in \Delta_i} \mathbb{E}_{\hat{\mathbb{Q}}^{(N)}} \left[c_i(\mathbf{x}_i, \mathbf{x}_{-i}; \xi) \right].$$

Then, for every $\mathbf{x}_{-i} \in \Delta_{-i}$,

$$\mathbb{E}_{\mathbb{P}} \left[c_i(\zeta_i^*(\mathbf{x}_{-i}), \mathbf{x}_{-i}; \xi) \right] \geqslant \min_{\mathbf{x}_i \in \Delta_i} \mathbb{E}_{\mathbb{P}} \left[c_i(\mathbf{x}_i, \mathbf{x}_{-i}; \xi_i) \right].$$

As shown above, given the other players' strategies, a player inclines to be *overoptimistic* due to the optimizer's curse. Therefore, it is reasonable to employ some "robustness" to deal with this overoptimism. In this work, given a tuple of his counterparts' strategies, we suppose that each player formulates the best response as the solution of a distributionally robust optimization problem.

Note that, in our framework, we assume that a player's opponents are outside the scope of the player's viewpoint. That is, the player takes the distributionally robust view only of the uncertainties of his cost function, with a tuple of the other players' strategies given. From this perspective, each player does not take a distributionally robust approach to his uncertainty with respect to this tuple itself. Moreover, we assume that each player's distributionally robust view of the game is common knowledge, which allows the players to predict each other's best-response correspondences. Thus, the players in the game defined by (4) can reach consistent predictions of what each other will play.

We interpret the distributionally robust game in a security setting. Suppose the players (defender and attacker) have the access to the same open-source dataset. On one hand, the players aim to obtain useful information from this dataset to achieve better defend/attack results. On the other hand, the dataset may not be reliable. It is natural for the players to be robust to the inference of the dataset. Hence, the distributionally robust formulation is a reasonable choice in a security problem in order to balance the optimism and conservativeness. However, one may have the concern over the reason why the players are assumed to know the same dataset. Indeed, in real world, the defender and the attacker oftentimes have different information (knowledge) due to different financial capabilities, backgrounds, identities, etc. In such cases, one may need to resort to Bayesian game framework. The information-asymmetric case is beyond the scope of this work and we leave it to future work.

Why Wasserstein Distance? In this work, we assume that each player adopts *Wasserstein Distance* as the metric measuring the difference between two distributions. Formally, a distributionally robust game using Wasserstein distance is defined by the following vector

$$\mathcal{G}_\epsilon^{(N)} = \left(\mathcal{I}, \tilde{\mathcal{S}}, \mathbb{P}, \hat{\Xi}^{(N)} \right), \tag{4}$$

where $\tilde{s} := (\mathcal{I}, (\mathcal{A}_i)_{i\in\mathcal{I}}, (c_i)_{i\in\mathcal{I}}, \epsilon)$ and $\tilde{s} \in \tilde{\mathcal{S}}$. The parameter ϵ is the radius of the Wasserstein ball, which stands for the *robustness* of the players. It is determined by the nature and assumed to be common knowledge and the same for all the players. The key feature distinguishing Wasserstein distance as a distribution metric from other distribution metrics is that the worst-case distribution can be supported outside the dataset. In a game setting, the utilization of Wasserstein distance can be interpreted as the following: the knowledge of the support set the types are common knowledge shared between the players. Using Wasserstein distance as distribution metric enables the players to utilize this support information. Moreover, this allows the players to be robust against perturbations of the data points [4]. It also makes sense in a security scenario: both of the defender and the attacker want to use every bit of information available to improve their performance while maintaining certain level of robustness.

5.2   Equilibrium Concept

With the empirical distribution $\hat{\mathbb{Q}}^{(N)}$ being centered, we construct a Wasserstein ball as follows:

$$\mathcal{B}_\epsilon\left(\hat{\mathbb{Q}}^{(N)}\right) = \left\{\mathbb{Q} \in \mathcal{M}(\Xi) : d(\mathbb{Q}, \hat{\mathbb{Q}}^{(N)}) \leqslant \epsilon\right\},$$

which contains all the possible probability measures, whose Wasserstein distance with the empirical distribution is less than ϵ. Here, $\mathcal{M}(\Xi)$ is the set of all the possible distributions whose support is Ξ.

Definition 3. *A mixed strategy profile* $\mathbf{x} = (\mathbf{x}_i^*, \mathbf{x}_{-i}^*)$ *is an **distributionally robust equilibrium (DRE)** solution if no player can decrease their interim expected cost by unilaterally changing their strategy: for* $i \in \mathcal{I}$ *and every mixed strategy* $\mathbf{x}_i \in \Delta_i$,

$$\sup_{\mathbb{Q}\in\mathcal{B}_\epsilon(\hat{\mathbb{Q}}^{(N)})} \mathbb{E}_\mathbb{Q}\left[c_i(\mathbf{x}_i^*, \mathbf{x}_{-i}^*; \xi)\right] \leqslant \sup_{\mathbb{Q}\in\mathcal{B}_\epsilon(\hat{\mathbb{Q}}^{(N)})} \mathbb{E}_\mathbb{Q}\left[c_i(\mathbf{x}_i, \mathbf{x}_{-i}^*, ; \xi)\right]. \tag{5}$$

Remark 1. By definition, DRE is a relaxation of *Knightian equilibrium*. In a homogeneous game where each player has the same objective function and action set, DRE falls in the category of *Knightian equilibrium*. The DRE exhibits several advantageous features:

1. The proposed DRE can be used as a solution concept in mechanism design and characterize the incentive compatibility such that each player has the incentive to truthfully reveal his private information in DRE. The players' uncertainty about their cost functions provides a potential opportunity for the mechanism designer to strategically design the ambiguity set as an additional rule of encounter to achieve the designer's social goal.
2. Suppose that the ambiguity set is given and not a part of the design. When the ambiguity set is different, one will need to solve the design problem all over again. The ambiguity set in DRE being induced by a dataset enables one to design a data-driven mechanism sequentially, as the only difference in ambiguity sets is the center of the Wasserstein ball.

When the robustness parameter ϵ goes to 0, then the Wasserstein ball collapses inward to $\{\hat{\mathbb{Q}}^{(N)}\}$. Consequently, a data-driven DRG becomes a data-driven EG, i.e.,

$$\lim_{\epsilon \to 0} \mathcal{G}_\epsilon^{(N)} = \mathcal{G}^{(N)}.$$

On the other hand, when ϵ goes to infinity, Data-Driven DRG becomes a classical robust game, as all the probability mass will concentrate on the worst-case support, i.e.,

$$\lim_{\epsilon \to \infty} \mathcal{G}_\epsilon^{(N)} = \mathcal{G}.$$

If we see ϵ as a tuning parameter, then $\mathcal{G}_\epsilon^{(N)}$ can be regarded as a generalization which bridges the robust game and data-driven EG.

5.3   Existence of DRE

In this section, we give the theoretical guarantee of the existence of DRE, which largely follows from Theorem 1 in [1]. In order to prove the existence of DRE in the game defined by $\mathcal{G}^{(N)}$, we first define the mapping $\rho_{i,\epsilon}^{(N)} : \Delta \times \Xi^N \to \Delta_i$ as the following

$$\rho_{i,\epsilon}^{(N)}(\mathbf{x}_i, \mathbf{x}_{-i}, \hat{\Xi}^{(N)}) = \sup_{\mathbb{Q} \in \mathcal{B}_\epsilon(\hat{\mathbb{Q}}^{(N)})} \mathbb{E}_{\mathbb{Q}} \left[c_i(\mathbf{x}_i, \mathbf{x}_{-i}; \xi) \right]. \tag{6}$$

Moreover, we define the following "point-to-set" mapping for game $\mathcal{G}^{(N)}$,

$$\Phi_\epsilon^{(N)} : \Delta \times \Xi^N \to \Delta.$$

Specially, we choose $\Phi_\epsilon^{(N)}$ to be the following

$$\Phi_\epsilon^{(N)}(\mathbf{x}, \hat{\Xi}^{(N)}) = \left\{ \tilde{\mathbf{x}} = (\tilde{\mathbf{x}}_i, \tilde{\mathbf{x}}_{-i}) \mid \tilde{\mathbf{x}}_i \in \arg\min_{\mathbf{u}_i \in \Delta_i} \rho_{i,\epsilon}^{(N)}(\mathbf{u}_i, \mathbf{x}_{-i}, \hat{\Xi}^{(N)}), i \in \mathcal{I} \right\}, \tag{7}$$

which is the set of all the best response strategies given the strategy profile $\mathbf{x}$.

Theorem 3. *Let Ξ be finite, and $C_i(a_i, a_{-i}; \xi)$ be bounded for all $\xi \in \Xi$. There exists at least one DRE in the game defined by $\mathcal{G}_\epsilon^{(N)}$.*

Sketch of Proof. We start the proof by proving that $\rho_{i,\epsilon}^{(N)}(\mathbf{x}_i, \mathbf{x}_{-i}, \hat{\Xi}^{(N)})$ is continuous on Δ, and that for each $i \in \mathcal{I}$, $\rho_{i,\epsilon}^{(N)}(\mathbf{x}_i, \mathbf{x}_{-i}, \hat{\Xi}^{(N)})$ is convex in $\mathbf{x}_i$. Then, the mapping $\Phi_\epsilon^{(N)}$ can be shown to be non-empty, convex and upper semicontinuous. Applying Kakutani's fixed-point theorem immediately gives us the theorem. $\square$

5.4   Asymptotic Consistency

We must notice that there may exist more than one equilibrium, i.e., the equilibrium may not be unique. Then, from now on, it will be reasonable to work on the set of equilibriums, which is given by

$$\mathcal{E}_\epsilon^{(N)}(\hat{\Xi}^{(N)}) = \left\{ \mathbf{x} \mid \mathbf{x} \in \Phi_\epsilon^{(N)}(\mathbf{x}, \hat{\Xi}^{(N)}) \right\}.$$

This set is non-empty due to Theorem 3.

When the true distribution of ξ is known to all the players, the problem boils down to a standard Nash game. This Nash game can be represented by a tuple $\mathcal{G}_{\text{Nash}} = (\mathcal{I}, \mathcal{S}, \mathbb{P})$. Similar to (6) and (7), define

$$\rho_i(\mathbf{x}_i, \mathbf{x}_{-i}) = \mathbb{E}_\mathbb{P} \left[c_i(\mathbf{x}_i, \mathbf{x}_{-i}; \xi) \right],$$

and

$$\Phi(\mathbf{x}) = \left\{ \tilde{\mathbf{x}} = (\tilde{\mathbf{x}}_i, \tilde{\mathbf{x}}_{-i}) \mid \tilde{\mathbf{x}}_i \in \arg \min_{\mathbf{u}_i \in \Delta_i} \rho_i(\mathbf{u}_i, \mathbf{x}_{-i}), \ i \in \mathcal{I} \right\},$$

respectively. Characterized by fixed points, the set of equilibria in $\mathcal{G}_{\text{Nash}}$ is given by

$$\mathcal{E} = \{ \mathbf{x} \mid \mathbf{x} \in \Phi(\mathbf{x}) \}.$$

It is not hard to see that $\mathcal{E}$ is non-empty.

Proposition 1. *Define a sequence of Wasserstein ball radius $\{\epsilon_N\}_{N=1}^\infty$ with the following property*

$$\lim_{N \to \infty} \epsilon_N = 0.$$

Then,

$$\lim_{N \to \infty} \mathcal{E}_{\epsilon_N}^{(N)}(\hat{\Xi}^{(N)}) = \mathcal{E}, \quad a.\ s.$$

Proof. When N goes to infinity, by using Lemma 3.7 from [4], we obtain that

$$\mathbb{Q}^\infty \left[\lim_{N \to \infty} d(\mathbb{P}, \hat{\mathbb{Q}}^{(N)}) = 0 \right] = 1.$$

Hence,

$$\lim_{N \to \infty} \rho_{i,\epsilon}^{(N)}(\mathbf{x}_i, \mathbf{x}_{-i}, \hat{\Xi}^{(N)}) = \lim_{N \to \infty} \sup_{\mathbb{Q} \in \mathcal{B}_\epsilon(\hat{\mathbb{Q}}^{(N)})} \mathbb{E}_\mathbb{Q} \left[c_i(\mathbf{x}_i, \mathbf{x}_{-i}; \xi) \right]$$

$$= \mathbb{E}_\mathbb{P} \left[c_i(\mathbf{x}_i, \mathbf{x}_{-i}; \xi) \right]$$

$$= \rho_i(\mathbf{x}_i, \mathbf{x}_{-i}), \quad a.\ s.$$

Then, it is clear that

$$\lim_{N \to \infty} \Phi_\epsilon^{(N)}(\mathbf{x}, \hat{\Xi}^{(N)}) = \Phi(\mathbf{x}), \quad a.\ s.$$

The argument in the proposition follows.

□

Remark 2. Proposition 1 exhibits the convergence result concerning the equilibrium set. As the number of data points goes to infinity, the distributionally robust game $\mathcal{G}^{(N)}$ is equivalent to the standard Nash game $\mathcal{G}$ in terms of the equilibria.

5.5   Tractable Formulations

In this section, we derive a tractable formulation using which one can solve for the DRE (as defined in (5)) in $\mathcal{G}_\epsilon^{(N)}$. Without loss of generality, we study a two-player game, i.e., $\mathcal{I} = \{1, 2\}$. Denote the cost matrix of the i-th player by

$$\mathbf{C}_i(\xi) = [C_i(a_1, a_2; \xi)]_{a_1 \in \mathcal{A}_1, a_2 \in \mathcal{A}_2}, \quad i \in \mathcal{I}.$$

Recall that the i-th player faces the following optimization problem:

$$\min_{\mathbf{x}_i \in \Delta_i} \sup_{\mathbb{Q} \in \mathcal{B}_\epsilon(\hat{\mathbb{Q}}^{(N)})} \mathbb{E}_\mathbb{Q} \left[\mathbf{x}_1^\mathsf{T} \mathbf{C}_i(\xi) \mathbf{x}_2\right]. \tag{8}$$

We drop the outer minimization for the clarity of notations. By the definition of Wasserstein ball, (8) can be rewritten as

$$\begin{aligned} \sup_\mathbb{Q} \quad & \sum_{\xi \in \Xi} \mathbf{x}_1^\mathsf{T} \mathbf{C}_i(\xi) \mathbf{x}_2\, \mathbb{Q}(\xi) \\ \text{s.t.} \quad & d(\hat{\mathbb{Q}}^{(N)}, \mathbb{Q}) \leqslant \epsilon. \end{aligned} \tag{9}$$

By the definition of Wasserstein distance,

$$\begin{aligned} \sup_\mathbb{Q} \quad & \sum_{\xi \in \Xi} \mathbf{x}_1^\mathsf{T} \mathbf{C}_i(\xi) \mathbf{x}_2\, \mathbb{Q}(\xi) \\ \text{s.t.} \quad & \min_\Pi \sum_{\xi; \xi' \in \Xi} |\xi - \xi'| \Pi(\xi; \xi') \leqslant \epsilon \\ & \sum_{\xi \in \Xi} \Pi(\xi; \xi') = \hat{\mathbb{Q}}^{(N)}(\xi') \\ & \sum_{\xi' \in \Xi} \Pi(\xi; \xi') = \mathbb{Q}(\xi). \end{aligned} \tag{10}$$

By eliminating the variable $\mathbb{Q}$, we reduce (9) equivalently to

$$\begin{aligned} \sup_\Pi \quad & \sum_{\xi; \xi' \in \Xi} \mathbf{x}_1^\mathsf{T} \mathbf{C}_i(\xi) \mathbf{x}_2\, \Pi(\xi; \xi') \\ \text{s.t.} \quad & \sum_{\xi; \xi' \in \Xi} |\xi - \xi'| \Pi(\xi; \xi') \leqslant \epsilon \\ & \sum_{\xi \in \Xi} \Pi(\xi; \xi') = \hat{\mathbb{Q}}^{(N)}(\xi'), \quad \forall\, \xi' \in \Xi. \end{aligned} \tag{11}$$

The dual optimization of (11) is given by

$$\begin{aligned} \min_{\lambda \geqslant 0} \quad & \lambda \epsilon + \sum_{\xi' \in \Xi} \hat{\mathbb{Q}}^{(N)}(\xi') s(\xi') \\ \text{s.t.} \quad & s(\xi') + \lambda |\xi - \xi'| \geqslant \mathbf{x}_1^\mathsf{T} \mathbf{C}_i(\xi) \mathbf{x}_2, \quad \forall\, \xi; \xi' \in \Xi. \end{aligned} \tag{12}$$

It is worth noting that there is no duality gap between (11) and (12) as (11) is essentially a linear programming. We can also write (12) as

$$\min_{\lambda \geqslant 0} \quad \lambda\epsilon + \sum_{\xi' \in \Xi} \hat{\mathbb{Q}}^{(N)}(\xi')s(\xi')$$

$$\text{s.t.} \quad s(\xi') \geqslant \max_{\xi \in \Xi}\left[\mathbf{x}_1^{\mathrm{T}}\mathbf{C}_i(\xi)\mathbf{x}_2 - \lambda|\xi - \xi'|\right], \quad \forall\, \xi' \in \Xi$$

So far, we have reduced the robust formulation using Wasserstein to a simpler form.

5.6　Mathematical Programming for DRE

By expanding the constraint that $\mathbf{x}_i \in \Delta_i$ and writing down (12) in the epigraph form, we have that for Player i,

$$\min_{\mathbf{x}_i,\lambda_i \geqslant 0,\eta_i,\{s(\xi')\}_{\xi' \in \Xi}} \quad \eta_i$$

$$\text{s.t.} \quad \lambda_i\epsilon + \sum_{\xi' \in \Xi} \hat{\mathbb{Q}}^{(N)}(\xi')s_i(\xi') \leqslant \eta_i$$

$$s_i(\xi') + \lambda_i|\xi - \xi'| \geqslant \sum_{a_1 \in \mathcal{A}_1}\sum_{a_2 \in \mathcal{A}_2} C_i(a_1,a_2;\xi)x_1(a_1)x_2(a_2),$$

$$\forall\, \xi; \xi' \in \Xi$$

$$x_i(a_i) \geqslant 0, \quad \forall\, a_i \in \mathcal{A}_i$$

$$\sum_{a_i \in \mathcal{A}_i} x_i(a_i) = 1.$$

$$(13)$$

The Lagrange function of (13) is given by

$$\mathcal{L}_i(\mathbf{x}_i,\lambda_i,\eta_i,\{s(\xi')\}_{\xi' \in \Xi},\{\omega_i(\xi,\xi')\}_{\xi,\xi' \in \Xi},\theta_i,\sigma_i)$$

$$=\eta_i + \sum_{\xi;\xi' \in \Xi} \omega_i(\xi,\xi')\left(\mathbf{x}_1^{\mathrm{T}}\mathbf{C}_i(\xi)\mathbf{x}_2 - s_i(\xi') - \lambda_i|\xi - \xi'|\right)$$

$$+ \theta_i\left(\lambda_i\epsilon + \sum_{\xi' \in \Xi}\hat{\mathbb{Q}}^{(N)}(\xi')s(\xi') - \eta_i\right) + \sigma_i\left(1 - \sum_{a_i \in \mathcal{A}_i}x_i(a_i)\right)$$

$$=(1-\theta_i)\eta_i + \lambda_i\left(\theta_i\epsilon - \sum_{\xi;\xi' \in \Xi}\omega_i(\xi,\xi')|\xi - \xi'|\right) + \sigma_i$$

$$+ \sum_{a_i \in \mathcal{A}_i}\left(\sum_{a_{-i} \in \mathcal{A}_{-i}}\sum_{\xi;\xi' \in \Xi}\omega_i(\xi,\xi')C_i(a_1,a_2;\xi)x_{-i}(a_{-i}) - \sigma_i\right)x_i(a_i)$$

$$+ \sum_{\xi' \in \Xi}\left(\theta_i\hat{\mathbb{Q}}^{(N)}(\xi') - \sum_{\xi \in \Xi}\omega_i(\xi,\xi')\right)s_i(\xi').$$

Here, $x_i(a_i) \geqslant 0, \lambda_i \geqslant 0$, and η_i and $\{s_i(\xi')\}_{\xi' \in \Xi}$ are free variables. Thus, we need

$$1 - \theta_i = 0,$$

$$\theta_i \epsilon - \sum_{\xi; \xi' \in \Xi} \omega_i(\xi, \xi') |\xi - \xi'| \geqslant 0,$$

$$\theta_i \hat{\mathbb{Q}}^{(N)}(\xi') - \sum_{\xi \in \Xi} \omega_i(\xi, \xi') = 0,$$

$$\sum_{a_{-i} \in \mathcal{A}_{-i}} \sum_{\xi; \xi' \in \Xi} \omega_i(\xi, \xi') C_i(a_1, a_2; \xi) x_{-i}(a_{-i}) \geqslant \sigma_i.$$

After some algebraic operations, we can write the dual problem to (13) as

$$\max_{\{\omega_i(\xi, \xi') \geqslant 0\}_{\xi, \xi' \in \Xi}, \sigma_i} \quad \sigma_i$$

$$\text{s.t.} \quad \sum_{\xi; \xi' \in \Xi} \omega_i(\xi, \xi') |\xi - \xi'| \leqslant \epsilon,$$

$$\hat{\mathbb{Q}}^{(N)}(\xi') = \sum_{\xi \in \Xi} \omega_i(\xi, \xi'), \quad \forall \xi \in \Xi,$$

$$\sum_{a_{-i} \in \mathcal{A}_{-i}} \sum_{\xi; \xi' \in \Xi} \omega_i(\xi, \xi') C_i(a_1, a_2; \xi) x_{-i}(a_{-i}) \geqslant \sigma_i, \quad \forall a_i \in \mathcal{A}_i.$$

The mathematical problem used to solve for DRE is given by the following,

$$\max_{\kappa} \quad \sum_{i \in \mathcal{I}} (\sigma_i - \eta_i)$$

$$\text{s.t.} \quad \lambda_i \epsilon + \sum_{\xi; \xi' \in \Xi} \omega_i(\xi, \xi') s_i(\xi') \leqslant \eta_i, \quad \forall i \in \mathcal{I},$$

$$s_i(\xi') + \lambda_i |\xi - \xi'| \geqslant \sum_{a_1 \in \mathcal{A}_1} \sum_{a_2 \in \mathcal{A}_2} C_i(a_1, a_2; \xi) x_1(a_1) x_2(a_2),$$

$$\forall \xi, \xi' \in \Xi$$

$$\sum_{a_i \in \mathcal{A}_i} x_i(a_i) = 1, \quad \forall i \in \mathcal{I},$$

$$\sum_{\xi; \xi' \in \Xi} \omega_i(\xi, \xi') |\xi - \xi'| \leqslant \epsilon, \quad \forall i \in \mathcal{I},$$

$$\sum_{a_{-i} \in \mathcal{A}_{-i}} \sum_{\xi; \xi' \in \Xi} \omega_i(\xi, \xi') C_i(a_1, a_2; \xi) x_{-i}(a_{-i}) \geqslant \sigma_i, \quad \forall a_i \in \mathcal{A}_i, i \in \mathcal{I},$$

$$\hat{\mathbb{Q}}^{(N)}(\xi') = \sum_{\xi \in \Xi} \omega_i(\xi, \xi'), \quad \forall \xi' \in \Xi, i \in \mathcal{I},$$

$$(14)$$

where

$$\kappa = \{x_i(a_i) \geqslant 0, \lambda_i \geqslant 0, \eta_i, \{s_i(\xi')\}_{\xi' \in \Xi}, \{\omega_i(\xi, \xi') \geqslant 0\}_{\xi, \xi' \in \Xi}, \sigma_i\}_{i \in \mathcal{I}}$$

is the collection of decision variables.

Theorem 4. *Solving the mathematical programming above is equivalent to finding the DRE (as defined in (5)) in $\mathcal{G}_\epsilon^{(N)}$.*

Proof. "$\Leftarrow$" Let $(\mathbf{x}_1^*, \mathbf{x}_2^*)$ be an DRE. Then, for $i \in \mathcal{I}$, $\mathbf{x}_i^*$ is the best response to $\mathbf{x}_{-i}^*$. As there is no duality gap between dual and primal, $\sum_{i\in\mathcal{I}}(\sigma_i^* - \eta_i^*) = 0$. Show κ^* is global maximum. We first notice that

$$\sum_{a_1\in\mathcal{A}_1, a_2\in\mathcal{A}_2} \sum_{\xi;\xi'\in\Xi} \omega_i(\xi,\xi')C_i(a_1, a_2; \xi)x_2(a_2)x_1(a_1) \geqslant \sigma_i.$$

By the second, the fourth and the fifth constraints in (14),

$$\eta_i = \sum_{\xi;\xi'\in\Xi} \omega_i(\xi,\xi')s_i(\xi') + \lambda_i\epsilon$$

$$\geqslant \sum_{\xi;\xi'\in\Xi} \omega_i(\xi,\xi')s_i(\xi') + \sum_{\xi;\xi'\in\Xi}\omega_i(\xi,\xi')\lambda_i|\xi - \xi'|$$

$$\geqslant \sum_{a_1\in\mathcal{A}_1}\sum_{a_2\in\mathcal{A}_2}\sum_{\xi;\xi'\in\Xi} \omega_i(\xi,\xi')C_i(a_1, a_2;\xi)x_1(a_1)x_2(a_2).$$

Thus,

$$\eta_i \geqslant \sigma_i.$$

"$\Rightarrow$" Let κ^* be the maximizer of (14). Then, we show that

$$\sigma_i^* = \eta_i^*, \quad i \in \mathcal{I}. \tag{15}$$

From the first, the second and the fourth constraints, we have

$$\sigma_i^* = \eta_i^*$$

$$\geqslant \lambda_i^*\epsilon + \sum_{\xi;\xi'\in\Xi}\omega_i^*(\xi;\xi')\left[\mathbf{x}_1^{*\mathrm{T}}\mathbf{C}_i(\xi)\mathbf{x}_2^* - \lambda_i^*|\xi - \xi'|\right]$$

$$\geqslant \lambda_i^*\sum_{\xi;\xi'\in\Xi}\omega_i(\xi,\xi')|\xi - \xi'| + \sum_{\xi;\xi'\in\Xi}\omega_i^*(\xi;\xi')\left[\mathbf{x}_1^{*\mathrm{T}}\mathbf{C}_i(\xi)\mathbf{x}_2^* - \lambda_i^*|\xi - \xi'|\right],$$

$$s^*(\xi') \geqslant \max_\xi \sum_{a_1\in\mathcal{A}_1}\sum_{a_2\in\mathcal{A}_2} C_i(a_1, a_2;\xi)x_1^*(a_1)x_2^*(a_2) - \lambda_i^*|\xi - \xi'|,$$

and

$$\eta_i^* \geqslant \lambda_i^*\epsilon + \sum_{\xi;\xi'\in\Xi}\omega_i^*(\xi;\xi')s_i^*(\xi')$$

$$\geqslant \lambda_i^*\epsilon + \sum_{\xi;\xi'\in\Xi}\omega_i^*(\xi;\xi')\max_\xi\sum_{a_1\in\mathcal{A}_1}\sum_{a_2\in\mathcal{A}_2} C_i(a_1, a_2;\xi)x_1^*(a_1)x_2^*(a_2) - \lambda_i^*|\xi - \xi'|.$$

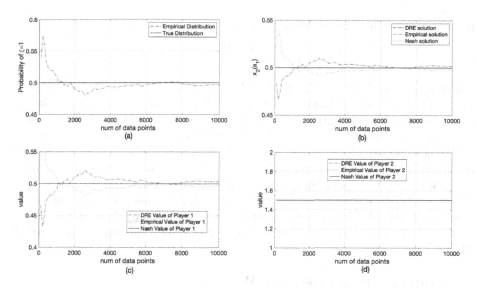

Fig. 2. The comparison of data-driven EG, Nash Game, and data-driven DRG.

From the last constraint,

$$\sigma_i^*$$

$$\leqslant \sum_{a_1 \in \mathcal{A}_1} \sum_{a_2 \in \mathcal{A}_2} \sum_{\xi;\xi' \in \Xi} \omega_i^*(\xi;\xi') C_i(a_1, a_2; \xi) x_1(a_1) x_2^*(a_2)$$

$$= \sum_{a_1 \in \mathcal{A}_1} \sum_{a_2 \in \mathcal{A}_2} \sum_{\xi' \in \Xi} \mathbb{Q}^{*(N)}(\xi') C_i(a_1, a_2; \xi) x_1(a_1) x_2^*(a_2)$$

$$\leqslant \lambda_i^* \epsilon + \sum_{\xi;\xi' \in \Xi} \omega_i^*(\xi;\xi') \left(\sum_{a_1 \in \mathcal{A}_1} \sum_{a_2 \in \mathcal{A}_2} C_i(a_1, a_2; \xi) x_1(a_1) x_2^*(a_2) - \lambda_i^* |\xi - \xi'| \right)$$

$$\leqslant \lambda_i \epsilon + \sum_{\xi;\xi' \in \Xi} \omega_i^*(\xi;\xi') \max_\xi \left(\sum_{a_1 \in \mathcal{A}_1} \sum_{a_2 \in \mathcal{A}_2} C_i(a_1, a_2; \xi) x_1(a_1) x_2^*(a_2) - \lambda_i^* |\xi - \xi'| \right)$$

Thus, we have

$$\sup_{\mathbb{Q} \in \mathcal{B}_\epsilon(\hat{\mathbb{Q}}^{(N)})} \mathbb{E}_\mathbb{Q}\left[c_i(\mathbf{x}_i^*, \mathbf{x}_{-i}^*; \xi) \right] \leqslant \sigma_i^* = \eta_i^* \leqslant \sup_{\mathbb{Q} \in \mathcal{B}_\epsilon(\hat{\mathbb{Q}}^{(N)})} \mathbb{E}_\mathbb{Q}\left[c_i(\mathbf{x}_i, \mathbf{x}_{-i}^*; \xi) \right].$$

Therefore, $(\mathbf{x}_1^*, \mathbf{x}_2^*)$ is a DRE.

□

6   Numerical Example

Consider a security game which is captured by a nonzero-sum game. The uncertainty parameter ξ represents the security environment, which influences the payoff. Assume that the payoff matrices are given by the following:

$$\begin{bmatrix} (1+\xi,3) & (0,2) \\ (2,0) & (-1,1) \end{bmatrix},$$

where $\xi \in \Xi = \{-1,1\}$. The true distribution of ξ is $\mathbb{P}[\xi = 1] = 1/2$, and $\mathbb{P}[\xi = 1] = 1/2$. When there is perfect distribution information (both players know the true distribution), the Nash equilibrium is $(1/2, 1/2)$, and the expected value of the game is $(1/2, 3/2)$. For the distributionally robust case, let the radius of Wasserstein ball be $\epsilon_N = 1/N$. As illustrated in Fig. 2, the value and equilibrium of both data-driven EG and data-driven DRG converge to the ones in Nash Game. We notice that the strategy of Player 1 and the value of Player 2 stay unaltered. By the indifferent principle [13], the bimatrix game considered here is fully mixed. In this case, the strategy of Player 1 only depends the payoff matrix of Player 2, and the value of Player 2 only depends on the strategy of Player 1.

7 Conclusions and Future Work

7.1 Conclusions

In this paper, we have proposed a new type of data-driven game model in which the players are capable of exploiting the information in the dataset. We have adopted the distributionally robust formulation to address the issue arising from the curse of the optimizer. We have used Wasserstein ball as the ambiguity set with the empirical distribution centered. By tuning the radius of the Wasserstein ball, we have demonstrated the relations between the proposed game and the existing games. We have also given the mathematical programming whose solutions are a subset of data-driven DRE.

7.2 Future Work

1. **Data-Driven Distributionally Robust Bayesian Game** In this work, we did not consider the case where there exists private information. As Harsanyi pointed out, the incomplete information is quite involving as there is *belief hierarchy*. We can use the information from the dataset to form the player's beliefs. As the belief are not generated from the common prior, the players are suspicious about the data-based belief. Therefore, it is reasonable to introduce robustness.
2. **Data-Driven Dynamic Game** It is also possible to extend the data-driven dynamic game. In a dynamic system, the agents do not have perfect nor complete knowledge of the system. While making decisions, they observe the outcomes of the system and update their knowledge. And with the updated knowledge, the agents are able to make *better* decisions.
3. **One-Sided Data-Driven Game** Consider a two-player game. One player has the access to the dataset $\hat{\Xi}$ and the other player has the access to the dataset $\tilde{\Xi}$. If $\tilde{\Xi} \subseteq \hat{\Xi}$, this becomes a one-sided information game, in which one player has more information than the other [7].

References

1. Aghassi, M., Bertsimas, D.: Robust game theory. Math. Program. **107**(1–2), 231–273 (2006). https://doi.org/10.1007/s10107-005-0686-0
2. Aumann, R.J.: Correlated equilibrium as an expression of Bayesian rationality. Econometrica J. Econometric Soc. **55**, 1–18 (1987)
3. Bauso, D., Gao, J., Tembine, H.: Distributionally robust games: f-divergence and learning. In: Proceedings of the 11th EAI International Conference on Performance Evaluation Methodologies and Tools, pp. 148–155 (2017)
4. Esfahani, P.M., Kuhn, D.: Data-driven distributionally robust optimization using the Wasserstein metric: performance guarantees and tractable reformulations. Math. Program. **171**(1–2), 115–166 (2018). https://doi.org/10.1007/s10107-017-1172-1
5. Farooq, M.J., Zhu, Q.: On the secure and reconfigurable multi-layer network design for critical information dissemination in the internet of battlefield things (IoBT). IEEE Trans. Wirel. Commun. **17**(4), 2618–2632 (2018)
6. Harsanyi, J.C.: Games with incomplete information played by "Bayesian" players part ii. Bayesian equilibrium points. Manag. Sci. **14**(5), 320–334 (1968)
7. Horák, K., Bošanský, B., Péchouček, M.: Heuristic search value iteration for one-sided partially observable stochastic games. In: Proceedings of the Thirty-First AAAI Conference on Artificial Intelligence, pp. 558–564 (2017)
8. Kakutani, S., et al.: A generalization of Brouwer's fixed point theorem. Duke Math. J. **8**(3), 457–459 (1941)
9. Koçyiğit, Ç., Iyengar, G., Kuhn, D., Wiesemann, W.: Distributionally robust mechanism design. Manage. Sci. **66**(1), 159–189 (2020)
10. Liang, A.: Games of incomplete information played by statisticians. arXiv preprint arXiv:1910.07018 (2019)
11. Liu, S., Zhu, Q.: Robust and stochastic optimization with a hybrid coherent risk measure with an application to supervised learning. IEEE Control Syst. Lett. **5**(3), 965–970 (2020)
12. Loizou, N.: Distributionally robust game theory. arXiv preprint arXiv:1512.03253 (2015)
13. Maschler, M., Solan, E., Zamir, S.: Game Theory (translated from the Hebrew by Ziv Hellman and edited by Mike Borns), pp. xxvi 979, 4. Cambridge University Press, Cambridge (2013)
14. Peng, G., Zhu, Q.: Game-theoretic analysis of optimal control and sampling for linear stochastic systems. In: 2019 57th Annual Allerton Conference on Communication, Control, and Computing (Allerton), pp. 647–654. IEEE (2019)
15. Peng, G., Zhu, Q.: Sequential hypothesis testing game. In: 2020 54th Annual Conference on Information Sciences and Systems (CISS), pp. 1–6. IEEE (2020)
16. Provost, F., Fawcett, T.: Data science and its relationship to big data and data-driven decision making. Big data **1**(1), 51–59 (2013)
17. Singh, V.V., Jouini, O., Lisser, A.: Distributionally robust chance-constrained games: existence and characterization of Nash equilibrium. Optim. Lett. **11**(7), 1385–1405 (2017). https://doi.org/10.1007/s11590-016-1077-6
18. Smith, J.E., Winkler, R.L.: The optimizer's curse: skepticism and postdecision surprise in decision analysis. Manag. Sci. **52**(3), 311–322 (2006)
19. Villani, C.: Optimal Transport: Old and New, vol. 338. Springer, Heidelberg (2008)
20. Zhang, Q., Zhu, Q., Boutaba, R.: Dynamic resource allocation for spot markets in cloud computing environments. In: 2011 Fourth IEEE International Conference on Utility and Cloud Computing, pp. 178–185. IEEE (2011)

Security Games over Lexicographic Orders

Stefan Rass[1]([✉])[iD], Angelika Wiegele[2][iD], and Sandra König[3][iD]

[1] Universitaet Klagenfurt, Institute of Applied Informatics, Klagenfurt, Austria
stefan.rass@aau.at
[2] Department of Mathematics, Universitaet Klagenfurt, Klagenfurt, Austria
angelika.wiegele@aau.at
[3] Austrian Institute of Technology, Center for Digital Safety & Security,
Vienna, Austria
sandra.koenig@ait.ac.at

Abstract. Security is rarely single-dimensional and is in most practical instances a tradeoff between dependent, and occasionally conflicting goals. The simplest method of multi-criteria optimization and games with vector-valued payoffs, is transforming such games into ones with scalar payoffs, and looking for Pareto-optimal behavior. This usually requires an explicit weighting of security goals, whereas practice often only lets us rank security goals in terms of importance, but hardly admits a crisp numerical weight being assigned. Our work picks up the issue of optimizing security goals in descending order of importance, coming to the computation of an optimal solution w.r.t. lexicographic orders. This is interesting in two ways, as it (i) is theoretically nontrivial since lexicographic orders do not generally admit representations by continuous utility functions, hence render Nash's classical result inapplicable, and (ii) practically relevant since it avoids ambiguities by subjective (and perhaps unsupported) importance weight assignments. We corroborate our results by giving numerical examples, showing a method to design zero-sum games with a set of a-priori chosen Nash equilibria. This simple instance of mechanism design may be of independent interest.

Keywords: Lexicographic order · multi-criteria optimization · Mechanism design · Security economics

1 Introduction and Motivation

Security is in many practical instances a multi-dimensional matter. Basic security goals like confidentiality, integrity and availability (CIA) are known to be potentially conflicting. For example, encryption serves confidentiality but can be problematic for availability. Likewise, keeping systems or data redundant to increase availability makes confidentiality more complex and may add to the attack surface. Generally, the different dimensions of security can depend on parameter settings (for example, threshold secret sharing has different resilience

© Springer Nature Switzerland AG 2020
Q. Zhu et al. (Eds.): GameSec 2020, LNCS 12513, pp. 422–441, 2020.
https://doi.org/10.1007/978-3-030-64793-3_23

against passive or active adversaries, regarding recoverability of the secret but also its confidentiality [16,21,26,35]), or security properties themselves (such as is the case for sanitizable signatures [4]). The general problem reaches much beyond basic cryptographic matters, since also risk management is by default a multi-dimensional challenge [28] of keeping financial losses, damages to reputation, legal liabilities and many more under control.

Generally, the priority of security goals depends on the application domain, and we can broadly distinguish two example domains with opposite priorities regarding CIA (we spare the full spectrum of security requirements here, as it would take us much beyond the scope of this section and work):

- data-processing enterprises will have confidentiality as their highest good, followed by integrity, and lastly followed by availability of the personal data in their possession.
- production-oriented enterprises, on the contrary, will not necessarily rely on continuous processing of personal data, but rather will protect their production lines, i.e., availability is their top priority. Likewise, production control signals need integrity protection (as second priority goal), followed by confidentiality as the least important among the three goals.

We will later illustrate our methods by showing how to apply them in an enterprise whose main business is processing personal data, or producing goods. It will turn out that the results are somewhat different, yet the method of computing them is the same in both cases, without the need to become explicit on a numeric difference in terms of importance of the security goals.

1.1 Related Work

Our work addresses the problem of multi-criteria optimization and -game theory, which is traditionally approached by scalarizing the vector-valued revenues gained by each player. While the concept of a Nash equilibrium is straightforward to generalize to a Pareto-Nash equilibrium [19] or -security strategy, the hereby involved importance weights put practitioners to the challenge of finding a meaningful quantification of importance for the relevant goals, or more generally, prioritization of security requirements [14,24], whose importance is widely recognized throughout security practitioners [18,25,34]. Sophisticated methods and heuristics to do this include the Choquet integral [12], fuzzy logic [31], or resorting to Pareto-optimality [33].

The problem of optimization over lexicographic orders itself is in fact not new, yet has seen surprisingly little attention for security applications, despite the fact that security goals are often in a very strict order of importance. The theoretical toolbox is rich, and includes axiomatic studies and characterizations [8–10,15] and questions of equilibria in lexicographically ordered vector-payoffs [17] and min-max optimization [22,23]. The latter is most closely related to our work, yet ours is conceptually different and uses a sequential application of criteria. Essentially, we adapt the "lexicographic method" (also called preemtive approach; see [5]) used in multi-criteria optimization, to the computation of equilibria in zero-sum games for security in a new form.

1.2 Our Contribution

The main contribution made in this work is the description of a simple method to compute a game-theoretic optimum if several goals are involved that obey a total order of priority without resorting to scalarization by using importance weights. As an implied consequence, we get a method to thereby refine ambiguous equilibria if they are intended as defense strategies, or as pointers to neuralgic spots in a system; the latter occurring if we interpret the optimal attack strategies in this way.

Independently, we corroborate our results by illustrating the computation using a method of mechanism design, allowing us to construct zero-sum games with a set of defined, i.e., designed, equilibria for both players. We remark that our focus on two-person zero-sum games is what makes the construction challenging, as it is conceptually not difficult to construct certain multi-player nonzero-sum games with desired optima: in the most trivial instance, we can just let the payoff for a player be independent of the other player's actions, and let it attain a maximum at the desired location(s). More generally, we may look for functions (e.g., polynomials) that, when having their domain restricted to points where the opponents have their optima, still have optima at desired positions. While this is, strictly speaking, no longer a strategic interaction with conflicts, and hence an uninteresting case for game theory or security, it nonetheless yields a theoretically valid instance of a general game. The most extreme instance is thus with exactly opposite goals of the players that depend on the player's mutual actions, i.e., a zero-sum game. This class of games is also useful in security modeling, since it delivers worst-case defenses without the need for accurate adversary models or -profiling [29, 30, 32, 36].

2 Preliminaries

2.1 Notation

We let vectors appear as bold-printed lower-case letters, and matrices will use uppercase bold printed letters. Sets will appear as upper case letters in normal font. Families of sets are written in calligraphic font. Let $\leq_{lex}$ be the lexicographic order over $\mathbb{R}^n \times \mathbb{R}^n$, defined in the usual way by setting $\mathbf{a} = (a_1, \ldots, a_n) \leq_{lex} (b_1, \ldots, b_n)$ if and only if $[a_1 < b_1] \vee [(a_1 = b_1) \wedge (a_2, \ldots, a_n) \leq_{lex} (b_2, \ldots, b_n)]$. In the following, let U be a metric vector space, and let $\leq$ be an ordering relation on it. Typically, U will be a space spanned over $\mathbb{R}$.

For a finite set $X = \{x_1, \ldots, x_n\}$, we let the symbol $\Delta(X)$ be the simplex over X, i.e., the set $\Delta(X) := \{\sum_{i=1}^n \lambda_i \cdot x_i | \lambda_i \geq 0$ for all i, and $\sum_{i=1}^n \lambda_i = 1\}$. Games are triples $(N, \mathcal{S}, H)$, with N being a finite set of players, $\mathcal{S}$ being a family of finite sets, one $S_i \in \mathcal{S}$ associated with each player giving its actions, and H is a collection of functions $u_i : S_i \times S_{-i} \to \mathbb{R}$ of utility functions. Herein, the notation S_{-i} is the cartesian product of all elements in $\mathcal{S}$, excluding S_i. It expresses the joint actions taken by player i's opponents. Throughout this work, we will have $N = \{1,2\}$, $\mathcal{S} = \{S_1 = \Delta(AS_1), S_2 = \Delta(AS_2)\}$ for finite action spaces AS_1, AS_2 with n elements for player 1, and m elements for player 2. In this special case, we can represent the whole game by an $(n \times m)$-payoff matrix $\mathbf{A}$, and abbreviate our notation by referring to the matrix $\mathbf{A}$ to synonymously mean the game that it defines.

2.2 Representability of the Lexicographic Order

Given an ordering relation $\leq$ on a set $U \times U$, we say that $\leq$ is *representable* by a function $f : U \to \mathbb{R}$ if, $[a \leq b] \iff [f(a) \leq f(b)]$ for all $a, b \in U$ that are comparable under $\leq$.

It is well known that the lexicographic order, in general, does *not* lend itself to a representation by any continuous function. This folklore result is made precise as Proposition 1, whose proof we let follow in Appendix A for convenience of the reader.

Proposition 1. *On the totally ordered set $([0,1]^2, \leq_{lex})$, there is no continuous function $f : [0,1]^2 \to \mathbb{R}$ with the property that $(x_1, x_2) \leq_{lex} (y_1, y_2) \iff f(x_1, x_2) \leq f(y_1, y_2)$.*

Proposition 1 makes lexicographic orders generally difficult to handle in optimization algorithms, since it lacks the minimal requirement of continuity, assumed in many optimization methods (up to the stronger requirement of differentiability). On the bright side, this lack of continuity only holds in the most general setting, and special situations may still admit a continuous representation, or other means of efficient optimization, as we outline next.

3 Finding Lex-Order Optimal Strategies

Our algorithm to compute equilibria over lexicographic orders will decompose a vector-valued game matrix into a sequence of games, in which the i-th game has a payoff matrix composed from the respective i-th coordinates in each vector. That is, given the vector-valued utility function $u : S_1 \times S_2 \to \mathbb{R}^d$ for a player, on the discrete strategy spaces S_1, S_2, we define the k-th game for $k = 1, 2, \ldots, d$ via the matrix $\mathbf{A}_k = (u_k(r,c))_{(r,c) \in S_1 \times S_2}$. Note that all game matrices have the same $n \times m$-shape.

Towards finding an optimum, i.e., an equilibrium, over the lex-order, we induct over the coordinate $k = 1, 2, \ldots, d$, and prove the existence of equilibria along the way. The goal is finding strategies that are lex-order optimal for each player, in light of unilateral deviation.

Induction start $\underline{k = 1}$: The game $\mathbf{A}_1$ is only about scalar payoffs, and the equilibrium w.r.t. the $\leq$-order over $\mathbb{R}$ is also lex-order optimal, since the two relations coincide on scalars.

Remark 1. We emphasize that the solution for $k = 1$ is the only stage at which the optima are the same as equilibria, since the lex-order and the real-valued $\leq$ coincide only in that case. As the idea will be seeking optima in the next stage among the optima found for (all of the) previous games, the term "equilibrium" will hereafter be understood *conditional* on the strategies constrained to be also equilibria for previous games (namely $\mathbf{A}_{k-1}, \mathbf{A}_{k-2}, \ldots$). Clearly, the solution may not be an equilibrium for any of the games when considered in isolation and independent of the others.

Remark 2. (Number of optima is finite). The characterization of equilibria by linear programs (appearing in Appendix B in the context of constructing games with desired equilibria) defines the feasible set of solutions via a finite number of inequalities. Therefore, the overall solution set, though generally infinite (as all convex combinations of optima are themselves also optimal; cf. Lemma 1), is representable by a finite (though in the worst case exponentially large) number of points, whose convex combination represents all feasible solutions, and hence also all optima therein. This finiteness property in fact holds in a measure-theoretic sense for almost all games [13].

Induction step $\underline{k - 1 \to k}$: For the induction until $k - 1$, we can assume a finite set $E_{k-1} = \left\{ (\mathbf{x}_{k-1,1}^*, \mathbf{y}_{k-1,1}^*), \ldots, (\mathbf{x}_{k-1,n_{k-1}}^*, \mathbf{y}_{k-1,n_{k-1}}^*) \right\}$ of optima (cf. Remark 1). For the induction hypothesis, assume that all of them are also optima of the $(k - 1)$-th game $\mathbf{A}_{k-1}$.

Our <u>goal</u> for the induction step is refining the equilibria into an optimum for the game $\mathbf{A}_k$ on the k-th coordinate. The basic idea is to play the game $\mathbf{A}_k$ restricted only to strategies that are already optimal for $\mathbf{A}_{k-1}$, so as to retain optimality in the previous games, when optimizing our behavior in the next game $\mathbf{A}_k$. We materialize this plan now.

From the set E_{k-1}, we define an auxiliary game $\mathbf{B}_k$: its strategy spaces are $S_{k,1} = \left\{ \mathbf{x}_{k-1,i}^* | i = 1, \ldots, n_{k-1} \right\}$ and $S_{k,2} = \left\{ \mathbf{y}_{k-1,i}^* | i = 1, \ldots, n_{k-1} \right\}$. The implied $(n_{k-1} \times n_{k-1})$-payoff structure is the matrix

$$\mathbf{B}_k := ((\mathbf{x}_{k-1,i}^*)^T \cdot \mathbf{A}_k \cdot \mathbf{y}_{k-1,j}^*)_{i,j=1}^{n_{k-1}}. \tag{1}$$

The so-constructed zero-sum game has its own equilibria, the entire set of which is enumerable by known algorithms [1]. Moreover, we have convenient topological properties, assuring that the set among which we look for optima is convex and closed, and the strategy spaces of $\mathbf{B}_k$ are compact sets. This is Lemma 1.

Lemma 1. *Let $\mathbf{A}$ be a matrix inducing a zero-sum game, on the strategy spaces $S_1 \subset \Delta(\mathbb{R}^n), S_2 \subset \Delta(\mathbb{R}^m)$. If $\leq$ is a continuous ordering[1], and $u : S_1 \times S_2 \to \mathbb{R}$*

---

[1] An ordering $\leq$ is called *continuous*, if all bounded sequences (a_n) with $a_n \leq b$ for all $n \in \mathbb{R}$, have a limit that also satisfies the same bound $\lim_{n\to\infty} a_n \leq b$, if that limit exists. The lexicographic order is discontinuous w.r.t. this definition, since the sequence $(1/n, 0) \geq_{lex} (0, 1)$ for all $n \in \mathbb{N}$, but $\lim_{n\to\infty}(1/n, 0) = (0, 0) \leq_{lex} (0, 1)$.

is continuous w.r.t. a norm on $\mathbb{R}^n$ and the order topology induced by $\leq$, then the set of mixed Nash equilibria for the zero sum game $\mathbf{A}$ is nonempty, convex and compact.

Combining Lemma 1 with Glicksberg's theorem [11] yields an equilibrium $(\boldsymbol{\alpha}_k^*, \boldsymbol{\beta}_k^*) \in \mathbb{R}^{n_{k-1}} \times \mathbb{R}^{n_{k-1}}$ in the game $\mathbf{B}_k$, which by definition satisfies the saddle point condition $\boldsymbol{\alpha}^T \cdot \mathbf{B}_k \cdot \boldsymbol{\beta}_k^* \leq (\boldsymbol{\alpha}^*)^T \cdot \mathbf{B}_k \cdot \boldsymbol{\beta}_k^* \leq (\boldsymbol{\alpha}^*)^T \cdot \mathbf{B}_k \cdot \boldsymbol{\beta}$, for all $\boldsymbol{\alpha}, \boldsymbol{\beta}$.

By the same token as in Remark 2, we can assume a finite number n_k of equilibria in $\mathbf{B}_k$, and let us put these as rows into two matrices $\mathbf{X}_{k-1} \in \mathbb{R}^{n_k \times n_{k-1}}$ and $\mathbf{Y}_{k-1}^{n_k \times n_{k-1}}$. These two relate to $\mathbf{B}_k$ via $\mathbf{B}_k = \mathbf{X}_{k-1} \cdot \mathbf{A}_k \cdot \mathbf{Y}_{k-1}^T$.

Since the pure strategies in $\mathbf{B}_k$ are all equilibria in $\mathbf{A}_{k-1}$, any mixed strategy pair $(\boldsymbol{\alpha}_k^*, \boldsymbol{\beta}_k^*) \in \Delta(S_{k,1}) \times \Delta(S_{k,2})$ played in $\mathbf{B}_k$ induces an equilibrium

$$\mathbf{x}_k' := (\boldsymbol{\alpha}_k^*)^T \cdot \mathbf{X}_{k-1}, \quad \text{and} \quad \mathbf{y}_k' := (\boldsymbol{\beta}_k^*)^T \cdot \mathbf{Y}_{k-1} \tag{2}$$

for the game $\mathbf{A}_{k-1}$ by Lemma 1 (note that the payoff is continuous, since the auxiliary game $\mathbf{B}_k$ is a standard matrix game and as such with continuous payoffs over mixed strategies). Thus, the pair $(\mathbf{x}_k', \mathbf{y}_k')$ satisfies the saddle point condition in $\mathbf{A}_{k-1}$, being $\mathbf{x}^T \cdot \mathbf{A}_{k-1} \cdot \mathbf{y}_k' \leq (\mathbf{x}_k')^T \cdot \mathbf{A}_{k-1} \cdot \mathbf{y}_k' \leq (\mathbf{x}_k')^T \cdot \mathbf{A}_{k-1} \cdot \mathbf{y}$ for all $\mathbf{x}, \mathbf{y}$.

Our goal is showing that the pair $(\mathbf{x}_k', \mathbf{y}_k')$ is also optimal in the game $\mathbf{A}_k$. To this end, we will adopt player 1's perspective, playing some arbitrary but fixed $\mathbf{x} \neq \mathbf{x}_k'$, while player 2 sticks to $\mathbf{y}_k'$.

Towards a contradiction, suppose that player 1 could improve in $\mathbf{A}_k$ by playing $\mathbf{x}$,

$$\mathbf{x}^T \cdot \mathbf{A}_k \cdot \mathbf{y}_k' > \mathbf{x}_k' \cdot \mathbf{A}_k \cdot \mathbf{y}_k'. \tag{3}$$

Substituting the definition of $\mathbf{x}_k'$ and $\mathbf{y}_k'$ by means of $\mathbf{X}_{k-1}, \mathbf{Y}_{k-1}$ gives on the left side of (3)

$$(\boldsymbol{\alpha}_k^*)^T \cdot \underbrace{\mathbf{X}_{k-1} \cdot \mathbf{A}_k \cdot \mathbf{Y}_{k-1}^T}_{=\mathbf{B}_k} \cdot \boldsymbol{\beta}_k^* = (\boldsymbol{\alpha}_k^*)^T \cdot \mathbf{B}_k \cdot \boldsymbol{\beta}_k^*.$$

With the same substitution on the right side of (3), we get $\mathbf{x}^T \cdot \mathbf{A}_k \cdot \mathbf{Y}_{k-1}^T \cdot \boldsymbol{\beta}_k^* > \boldsymbol{\alpha}_k^* \cdot \mathbf{B}_k \cdot \boldsymbol{\beta}_k^*$. Now, if there were some $\tilde{\mathbf{x}}$ such that $\mathbf{x}^T = \tilde{\mathbf{x}}^T \cdot \mathbf{X}_{k-1}$, we could rewrite the last inequality into $\tilde{\mathbf{x}}^T \cdot \mathbf{X}_{k-1} \cdot \mathbf{A}_k \cdot \mathbf{Y}_{k-1}^T \cdot \boldsymbol{\beta}_k^* = \tilde{\mathbf{x}}^T \cdot \mathbf{B}_k \cdot \boldsymbol{\beta}_k^* > \boldsymbol{\alpha}_k^* \cdot \mathbf{B}_k \cdot \boldsymbol{\beta}_k^*$, to contradict the fact that $(\boldsymbol{\alpha}_k^*, \boldsymbol{\beta}_k^*)$ is an equilibrium in $\mathbf{B}_k$, and thereby finally refute (3). But such an $\tilde{\mathbf{x}}$ is in fact easy to find, since the possible actions are restricted to equilibrium strategies in $\mathbf{A}_{k-1}$. The vector $\mathbf{x}$ must thus be a mix of rows from the matrix $\mathbf{X}_{k-1}$, putting $\mathbf{x}$ into the row-space of $\mathbf{X}_{k-1}$. In that case, the equation system $\mathbf{x}^T = \tilde{\mathbf{x}}^T \cdot \mathbf{X}_{k-1}$, even if over-determined, has a solution being the sought $\tilde{\mathbf{x}}$. Hence, (3) cannot hold, and $\mathbf{x}_k'$ is also optimal in the game $\mathbf{A}_k$, when the opponent plays $\mathbf{y}_k'$. By symmetry, the argument for the second player works analogously, and the induction step is complete, delivering the sought simultaneous optimum $(\mathbf{x}_k', \mathbf{y}_k')$ as given by (2). Figure 1 summarizes the construction as an algorithm.

Remark 3. From another angle, the above procedure is viewable as starting in the game on the first coordinate, with a possibly large set E_1 of equilibria, and then narrowing down, resp. *refining*, this set to those elements $E_2 \subseteq E_1$ that are also optimal in the game $\mathbf{A}_2$. Repeating this procedure, we then further restrict the set to $E_3 \subseteq E_2$, in which only those strategies are retained that are also optimal in the game $\mathbf{A}_3$, etc. It is obvious that the equilibria in $\mathbf{A}_1$ can be disjoint from those in $\mathbf{A}_2$, which means that a strategy carried over from E_k to E_{k+1} may no longer be an equilibrium in $\mathbf{A}_{k+1}$. This brings us back to the initial remark made at the induction step, calling the solutions "conditional optimal" rather than equilibria. However, since we are after optimality w.r.t. a lexicographic order, all we count is the chances of worsening the outcome upon an unilateral deviation from the final solution. Since the final set $E_d \subseteq E_{d-1} \subseteq \cdots \subseteq E_1 = \{$ all equilibria in $\mathbf{A}_1\}$ contains only equilibria for the first game, deviating from it would worsen our situation on the first coordinate, and hence irrespectively of the other coordinates, would make the result lex-order worse. Upon equality, the second coordinate kicks in, and so on.

Now, let us wrap up by putting the result in the context of security: like a conventional, scalar-valued, zero-sum game, our lex-ordered optima here have the same property of being a worst-case defense against any adversarial behavior, as long as the defender adheres to the final optimum.

Input: A set of payoff matrices $\mathbf{A}_1, \ldots, \mathbf{A}_d \in \mathbb{R}^{n \times m}$,
Output: A lex-order optimal strategy $\mathbf{x}^*, \mathbf{y}^*$ with the properties told by Prop. 2
Procedure:

1. Compute all equilibria in the game $\mathbf{A}_1$ (e.g., using the algorithm from [1]), and collect the optima for player 1 in the set $S_{1,1}$ and the optima for player 2 in the set $S_{1,2}$.
2. Put $k \leftarrow 1$
3. **if** $k = d$, **then return** any $(\mathbf{x}^*, \mathbf{y}^*) \in S_{k,1} \times S_{k,2}$ as the final result and **terminate**.
4. Otherwise (if $k < d$), update $k \leftarrow k + 1$
5. Arrange the elements of $S_{k-1,1}$ as rows of a matrix $\mathbf{X}$ and arrange the elements of $S_{k-1,2}$ as rows of a matrix $\mathbf{Y}$, and compute the matrix $\mathbf{B}_k = \mathbf{X} \cdot \mathbf{A}_k \cdot \mathbf{Y}^T$.
6. Compute all equilibria in the matrix game $\mathbf{B}_k$ and collect them in a set $E_k := \{(\boldsymbol{\alpha}_1^*, \boldsymbol{\beta}_1^*), \ldots, (\boldsymbol{\alpha}_{n_k}^*, \boldsymbol{\beta}_{n_k}^*)\}$.
7. Iterate over $i = 1, 2, \ldots, n_k$ pairs $(\boldsymbol{\alpha}_i, \boldsymbol{\beta}_i) \in E_k$ and for each pair, compute $\mathbf{x}_i' = (\boldsymbol{\alpha}_i)^T \cdot \mathbf{X}, \mathbf{y}_i' = (\boldsymbol{\beta}_i)^T \cdot \mathbf{Y}$. Put all the resulting $\mathbf{x}_i'$ into the set $S_{k,1}$ and the resulting $\mathbf{y}_i'$ into the set $S_{k,2}$.
8. go back to step 3.

Fig. 1. Computation of lexicographically optimal multi-goal security strategies

More formally, we have:

Proposition 2. *Let* $\mathbf{A}_1, \ldots, \mathbf{A}_d$ *be a series of game-matrices, all of* $(n \times m)$-*shape, describing a security game between a defender as player 1, and an attacker as player 2, whose unknown payoffs may be* $\mathbf{U}_1, \ldots, \mathbf{U}_d$, *in the same game.*

Let the defending player 1 substitute $\mathbf{U}_k := -\mathbf{A}_k$ *for all* $k = 1, 2, \ldots, d$, *in lack of better knowledge, and let* $\mathbf{x}^* = \mathbf{x}'_d, \mathbf{y}^* = \mathbf{y}'_d$ *be the output computed by the lexicographic method as described in Fig. 1.*

Then, conditional on the attacker acting within its own action space (i.e., not playing any strategy whose payoff is not captured by the columns in the $\mathbf{A}_k$'s), *we have the actual payoff in the* k-*th game for* $k = 1, 2, \ldots, d$ *for the defender satisfy*

$$\mathbf{x}^* \cdot \mathbf{A}_k \cdot \mathbf{y}^* \leq \mathbf{x}^* \cdot \mathbf{A}_k \cdot \mathbf{y},$$

for any true behavior $\mathbf{y}$ *of the attacker.*

The proof is a simple consequence of the equilibrium property that we have shown to hold for each $\mathbf{A}_k$: it means that each $\mathbf{x}'_d, \mathbf{y}'_d$ is a saddle point

$$\mathbf{x} \cdot \mathbf{A}_k \cdot \mathbf{y}'_d \leq \mathbf{x}'_d \cdot \mathbf{A}_k \cdot \mathbf{y}'_d \leq \mathbf{x}'_d \cdot \mathbf{A}_k \cdot \mathbf{y},$$

for all $k = 1, 2, \ldots, d$, since each $\mathbf{x}'_k, \mathbf{y}'_k$ is a convex combination of saddle points. If player 2 has a different incentive than engaging in a zero-sum competition, then the saddle point property will ensure that player 1's revenue can only increase by the unilateral deviation of player 2. The worst case is attained for exactly opposite intentions, i.e., a zero-sum regime.

4 Applications and Examples

4.1 Refining Ambiguous Attack or Defense Strategies

One appeal of using game theory to analyze attacker/defender scenarios is its simultaneous account for the natural opposition of interests. Thereby, it delivers optimal defenses and optimal attacks, but their practical value depends on matters of plausibility (e.g., for attacks), or feasibility (e.g., for defenses).

Implausible equilibria arise in models that neglect certain interests of the attacker, or under oversimplifying assumptions on the attack models. Likewise, infeasible defenses can result from models missing on certain cost or efforts imposed on the defender if it were to implement the game-theoretically optimal choice. The existence of ambiguities in Nash equilibria is well documented, and we can state the following explicit result for security games as zero-sum competitions:

Lemma 2. *Pick any set of vectors* $E_1 = \left\{\mathbf{x}_1^*, \ldots, \mathbf{x}_{k_1}^*\right\} \subset \mathbb{R}^n$ *and* $E_2 = \{\mathbf{y}_1^*, \ldots, \mathbf{y}_{k_2}^*\} \subset \mathbb{R}^m$, *where* $k_1 < n$ *and* $k_2 < m$. *Then, there is a finite two-person zero-sum game whose equilibria are exactly the set* $\Delta(E_1) \times \Delta(E_2)$.

Lemma 2 is proven in Appendix B. It essentially tells that any desired equilibrium for both, the defender and the attacker can be "enforced" by a proper mechanism designed, which is not per se surprising, but this mechanism can take the form of a simple security game. Conversely, this means that we may expect either a unique or an infinitude of equilibria in even the simplest instances of security games, making a method of refining them necessary. The usual way of resorting to more advanced concepts of equilibria is not necessarily also a practical way to go, since it still can leave practically relevant aspects untouched, see some examples following below.

The lexicographic method of computing equilibria does not require a priori knowledge of all relevant dimensions, and can refine ambiguous or implausible results "as needed" by bringing in further utility values. For example, several ways of defending a system by randomization of actions can be judged upon the following additional criteria:

Cost of Changing from Between Strategies: Randomization itself causes friction losses, and this is in conflict with the common practice of "never touch a running system". Thus, changing configurations requires efforts (e.g., people can be reluctant to change their password) and proper modeling [6] that can lead to further utility values for the lexicographic optimization.

Predictability of a Defense for the Attacker: Since a randomized action is essentially describing a random variable, we can – as an additional "utility" – ask for the uncertainty that our defense has against a guessing adversary. To measure this, we could define the randomized choice rule's min-entropy as another utility of interest (not Shannon-entropy, since this is in general not a good measure of unpredictability against guessing).

Cost or Times to Exploit: For the attacker, even if there is a vulnerability to exploit, it is typically a complex choice to pick the "easiest" one. Methods like the Common Vulnerability Scoring (CVSS) associate several scores with a vulnerability, such as required background knowledge, necessary form and duration of access, etc. All these lend themselves to defining their own utility values for the attacker, and can be brought into a lexicographic optimization for the defender to narrow down the set of optimal defenses in such multiple dimensions.

4.2 Example 1: The Pure Algorithm (Numerical Illustration)

Let us now give a numerical example of the computational method from Sect. 3 on a game with two payoffs per player. We start with a constructed matrix $\mathbf{A}_1$ (obtained by application of the techniques to prove Lemma 2; see Appendix B),

$$\mathbf{A}_1 = \begin{pmatrix} 0.955986 & -0.272557 & 0.316327 & -0.405844 & 0.102397 & -0.662056 \\ 0.0454297 & -0.0580642 & -0.178636 & -0.187195 & 0.130912 & 0.204854 \\ -0.298982 & 0.05127 & -0.17908 & 0.0170827 & 0.0593234 & 0.292065 \\ -0.436331 & 0.223209 & -0.113101 & 0.453724 & -0.301461 & 0.340507 \\ -0.558309 & 0.0324137 & 0.0676309 & -0.0335246 & 0.251095 & -0.076376 \end{pmatrix}, \quad (4)$$

known to have three equilibria $\mathbf{x}_1^*, \ldots, \mathbf{x}_3^*$ for player 1, and 2 optimal strategies $\mathbf{y}_1^*, \mathbf{y}_2^*$ for player 2 (given explicitly in Appendix B as (5) and (6)), and another matrix

$$\mathbf{A}_2 = \begin{pmatrix} 5 & 4 & 5 & 3 & 3 & 2 \\ 5 & 5 & 3 & 2 & 5 & 1 \\ 3 & 3 & 1 & 1 & 2 & 4 \\ 2 & 2 & 5 & 5 & 2 & 3 \\ 2 & 3 & 2 & 4 & 3 & 2 \end{pmatrix}$$

chosen purely at random, but with the same shape as $\mathbf{A}_1$. A systematic construction of $\mathbf{A}_2$ would be possible (e.g., using a selection of the vectors used above to construct $\mathbf{A}_1$), but the optimization does not hinge on such constructed input(s).

Now, the auxiliary game matrix $\mathbf{B}_2$ arises from computing the equilibria of the scalar-valued matrix game $\mathbf{A}_1$, which we know to be given by any combination of $\{\mathbf{x}_1^*, \mathbf{x}_2^*, \mathbf{x}_3^*\} \times \{\mathbf{y}_1^*, \mathbf{y}_2^*\} = \{(\mathbf{x}_{1,i}^*, \mathbf{y}_{1,i}^*)\}_{i=1}^{n_1=6}$. The matrix has as many rows as player 1 has equilibria, and as many columns as player 2 has equilibria, being

$$\mathbf{B}_2 = \begin{pmatrix} 3.27905 & 3.35008 & 3.31098 \\ 3.0755 & 3.1093 & 3.00523 \end{pmatrix}.$$

In this game, an equilibrium is computable by linear programming, explicitly stated as primal (P) and dual problem (D) in Appendix B, using the GNU linear programming kit [20]. An equilibrium is found as

$$\alpha_2^* = (1, 0), \quad \text{and} \quad \beta_2^* = (1, 0, 0),$$

so that the final optimum for both players is obtained by evaluating (2), giving

$$\mathbf{x}_{2,1}' = (0.236624, 0.259513, 0.011683, 0.330247, 0.161933) \quad (= \mathbf{x}_1^*)$$

and

$$\mathbf{y}_{2,1}' = (0.11090, 0.13516, 0.22033, 0.12635, 0.23811, 0.16914) \quad (= \mathbf{y}_1^*).$$

From here onwards, the process would continue likewise by enumerating all equilibria that exist in the game $\mathbf{B}_2$, to make up a list of strategies $\mathbf{x}_{2,1}', \ldots, \mathbf{x}_{2,n_2}'$ and $\mathbf{y}_{2,1}', \ldots, \mathbf{y}_{2,n_2}'$ to define the game $\mathbf{B}_3$ and so on. Since the process is repetitive, we let our example stop here, with a unique solution obtained for the second coordinate already. Once we are left with a single solution, the iteration may safely stop, since considering further payoff matrices for higher coordinates cannot further narrow down the set of equilibria; it would remain the same optimum over all coordinates $> k$, once the solution is unique at stage k.

4.3   Example 2: Data Download

Let us recap the two distinct settings of a company processing personal data or running a production line. In both cases, we assume that data is being downloaded from redundant servers, some of which may be compromised by an adversary. The settings are different for the two companies in the following way:

- for the *production-oriented* enterprise, Alice will download software or control scripts, neither of which has a particular demand for confidentiality, but must be available and integrity protected, in this order of importance for the two. The overall goals are thus

"Availability" > "Integrity" > "Confidentiality".
– for the *personal data processing* enterprise, it may not matter too much if the data of a particular person is not instantly accessible, but it must remain confidential in all cases, and needs protection from manipulation. The priorities are thus

"Confidentiality" > "Integrity" > "Availability".

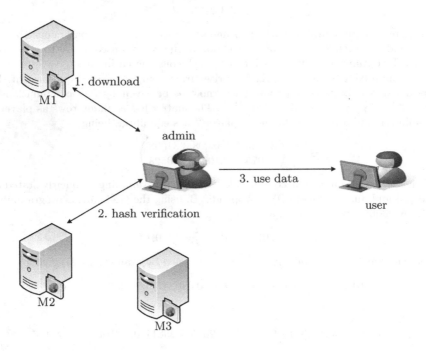

Fig. 2. Example scenario for data download

Towards a specific example, suppose that an administrator has three servers to potentially retrieve data from (where "data" can be a software or personal data), and that the policy prescribes to do a majority vote verification. That is, data retrieved from one server M_i needs to be checked against another redundant server M_j[2]; if the results are consistent, we have a 2-out-of-3 majority pointing to the downloaded data as correct, since the data is apparently the same as if it were when downloaded from the verification server M_j and checked against the other server M_i. If the verification fails, the data could be checked for consistency with a third server.

Let the situation be as depicted in Fig. 2, and consider the following likelihoods for a man-made hacker attack (probabilities p_1, p_2, p_3) or a natural outage of a server. Natural failures are hereby considered individually different, e.g., due to varying traffic

---

[2] This is indeed the standard idea behind putting cryptographic hash fingerprints on download sites for open-source software, addressing the possibility of a forged installation bundle. The package's fingerprint as put on the website next to the download is for verification against independent other mirrors that offer the same download.

loads, distinct hard- and software configurations, different administrative procedures applying to a server and its mirror, or similar, leading to different probabilities q_1, q_2 and q_3 assumed here:

mirror	M_1	M_2	M_3
probability of being hacked	$p_1 = 0.1$	$p_2 = 0.05$	$p_3 = 0.01$
probability of failure (reliability)	$q_1 = 0.1$	$q_2 = 0.2$	$q_3 = 0.15$

With this, we can set up a payoff structure with the strategies $\{M_1, M_2\}$, $\{M_2, M_3\}$ and $\{M_1, M_3\}$, meaning that both servers are used by the players; for player 1, using $\{M_i, M_j\}$ means download from M_i and verify against M_j. The same strategy for the attacker means that exactly M_i and M_j are being attacked, with success chances as given in the table above.

Assuming stochastic independence, we get the following generic payoff structure, where ℓ_i is a likelihood later to be substituted by either p_i or q_i,

	$\{M_1, M_2\}$	$\{M_1, M_3\}$	$\{M_2, M_3\}$
$\{M_1, M_2\}$	$(1 - \ell_1)(1 - \ell_2)$	$1 - \ell_1$	$1 - \ell_2$
$\{M_1, M_3\}$	$1 - \ell_1$	$(1 - \ell_1)(1 - \ell_3)$	$1 - \ell_3$
$\{M_2, M_3\}$	$1 - \ell_2$	$1 - \ell_3$	$(1 - \ell_2)(1 - \ell_3)$

which, upon substituting the values $\ell_i = p_i$ or $\ell_i = q_i$ values, gives the confidentiality game $\mathbf{A}_{conf}$ and availability game $\mathbf{A}_{avail}$

$$\mathbf{A}_{conf} := \begin{pmatrix} 0.855 & 0.9 & 0.95 \\ 0.9 & 0.891 & 0.99 \\ 0.95 & 0.99 & 0.9405 \end{pmatrix}, \quad \text{and} \quad \mathbf{A}_{avail} = \begin{pmatrix} 0.72 & 0.9 & 0.8 \\ 0.9 & 0.765 & 0.85 \\ 0.8 & 0.85 & 0.68 \end{pmatrix}.$$

Now, the optimization is either w.r.t. the goal priorities "Confidentiality" > "Availability", coming to the payoff vector $(\mathbf{x}^T \cdot \mathbf{A}_{conf} \cdot \mathbf{y}, \mathbf{x}^T \cdot \mathbf{A}_{avail} \cdot \mathbf{y})$, or with the reversed goal priorities "Availability" > "Confidentiality", giving the (reversed) payoff vector $(\mathbf{x}^T \cdot \mathbf{A}_{avail} \cdot \mathbf{y}, \mathbf{x}^T \cdot \mathbf{A}_{conf} \cdot \mathbf{y})$.

Let us compute the results in both cases separately:

1. For confidentiality as the highest goal, we find only a single equilibrium being

$$\mathbf{x}_1^* = (0, 0.09548, 0.90452), \quad \text{and} \quad \mathbf{y}_1^* = (0.49749, 0, 0.50251)$$

with the saddle point value $v_1 = 0.94523$, i.e., an $\approx 94\%$ chance of the data being not compromised (w.r.t. confidentiality).

Since this equilibrium is unique, it carries through to the second coordinate without any further change, giving the 1×1-payoff structure $B_2 = (0.7526)$. This is, at the same time, the best achievable payoff regarding availability, so we have the lex-order optimum being (Pr(Confidentiality), Pr(Availability)) = $(0.94523, 0.7526)$.

2. If availability is the highest-priority goal, we first look for a saddle point on $\mathbf{A}_{avail}$, giving

$$\mathbf{x}_2^* = \mathbf{y}_2^* = (0.40564, 0.55531, 0.03905),$$

with the availability likelihood being the saddle point value $v_2 = 0.82308$, i.e., an $\approx 82\%$ chance for the data to be downloadable.

As before, this equilibrium is unique, and hence no change upon proceeding to further coordinates will happen. The game $\mathbf{B}_2$ is again 1×1 and rewards the (constant) value 0.89537. The lex-order optimum is thus (Pr(Availability), Pr(Confidentiality)) $= (0.82308, 0.89537)$.

Generally, the procedure will make the goal with highest priority matter most, with the multi-criteria optimization subsequently refining the set of equilibria existing for the first goal. This is in contrast to other instances of multi-goal treatment, where the goals may play equally important roles. From the complexity perspective, the enumeration of equilibria per goal can take worst-case exponential time (in the number of strategies), but practically, there may not be a need to compute all equilibria in all cases; the method will never shrink the set towards emptiness, since once the set is singleton at stage k, it will remain unchanged for $k + 1, k + 2, \ldots, d$. Thus, as long as equilibria remain plausible in the context at hand, the computational burden may be kept in feasible bounds. Nonetheless, this may still call for other refinements like perfect equilibria or others. Imposing such additional constraints on the equilibria per stage is a straightforward matter.

5   Conclusion

We described a simple method to do multi-criteria optimization with goal priorities as optimization over lexicographic orders. As a natural side-effect, our algorithm narrows down a potentially large set of ambiguous Nash equilibria to fewer ones, and therefore is a natural refinement of the general Nash equilibrium in case of multiple criteria. It is, however, fair to admit that this process is in general not guaranteed to establish ultimate uniqueness of the equilibrium. In general, the so-found optimum depends on the specific goal prioritization, reflecting the fact that security strategies are expectedly different depending on the application domain. The method is algorithmically simple, and implemented as open source and freely available (see [2] for a software to enumerate equilibria, and [27] for the source code behind the examples given in this work).

While our method to construct games with desired ambiguous equilibria (see Appendix B) is here used only for the sake of illustrating, it may be of independent interest, e.g., for teaching general game theory to construct examples.

Acknowledgement. The authors would like to thank the anonymous reviewers for valuable and constructive feedback on this work.

A   Proof of Proposition 1

Towards a contradiction, suppose there were such a function f then, it obviously cannot be constant, for otherwise, it were meaningless. Thus, there must be some value x for which $f(x, 0) \neq f(x, 1)$, and the interval $I(x) := [f(x, 0), f(x, 1)]$ has nonzero width.

Furthermore, any two such intervals $I(x), I(y)$ are disjoint: if there were x, y such that the intervals overlap, then we would have $f(x, 0) < f(y, 0) < f(x, 1) < f(y, 1)$, which, since f represents the ordering, entails $(x, 0) <_{lex} (y, 0) <_{lex} (x, 1) <_{lex} (y, 1)$, in which the first $<_{lex}$ implies $x < y$ and the second implies $y < x$, which is not possible at the same time.

Let us pick some particular (arbitrary) x for which $f(x, 0) \neq f(x, 1)$ in the following. Since f is continuous, so is the function $f(h) := f(x + h, 0) - f(x + h, 1)$. Our choice of x makes $f(0) > 0$, and this relation holds in an entire compact neighborhood f of 0. The compactness of f implies that f attains a minimum $\varepsilon > 0$ on f.

Each $h \in f$ gives rise to a set $I(x + h)$, whose length is by construction $\geq \varepsilon$. Furthermore, all these uncountably many sets are pairwise disjoint, so that adding up their lengths would add up to infinity.

This is, however, impossible given the fact that this all happens within the unit interval $[0, 1]$, whose length is 1. This final contradiction refutes the initial assumption on the existence of a continuous function f to represent the lexicographic order.

B   Proof of Lemma 2

Suppose that we have picked a set of vectors $0 \leq \mathbf{x}_1^*, \ldots, \mathbf{x}_{k_1}^* \in \mathbb{R}^n$ for $k_1 < n$, to be equilibrium strategies for player 1, and likewise, let $0 \leq \mathbf{y}_1^*, \ldots, \mathbf{y}_{k_2}^* \in \mathbb{R}^m$ with $k_2 < m$ be a set of chosen equilibria for player 2 in our zero-sum game to be constructed.

Let the matrix $\mathbf{X}$ be such that all $\mathbf{x}_i^* \in N(\mathbf{X})$, when $N(\mathbf{X})$ denotes the null-space of the matrix $\mathbf{X}$. This matrix is directly constructible by taking the singular value decomposition of the matrix whose rows are exactly the desired $\mathbf{x}_i^*$. In defining $\mathbf{X}$ in this way, each (mixed) strategy $\mathbf{x}_i^*$ makes the other player indifferent in its response, since $\mathbf{X} \cdot \mathbf{x}_i^* = 0$.

Analogously, we can construct a matrix $\mathbf{Y}$ whose null-space is spanned by $\{\mathbf{y}_1^*, \ldots, \mathbf{y}_{k_2}^*\}$, thus achieving $(\mathbf{y}_i^*)^T \cdot \mathbf{Y}^T = 0$ for all $i = 1, 2, \ldots, k_2$.

Finally, pick any random matrix $\mathbf{Z}$ with a conformable shape to have the matrix product $\mathbf{A} = \mathbf{X}^T \cdot \mathbf{Z} \cdot \mathbf{Y} \in \mathbb{R}^{n_A \times m_A}$ well-defined[3]. By associativity, $\mathbf{A}$ retains the properties of $\mathbf{X}$ and $\mathbf{Y}$, so that we still have $(\mathbf{x}_i^*)^T \cdot \mathbf{A} = 0$ and $\mathbf{A} \cdot \mathbf{y}_j^* = 0$ for all i, j. Now, take $\mathbf{A}$ as the $(n_A \times m_A)$-payoff matrix in the game. It is well known that we can obtain an equilibrium for a maximizing player by solving the linear program

$$(P) \quad \min \overbrace{\begin{pmatrix} \mathbf{0} \\ 1 \end{pmatrix}}^{=:\mathbf{c}^T}{}^T \cdot \overbrace{\begin{pmatrix} v \\ \mu \end{pmatrix}}^{=:\mathbf{x}} \quad \text{s.t.} \quad \overbrace{\left(\begin{array}{c|c} -\mathbf{A}^T & \mathbf{1} \\ \hline \mathbf{1} & 0 \end{array} \right)}^{=:\mathbf{B}} \cdot \begin{pmatrix} \mu \\ v \end{pmatrix} \overset{\geq}{=} \overbrace{\begin{pmatrix} \mathbf{0} \\ 1 \end{pmatrix}}^{=:\mathbf{b}}$$

and $\mu_i \geq 0$ for all $i = 1, \ldots, n_A$

in which the conditions given here in matrix notation evaluate to the minimization of the saddle-point value v, upper-bounding the payoff obtained from the matrix $\mathbf{A}$ by playing the i-th row with probability μ_i, i.e., $\mu^T \cdot \mathbf{A} \cdot \mathbf{e}_i \leq v$ for all i when $\mathbf{e}_i$ is the i-th unit vector. The lower block in the product $\mathbf{B} \cdot \mu = 1$ is then just the condition that the sum of all μ_i should equal 1.

Now, look at the dual program for the other player being

---

[3] Here, n_A and m_A are new variables to describe the shape; their values depend on how many equilibria we want to enforce, and whether these are linearly dependent. This determines the dimension of the nullspaces, which sets the values for n_A, m_A.

$$(D) \quad \max \mathbf{b}^T \cdot \overbrace{\begin{pmatrix} \nu \\ v \end{pmatrix}}^{=:\mathbf{y}}, \text{ s.t. } \mathbf{y}^T \cdot \left(\begin{array}{c|c} -\mathbf{A} & 1 \\ \hline 1 & 0 \end{array} \right) \overset{\leq}{=} \overbrace{\begin{pmatrix} 0 \\ 1 \end{pmatrix}}^{=\mathbf{c}^T}{}^T$$

and $\nu_i \geq 0$ for all $i = 1, \dots, m_A$.

The point of our construction is that in the matrix products $\mathbf{B} \cdot \mathbf{x}$ and $\mathbf{y}^T \cdot \mathbf{B}$, the following happens:

- in (P), we get the expression $-\mathbf{A} \cdot \boldsymbol{\mu} = 0$ for every $\boldsymbol{\mu} \in \{\mathbf{x}_1^*, \dots, \mathbf{x}_{k_1}^*\}$ or linear combinations thereof. Thus, the constraint ≥ 0 on this row is satisfied with equality if $v = 0$.
- Likewise, evaluating the constraints in (D) creates the inner term $-\boldsymbol{\nu}^T \mathbf{A} = 0$ for all $\boldsymbol{\nu} \in \{\mathbf{y}_1^*, \dots, \mathbf{y}_{k_2}^*\}$ (and any linear combinations thereof). Thus, the dual constraint ≤ 0 is also satisfied with equality.

Now, an equilibrium $(\boldsymbol{\mu}, \boldsymbol{\nu})$ in the zero-sum game $\mathbf{A}$ is characterized by $\boldsymbol{\mu}$ being an optimum in (P) and $\boldsymbol{\nu}$ being an optimum in (D), and by strong duality, this happens if both are feasible for the respective constraints, and the respective optima are equal. Putting these conditions together, we find $(\boldsymbol{\mu}, \boldsymbol{\nu})$ to be an equilibrium if and only if the following conditions are all satisfied:

1. $\mathbf{B} \cdot \mathbf{x} \geq \mathbf{b}$, i.e., feasibility for (P): this holds by construction, even with equality in all rows.
2. $\mathbf{y}^T \cdot \mathbf{B} \leq \mathbf{c}^T$, i.e., feasibility for (D): this also holds by construction with equality.
3. $\mathbf{c}^T \cdot \mathbf{x} \leq \mathbf{y}^T \cdot \mathbf{b}$, which can only hold if the two values are equal. But we constructed all equilibria to create the value $v = \boldsymbol{\mu}^T \cdot \mathbf{A} = \mathbf{A} \cdot \boldsymbol{\nu} = 0$, so equality holds here too.

Thus, all pairs $(\mathbf{x}_i^*, \mathbf{y}_j^*)$ are equilibria of our matrix game $\mathbf{A}$.

Remark 4. Switching the players's directions between minimization and maximization, as well as changing the saddle-point value from $v = 0$ into some chosen $v' \neq 0$ is easy by a proper affine transformation $\mathbf{A}' \mapsto \pm\mathbf{A} + v'$.

It is easy to see that the so-constructed game has the designed equilibria, but also many others, since not only the convex-combination, but any linear combination of the chosen vectors will be in the nullspace. Let us take a short break here to numerically illustrate the intermediate construction.

B.1 Example

We implemented the algorithm in GNU Octave [7], with sources are available from [27]: for the example, let us fix the strategy spaces for player 1 and 2 to have five, resp. six, actions. Furthermore, let us pick two equilibria for player 1, and three equilibria (all mixed for both players) at random, sampling uniformly random values from $[0, 1]$, and normalizing the vector to unit sum. For a random instance, these equilibria were

$$\begin{array}{cccccc} \text{strategy} & 1 & 2 & 3 & 4 & 5 \\ \mathbf{x}_1^* = & (0.236624, & 0.259513, & 0.0116831, & 0.330247, & 0.161933) \\ \mathbf{x}_2^* = & (0.26241, & 0.117688, & 0.21289, & 0.284324, & 0.122688) \end{array} \quad (5)$$

and

$$\text{strategy} \quad 1 \qquad\quad 2 \qquad\quad 3 \qquad\quad 4 \qquad\; 5 \qquad\quad 6$$
$$\mathbf{y}_1^* = (0.110901, \quad 0.13516, \quad 0.220331, 0.126352, 0.238114, \quad 0.169142)$$
$$\mathbf{y}_2^* = \quad (0.1328, \quad 0.45488, \, 0.0802542, 0.040265, 0.236992, 0.0548095) \qquad (6)$$
$$\mathbf{y}_3^* = (0.148226, 0.0651162, 0.0286501, \quad 0.31977, 0.375297, 0.0629404)$$

With these values, the matrices $\mathbf{X}_1$ and $\mathbf{Y}_1$ from the previous section are easily found using the `null` function in Octave (that internally computes a singular value decomposition), to find

$$\mathbf{X} = \begin{pmatrix} -0.490976 & 0.689481 & 0.497453 & -0.183545 & -0.0490909 \\ -0.617055 & -0.273987 & 0.0243345 & 0.724245 & -0.138025 \\ -0.263877 & -0.192006 & 0.0534469 & -0.120881 & 0.935967 \end{pmatrix}$$

and

$$\mathbf{Y} = \begin{pmatrix} -0.554165 & 0.271458 & 0.237081 & 0.640731 & -0.372757 & -0.116278 \\ -0.72375 & -0.0592711 & 0.0703592 & -0.314963 & 0.585821 & -0.159171 \\ -0.278293 & 0.0898957 & -0.51704 & 0.0385987 & -0.0337394 & 0.802816 \end{pmatrix}$$

and with a randomly chosen matrix $\mathbf{Z}$, we find the payoff structure

$$\mathbf{A} = \begin{pmatrix} 0.955986 & -0.272557 & 0.316327 & -0.405844 & 0.102397 & -0.662056 \\ 0.0454297 & -0.0580642 & -0.178636 & -0.187195 & 0.130912 & 0.204854 \\ -0.298982 & 0.05127 & -0.17908 & 0.0170827 & 0.0593234 & 0.292065 \\ -0.436331 & 0.223209 & -0.113101 & 0.453724 & -0.301461 & 0.340507 \\ -0.558309 & 0.0324137 & 0.0676309 & -0.0335246 & 0.251095 & -0.076376 \end{pmatrix}$$

which is exactly the matrix (4) used in Sect. 4.2.

Solving the linear programs (P) and (D), we find the following mixed equilibrium for the game $\mathbf{A}$:

$$\mathbf{x}^* = (0.28381, 0, 0.37985, 0.24622, 0.09012),$$
$$\text{and } \mathbf{y}^* = (0.06237, 0, 0.48687, 0, \qquad 0.11092, 0.33984)$$

which is not among the equilibria listed in (5) or (6). However, it is a simple matter to put the vectors $\mathbf{x}^*, \mathbf{y}^*$ into span $\{\mathbf{x}_1^*, \mathbf{x}_2^*\}$ and span $\{\mathbf{y}_1^*, \mathbf{y}_2^*, \mathbf{y}_3^*\}$ via

$$\mathbf{x}^* = -0.8298 \cdot \mathbf{x}_1^* + 1.8298 \cdot \mathbf{x}_2^* \quad \text{and}$$
$$\mathbf{y}^* = 2.55931 \cdot \mathbf{y}_1^* - 0.62699 \cdot \mathbf{y}_2^* - 0.93232 \cdot \mathbf{y}_3^*.$$

B.2 Restricting the Equilibria to the Desired Set

Now, to complete the proof of Lemma 2, it remains to modify the game so that no solution outside the convex hull of our chosen equilibrium points is possible.

The simplest method of to exclude equilibria outside the desired set is adding a penalty term to the goal function that vanishes on the desired set of optima. An obvious choice is letting δ be a distance measure, such as

$$\delta(M, \mathbf{y}) := \inf \{\|\mathbf{x} - \mathbf{y}\| : \mathbf{x} \in M\},$$

for a set $M \subset \mathbb{R}^n$ and a point $\mathbf{x} \in \mathbb{R}^n$, using any norm $\|\cdot\|$ on $\mathbb{R}^n$. Put E_1 as the set of desired equilibria of player 1, and let E_2 be the set of desired equilibria for player 2.

Then, any action outside E_1 shall decrease the revenue for player 1, while any deviation to the exterior of E_2 shall increase the payoff for player 1, so that there is an incentive for player 1 to stay within the desired set of equilibria, and another incentive for player 2 to do the same (zero-sum game). Thus, we change the expected payoff function from $u(\mathbf{x}, \mathbf{y}) = \mathbf{x}^T \cdot \mathbf{A} \cdot \mathbf{y}$ into

$$u(\mathbf{x}, \mathbf{y}) = \mathbf{x}^T \cdot \mathbf{A} \cdot \mathbf{y} + \delta(\mathbf{y}, \Delta(E_2)) - \delta(\mathbf{x}, \Delta(E_1)). \tag{7}$$

This function is no longer linear, and hence the optimization problems (P) and (D) no longer apply as such. But strong duality still holds, since Slater's condition [3] is satisfied: note that the change in the payoff functional manifests itself in the primal problem (P) as the inequality $u(\mathbf{x}, \mathbf{e}_i) \leq v$ for $\mathbf{e}_i$ being the i-th unit vector running over all strategies of the second player (the likewise converse inequality would arise in the dual problem (D)). This is due to the fact that we still do a min-max optimization $\max_{\mathbf{x}} \min_{\mathbf{y}} u(\mathbf{x}, \mathbf{y})$, where the inner optimization is easy because we have only a finite number of choices (or any convex combination of them), making $\min_{\mathbf{y}} u(\mathbf{x}, \mathbf{y}) = \min_{i=1,\dots,m} u(\mathbf{x}, \mathbf{e}_i)$.

More formally, let $B^o := \{(\mathbf{x}, \mathbf{y}) : \|\mathbf{x}\|_1 < 1, \|\mathbf{y}\|_1 < 1\}$ be the interior of the unit balls defining the feasible set of probability distributions, i.e., mixed strategies for both players. Moreover, let E be the convex hull of all equilibria that are admissible by design. For Slater's condition, we look for an inner point that satisfies the constraints with strict inequality. Note that the affine hull $\text{aff}(E)$ is unbounded, and therefore extends over the bounded convex set E. Moreover, by construction of the penalized utility (7), we have nonzero contributions of the distance terms outside E. Now, distinguish two cases:

Case 1: If $B^o \setminus E = \emptyset$, then all probability distributions are admissible equilibria by design, and there is nothing to restrict (the penalty terms never become active, and always add zero to the overall utility).

Case 2: Otherwise, the affine hull $\text{aff}(E)$ must contain a point $(\mathbf{x}_0, \mathbf{y}_0) \in (B^o \cap \text{aff}(E)) \setminus E$ outside the admissible set E but in the interior of the unit ball. Look at the terms that sum up to the penalized utility:

$$\mathbf{x}^T \cdot \mathbf{A} \cdot \mathbf{y} = 0, \quad \text{because } (\mathbf{x}_0, \mathbf{y}_0) \text{ are still in the nullspace of } \mathbf{A};$$
$$\delta(\mathbf{x}_0, \Delta(E_1)) > 0, \quad \text{because we are outside } \Delta(E_1) \subset E;$$
$$\delta(\mathbf{y}_0, \Delta(E_2)) > 0, \quad \text{because we are outside } \Delta(E_2) \subset E.$$

So, whenever $\delta(\mathbf{x}, \Delta(E_1)) \neq \delta(\mathbf{y}, \Delta(E_2))$, we are done since we have a nonzero utility for the respective player and hence a Slater point (for one of the players, i.e., either the primal or the dual problem). Otherwise, if $\delta(\mathbf{x}, \Delta(E_1)) = \delta(\mathbf{y}, \Delta(E_2))$, we can slightly move $\mathbf{x}$ farer away from E, since B^o is an open set. This move from $\mathbf{x}_0$ to $\mathbf{x}_0'$ with $\delta(\mathbf{x}_0, \Delta(E_1)) \neq \delta(\mathbf{x}_0', \Delta(E_1))$ again makes the penalty term overall negative, and we have $(\mathbf{x}_0', \mathbf{y}_0)$ as the sought Slater point. The existence of a Slater point certifies strong duality to hold for the optimization problems. The design of the respective utilities (having opposite signs since we are playing a zero-sum regime) then assures that all feasible solutions must be inside the set $\Delta(E_1) \times \Delta(E_2)$. By strong duality, no solution outside this region is possible, and Lemma 2 is proven.

References

1. Avis, D., Rosenberg, G., Savani, R., Stengel, B.: Enumeration of nash equilibria for two-player games. Econ. Theory **42**, 9–37 (2010)

2. Avis, D.: lrs home page (2020). http://cgm.cs.mcgill.ca/~avis/C/lrs.html
3. Boyd, S.P., Vandenberghe, L.: Convex Optimization. Cambridge University Press, Cambridge (2004)
4. Brzuska, C., et al.: Security of sanitizable signatures revisited. In: Jarecki, S., Tsudik, G. (eds.) PKC 2009. LNCS, vol. 5443, pp. 317–336. Springer, Heidelberg (2009). https://doi.org/10.1007/978-3-642-00468-1_18
5. Cococcioni, M., Pappalardo, M., Sergeyev, Y.D.: Lexicographic multi-objective linear programming using grossone methodology: theory and algorithm. Appl. Math. Comput. **318**, 298–311 (2018). https://doi.org/10.1016/j.amc.2017.05.058, https://linkinghub.elsevier.com/retrieve/pii/S0096300317303703
6. Davidson, C.C., Andel, T.R.: Feasibility of applying Moving Target Defensive Techniques in a SCADA System. ACPI, Boston University, Boston (2016). https://doi.org/10.13140/RG.2.1.5189.5441, http://rgdoi.net/10.13140/RG.2.1.5189.5441
7. Eaton, J.W., Bateman, D., Hauberg, S., Wehbring, R.: GNU Octave version 5.2.0 manual: a high-level interactive language for numerical computations (2020). https://www.gnu.org/software/octave/doc/v5.2.0/
8. Ehrgott, M.: Discrete decision problems, multiple criteria optimization classes and lexicographic max-ordering. In: Fandel, G., Trockel, W., Stewart, T.J., van den Honert, R.C. (eds.) Trends in Multicriteria Decision Making. Lecture Notes in Economics and Mathematical Systems, vol. 465, pp. 31–44. Springer, Heidelberg (1998). https://doi.org/10.1007/978-3-642-45772-2_3
9. Ehrgott, M.: A Characterization of Lexicographic Max-Ordering Solutions (1999). https://kluedo.ub.uni-kl.de/frontdoor/index/index/docId/484
10. Fishburn, P.C.: Exceptional paper-lexicographic orders, utilities and decision rules: a survey. Manag. Sci. **20**(11), 1442–1471 (1974). https://doi.org/10.1287/mnsc.20.11.1442, http://pubsonline.informs.org/doi/abs/10.1287/mnsc.20.11.1442
11. Glicksberg, I.L.: A further generalization of the kakutani fixed point theorem, with application to nash equilibrium points, vol. 3, pp. 170–174 (1952). http://dx.doi.org/10.2307/2032478
12. Grabisch, M.: The application of fuzzy integrals in multicriteria decision making. Eur. J. Oper. Res. **89**(3), 445–456 (1996). https://doi.org/10.1016/0377-2217(95)00176-X, https://linkinghub.elsevier.com/retrieve/pii/037722179500176X
13. Harsanyi, J.C.: Oddness of the number of equilibrium points: a new proof. Int. J. Game Theory **2**(1), 235–250 (1973). https://doi.org/10.1007/BF01737572, http://link.springer.com/10.1007/BF01737572
14. Herrmann, A., Morali, A., Etalle, S., Wieringa, R.: Risk and business goal based security requirement and countermeasure prioritization. In: Niedrite, L., Strazdina, R., Wangler, B. (eds.) BIR 2011. LNBIP, vol. 106, pp. 64–76. Springer, Heidelberg (2012). https://doi.org/10.1007/978-3-642-29231-6_6
15. Isermann, H.: Linear lexicographic optimization. Oper. Res. Spektrum **4**(4), 223–228 (1982). https://doi.org/10.1007/BF01782758, http://link.springer.com/10.1007/BF01782758
16. Karnin, E.D., Greene, J.W., Hellman, M.E.: On secret sharing systems. IEEE Trans. Inf. Theory IT **29**(1), 35–41 (1983). http://ieeexplore.ieee.org/document/1056621/
17. Konnov, I.: On lexicographic vector equilibrium problems. J. Optim. Theory Appl. **118**(3), 681–688 (2003). https://doi.org/10.1023/B:JOTA.0000004877.39408.80
18. Kotler, R.: How to prioritize IT security projects (2020). https://www.helpnetsecurity.com/2020/01/30/prioritize-it-security-projects/, library Catalog: www.helpnetsecurity.com

19. Lozovanu, D., Solomon, D., Zelikovsky, A.: Multiobjective games and determining pareto-nash equilibria. Buletinul Academiei de Stiinte a Republicii Moldova Matematica **3**(49), 115–122 (2005)
20. Makhorin, A.: GLPK - GNU Project - Free Software Foundation (FSF) (2012) https://www.gnu.org/software/glpk/
21. McElice, R.J., Sarwate, D.V.: On sharing secrets and reed-solomon codes. Commun. ACM **24**(9), 583–584 (1981)
22. Ogryczak, W.: Lexicographic max-min optimization for efficient and fair bandwidth allocation. In: International network optimization conference (INOC) (2007)
23. Ogryczak, W., Śliwiński, T.: On direct methods for lexicographic min-max optimization. In: Gavrilova, M., et al. (eds.) ICCSA 2006. LNCS, vol. 3982, pp. 802–811. Springer, Heidelberg (2006). https://doi.org/10.1007/11751595_85
24. Park, K.-Y., Yoo, S.-G., Kim, J.: Security requirements prioritization based on threat modeling and valuation graph. In: Lee, G., Howard, D., Ślęzak, D. (eds.) ICHIT 2011. CCIS, vol. 206, pp. 142–152. Springer, Heidelberg (2011). https://doi.org/10.1007/978-3-642-24106-2_19
25. Perkowski, M.: Why You Need To Prioritize Cyber Risks (2018). https://www.securityroundtable.org/everything-cant-be-urgent-why-you-need-to-prioritize-cyber-risks/
26. Rabin, T., Ben-Or, M.: Verifiable secret sharing and multiparty protocols with honest majority. In: STOC 1989, pp. 73–85. ACM (1989). http://dx.doi.org/10.1145/73007.73014
27. Rass, S., Wiegele, A., König, S.: Source code to run the examples in Appendix B.1 available from https://www.syssec.at/de/publikationen/description/games-over-lex-orders. online (2020)
28. Rass, S., Schauer, S.: Game Theory for Security and Risk Management: From Theory to Practice. Springer, Heidelberg (2018). https://doi.org/10.1007/978-3-319-75268-6
29. Rios Insua, D., Couce-Vieira, A., Rubio, J.A., Pieters, W., Labunets, K., Rasines, D.G.: An Adversarial Risk Analysis Framework for Cybersecurity. Risk Analysis (2019). https://doi.org/10.1111/risa.13331, https://onlinelibrary.wiley.com/doi/abs/10.1111/risa.13331
30. Rios Insua, D., Rios, J., Banks, D.: Adversarial Risk Analysis. J. Am. Stat. Assoc. **104**(486), 841–854 (2009). http://pubs.amstat.org/doi/abs/10.1198/jasa.2009.0155
31. Ross, T., Booker, J.M., Parkinson, W.J.: Fuzzy logic and probability applications: bridging the gap. In: ASA SIAM (2002)
32. Rothschild, C., McLay, L., Guikema, S.: Adversarial risk analysis with incomplete information: a level-k approach. Risk Anal. **32**(7), 1219–1231 (2012). https://doi.org/10.1111/j.1539-6924.2011.01701.x, http://doi.wiley.com/10.1111/j.1539-6924.2011.01701.x
33. Stanimirovic, I.P.: Compendious lexicographic method for multi-objective optimization. Facta Universitatis **27**(1), 55–66 (2012), https://pdfs.semanticscholar.org/25c6/8b5d4d9adfef3684dddbf0096a38fcbd1923.pdf?_ga=2.42418213.1664777629.1591959638-2095801372.1591959638
34. The Recorded Future Team: You Can't Do Everything: The Importance of Prioritization in Security (2018). https://www.recordedfuture.com/vulnerability-threat-prioritization/, library Catalog: www.recordedfuture.com Section: Cyber Threat Intelligence

35. Tompa, M., Woll, H.: How to share a secret with cheaters. J. Cryptol. **1**(3), 133–138 (1989). https://doi.org/10.1007/BF02252871, http://link.springer.com/10.1007/BF02252871
36. Yuan, X., He, P., Zhu, Q., Li, X.: Adversarial examples: attacks and defenses for deep learning. arXiv:1712.07107 [cs, stat] (2018), http://arxiv.org/abs/1712.07107, arXiv: 1712.07107

Emerging Topics

Game Theory on Attack Graph for Cyber Deception

Ahmed H. Anwar🆔 and Charles Kamhoua⁽✉⁾ 🆔

US Army Research Laboratory, Adelphi, MD 20783, USA
`charles.a.kamhoua.civ@mail.mil`

Abstract. Game Theory provides a set of tools and a framework suitable to study security problems. In this paper, a class of games is developed to study cyber deception and the interactions between the network defender who is deceiving an adversary to mitigate the damage of the attack. In order to capture network topology, each game is played over an attack graph that can be generated according to the vulnerabilities associated with each node. The defender's goal is to take deceptive actions to prevent the attacker from taking control over the network resources exploiting the incomplete information of the attacker regarding the deceptive network gained through the attack reconnaissance stage. To this end, we present several games such as normal form static, dynamic, hypergame, and a partially observable stochastic game (POSG) to study the game dynamics at different information structures. For the most general class of games, (i.e., POSG), we provide multiple solution approaches to overcome the intractability of the game model and finally present numerical result samples to show the effectiveness of each solution approach.

Keywords: Game theory · Cyber deception · Network security · Attack graph · Hypergame · Partial observable stochastic game

1 Introduction

Cyber deception refers to a set of techniques that can be implemented to give attackers false beliefs. Such set includes information masking, dazzling, hiding, decoying, false information, and camouflaging [2, 5]. In fact, cyber deception is used from both sides, the attacker implements deception techniques to hide his true identity, strategy, and payoff and let the defender believe that the attacker is a legitimate user. However, the focus of this paper is to study cyber deception as a defense technique implemented by network admin [1]. In a real threat scenario, the identities of adversaries are unknown to the defender, which is a huge advantage to the attackers that allows them to collect information about the network until an intrusion detection system (IDS) catches them [17]. Therefore, to suppress this advantage from attackers, a defender needs to implement cyber deception techniques to misrepresent the network and alter its true state, and hence the outcome of the attackers' reconnaissance will be useless and misleading. To this end,

Q. Zhu et al. (Eds.): GameSec 2020, LNCS 12513, pp. 445–456, 2020.
https://doi.org/10.1007/978-3-030-64793-3_24

deception techniques such as honeynets [4, 7, 16], data, and file obfuscation techniques [11, 12, 21, 25], and moving target defense (MTD) [8, 44, 45] have been proposed. Although, MTD and cyber deception techniques aim to thwart the attackers' attempts to collect the system information via changing the attack space and the true state of the network, however, MTD techniques do not introduce any false information that can actively mislead attackers. On the other hand, cyber deception may use false objects or information for the attackers to form false beliefs that affect the decision of the attackers.

Security games literature studied strategic decision-making problems in a game-theoretic framework between two players, specifically, the network defender and the attacker [3, 14, 43, 46]. Security games applications includes the protection of critical infrastructures, [14, 22, 23], computer networks [6, 10, 15, 19, 24, 38, 39, 44, 45]. The success of strategic deception hinges on the information observed by both players. The defender may strategically leak or let the attacker access manipulated information about the network that lures the attacker to behave in a certain way that may or may not be observed by the defender. How information observability is classified leads to different classes of the game as discussed in detail in Sect. 2.

In this paper, we present the state-of-the-art game-theoretic models to address cyber deception and develop a partially observable stochastic game as a generalized framework to study this problem. Secondly, we discuss the complexities and intractability of POSG games and present several approaches and relaxations to overcome the game model complexities. Finally, numerical results are presented to validate the proposed approaches to solve the game.

The rest of the paper is organized as follows: In Sect. 2, we present a line of related cyber deception work on attack graphs and game theory. After that, in Sect. 3, we discuss different game classes. In Sect. 4, several approaches are presented to solve the game. We present numerical results in Sect. 5 and conclude our work in Sect. 6.

2 Related Work

2.1 Attack Graph

An attack graph is a tool used to model network security by capturing network connectivity and vulnerabilities. Attack graphs could be generated in several ways. For instance, Kamdem et al. [30] generated a vulnerability multi-graph in which node are vulnerable hosts, and edges represent the vulnerabilities between nodes. Authors in [31] used attack graphs to model the causal relationship of different vulnerabilities and proposed a probabilistic metric for network security. Stochastic games played on attack graphs facilitate cyber deception automation and deception policy implementation on networks. However, the dimension of strategy space explodes for attack graph games in the size of the attack graph. Moreover, partial observability regarding attacker dynamics is a struggle against developing deception policy.

A defender can model the behavior of a partially observable attacker using one of two approaches. A simple but naïve approach is to model the actions of the attacker as exogenous noise. The second approach is to take into account the attacker's actions as observations that are induced given her actions. Finally, the defender can assume that the attacker is also monitoring the system partially and is maximizing his long-term reward symmetrically. The latest model is known as POSG and is the most general framework.

Attack graph is adopted extensively to study cybersecurity problems [32–36]. More specifically, it is used to study cyber deception using different game-theoretic models. These models include normal form games, Stackelberg games, hypergames, and partially observable stochastic games.

In [32], a full information normal form game is played on an attack graph to study the effect of software diversity to deceive adversaries and enhance network security. The goal of the defender is to diversify the network attack graph to prevent the attacker from launching a full-scale zero-day attack exploiting a single vulnerability. Moreover, a diversified network requires a larger number of probes to collect information. Hence the attacker interacts more with the network which leads to early detection. The attack graph captures the network topology and the relation between the set of vulnerabilities associated with each node. Our results show that diversity limited the attacker's ability to control the network.

In a social network, a malicious user attacks the network through influencing its node. Therefore, one way to counter his negative influence is by blocking a subset of edges (i.e., a subgraph) [33]. We formulated the interaction between the defender and the attacker as a Stackelberg game where the defender first chooses a set of nodes to block in order to minimize the attacker's influence. After observing the modified network, the attacker selects a set of seeds to spread negative information from. To avoid the computational complexity of this bi-level game theoretic optimization problem, an approximate method models the attacker's problem as the maximum node domination problem. To solve this problem, we first develop a method to formulate the problem as an integer programming combined with constraint generation. Also, proposed an approximate solution to enhance scalability [33]. Considering a Stackelberg game, the defender in [34] is assumed to allocate defensive resources and manipulate the attack graph. We provided techniques for efficiently solving the problem as a mixed-integer linear program.

In a more sophisticated attack scenario, the network suffers an outbreak of a spreading virus. An epidemic game-theoretic model is developed in [36] to study these types of attacks. Epidemic models are used in cybersecurity to model the change of nodes' states over time. In other words, at each time slot, a node could be infected, vulnerable, or recovered. The epidemic model captures the transition of nodes between the mentioned three states. In [36], we proposed a POSG game with one-sided information where players don't observe the actions of each other. In this epidemic-game model, the attacker at any time-slot selects a subset of neighbors of infected nodes to propagate the malware from via connecting edges. On the other hand, the defender distributes a limited number of honeypots over selected edges of the network. We show that the heuristic search value iteration (HSVI) algorithm developed initially to solve partially observable Markov decision process (POMDP) [40], can be used to efficiently solve this class of POSGs. To this end, we show that the value function operator of the epidemic game model has the necessary properties such that it can be solved using an HSVI-like algorithm.

2.2 Hypergame

Another approach to handle uncertainty is the hypergame framework [35, 37, 41]. Hypergame theory studies the case where the game players have different views of the game model including the strategies of their opponents therefore it fits perfectly to study cyberdeception. Although Hypergame theory can be used to study multiple players, we restrict our discussion for the two-player Hypergame for cyber deception.

A Hypergame $G = (V_1, V_2)$ consists of two preference vectors for each player. Each vector represents the player's perspective of the game. In a fully observed game, each player knows his opponent's preference vector. On the other hand, practically player p can perceive player q's preferences partially, in terms of V_{21} and V_{12} as the perspective of player 1 of player 2 preference and vice versa. In hypergame, players play two different games according to how each player perceives the game. Therefore, a player makes his own decision based on his perceived game. In cyber deception, the attacker is unaware of the induced network state after the deceptive actions have been implemented by the network defender. To solve for an equilibrium of hypergame with a first-level perception, each player plays their own perceived game. First, the attacker solves his perceived game and find the equilibrium of the adversary perceived game as denoted by $(a^e(A), d^e(A))$. Similarly, the defender solves his perceived game, and find the equilibrium $(a^e(D), d^e(D))$ of the game. Finally, the hypergame equilibrium is $(a^e(A), d^e(D))$.

In [37], we developed a hypergame model that examines how attacks spread inside the network using attack graphs. In this mode, the defender installs honeypots on well-selected nodes to thwart the attack. Based on the formulated hypergame, the defender decides where to place honeypots. The game is repeated after players receive the payoff of their actions. According to her payoff, the attacker could choose to cover the maximum number of nodes to increase his reward at the current stage. However, the attacker could also decide to explore other unvisited nodes. We estimate the amount of time needed for an attacker to reach the target nodes through experiments, which provides a quantitative measure to determine when it is necessary to disable all the connections to the target nodes.

In [35], we focused on the problem of joint designing a decoy placement strategy and a deceptive defense strategy that maximally exploits the fact that decoy locations are partially observable by the attacker to ensure that the defender can satisfy his/her goal in temporal logic. Given the large space searching for optimal decoy placement policy, we use formal methods to show that the utility function is non-decreasing and monotone. We formulated a deception hypergame to place decoy devices. In this game, the defender allocates decoys to deceive and trap the attacker. We have also synthesized stealthy deceptive strategies with temporal logic specifications using hypergame theory in [41] to develop sure winning and almost-sure winning strategies for the defender.

3 Information Model and Game Formulation

3.1 On the Complexity of POSG

Information monitoring determines the class of the game to be played between the attacker and the defender. In a complete information game, the game reward function, possible actions, and player identity is common knowledge. However, if players don't know all the information about their opponent, then we are dealing with an incomplete information game. This arises if, for example, the defender does not know the reward function or the possible strategies of the attacker. In a game of perfect monitoring, each player fully observes the actions taken by the other players. This is different from a class of game of imperfect monitoring in which, a player does not know what specific action is played by his/her opponent after any stage. Therefore, poker is studied under the latter class of games. A stochastic game is played in a sequence of stages with the game dynamically evolving from one state to another depending on the actions taken by all players. The most general framework that combines an evolving game, with imperfect monitoring is the partially observable stochastic game (POSG). In this class, the game information is known to both players, however, each player observes the game evolution and/or his opponent's actions partially. POSGs are the most general framework in game theory literature. A single-agent dynamic game resort to a Markov decision process (MDP). The optimal policy of an MDP can be obtained efficiently in polynomial time as shown in [20]. On the other side, Conitzer and Sandholm have shown that hardness of determining whether a pure-strategy Nash equilibrium exists in a Markov (stochastic) game is PSPACE-hard [9]. Adding uncertainty to an MDP results in a partially observable MDP (POMDP) where an optimal policy cannot be obtained in polynomial time anymore. Eventually, the complexity of solving a POMDP is known to be PSPACE-complete [20]. A POMDP is considered a single-agent POSG. Goldsmith and Mundhenk [13] have shown that extending a POMDP to a noncooperative multi-agent scenario (i.e., POSG) results in a NEXPNP-complete problem to determine whether there is a "good" strategy for that game and optimal policy existence problem associated with POSGs is undecidable [18].

3.2 Game Model

A zero-sum partially observable stochastic game is a tuple $(S, A_1, A_2, O_1, O_2, T, R, b^{init})$ where S is a finite set of states, A_1, A_2 are finite sets of actions of player 1 and player 2, respectively. O_1, O_2 denote observation sets of player 1 and player 2, respectively. $T(o_1, o_2, s \mid s_0, a_1, a_2)$ is the probability of transition from s_0 to s, while observing (o_1, o_2), under action profile (a_1, a_2). $R(s, a_1, a_2)$ denotes the reward of player 1 under (a_1, a_2) at state s, and $b^{init} \in \Delta(S)$ is some initial state-belief vector. To study cyber deception within a POSG we need to define the game components regarding our system model.

Let the defender be player 1 and the attacker be player 2. Assuming that the game is played over an attack graph G(V, E), where V is the set of nodes and E is the set of edges. A node represents a vulnerability that can be exploited by the attacker, while an edge connecting two nodes v_1 and v_2 means that a vulnerability v_2 can be exploited only if the attacker can reach it through exploiting v_1. In other words, the set of edges manifests the dependencies between the network vulnerabilities based on the network topology. The attacker decides which vulnerability or a subset of vulnerabilities to exploit. The defender, on the other side, inserts fake vulnerabilities along the graph edges such as honeypots to deceive the attacker. The defender decides the locations of the honeypots to maximize his long-term expected reward. The attacker does not observe the actions of the defender and vice versa. The state of the game, s, represents the current location of the attacker as well as the locations of the honeypots. In other words, the state captures the joint history of actions taken by the players. However, each player observes the state partially through observing (o_1, o_2) instead. As mentioned above, for the general stochastic game, a no-regret policy is not tractable [13], set aside the partially observable case. Therefore, in the next section, we discuss solution approaches for POSG under some natural assumptions and relaxations.

4   Game Solving Techniques

In this section, we propose different techniques and approaches to solve POSG formulations for cyber deception. This includes solving POMDP + embedded game approach [42], and One-sided POSG [29].

4.1   POMDP Embedded Game

In the first approach, we adopt the POMDP game model and leverage the rich literature of efficient solving algorithms [26]. In this approach, we solely focus on the defender's cyber deception strategy to maximize his long-term discounted reward. The attacker is assumed to have local knowledge about the network structure, and hence she can only reason about her immediate reward.

$$V^*(b) = max_{a_1 \in A_1} \left[R(a_1, b) + \gamma \sum_{b' \in B} \tau(b', a_1, b) V^*(b') \right] \tag{1}$$

Adopting the conventional POMDP notations, Eq. (1) represents the value function under the optimal policy that maps the belief space to action space. A key component of the above equation is the belief update function, $\tau(b', a_1, b)$. In order to calculate that function, one needs to know the state transition dynamic as well as the observation associated with each transition. The state transition model, $T(s', a_1, s)$, is known by the defender.

On the other hand, observations are directly related to the action played by the attacker. Let $O(o, s', a_1) = Pr(o|s', a_1, b)$ denote the probability of observing observation o with the system transitioning from state belief b under action a to state belief b(s'). Using game-theoretic reasoning, the defender can exploit Nash equilibrium strategies adopted by the attacker to estimate the probability that the attacker has played a specific action given any state, $s \in S$. The defender can then calculate the belief update function as follows:

$$P(o|s', a_1, b) = \sum_{s \in S} P(o|s', a_1, s) b(s)$$

Where,

$$P(o|s', a_1, s) = \sum_{a_2 \in A_2} P(o|a_2, s', s) P(a_2|s', s)$$

$$\tau(b', a_1, b) = \sum_{\{o \in O | SE(b, a_1, o) = b'\}} P(o|a_1, b)$$

for every possible future belief, b', where $SE(b, a_1, o)$, denotes the state estimate computed as the probability $P(s'|a_1, o, b)$.

4.2   One-sided POSG

In the second approach we focus on a class of one-sided partially observable stochastic games (OS-POSGs). In this model, the attacker is assumed to be perfectly informed about the current state. Along the same lines of POMDP, the belief space is a simplex are over state space and the value function defined over the belief space is convex. The class of one-sided POSGs has been studied previously in [27] as Level-1 stochastic games with incomplete information. Therefore, one-sided POSG's value function has similar structure to the value function of POMDPs. Let $G = (S, A_1, A_2, O, T, R, \gamma)$ where, S is a finite set of game states, and O denotes the observation set. The function $T(.| s, a_1, a_2) \in \Delta(O \times S)$ represents probabilistic transition function between states under action profile (a_1, a_2). The current state of the game is revealed to the attacker only. The goal is to find a defense strategy that maximizes the expected discounted reward over an infinite number of stages. Numerical results showed that active deception significantly enhanced the security of the network. A strategy that maps the history of actions and observations for player, i, is called 'behavioral strategy' and denoted by, σ^i.

In OS-POSG, the attacker observes the current state, s. Therefore, his decision rule at each state, s, is $\pi_2(a_2|s)$, while the defender (player 1) decision rule is not conditional over the state, and is denoted by, $\pi_1(a_1)$. If player 1 played $a_1 \in A_1$ and observed $o \in O$, his updated belief $\tau(b, a_1, \pi_2, o)$ over state future state, s', can be expressed as:

$$\tau(b, a_1, \pi_2, o)(s') = \frac{1}{P_{b,\pi_1,\pi_2}[a_1, o]} \sum_{s,a_2} b(s)\pi_1(a_1)\pi_2(a_2|s)T(o, s'|s, a_1, a_2).$$

The value of strategy σ_1 is

$$val^{\sigma_1}(b) = inf_{\sigma_2 \in \Sigma_2} E_{b,\sigma_1,\sigma_2}(Disc^\gamma)$$

Where $Disc^\gamma$ is the infinite discounted reward, for some $0 \le \gamma < 1$. The optimal value function can hence be expressed as:

$$V^*(b) = sup_{\sigma_1 \in \Sigma_1} val^{\sigma_1}(b)$$

Although we have defined the value function V^* as the supremum over the strategies of player 1 at each the belief point, however finding the value for the given belief is as hard as solving the game itself. Our approach relies on an alternative characterization of the optimal value function V^* to follow the structure of the optimal value function of a POMDPs. The idea behind this approach is to start with a coarse approximation $V_0: \Delta(S) \to \mathbf{R}$ of the value function V^*, and then iteratively improve the approximation by applying the Bellman's operator H, iteratively, $V_{i+1} = HV_i$. One can show that the function HV resulting from applying H on a convex continuous function V as formulated above is also convex and continuous. Hence, we can apply the operator H iteratively. Operator H can be used to approximate the optimal value function V^*. The bellman operator, H, is a contraction mapping, and hence converges to the unique fixpoint, and which is the optimal value function V^*, therefore [HV](b) leads to the Nash equilibrium of the corresponding stage game. The described structure of the H operator and the value function V(b), we can hence adopt POMDP solving approaching such as value iterations and Heuristic Search Value Iteration (HSVI) for better performance.

5 Results

To show the efficiency of the developed algorithms in Sects. 3.1 and 3.2, we present sample results that show the effectiveness of the cyber deception strategies developed via the proposed POSG algorithms.

First, we present results for the model introduced in Sect. 3.1, [42]. In this context, the attacker can only reason his actions based on local information, not the whole network. However, the defender is solving his imperfect information game with the defender assuming that the attacker is rational and following Nash strategies at equilibrium for each subgame (i.e., game stage). For a 7-node network, the defender decides where to place a honeypot, while the attacker is evading honeypots to stay stealthy as long as possible and attack real nodes. The defender receives a reward if capturing the attacker in a honeypot while losses if the attacker escaped honeypots. The defender incurs a cost for placing honeypots, and there is a cost per attack paid by the attacker. Both players can choose to stay idle to avoid the cost associated with each action. In Fig. 1, the defender reward is plotted versus the capture cost. As shown, the proposed deception algorithm outperforms other schemes. Defender's reward increases as the capture cost incurred by the attacker when caught increases. However, if the cost is very high, it forces the attacker to back off to avoid the high-risk action, the defender reward goes down. Note that, in this scenario, we mainly focus on the capture reward due to successful deception. As shown in Fig. 1, a fixed allocation policy does not recognize game dynamics, and hence ignores all observations that are available through the network monitoring systems, IDS, etc. On the other hand, random deception strategies do not consider the network structure, it randomly allocates honeypots as the game evolves.

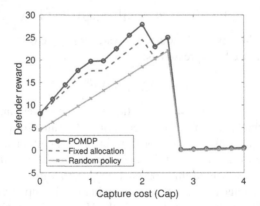

Fig. 1. Defender reward against capture cost for a 7-node network

For the second approach described in Sect. 3.2 [29], we developed an algorithm for the OS-POSG. Specifically, a Heuristic Search Value Iteration (HSVI) is used to solve a OS-POSG game modeling a lateral movement problem. The HSVI algorithm leverage a double-oracle algorithm for strategy generation [28].

The game is played over a synthesized computer network. The attacker aims to reach a target node from a source node through the graph edges while minimizing the cost of controlling each of the interconnecting nodes. The attacker can gain control over any of the visited nodes unless countermeasures were taken by the defender, such as the deception mechanism. Using this mechanism, the defender can discover the attacker's location via honeypots. In Fig. 2, we compare three HSVI-based algorithms, also showing the percentage of instances where the algorithms failed to terminate within 2 h are shown in the bottom. NH is the number of honeypots used, and k is the average node degree. Figure 2, clearly illustrates the scalability of the developed heuristic defender algorithm. Our novel algorithms scale several orders of magnitude better compared to the existing state of the art.

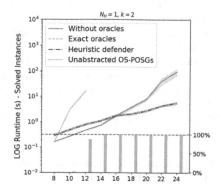

Fig. 2. Number of vertices in the network and confidence intervals mark the standard error.

6 Conclusion

In this paper, we presented a body of work covering cyber deception over attack graphs. We presented several game-theoretic models considering different information structures to capture players' uncertainties. Attack graphs have been used to map out the network topologies along with vulnerabilities of nodes. We highlighted the computational complexity of each game model, especially the partially observable stochastic game model. Solution approaches have been discussed to overcome the intractability of POSGs under specific conditions. Solution approaches have been implemented to solve the proposed game models to generate deception strategies that enhanced network security. To show the effectiveness of cyber deception using the game model, we presented sample numerical results. Our ongoing research focuses on implementing the developed cyber deception in real network settings to refine the model parameters and quantify the deception overhead. We are extending the game model to account for time-varying vulnerabilities.

Acknowledgment. Research was sponsored by the Army Research Laboratory and was accomplished under Cooperative Agreement Number W911NF-19-2-0150. The views and conclusions contained in this document are those of the authors and should not be interpreted as representing the official policies, either expressed or implied, of the Army Research Laboratory or the

U.S. Government. The U.S. Government is authorized to reproduce and distribute reprints for Government purposes notwithstanding any copyright notation herein.

References

1. De Gaspari, F., Jajodia, S., Mancini, L.V., Pagnotta, G.: Towards intelligent cyber deception systems. In: Al-Shaer, E., Wei, J., Hamlen, K.W., Wang, C. (eds.) Autonomous Cyber Deception, pp. 21–33. Springer, Cham (2019). https://doi.org/10.1007/978-3-030-02110-8_2
2. Almeshekah, M.H., Spafford, E.H.: Cyber security deception. In: Jajodia, S., Subrahmanian, V.S.S., Swarup, V., Wang, C. (eds.) Cyber Deception, pp. 25–52. Springer, Cham (2016). https://doi.org/10.1007/978-3-319-32699-3_2
3. Anwar, A.H., Atia, G., Guirguis, M.: Game theoretic defense approach to wireless networks against stealthy decoy attacks. In: 2016 54th Annual Allerton Conference on Communication, Control, and Computing (Allerton), pp. 816–821. IEEE (2016)
4. Anwar, A.H., Kamhoua, C., Leslie, N.: Honeypot allocation over attack graphs in cyber deception games. In: 2020 International Conference on Computing, Networking and Communications (ICNC), pp. 502–506. IEEE (2020)
5. Bell, J.B., Whaley, B.: Cheating and Deception. Transaction, New York (1991)
6. Cai, W., et al.: A survey on cloud gaming: future of computer games. IEEE Access 4, 7605–7620 (2016)
7. Carroll, T.E., Grosu, D.: A game theoretic investigation of deception in network security. Secur. Commun. Netw. 4(10), 1162–1172 (2011)
8. Cho, J.H., et al.: Toward proactive, adaptive defense: a survey on moving target defense. IEEE Commun. Surveys Tutorials 22(1), 709–745 (2020)
9. Conitzer, V., Sandholm, T.: New complexity results about nash equilibria. Games Econ. Behav. 63(2), 621–641 (2008)
10. Durkota, K., Lisy, V., Bosansky, B., Kiekintveld, C.: Optimal network security hardening using attack graph games. In: Proceedings of the 24th International Joint Conference on Artificial Intelligence (2015)
11. Farhang, S., Hayel, Y., Zhu, Q.: Phy-layer location privacy-preserving access point selection mechanism in next-generation wireless networks. In: 2015 IEEE Conference on Communications and Network Security (CNS), pp. 263–271. IEEE (2015)
12. Fraunholz, D., Schotten, H.D.: Defending web servers with feints, distraction and obfuscation. In: 2018 International Conference on Computing, Networking and Communications (ICNC), pp. 21–25. IEEE (2018)
13. Goldsmith, J., Mundhenk, M.: Competition adds complexity. In: Advances in Neural Information Processing Systems, pp. 561–568 (2008)
14. Kiekintveld, C., Jain, M., Tsai, J., Pita, J., Ordonez, F., Tambe, M.: Computing optimal randomized resource allocations for massive security games. In: Proceedings of the 8th International Conference on Autonomous Agents and Multiagent Systems, vol. 1, pp. 689–696 (2009)
15. Kiekintveld, C., Lisý, V., Píbil, R.: Game-theoretic foundations for the strategic use of Honeypots in network security. In: Jajodia, S., Shakarian, P., Subrahmanian, V.S., Swarup, V., Wang, C. (eds.) Cyber Warfare. AIS, vol. 56, pp. 81–101. Springer, Cham (2015). https://doi.org/10.1007/978-3-319-14039-1_5
16. La, Q.D., Quek, T.Q., Lee, J., Jin, S., Zhu, H.: Deceptive attack and defense game in honeypot-enabled networks for the internet of things. IEEE Internet Things J. 3(6), 1025–1035 (2016)
17. Liao, H.J., Lin, C.H.R., Lin, Y.C., Tung, K.Y.: Intrusion detection system: a comprehensive review. J. Netw. Comput. Appl. 36(1), 16–24 (2013)

18. Madani, O., Hanks, S., Condon, A.: On the undecidability of probabilistic planning and infinite-horizon partially observable Markov decision problems. In: AAAI/IAAI, pp. 541–548 (1999)
19. Nguyen, T., Wellman, M.P., Singh, S.: A stackelberg game model for botnet data exfiltration. In: International Conference on Decision and Game Theory for Security, pp. 151–170. Springer (2017). https://doi.org/10.1007/978-3-319-68711-7_9
20. Papadimitriou, C.H., Tsitsiklis, J.N.: The complexity of Markov decision processes. Mathe. Oper. Res. **12**(3), 441–450 (1987)
21. Pawlick, J., Zhu, Q.: A Stackelberg game perspective on the conflict between machine learning and data obfuscation. In: 2016 IEEE International Workshop on Information Forensics and Security (WIFS), pp. 1–6. IEEE (2016)
22. Pita, J., et al.: Deployed armor protection: the application of a game theoretic model for security at the Los Angeles international airport. In: Proceedings of the 7th International Joint Conference on Autonomous Agents and Multiagent Systems: Industrial Track, pp. 125–132 (2008)
23. Shieh, E., et al.: Protect: a deployed game theoretic system to protect the ports of the united states. In: Proceedings of the 11th International Conference on Autonomous Agents and Multiagent Systems, vol. 1, pp. 13–20 (2012)
24. Vanek, O., Yin, Z., Jain, M., Bosansky, B., Tambe, M., Pechoucek, M.: Game theoretic resource allocation for malicious packet detection in computer networks. In: AAMAS, pp. 905–912 (2012)
25. Zhang, T., Zhu, Q.: Distributed privacy-preserving collaborative intrusion detection systems for vanets. IEEE Trans. Signal Inf. Process. Netw. **4**(1), 148–161 (2018)
26. Shani, G., Pineau, J., Kaplow, R.: A survey of point-based POMDP solvers. Auton. Agent. Multi-Agent Syst. **27**(1), 1–51 (2013)
27. Neyman, A., Sorin, S., Sorin, S.: Stochastic Games and Applications, vol. 570. Springer Science and Business Media, Heidelberg (2003). https://orcid.org/10.1007/978-94-010-0189-2
28. Jain, M., Conitzer, V., Tambe, M.: Security scheduling for real-world networks. In: Proceedings of the 2013 International Conference on Autonomous Agents and Multi-agent Systems, International Foundation for Autonomous Agents and Multiagent Systems, pp. 215–222 (2013)
29. Horák, K., Bošanský, B., Tomášek, P., Kiekintveld, C., Kamhoua, C.: Optimizing honeypot strategies against dynamic lateral movement using partially observable stochastic games. Comput. Secur. **87**, 101579 (2019)
30. Kamdem, G., Kamhoua, C., Lu, Y., Shetty, S., Njilla, L.: A Markov game-theoretic approach for power grid security. In: 2017 IEEE 37th International Conference on Distributed Computing Systems Workshops (ICDCSW), pp. 139–144. IEEE (2017)
31. Wang, L., Islam, T., Long, T., Singhal, A., Jajodia, S.: An attack graph-based probabilistic security metric. In: Atluri, V. (ed.) DBSec 2008. LNCS, vol. 5094, pp. 283–296. Springer, Heidelberg (2008). https://doi.org/10.1007/978-3-540-70567-3_22
32. Anwar, A.H., Kamhoua, C., Leslie, N., Kiekintveld, C.: A game theoretic framework for software diversity for network security. In: International Conference on Decision and Game Theory for Security. Springer (2020)
33. Jia, F., Zhou, K., Kamhoua, C., Vorobeychik, Y.: Blocking adversarial influence in social networks. In: International Conference on Decision and Game Theory for Security. Springer (2020)
34. Milani, S., et al.: Harnessing the power of deception in attack graph games. In: International Conference on Decision and Game Theory for Security. Springer (2020)

35. Kulkarni, A.N., Fu, J., Luo, H., Kamhoua, C.A., Leslie, N.O.: Decoy placement games on graphs with temporal logic objectives. In: International Conference on Decision and Game Theory for Security. Springer (2020)

36. Tsemogne, O., Hayel, Y., Kamhoua, C.A., Deugoue, G.: Partially observable stochastic games for cyber deception against epidemic process. In: International Conference on Decision and Game Theory for Security. Springer (2020)

37. Xi, B., Kamhoua, C.A.: A hypergame-based defense strategy toward cyber deception in internet of battlefield things (IoBT). Model. Des. Secure Internet Things Chapter **3**, 59–77 (2020)

38. Kamhoua, C.A., Kiekintveld, C.D., Fang, F., Zhu Q.: Game Theory and Machine Learning for Cyber Security. Wiley-IEEE Press, April (2021). ISBN: 978-1-119-72392-9

39. Kamhoua, C.A., Njilla, L., Kott, A., Shetty, S.: Modeling and Design of Secure Internet of Things. Wiley-IEEE Press, August (2020). ISBN: 978-1-119-59336-2

40. Smith, T., Simmons, R.: Heuristic search value iteration for POMDPs. In: Proceedings of UAI (2012)

41. Kulkarni, A.N., Luo, H., Leslie, N.O., Kamhoua, C.A., Fu, J.: Deceptive labeling: hypergames on graphs for stealthy deception. IEEE Control Syst. Lett. **5**(3) (2021)

42. Anwar, A.H., Kamhoua, C., Leslie, N.: A game-theoretic framework for dynamic cyber deception in internet of battlefield things. In: Proceedings of the 16th EAI International Conference on Mobile and Ubiquitous Systems: Computing, Networking and Services, pp. 522–526 (2019)

43. Do, C.T.: Game theory for cyber security and privacy. ACM Comput. Surv. (CSUR) **50**(2), 1–37 (2017)

44. Anwar, A.H., Kelly, J., Atia, G., Guirguis, M.: Stealthy edge decoy attacks against dynamic channel assignment in wireless networks. In: IEEE Military Communications Conference (MILCOM), pp. 671–676 (2015)

45. Anwar, A.H., Kelly, J., Atia, G., Guirguis, M.: Pinball attacks against dynamic channel assignment in wireless networks. Comput. Commun. **140**, 23–37 (2019)

46. Anwar, A.H., Atia, G., Guirguis, M.: Adaptive topologies against jamming attacks in wireless networks: a game-theoretic approach. J. Netw. Comput. Appl. **121**, 44–58 (2018)

Attacking Machine Learning Models for Social Good

Vibha Belavadi, Yan Zhou, Murat Kantarcioglu$^{(\boxtimes)}$,
and Bhavani Thuriasingham

University of Texas at Dallas, Richardson, TX 75080, USA
muratk@utdallas.edu

Abstract. As machine learning (ML) techniques are becoming widely used, awareness of the harmful effect of automation is growing. Especially, in problem domains where critical decisions are made, machine learning-based applications may raise ethical issues with respect to fairness and privacy. Existing research on fairness and privacy in the ML community mainly focuses on providing remedies during the ML model training phase. Unfortunately, such remedies may not be voluntarily adopted by the industry that is concerned about the profits. In this paper, we propose to apply, from the user's end, a fair and legitimate technique to "game" the ML system to ameliorate its social accountability issues. We show that although adversarial attacks can be exploited to tamper with ML systems, they can also be used for social good. We demonstrate the effectiveness of our proposed technique on real world image and credit data.

Keywords: Adversarial machine learning · Adversarial attacks · Artificial intelligence fairness · Data privacy

1 Introduction

Increasingly, machine learning (ML) models have been deployed in many critical applications ranging from credit scoring to triaging patients for emergency care (e.g., [19]). Unfortunately, using ML models for critical decision-making tasks can raise fairness and privacy concerns. For example, an ML model used to predict criminal recidivism has been shown to be biased against a certain subgroup [25]. In other cases, ML models could be used to predict some sensitive information. For instance, it has been shown that ML models could predict sexual orientation based on Facebook likes and/or profile images [30]. The sexual orientation information by itself may be sensitive and even the existence of an accurate ML model could result in significant privacy loss.

The research reported herein was supported in part by NIH award 1R01HG006844, NSF awards CNS-1837627, OAC-1828467, IIS-1939728 and ARO award W911NF-17-1-0356.

Q. Zhu et al. (Eds.): GameSec 2020, LNCS 12513, pp. 457–471, 2020.
https://doi.org/10.1007/978-3-030-64793-3_25

To address some of these issues, there is an active ongoing research on fairness and privacy in ML. The proposed techniques range from new algorithms that produce fair ML models (see the survey for more details [8]) to differentially private machine learning models that protect individual privacy (see the survey for more details [15]). Unfortunately, most of these techniques require the buy-in of the organization that is deploying the ML model and may not be easily leveraged by end users in the already deployed ML models.

Although, some existing privacy regulations such as GDPR [9], if requested, require ML based decisions to be audited by humans. Still, as the recent research indicates, it is not always possible for humans to detect potential biases in the ML models (e.g., [2]) even if the ML decisions are explained using explainable AI techniques.

In this work, we propose a complementary approach that tries to protect individual privacy and increase fairness by "attacking" the ML model directly. In other words, the user may modify some of his/her data, the input to the ML model, so that the privacy sensitive decisions that could be generated by the ML model are impacted and the potential bias of the ML model is reduced. Our approach is based on the observation that many of the ML models are not robust against adversarial attacks that modify inputs to the ML models (e.g., adding background noise to deceive an image classifier). Therefore, such approach can be used to hinder ML models that try to predict sensitive information and increase fairness by changing "biased" decisions without any cooperation from the organizations that deploy the ML models.

Compared to traditional adversarial machine learning settings, in this context, we want to make sure that our attacks are ethical and legal. In other words, it may be illegal to lie about your income in a credit card application but it is acceptable to get a free checking account from a bank to improve your credit score. To address this challenge, we carefully define the *cost of data modification* in the developed "adversarial" attacks so that illegal, unethical, and unfeasible modifications are not considered during the "attack".

The main contributions of this paper could be summarized as follows:

- We provide a framework that improves privacy and fairness without the cooperation of the ML model owners.
- Our framework is carefully designed by specifying appropriate cost functions to only consider data modifications that are legal and ethical.
- We empirically show the utility of this framework in two different applications (image classification and credit application).

The rest of the paper is organized as follows: in Sect. 2, we discuss the related work. In Sect. 3, we provide a generic framework that shows how to deploy adversarial attacks for improving privacy and fairness and show the initiation of this generic model in two application domains. In Sect. 4, we show the utility of the proposed framework in two different applications via extensive empirical evaluation. Finally, in Sect. 5, we conclude with the discussion of our results and the future work.

2   Related Work

Adversarial attacks have become a major threat to applications that heavily rely on the integrity and accuracy of machine learning models. Adversarial learning has been an active research area for years [4,10,17,21,34,35], but only catches more awareness as the deep learning technique becomes popular. Recent studies on adversarial attacks mainly target gradient-based attacks against deep neural networks for image classification [5,6,13,23,28].

More recently, concerns on adversarial attacks are being raised in other machine learning application domains such as finance and health care where modifying data is more restricted by data domain constraints [14,24]. Ballet et al. [3] demonstrate how adversarial samples can be crafted for tabular data in the finance domain. They discuss the unique challenge specific to models trained on tabular data: how to make the modified sample, such as a loan application, remain credible and relevant for a potential expert eye? Unlike image data, tabular features are not interchangeable and less readable. For people with expert knowledge, only a small subset of features is most critical when making decisions. Therefore, adversarial attacks should avoid this subset of important features when modifying samples. An empirical study on tabular data attacks and their detection and mitigation by model interpretation and reducing attack vector size has been presented in [16].

The influence of adversarial attacks has also been investigated in the context where users can game machine learning systems to gain or protect for better social, economic, moral, and political advantages [18,24]. For example, Protective Optimization Technologies (POTs) provide the users of machine learning systems with tools to counter or contest the biases and discriminatory harms caused by these systems [18]. For dishonest users gaming the system to gain advantages, such as the approval of a loan application, features critical to the final decisions can be identified and verified to mitigate this kind of attack against the decision-making systems [24].

The threat of adversarial attacks in the applications of computer vision, ranging from self-driving cars to surveillance and security, has become a heated topic recently. A detailed survey can be found in [1]. For the purpose of poisoning attacks, backdoors and patches—digital patterns and their physical realizations deliberately inserted into images to cause misclassification—have been heavily studied in image classification [12,22,31].

Deep Learning has become the backbone of various face recognition systems offered by Amazon, IBM, Google, Microsoft and other companies like FacePlusPlus. Wang & Kosinski [30] applied Deep Learning to test whether the sexual orientation of a person can be accurately predicted better than a human predicting it. They claim that upon transfer learning with VGGFace, they are able to predict sexual orientation with a better accuracy than the human. In wake of such claims, it becomes imperative to be able to safeguard sensitive attributes identifiable from images from such black box models. One such approach is using adversarial examples for good as done by [27]. They have used DCGAN to generate glasses to fool the state-of-the-art face recognition systems. They have also proposed a general framework where anyone can train their model with a set of generator and a discriminator to create adversarial examples that can fool any machine recognition systems of choice for face images.

Our work is different from these major lines of research in that our "attacks" are strictly constrained to the set of *feasible instances* to which a user data profile can be legitimately modified to achieve fairness and protect privacy. In addition, we take into account the cost of data modification so that changes made to the data would be most feasible and least expensive to the end user. Our objective is to legitimately "attack" the system to mitigate its inherent biases with the least disruption to both parties that must adhere the terms of the contract.

3   Modeling Socially Good Adversarial Attacks

Given a machine learning model f, an instance (x, y) where x is the feature vector for the instance (e.g., a vector of real numbers representing an image) and y is the class value (e.g., $y = $ 'Heterosexual'). x can be modified to x' by the user such that

$$\arg\min_{x'} \quad c(x, x')$$
$$subject\ to\ x' \in F_x, f(x') = t \tag{1}$$

for a set of feasible instances F_x, cost function c that measures the cost of modifying the original instance x by the user, and the desired target class t.

It is important that the instance x' can only adopt modifications that are ethical. Therefore, for a given context, we want to make sure that the set of possible modification F_x is carefully defined. For example, in the case of image processing, we may want to find x' so that the changes to x can be done by adding "eyeglasses". In other words, we may want to make sure that by putting a pair of eyeglasses to an image, a ML model that predicts sexual orientation can be fooled without significantly changing the overall image.

In other domains, there may be other constraints. For example, for a credit card application, it may be illegal to lie about your income. At the same time, opening a new free checking account may be a totally valid and ethical change, especially if this change improves the chance of getting the credit application approved. Therefore, it will be crucial to define the F_x correctly in different contexts.

In addition, to correctly identify F_x, we need to carefully define the cost function c that guides the modification. For example, in credit card application, reducing the existing debt to income ratio may help with the application but it may not be feasible due to the associated monetary cost.

Finally, the attack target t should be carefully designed. For example, for credit application, the t could be the "approved" status. Below, we discuss how our framework could be applied in two important application domains: image classification and credit application evaluation.

3.1 Ethical and Practical Adversarial Attacks for Image Classification

In the case of image classification, we would like to achieve multiple goals. First, we would like the modifications to be concentrated on only certain parts of the images. For example, we may want the modification to be able to printed on a face covering that is commonly worn during covid-19 pandemic. Alternatively, we may want to consider modifications that can be printed and shown on eyeglasses. Therefore, we require the modification to be part of a set $\mathcal{X}_m$ (i.e., modifications concentrated around the eye of the user). In addition, we would like to make sure that the modification ϵ is bounded appropriately in some norm.

$$\arg\min_\epsilon \quad f(x + \epsilon) = t$$
$$subject\ to\ \|\epsilon\| \leq \delta, \epsilon \in \mathcal{X}_m \tag{2}$$

3.2 Ethical and Practical Adversarial Attacks for Classification with Discrete Attributes

In many domains such as credit application, many of the attributes could be discrete. In addition, due to legal and ethical concerns, we may want to avoid changing certain attributes. In such settings, for each attribute k that could be legally modified, we define the cost of those feasible modifications via cost matrix $C_{i,j}^k$. For attribute k, keeping A_i^k the same has zero cost (i.e., $C_{i,i}^k = 0$). On the other hand, infeasible modifications would have cost of infinity ∞, and the remaining modifications could be assigned appropriate cost value $C_{i,j}^k$ (i.e., cost of changing attribute A_i^k to A_j^k). For example, if the credit applicant has no cell phone, getting a cell phone could be a costly but a feasible transformation. On the other hand, getting rid of the cell phone subscription may not be feasible.

Using these observations, we can rewrite Eq. (1) as follows:

$$\arg\min_{\bigcup_{k=1}^K (\{i_k, j_k\})} \sum_{k=1}^K w_k \cdot C_{i_k, j_k}^k$$
$$subject\ to\quad f(M(x)) = t$$

where M represent the set of modifications that is applied to each attribute (i.e., $M = \bigcup_{k=1}^K (\{i_k, j_k\})$), K is the total number of attributes, and w_k is the relative weight of the attribute.

4 Experiments

In the next two Sects. 4.1 and 4.2, we present the experimental results on the CelebA dataset and the German Credit dataset that illustrate how our proposed framework can be applied in practice.

4.1   Methodology and Experimentation for CelebA Dataset

Dataset Creation

We train our image classifier on a subset of data from the public CelebA dataset
[20]. CelebA dataset is a large scale face-attribute dataset of 202,599 face images
from 10,177 celebrity identities with large pose and background variations. The
CelebA dataset is richly annotated with 5 landmark locations and 40 binary
attributes like 'Arched Eyebrows', 'Eyeglasses', 'Gender', 'Smiling', 'Wearing
Hat' etc. We preprocess our training dataset by first extracting 68 facial landmarks using the dlib features from the target image. If an image has no dlib
features: either because the image has no facial landmarks or because the face
is too small to be detected, we eliminate the image. We then scale the image for
convergence during the training process. We also augment our dataset to consider rotation, random cropping, and horizontal flip variants of the same image.
By data augmentation, we intend to artificially increase the data size and thus
ensure our target model is generalizable on real data. Figure 1 demonstrates the
different image augmentation techniques used. For each original image, we use
four augmented images for the training process.

Fig. 1. Data augmentation used to improve classifier accuracy.

Model Training

For our experiments, we have chosen the concept of Gender to train and generate
our ethical adversarial examples.[1] We trained our gender model with 20,000 male
and 20,000 female examples using transfer learning [33] on the VGGFace model
with VGG16 architecture [29]. We chose to transfer learn on the VGGFace model
as it has been trained on 2.6 million faces of 2,622 celebrities and hence can
robustly extract the high level facial features from our images. In our custom
model, we first extract the model features from the penultimate layer in our
model. We do so by freezing the blocks (specifying their learning rate to be 0).

---

[1] Although the gender information is not privacy sensitive, we use this as a substitute
for more privacy-sensitive concept such as sexual orientation.

These features are then fine-tuned and further trained by passing them through the final convolution block and the three custom convolution blocks defined on top of it. The final convolution block has relatively smaller learning rate for fine-tuning purposes compared to the custom convolution layers. We train our model using softmax loss. For comparison purposes, we have also trained a gender model on the inception_v3 architecture, though our adversarial attacks will be primarily on our custom VGG16 model. Table 1 presents the training and validation accuracy of the VGG16 and the inception_v3 architectures. As can be observed, the gender concept is successfully learned for the CelebA dataset.

Table 1. Determining gender on the basis of the image

Model	f_train_acc	f_val_acc
inception_v3_model	97%	93%
VGG16_model	94.75%	94.44%

Attack Mechanism

We use the attack mechanism developed in [26] to attack the gender concept using the artifact of eyeglasses. We first align our data sample to be attacked using target landmarks (canonical pose marks). Once the data is aligned, we choose good candidate images for attack and preprocess them. In our setting, an image is a good candidate image if 1) it is classified correctly without any perturbation and 2) the difference in probability between the correct and incorrect classes is more than 3%. We chose the 3% threshold as we want the classifier to be able to confidently predict the class better than random guessing (50% probability). 3% ensures that the winning probability of the correct class is 51.5% and the other class is 48.5%. We then normalize our images by subtracting the standard normalization constant from them.

Fig. 2. Random color initialization of our artifact

To satisfy the constraint based nature of our attack, we perform modifications only on our artifact (eyeglasses) added to the face. We ensure this by limiting

perturbation area on the artifact's location on the image. In the case of our artifact, i.e eyeglasses, we focus around the eyes in the specific location of eyeglasses.
Before performing the attack, we first initialize our artifact (eyeglasses) to a set
of random starting colors to provide an "easy" starting point for perturbation.
If any of the starting colors causes change in the original classification, we hold
on to that specific initialization for our attack, else we randomly choose one
from the set. We show an example of initialization in Fig. 2, where we have the
eyeglasses artifact before and after initialisation. Given the exact location of our
artifact, we selectively normalize the gradients by replacing them with 0 in non-
artifact areas of the input and normalizing them with respect to the maximum
gradient value otherwise. Once our gradients are normalized, we then perturb
them by taking a small step-size in the direction of the gradient. We keep adding
the perturbations to the gradient till we flip at least half of the images of the
batch. Since we previously initialized the gradients of non-artifact based areas
with 0, we guarantee to perturb only the gradients of the artifact region. For
this experiment, we chose 279 female candidate images and 266 male candidate
images. In both cases, we were able to successfully attack all the chosen images
and achieve an attack success rate of 100%. Some of the adversarial examples
and their corresponding base images are shown in Figs. 3 and 4.

Fig. 3. Examples of base images

Fig. 4. Examples of adversarial attack images with glasses

Our results indicate that the adversarial attacks in the context of image
classification can be easily used to hide sensitive information (e.g., gender information) that can be inferred by the image classification models.

4.2   Methodology and Experimentation for German Credit Dataset

Dataset Creation

For evaluating our framework on discrete data, we chose Statlog (German Credit Dataset) [11]. The German Credit dataset has clearly defined attributes with respect to the ground truth. The dataset, however, is highly imbalanced with 70% of the attributes being good credit and 30% being bad credit and this imbalance needs to be handled with over/under sampling techniques. For the preprocess step, we encode the categorical features with one-hot encoding and normalize the numerical attributes. After the preprocessed data is fed to the pipeline, we handle the data imbalance by first over-sampling using SMOTE [7] and then under-sampling using the Edited Nearest Neighbours [32] technique. We train our models on this pipeline using 10-fold cross validation. Table 2 lists the best case validation accuracy of the select ML models on the German Credit dataset:

Table 2. Complete training data balanced with SMOTEENN

Classifier	Validation accuracy	F1 score
RandomForest	76%	84%
AdaBoost	73%	82%
XGBoost	75%	84%
SVM	75%	83%
RidgeClassifier	72%	80%

Attack Mechanism

We choose 125 samples from the original test data that have been correctly classified as "Bad Credit". Our objective is to find the minimum cost multi-attribute change that will flip the classification of our examples to "good credit". We start by changing only one attribute at a time. After that we keep adding other attributes to be changed simultaneously. For example, in our first pass, we modify only attribute i_1 and record which samples change their classification. In the second pass of our algorithm, we change attributes i_1 and i_2 together and record the flipped samples. In the nth pass, we will be changing n attributes $i_1 \ldots i_n$. We are only allowed to change an attribute from one of it's legitimate domain values to another. At each pass, we also record the transformation tuple set that caused target classification. Suppose we are changing two attributes i_1 (with subclasses j and k) and i_2 (with subclasses m and n). A possible transformation instance for n = 2 attributes may look like: $((A_j^{i_1}, A_k^{i_1}),(A_m^{i_2}, A_n^{i_2}))$. We discuss in detail about our cost functions for feasible transformations in the next section.

A transformation tuple based attack is similar to the adversarial example creation for images, in the sense that we cause imperceptible changes to the pixel values of our image to change the classification of our model. The difference between the two is that in the discrete scenario we change our data one attribute at a time: initially changing one attribute and recording if the classification changes, then, changing two attributes simultaneously and recording the classification change and so forth. Our algorithm is model agnostic and does not depend on the ML model's internal loss function formulation to work.

In this setting, we define the feasible instance space that includes only the following six modifiable attributes: Duration, Credit_amount, Purpose, Savings, Other_installment_plans, and Telephone. Since our algorithm involves multi-step multi-attribute change, the order of attribute change has impact on both speed and efficacy. We prefer the more sensitive attributes (attributes that easily cause change in the classification) to be changed early in our algorithm to ensure that we have the minimum attribute change for our examples. A simple way to decide the sensitivity of the attributes is to change each of the attributes individually and see which attributes have the highest attack success rate. Table 3 shows the attack success rate for our six attributes ordered from the highest success rate to the lowest success rate.

Table 3. Success rate of flipping classification result when one attribute is changed (out of 125)

Attribute	Attack success rate
Purpose	20%
Duration	10.4%
Savings	8.8%
Credit_amount	6.4%
Telephone	4.8%
Other_installment_plans	4%

Given the ordering of the attributes as shown in the table above, we run the multi-pass attack. We store those transformation tuples that cause the model to flip classification from "Bad" credit to "Good" credit. Table 4 gives us the attack success rate when we change more than one attribute. As we can see in the results, as the number of attributes changed increases, the attack success rate also increases. When we change six attributes, our attack success rate is 90%. However, this doesn't capture the cheapest possible attribute change for any given example which will be described in the next section.

Cost Formulation
Given a list of transformations that can be performed on an example, we also have the constraint that our attribute-changes should be drawn from a pool of feasible and ethical attribute modifications. To get a list of feasible transformations for each of the attributes, please refer to the appendix. To address the feasibility of individual attribute changes, we formulate a cost matrix C and assign a cost penalty to every attribute change. This cost penalty will be extremely large (close to infinity ∞) to discourage certain attribute change and

Table 4. Success rate of number of examples flipped (out of 125)

Num attr changed	Attack success rate
2	52.8%
3	60.8%
4	69.64%
5	80.8%
6	90.4%

certain sub-attribute changes. For other changes, the cost matrix formulation assigns small non-negative float value (between 0 and 1) as the cost. For example, for attribute i (with three subclasses j, k and z), the feasible attribute changes are: j to k, k to z, then $C^i_{j,z}$, $C^i_{z,k}$, $C^i_{k,j}$ and $C^i_{z,j}$ are all ∞ since they are infeasible changes. We also assign a weight w_i to each attribute i to weigh the influence of that particular attribute in our cost formulation. Assume, each example e can have a set of transformation tuples $M = (m_1, m_2, ...)$ such that $f(M(x)) = t$, where t is good credit. Given our cost formulation mechanism, (C and w), the cost required to get a classification flip from bad credit to good credit is $\arg\min_{\bigcup_{k=1}^{K}(\{i_k, j_k\})} \sum_{k=1}^{K} w_k \cdot C^k_{i_k, j_k}$, where K is the total number of attributes. We have three different cost formulation mechanisms for C and w that will be discussed below.

To understand the impact of the cost function, we experimented with three types of cost functions for the cost matrix formulation of attribute change. In all the three formulations, the infeasible attribute changes are assigned ∞ cost. The first cost function f_1 treats every feasible attribute change as equal. For example, if in one of our transformation tuple M, we are changing attribute i from subclass j to subclass k and attribute l from subclass m to n, then our cost function will ensure $C^i_{j,k} = C^l_{m,n}$ and $w_i = w_l$. The second cost function f_2 treats different attribute change differently, however each individual attribute will have a fixed cost for changes within the sub-classes. Going back to our example of attribute i with three subclasses (i, j and z), if the feasible modifications for i are j to k, and k to z, then $C^i_{j,k} = C^i_{k,z}$. However, for different attributes i and l, $C^i_{j,k} \neq C^l_{m,n}$ and $w_i \neq w_l$. The third cost function f_3 treats every attribute and sub-attribute change independently. The motivation behind this cost function formulation is that it might be easy to move between specific changes in sub-attribute classes for the same attribute class compared to others. So in the third case, $C^i_{j,k} \neq C^i_{j,z}$, $C^i_{j,k} \neq C^l_{m,n}$ and $w_i \neq w_l$. Figure 5 shows the relationship between minimum attributes required to be changed and the percentage of examples that can be flipped. We have plotted this comparison for our three different cost formulations. As we can see the distribution of the percentage has flattened with the introduction of variable weighting component into cost function formulation. Figure 6 gives the percentage of examples flipped as a function of the maximum cost possible (i.e., the maximum allowed cost of changing all the feasible attributes without considering transformations with infinite costs). The fixed cost formulation has a very bumpy and uneven plot. As we introduce attribute weighting and non-uniform cost formulation for attribute changes, the graph becomes more smooth. As expected, as the "transformation cost" increases, more of total instances can flipped.

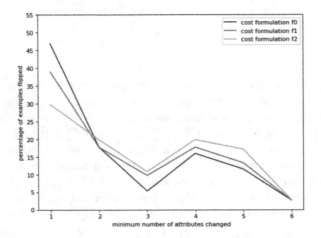

Fig. 5. Percentage of total attributes flipped vs min. attributes changed)

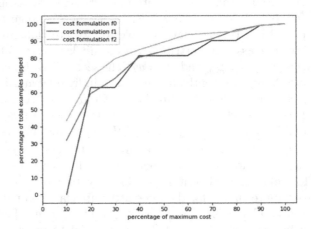

Fig. 6. Percentage of total attributes flipped vs percentage of maximum cost

5   Conclusion

In this paper, we present an approach to protecting individuals' privacy and fair opportunity by encouraging the end user to "game" a machine learning system in a legitimate manner. The idea is adapted from the adversarial learning problem that studies the vulnerability of machine learning systems to adversarial attacks—modifying data to foil the learning system. By incentivizing positive changes to the user's data profile, we can "convince" the learning system to make a different but fairer decision. If used properly, we show that this hostility against machine learning systems can become a powerful tool at the end user's disposal to protect and improve privacy and fairness. Our empirical results indicate that this idea can be successfully used, in a constrained way, to protect individuals against potentially harmful biases embedded in ML systems.

Appendix A

We consider the following attributes to change in our German Credit data:

1. Purpose: For getting the loan ex. car(new), car(old), repairs, education, etc.
2. Duration: Increase/decrease the duration (in months) to see the change in granting loan.
3. Credit amount: Increase and decrease the credit amount granted as a matter of percentage of original amount. ex: 1.05x, 1.10x, 0.90x, 0.85x where x is the current amount.
4. Savings account/bonds: Change the number of savings and bonds from None (A65) to '...100 DM' (A61).
5. Other installment plans: Change from None (A143) to Bank/Store (A141/A142).
6. Telephone: Change the ownership of telephone from None (A191) to registered in user's name (A192).

References

1. Akhtar, N., Mian, A.: Threat of adversarial attacks on deep learning in computer vision: a survey. IEEE Access **6**, 14410–14430 (2018)
2. Alufaisan, Y., Marusich, L.R., Bakdash, J.Z., Zhou, Y., Kantarcioglu, M.: Does explainable artificial intelligence improve human decision-making? (2020)
3. Ballet, V., Renard, X., Aigrain, J., Laugel, T., Frossard, P., Detyniecki, M.: Imperceptible adversarial attacks on tabular data. arXiv e-prints arXiv:1911.03274, November 2019
4. Bruckner, M., Scheffer, T.: Stackelberg games for adversarial prediction problems. In: Proceedings of the 17th ACM SIGKDD International Conference on Knowledge Discovery and Data Mining. ACM (2011)
5. Carlini, N., Wagner, D.: Adversarial examples are not easily detected: bypassing ten detection methods. In: Proceedings of the 10th ACM Workshop on Artificial Intelligence and Security, pp. 3–17. Association for Computing Machinery, New York (2017). https://doi.org/10.1145/3128572.3140444

6. Carlini, N., Wagner, D.A.: Towards evaluating the robustness of neural networks. In: 2017 IEEE Symposium on Security and Privacy (SP), pp. 39–57 (2017)

7. Chawla, N.V., Bowyer, K.W., Hall, L.O., Kegelmeyer, W.P.: SMOTE: synthetic minority over-sampling technique. J. Artif. Int. Res. 16(1), 321–357 (2002)

8. Chouldechova, A., Roth, A.: A snapshot of the frontiers of fairness in machine learning. Commun. ACM 63(5), 82–89 (2020). https://doi.org/10.1145/3376898

9. Commission, E.: 2018 reform of EU data protection rules

10. Dalvi, N., Domingos, P., Mausam, Sanghai, S., Verma, D.: Adversarial classification. In: Proceedings of the Tenth ACM SIGKDD International Conference on Knowledge Discovery and Data Mining, pp. 99–108. KDD 2004. ACM, New York (2004)

11. Dua, D., Graff, C.: UCI machine learning repository (2017). http://archive.ics.uci.edu/ml

12. Eykholt, K., et al.: Robust physical-world attacks on deep learning visual classification. In: Computer Vision and Pattern Recognition (CVPR)

13. Goodfellow, I., Shlens, J., Szegedy, C.: Explaining and harnessing adversarial examples. In: International Conference on Learning Representations (2015)

14. Hashemi, M., Fathi, A.: PermuteAttack: counterfactual explanation of machine learning credit scorecards (2020)

15. Ji, Z., Lipton, Z.C., Elkan, C.: Differential privacy and machine learning: a survey and review. CoRR abs/1412.7584 (2014). http://arxiv.org/abs/1412.7584

16. Kanerva, A., Helgesson, F.: On the use of model-agnostic interpretation methods as defense against adversarial input attacks on tabular data. Master's thesis, Department of Computer Science (2020)

17. Kantarcioglu, M., Xi, B., Clifton, C.: Classifier evaluation and attribute selection against active adversaries. Data Min. Knowl. Discov. 22, 291–335 (2011)

18. Kulynych, B., Overdorf, R., Troncoso, C., Gürses, S.: POTs: protective optimization technologies. In: Proceedings of the 2020 Conference on Fairness, Accountability, and Transparency, pp. 177–188. FAT* 2020. Association for Computing Machinery, New York (2020). https://doi.org/10.1145/3351095.3372853

19. Levin, S., et al.: Machine-learning-based electronic triage more accurately differentiates patients with respect to clinical outcomes compared with the emergency severity index. Ann. Emerg. Med. 71(5), 565–574.e2. https://doi.org/10.1016/j.annemergmed.2017.08.005

20. Liu, Z., Luo, P., Wang, X., Tang, X.: Deep learning face attributes in the wild. In: Proceedings of International Conference on Computer Vision (ICCV), December 2015

21. Lowd, D., Meek, C.: Adversarial learning. In: Proceedings of the eleventh ACM SIGKDD International Conference on Knowledge Discovery in Data Mining, pp. 641–647. KDD 2005 (2005)

22. Luo, J., Bai, T., Zhao, J., Li, B.: Generating adversarial yet inconspicuous patches with a single image (2020)

23. Papernot, N., McDaniel, P., Goodfellow, I., Jha, S., Celik, Z.B., Swami, A.: Practical black-box attacks against machine learning. In: Proceedings of the 2017 ACM on Asia Conference on Computer and Communications Security, pp. 506–519. ASIA CCS 2017. ACM, New York (2017)

24. Renard, X., Laugel, T., Lesot, M.J., Marsala, C., Detyniecki, M.: Detecting potential local adversarial examples for human-interpretable defense. In: Workshop on Recent Advances in Adversarial Learning (Nemesis) of the European Conference on Machine Learning and Principles of Practice of Knowledge Discovery in Databases (ECML-PKDD), Dublin, Ireland, September 2018. https://hal. sorbonne-universite.fr/hal-01905948, presented at: ECML/PKDD Workshop on Recent Advances in Adversarial Machine Learning (Nemesis 2018), Dublin, Ireland (2018)

25. Rudin, C., Wang, C., Coker, B.: The age of secrecy and unfairness in recidivism prediction. Harvard Data Sci. Rev. (1) (2020). https://doi.org/10.1162/99608f92. 6ed64b30

26. Sharif, M., Bhagavatula, S., Bauer, L., Reiter, M.K.: Accessorize to a crime: real and stealthy attacks on state-of-the-art face recognition. In: Proceedings of the 23rd ACM SIGSAC Conference on Computer and Communications Security (2016)

27. Sharif, M., Bhagavatula, S., Bauer, L., Reiter, M.K.: A general framework for adversarial examples with objectives. ACM Trans. Priv. Secur. (2019)

28. Szegedy, C., et al.: Intriguing properties of neural networks. In: International Conference on Learning Representations (2014). http://arxiv.org/abs/1312.6199

29. Vedaldi, A., Lenc, K.: MatConvNet - convolutional neural networks for MATLAB. In: Proceeding of the ACM International Conference on Multimedia (2015)

30. Wang, Y., Kosinski, M.: Deep neural networks are more accurate than humans at detecting sexual orientation from facial images, October 2018. http://www.osf.io/zn79k

31. Wenger, E., Passananti, J., Yao, Y., Zheng, H., Zhao, B.Y.: Backdoor attacks on facial recognition in the physical world. CoRR abs/2006.14580 (2020). https://arxiv.org/abs/2006.14580

32. Wilson, D.L.: Asymptotic properties of nearest neighbor rules using edited data. IEEE Trans. Syst. Man Cybern. 408–421 (1972)

33. Yosinski, J., Clune, J., Bengio, Y., Lipson, H.: How transferable are features in deep neural networks? In: Ghahramani, Z., Welling, M., Cortes, C., Lawrence, N.D., Weinberger, K.Q. (eds.) Advances in Neural Information Processing Systems 27: Annual Conference on Neural Information Processing Systems 2014, 8–13 December 2014, Montreal, Quebec, Canada, pp. 3320–3328 (2014). http://papers. nips.cc/paper/5347-how-transferable-are-features-in-deep-neural-networks

34. Zhou, Y., Kantarcioglu, M.: Modeling adversarial learning as nested Stackelberg games. In: Bailey, J., Khan, L., Washio, T., Dobbie, G., Huang, J.Z., Wang, R. (eds.) PAKDD 2016. LNCS (LNAI), vol. 9652, pp. 350–362. Springer, Cham (2016). https://doi.org/10.1007/978-3-319-31750-2_28

35. Zhou, Y., Kantarcioglu, M., Thuraisingham, B., Xi, B.: Adversarial support vector machine learning. In: Proceedings of the 18th ACM SIGKDD International Conference on Knowledge Discovery and Data Mining. ACM, New York (2012)

A Review of Multi Agent Perimeter Defense Games

Daigo Shishika[1](✉)(iD) and Vijay Kumar[2](iD)

[1] George Mason University, Fairfax, VA 22030, USA
dshishik@gmu.edu
[2] University of Pennsylvania, Philadelphia, PA 19104, USA
kumar@seas.upenn.edu

Abstract. This paper reviews a series of works done on the multi-agent perimeter defense scenario, in which a team of intruders try to score by reaching the target region while a team of defenders try to minimize the score by intercepting those intruders. We describe how the small-scale differential games are solved and are leveraged to design team strategies in the large-scale swarm versus swarm scenarios. Three different approaches to analyze the large-scale games (MM, MIS, and LGR) are introduced with comments on their relative strengths and weaknesses. As a unique contribution of this paper, we discuss how the existing results can be extended into more general problem formulations. Furthermore, we point out the limitations of the current work and suggest potential directions for future research.

Keywords: Pursuit-evasion games · Multi-agent systems ·
Cooperative control · Reach-avoid games · Perimeter defense

1 Introduction

Multi-robot systems (MRS) have gained significant attention in the past few decades. Since MRS are naturally robust due to their redundancy, and are also able to distribute into large areas, there are various application spaces that are anticipated. Of particular relevance to this paper is a class of scenarios related to security and defense applications. Specifically, we discuss a scenario in which a group of defenders is tasked to protect a region from a group of intruders.

Since we are concerned with two parties with conflicting objectives, the study of effective strategies naturally fits into game-theoretic analyses. The problem which we call the *perimeter defense game* considers a scenario where intruders try to reach the perimeter of a target region without being intercepted by the defenders, whereas a team of defenders seek to intercept or capture those intruders before they reach the perimeter. This is a variant of pursuit-evasion games for which various versions of one pursuer vs. one evader scenarios have been

Supported by ARL grant ARL DCIST CRA W911NF-17-2-0181.

Q. Zhu et al. (Eds.): GameSec 2020, LNCS 12513, pp. 472–485, 2020.
https://doi.org/10.1007/978-3-030-64793-3_26

considered, and the differential-game approach has been applied successfully to derive equilibrium strategies [1, 16].

In the past decade, there have been increasing efforts in solving pursuit-evasion games that involve multiple pursuers or multiple evaders. When the game is set up so that a group of agents faces a single opponent, the optimal solution leads to coordination strategies for the group. There are works that look at the problem from the perspective of the pursuers [29, 30, 35], and also those that consider the problem from the evaders' side [6, 12, 24].

The derivation of the optimal strategies becomes more challenging when the game is played between teams of agents: i.e., multiple pursuers and multiple evaders [11]. The main challenge is in the dimensionality of the state space that prohibits us from naively applying the differential-game techniques. Similar to other multi-agent problems, the Voronoi tessellation has been widely employed to reduce the large-scale problems into a local area-minimization problem, or to assign pursuers to evaders [15, 18, 20, 39].

When there is a target region to be protected, the problem becomes a variant of the *target guarding problem*, originally introduced in [16]. A version of this problem is called the target-attacker-defender game [9, 17, 22], which has relevance to missile guidance applications [9, 21]. A similar scenario is also called the reach-avoid game [5, 37, 38], and it has been studied in many different variants [2, 3, 14, 34–36], including coast-line guarding or boarder defense [7, 10, 13, 31], and three-dimensional environments [8, 33].

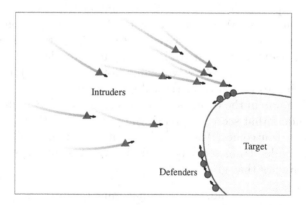

Fig. 1. Illustration of a perimeter defense game. Multiple intruders are approaching the target, while the defenders are tasked to intercept them.

This paper is concerned with the perimeter defense game, which is a variant of the target guarding problem where defenders are constrained to move on a convex target region [25–28]. This additional constraint leads to convenient closed-form solutions, as well as their interesting geometric interpretations. Moreover, the problem has high relevance to scenarios involving ground vehicles defending a building, or aerial vehicles patrolling around a no-fly zone.

This paper serves as an overview of various results and developments presented in our previous publications [25–28]. After formulating the perimeter defense problem in Sect. 2, we review solution methods and the associated results in Sect. 3. The potential extensions and generalizations of those results are considered in Sect. 4. Finally, Sect. 5 discusses the limitations in the current work and suggests directions for future research.

2   Problem Statement

We consider planer dynamics of point particles representing N_A intruders and N_D defenders. The symbols $_A$ and $_D$ are reserved to denote the intruders and the defenders respectively. The agents all have simple dynamics (i.e., first-order integrator), implying that they can change their velocity instantaneously, and this velocity vector is the control variable for each agent. Without the loss of generality, the intruders and the defenders have bounds on there speed, ν and 1, respectively. The parameter ν has a constraint $\nu \leq 1$, implying that the intruders are at most as fast as the defenders.

We make the following assumptions: (A1) the defenders move along the perimeter of the target region; (A2) the target region is convex; (A3) each agent has access to full-state information (i.e., positions of all agents); and (A4) intercept or capture occurs when the distance between the intruder and the defender becomes zero.

Viewing the game from an individual intruder's perspective, either one of the following three happens: (i) it reaches the perimeter without being intercepted by any of the defenders (ii) the distance with the defender becomes zero when it reaches the perimeter, or (iii) it does not reach the perimeter in finite time. The third case is caused by the defender's maneuver to place itself between the target and the intruder. Therefore, we define both (ii) and (iii) as *capture*. Any intruder that achieves the outcome (i) will score a point.

Viewing the game in the team vs. team level, the objective function Q is the number of intruders that score, i.e., reach the perimeter without being captured by the defenders (outcome (i) above). The intruder team seeks to maximize Q while the defender team seeks to minimize Q. The problem is to find the equilibrium strategies that give

$$\min_{\Gamma_D} \max_{\Gamma_A} Q = \max_{\Gamma_A} \min_{\Gamma_D} Q,$$

where Γ_D and Γ_A denote the defender and intruder team strategies respectively.

3   Solution Method

A common approach in the variants of the multi-player target guarding problem is to leverage the results of the games played between a small number of players. The low-level velocity control strategies obtained in this small-scale game are combined with the high-level assignment policies to design the team-level strategies.

3.1   Agent-Level Control Policy

One vs. One. The smallest problem is the game played between one defender and one intruder. The key result that we need from this small-scale problem is the solution to the *game of kind*, which consists of the *barrier* surface and the corresponding control strategies. The barrier surface divides the state space into two regions: the intruder-winning region and the defender-winning region. If the initial configuration of the game falls in the intruder-winning region, then the intruder has a strategy to score, whereas if the game starts in the defender-winning region, then the defender has a strategy to guarantee capture.

To derive the barrier surface, one can consider a *game of degree* in which the payoff J is defined as the distance between the defender and the intruder at the time of breaching, i.e., when the intruder reaches the perimeter. The intruder tries to maximize this distance while the defender tries to minimize it. If an equilibrium exists, the Value function is defined as

$$V = \min_{\omega_D} \max_{\mathbf{v}_A} J = \max_{\mathbf{v}_A} \min_{\omega_D} J, \tag{1}$$

where ω_D denotes the defender's control on a one-dimensional space, and $\mathbf{v}_A$ denotes intruder's velocity. Once the equilibrium strategies ω_D^* and $\mathbf{v}_A^*$ are derived, the Value V is a function of the player positions, and the barrier surface can be identified as the level set $V = 0$.

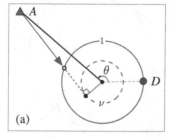 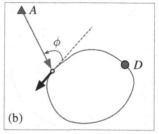

Fig. 2. Construction of the intruder strategies. (a) For circular perimeters, circles scaled by ν are used. (b) For non-circular perimeters, the approach angle ϕ is used.

The barrier for a circular perimeter was first derived in [25] using geometric approach, and later verified with differential game approach in [32]. The equilibrium defender strategy is to simply move in the direction of the intruder. Using the polar angle shown in Fig. 2, the equilibrium defender strategy is

$$\omega_D^* = \text{sign}(\theta).$$

The intruder's equilibrium strategy is to move towards the tangent point on a circle scaled by the speed ratio ν [25,32].

The above defender strategy for the circular perimeter is almost trivial since any intruder position that gives $\theta = 0$ clearly defines the "front" of the defender's position. When considering a non-circular perimeter (e.g.., polygon), this surface that divides the left and the right side from the defender's position is not immediately obvious. In addition, the intruder strategy can no longer be parameterized by the polar angle.

In [26], these issues are addressed by parameterizing the intruder strategies based on the *approach angle*, which is defined by the angle between the intruder's direction of motion and the tangent vector of the curve at the breach point. The optimal approach angle was derived to be

$$\phi = \cos^{-1} \nu.$$

This result tells us that the intruder should approach the tangent point on the target when $\nu = 1$, whereas it should approach the closest point on the target when $\nu \to 0$. It is easy to verify that this result matches with the special case where the target is circular.

The barrier is also obtained for the case when the perimeter is some arbitrary convex shape [26]. A convenient way to visualize the barrier surface is to look at the slice of the state space at a particular defender position. Then the barrier for that particular defender position is shown as a closed curve that completely surrounds the target region (Fig. 3a).

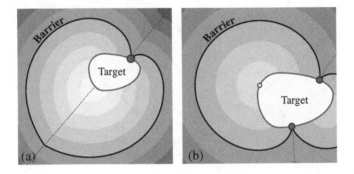

Fig. 3. Contour of the value function and the barrier curve for a non-circular perimeter. The region enclosed by the barrier is the intruder-winning region, and the region outside is the defender-winning region. (a) One vs. one game. (b) Two vs. one game.

The results obtained in the above accommodate any value of the speed ratio $\nu \in (0, 1]$, however, the result for the case with $\nu = 1$ lends itself to a nice geometric interpretation. Firstly, the intruder's equilibrium strategy is to move towards the tangent of the target region (for both circular and non-circular perimeters). Secondly, the barrier curve is constructed by pieces of geometry called the *involute*. An involute of a convex shape is the locus of a point on a piece of taut string as the string is either unwrapped from or wrapped around the shape. In our case, the shape of interest is the target region.

Two vs. One. To consider an explicit form of cooperation among the defenders, we extended the one vs. one results into a game played between two defenders and one intruder [25, 26, 32]. Since the intruder must avoid both defenders, the optimal breach point against one defender may be suboptimal against anoteher defender. Depending on the configuration, the safest breach point now becomes either the optimal breach point against the closer defender or the mid-point between the two defenders. The defender pair's optimal strategy is to approach the intruder from both sides, which we call the *pincer movement*. Importantly, the defender-winning region provided by the pincer movement is larger than the union of the winning regions provided by the individual defenders [25, 28, 32]. The barrier derived for the two vs. one game has a greater implication beyond the additional consideration in the assignment strategy. The intruder-winning regions for the two vs. one game gives us a way to directly analyze an arbitrary size of the game played between n_D defenders and n_A intruders, which will be discussed at the end of Sect. 3.2.

3.2   Team-Level Coordination Policies

The results from small scale games are used to develop team strategies when there are N_D defenders and N_A intruders. Let Q denote the number of intruders that reach the perimeter without being captured. Let the team strategies Γ_D and Γ_A denote the mappings from the current states (positions of all the agents) to the control actions $\omega_D = [\omega_{D_1}.., \omega_{D_{N_D}}]$ and $\mathbf{v}_A = [\mathbf{v}_{A_1}.., \mathbf{v}_{A_{N_A}}]$ respectively. The large-scale game uses this score Q as the payoff function, which the defender team minimizes and the intruder team maximizes. If an equilibrium exists, the Value function is

$$Q^* = \min_{\Gamma_D} \max_{\Gamma_A} Q = \max_{\Gamma_A} \min_{\Gamma_D} Q. \tag{2}$$

The goal is to find the equilibrium team strategies (Γ_D^*, Γ_A^*) and the Value Q^*.

Since directly solving this large-scale game is very challenging, various approximation methods have been proposed. We describe three approaches in analyzing the multi-player games represented by: maximum matching (MM), maximum independent set (MIS), and the local game regions (LGR).

Man-to-man Defense. The results of the one-defender vs. one-intruder game immediately leads to a naive coordination strategy for the defender team. We can assign each defender to an intruder that it can capture, i.e., one in the corresponding defender-winning region. What we must avoid in these assignments is any overlap in the defenders or the intruders. More specifically, we must not assign a single defender to multiple intruders, since capture is only guaranteed against one intruder. In addition, we must not assign multiple defenders to a single intruder, since such redundant assignments will reduce the overall number of capture, leading to a higher score.

The optimal assignment of defenders to intruders in the man-to-man defense framework is provided by *matching* in graph theory. Considering a bipartite graph, where one set of nodes represents the defenders and the other represents the intruders, we draw edges from each defender to all the intruders that it can capture. By performing *maximum-cardinality matching* (MM) on this bipartite graph, we obtain the optimal man-to-man defense that gives us an upper-bound on the score

$$Q^* \leq Q_{\text{MM}} = N_A - N_{\text{MM}}, \tag{3}$$

where N_{MM} denotes the number of matches.

This general approach was originally proposed in [3,4], and it has been applied to other variants of the problems [25,36]. Due to its simplicity, there is a potential for application to many other scenarios, which will be discussed further in Sect. 4.1. The downside of this approach is that this naive coordination strategy does not account for a tighter cooperation that can happen between the defenders or the intruders. The cooperation between the defenders was incorporated by leveraging the result of two-defender vs. one-intruder game.

Two-on-one Defense. A naive extension of the maximum-cardinality matching approach is to incorporate the results of the two vs. one game by assigning pairs of defenders to intruders. We are tempted to simply augment the bipartite graph with nodes representing the pairs of defenders, and adding edges from each defender pair to all the intruders that it can capture. However, we cannot perform maximum-cardinality matching on this bipartite graph since a node representing a single defender and one that represents a pair may share the same defender, which leads to an overlapping assignment.

To circumvent this problem, we can construct a new graph in which each node represents an assignment in the original graph, and the edges represent any conflict between the assignments: i.e., whenever two assignments share any defender or intruder, they are connected. By solving the Maximum Independent Set (MIS) problem on this transformed graph, we obtain the set of assignments without any overlapping defenders or intruders. This assignment method guarantees that the number of capture is greater than the one provided by the maximum matching, i.e., the provided upper bound is tighter:

$$Q^* \leq Q_{\text{MIS}} = N_A - N_{\text{MIS}} \leq Q_{\text{MM}}, \tag{4}$$

where N_{MIS} denotes the cardinality of the maximum independent set. However, the down side of this method is its computational complexity. Since MIS problem is NP-hard, it does not scale well with large number of agents. An improvement over the MM and MIS approaches is presented next.

Local Game Decomposition. As was mentioned in Sect. 3.1, the barrier curve for the two vs. one game leads to a stronger coordination policy beyond two-on-one assignments. Consider a specific pair of defenders and the intruder-winning region that it defines (Fig. 3b or Fig. 4). We call it the *Local Game Region* (LGR) as it leads to a region-based decomposition method [28].

The results of the two vs. one game tell us that the n_A^k intruders contained in this LGR can win against the defender pair, by approaching near the mid-point. Additionally, this result implies that any defender outside of this LGR cannot capture any of those intruders. Therefore, only those n_D^k defenders contained

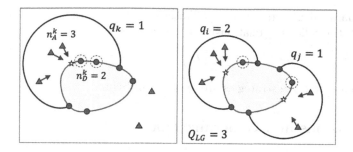

Fig. 4. Local game regions (LGRs) and the associated subteams. (a) An LGR that contains three intruders and two defenders. (b) The intruder team's optimal selection of the LGRs, $\mathbf{G}^*$, leading to the overall score of $Q = 3$.

in the LGR can possibly contribute to capture. If the intruders have a local numerical advantage, i.e., $q_k = n_A^k - n_D^k > 0$, then the intruders can achieve a score of q_k. The subscript k denotes the indexing of the defender pairs, or the LGRs.

Now, the intruder team can maximize the guaranteed score by intelligently selecting the set of LGRs in which they play the local game [28]. Let $\mathbf{G}$ denote the set of disjoint LGRs, then the intruder team can consider the following optimization problem:

$$Q_{\mathrm{LG}} = \max_{\mathbf{G}} \sum_{k \in \mathbf{G}} q_k', \tag{5}$$

where $q_k' = \max\{0, q_k\}$.

Theorem 1 (From [28]). *Let $\boldsymbol{\Gamma}_A^*$ denote the intruder strategy corresponding to the teaming into $\mathbf{G}^*$ and then playing the two vs. one game against the defender pair associated to each LGR. The strategy $\boldsymbol{\Gamma}_A^*$ guarantees*

$$Q^* \geq Q_{LG} \tag{6}$$

for all permissible defender strategies. ■

Importantly, this is the first result in the team-level coordination policy that gives an intruder team strategy and a corresponding lower bound on the score. In [28] we also propose a defender team strategy $\boldsymbol{\Gamma}_D^*$ based on the local game decomposition. The strategy first removes any uncapturable intruders based on the result of Theorem 6. Then the two-on-one defense are assigned to intruders that are near the boundary of the LGRs with the score $q_k = 0$. Intuitively, this assignment is used to ensure that no additional intruder enters the LGRs that already has an equal number of intruders and defenders, which we call the *occupied* LGRs [28]. Finally, one-on-one defense is assigned to the remaining agents. In [28], we explain how this strategy accounts for the sequence of captures that occur in time, in contrast to the MM and MIS approaches that are ignorant of such dynamical aspects. Finally, [28] discusses the class of initial configurations from which the following relationship is guaranteed

$$Q(\Gamma_D^*, \Gamma_A) \leq Q(\Gamma_D^*, \Gamma_A^*) \leq Q(\Gamma_D, \Gamma_A^*), \tag{7}$$

which implies that the strategies are at an equilibrium.

4   Extensions and Generalizations

This section discusses potential extensions and generalizations of the results described in the previous section.

4.1   Assignment-Based Defense Policies

The solution method involving the one vs. one results and the maximum-cardinality matching (MM) gives us a generic framework to solve various swarm vs. swarm problems. An immediate extension of the perimeter defense problem is the engagement between intruders and defenders that can move in three-dimensional space. A similar problem has been considered for agents that can freely move in three-dimensional space, with target region defined as a plane [33].

A direct extension of the perimeter defense scenario is the *hemisphere guarding problem*, in which defenders that move on a hemisphere seek to intercept aerial intruders. An initial step to solve this problem is presented in [23], where one vs. one engagement between an aerial defender and a ground intruder is considered. This is an intermediate step towards intruders that can freely move in three-dimensional space. Once we have the barrier surface from this small-scale problem, we can determine whether the intruder is capturable or not for every defender-intruder pair. This information allows us to convert the design of strategies in continuous velocity space into a matching problem, as was discussed in Sect. 3.2.

Heterogeneous Speed. The assignment approach also extends to teams with heterogeneous capabilities. For example, defenders may have various speed limits. In this case, the barrier surface will be different for every defender. However, this variation does not affect the assignment method, since all we need in the high-level matching algorithm is the pair-wise information of whether a given defender can capture a given intruder or not. Similarly, the intruders may have different speeds without affecting the overall solution method. It is worth noting that the closed-form solution for the one vs. one game provided in our work becomes useful in the presence of these speed variations, since the required win/loss information can be obtained computationally efficiently. When the numerical approach with HJI PDE is used (as in [3,4]), the extension becomes more challenging because the barrier surfaces for all possible values of ν have to be computed a priori and be stored to be used as a look-up table.

Intruder Weights. Another immediate extension of the assignment based approach is the case when different intruders carry different weights in terms of the damage they incur when the perimeter is breached. For example, the threat level of each intruder may be described by some weighting factor. In this case, the maximum cardinality matching will be modified to a Linear Sum Assignment Problem that can be solved by the well-known Hungarian Algorithm.

MIS Approach. The solutions to the two-defender vs. one-intruder game were used to improve the defender team's performance by considering explicit cooperation among pairs of defenders. A similar approach will apply for other problems if any n-defender vs. m-intruder subproblem is identified and solved. In the transformed graph, each node represents an assignment of a team of n defenders to a group of m intruders, and each edge represents a conflict. Each node (assignment) also carries a weight based on the number of intruders or their weighted sum according to the relative threat level as was discussed with intruder weights. Each edge represents a conflict whenever two different assignments contain the same defender or the intruder. By finding the Maximum-weight Independent Set on this graph, we can optimize the defender to intruder assignments that account for explicit cooperation.

4.2   Cooperative Intruder Strategies

The tasks given to the defender team and the intruder team are fundamentally different, and it is easy to see that the assignment-based approaches do not work well for the intruder team. More specifically, each intruder cannot simply select a single defender and play a one vs. one game against it. Instead, an intruder has to avoid all defenders in order to reach the target and score a point. This asymmetry makes it difficult for us to design a cooperative team strategy for the intruders.

The decomposition method using the local game regions (LGRs) presented in [28] was most useful in the sense that it led to a cooperative intruder strategy, which was not provided by either the MM or the MIS formulations. The essence of this approach is in the analysis based on local *numerical advantages*. In the perimeter defense game, a local overmatch situation was created by the intruder subteams that simultaneously attack a single point on the perimeter.

A similar strategy will likely to appear in the multi-player reach avoid game if it is assumed that the defender is consumed by the intruder whenever a capture occurs, i.e., a single defender cannot capture multiple intruders. The main challenge in extending the LGR decomposition to the reach avoid game or any other variants of the target guarding problem is in the definition of the regions that leads to an efficient combinatorial optimization. Each region must have two elements: (a) an associated intruder subteam that, and (b) a set of defenders that every intruder in the subteam can win against. The latter gives us the complement of the defender subteam associated to the region, which leads to the sufficient condition for the intruder subteam to score: $n_A^k > n_D^k$.

5   Limitations and Future Directions

In this section we discuss the limitations in the existing works and consider directions for future developments.

Defender Dynamics. We assumed that the defender's motion is constrained on the perimeter. The most significant consequence of this constraint is the fact that the intruders can ensure no defender captures more than one intruder, by approaching the perimeter simultaneously. This property makes the perimeter defense game to be interesting only when $N_A < N_D$, since the intruder team can always guarantee a score otherwise.

Sequential Capture. If we allow the defenders to leave the perimeter and pursue the intruder, there is a possibility of multiple captures achieved by a single defender. Such scenario leads to several interesting avenues for future work. First, the defender team strategy will now contain a *vehicle routing problem*, which is a complex combinatorial optimization problem even in the case where the locations to be visited by the agents are stationary. Secondly, the intruder behavior will now have a more meaningful distinction between an evasive maneuver and an offensive maneuver. More specifically, some of the intruders may try to lure the defenders away from the perimeter so that other intruders can successfully reach the target. Such cooperation schemes have been considered for small-scale games, e.g.., [29]. The design of defender's strategy will also become complex because there is a potential conflict between (i) pursuing an intruder, and (ii) staying close to the target for subsequent captures. The design of coordination strategies for large teams is therefore an interesting problem from the perspective of both the defenders and the intruders.

Fast Intruders. The existing results are provided for any speed ratio $\nu \in (0, 1]$, i.e., the intruders cannot be faster than the defenders. It is easy to see that this assumption is necessary for one vs. one game since if the intruder has a speed advantage, then it can come arbitrarily close to the perimeter and outrun the defender to always guarantee intrusion. This is still the case even when there are multiple defenders. The degeneracy arises due to the combination of assumptions (A1) and (A4) in Sect. 2. To consider a faster intruder scenario, we must relax either or both of those two assumptions (e.g.., consider nonzero capture radius) and design strategies for the defenders to coordinate their motion.

Partial Information. Finally, one of the strongest assumptions in the existing variants of the target guarding problems is the assumption that each agent knows the location of all other agents (i.e., full state information). In a realistic setting the detection of the intruders is an important consideration. As a step towards a more holistic solution, [27] considers the design of a patroller team that ensures the detection of any agent that approaches a certain distance from the perimeter. Additionally, for large-scale problems, the defenders must be able to act on locally collected information. The work in [19] developed a training methodology to learn communication strategies from a centralized expert policy. The proposed method was used to design a decentralized version of the MM assignment strategy without any centralized coordination mechanism.

Importantly, neither of the above works directly addressed the issue of unseen intruders. The consideration of such partial information will make any pursuit-evasion game much more difficult to solve. When an equilibrium is infeasible to obtain, a design of reasonable team strategies will be of great importance to the field.

6 Conclusion

This paper presented an overview of the works done on the multi-agent perimeter defense game, in which a team of intruders seek to reach a target region while a team of defenders try to intercept those intruders. The multi-player game can be solved by first deriving the strategies for the games played between a small number of agents (one vs. one and two vs. one) and leveraging those results in the team-level coordination strategies. Three different analysis methods (maximum matching, maximum independent set, and local-game decomposition) have varying levels of cooperation. While the local-game decomposition generates the most sophisticated team behavior, the maximum matching has the most straightforward ways of being applied to other problems. There are several limitations in the current problem formulation that lead us to future developments in the aspects related to the agent dynamics, payoff function, and the information structure.

References

1. Basar, T., Olsder, G.J.: Dynamic Noncooperative Game Theory, 2nd edn. Society for Industrial and Applied Mathematics, Philadelphia (2011)
2. Chen, M., Zhou, Z., Tomlin, C.J.: A path defense approach to the multiplayer reach-avoid game. In: IEEE Conference on Decision and Control (CDC), pp. 2420–2426 (2014)
3. Chen, M., Zhou, Z., Tomlin, C.J.: Multiplayer reach-avoid games via low dimensional solutions and maximum matching. In: Proceedings of the American Control Conference (ACC), pp. 1444–1449 (2014)
4. Chen, M., Zhou, Z., Tomlin, C.J.: Multiplayer reach-avoid games via pairwise outcomes. IEEE Trans. Autom. Control 62(3), 1451–1457 (2017)
5. Fisac, J.F., Chen, M., Tomlin, C.J., Sastry, S.S.: Reach-avoid problems with time-varying dynamics, targets and constraints. In: Proceedings of the 18th International Conference on Hybrid Systems: Computation and Control (ACM), pp. 11–20 (2015)
6. Fuchs, Z.E., Khargonekar, P.P., Evers, J.: Cooperative defense within a single-pursuer, two-evader pursuit evasion differential game. In: IEEE Conference on Decision and Control (CDC), pp. 3091–3097 (2010)
7. Garcia, E., Casbeer, D.W., Pachter, M.: The barrier surface in the cooperative football differential game. arXiv preprint arXiv:2006.03682 (2020)
8. Garcia, E., Casbeer, D.W., Pachter, M.: Optimal strategies for a class of multiplayer reach-avoid differential games in 3d space. IEEE Rob. Autom. Lett. 5(3), 4257–4264 (2020)

9. Garcia, E., Casbeer, D.W., Pham, K., Pachter, M.: Cooperative aircraft defense from an attacking missile. J. Guid. Control Dyn. **38**(8), 1510–1520 (2015)
10. Garcia, E., Casbeer, D.W., Von Moll, A., Pachter, M.: Cooperative two-pursuer one-evader blocking differential game. In: Proceedings American Control Conference (ACC), pp. 2702–2709. IEEE (2019)
11. Garcia, E., Casbeer, D.W., Von Moll, A., Pachter, M.: Multiple pursuer multiple evader differential games. IEEE Transactions on Automatic Control (2020)
12. Garcia, E., Von Moll, A., Casbeer, D.W., Pachter, M.: Strategies for defending a coastline against multiple attackers. In: IEEE Conference on Decision and Control (CDC), pp. 7319–7324. IEEE (2019)
13. Garcia, E., Von Moll, A., Casbeer, D.W., Pachter, M.: Strategies for defending a coastline against multiple attackers. In: IEEE Conference on Decision and Control (CDC), pp. 7319–7324 (2019)
14. Huang, H., Ding, J., Zhang, W., Tomlin, C.J.: A differential game approach to planning in adversarial scenarios: a case study on capture-the-flag. In: IEEE International Conference on Robotics and Automation (ICRA), pp. 1451–1456 (2011)
15. Huang, H., Zhang, W., Ding, J., Stipanović, D.M., Tomlin, C.J.: Guaranteed decentralized pursuit-evasion in the plane with multiple pursuers. In: IEEE Conference on Decision and Control (CDC), pp. 4835–4840 (2011)
16. Isaacs, R.: Differential games: a mathematical theory with applications to warfare and pursuit, control and optimization. Courier Corporation (1999)
17. Liang, L., Deng, F., Peng, Z., Li, X., Zha, W.: A differential game for cooperative target defense. Automatica **102**, 58–71 (2019)
18. Makkapati, V.R., Tsiotras, P.: Optimal evading strategies and task allocation in multi-player pursuit–evasion problems. Dyn. Games Appl. **9**(4), 1168–1187 (2019). https://doi.org/10.1007/s13235-019-00319-x
19. Paulos, J., Chen, S.W., Shishika, D., Kumar, V.: Decentralization of multiagent policies by learning what to communicate. In: IEEE International Conference on Robotics and Automation (ICRA), pp. 7990–7996. IEEE (2019)
20. Pierson, A., Wang, Z., Schwager, M.: Intercepting rogue robots: an algorithm for capturing multiple evaders with multiple pursuers. IEEE Rob. Autom. Lett. **2**(2), 530–537 (2017)
21. Prokopov, O., Shima, T.: Linear quadratic optimal cooperative strategies for active aircraft protection. J. Guid. Control Dyn. **36**(3), 753–764 (2013)
22. Rubinsky, S., Gutman, S.: Three-player pursuit and evasion conflict. J. Guid. Control Dyn. **37**(1), 98–110 (2014)
23. Lee, S.E., Shishika, D., Kumar, V.: Perimeter-defense game between aerial defender and ground intruder. In: To Appear in IEEE Conference on Decision and Control (CDC). IEEE (2020)
24. Scott, W.L., Leonard, N.E.: Optimal evasive strategies for multiple interacting agents with motion constraints. Automatica **94**, 26–34 (2018)
25. Shishika, D., Kumar, V.: Local-game decomposition for multiplayer perimeter-defense problem. In: IEEE Conference on Decision and Control (CDC), pp. 2093–2100 (2018)
26. Shishika, D., Kumar, V.: Perimeter-defense game on arbitrary convex shapes. arXiv arXiv:190903989 (2019)
27. Shishika, D., Paulos, J., Dorothy, M.R., Hsieh, M.A., Kumar, V.: Team composition for perimeter defense with patrollers and defenders. In: IEEE Conference on Decision and Control (CDC), pp. 7325–7332 (2019)
28. Shishika, D., Paulos, J., Kumar, V.: Cooperative team strategies for multi-player perimeter-defense games. IEEE Rob. Autom. Lett. **5**(2), 2738–2745 (2020)

29. Von Moll, A., Casbeer, D., Garcia, E., Milutinović, D., Pachter, M.: The multi-pursuer single-evader game. J. Intel. Rob. Syst. **96**(2), 193–207 (2019)
30. Von Moll, A., Casbeer, D.W., Garcia, E., Milutinović, D.: Pursuit-evasion of an evader by multiple pursuers. In: International Conference on Unmanned Aircraft Systems (ICUAS), pp. 133–142. IEEE (2018)
31. Von Moll, A., Garcia, E., Casbeer, D., Suresh, M., Swar, S.C.: Multiple-pursuer, single-evader border defense differential game. J. Aero. Info. Syst. **17**(8), 1–10 (2019)
32. Von Moll1, A., Pachter, M., Shishika, D., Fuchs, Z.: Guarding a circular target by patrolling its perimeter. In: To Appear in IEEE Conference on Decision and Control (CDC). IEEE (2020)
33. Yan, R., Duan, X., Shi, Z., Zhong, Y., Bullo, F.: Maximum-matching capture strategies for 3d heterogeneous multiplayer reach-avoid games. arXiv preprint arXiv:1909.11881 (2019)
34. Yan, R., Shi, Z., Zhong, Y.: Escape-avoid games with multiple defenders along a fixed circular orbit. In: 13th IEEE International Conference on Control & Automation (ICCA), pp. 958–963. IEEE (2017)
35. Yan, R., Shi, Z., Zhong, Y.: Reach-avoid games with two defenders and one attacker: an analytical approach. IEEE Trans. Cybern. **49**(3), 1035–1046 (2018)
36. Yan, R., Shi, Z., Zhong, Y.: Task assignment for multiplayer reach-avoid games in convex domains via analytical barriers. IEEE Trans. Rob. **36**(1), 107–124 (2019)
37. Zhou, Z., Ding, J., Huang, H., Takei, R., Tomlin, C.: Efficient path planning algorithms in reach-avoid problems. Automatica **89**, 28–36 (2018)
38. Zhou, Z., Takei, R., Huang, H., Tomlin, C.J.: A general, open-loop formulation for reach-avoid games. In: IEEE Conference on Decision and Control (CDC), pp. 6501–6506 (2012)
39. Zhou, Z., Zhang, W., Ding, J., Huang, H., Stipanović, D.M., Tomlin, C.J.: Cooperative pursuit with Voronoi partitions. Automatica **72**, 64–72 (2016)

Hardware Security and Trust: A New Battlefield of Information

Gang Qu[✉]

University of Maryland, College Park, MD 20742, USA
gangqu@umd.edu

Abstract. Hardware security and trust has received a lot of attention in the past 25 years. The purpose of this paper is to introduce the fundamental problems related to hardware security and trust to audiences who do not necessarily have hardware design background. In order to do that, we first discuss the evolving roles of hardware in security from an *enable* to an *enhancer* and now an *enforcer* as it get involves more and more in system security. Then we review the following key problems in hardware security, physical attacks, side channel analysis, intellectual property protection, hardware Trojan, hardware security primitives, and applications in security and trust. We provide a novel view of these problems and the corresponding solutions from the perspective of information battle between the attackers and designers, where we consider three types of information: data collected, processed, and stored by the hardware; information hidden in the design as watermark, fingerprint, and Trojans; and the chip fabrication variations that can be extracted and utilized. It is interesting to see how the hardware security and trust problems can be unified under this framework of information battle (stealing and protection). Unfortunately, there are more unknowns and challenges than what we have discovered on this framework as we illustrated in the section of open problems. However, the emerging Internet of Things and cyber physical systems have provided a large application field for researchers and practitioners to work on hardware based lightweight security.

Keywords: Hardware security · Trusted IC · Intellectual property protection · Reverse engineering · Side channel analysis · Physical unclonable function · Hardware trojan · Logic obfuscation · Hardware security primitives · Information hiding · Lightweight authentication

1 Introduction

The year of 1996 saw two important events in what we now know as hardware security and trust. First, timing attack was reported as a computationally inexpensive method to break cryptosystems including Diffie-Hellman, RSA, and DSS [1]. This leads to the discovery of various side channel analysis (SCA) attacks, which take advantage of system's different execution time, power consumption, electromagnetic emission or other physically measureable characteristics while running same operations with different values (such as bit '0' and bit '1') to reveal the cryptographic keys. Second, the Virtual

© Springer Nature Switzerland AG 2020
Q. Zhu et al. (Eds.): GameSec 2020, LNCS 12513, pp. 486–501, 2020.
https://doi.org/10.1007/978-3-030-64793-3_27

Socket Interface Alliance (VSIA) was founded to enhance semiconductor industry's design productivity by establishing standards for the adoption of intellectual property (IP). The alliance attracted more than 200 companies worldwide and was dissolved in 2008 after accomplishing it mission. VSIA identified six challenges and built development and working groups (DWG) for each of them in 1997. IP protection was one of the most technically challenging with the goals to 1) enable IP providers to protect their IPs against unauthorized use, 2) protect all types of design data used to produce and deliver IPs, 3) detect use of IPs, and 4) trace use of IPs [2]. Most reported research efforts were on side channel attacks and IP protection for about a decade before several other important discoveries in hardware security and trust.

The problems of trusted integrated circuit (IC) design and hardware Trojan detection were proposed around 2005 and 2007, respectively. One of the most notable efforts on these problems is a sequence of DARPA programs: trusted integrated circuits (TRUST), integrity and reliability of integrated circuits (IRIS), supply chain hardware integrity for electronics defense (SHIELD), and Automatic Implementation of Secure SoCs (AISS). Trusted IC was defined as *doing exactly what it is asked, no more and no less* [3] and was recommended to be re-defined more precisely as "*no less and no malicious more*" [4]. One way to make ICs untrusted is to embed hardware Trojans (HT), which is a piece of circuit that is added to the design or modified from the original design for malicious purposes. HT was first reported in [5]. Also in 2007, silicon physical unclonable function (PUF) got a great deal of attention. PUF is a device or sub-circuit embedded on chip to capture the fabrication variations in the forms of path delay, device voltage transfer, or other characteristics. Such variations exist in the silicon manufacturing process and are considered to be unpredictable and uncontrollable. PUF can generate and store secret that can be used as keys or seeds to generate random numbers; and create challenge-response pairs that can be used for chip authentications [6].

These are just a few key topics in the emerging field of hardware security and trust. In 1999, the Cryptographic Hardware and Embedded Systems (CHES) conference was founded "for research on both design and analysis of cryptographic hardware and software implementations". In 2008, the International Symposium on Hardware Oriented Security and Trust (HOST) was established "for researchers and practitioners to advance knowledge and technologies related to hardware security and assurance". Nowadays, all the major conferences on hardware, architecture, and system design cover the topics of hardware security and trust, which is also listed in the leading security conferences. For instance, Crypto solicits submissions on "secure implementation and optimization in hardware". USENIX Security has an area of "hardware security" with topics on secure computer architecture, embedded system security, malicious and counterfeit hardware detection, and side channels.

In this paper, we will discuss the evolving role of hardware in security and cybersecurity in Sect. 2. We will introduce the key problems in hardware security and trust and the state-of-the-art approaches in Sects. 3. The synergy of these problems and solutions will be analyzed in Sect. 4. Unlike a comprehensive survey for hardware engineers, we will provide the researchers with little hardware design background the perspectives of information battle between the attackers and defenders. We discuss the open problems in hardware security and conclude the paper in Sect. 5.

2 The Role of Hardware in Cybersecurity

In 2009, I was invited to give a talk to a group of audience who are not computer engineers about hardware's role in security and trustworthy computing. I used the terms *enabler, enhancer*, and *enforcer* to describe this evolving role and I also questioned whether hardware has become the weakest link in security and trust.

Security starts with cryptography which is built on sound mathematics foundations and implemented either in software or hardware. But ultimately it is the computer hardware that enables us to realize all the security protocols. Consider the extremely high computational complexity of the modern cryptography schemes, it is impossible for human to do the computation manually without the help of computing devices. For example, in the modular exponentiation operation which computes $a^e (mod n)$, all the values are huge number with the exponent e suggested to be 1024-bit or longer. In such cases, hardware is absolutely needed as an enabler.

It is well known that many applications, security related or not, have better performance when implemented in hardware comparing to their software based implementation. Dedicated hardware, sometimes called accelerators, are built for the purpose of performance enhancement. Ironically, hardware is also used to break the security protocols (e.g. through brute-force attacks). Indeed, it was the increasing computation power that made data encryption standards (DES) unsecure and motivated the establishment of the advanced encryption standard (AES). In 2001, Rijndael ciphers was selected from many AES candidates in part because of its efficiency and implementation details [7].

Then computer hardware becomes more actively involved in security and trustworthy computing. The first line of defense is built in hardware to protect the CPU, memory and data. For example, a biometric coprocessor checks user's biological features such as fingerprint, iris, and pulse to authenticate the user before giving user the permission to access the computer or the network. Another example is the trusted platform module (TPM) chips that are embedded to all the laptops and smart phones. A TPM chip helps system to manage all the security and trusted computing functions.

However, the high involvement of hardware in security also introduces the new attacking surface in hardware implementation of the cryptographic systems. Hardware engineers are traditionally trained to optimize performance and security is not considered when hardware is designed and built. This gives attackers another target, in particular when there is no flaw in the crypto algorithms, software vulnerabilities have been patched, and network communication becomes secure. The side channel attack we mentioned earlier is one example. More security and trust vulnerabilities in hardware will be discussed later, which prompts me to ask the question whether hardware is the weakest link (after human) in cybersecurity (Fig. 1).

From the information standpoint, an enabler is a passive information processor; an enhancer is a dedicated processor for specific information process; and an enhancer is one that collects information, processes information, and makes decisions (such as authentication and access control) accordingly. Information may leak during the process on hardware, causing security vulnerabilities that we will elaborate next.

Fig. 1. A slide that illustrates the role of hardware in security and trust (2011).

3 Key Problems in Hardware Security and Trust

In this section, we review the key research problems and practices in hardware security and trust. We will also discuss the existing countermeasures. More detailed and conclusive list of topics can be found in the call for papers of the recent conferences focusing on hardware security in the Appendix.

3.1 Physical Attacks

As the name suggests, physical attacks refer to the attacks where an attacker has physical access to a system or is within its proximity to collet certain physical information. The goal of physical attacks is to break or "learn" the system without authorization. Unlike cryptanalysis which uses mathematical analysis on the cryptographic algorithms to find flaws, physical attacks attempt to exploit the vulnerabilities in the implementation of the system. Based on whether the target system will be damaged during and after the attack, physical attacks can be classified in three groups: invasive attacks where the attacker "breaks" the system physically to learn, the system will be damaged and there will be tampering evidence left; non-invasive attacks where the attacker learns by "using" the system without causing any damage or leaving any trace of tampering; and semi-invasive attacks where the attacker needs to access the surface of the system without "breaking" or "damaging" it, there will be no or very little tamper evidence.

In hardware, invasive physical attacks are also known as reverse engineering where an attacker will depackage the chip or device to expose the silicon die to learn the inner structure and the functionality of the chip. For modern multi-layer chips, the attacker will remove layer by layer to study features in each layer. Reverse engineering is legal and very common in industry as companies use it to learn from their competitors and legacy systems where the detailed design information is unavailable. There are commercial advanced reverse engineering tools available, which makes reverse engineering based attacks possible. Reverse engineering will cause damage to the chip or device and thus cannot be repeated on the same device. More about reverse engineering and the countermeasures will be discussed in the section of design IP protection.

Common non-invasive attacks include side channel analysis (which we will elaborate in details in the next subsection), fault based attacks, data remanence, and brute force. The idea of fault based attacks is to put the system into abnormal and unexpected execution state in the hope that such states are not well protected by design. This can be achieved by injecting faulty data or unexpected instructions, or changing the execution environment such as lowing the voltage. Data remanence are attacks on the data stored in the SRAM, EEPROM, or flash memory. Because of certain physical features of these memory, data stored for a long time may leave some trace even after it is removed or powered down, protected data may also become readable at extreme environment such as low temperature or frequently changed voltage. When the search space is not sufficiently huge, brute force search for the cryptographic keys or backdoor access to a system becomes possible with the help of today's powerful computers.

Semi-invasive attacks to hardware normally require depackaging the chip but will not need the reverse engineering steps to learn and will not make physical contacts with the internal wires. This normally helps to launch more powerful attacks such as fault injection or side channel analysis because now the silicon die is decapsulated and exposed to the attackers.

3.2 Side Channel Analysis

An attacker can observe a system's physical characteristics from side channels during execution and uses such characteristics to reveal the system's secret information such as the cryptographic keys. These physical features can be power, current, timing or delay, electromagnetic emission, acoustic and optical information, and even the system's output values. Side channel analysis (SCA) attacks have two phases: measuring and data analysis. During the first phase, the attacker will monitor the system's execution and collect the physical features of interest. Then, the attacker will perform data analysis on the collected side channel information to determine the on-chip secret information.

SCA attacks are perhaps the most successful attacks to modern cryptographic systems for two main reasons. First, they target the weakness of the implementation of the crypto algorithms, not the algorithms themselves. Therefore, a mathematically sound algorithm can become vulnerable against SCA attacks. Second, these attacks are non-invasive, passive, and will not leave any trace of attack. They use the signals leaked from side channels during system's normal execution and thus it will be hard to detect and catch such attacks.

SCA attacks rely on the fact that the execution of the same operations with different input values will generate different trace on the side channels. For example, in the popular square and multiply implementation of modular exponentiation, the computation will be performed iteratively on each of the key bit with the multiplication being carried out only when the key bit is '1'. This will create asymmetric information in terms of the execution time and power consumption for different key bit values, enabling the timing and power analysis attacks.

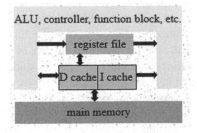

Fig. 2. Side channels in a simplified microprocessor.

Figure 2 illustrates a simplified architecture of a standard microprocessor or a computing device. It has its memory hierarchy of the main memory, data cache, instruction cache, and register files. This is the central processing unit, or CPU, with control logics, function blocks, and the arithmetic and logic unit (ALU). In a typical flow of the execution of a software or program, instructions and data will be loaded from the main memory to I-cache and D-cache. The registers are the closest storage to the CPU and thus have the fastest access time. The CPU will take instructions and data from these memory units and process them accordingly. The result will be written back to the memory, either cache or the main memory.

Now assume that we store some secret data in the registers during the execution and revisit the typical execution blow to identify the side channel vulnerabilities. First, memory load operation will get data from D cache to the register file. This needs the memory address of the data. If the address is determined by or related to the secret data, the secret might leak from the memory address. When the secret data is overwritten by the data from the memory, there will also be information leak. For example, when the register file is reset to be all 0s, it requires power to overwrite all the 1s, but there is almost zero power consumption on the bit that was previously 0. Similarly, when a memory store operation is performance, information might leak from either the memory address or the data to be written to the memory. During arithmetic and logic operations, particularly when the operation is performed at bit-level, the secret data may be exposed through side channel. For example, the execution of a multiplication with two random large numbers and the same multiplication with one operand equal to one will have quite different behaviors that can be observed through power or timing side channels. Finally, data might leak from the control flow of the execution as we have seen from the example of modular exponentiation where whether the multiplication is executed will depend on the key bit values.

Common countermeasures to SCA attacks either try to hide side channel information or remove its dependency on the secret data. Crypto algorithms can be modified, typically by randomization, to remove the correlation between the cryptographic key values and the side channel information generated while running the crypto algorithm using the key. Second, physical security can be used to keep the attackers away from the proximity, access, and possession of the system under attack. For example, acoustic shielding can protect acoustic emission and the secure construction zoning is common to prevent potential EM emission attacks. Third, design partitioning, in particular the emerging 2.5D and 3D fabrication and split manufacturing, can help to mitigate SCA attacks. Separating on-chip infrastructures such as power supply rails, clock networks, and testing facilities from crypto operations and other applications will make it more challenging for side channel information collection. Masking and blinding is another approach to remove the correlation between the secret data and the side channel signals. For instance, XORing the output of a logic unit with some pre-selected data will mask the real output, which can be retrieved only when the pre-selected data is known. Finally, hiding is the most common methods to increase the difficulty for the SCA attackers to gather side channel data. This can be achieved by careful design that will leak identical information on different key values, by using asynchronous logic, or by generating random noise.

3.3 Intellectual Property Protection

Design intellectual properties (IP) are the components or units that can be considered as stand-alone for being reused or integrated into a larger design with efforts much lower than redesigning the component. IPs are the most valuable for the company who designs, manufactures, and owns them. However, an adversary can steal or misuse IPs by forging, tampering, counterfeiting, overbuilding, and so on. Most of these IP infringements require reserve engineering to some extent.

The VISA has identified three major IP protection methods: **Deterrent** methods enable an IP owner to deter the infringer from contemplating IP theft by using proper legal means including patents, copyrights, contracts, trademarks, and trade secrets. **Protection** mechanisms use means such as encryption, licensing agreements, obfuscation, dedicated hardware, or chemicals to prevent unauthorized access to the IP. **Detection** approaches such as digital watermarking, fingerprinting, and metering, help the IP owners to detect and trace both legal and illegal use of their IPs.

Most protection mechanisms are mature and could be effective, but they incur additional design cost such as the computational expensive encryption/decryption, the integration and packaging of chemicals and dedicated hardware ware. Deterrent methods do not directly prevent IP piracy from happening, but rather discourage the misuse of IPs because the attackers, once being caught, may face lawsuits and severe penalty to recover the financial loss of the IP owner. However, all of the aforementioned means except trade secrets are affirmative rights, which means that it is the IP owner's responsibility to identify IP infringement and catch the IP infringer. Therefore, majority of efforts in IP protection in the past couple of decades are on the detection approaches.

Digital watermarking embeds IP owner's signature into the IP during its design, integration, and testing phases. The watermark, if needed, can be retrieved from the IP to prove the authorship. Digital fingerprinting incorporates IP buyer's unique information into the IP in order to identify the traitor should any IP infringement happens. Metering is a means to create/insert tags into each copy of the IP or chip, making them unique to facilitate the trace chip. Recently developed IP protection methods have made the distinction between protection and detection approached vague. For example, active metering and logic locking techniques are protection mechanisms that provide chip owners post-fabrication control of the fabricated chips (because they can disable the normal usage of the chip). Meanwhile, circuit obfuscation method intentionally introduces ambiguity to chip design to confuse reverse engineering attackers and should be considered as detection approach. Split manufacturing and 3D integration technologies also facilitate IP protection by giving designers the option of fabricating chips in multiple foundries and serve both the purposes of protection and detection.

3.4 Hardware Trojan

A hardware Trojan is any modification or addition to a circuit for malicious purpose. Common malicious goals of hardware Trojan include leaking sensitive information, changing or controlling the functionality of the circuit, and reducing circuit reliability. Based on different criteria, hardware Trojans can be categorized in many different ways. We list a few below as we discuss more features of hardware Trojan.

First, hardware Trojans can be as small as only a few logic gates (e.g. malicious on-chip sensors and the killer switch) and can be as large as a functional block such as a powerful antenna which is capable of sending out sensitive information. An external disable/enable signal combined with a simple 2-input logic AND gate can be used to control any functional units (e.g. the encryption engine) on the chip.

These small and large hardware Trojans can be inserted almost all over the system. Trojans in the on-chip clock (or power) network can change system's clock frequency (or operating voltage) to launch fault attacks or timing (or power) side channel information leaking. Trojans in the system's memory structure can maliciously change data or leak information. Trojans in the CPU or functional units can create faulty output or disable the functional units. Trojans in the input-output periphery can facilitate fault injection attacks or provide misleading results.

Hardware Trojans normally are triggered by specific signals or events that are rare to occur under normal execution mode (in order to minimize the chance of being detected or accidentally activated). These triggers can be from inside the chip such as whether the counter has reached a specific value (time bomb) or certain on-chip temperature has been sensed by the temperature sensor. They can also be controlled externally by triggers hidden behind user input or environmental conditions.

Hardware Trojans can be embedded during any untrusted phase in the chip design, fabrication, and testing process, or any stage of the IC supply chain. This makes hardware Trojan detection and prevention a very challenging task. It is important to mention that the goal of hardware Trojan detection is determine whether a chip or system contains any hardware Trojan. If a Trojan is found, we can conclude that the chip or system cannot be trusted. But unfortunately, one can never claim a chip is Trojan free because a system's functionality can never be completely specified and thus there are always unspecified functionality being implemented in the chip [10].

Hardware Trojan detection can be done at chip test time followed by run-time monitoring. At test time, one can use logic test-based approaches to run different input and verify the corresponding output generated by the chip while monitoring chip's execution behavior. Since we have mentioned earlier that Trojans are triggered by rare signals or events, such logic test detection methods could fail. Monitoring side channels during the test can help to capture some Trojans but it may have high false alarm rate due to measurement errors, noise, and hardware fabrication variations. Such SCA based monitoring should be kept during the normal execution of the chip because test time detection methods can never discover all the Trojans.

3.5 Hardware Security Primitives

It is well know that chips, even identical designed and fabricated with the same mask on the same wafer, exhibit the intrinsic manufacturing variations from the complicated semiconductor fabrication process. Such variations are believed to be random and cause the unpredictable chip performance. However, it is extremely difficult, if not impossible, to model or control the manufacturing variations as the semiconductor industry has failed to do so in the past half century. The concept of physical unclonable function (PUF) takes advantage of the randomness, unclonability, and uncontrollability of such intrinsic variations to deliver security primitives. The most popular applications of PUF are to create and store cryptographic keys, to facilitate random number generation, and to generate challenge-response pairs for authentication.

Figure 3 shows the basic ring oscillator (RO) PUF structure. As we can see, N identical ROs are implemented but the fabrication variations will make them have different delays. The two multiplexers (MUX) will select two ROs and compare their delay through the readings of the two counters. For example, one can define a bit '0' is the RO on the top is faster and a bit '1' if the one at the bottom is faster. There are numerous reports on how to create PUF bits, make them robust against operation environments, optimize the amount of bits generated from a given hardware resource, and how to use PUF for security applications.

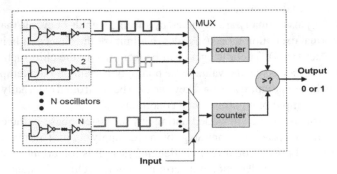

Fig. 3. The architecture of ring oscillator PUF [6].

3.6 Applications in Security and Trust

There are many research efforts to connect circuit level hardware security with lower level such as memory and new materials (resistive RAM, phase change memory, Spin-transfer torque magnetic RAM, etc.), and with upper level at architecture, software, communication and physical layer. We give two examples on how hardware can help security at system or device level.

As hardware is the root of all systems ranging from the sensors, smart portable devices, and medical implants to vehicle components, smart home appliances, smart grid, cloud computing servers, and the general Internet of Things (IoT) and cyber physical systems (CPS), it is not surprising to see that they are used not only to implement system security protocols, but also contribute to improve system security. This is particularly true for the recent IoT and CPS applications where the devices may be resource constrained and cannot afford to the computational and resource expensive cryptographic solutions. For example, many hardware based lightweight authentication schemes have been proposed to authenticate device, user, and computation.

Figure 4 shows how silicon PUF can be used to enhance the entropy of a random variable [8]. The bell-look curve at the bottom is the Shannon entropy when a random input bit is generated with a given percentage of 1's. For example, in the middle when there are 50% 1's and 50% 0's, perfect entropy is reached. But on both ends when there are very few 1's or a lot of 1's, the entropy will be very low. With the assist of RO PUF, we can see that the entropy is improved significantly. The top curve is the case when PUF is combined with XOR. This indicates a cost effective way to convert data from a poor entropy source to high entropy bit-stream.

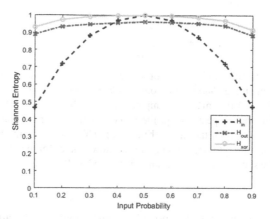

Fig. 4. Bit entropy enhanced by silicon PUF [8].

As another example, Fig. 5 shows how the benchmark images "snowflakes" and "trees" can be superimposed to generate the image of "snowfall", where each pixel value of the "snowfall" is obtained by adding the pixel values of "snowflakes" and "trees" at the same pixel position [9]. We design an adder in hardware to perform this operation. When the same adder design is implemented on two different FPGA boards, we reduce the operating voltage for both FPGA to force addition errors as shown in Fig. 6. Clearly we can see the visual difference between these erroneous images and the original one. More importantly, different adders create different errors, making it possible to use such fabrication variation induced errors for device authentication [9].

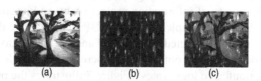

Fig. 5. Creation of "snowfall" (c) by superimposing "snowflakes" (b) on top of "trees" (a) [9].

4 Information Battle Perspective of Hardware Security

We analyze the key problems in hardware security and trust listed in the previous section from the perspective of information.

Consider the role that hardware plays as an enabler and an enhancer, it may process and store sensitive information of the attacker's interest. Through different types of

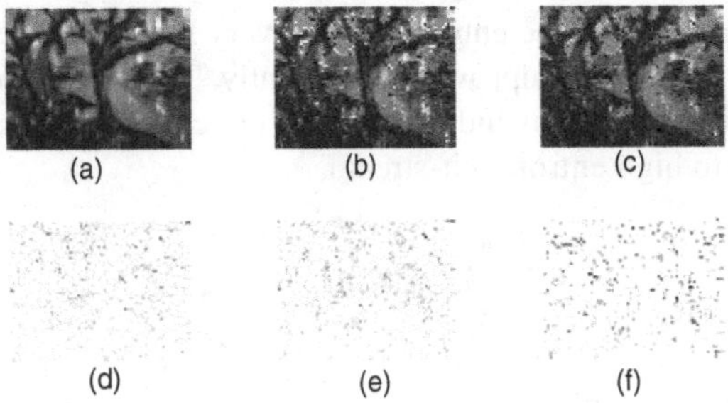

Fig. 6. An example of the effect of fabrication variations in voltage over-scaling based computation. In (a) the gray scale image *Snowfall* is computed using *trees* and *snowflakes* without voltage over-scaling; in (b) and (c) the image is computed under voltage over-scaling with two adders which are identical in every aspect, except the process variation of the transistors; (d) and (e) shows the error pattern found in the figure (b) and (c). This error pattern shows the deviations for each adder from the correct image. Subfigure (f) shows the difference between the two error pattern (d) and (e). The source images were downsized to 52×40 pixels for reducing computation time.

attacks that include physical attacks and side channel analysis, the attacker attempts to obtain the desired information directly or indirectly. For example, invasive attack to a smartcard can reveal the contents stored in the memory, analyzing timing or power side channel information can help the attacker to reveal the cryptographic key used in the crypto algorithm. Consequently, all the countermeasures against such attacks try to hide the sensitive information, to disable the attacker's access to side channels, or to remove the correlation between the sensitive information and the side channel information.

For design IP protection, the design and implementation details are the value of the IP and take the forms of hardware device, IP cores, gate layout, FPGA configurable bit streams, Verilog code, optimization algorithms, and so on. Reverse engineering is one vehicle for the attackers to retrieve these information from a IP product. IP protection methods either protect such information, making them inaccessible, or embed more information into the IP as watermark, fingerprint, and tags for detection purpose. So here we see a new dimension of information protection by adding more proof-carrying information into the design and implementation of IPs. This can be done as encryption (where the information to be protected is encrypted and the encryption key becomes the vital information for decryption) or obfuscation (where the original design information is hidden behind the camouflaged logic gates). Figure 7 illustrates the basic idea of digital watermarking as a steganography system [11]. Digital fingerprint and metering tags can be embedded in the same way.

Unlike watermarking multimedia contents, adding digital watermark into hardware IP has a fundamentally different challenge: the contents of the multimedia artifacts can change as long as the end consumer, which is human, cannot tell or can tolerate the difference between the original and the watermarked copy. However, for hardware IP, changes to the design and implementation of the IP are normally unacceptable because they may cause malfunctions. As depicted in Fig. 6, we view the creation of IP as solving a constraint optimization problem, where system's specifications and design requirements are

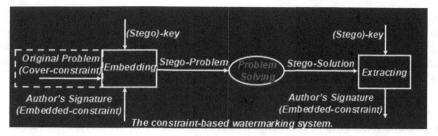

Fig. 7. Digital watermarking for IP protection as a steganography system [11].

considered to be the original constraints. We convert IP author's signature into constraints that will not cause any conflicts or violation to the original constraints. The proposed digital watermarking system is a steganography system where the original constraints serve as the cover-constraint and the author's signature is the embedded-constraint. The stego-problem to solve is both sets of constraints. Now we solve this stego-problem, that is, design and implement the IP to satisfy both the original and the embedded constraints. The solution, or the developed IP, will have the property to meet not only the original constraints, but also a set of seemingly random constraints that we embedded as watermark, or the proof of author's signature. It is crucial to extract the watermarking information from the stego-solution.

Interestingly, hardware Trojan also can be considered as information embedded into the system, but for malicious purposes. Trojan detection becomes the process of finding such hidden information and evidently attacker's physical attack and SCA methods has be utilized.

The intrinsic fabrication variation information carried by the chip is another type of interesting information. PUF is the circuitry that collects such information and converts it to data that can be used for security such as cryptographic keys. As we have discussed earlier, one of the biggest challenge in PUF is its usability as most of the fabrication variations are very sensitive to the chip's operating environment including power, voltage, and temperature. If we consider PUF as the noise introduced during the manufacturing process, PUF information's sensitivity to environmental factors is the "measurement" error/noise when the PUF circuitry collects the fabrication variation. When PUF is used in the system, various security concerns, such as how to steal PUF information or forge the challenge-response pair, share the same core of how to protect the PUF information from unauthorized access or usage. This brings us back to the start of this section where we discussed securing data and data processing against attacks.

5 Open Problems and Conclusions

Security becomes one vital concern for almost all systems. Hardware, as the player to collect, process, store, and transmit information, not only causes various security vulnerabilities, largely due to the lack of consideration of security and trust in hardware design flow, but can also makes the system more security at lower cost. So the first and most important challenge for hardware security is how to convince the users that *the hardware system is secure and trusted*. For example, when a sensor collects data and sends the sensor readings to the network, how to check whether the right and accurate data is collected? Are the sensor's data calibration and other pre-processing schemes executed in a secure and trusted execution environment? Is the data storage secure and uncompromised? Does the sensor have any Trojan or side channel that might leak the data?

Secondly, *how to utilize hardware to build and enhance system security and trust?* We already know hardware security primitives have this potential with the advantage of low cost and sometimes better security (e.g. unclonability of the fabrication variations and requirement of the physical presence of or close proximity to the hardware). Such hardware based lightweight schemes are good for applications such as authentication when the security level is low. How to establish a formal foundation for the hardware base lightweight security protocols? This seems to be a very challenging task as the semiconductor industry still does not have any accurate models for various fabrication variations and it will be impossible to conduct any quantitative study on the security protocols built on such variations. For example, the randomness and unclonability of variations are just the general belief without any proof or validation. Nevertheless, finding new security applications based on hardware is still of great interest.

Finally, from the perspective of hardware designer, *IP protection is still an important yet open problem.* As one of the earliest challenges from the industry, IP protection is a real problem and still has not received the attention it deserves. In part, this is due to the complexity of IP validation and integration as well as other challenges for IP reuse. Before IP reuse becomes a common design practice, we cannot see the true value of IPs and how serve IP infringement could be. Fortunately, the incidents of tampering, reverse engineering based IP stealing, and counterfeiting reported in the recent years have raised the global awareness of IP protection. The existing IP protection techniques are not adequate. For example, two the most well-studied active IP protection methods, logic locking and circuit obfuscation are vulnerable to SAT-based attacks. Digital watermarking and fingerprinting methods are relatively mature and there is the ongoing efforts to integrate them into the hardware design flow. However, the impact to the system performance caused by embedding watermark and fingerprint is still unknown.

Acknowledgement. This work is supported in part by the DARPA project entitled "INDEPENDENT VERIFICATION & VALIDATION (IV&V) OF THE AISS PROGRAM".

Appendix

CHES 2021 list of topics in the call for paper (https://ches.iacr.org/2021/callforpapers.php)

Cryptographic implementations:

- Hardware architectures
- Cryptographic processors and co-processors
- True and pseudorandom number generators
- Physical unclonable functions (PUFs)
- Efficient software implementations

Attacks against implementations, and countermeasures:

- Side-channel attacks and countermeasures
- Micro-architectural side-channel attacks
- Fault attacks and countermeasures
- Hardware tampering and tamper-resistance
- White-box cryptography and code obfuscation
- Hardware and software reverse engineering

Tools and methodologies:

- Computer-aided cryptographic engineering
- High-assurance crypto
- Verification methods and tools for secure design
- Domain-specific languages for cryptographic systems
- Metrics for the security of embedded systems
- Secure programming techniques
- FPGA design security

Interactions between cryptographic theory and implementation issues:

- New and emerging cryptographic algorithms and protocols targeting embedded devices
- Special-purpose hardware for cryptanalysis
- Leakage resilient cryptography

Applications:

- Cryptography and security for the Internet of Things (RFID, sensor networks, smart devices, smart meters, etc.)
- Hardware IP protection and anti-counterfeiting
- Reconfigurable hardware for cryptography
- Smartcard processors, systems and applications
- Security for cyberphysical systems (home automation, medical implants, industrial--control systems, etc.)
- Automotive security
- Secure storage devices (memories, disks, etc.)
- Technologies and hardware for content protection
- Trusted computing platforms

HOST 2021 list of topics in the call for paper (http://www.hostsymposium.org/call-for-paper.php).

Hardware

- Security primitives
- Computer-aided design (CAD) tools
- Emerging and nanoscale devices
- Trojans and backdoors
- Side-channel attacks and mitigation
- Fault injection and mitigation
- (Anti-)Reverse engineering and physical attacks
- Anti-tamper
- Anti-counterfeit
- Hardware Obfuscation

Architecture

- Trusted execution environments
- Cache-side channel attacks and mitigation
- Privacy-preserving computation
- System-on-chip (SoC)/platform security
- FPGA and reconfigurable fabric security
- Cloud computing
- Smart phones and smart devices

System

- Internet-of-things (IoT) security
- Sensors and sensor network security
- Smart grid security
- Automotive/autonomous vehicle security
- Cyber-physical system security
- (Adversarial) Machine learning and cyber deception
- Security and trust for future pandemics
- Blockchain and cryptocurrencies

AsianHOST 2020 list of topics in the call for paper (http://asianhost.org/2020/authors.htm#cfp)

- Hardware-intrinsic security primitives (e.g., PUF and TRNG)
- Architectural and microarchitectural attacks and defenses
- Secure system-on-chip (SoC) architecture
- Trusted platform modules and hardware virtualization
- Side-channel attacks and countermeasures
- Hardware Trojan attacks and detection techniques
- Security analysis and protection of Internet of Things (IoT)
- Hardware IP core protection and trust for consumer electronics systems and IoT
- Security and trust of machine learning and artificial intelligence
- Automobile, self-drive and autonomous vehicle security
- 5G and physical layer security
- Hardware-assisted cross-layer security
- Cyber-physical system (CPS) security and resilience
- Metrics, policies, and standards related to hardware security
- Security verification at IP, IC, and system levels
- Reverse engineering and hardware obfuscation
- Supply chain risks mitigation including counterfeit detection & avoidance
- Trusted manufacturing including split manufacturing, 2.5D, and 3D ICs
- Emerging nanoscale technologies in hardware security applications

References

1. Kocher, P.: Timing attacks on implementations of Diffie-Hellman, RSA, DSS, and other systems. In: Crypto 1996, pp. 104–113 (1996)
2. Virtual Socket Interface Alliance: Intellectual Property Protection White Paper: Schemes, Alternatives and Discussion, Version 1.1, January 2001
3. Report of the Defense Science Board Task Force on High Performance Microchip Supply, February 2005
4. Qu, G., Yuan, L.: Design THINGS for the internet of things – an EDA perspective. In: Proceedings of IEEE/ACM International Conference on Computer-Aided Design, pp. 411–416, November 2014
5. Agrawal, D., Baktir, S., Karakoyunlu, D., Rohatgi, P., Sunar, B.: Trojan Detection using IC Fingerprint. In: IEEE Symposium on Security and Privacy, pp. 296–310, May 2007
6. Suh, G.E., Devadas, S.: Physical unclonable functions for device authentication and secret key generation. In: Proceedings of 44th ACM/IEEE Design Automation Conference, pp. 9–14, June 2007
7. United States National Institute of Standards and Technology (NIST): Announcing the ADVANCED ENCRYPTION STANDARD (AES), Federal Information Processing Standards Publication 197, 26 November 2001
8. Wang, Q., Qu, G.: A silicon PUF based entropy pump. IEEE Trans. Dependable Secure Comput. **16**(3), 402–414 (2018)
9. Arafin, M., Gao, M., Qu, G.: VOLtA: voltage over-scaling based lightweight authentication for IoT applications. In: Proceedings of 22nd Asia and South Pacific Design Automation Conference (ASP-DAC), pp. 336–341, January 2017
10. Gu, J., Qu, G., Zho, Q.: Information hiding for trusted system design. In: Proceedings of the 46th ACM/IEEE Design Automation Conference, pp. 698–701, June 2009
11. Qu, G., Potkonjak, M.: Intellectual Property Protection in VLSI Design: Theory and Practice. Springer Science and Business Media, Berlin, May 2007. https://orcid.org/10.1007/b105846

Security Games with Insider Threats

Derya Cansever[✉]

Army Research Office, Durham, NC 27703, USA
derya.h.cansever.civ@mail.mil

Abstract. Many cyber-security defense strategies rely on the information asymmetry between the defender and the attacker. Examples of information asymmetry include passwords and network configuration parameters. Using private information, defenders can drastically increase the computation complexity of the attacker and render his/her attacks inefficient. Availability of insider information can alter the equilibrium and favor the attacker. This paper discusses some of the attributes of private information and describes a three-player game with a partially collaborating insider to illustrate its impact.

Keywords: Insider threat · Stackelberg games · Cyber security

1 Introduction

Protection of infrastructure and information technology systems from advanced and ever more sophisticated cyber-attacks is a major concern. These attacks, often called Advanced Persistent Threat (APT), are launched by well-funded entities and are persistent in pursuing their objectives. Moreover, they often act in a stealthy way to avoid being detected to maximize the long-term payoffs. In fact, it is well documented that cyber-attacks can remain undetected for months or even longer. APT attacks cause staggering amounts of costs to nation states as well as to corporations. Advances in technologies can in principle benefit both sides. However, attackers seem to remain one step ahead in many cases.

A main attribute of the conflict between APT, termed the Attacker, and the defending entity, termed the Defender, is the asymmetry in their respective information structures. The defender does not know when and where the attack will occur. Even with advanced network monitoring systems, attacks may occur without the defender's knowledge. The Defender has an advantage in the asymmetry of information on the actual architecture, configuration attributes and parameters of the system to be defended. This advantage can provide definitive advantage to the defender. However, if an entity in the Defender's organization is compromised and discloses some of the private information for personal gain, this potential advantage can turn into significant vulnerability. In fact, it is reported that [1] in 2018, 44% of data breaches are attributable to insiders. We discuss private information and insider threats in Sect. 2. In Sect. 3, we describe a three-player game with a compromised insider. Potential open research areas are discussed in Sect. 4.

Q. Zhu et al. (Eds.): GameSec 2020, LNCS 12513, pp. 502–505, 2020.
https://doi.org/10.1007/978-3-030-64793-3_28

2 Private Information

Information asymmetry is a foundational aspect of cyber defense. Defenders use private information to make it more difficult for the Attacker to accomplish his/her goal. Examples of information asymmetry include encryption and Moving Target Defense (MTD) [2]. In symmetric encryption, lack of knowledge of the key by the Attacker makes it extremely difficult for the attacker to decrypt the text of interest. Similarly, lack of the knowledge of the pattern, or the algorithm, that governs the change in configuration parameters makes it very difficult for the Attacker to accomplish his/her goals.

The conflict between the Attacker and the Defender can be modeled as a game where each player pursues conflicting interests. If we neglect for a moment the penalties on their respective controls, the conflict can be approximated by a zero-sum game. For example, the Attacker may be trying to maximize the probability of breaching the IT system, while the Defender is attempting to minimize that probability. Let X denote the state of the system, Y_A denote the information of the Attacker, and Y_D denote the information of the Defender, α_A the strategy of the Attacker and l_D denote the strategy of the defender, and $P(.)$ the probability of breach. Assume that $P(.)$ is strictly concave in the actions of the Attacker and the Defender. The Defender is trying to minimize

$E\{P(X, \alpha_A, l_D| Y_D\}$, while the attacker is trying to maximize

$E\{E\{P(X, \alpha_A, l_D| Y_D\}| Y_A\}$. Assuming that the probability space of Y_A is coarser than the one of Y_D, $E\{P(X, \alpha_A, l_D| Y_D\}$ is a random variable from the point of view of the Attacker. Let us call it φ. Let us assume that Y_D has finite support. Then, for each realization of the random variable φ, the Attacker faces a different optimization problem. The Attacker will maximize the conditional expectation of φ given Y_A. Let $P*$ denote the actual outcome of this game for a given realization of φ, and P^0 denote the expected outcome of the game relative to the Attacker. Assume that $P(.)$ is a monotonous function of Y_D and it is strictly concave in α_A, l_D for each value of φ. Then, $P*$ will be smaller than P^0 unless the Attacker has access to the actual realization of φ. The defender wants to make the absolute value of the difference between $P*$ and P^0 for each possible realization of φ as large as possible, weighted by its probability of occurrence. One way to accomplish this goal is to maximize the entropy of Y^D. That is, to ensure that Y^D can take values that are wide spread from its mean, and the respective probabilities of such occurrences are not relatively small. Thus, it is in the best interest of the Defender to ensure that the entropy of its private information is maximized. This can be accomplished by choosing a complex and long password, or increasing the rate of the change of configuration parameters in MTD systems. In addition to maximize the difference between the actual and expected values of the payoff function, the Defender will also try to make the solution of this optimization problem as hard as possible to obtain for the Attacker. This can be accomplished by maximizing the Kolmogorov complexity of the optimization problem of the Attacker in computing its solution. But Kolmogorov complexity and entropy are related. In fact, the Kolmogorov complexity of an i.i.d. sequence converges to its entropy [3]. Thus, maximizing the entropy of its private information is advantageous for the defender in several aspects: make it difficult for the Attacker to compute optimal strategy, and also ensure that the expected outcome of optimal strategy of its adversary is relatively mediocre compared with what it could have been if he/she had access to the Defender's private information. The Defender's advantage can be reduced when an agent that functions in the defending team is compromised and is willing to share parts of the Defender's private information with the Attacker for his/her own benefit. We discuss such a setting in the next Section.

3   Stealthy Attacks with Insider Information

Consider a security game obtain control of IT resources. This game is described in detail in [4]. Figure 1 describes the evolution of the game when there is no Insider in play.

Fig. 1. A two players stealthy game. Blue circles and red circles represent defender's and attacker's actions, respectively. A blue segment denotes that the resource is under protection, and a red segment denotes that the resource is compromised. (Color figure online)

This is is a variation of the FlipIt game, [5], where an agent that decides to make a move will have control of the resources. We assume that the defender does not know when the attacker moves, while the Attacker can find out when the Defender made the last move with a random delay ω called the "awareness time". The awareness time represents the period of time it takes for the attacker to find out that the Defender has in fact moved to control the resource. A reasonable strategy for the Defender is to move to control the resource on pints in time that are exponentially distributed to avoid learning by the adversary. The Attacker's corresponding best strategy is to act immediately after ω seconds elapsed. When there is a compromised insider in the defense team, the outcome of the game can change significantly. The insider can help the attacker in reducing the awareness time ω by partially disclosing insider information, and obtain personal benefit by doing so. On the other hand, being a part of the organization, the insider shares its revenue; hence, it may also choose to help the defender against the attacker. In both cases, however, the insider will try to hide its adversary actions from the defender. The insider can inform the Attacker to reduce the awareness time by notifying the Attacker after the Defender's last action (immediately or with a judiciously chosen delay). The sooner it notifies the Attacker, the more it gets paid by the Attacker, but also incurs a higher risk of being detected by the Defender. In this three-person game, the defender first determines and declares its strategy β. After observing β, the insider then decides whether to help the attacker or the defender. In the former case, it makes a "take-it-or-leave-it" offer $\gamma > 0$ to the attacker. In the latter case, it helps the defender by choosing a $\gamma < 0$. Finally, given β and γ, the attacker decides its strategy α. The defender determines the optimal strategy based on the above considerations, which makes the multi-person optimization problem a three level Stackelberg game. Figure 2 below shows the impact of the presence of the insider on the Defender's and Attacker's payoff functions as a function of unit cost C_D for the Defender. With partial disclosure of private information by the insider, the Attacker and the Defender can face significant changes in their respective payoffs, depending on the values of the game parameters.

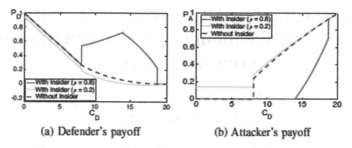

(a) Defender's payoff   (b) Attacker's payoff

Fig. 2. Change in payoff functions under the presence of an insider.

4 Conclusions and Future Research

Increasing the entropy of the externally observable entities that are related to the state of a system appears to be good strategy for the defenders of cyber systems. Such strategies can be implemented as publicly available security policies, or as actions that amount to intentional signaling to malicious entities that are trying to learn from the actions of the defenders. Design of policies that induce uncertainty for the attackers and that also have robustness properties against actions of insiders could pave fruitful research areas. This is in contrast to the problem of reinforcement learning, where the goal is to learn about the system and to control it efficiently. Analysis of the trade-offs among exploring, mis(signaling) and exploiting functions of control policies for multi-agent systems with asymmetric information could amount to challenging and fertile research topics.

References

1. PWC Homepage. https://www.pwc.co.uk/audit-assurance/assets/pdf/insider-threat-for-goo gle.pdf. Accessed 12 Act 2020
2. Fink, R.A., Gunduzhan, E., Benjamin, B.P., Cansever, D., Gralia, M., Dinsmore, P.: IPsec tunnels vs. identity-only obfuscation techniques for moving target networks. In: MILCOM 2012–2012 IEEE Military Communications Conference, Orlando, FL, pp. 1–6 (2012)
3. Cover, T., Thomas, J.: Elements of Information Theory, 2nd edn. Wiley, Hoboken (2006)
4. Feng, X., Zheng, Z., Cansever, D., Swami, A., Mohapatra, P.: Stealthy attacks with insider information: a game theoretic model with asymmetric feedback. In: MILCOM 2016–2016 IEEE Military Communications Conference, Baltimore, MD, pp. 277–282 (2016)
5. van Dijk, M., Juels, A., Oprea, A., Rivest, R.L.: FlipI: the game of Stealthy Takeover. J. Cryptol. **26**(4), 655–713 (2012). https://doi.org/10.1007/s00145-012-9134-5

Securing Next-Generation Wireless Networks: Challenges and Opportunities (Extended Abstract)

Alex Sprintson[✉] [iD]

Texas A&M University, College Station, TX 77843, USA
spalex@tamu.edu

Abstract. This paper focuses on the security issues in next-generation wireless broadband networks. As such networks are expected to play a critical role in modern society, there is an increasing focus on their security and robustness. Such networks are expected to satisfy stringent security requirements and guarantee uninterrupted end-to-end service for diverse applications. The goal of this paper is to discuss long-term challenges in the design of such networks as well as new research opportunities in developing security mechanisms for such networks.

Keywords: Wireless broadband networks · Network security · Network privacy

1 Introduction

Wireless broadband networks have seen continuous development and evolution over the last two decades. Each new generation of cellular technology has brought new capabilities, including increasing data rates, lower latencies, and increased coverage.

It is widely recognized that broadband wireless networks have reached a turning point in their evolution. Next generation cellular networks are expected to connect billions of heterogeneous Internet of Thing (IoT) devices, enable machine-to-machine communications, and support a variety of mission-critical services in multiple application domains, including transportation, public safety, and defense. This is in contrast to today's cellular systems which are designed to support voice and data communications for individual customers. The next-generation networks are expected to have a high degree of reliability and availability, and meet strict requirements on performance and service assurance. The new capabilities are expected to enable exciting new applications such as Augmented Reality/Virtual Reality (AR/VR) and video analytics.

Future wireless broadband networks constitute a complex system that leverages modern technologies, including software-defined networking (SDN) and Network Function Virtualization (NFV). The transition to SDN leads to an emphasis

Q. Zhu et al. (Eds.): GameSec 2020, LNCS 12513, pp. 506–510, 2020.
https://doi.org/10.1007/978-3-030-64793-3_29

on software implementation, including at the base station radio level. Moreover, future broadband networks are expected to rely on cloud technologies, including edge cloud, to support network operation. Furthermore, such networks can benefit from the convergence and maturation of multiple technologies, such as massive MIMO, and from the ability to utilize higher frequency bands, such as mmWave, to achieve high data rate, ultra-low latency, and increased coverage (such as reaching mobile end-points inside the buildings).

Future mobile networks are expected to attract new groups of users and stakeholders that can use different slices of the networks for their unique applications. Service providers can offer mobile infrastructure as a service to various industries such as defense, power grid, transportation, and smart agriculture, that have unique security and reliability requirements. In addition, future networks are expected to provide real-time compute capabilities and facilitate content distribution, in addition to supporting traditional connectivity and data delivery services.

Due to the increasing reliance of many sectors of modern society on mobile broadband services, their security and reliability have become issues of paramount importance. However, the current focus of developers, standard bodies, and network operators is on performance and functionality, while security and resilience remain a secondary consideration. Today's tools and technique for system design lack principled approaches, which could result in security vulnerabilities and unpredictable behaviors.

The goal of this paper is to highlight fundamental longer-term security challenges for next-generation networks. We will also outline several approaches that have the potential to address these challenges.

2 Security Goals and Challenges

Securing a complex system that spans a very large geographical area is a formidable task. The mobile broadband system is expected to be one of the largest engineering systems in the world. The complex structure of the system, its reliance on the wireless medium for user access and backhaul, as well as its large user base creates many attack surfaces for malicious agents. Furthermore, the limited capabilities of IoT devices make it harder to deploy sophisticated security functions, which will force network designers to rely on light-weight security methods. It is likely that some elements of the system will remain unprotected and highly vulnerable to attacks.

2.1 Goals

The main goal of the mobile broadband system is to provide *end-to-end* security, which will ensure that every network application can function in a reliable and predictable manner. This goal can only be achieved through holistic solutions that coordinate security functions among various network elements.

Another important goal for the next-generation wireless broadband networks is to achieve a drastic reduction (several orders of magnitude) in the overall number of vulnerabilities compared to the current systems. This is due to the fact that future networks can be used in life-critical systems and any interruption in network service may lead to very significant consequences.

The security requirements can be different for different groups of users. For example, the network slices that are used for industrial control applications or intelligent transportation systems must have higher levels of security and reliability than slices that serve traditional consumers.

Furthermore, future networks can offer security as a service. This could include a formal specification of the provided security guarantees as well as the consequences of not meeting these security guarantees.

Enabling high levels of security should come at a reasonable cost and incur minimum overhead in terms of system efficiency. Accordingly, the major goal of the system designers is to strike a reasonable trade-off between security and efficiency.

2.2 Challenges

In general, the more complex the system, the more difficult it is to secure. In particular, the large number of configuration parameters will result in a larger attack surface. Next-generation systems are expected to offer great flexibility, which makes the task of securing them more difficult.

Securing next-generation systems requires appropriate solutions to the following challenges:

Physical Layer Security. The air-interface and radio access networks use a shared medium, and hence are vulnerable to intentional interference and jamming. Next-generation systems are expected to share spectrum among multiple service providers and technologies, which can make it harder to detect malicious attacks.

Hardware and Supply Chain Security. This includes a trustworthy hardware design that ensures that each hardware component of the system functions according to the specification. Since the network devices are expected to be manufactured by different providers, factory device identity management tools can be used to mitigate potential risks.

Software/ Software-Defined Networking (SDN) Security. With the advent of the SDN approach, more network functions will be implemented in software. SDN frameworks, however, are prone to their own vulnerabilities (see, e.g.., [6]).

Slicing/Virtualization Security. Since the future networks support different slices, there is a need to properly separate them so the users or different slices cannot adversely affect each other. The orchestration mechanisms should include security features to eliminate attack doors at the time of slice creation and resource allocation.

IoT Security. The large number of IoT devices connected to the future wireless broadband networks will likely be the weakest link in the entire system.

Light-weight tools will be required to support end-to-end encryption and identify management for such devices. Developing scalable security mechanisms will be the key to addressing this problem. The attacker can also exploit the fact that the IoT devices have severe energy constraints due to limitation on the battery capacity or on the amount of energy that can be harvested from the environment.

Security challenges are exacerbated by the fact that the currently adopted standards (including these developed by the 3GPP) leave many critical security enhancements as optional. Furthermore, the ambiguity and the lack of formal representation open the door for different interpretations by vendors, which weakness the security properties of the operational systems. Furthermore, the networks are designed to support backward compatibility with older generations, which weakens the impact of newer security enhancements.

Open Source. In today's networks, the networking solutions are provided by individual vendors that follow a "closed source" approach for their software stacks and utilize closed ("black box") hardware. The closed nature of their systems makes it harder to secure these networks due to the lack of visibility inside the black box devices as well as due to the lack of certainty in their behavior. However, open source solutions may introduce additional security challenges [1].

3 Opportunities

Security challenges present unique opportunities for researchers and developers. This section presents some of the concepts and tools that have the potential to address the challenges referenced in Sect. 2.2.

Provable Security/Security by Design. In most engineering systems, the performance and flexibility of the systems are prioritized while security and privacy are treated as an afterthought. By addressing security requirements at the early stages of the design process, the developers and the system architects can eliminate entire categories of threats. Security by design can be coupled with the *clean slate* approach while the system architects are not constrained by compatibility requirements or by the requirements to be compatible with the existing systems.

Composable Security. The services provided by next generation wireless broadband systems cut across multiple layers and include multiple network components. Indeed, fifth-generation networks are expected to provide end-to-end slicing capabilities. Accordingly, there is a need to coordinate the security functions be provided by multiple layers and network components. This, in turn, will require tools to reason and analyze the joint behavior of distributed security mechanisms to ensure the correctness of operations, eliminating redundant security functions, and minimizing the performance overhead.

Machine Learning (ML)/Artificial Intelligence (AI) Security. ML/AI tools and techniques are expected to play a significant role in the next-generation wireless systems. Due to their reliance on training data sets, ML/AI tools can be exploited by the attacker to steer the system to an unstable state [5].

Programmable Security. It is highly desirable to move from the static (decided in advance) security policies to dynamic policies that can be easily updated during the operation of the system. Security functions can also be programmed by following the SDN approach, as opposed to the current practices in which security policies are configured. Programmable security provides more flexibility in responding to highly dynamic and evolving threats [3].

Developing Security Metrics and Indices. While there exists a large body of research on assessing reliability of engineering systems in the presence of conventional failures, assessing risk in the case of directed attacks is not well understood. Accordingly, it would be useful to develop a probabilistic methodology for assessing the ability of systems to withstand directed attacks aimed at the different system components. This methodology would lead to the development of security indices that can quantify the degree of resilience of the given system.

Leveraging Formal Methods. Formal methods can be leveraged to enable provable security guarantees about systems at specification and design time as well as to enable security measurement, verification, and validation at deployment time [2]. In addition, the formal methods can benefit the network standardization process through the development of a methodology to formally specify and reason about the network protocols. This methodology will address the problems associated with traditional ways of describing protocols using a natural language [4].

References

1. Boswell, J., Poretsky, S.: Security considerations of open ran. https://www.ericsson.com/en/security/security-considerations-of-open-ran. Accessed 19 Oct 2020
2. Chong, S., et al.: Report on the nsf workshop on formal methods for security. arXiv preprint arXiv:1608.00678 (2016)
3. Gu, G., et al.: Programmable system security in a software-defined world-research challenges and opportunities (2018)
4. McMillan, K.L., Zuck, L.D.: Formal specification and testing of quic. In: Proceedings of the ACM Special Interest Group on Data Communication, pp. 227–240 (2019)
5. Papernot, N., McDaniel, P., Sinha, A., Wellman, M.: Towards the science of security and privacy in machine learning. arXiv preprint arXiv:1611.03814 (2016)
6. Shin, S., Gu, G.: Attacking software-defined networks: a first feasibility study. In: Proceedings of the Second ACM SIGCOMM Workshop on Hot Topics in Software Defined Networking, pp. 165–166 (2013)

Short Paper

A Data Mining Friendly Anonymization Scheme for System Logs using Distance Mapping

Gabriela Limonta and Yoan Miche$^{(\boxtimes)}$ (iD)

Nokia Bell Labs, Espoo Finland
{gabriela.limonta,yoan.miche}@nokia-bell-labs.com

Abstract. In this document, we investigate the use of Distance Mapping ideas and what they enable for system logs. In the field of telecommunication networks, log files are used for service quality assurance, and are coming from various devices, back end systems, and general usage of the network. Typically, these log files are not allowed to be monetized or shared with third parties, thanks to legal restrictions on privacy issues. While there are some existing early solutions to this, such as Differential Privacy or Homomorphic Encryption, we propose here to look at Distance Mapping to transform the raw data (the system log files) into highly usable but anonymized data. The resulting data can be used directly by Machine Learning algorithms, visualization algorithms, or be considered for re-embedding. While this approach transforms the data format significantly and limits its usage only for distance-based data mining and machine learning tools, it is an elegant and computationally feasible methodology for such applications.

1 Motivation

Logs are generated by applications to record important information and events during the runtime of a system. Automated log analysis has been an active area of research [5, 8] focusing on how to use logs effectively. These event logs can be used in combination with machine learning techniques for different purposes, including forensic analysis [2] and anomaly detection [1].

5G telecommunications enable increased connectivity and the deployment of diverse Internet of Things (IoT) applications. By combining logs from different sources of a distributed system, we can build an overview of its state, which provides situational awareness when investigating an incident. Logs play a crucial role in analyzing the state of both 5G infrastructure [6] and the IoT applications built on top of it [4].

Log files can also be used for data mining. For example, telecommunications operators hold large amounts of log data, which often includes information related to the traffic, location and movement of connected mobile equipment. This data can be monetized by mining it internally to build better services or by selling it to external parties for commercial purposes. However, the latter is often not possible due to

© Springer Nature Switzerland AG 2020
Q. Zhu et al. (Eds.): GameSec 2020, LNCS 12513, pp. 513–515, 2020.
https://doi.org/10.1007/978-3-030-64793-3

regulations on privacy and data protection rules and the risks of re-identification of users or systems.

2 Problem and Proposed Solution

To use the contents of log files in machine learning, data is transformed typically to a format that can be used by an algorithm, i.e. numerical data, (often arbitrarily mapping values to integers). This raises issues, as detailed in [3], and falls short with text fields as in log files. We propose to use the technique in [3], named Distance Mapping, followed by neighbor re-embedding [7].

The idea in Distance Mapping is to create a function that maps probabilistically the distances between elements in the original metric space $(\mathbb{X}, d)$ (with $\mathbb{X}$ a set of values, and d a distance function over that set) to distances in a well-known space, such as the canonical Euclidean $(\mathbb{R}, d_{\text{EUC}})$: Distances between log entries (across all fields: timestamp, message,…) are mapped to distances between points in a Euclidean space that are as likely (probabilistically) to be at that distance. The goal is to preserve the structure of the data, specifically distance-based, such as density, separation of clusters and classes,…

With pairwise distances between log entries mapped, the mapped distances can be used by distance based machine learning, e.g. K-Means. Some techniques do not use directly distances, so we perform re-embedding of the data into another space [3]: We convert pairwise distances between points to a set of points that respects those pairwise distances. For outlier detection, visualization, and machine learning, re-embedding the mapped distances into $\mathbb{R}^d$ is ideal. For privacy, and having data of the same format as the original, we can decide to re-embed the mapped distances into the original space. We obtain a data set of the same format as the original, with log entries that relate to each other (in terms of pairwise distances) as in the original data, and yet none of the entries are the same as in the original data.

We theorize that this last approach allows for generating synthetic data that preserves (statistically) pairwise distances between original data points, and the structure of the data (understood here as based on distances).

References

1. Du, M., Li, F., Zheng, G., Srikumar, V.: DeepLog: anomaly detection and diagnosis from system logs through deep learning. In: Proceedings of the 2017 ACM SIGSAC Conference, pp. 1285–1298. ACM, Dallas Texas, October 2017
2. Kahles, J., Törrönen, J., Huuhtanen, T., Jung, A.: Automating root cause analysis via machine learning in agile software testing environments. In: 12th IEEE Conference on Software Testing, Validation and Verification (ICST), pp. 379–390, April 2019
3. Miche, Y., Ren, W., Oliver, I., Holtmanns, S., Lendasse, A.: A framework for privacy quantification: measuring the impact of privacy techniques through mutual information, distance mapping, and machine learning. Cogn. Comput. 11(2), 241–261 (2019)

4. Noura, H.N., Salman, O., Chehab, A., Couturier, R.: DistLog: a distributed logging scheme for IoT forensics. Ad Hoc Netw. **98**, 102061 (2020)
5. Oliner, A., Stearley, J.: What supercomputers say: a study of five system logs. In: 37th Annual IEEE/IFIP International Conference on Dependable Systems and Networks (DSN 2007), pp. 575–584, June 2007
6. Sundqvist, T., Bhuyan, M.H., Forsman, J., Elmroth, E.: Boosted ensemble learning for anomaly detection in 5G RAN. In: Maglogiannis, I., Iliadis, L., Pimenidis, E. (eds.) AIAI 2020. IFIP Advances in Information and Communication Technology, vol. 583, pp. 15–30. Springer, Cham (2020). https://doi.org/10.1007/978-3-030-49161-1_2
7. Yang, Z., Peltonen, J., Kaski, S.: Scalable optimization of neighbor embedding for visualization. In: International Conference on Machine Learning, pp. 127–135. PMLR, May 2013
8. Zhu, J., et al.: Tools and benchmarks for automated log parsing. In: IEEE/ACM 41st International Conference on Software Engineering: Software Engineering in Practice (ICSE-SEIP), pp. 121–130, May 2019

Author Index

Printed in the United States
By Bookmasters